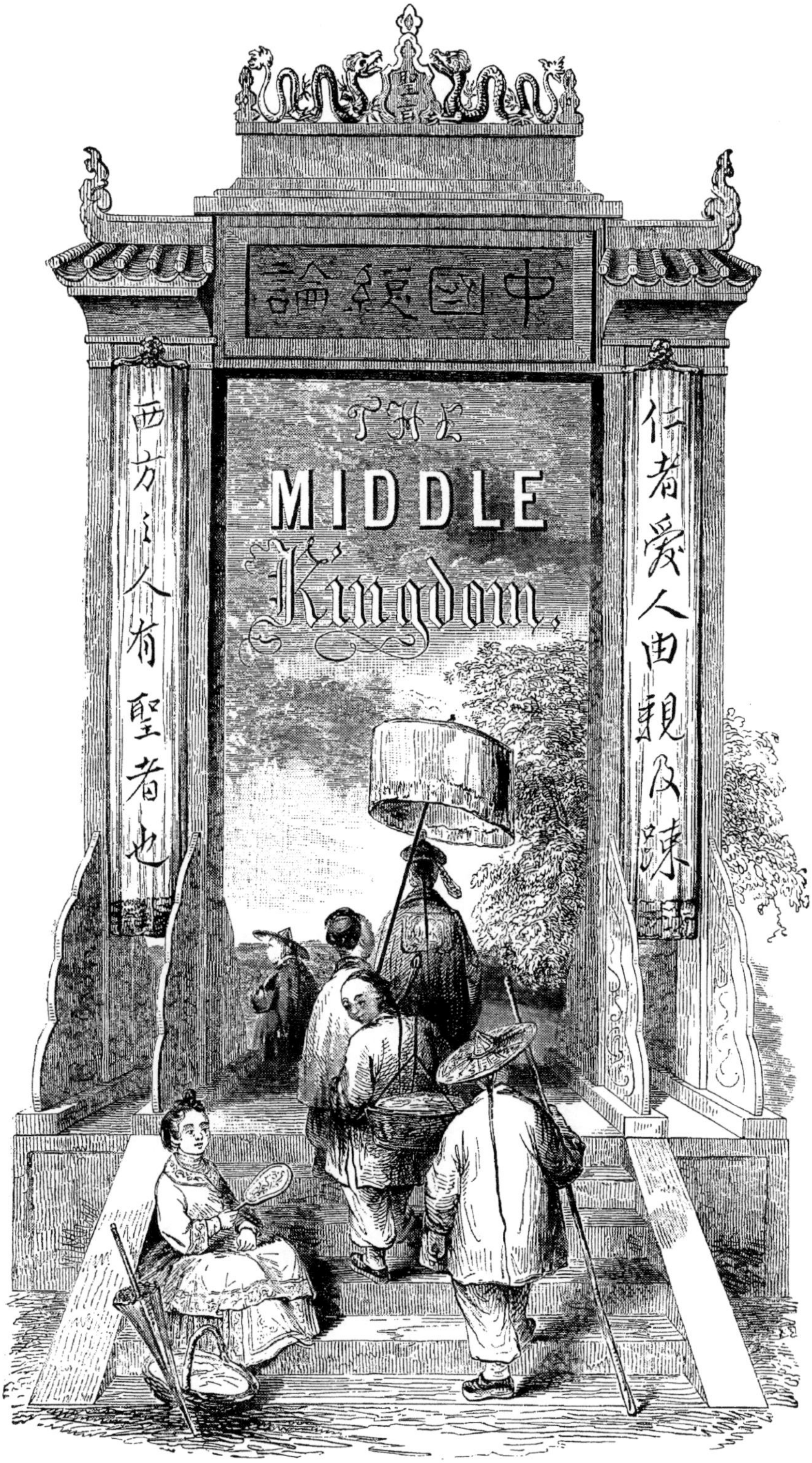
中國總論
THE
MIDDLE
Kingdom,
西方之人有聖者也
仁者愛人由親及疎

IMPERIAL WORSHIP OF SHANGTI ON THE ALTAR OF HEAVEN AT PEKING.

FROM A CHINESE PAINTING

In the drawing is represented the Emperor Hienfung, attended by his principal ministers, kneeling before the shrine of HWANG-TIEN SHANGTÍ. *Though no foreigner has witnessed this ceremony, a few words concerning this native representation will make plain the chief objects of worship.*

Upon the triple altar, or TIÉN TAN *(Volume I., p.* 76), *the central temporary shrine is dedicated to* HWANG-TIEN SHANGTÍ, *or 'Imperial Heaven's Ruler above.' Upon the Emperor's right, nearest the chief pavilion, are tablets to his ancestors, Tienming, Shunchí, Yungching, and Kiaking; the corresponding opposite house is similarly devoted to Tientsung, Kanghí, Kienlung, and Taukwang. The small buildings behind and below these are the* TAMING CHÍ WEI, *the 'Altar of the Sun' or 'Great Luminary' (on the right), and the* YE-MING CHÍ WEI, *or 'Altar of the Night Luminary.' The last structure on the worshipper's right contains tablets to the* CHAU-TIEN SING, *or 'All Stars;' to the* URH-SHIH PAT SUH-SING, *or 'Twenty-eight Constellations in the Ecliptic;' to the* PEH-TAN SING, *or Ursa Major; and to the* MUH, KIN, SHUI, FO, *and* TU, *or Five Elements—'Wood, Metal, Water, Fire, and Earth.' Facing this building on the left are shrines to* SIUEH-SZ', YÜ-SZ', FUNG-SZ', *and* LUI-SZ', *the superintendents of Snow, Rain, Wind, and Thunder.*

THE MIDDLE KINGDOM

This work by S. Wells Williams is a complete look at the Chinese Empire during the mid-nineteenth century. Subjects include the divisions of the Empire, geographical descriptions, religion and art, literature, the second war between Great Britain and China and social life among the Chinese.

www.keganpaul.com

THE KEGAN PAUL CHINA LIBRARY

WANDERINGS IN CHINA
Robert Fortune

VILLAGE LIFE IN CHINA
Arthur H. Smith

CHINA
Mortimer Menpes and Henry Arthur Blake

SOCIAL LIFE OF THE CHINESE
Justus Doolittle

RULERS OF CHINA
A. C. Moule

BEYOND THE GOLDEN LOTUS
Ko Lien Hua Ying

JADE
Berthold Laufer

THE GOLDEN PEACHES OF SAMARKAND
Edward H. Schafer

OLD BUDDHA
Der Ling

SUN TZU ON THE ART OF WAR
Lionel Giles

THINGS CHINESE
J. Ball Dyer

TWO YEARS IN THE FORBIDDEN CITY
Der Ling

THE MIDDLE KINGDOM, VOL. 1 & 2
S. Wells Williams

THE MIDDLE KINGDOM

A SURVEY OF THE GEOGRAPHY, GOVERNMENT, LITERATURE, SOCIAL LIFE, ARTS AND HISTORY OF THE CHINESE EMPIRE AND ITS INHABITANTS

VOLUME I

BY

S. WELLS WILLIAMS

KEGAN PAUL
London · New York · Bahrain

First published in 2005 by
Kegan Paul Limited
UK: P.O. Box 256, London WC1B 3SW, England
Tel: 020 7580 5511 Fax: 020 7436 0899
E-Mail: books@keganpaul.com
Internet: http://www.keganpaul.com
USA: 61 West 62nd Street, New York, NY 10023
Tel: (212) 459 0600 Fax: (212) 459 3678
Internet: http://www.columbia.edu/cu/cup
BAHRAIN: bahrain@keganpaul.com

Distributed by:
Marston Book Services Ltd
160 Milton Park
Abingdon
Oxfordshire OX14 4SD
United Kingdom
Tel: (01235) 465500 Fax: (01235)465555
Email: direct.enqiries@marston.co.uk

Columbia University Press
61 West 62nd Street, New York, NY 10023
Tel: (212) 459 0600 Fax: (212) 459 3678
Internet: http://www.columbia.edu/cu/cup

Printed in Great Britain

ISBN: 0-7103-1167-2

British Library Cataloguing in Publication Data

Library of Congress Cataloging-in-Publication Data
Applied for.

PREFACE.

During the thirty-five years which have elapsed since the first edition of this work was issued, a greater advance has probably been made in the political and intellectual development of China than within any previous century of her history. While neither the social habits nor principles of government have so far altered as to necessitate a complete rewriting of these pages, it will be found, nevertheless, that the present volumes treat of a reformed and in many respects modern nation. Under the new régime the central administration has radically increased its authority among the provincial rulers, and more than ever in former years has managed to maintain control over their pretentions. The Empire has, moreover, established its foreign relations on a well-understood basis by accredited envoys; this will soon affect the mass of the people by the greater facilities of trade, the presence of travellers, diffusion of education, and other agencies which are awaking the people from their lethargy. Already the influences which will gradually transform the face of society are mightily operating.

The changes which have been made in the book comprise such alterations and additions as were necessary to describe the country under its new aspects. In the constant desire to preserve a convenient size, every doubtful or superfluous sentence has been erased, while the new matter incorporated has increased the bulk of the present edition about one-third. The arrangement of chapters is the same. The first four, treating of the geography, combine as many and accurate details of recent explorers or residents as the proportions of this section will permit. The extra-provincial regions are described from the researches of Russian, English, and Indian travellers of the last twenty years. It is a waste, mountainous territory for the most part and can never support a large population. Great pains have been taken by the cartographer, Jacob Wells, to consult the most authentic charts in the construction of the map of the Empire. By collating and reducing to scale the surveys and route charts of reliable travellers throughout the colonies, he has produced in all respects as accurate a map of Central Asia as is at this date possible. The Eighteen Provinces are in the main the same as in my former map.

The chapter on the census remains for the most part without alteration, for until there has been a methodical inspection of the Empire, important questions concerning its population must be held in abeyance. It is worth noticing how generally the estimates in this chapter—or much larger figures—have since its first publication been accepted for the population of China. Foreign students of natural history in China have, by their researches in every department, furnished material for more extensive and precise descriptions under this subject than could possibly have been gathered twoscore years ago. The sixth chapter has, therefore, been almost wholly rewritten, and embraces as complete a summary of this wide field as space would allow or the general reader tolerate. The specialist will, however, speedily recognize the fact that this rapid glance serves rather to indicate how immense and imperfectly explored is this subject than to describe whatever is known.

That portion of the first volume treating of the laws and their administration does not admit of more than a few minor changes. However good their theory of jurisprudence, the people have many things to bear from the injustice of their rulers, but more from their own vices. The *Peking Gazette* is now regularly translated in the Shanghai papers, and gives a *coup d'œil* of the administration of the highest value.

The chapters on the languages and literature are considerably improved. The translations and text-books which the diligence of foreign scholars has recently furnished could be only partially enumerated, though here, as elsewhere in the work, references in the foot-notes are intended to direct the more interested student to the bibliography of the subject, and present him with the materials for an exhaustive study. The native literature is extensive, and all branches have contributed somewhat to form the résumé which is contained in this section, giving a preponderance to the Confucian classics. The four succeeding chapters contain notices of the arts, industries, domestic life, and science of the Chinese—a necessarily rapid survey, since these features of Chinese life are already well understood by foreigners. Nothing, however, that is either original or peculiar has been omitted in the endeavor to portray their social and economic characteristics. The emigration of many thousands of the people of Kwangtung within the last thirty years has made that province a representative among foreign nations of the others; it may be added that its inhabitants are well fitted, by their enterprise, thrift, and maritime habits, to become types of the whole.

The history and chronology are made fuller by the addition of several facts and tables;[1] but the field of research in this direction has as yet scarcely been defined, and few certain dates have been determined prior to the Confucian era.

[1] An alphabetical arrangement of all the tables scattered throughout the work may be found under this word in the Index.

The entire continent of Asia must be thoroughly investigated in its geography, antiquities, and literature in order to throw light on the eastern portion. The history of China offers an interesting topic for a scholar who would devote his life to its elucidation from the mass of native literature.

The two chapters on the religions, and what has been done within the past half century to promote Christian missions, are somewhat enlarged and brought down to the present time. The study of modern scholars in the examination of Chinese religious beliefs has enabled them to make comparisons with other systems of Asiatics, as well as discuss the native creeds with more certainty.

The chapter on the commerce of China has an importance commensurate with its growing amount. Within the past ten years the opium trade has been attacked in its moral and commercial bearings between China, India, and England. There are grounds for hope that the British Government will free itself from any connection with it, which will be a triumph of justice and Christianity. The remainder of Volume II. describes events in the intercourse of China with the outer world, including a brief account of the Tai-ping Rebellion, which proximately grew out of foreign ideas. No connected or satisfactory narrative of the events which have forced one of the greatest nations of the world into her proper position, so far as I am aware, has as yet been prepared. A succinct recital of one of the most extraordinary developments of modern times should not be without interest to all.

The work of condensing the vast increase of reliable information upon China into these two volumes has been attended with considerable labor. Future writers will, I am convinced, after the manner of Richthofen, Yule, Legge, and others, confine themselves to single or cognate subjects rather than attempt such a comprehensive synopsis as is here presented. The number of illustrations in this edition is nearly doubled, the added ones being selected with particular reference to the subject-matter. I have availed myself of whatever sources of information I could command, due acknowledgment of which is made in the foot-notes, and ample references in the Index.

The revision of this book has been the slow though constant occupation of several years. When at last I had completed the revised copy and made arrangements as to its publication, in March, 1882, my health failed, and under a partial paralysis I was rendered incapable of further labor. My son, Frederick Wells Williams, who had already looked over the copy, now assumed entire charge of the publication. I had the more confidence that he would perform the duties of editor, for he had already a general acquaintance with China and the books which are the best authority. The work has been well done, the last three chapters particularly having been improved under his careful revision and especial study of the recent political history of China. The Index is his work, and throughout the book I am indebted to his careful supervision, especially on the chapters treating of geography and literature. By the opening of this year I had so far recovered as to be able to superintend the printing and look over the proofs of the second volume.

My experiences in the forty-three years of my life in China were coeval with the changes which gradually culminated in the opening of the country. Among the most important of these may be mentioned the cessation of the East India Company in 1834, the war with England in 1841–42, the removal of the monopoly of the hong merchants, the opening of five ports to trade, the untoward attack on the city of Canton which grew out of the lorcha Arrow, the operations in the vicinity of Peking, the establishment of foreign legations in that city, and finally, in 1873, the peaceful settlement of the *kotow*, which rendered possible the approach of foreign ministers to the Emperor's presence. Those who trace the hand of God in history will gather from such rapid and great changes in this Empire the foreshadowing of the fulfilment of his purposes; for while these political events were in progress the Bible was circulating, and the preaching and educational labors of missionaries were silently and with little opposition accomplishing their leavening work among the people.

On my arrival at Canton in 1833 I was officially reported, with two other Americans, to the hong merchant Kingqua as *fan-kwai*, or 'foreign devils,' who had come to live under his tutelage. In 1874, as Secretary of the American Embassy at Peking, I accompanied the Hon. B. P. Avery to the presence of the Emperor Tungchí, when the Minister of the United States presented his letters of credence on a footing of perfect equality with the 'Son of Heaven.' With two such experiences in a lifetime, and mindful of the immense intellectual and moral development which is needed to bring an independent government from the position of forcing one of them to that of yielding the other, it is not strange that I am assured of a great future for the sons of Han; but the progress of pure Christianity will be the only adequate means to save the conflicting elements involved in such a growth from destroying each other. Whatever is in store for them, it is certain that the country has passed its period of passivity. There is no more for China the repose of indolence and seclusion—when she looked down on the nations in her overweening pride like the stars with which she could have no concern.

In this revision the same object has been kept in view that is stated in the Preface to the first edition—to divest the Chinese people and civilization of that peculiar and indefinable impression of ridicule which has been so generally given them by foreign authors. I have endeavored to show the better traits of their national character, and that they have had up to this time no opportunity of learning many things with which they are now rapidly becoming acquainted. The time is speedily passing away when the people of the Flowery Land can fairly be classed among uncivilized nations. The stimulus which in this labor of my earlier and later years has been ever present to my mind is the hope that the cause of missions may be promoted. In the success of this cause lies the salvation of China as a people, both in its moral and political aspects. This success bids fair to keep pace with the needs of the people. They will become fitted for taking up the work themselves and joining in the multiform operations of foreign civilizations. Soon railroads, telegraphs, and manufactures will be introduced, and these must be followed by whatsoever may conduce to enlightening the millions of the people of China in every department of religious, political, and domestic life.

The descent of the Holy Spirit is promised in the latter times, and the preparatory work for that descent has been accomplishing in a vastly greater ratio than ever before, and with increased facilities toward its final completion. The promise of that Spirit will fulfil the prophecy of Isaiah, delivered before the era of Confucius, and God's people will come from the land of Sinim and join in the anthem of praise with every tribe under the sun.

S. W. W.

NEW HAVEN, July, 1883.

CONTENTS OF VOLUME I.

CHAPTER I.

CHAPTER II.

CHAPTER IV.

CHAPTER V.

CHAPTER XIII.

CHAPTER XIV.

LIST OF ILLUSTRATIONS IN VOLUME I.

NOTE RESPECTING THE SYSTEM OF PRONUNCIATION ADOPTED IN THIS WORK.

In this the values of the vowels are as follows:

1. *a* as the italicized letters in f*a*ther, f*a*r (never like *a* in h*a*t); e.g., *chang*, *hang*—sounded almost as if written *chahng*, *hahng*, not flat as in the English words *sang*, *bang*, *man*, etc.
2. *ă* like the short *u* in b*u*t, or as any of the italicized vowels in *A*meric*a*n, s*u*mm*e*r, moth*e*r; the German *ö* approaches this sound, while Wade writes it *ê*; e.g., *păn*, *tăng*, to be pronounced as *pun*, *tongue*.
3. *e* as in m*e*n, d*e*ad, s*ai*d; as *teh*, *shen*, *yen*.
4. *é*, the French *é*, as in th*ey*, n*eigh*, pr*ay*; as ch*é*, y*é*, pronounced *chay*, *yay*.
5. *i* as in p*i*n, f*i*n*i*sh; as *sing*, *lin*, *Chihlí*.
6. *í* as in mach*i*ne, bel*ie*ve, f*ee*l, m*e*; as *lí*, *Kíshen*, *Kanghí*.
7. *o* as in l*o*ng, l*aw*n; never like n*o*, cr*ow*; as *to*, *soh*, *po*.
8. *u* as in r*u*le, t*oo*, f*oo*l; as *Turk*, *Belur*, *ku*, *sung*; pronounced *Toork*, *Beloor*, *koo*, *soong*. This sound is heard less full in *fuh*, *tsun*, and a few other words; this and the next may be considered as equivalent to the two *u*-sounds found in German.
9. *ü* nearly as in l'*u*ne (French), or *u*nion, rh*eu*m; as *hü*, *tsü*.
10. *ai* as in *ai*sle, h*igh*, or longer than *i* in p*i*ne; as *Shanghai*, *Hainan*. The combination *ei* is more slender than *ai*, though the difference is slight; e.g., *Kwei-chau*.
11. *au* and *ao* as in r*ou*nd, *ou*r, h*ow*; as *Fuhchau*, *Macao*, *Taukwang*.
12. *éu* as in the colloquial phrase *say 'em*; e.g., *chéung*. This diphthong is heard in the Canton dialect.

13. *ia* as in *yard*; e.g., *hia, kiang;* not to be sounded as if written *high-a, kigh-ang,* but like *heä, keäng.*
14. *iau* is made by joining Nos. 5 and 11; *hiau, Liautung.*
15. *ie* as in s*ie*rra (Spanish), R*ie*nzi; e.g., *hien, kien.*
16. *iu* as in p*ew*, p*u*re, lengthened to a diphthong; *kiu, siun.*
17. *iue* is made by adding a short *e* to the preceding; *kiuen, hiuen.*
18. *ui* as in Lo*ui*siana, s*ui*cide; e.g., *sui, chui.*

The consonants are sounded generally as they are in the English alphabet. *Ch* as in *ch*urch; *hw* as in *wh*en; *j* soft, as *s* in pleasure; *kw* as in aw*kw*ard; *ng*, as an initial, as in si*nging*, leaving off the first two letters; *sz'* and *tsz'* are to be sounded full with one breathing, but none of the English vowels are heard in it; the sound stops at the *z*; Dr. Morrison wrote these sounds *tsze* and *sze*, while Sir Thomas Wade, whose system bids fair to become the most widely employed, turns them into *ssŭ* and *tzŭ*. The *hs* of the latter, made by omitting the first vowel of *hissing*, is written simply as *h* by the author.' *Urh*, or *'rh*, is pronounced as the three last letters of *purr*.

All these, except No. 12, are heard in the court dialect, which has now become the most common mode of writing the names of places and persons in China. Though foreign authors have employed different letters, they have all intended to write the same sound; thus *chan, shan,* and *xan*, are only different ways of writing 閂; and *tsse, tsze, tsz', ʒh, tzŭ,* and *tzu*, of '子. Such is not the case, however, with such names as *Macao, Hongkong, Amoy, Whampoa,* and others along the coast, which are sounded according to the local patois, and not the court pronunciation—*Ma-ngau, Hiangkiang, Hiamun, Hwangpu,* etc. Many of the discrepancies seen in the works of travellers and writers are owing to the fact that each is prone to follow his own fancy in transliterating foreign names; uniformity is almost unattainable in this matter. Even, too, in what is called the court dialect there is a great diversity among educated Chinese, owing to the traditional way all learn the sounds of the characters. In this work, and on the map, the sounds are written uniformly according to the pronunciation given in Morrison's Dictionary, but not according to his orthography. Almost every writer upon the Chinese language seems disposed to propose a new system, and the result is a great confusion in writing the same name ; for example, *eull, olr, ul, ulh, lh, urh, 'rh, í, e, lur, nge, ngí, je, jí,* are different ways of writing the sounds given to a single character. Amid these discrepancies, both among the Chinese themselves and those who endeavor to catch their pronunciation, it is almost impossible to settle upon one mode of writing the names of places. That which seems to offer the easiest pronunciation has been adopted in this work. It may, perhaps, be regarded as an unimportant matter, so long as the place is known, but to one living abroad, and unacquainted with the language, the discrepancy is a source of great confusion. He is unable to decide, for instance, whether *Tung-ngan, Tungon hien, Tang-oune,* and *Tungao,* refer to the same place or not.

In writing Chinese proper names, authors differ greatly as to the style of placing them ; thus, Fuhchaufu, Fuh-chau-fu, Fuh Chau Fu, Fuh-Chau fu, etc., are all seen. Analogy affords little guide here, for New York, Philadelphia, and Cambridge are severally unlike in the principle of writing them : the first, being really formed of an adjective and a noun, is not in this case united to the latter, as it is in Newport, Newtown, etc. ; the second is like the generality of Chinese towns, and while it is now written as one word, it would be written as two if the name were translated—as 'Brotherly Love ;' but the third, *Cambridge,* despite its derivation, is never written in two words, and many Chinese names are like this in origin. Thus applying these rules, properly enough, to Chinese places, they have been written here as single words, *Suchau, Peking, Hongkong ;* a hyphen has been inserted in some places only to avoid mispronunciation, as *Hiau-í, Sí-ngan,* etc. It is hardly supposed that this system will alter such names as are commonly written otherwise, nor, indeed, that it will be adhered to with absolute consistency in the following pages ; but the principle of the arrangement is perhaps the simplest possible. The additions *fu, chau, ting,* and *hien,* being classifying terms, should form a separate word. In conclusion, it may be stated that this system could only be carried out approximately as regards the proper names in the colonies and outside of the Empire.

THE

MIDDLE KINGDOM.

CHAPTER I.

GENERAL DIVISIONS AND FEATURES OF THE EMPIRE.

THE possessions of the ruling dynasty of China,—that portion of the Asiatic continent which is usually called by geographers the CHINESE EMPIRE,—form one of the most extensive dominions ever swayed by a single power in any age, or any part of the world. Comprising within its limits every variety of soil and climate, and watered by large rivers, which serve not only to irrigate and drain it, but, by means of their size and the course of their tributaries, affording unusual facilities for intercommunication, it produces within its own borders everything necessary for the comfort, support, and delight of its occupants, who have depended very slightly upon the assistance of other climes and nations for satisfying their own wants. Its civilization has been developed under its own institutions; its government has been modelled without knowledge or reference to that of any other kingdom; its literature has borrowed nothing from the genius or research of the scholars of other lands; its language is unique in its symbols, its structure, and its antiquity; its inhabitants are remarkable for their industry, peacefulness, numbers, and peculiar habits. The examination of such a people, and so extensive a country, can hardly fail of being both instructive and entertaining, and if rightly pursued, lead to a stronger conviction of the need of the precepts and sanctions of the Bible to the highest development of every nation in its personal, social, and political relations in this world, as well as to individual happiness in another. It is to be hoped, too, that at this date in the world's history, there are many more than formerly, who desire to learn the condition and wants of others, not entirely for their own amusement and congratulation at their superior knowledge and advantages, but also to promote the well-being of their fellow-men, and impart liberally of the gifts they themselves enjoy. Those who desire to do this, will find that few families of mankind are more worthy of their greatest efforts than those comprised within the limits of the Chinese Empire; while none stand in more need of the purifying, ennobling, and invigorating principles of our holy religion to develop and enforce their own theories of social improvement.

The origin of the name *China* has not yet been fully settled. The people themselves have now no such name for their country, nor is there good evidence that they ever did apply it to the whole land. The occurrence in the *Laws of Manu* and in the *Mahâbhârata* of the name *China*, applied to a land or people with whom the Hindus had intercourse in the twelfth century B.C., and who were probably the Chinese, throws the origin far back into the remotest times, where probability must take the place of evidence. The most credible account ascribes its origin to the family of Tsin, whose chief first obtained complete sway, about B.C. 250, over all the other feudal principalities in the land, and whose exploits rendered him famous in India, Persia, and other Asiatic states. His sept had, however, long been renowned in Chinese history, and previous to this conquest had made itself widely known, not only in China, but in other countries. The kingdom lay in the northwestern parts of the empire, near the Yellow River, and according to Visdelou, who has examined the subject, the family was illustrious by its nobility and power. "Its founder was Tayé, son of the emperor Chuen-hü. It existed in great splendor for more than a thousand years, and was only inferior to the royal dignity. Feitsz', a prince of this family, had the superintendence of the stud of the emperor Hiao, B.C. 909, and as a mark of favor his majesty conferred on him the sovereignty of the city of Tsinchau in *mesne tenure*, with the title of sub-tributary king. One hundred and twenty-two years afterwards, B.C. 770, Siangkwan, *petit roi* of Tsinchau (having by his bravery revenged the insults offered to the emperor Ping by the Tartars, who slew his father Yu), was created king in full tenure, and without limitation or exception. The same monarch, abandoning Sí-ngan (then called Hao-king, the capital of his empire) to transport his seat to Lohyang, Siangkwan was able to make himself master of the large province of Shensí, which had composed the proper kingdom of the emperor. The king of Tsin thus became very powerful, but though his fortune changed, he did not alter his title, retaining always that of the city of Tsinchau, which had been the foundation of his elevation. The kingdom of Tsin soon became celebrated, and being the place of the first arrival by land of people from western countries, it seems probable that those who saw no more of China than the realm of Tsin, extended this name to all the rest, and called the whole empire Tsin or Chin."[1]

This extract refers to periods long before the dethronement of the house of Chau by princes of Tsin; the position of this latter principality, contiguous to the desert, and holding the passes leading from the valley of the Tarim across the desert eastward to China, renders the supposition of the learned Jesuit highly probable. The possession of the old imperial capital would strengthen this idea in the minds of the traders resorting to China from the West; and when the same family did obtain paramount sway over the whole empire, and its head render himself celebrated by his conquests, and by building the Great Wall, the name Tsin was still more widely diffused, and regarded as the name of the country. The Malays and Arabians, whose vessels were early found between Aden and Canton, knew it as China, and probably introduced the name into Europe before 1500. The Hindus contracted it into *Machin*, from *Maha-china*, *i.e.*, 'Great China;' and the first of

[1] D'Herbelot, *Bibliothèque Orientale*, quarto edition, 1779, Tome IV., p. 8. Yule, *Cathay and the Way Thither*, Vol. I., pp. xxxiv., lxviii. Edkins, *Chinese Buddhism*, p. 93.

these was sometimes confounded with *Manji*, a term used for the tribes in Yunnan. Thus it appears that these and other nations of Asia have known the country or its people by no other terms than *Jin*, *Chin*, *Sin*, *Sinæ*, or *Tzinistæ*. The Persian name *Cathay*, and its Russian form of *Kitai*, is of modern origin; it is altered from *Ki-tah*, the race which ruled northern China in the tenth century, and is quite unknown to the people it designates. The Latin word *Seres* is derived from the Chinese word *sz'* (silk), and doubtless first came into use to denote the people during the Han dynasty.

The Chinese have many names to designate themselves and the land they inhabit. One of the most ancient is *Tien Hia*, meaning 'Beneath the Sky,' and denoting the World; another, almost as ancient, is *Sz' Hai*, *i.e.*, '[all within] the Four Seas,' while a third is *Chung Kwoh*, or 'Middle Kingdom.' This dates from the establishment of the Chau dynasty, about B.C. 1150, when the imperial family so called its own special state in Honan because it was surrounded by all the others. The name was retained as the empire grew, and thus has strengthened the popular belief that it is really situated in the centre of the earth; *Chung Kwoh jin*, or 'men of the Middle Kingdom,' denotes the Chinese. All these names indicate the vanity and ignorance of the people respecting their geographical position and their rank among the nations; they have not been alone in this foible, for the Egyptians, Greeks and Romans all had terms for their possessions which intimated their own ideas of their superiority; while, too, the area of none of those monarchies, in their widest extent, equalled that of China Proper. The family of Tsin also established the custom, since continued, of calling the country by the name of the dynasty then reigning; but, while the brief duration of that house of forty-four years was not long enough to give it much currency among the people, succeeding dynasties, by their talents and prowess, imparted their own as permanent appellations to the people and country. The terms *Han-jin* and *Han-tsz'* (*i.e.*, men of Han or sons of Han) are now in use by the people to denote themselves; the last also means a "brave man." *Tang-jin*, or 'Men of Tang,' is quite as frequently heard in the southern provinces, where the phrase *Tang Shan*, or 'Hills of Tang,' denotes the whole country. The Buddhists of India called the land *Chin-tan*, or the 'Dawn,' and this appellation has been used in Chinese writings of that sect.

The present dynasty calls the empire *Ta Tsing Kwoh*, or 'Great Pure Kingdom;' but the people themselves have refused the corresponding term of *Tsing-jin*, or 'Men of Tsing.' The empire is also sometimes termed *Tsing Chau*, *i.e.*, '[land of the] Pure Dynasty,' by metonymy for the family that rules it. The term now frequently heard in western countries—the Celestial Empire—is derived from *Tien Chau*, *i.e.*, 'Heavenly Dynasty,' meaning the kingdom which the dynasty appointed by heaven rules over; but the term *Celestials*, for the people of that kingdom, is entirely of foreign manufacture, and their language could with difficulty be made to express such a patronymic. The phrase *Lí Min*, or 'Black-haired Race,' is a common appellation; the expressions *Hwa Yen*, the 'Flowery Language,' and *Chung Hwa Kwoh*, the 'Middle Flowery Kingdom,' are also frequently used for the written language of the country, because the Chinese consider themselves to be among the most polished and civilized of all nations—which is the sense of *hwa* in these phrases. The phrase *Nui Tí*, or 'Inner Land,' is often employed to distinguish it from countries beyond their borders, regarded as the desolate and barbarous regions of the earth. *Hwa Hia* (the Glorious Hia) is an ancient term for China, the Hia dynasty being the first of the series; *Tung Tu*, or "Land of the East," is a name used in Mohammedan writings alone.

The present ruling dynasty has extended the limits of the empire far beyond what they were under the Ming princes, and nearly to their extent in the reign of Kublai, A.D. 1290. In 1840, its borders were well defined, reaching from Sagalien I. on the north-east, in lat. 48° 10′ N. and long. 144° 50′ E., to Hainan I. in the China Sea, on the south, in lat. 18° 10′ N., and westward to the Belur-tag, in long. 74° E., inclosing a continuous area, estimated, after the most careful valuation by McCulloch, at 5,300,000 square miles. The longest line which could be drawn in this vast region, from the south-western part of Îlí, bordering on Kokand, north-easterly to the sea of Okhotsk, is 3,350 miles; its greatest breadth is 2,100 miles, from the Outer Hing-an or Stanovoi Mountains to the peninsula of Luichau in Kwangtung:—the first measuring 71 degrees of longitude, and the last over 34 of latitude.

Since that year the process of disintegration has been going on, and the cession of Hongkong to the British has been followed by greater partitions to Russia, which have altogether reduced it more than half a million of square miles on the north-east and west. Its limits on the western frontiers are still somewhat undefined. The greatest breadth is from Albazin on the Amur, nearly south to Hainan, 2,150 miles; and the longest line which can be drawn in it runs from Sartokh in Tibet, north-east to the junction of the Usuri River with the Amur.

The form of the empire approaches a rectangle. It is bounded on the east and south-east by various arms and portions of the Pacific Ocean, beginning at the frontier of Corea, and called on European maps the gulfs of Liautung and Pechele, the Yellow Sea, channel of Formosa, China Sea, and Gulf of Tonquin. Cochinchina and Burmah border on the provinces of Kwangtung, Kwangsí, and Yunnan, in the south-west; but most of the region near that frontier is inhabited by half-independent tribes of Laos, Kakyens, Singphos, and others. The southern ranges of the Himalaya separate Assam, Butan, Sikkim, Nípal and states in India from Tibet, whose western border is bounded by the nominally dependent country of Ladak, or if that be excluded, by the Kara-korum Mountains. The kingdoms or states of Cashmere, Badakshan, Kokand, and the Kirghís steppe, lie upon the western frontiers of Little Tibet, Ladak, and Îlí, as far north as the Russian border; the high range of the Belur-tag or Tsung-ling separates the former countries from the Chinese territory in this quarter. Russia is conterminous with China from the Kirghís steppe along the Altai chain and Kenteh range to the junction of the Argun and the Amur, from whence the latter river and its tributary, the Usuri, form the dividing line to the border of Corea, a total stretch of 5,300 miles. The circuit of the whole empire is 14,000 miles, or considerably over half the circumference of the globe. These measurements, it must be remembered, are of the roughest character. The coast line from the mouth of the river Yaluh in Corea to that of the Annam in Cochinchina is not far from 4,400 miles. This immense country comprises about one-third of the continent, and nearly one-tenth of the habitable part of the globe; and, next to Russia, is the largest empire which has existed on the earth.

It will, perhaps, contribute to a better comprehension of the area of the Chinese Empire to compare it with some other countries. Russia is nearly 6,500 miles in its greatest length, about 1,500 in its average breadth, and measures 8,369,144[1] square miles, or one-seventh of the land on the globe. The United States of America extends about 3,000 miles from Monterey on the Pacific in a north-easterly direction to Maine, and about 1,700 from Lake of the Woods to Florida. The area of this territory is now estimated at 2,936,166 square miles, with a coast line of 5,120 miles. The area of the British Empire is not far from 7,647,000 square miles, but the boundaries of some of the colonies in Hindostan and South Africa are not definitely laid down; the superficies of the two colonies of Australia and New Zealand is nearly equal to that of all the other possessions of the British crown.

The Chinese themselves divide the empire into three principal parts, rather by the different form of government in each, than by any geographical arrangement.

I. The *Eighteen Provinces*, including, with trivial additions, the country conquered by the Manchus in 1664.

II. *Manchuria*, or the native country of the Manchus, lying north of the Gulf of Liautung as far as the Amur and west of the Usuri River.

III. *Colonial Possessions*, including Mongolia, Îlí (comprising Sungaria and Eastern Turkestan), Koko-nor, and Tibet.

The first of these divisions alone is that to which other nations have given the name of China, and is the only part which is entirely settled by the Chinese. It lies on the eastern

---

[1] Or 21,759,974 sq. km.—*Gotha Almanach.*

slope of the high table-land of Central Asia, in the south-eastern angle of the continent; and for beauty of scenery, fertility of soil, salubrity of climate, magnificent and navigable rivers, and variety and abundance of its productions, will compare with any portion of the globe. The native name for this portion, as distinguished from the rest, is *Shih-pah Săng* or the 'Eighteen Provinces,' but the people themselves usually mean this part alone by the term *Chung Kwŏh*. The area of the Eighteen Provinces is estimated by McCulloch at 1,348,870 square miles, but if the full area of the provinces of Kansuh and Chihlí be included, this figure is not large enough; the usual computation is 1,297,999 square miles; Malte Brun reckons it at 1,482,091 square miles; but the entire dimensions of the Eighteen Provinces, as the Chinese define them, cannot be much under 2,000,000 square miles, the excess lying in the extension of the two provinces mentioned above. This part, consequently, is rather more than two-fifths of the area of the whole empire.

The old limits are, however, more natural, and being better known may still be retained. They give nearly a square form to the provinces, the length from north to south being 1,474 miles, and the breadth 1,355 miles; but the diagonal line from the north-east corner to Yunnan is 1,669 miles, and that from Amoy to the north-western part of Kansuh is 1,557 miles. China Proper, therefore, measures about seven times the size of France, and fifteen times that of the United Kingdom; it is nearly half as large as all Europe, which is 3,650,000 square miles. Its area is, however, nearer that of all the States of the American Union lying east of the Mississippi River, with Texas, Arkansas, Missouri and Iowa added; these all cover 1,355,309 square miles. The position of the two countries facing the western borders of great oceans is another point of likeness, which involves considerable similarity in climate; there is moreover a further resemblance between the size of the provinces in China and those of the newer States.

Before proceeding to define the three great basins into which China may be divided, it will give a better idea of the whole subject to speak of the mountain ranges which lie within and near or along the limits of the country. The latter in themselves form almost an entire wall inclosing and defining the old empire; the principal exceptions being the western boundaries of Yunnan, the border between Ílí and the Kirghís steppe, and the trans-Amur region.

Commencing at the north-eastern corner of the basin of the Amur above its mouth, near lat. 56° N., are the first summits of the Altai range, which during its long course of 2,000 miles takes several names; this range forms the northern limit of the table-land of Central Asia. At its eastern part, the range is called Stanovoi by the Russians, and *Wai Hing-an* by the Chinese; the first name is applied as far west as the confluence of the Songari with the Amur, beyond which, north-west as far as lake Baikal, the Russians call it the Daourian Mountains. The distance from the lake to the ocean is about 600 miles, and all within Russian limits. Beyond lake Baikal, westward, the chain is called the Altai, *i.e.*, Golden Mountains, and sometimes *Kin shan*, having a similar meaning. Near the head-waters of the river Selenga this range separates into two nearly parallel systems running east and west. The southern one, which lies mostly in Mongolia, is called the Tangnu, and rises to a much higher elevation than the northern spur. The Tangnu Mountains continue under that name on the Chinese maps in a south-westerly direction, but this chain properly joins the Tien shan, or Celestial Mountains, in the province of Cobdo, and continues until it again unites with the Altai further west, near the junction of the Kirghís steppe with China and Russia. The length of the whole chain is not far from 2,500 miles, and except near the Tshulyshman River, does not, so far as is known, rise to the snow line, save in detached peaks. The average elevation is supposed to be in the neighborhood of 7,000 feet; most of it lies between latitudes 47° and 52° N., largely covered with forests and susceptible of cultivation.

The next chain is the Belur-tag, Tartash ling, in Chinese *Tsung ling*, Onion Mountains, or better, Blue Mountains, so called from their distant hue.[1] This range lies in the south-west of Son-

[1] Klaproth (*Mémoires sur l'Asie*, Tome II., p. 295) observes that the name is derived from the abundance of onions found upon these mountains. M. Abel-Rémusat prefers to attribute it to the "bluish tint of onions."

garia, separating that territory from Badakshan; it commences about lat. 50° N., nearly at right angles with the Tien shan, and extends south, rising to a great height, though little is known of it. It may be considered as the connecting link between the Tien shan and the Kwănlun; or rather, both this and the latter may be considered as proceeding from a mountain knot, detached from the Hindu-kush, in the south-western part of Turkestan called Pushtikhur, the Belur-tag coming from its northern side, while the Kwănlun issues from its eastern side, and extends across the middle of the table-land to Koko-nor, there diverging into two branches. This mountain knot lies between latitudes 36° and 37° N., and longitudes 70° and 74° E. The Himalaya range proceeds from it south-easterly, along the southern frontier of Tibet, till it breaks up near the head-waters of the Yangtsz', Salween, and other rivers between Tibet, Burmah, and Yunnan, thus nearly completing the inland frontier of the empire. A small spur from the Yun ling, in the west of Yunnan, in the country of the Singphos and borders of Assam, may also be regarded as forming part of the boundary line. The *Chang-peh shan* lies between the head-waters of the Yaluh and Toumen rivers, along the Corean frontier, forming a spur of the lower range of the Sihota or *Sih-hih-teh* Mountains, east of the Usuri.

Within the confines of the empire are four large chains, some of the peaks in their course rising to stupendous elevations, but the ridges generally falling below the snow line. The first is the Tien shan or Celestial Mountains, called Tengkiri by the Mongols, and sometimes erroneously Alak Mountains. This chain begins at the northern extremity of the Belur-tag in lat. 40° N., or more properly comes in from the west, and extends from west to east between longitudes 76° and 90° E., and generally along the 22° of north latitude, dividing Îlí into the Northern and Southern Circuits. Its western portion is called Muz-tag; the Muz-daban, about long. 79° E., between Kuldja and Aksu, is where the road from north to south runs across, leading over a high glacier above the snow line. East of this occurs a mass of peaks among the highest in Central Asia, called Bogdo-ula; and at the eastern end, near Uramtsi, as it declines to the desert, are traces of volcanic action seen in solfataras and spaces covered with ashes, but no active volcanoes are now known. The doubtful volcano of Pí shan, between the glacier and the Bogdo-ula, is the only one reported in continental China. The Tien shan end abruptly at their eastern point, where the ridge meets the desert, not far from the meridian of Barkul in Kansuh, though Humboldt considers the hills in Mongolia a continuation of the range eastward, as far as the Nui Hing-an. The space between the Altai and Tien shan is very much broken up by mountainous spurs, which may be considered as connecting links of them both, though no regular chain exists. The western prolongation of the Tien shan, under the name of the Muz-tag, extends from the high pass only as far as the junction of the Belur-tag, beyond which, and out of the Chinese Empire, it continues nearly west, south of the river Sihon toward Kodjend, under the names of Ak-tag and Asferah-tag; this part is covered with perpetual snow.

Nearly parallel with the Tien shan in part of its course is the Nan shan, Kwănlun or Koulkun range of mountains, also called *Tien Chu* or 'Celestial Pillar' by Chinese geographers. The Kwănlun starts from the Pushtikhur knot in lat. 36° N., and runs along easterly in nearly that parallel through the whole breadth of the table-land, dividing Tibet from the desert of Gobi in part of its course. About the middle of its extent, not far from long. 90° E., it divides into several ranges, which decline to the south-east through Koko-nor and Sz'chuen, under the names of the Bayan-kara, the Burkhan-buddha, the Shuga and the Tangla Mountains,—each more or less parallel in their general south-east course till they merge with the Yun ling (*i.e.*, Cloudy Mountains), about lat. 33° N. Another group bends northerly, beyond the sources of the Yellow River, and under the names of Altyn-tag, Nan shan, Ín shan, and Ala shan, passes through Kansuh and Shensí to join the Nui Hing-an, not far from the great bend of the Yellow River. Some portion of the country between the extremities of these two ranges is less elevated, but no plains occur, though the parts north of Kansuh, where the Great Wall runs, are rugged and unfertile. The large tract between the basins of the Tarim River and that of the Yaru-tsang . ı, including the Kwănlun range, is mostly occupied by the desert of Gobi, and is now one of the least known parts of the globe. The mineral treasures of the Kwănlun are probably great, judging from the many precious stones ascribed to it; this desolate region is the favorite arena for the monsters, fairies, genii, and other beings of Chinese legendary lore, and is the Olympus where the Buddhist and Taoist divinities hold their mystic sway, strange voices are heard, and marvels accomplished.[1]

From near the head-waters of the Yellow River, the four ridges run south-easterly, and converge hard by the confines of Burmah and Yunnan, within an area about one hundred miles in breadth. The Yun ling range constitutes the western frontier of Sz'chuen, and going south-east into Yunnan, thence turns eastward, under the names of Nan ling, Mei ling, Wu-í shan, and other local terms, passing through Kweichau, Hunan, and dividing Kwangtung and Fuhkien from Kiangsí and Chehkiang, bends north-east till it reaches the sea opposite Chusan. One or two spurs branch off north from this range through Hunan and Kiangsí, as far as the Yangtsz', but they are all of moderate elevation, covered with forests, and susceptible of cultivation. The descent from the Siueh ling or Bayan-kara Mountains, and the western part of the Yun ling, to the Pacific, is very gradual. The Chinese give a list of fifty peaks lying in the provinces which are covered with snow for the whole or part of the year, and describe glaciers on several of them.

Another less extensive ridge branches off nearly due east from the Bayan-kara Mountains in Koko-nor, and forms a moderately high range of mountains between the Yellow River and Yangtsz' kiang as far as long. 112° E., on the western borders of Nganhwui; this range is called Ko-tsing shan, and Peh ling (*i.e.*, Northern Mountains), on European maps. These two chains, viz., the Yun ling—with its continuation of the Mei ling—and the Peh ling, with their numerous offsets, render the whole of the western part of China very uneven.

---

[1] Compare Rémusat, *Histoire de la Ville de Khotan*, p. 65, ff.

On the east of Mongolia, and commencing near the bend of the Yellow River, or rather forming a continuation of the range in Shansí, is the Nui Hing-an ling or Sialkoi, called also Soyorti range, which runs north-east on the west side of the basin of the Amur, till it reaches the Wai Hing-an, in lat. 56° N. The sides of the ridge toward the desert are nearly naked, but the eastern acclivities are well wooded and fertile. On the confines of Corea a spur strikes off westward through Shingking, called Kolmin-shanguin alin by the Manchus, and Chang-peh shan (*i.e.*, Long White Mountains) by the Chinese. Between the Sialkoi and Sihota are two smaller ridges defining the basin of the Nonni River on the east and west. Little is known of the elevation of these chains except that they are low in comparison with the great western ranges, and under the snow line.

The fourth system of mountains is the Himalaya, which bounds Tibet on the south, while the Kwănlun and Burkhan Buddha range defines it on the north. A small range runs through it from west to east, connected with the Himalaya by a high table-land, which surrounds the lakes Manasa-rowa and Ravan-hrad, and near or in which are the sources of the Indus, Ganges, and Yaru-tsangbu. This range is called Gang-dis-ri and Zang, and also Kailasa in Dr. Buchanan's map, and its eastern end is separated from the Yun ling by the narrow valley of the Yangtsz', which here flows from north to south. The country north of the Gang-dis-ri is divided into two portions by a spur which extends in a north-west direction as far as the Kwănlun,[1] called the Kara-korum Mountains. On the western side of this range lies Ladak, drained by one of the largest branches of the Indus, and although included in the imperial domains on Chinese maps, has long been separated from imperial cognizance. The Kara-korum Mountains may therefore be taken as composing part of the boundary of the empire; Chinese geographers regard them as forming a continuation of the Tsung ling.

[1] One among many native names given to the Kwănlun, or Koulkun Mountains, is *Tien chu*, 天柱 'Heaven's Pillar,' which corresponds precisely with the *Atlas* of China.

This hasty sketch of the mountain chains in and around China needs to be further illustrated by Pumpelly's outlines of their general course and elevation in what he suitably terms the *Sinian System*, applied "to that extensive northeast-southwest system of upheaval which is traceable through nearly all Eastern Asia, and to which this portion of the continent owes its most salient features." He has developed this system in the *Researches in China, Mongolia and Japan*, issued by the Smithsonian Institution in 1866. The mountains of China correspond in many respects to the Appalachian system in America, and its revolution probably terminated soon after the deposition of the Chinese coal measures. Mr. Pumpelly describes the principal anticlinal axes of elevation in China Proper, beginning with the Barrier Range, extending through the northern part of Chihlí and Shansí, where it trends W.S.W., prolonging across the Yellow River at Pao-teh, and hence S.W. through Shansí and Kansuh, coinciding with the watershed between the bend of that river, which traverses it through an immense gorge.

The next axis east begins at the Tushih Gate, and goes S.W. to the Nankau Pass, both of them in the Great Wall, and thence across Shansí to the elbow of the Yellow River, and onward to Western Sz'chuen, forming the watershed within the bend of the Yangtsz'. In the regions between these two axes are found coal deposits. A central axis succeeds this in Shansí, crossing the Yangtsz' near Íchang, and passing on S.W. through Kweichau to the Nan ling; going N.E., it runs through Honan and subsides as it gets over the Yellow River, till in Shantung and the Regent's Sword it rises higher and higher as it stretches on to the Chang-peh shan in Manchuria, and the ridge between the Songari and Usuri rivers. Between the last two ranges lie the great coal, iron, and salt deposits in the provinces, and each side of the central axis huge troughs and basins occur, such as the valley of the Yangtsz' in Yunnan, the Great Plain in Nganhwui and Chihlí, the Gulf of Pechele, and the basins of the Liao and Songari rivers.

The coast axis of elevation is indicated by ranges of granitic mountains between Kiangsí and Kiangsu on the north, and Chehkiang and Fuhkien on the south, extending S.W. through

Kwangtung into the Yun ling, and N.E. into the Chusan Archipelago, thence across to Corea and the Sihota Mountains east of the Usuri River. An outlying granitic range, reaching from Hongkong north-easterly to Wănchau, and S.W. to Hainan Island, marks a fifth axis of elevation.

Crossing these anticlinal axes are three ranges, coming into China Proper from the west in such a manner as to prove highly beneficial to its structure. The northern is apparently a continuation of the Bayan-kara Mountains in a S.E. direction into Kansuh, and south of the river Wei into Honan, under the name of the Hiung shan or 'Bear Mountains.' The centre is an offset from this, going across the north of Hupeh. The southern appears to be a prolongation of the Himalaya into Yunnan and Kwangsí, making the watershed between the Yangtsz' and Pearl river basins.

Between the Tien shan and the Kwănlun range on the southwest, and reaching to the Sialkoi on the north-east, in an oblique direction, lies the great desert of Gobi or Sha-moh, both words signifying a *waterless plain*, or *sandy floats*.[1] The entire length of this waste is more than 1,800 miles, but if its limits are extended to the Belur-tag and the Sialkoi, at its western and eastern extremity, it will reach 2,200 miles; the average breadth is between 350 and 400 miles, subject, however, to great variations. The area within the mountain ranges which define it is over a million square miles, and few of the streams occurring in it find their way to the ocean. The whole of this tract is not a barren desert, though no part of it can lay claim to more than comparative fertility; and the great altitude of most portions seems to be as much the cause of its sterility as the nature of the soil. Some portions have relapsed into a waste because of the destruction of the inhabitants.

The western portion of Gobi, lying east of the Tsung ling and north of the Kwănlun, between long. 76° and 94° E., and in lat. 36° and 41° N., is about 1,000 miles in length, and between 300 and 400 wide. Along the southern side of the

---

[1] Another interpretation makes Gobi (Kopi) to apply to the stony, while Sha-moh denotes the sandy tracks of this desert, in which case the name would more correctly read, "Great Desert of Gobi *and* Sha-moh."

Tien shan extends a strip of arable land from 50 to 80 miles in width, producing grain, pasturage, cotton, and other things, and in which lie nearly all the Mohammedan cities and forts of the *Nan Lu*. The Tarim and its branches flow eastward into Lob-nor, through the best part of this tract, from 76° to 89° E.; and along the banks of the Khoten River a road runs from Yarkand to that city, and thence to H'lassa. Here the desert is comparatively narrow. This part is called *Han hai*, or 'Mirage Sea,' by the Chinese, and is sometimes known as the desert of Lob-nor. The remainder of this region is an almost unmitigated waste, and north of Koko-nor assumes its most terrific appearance, being covered with dazzling stones, and rendered insufferably hot by the reflection of the sun's rays from these and numerous movable mountains of sand. Nor in winter is the climate milder or more endurable. "The icy winds of Siberia, the almost constantly unclouded sky, the bare saline soil, and its great altitude above the sea, combine to make the Gobi, or desert of Mongolia, one of the coldest countries in the whole of Asia." [1]

The sandhills—*kuzupchi*, as the Mongols call them—appear north of the Ala shan and along the Yellow River, and when the wind sets them in motion they gradually travel before it, and form a great danger to travellers who try to cross them. One Chinese author says, "There is neither water, herb, man, nor smoke;—if there is no smoke, there is absolutely nothing." The limits of the actual desert are not easily defined, for near the base of the mountain ranges, streams and vegetation are usually found.

Near the meridian of Hami, long. 94° E., the desert is narrowed to about 150 miles. The road from Kiayü kwan to Hami runs across this narrow part, and travellers find water at various places in their route. It divides Gobi into two parts—the desert of Lob-nor and the Great Gobi—the former being about 4,500 feet elevation, and the latter or eastern not higher than 4,000 feet. The borders of Kansuh now extend across this tract to the foot of the Tien shan.

---

[1] Col. Prejevalsky, *Travels in Mongolia*, etc. Vol. II., p. 22. London, 1876.

The eastern part, or Great Gobi, stretches from the eastern declivity of the Tien shan, in long. 94° to 120° E., and about lat. 40° N., as far as the Inner Hing-an. Its width between the Altai and the Ĭn shan range varies from 500 to 700 miles. Through the middle of this tract extends the depressed valley properly called Sha-moh, from 150 to 200 miles across, and whose lowest depression is from 2,600 to 2,000 feet above the sea. Sand almost covers the surface of this valley, generally level, but sometimes rising into low hills. The road from Urga to Kalgan, crossing this tract, is watered during certain seasons of the year, and clothed with grass. It is 660 miles, and forty-seven posts are placed along the route. The crow, lark, and sand-grouse are abundant on this road, the first being a real pest, from its pilfering habits. Such vegetation as occurs is scanty and stunted, affording indifferent pasture, and the water in the small streams and lakes is brackish and unpotable. North and south of the Sha-moh the surface is gravelly and sometimes rocky, the vegetation more vigorous, and in many places affords good pasturages for the herds of the Kalkas tribes. In those portions bordering on or included in Chihlí province, among the Tsakhars, agricultural labors are repaid, and millet, oats, and barley are produced, though not to a great extent. Trees are met with on the water-courses, but not to form forests. This region is called *tsau-ti*, or Grassland, and maintains large herds of sheep and cattle. It extends more or less northward towards Siberia. The Etsina is the largest inland stream in this division of Gobi, but on its north-eastern borders are some large tributaries of the Amur. On the south of the Sialkoi range the desert-lands reach nearly to the Chang-peh shan, about five degrees beyond those mountains. The general features of this portion of the earth's surface are less forbidding than Sahara, but more so than the steppes of Siberia or the pampas of Buenos Ayres. The whole of Gobi is regarded by Pumpelly as having formed a portion of a great ocean, which, in comparatively recent geological times, extended south to the Caspian and Black Seas, and between the Ural and Inner Hing an Mountains, and was drained off by an upheaval whose traces and effects can be detected in many parts. "It appears to me," he adds, "that the ancient physical geography of this region, and the effects of its elevation, present one of the most important fields of exploration." It will no doubt soon be more fully explored. Baron Richthofen describes Central Asia as properly a shallow trough, 1,800 miles long and about 400 miles wide, whose bottom is about 1,800 feet above the ocean; its ancient shore-line extended between the Kwănlun and Tien shan ranges on the west, from 5,000 to 10,000 feet high, and gradually falling to 3,600 feet in its eastern shore. This is the *Han-hai*; eastward is *Sha-moh*, and outside of both these wildernesses are the peripheral regions, where the waters flow to the ocean, carrying their silt, the erosions from the mountains. Inside of the shore-line nothing reaches the oceans, and these results of degradation are washed or blown into the valleys, and the country is buried in its own dust.[1]

The *rivers* of China are her glory, and no country can compare with her for natural facilities of inland navigation. The people themselves consider that portion of geography relating to their rivers as the most interesting, and give it the greatest attention. The four largest rivers in the empire are the Yellow River, the Yangtsz', the Amur, and the Tarim; the Yaru-tsangbu also runs more than a thousand miles within its borders.

The *Hwang ho*, or 'Yellow River,' rises in the plain of Odontala, called in Chinese *Sing-suh hai*, or 'Starry Sea,' from the numerous springs or lakelets found there between the Shuga and Bayan-kara Mountains, in lat. 35⅛°, and about long. 96° E., and not a hundred miles from the Yangtsz'. The Chinese popularly believe that the Yellow River runs underground from Lob-nor to Sing-suh hai. In this region are two lakes—the Dzaring and Oling, which are its fountains; and its course is very crooked after it leaves them. It turns first south 30 miles, then east 160, then nearly west about 120, winding through gorges of the Kwănlun; the river then flows north-east and east to Lanchau in Kansuh, having gone about 700 miles in its devious line. From Lanchau it turns northward along the

---

[1] Von Richthofen, *China. Ergebnisse eigener Reisen, Band I. Berlin*, 1877.

Great Wall for 430 miles, till deflected eastward by the Ĭn shan, on the edge of the plateau, and incloses the country of the Ortous Mongols within this great bend. A spur of the Peh ling forces it south, about long. 110° E., between Shansí and Shensí, for some 500 miles, till it enters the Great Plain, having run 1,130 miles from Lanchau. Through this loess region it becomes tinged with the soil which imparts both color and name to it. At the northern bend it separates in several small lakes and branches, and during this part of its course, for more than 500 miles, receives not a single stream of any size, while it is still so rapid, in descending from the plateau, as to demand much care when crossing it by boats. At the south-western corner of Shansí this river meets its largest tributary, the Wei, which comes in from the westward after a course of 400 miles, and is more available as a navigable stream than any other of the affluents. The area of the whole basin is less than that of the Yangtsz', and may be estimated at about 475,000 square miles; though the source of this stream is only 1,290 miles in a direct line from its mouth, its numerous windings prolong its course to nearly double that distance.

The great differences of level in winter and summer have always made this river nearly useless, except as a drain; while the effect of the long-continued deposit of silt along its lower level course has finally choked the mouth altogether. This remarkable result has been hastened, no doubt, by the dikes built along the banks to the east of Kaifung, which thus forced the floods to fill up the channel, and pushed the waters back over 500 miles to Honan-fu. Here the land is low, and the refluent waters gradually worked their way through marshes and creeks into the river Wei on the north bank, and thus found a north-east channel into the Canal and the Ta-tsing River, till they reached the Gulf of Pechele. A small part of these floods have perhaps gone south into the head-waters of the river Hwai, and thence into Hung-tsih Lake; but that lake has shrivelled, like its great feeder, and all its waters flow into the Yangtsz'. The history of the Yellow River furnishes a conclusive argument against diking a river's banks to restrain its floods. It has now reverted to the channel it occupied about fourteen centuries ago.[1]

Far more tranquil and useful is its rival, the Yangtsz' kiang, called also simply *Kiang* or *Ta kiang*, the 'River,' or 'Great River.' It is often erroneously named on western maps, Kyang Ku, which merely means 'mouth of the river.' The sources of the Kiang are in the Tangla Mountains and the Kwănlun range, and are placed on native maps in three streams flowing from the southern side of the Bayan-kara. This has been partly confirmed by Col. Prejevalsky. In January, 1873, he reached the Murui-ussu (Tortuous River) in lat. 35°, long. 94°, at its junction with the Napchitai, the northern of the three branches, and found it 750 feet wide at that season. In spring, the river's bed there is filled up a mile wide. Its course thence is south-east, receiving three other streams, all of which may be considered as its head-waters. All their channels are over ten thousand feet above the sea, but the ranges near them are under the snow-line. There is no authentic account of its course from this union till it joins the Yalung kiang in Sz'chuen, a distance of nearly 1,300 miles; but Chinese maps indicate a south-easterly direction through the gorges of the Yun ling, till it bursts out from the mountains in lat. 26° N., where it turns north-east. During much of this distance it bears the name of the Po-lai-tsz'. The Yalung River rises very near the Yellow River, and runs parallel with the Kiang in a valley further east, flowing upwards of 600 miles before they join. Great rafts of timber are floated down both these streams, for sale at the towns further east, but no large boats are seen on them before they leave the mountains. The town of Batang, in Sz'chuen, on the road from H'lassa, is the first large place on the river. The main trunk is called Kin-sha kiang (*i.e.*, Golden-sand River), until it receives the Yalung in the southern part of Sz'chuen, which the Chinese there regard as the principal stream of the two. Beyond the junction, the united river is called Ta kiang as far as Wuchang, in Hupeh, beyond which

[1] Report by Dr. W. A. P. Martin in *Journal of N. C. Branch of R. A. Society*, Vol. III., pp. 33–38; 1866. Same journal, Vol. IV., pp. 80–86; 1867; Notes by Ney Elias. Pumpelly's *Researches*, 1866, chap. v., pp. 41–51.

the people know it also as the Chang kiang, or 'Long River.' They do not often call it Yangtsz', which is properly applied only to the reach from Nanking out to sea, which lay within the old region of Yangchau. This name has been erroneously written in Chinese, and thence translated 'Son of the Ocean.' The French often call it the *Fleuve Bleu*, but the Chinese have no such name. Its general course from Wuchang is easterly, receiving various tributaries on both shores, until it discharges its waters at Tsungming Island, by two mouths, in lat. 32° N., more than 1,850 miles from its mouth in a direct line, but flowing nearly 3,000 miles in all its windings.[1]

One of the largest and most useful of its tributaries in its lower course is the Kan kiang in Kiangsí, which empties through the Poyang lake, and continues the transverse communication from north to south, connecting with the Grand Canal. The Tungting lake receives the Siang and Yuen, which drain the northern sides of the Nan ling in Hunan; and west of them is the Kungtan or Wu, which comes in with its surplus waters from Kweichau. These are on the south; the Han in Hupeh, and the Kialing, Min, and Loh in Sz'chuen, are the main affluents on the north, contributing the drainage south of the Peh ling. The Grand Canal comes in opposite Chinkiang, and from thence the deep channel, able to carry the largest men-of-war on its bosom, finds its way to the Pacific. No two rivers can be more unlike in their general features than these two mighty streams. While the Yellow River is unsteady, the Yangtsz' is uniform and deep in its lower course, and available for rafts from Batang in the western confines of Sz'chuen, and for boats from beyond Tungchuen in Yunnan, more than 1,700 miles from its mouth. Its great body and depth afford ample room for ocean steam-ships 200 miles, as far as Nanking, where in some places no bottom could be found at twenty fathoms, while the banks are not so low as to be often injured by the freshets, even when the flood is over thirty feet.

---

[1] See the account of Père Laribe's voyage on this river in 1843, *Annales de la Propagation de la Foi*, Tome XVII., pp. 207, 286, ff. *Five Months on the Yang-tsze*, by Capt. Thos. W. Blakiston; London, 1862. Pumpelly's *Researches*, chap. ii., pp. 4–10. Capt. Gill, *The River of Golden Sand*.

At Pingshan above Süchau in Sz'chuen, 1,550 miles from its mouth, Blakiston reckons the river to be 1,500 feet above tide-water, which gives an average fall of 12 inches to a geographical mile; the inclination is increased to 19 inches in some portions, and it is this force which carries the silt of this stream out to sea, but which is wanting in the Yellow River. The fall of the Yangtsz' is nearly double that of the Nile and Amazon, and half that of the Mississippi. The amount of water discharged is estimated at 500,000 cubic feet a second at Íchang, about 700 miles up, and it may reasonably be concluded that at Tsungming it discharges in times of flood a million cubic feet per second. Barrow calculated the discharge of the Yellow River in 1798 to be 11,616 cubic feet per second, when the current ran seven miles an hour. No river in the world exceeds the Yangtsz' for arrangement of subsidiary streams, which render the whole basin accessible as far as the Yalung. When a ship-canal has been dug around the gorges and rapids between Íchang and Kwei, steam-vessels can ascend nearly two thousand miles. The area of its basin is estimated at 548,000 square miles; and from its central course, and the number of provinces through which it passes, it has been termed the Girdle of China; while for its size, perennial and ample supply of water, and accessibility for navigation, it ranks with the great rivers of the world.[1]

Besides these two notable rivers, numerous others empty into the ocean along the coast from Hainan to the Amur, three of which drain large tracts of country, and afford access to many populous cities and districts. The third basin is that south of the Nan ling to the ocean; it is drained chiefly by the Chu kiang, and its form is much less regular than those of the Yellow River and Yangtsz'. The Chu kiang or Pearl River, like most of the rivers in China, has many names during its course, and is formed by three principal branches, respectively called East, North, and West rivers, according to the quarter from whence they come. The last is by far the largest, and all

---

[1] Staunton's *Embassy*, Vol. III., p. 233. Blakiston's *Yang-tsze*, p. 294, etc. *Chinese Repository*, Vol. II., p. 316.

of them are navigable most of their length. They disembogue together at Canton, and drain a region of not much less than 130,000 square miles, being all the country east of the Yun ling and south of the Nan ling ranges. The rivers in Yunnan, for the most part, empty into the Salween, Saigon, Meikon, and other streams in Cochinchina. The Min, which flows by Fuhchau, the Tsih, upon which Ningpo lies, the Tsientang, leading up to Hangchau, and the Pei ho, or White River, emptying into the Gulf of Pechele, are the most considerable among these lesser outlets in the provinces; while the Liau ho and Yahluh kiang, discharging into the Gulf of Liautung, are the only two that deserve mention in Southern Manchuria. The difference between the number of river-mouths cutting the Chinese coast and that of the United States is very striking, resulting from the different direction of the mountain chains in the interior.

The *lakes* of China are comparatively few and small; all those in the provinces of any size lie within the Plain, and are connected with the two great rivers. The largest is the Tungting in Hunan, about 220 miles in circumference, through which the waters of the Siang and Yuen rivers flow, and fill its channels and beds according to the season; it is now the silted-up bed of a former inland sea in Hupeh, lying on both sides of the Yangtsz', and through which countless lakes, creeks, and canals form a navigable network between that river and the Han. The lake receives the silt as the tributaries flow on through it, and discharge themselves along the deep outlet near Yohchau; this depression altogether is about 200 miles long and 80 broad. About 320 miles eastward lies the Poyang Lake in Kiangsí, which also discharges the surplus waters of the Kan into the Yangtsz'. It is nearly 90 miles long, and about 20 in breadth, inclosing within its bosom many beautiful and populous islets. The scenery around this lake is highly picturesque, and its trade and fisheries are more important than those of the Tungting. The Yangtsz' receives the waters of several other lakes as it approaches the ocean, the largest of which are the Ta hu or 'Great Lake' near Suchau, and the Tsau hu, lying on the northern bank, between Nganking and Nanking; both these lakes join the river by navigable streams.

and the former is connected with the ocean by more than one channel.

The only considerable lake connected with the Yellow River is the Hungtsih in Kiangsu, situated near the junction of that river and the Grand Canal, into which it discharges the drainings of the Hwai River; it is more remarkable for the fleets of boats upon it than for scenery in the vicinity. The larger part of the country between the mouths of the two rivers is so marshy and full of lakes, as to suggest the idea that the whole was once an enormous estuary where their waters joined, or else that their deposits have filled up a huge lake which once occupied this tract, leaving only a number of lesser sheets. Besides these, there are small lakes in Chihlí and Shantung; also the *Tien*, the *Sien*, and the *Tali*, of moderate extent, in Yunnan; all of them support an aquatic population upon the fish taken from their waters.

The largest lake in Manchuria is the Hinkai-nor in Kirin, near the source of the Usuri; the two lakes Hurun and Puyur, or Pir, in the basin of the Nonni River, give their name to Hurun-pir, the western district of Tsitsihar; but of the extent and productions of these sheets of water little is known.

The regions lying north and south of Gobi contain many salt lakes, none of them individually comparing with the Aral Sea, but collectively covering a much larger extent, and most of them receiving the waters of the streams which drain their own isolated basins. The peculiarities of these little known parts, especially the depression on each side of the Tien shan, are such as to render them among the most interesting fields for geographical and geological research in the world. The largest one in Turkestan is Lob-nor, stated to be a great marsh overgrown with tall reeds and having a length of 75 miles and width of 15 miles.[1] Bostang-nor, said to connect with this lake, is placed on Chinese maps some 30 miles north of it. North of the Tien shan the lakes are larger and more numerous; the Dzaisang, Kisil-bash and Issik-kul are the most important. All these lakes are salt.

[1] Prejevalsky, *From Kulja Across the Tien shan to Lob-nor*, p. 99.

The whole region of Koko-nor is a country of lakes. The Oling and Dzaring are among the sources of the Yellow River; and the *Tsing hai*, or Azure Sea, better known as Koko-nor, gives its name to the province. The Tengkiri-nor in Tibet lies to the north of H'lassa, and is the largest sheet of water within the frontiers of the empire. In its neighborhood are numerous small lakes extending northward into Koko-nor. The Palti or Yamorouk is shaped like a ring, an island in its centre occupying nearly the whole surface. Ulterior Tibet possesses many lakes on both sides of the Gang-dis-ri range; the Yik and Paha, near Gobi, are the largest, being only two of a long row of them south of the Kwănlun range.

The Eighteen Provinces are bounded on the north-east by the colony of Shingking, from which they are separated by the line of a former palisade marking the boundary from the town of Shan-hai kwan to the Hwang ho. Following this stream to its sources in the Ĭn shan, the boundary then crosses these mountains and pursues a west and south-west course, through the territories of roving Mongol tribes, until it finds the Yellow River at the settlement of Hokiuh in Shensí. West of this the Great Wall divides the provinces of Shensí and Kansuh from the Mongolian deserts as far as the Kiayü Pass, beyond which lies the desert of Gobi, called *Peh hai* (North Sea) and *Hah hai* (Black Sea). On the east are the Gulf of Pechele and the Yellow Sea or *Hwang hai*, also called *Tung hai* (Eastern Sea) as far south as the Channel of Formosa. This channel and the China Sea lie on the south-east and south, as far as the Gulf of Tongking and the confines of Annam. Kwangsí and Yunnan border on Annam and Siam on their south sides, while Burmah marks the western frontier, but nearly the whole south-west and western frontiers beyond Yunnan and Sz'chuen are possessed by small tribes of uncivilized people, over whom neither the Chinese nor Burmese have much real control. Koko-nor bounds Sz'chuen and Kansuh on their western and south-western sides.

The coast of China, from Hainan to the mouth of the Yangtsz', is bordered with multitudes of islands and rocky islets; from that point northward to Liautung, the shores are low, and, except in Shantung, the coast is rendered dangerous by shoals.

South of the Pei ho, along to the end of Shantung Promontory, the coast is bolder, increasing in height after passing the Miautau Islands, though neither side of the promontory presents any point of remarkable elevation; Cape Macartney, at the eastern end, is a conspicuous bluff when approaching it from sea. From this cape to the mouth of the Tsientang River, near Chapu, a distance of about 400 miles, the coast is low, especially between the mouths of the Yangtsz' and Yellow rivers, and has but few good harbors. Quicksands in the regions near these rivers and the Bay of Hangchau render the navigation dangerous to native junks. From Kitto Point, near Ningpo, down to Hongkong, the shores assume a bolder aspect, and numerous small bays and coves occur among the islands, affording safe refuge for vessels. The aspect along this part is uninviting in the extreme, consisting principally of a succession of yellowish cliffs and naked headlands, giving little promise of the highly cultivated country beyond them. This bleak appearance is caused by the rains washing the decomposed soil off the surface; the rock being granite in a state of partial and progressive disintegration, the loose soil is easily carried down into the intervals. Another reason for its treeless surface is owing to the practice of annually cutting the coarse grass for fuel, and after the crop is gathered setting the stubble on fire, in order to manure the ground for the coming year; the fire and thinness of the soil together effectually prevent any large growth of trees or shrubbery upon the hills.

The estuary of the Pearl River from the Bocca Tigris down to the Grand Ladrones, a distance of 70 miles, and from Hongkong westerly to the Island of Tungku, about 100 miles, is interspersed with islands. The strait which separates Hainan from the Peninsula of Luichau has been supposed to be the place called by Arabian travellers in the ninth century the Gates of China, but that channel was probably near the Chusan Archipelago. That group of fertile islands is regarded as the broken termination of the continental range of mountains running through Chehkiang.

The Island of Formosa, or Taiwan, connects the islands of Japan and Lewchew with Luçonia. Between Formosa and the coast lie the Pescadores or Panghu Islands, a group much less in extent and number than the Chusan Islands. The Chinese have itineraries of all the places, headlands, islands, etc., along the entire coast, but they do not afford much information respecting the names of positions.[1]

The first objects that invite attention in the general aspect of China Proper are the Great Plain in the north-east, and the three longitudinal basins into which the country is divided by mountain chains running east and west.[2] The three great rivers which drain these basins flow through them very irregularly, but by means of their main trunks and the tributaries, water communication is easily kept up, not only from west to east along the great courses, but also across the country. These natural facilities for inland navigation have been greatly improved by the people, but they still, in most cases, await the introduction of steam to assist them in stemming the rapid currents of some of their rivers, and bringing distant places into more frequent communication.

The whole surface of China may be conveniently divided into the mountainous and hilly country and the Great Plain. The mountainous country comprehends more than half of the whole, lying west of the meridian of 112° or 114° (nearly that of Canton), quite to the borders of Tibet. The hilly portion is that south of the Yangtsz' kiang and east of this meridian, comprising the provinces of Fuhkien, Kiangsí, Kwangtung, and sections of Hunan and Hupeh. The Great Plain lies in the north-east, and forms the richest part of the empire.

This Plain extends in length 700 miles from the Great Wall and Barrier Range north of Peking to the confluence of Poyang Lake with the Yangtsz' in Kiangsí, lat. 30° N. The latter river is considered as its southern boundary as far down

---

[1] *Chinese Repository*, Vol. V., p. 337; Vol. X., pp. 351, 371. Williams' *Chinese Commercial Guide*, fifth edition, second part, 1863.

[2] Rémusat (*Nouveaux Mélanges*, Tome I., p. 9) adds a fourth basin, that of the Sagalien. The latter, however, scarcely deserves the name, having so many interrupting cross-chains.

as Nganking in Nganhwui, whence to the sea it is formed by a line drawn nearly east through Hangchau. The western boundary may be marked by a line drawn from Kingchau in Hupeh (lat. 30° 36′), nearly north to Hwaiking, on the Yellow River, and thence due north to the Great Wall, 50 miles north-west of Peking. The breadth varies. North of lat. 35°, where it partly extends to the Yellow Sea, and partly borders on the western side of Shantung, thence across to the Bear Mountains and Shansí, its measure is between 150 and 250 miles; stating the average at 200 miles, this portion has an area of 70,000 square miles. Between 34° and 35° the Plain enlarges, and in the parallel of the Yellow River has a breadth of some 300 miles from east to west; while further south, along the course of the Yangtsz', it reaches nearly 400 miles inland. Estimating the mean breadth of this portion at 400 miles, there are 140,000 square miles, which, with the northern part, make an area of about 210,000 square miles—a surface seven times as large as that of Lombardy, and about the same area as the plain of Bengal drained by the Ganges. The northern portion in Chihlí up to the edge of the Plateau is mostly a deposit of the yellow loess and alluvial on the river bottoms; that lying near the coast in Kiangsu is low and swampy, covered by lakes and intersected by water-courses. This portion is extremely fertile, and furnishes large quantities of silk, tea, cotton, grain, and tobacco. The most interesting feature of this Plain is the enormous population it supports, which is, according to the census of 1812, not less than 177 millions of human beings, if the whole number of inhabitants contained in the six provinces lying wholly or partly in it be included; making it by far the most densely settled of any part of the world of the same size, and amounting to nearly two-thirds of the whole population of Europe.[1]

The public works of China are probably unequalled in any land or by any people, for the amount of human labor bestowed upon them; the natural aspect of the country has been

---

[1] *Penny Cyclopædia*, Vol. VII., p. 74. McCulloch's *Geographical Dictionary*, Vol. I., p. 596.

materially changed by them, and it has been remarked that the Great Wall is the only artificial structure which would arrest attention in a hasty survey of the surface of the globe. But their usefulness, or the science exhibited in their construction, is far inferior to their extent. The Great Wall, called *Wan-lí Chang Ching* (*i.e.*, Myriad-mile Wall), was built by Tsin Chí-hwangtí, in order to protect his dominions from the incursions of the northern tribes. Some portions of it were already in existence, and he formed the plan of joining and extending them along the whole northern frontier to guard it. It was finished B.C. 204, having been ten years in building, seven of which were done after the Emperor's death. This gigantic work was probably a popular one in the main, and still remains as its own chief evidence of the energy, industry, and perseverance of its builders, as well as their unwisdom and waste. Its construction probably cost less than the usual sums spent by European States for their standing armies. It commences at Shanhai wei or Shanhai kwan (lat. 40°, long. 119° 50′), a coast town of some importance as on the boundary between Chihlí and Shingking, and a place of considerable trade. Lord Jocelyn describes the wall, when observed from the ships, as "scaling the precipices and topping the craggy hills of the country, which have along this coast a most desolate appearance."

It runs along the shore for several miles, and terminates on the beach near a long reef. Its course from this point is west, a little northerly, along the old frontiers of the province of Chihlí, and then in Shansí, till it strikes the Yellow River, in lat. 39½° and long. 111½°. This is the best built part, and contains the most important gates, where garrisons and trading marts are established. Within the province of Chihlí there are two walls, inclosing a good part of the basin of the Sangkan ho west of Peking; the inner one was built by an emperor of the Ming dynasty. From the point where it strikes the Yellow River, near Pau-teh, it forms the northern boundary of Shensí, till it touches that stream again in lat. 37°, inclosing the country of the Ortous Mongols. Its direction from this point is north-west along the northern frontier of Kansuh to its termination near Kiayü kwan, through which the road passes leading to Hami.

From near the eastern extremity of the Wall in the province of Chihlí, extending in a north-easterly direction, there was once a wooden stockade or palisade, forming the boundary between Liautung and Kirin, which has been often taken from its representation on maps as a continuation of the Great Wall. It was erected by the Manchus, but has long since become decayed and disused.

The entire length of the Great Wall between its extremities is 22½ degrees of latitude, or 1,255 miles in a straight line; but its turnings and doublings increase it to fully 1,500 miles. It would stretch from Philadelphia to Topeka, or from Portugal to Naples, on nearly the same latitude. The construction of this gigantic work is somewhat adapted to the nature of the country it traverses, and the material was taken or made on the spot where it was used. In the western part of its course, it is in some places merely a mud or gravel wall, and in others earth cased with brick.

The eastern part is generally composed of earth and pebbles faced with large bricks, weighing from 40 to 60 lbs. each, supported on a coping of stone. The whole is about 25 feet thick at the base, and 15 feet at the top, and varying from 15 to 30 feet high; the top is protected with bricks, and defended by a slight parapet, the thinness of which has been taken as proof that cannon were unknown at the time it was erected. There are brick towers at different intervals, some of them more than 40 feet high, but not built upon the Wall. These are independent structures, usually about 40 feet square at the base, diminishing to 30 at the top; at particular spots the towers are of two stories.

The impression left upon the mind of a foreigner, on seeing this monument of human toil and unremunerative outlay, is respect for a people that could in any manner build it. Standing on the peak at *Ku-peh Kau* (Old North Gate), one sees the cloud-capped towers extending away over the declivities in single files both east and west, until dwarfed by miles and miles of skyward perspective as they dwindle into minute piles, yet stand with solemn stillness where they were stationed twenty centuries ago, as though condemned to wait the march of time till their builders returned. The crumbling dike at their feet may be followed, winding, leaping across gorges, defiles, and steeps, now buried in some chasm, now scaling the cliffs and slopes, in very exuberance of power and wantonness, as it vanishes in a thin, shadowy line, at the horizon. Once seen, the Great Wall of China can never be forgotten.

At present this remarkable structure is simply a geographical boundary, and except at the Gates nothing is done to keep it in repair. Beyond the Yellow River to its western extremity, the Great Wall, according to Gerbillon, is mostly a mound of earth or gravel, about fifteen feet in height, with only occasional towers of brick, or gateways made of stone. At Kalgan portions of it are made of porphyry and other stones piled up in a pyramidal form between the brick towers, difficult to cross but easy enough to pull down. The appearance of this rampart at Ku-peh kau is more imposing; the entire extent of the main and cross walls in sight from one of the towers there is over twenty miles. In one place it runs over a peak 5,225 feet high, where it is so steep as to make one wonder as much at the labor of erecting it on such a cliff as on the folly of supposing it could be of any use there as a defence. The wall is most visited at Nan-kau (South Gate), in the Ku-yung Pass, a remarkable Thermopylæ fifteen miles in length, which leads from the Plain at Peking up to the first terrace above it, and at one time was guarded by five additional walls and gates, now all in ruins. From this spot, the wall reaches across Shansí, and was built at a later period.

The other great public work is the Grand Canal, or *Chah ho* (*i.e.*, river of Flood-gates), called also *Yun ho* or 'Transit River,' an enterprise which reflects far more credit upon the monarchs who devised and executed it, than does the Great Wall, and if the time in which it was dug, and the character of the princes who planned it, be considered, few works can be mentioned in the history of any country more admirable and useful. When it was in order, before the inflow of the Yellow River failed, by means of its connection with its feeders, an uninterrupted water communication across the country from Peking to Canton existed, and goods and passengers passed from the capital to nearly every large town in the basins of the two great rivers. The canal was designed by Kublai to reach from his own capital as far as Hangchau, the former capital of the Sung dynasty, and cannot be better described than in Marco Polo's language: "You must understand that the Emperor has caused a water communication to be made from this city [Kwa-chau] to Cambaluc, in the shape of a wide and deep channel dug between stream and stream, between lake and lake, forming as it were a great river on which large vessels can ply."[1] The northern end is a channel fourteen miles long, from Tung-chau up to Peking, which, passing under the city walls, finishes its course of some 600 miles at the palace wall, close by the British Legation; here it is called *Yu ho*, or 'Imperial River,' but all boats now unlade at the eastern gate. An abridged account of Davis's observations[2] will afford a good idea of its construction and appearance.

"Early on the 23d September, we entered the canal through two stone piers and between very high banks. The mounds of earth in the immediate vicinity were evidently for the purpose of effecting repairs, which, to judge from the vestiges of inundation on either side, could not be infrequent. The canal joins the Yu ho, which we had just quitted, on its eastern bank, as that river flows towards the Pei ho. One of the most striking features of the canal is the comparative clearness of its waters, when contrasted with that of the two rivers on which we had hitherto travelled; a circumstance reasonably attributable to the depositions occasioned by the greater stillness of its contents. The course of the canal at this point was evidently in the bed of a natural river, as might be perceived from its winding course, and the irregularity and inartificial appearance of its banks. The stone abutments and flood-gates are for the purpose of regulating its waters, which at present were in excess and flowing out of it. As we proceeded on the canal, the stone flood-gates or sluices occurred

---

[1] Yule's *Marco Polo*, Vol. II., p. 136. [2] *Sketches of China*, Vol. I., p. 245.

at the rate of three or four a day, sometimes oftener, according as the inequalities in the surface of the country rendered them necessary. . . . . .

"As we advanced, the canal in some parts became narrower, and the banks had rather more of an artificial appearance than where we first entered it, being occasionally pretty high; but still the winding course led to the inference, that as yet the canal was for the most part only a natural river, modified and regulated by sluices and embankments. The distance between the stone piers in some of the flood-gates was apparently so narrow as only just to admit the passage of our largest boats. The contrivance for arresting the course of the water through them was extremely simple; stout boards, with ropes fastened to each end, were let down edgewise over each other through grooves in the stone piers. A number of soldiers and workmen always attended at the sluices, and the danger to the boats was diminished by coils of rope being hung down at the sides to break the force of blows. The slowness of our progress, which for the last week averaged only twenty miles a day, gave us abundant leisure to observe the country. . . . .

"We now began to make better progress on the canal than we had hitherto done. The stream, though against us, was not strong, except near the sluices, where it was confined. In the afternoon we stopped at Kai-ho chin (*i.e.*, River-opening mart), so called, perhaps, because the canal was commenced near here. On the 28th we arrived at the influx of the Yun ho, where the stream turned in our favor, and flowed to the southward, being the highest point of the canal, and a place of some note. The Yun ho flows into the canal on its eastern side nearly at right angles, and a part of its waters flow north and part south, while a strong facing of stone on the western bank sustains the force of the influx. At this point is the temple of the Dragon King, or genius of the watery element, who is supposed to have the canal in his special keeping. This enterprise of leading in this river seems to have been the work of Sung Lí, who lived under Hungwu, the first emperor of the Ming dynasty, about 1375. In his time, a part of the canal in Shantung became so impassable that the coasting passage by sea began to be most used. This was the very thing the canal had been intended to prevent; Sung accordingly adopted the plan of an old man named Píying, to concentrate the waters of the Yun ho and neighboring streams, and bring them down upon the canal as they are at present. History states that Sung employed 300,000 men to carry the plan into operation, and that the work was completed in seven months. On both sides of us, nearly level with the canal, were extensive swamps with a shallow covering of water, planted with the Nelumbium; they were occasionally separated by narrow banks, along which the trackers walked, and the width of the canal sometimes did not exceed twenty-five yards. On reaching the part which skirts the Tu-shan Lake, the left bank was entirely submerged, and the canal confounded with the lake. All within sight was swamp, coldness, and desolation—in fact, a vast inland sea, as many of the large boats at a distance were hull down. The swamps on the following day were kept out of sight by some decent villages on the high banks, which from perpetual accumulation assumed in some places the aspect of hills.

"A part of our journey on the first of October lay along a portion of the canal where the banks, particularly to the right, were elaborately and thoroughly faced with stone; a precaution which seemed to imply a greater than ordinary danger from inundations. In fact, the lakes, or rather floods, seemed to extend at present nearly to the feet of the mountains which lay at a distance on our left. We were now approaching that part of China which is exposed to the disastrous overflowings of the Yellow River, a perpetual source of wasteful expenditure to the government, and of peril and calamity to the people; it well deserves the name of China's Sorrow. We observed the repairs of the banks diligently proceeding under the superintendence of the proper officer. For this purpose they use the natural soil in combination with the thick stalks of the gigantic millet."

The canal reaches the Yellow River about 70 miles from its mouth; but before leaving the lakes in the southern part of Shantung, it used to run nearly parallel with that stream for more than a hundred miles, and between it and the New Salt River during a good part of this distance. It is hard to understand how, by natural causes, so powerful a river, as it is described to be by the historians of both the British embassies less than one hundred years ago, should have become so completely choked up. The difference of level near Kaifung is found to be so very little that the siltage there has been enough to turn the current into the river Wei and elsewhere. When Amherst's embassy passed, the boats struck right across the stream, and gained the opposite bank, about three-fourths of a mile distant, in less than an hour. They drifted about two miles down, and then slowly brought up against the current to the spot where the canal entered. This opening was a sluice nearly a hundred yards across, and through it the waters rushed into the river like a mill-race; the banks were constructed of earth, strengthened with sorghum stalks, and strongly bound with cordage. Sir John Davis remarks, with the instinct of a tradesman, as he commends the perseverance and industry which had overcome these obstacles, that if the science of a Brunel could be allowed to operate on the Yellow River and Grand Canal, "a benefit might be conferred on the Chinese that would more than compensate for all the evil that we have inflicted with our opium and our guns." The boats were dragged through and up the sluice close to the bank by ropes communicating with large windlasses worked on the bank, which safely, though slowly, brought them into still water.

The distance between the Yellow and Yangtsz' rivers is about ninety miles, and the canal here is carried largely upon a raised work of earth, kept together by retaining walls of stone, and not less that twenty feet above the surrounding country in some parts. This sheet of water is about two hundred feet wide, and its current nearly three miles an hour. South of the Hwang ho several large towns stand near the levees, below their level, whose safety wholly depends upon the care taken of the banks of the canal. Hwai-ngan and Pauying lie thus under and near them, in such a position as to cause an involuntary shudder at the thought of the destruction which would take place if they should give way. The level descends from these towns to the Yangtsz', and at Yangchau the canal is much below the houses on its sides. It also connects with every stream or lake whose waters can be led into it. There are two or three inlets into the Yangtsz' where the canal reaches the northern bank, but Chinkiang, on the southern shore, is regarded as the principal defence and post of its crossing. The canal leaves the river east of that city, proceeds south-east to Suchau, and thence southerly on the eastern side of lake Tai, with which it communicates, to Hangchau in Chehkiang. This portion is by far the most interesting and picturesque of the whole line, owing to its rich and populous cities, the fertility and high cultivation of the banks, and the lively aspect imparted by the multitude of boats. Though Kublai has had the credit of this useful work, it existed in parts of its course long before his day. The reach between the two great rivers was opened in the Han dynasty, and repaired by the wise founder of the Sui dynasty (A.D. 600). The princes of the Tang dynasty kept it open, and when the Sung emperors lived at Hangchau they made the extension up to Chinkiang the great highway which it is to this day. The work from Peking to the Yellow River was opened by the Mongols about 1289, in which they merely joined the rivers and lakes to each other as they now exist. The Ming and Tsing emperors have done all they could to keep it open throughout, and lately an attempt has been made to reopen the passage from Hungtsih Lake north into the old bed, so that boats can reach Tientsin from Kwachau. Its entire length is about 650 miles, or not quite twice that of the Erie Canal, but it varies in its breadth and depth more than any important canal either of America or Europe.

As a work of art, compared with canals now existing in western countries, the Transit River does not rank high; but even at this day there is no work of the kind in Asia which can compare with it, and there was none in the world equal to it when first put in full operation. It passes through alluvial soil in every part of its course, and the chief labor was expended in constructing embankments, and not in digging a deep channel. The junction of the Yun ho, about lat. 36° N., was probably taken as the summit level. From this point northward the trench was dug through to Lintsing to join the Yu ho, and embankments thrown up from the same place southward to the Yellow River, the whole being a line of two hundred miles. In some places the bed is cut down thirty, forty, and even seventy feet, but it encountered no material obstacle. The sluices which keep the necessary level are of rude construction, and thick planks, sliding in grooves hewn in stone buttresses, form the only locks. Still, the objects intended are all fully gained, and the simplicity of the means certainly does not derogate from the merit and execution of the plan.[1]

There are some other inferior canals in the empire. Kienlung constructed a waste-weir for carrying off the surplus waters of the Yellow River of about a hundred miles in length, by cutting a canal from Ifung hien in Honan, to one of the principal affluents of lake Hungtsih. It also answered as a drain for the marshy land in that part, and has probably recently served to convey the floods from the main stream into the lake. In the vicinity of Canton and Suchau are many channels cut through the plains, which serve both for irrigation and navigation, but they are not worthy the name of canals. Similar conveniences are more or less frequently met with in all parts of the provinces, notably those on the Plain and low coast-lands.

The public roads, in a country so well provided with navigable streams, are of minor consequence, but these media of travel are not neglected. "I have travelled near 600 leagues by land in China," observes De Guignes, "and have found many good roads, most of them wide and planted with trees. They are not usually paved, and consequently in rainy weather are either channelled by the water or covered with mud, and in dry weather so dusty that travellers are obliged to wear spectacles to protect their eyes. In Kwangtung transportation is performed almost wholly by water, the only roads being across the lines of navigation. The pass across the Mei ling is paved or filled up with stones; at Kih-ngan, in Kiangsí, are paved roads in good condition, but beyond the Yangtsz', in Nganhwui, they were

---

[1] Klaproth, *Mémoires*, Tome III., p. 312 *sqq*. De Guignes' *Voyages à Peking*, Tome II., p. 195. Davis's *Sketches*, Vol. I., *passim*.

almost impracticable, but became better as we proceeded northward, and in many places had trees on both sides. Beyond the Hwang ho they were broader, and we saw crowds of travellers, carts, mules, and horses. In Shantung and Chihlí they were generally broad and shady, and very dusty. This is, no doubt, disagreeable, but we went smoothly over these places, while in the villages and towns we were miserably jolted on the pavements. I hope, for the sake of those who may come after me, that the Chinese will not pave their roads before they improve their carriages. Some of the thoroughfares leading to Peking are paved with thick slabs of stone. One feature of the roads through the northern provinces which attracts attention is the great number that lie below the level of the country. It is caused by the wind sweeping along them, and carrying over

A Road-Cut in the Loess.

the fields the dust made and raised by the carts. As soon as the pools left by the rains dry enough to let the carts pass, the earth is reduced to powder; as the winds sweep through the passage and clear it out, the process in a few years cuts a defile through the loam often fifteen feet deep, which impedes travel by its narrow gauge, hindering the carts as they meet. The banks are protected by revetment walls or turf, if necessary. Those near Hangchau, and the great road leading from Chehkiang into Kiangsí, are all in good condition. Generally speaking, however, as is the case with most things in China, the roads are not well repaired, and large holes are frequently allowed to remain unfilled in the path, to the great danger of those who travel by night."[1]

Mountain passes have been cut for facilitating the transit of goods and people over the high ranges in many parts of the empire. The great road leading from Peking south-west through Shansí and Shensí, and thence to Sz'chuen, is carried across the Peh ling and the valley of the river Hwai by a mountain road, "which, for the difficulties it presents and the art and labor with which they have been overcome, does not appear to be inferior to the road over the Simplon."[2] At one place on this route, called Lí-nai, a passage has been cut through the rock, and steps hewn on both sides of the mountain from its base to the summit. The passage across the peak being only wide enough for one sedan, the guards are perched in little houses placed on poles over the pass. This road was in ancient times the path to the metropolis, and these immense excavations were made from time to time by different monarchs. The pass over the Mei ling, at Nan-ngan, is a work of later date, and so are most of the other roads across this range in Fuhkien and Kwangtung.

The general aspect of the country is perhaps as much modi-

---

[1] *Voyages à Peking*, Vol. II., p. 214. Compare the letter of a Jesuit missionary (*Annales de la Foi*, Tome VII., p. 377), who describes houses of rest on the wayside. These singular road-gullies of the loess region have been very thoroughly examined by Baron von Richthofen, from whose work the cut above is taken.

[2] *Penny Cyclopædia*, Vol. XXVII., p. 656.

fied by labor of man in China as in England, but the appearance of a landscape in the two kingdoms is unlike. Whenever water is available, streams are led upon the rice fields, and this kind of cultivation allows few or no trees to grow in the plats. Such fields are divided by raised banks, which serve for pathways across the marshy enclosure, and assist in confining the water when let in upon the growing crop. The bounds of other fields are denoted by stones or other landmarks, and the entire absence of walls, fences, or hedgerows, makes a cultivated plain appear like a vast garden.

The greatest sameness exists in all the cities. A wall encloses all towns above a *sz'* or township, and the suburbs are not unfrequently larger than their enceinte. The streets in large towns south of the Hwang ho are paved, and the sewers run under the cross slabs. What filth is not in them is generally in the street, as these drains easily become choked. The roadways are not usually over ten feet wide, but the low houses on each side make them appear less like alleys than would be the case in western cities. Villages have a pleasant appearance at a distance, usually embowered among trees, between which the whitewashed houses look prettily; but on entering them one is disappointed at their irregularity, dirtiness, and generally decayed look. The gardens and best houses are mostly walled in from sight, while the precincts of temples are the resort of idlers, beggars, and children, with a proportion of pigs and dogs.

Elegance or ornament, orderly arrangement and grandeur of design, cleanliness, or comfort, as these terms are applied in Europe, are almost unknown in Chinese houses, cities, or gardens. Commanding or agreeable situations are chosen for temples and monasteries, which are not only the abode of priests but serve for inns, theatres, and other purposes. The terrace cultivation sometimes renders the acclivities of hills beautiful in the highest degree, but it does not often impart a distinguishing feature to the landscape. A lofty solitary pagoda, an extensive temple shaded by trees in the opening of a vale, a commemorative *pai-lau*, or boats moving in every direction through narrow creeks or on broad streams, are some of the peculiar lineaments of Chinese scenery. No imposing mansions with beautiful grounds are found on the skirts of a town, for the people huddle together in hamlets and villages for mutual aid and security. No tapering spires pointing out the rural church, nor towers, pillars, domes, or steeples in the cities, indicating buildings of public utility, rise upon the low level of dun-tiled roofs. No meadows or pastures, containing herds and flocks, are visible from the hill-tops in China; nor are coaches or railroad cars observed hurrying across its landscapes. Steamers have just begun to course through some of its rivers, and disturb, by their whistles and wheels, the drowsy silence of past ages and the slow progress of unwieldy junks—the other changes have yet to come.

The condition and characteristics of the various families of man inhabiting this great empire, render its study far more interesting than anything relating to its physical geography or public works. The Chinese forms the leading family, but the Miaotsz', the Li-mu, the Kakyens, and other aborigines in the southern provinces, the Manchus, the Mongols, and various Tartar tribes, the Tibetans, and certain wild races in Kirin and Formosa, must not be overlooked. The sons of Han are indeed a remarkable race, whether regard be had to their antiquity, their numbers, their government, or their literature, and on these accounts deserve the study and respect of every intelligent student of mankind; while their unwearied industry, their general peaceableness and good humor, and their attainments in domestic order and mechanical arts, commend them to the notice of every one who sees in these points of character an earnest of their future position amid the great family of civilized nations when once they shall have attained the same.

The physical traits of the Chinese may be described as being between the light and agile Hindu, and the muscular, fleshy European. Their form is well built and symmetrical; their color is a brunette or sickly white, rather approaching to a yellowish than to a florid tint, but this yellow hue has been much exaggerated; in the south they are swarthy but not black, never becoming as dark even as the Portuguese, whose fifth or sixth ancestors dwelt near the Tagus. The shades of complexion differ much according to the latitude and degree of exposure to the weather, especially in the females. The hair of the head is lank, black, coarse, and glossy; beard always black, thin, and deficient; scanty or no whiskers; and very little hair on the body. Eyes invariably black, and apparently oblique, owing to the slight degree in which the inner angles of the eyelids open, the internal canthi being more acute than in western races, and not allowing the whole iris to be seen; this peculiarity in the eye distinguishes the eastern races of Asia from all other families of man. There is a marked difference between the features of the mixed race living south of the Mei ling, and the inhabitants of the Great Plain and in Shansí or further west; the latter are the finer appearing. The hair and eyes being always black, a European with blue eyes and light hair appears strange to them; one reason given by the people of Canton for calling foreigners *fan kwei*, or 'foreign devils,' is, that they have sunken blue eyes, and red hair like demons.

The cheek-bones are high, and the outline of the face remark ably round. The nose is rather small, much depressed, nearly even with the face at the root, and wide at the extremity; there is, however, considerable difference in this respect, but no aquiline noses are seen. Lips thicker than among Europeans, but not at all approaching those of the negro. The hands are small, and the lower limbs better proportioned than among any other Asiatics. The height of those living north of the Yangtsz' is about the same as that of Europeans. A thousand men taken as they come in the streets of Canton, will hardly equal in stature and weight the same number in Rome or New Orleans, while they would, perhaps, exceed these, if gathered in Peking; their muscular powers, however, would probably be less in either Chinese city than in those of Europe or America.

In size, the women are smaller than European females; and in the eyes of those accustomed to the European style of beauty, the Chinese women possess little; the broad upper face, low nose, and linear eyes, being quite the contrary of handsome. Nevertheless, the Chinese face is not destitute of beauty, and when animated with good humor and an expressive eye, and lighted by the glow of youth and health, the features lose much of their repulsiveness. Nor do they fade so soon and look as ugly and withered when old as some travellers say, but are in respect to bearing children and keeping their vigor, more like Europeans than the Hindus or Persians.

The mountainous regions in Yunnan, Kwangsí, and Kweichau, give lodgement to many clans of the Miaotsz' or "children of the soil," as the words may be rendered. It is singular that any of these people should have maintained their independence so long, when so large a portion of them have partially submitted to Chinese rule. Those who will not are called *săng Miaotsz'*, *i.e.*, wild or 'unsubdued,' while the others are termed *shuh* or 'subdued.' They present so many physical points of difference as to lead one to infer that they are a more ancient race than the Chinese around them, and the aborigines of Southern China. They are rather smaller in size and stature, have shorter necks, and their features are somewhat more angular. They are divided into many tribes, and have been described by Chinese travellers, who have illustrated their habits by paintings and sketches, from which a good idea can be obtained of their condition. Dr. Bridgman has translated such an account, written by a Chinese native traveller, in which he sketches the manners of eighty-two clans, especially those customs relating to worship and marriage, showing how little they have learned from their rulers or improved from the savage state. An examination of their languages shows that those of the Miaotsz' proper have strong affinities with the Siamese and Annamese, and those known as *Lolo* exhibit a decided likeness to the Burmese. The former of these are mentioned in Chinese history during 4,000 years; the latter about A.D. 250, when a Shan nation came under Chinese influence in Yunnan, and was the object of a warlike expedition. The same race still remain on the Upper Irrawadi and in Assam as Shans and Khamti, and in the basins of the Meinam and Mei-lung, all of them akin to the Tibetans and Burmese. They form together an interesting relic of the ancient peoples of the land, and further inquiries will doubtless develop something of their history and origin.[1]

[1] *Chinese Repository*, Vol. XIV., p. 105. *Shanghai Journal*, No. III., 1859. *Journal of Indian Archipelago*, 1852. *Missionary Recorder*, Vol. III., pp. 33, 62, 149, etc. T. T. Cooper, *Travels of a Pioneer of Commerce*, passim.

An aboriginal race—the *Li-mu*—exists in the centre of Hainan, an offset from the Miaotsz', judging by the little that is known of their language. The natives of Formosa seem to have more affinity with their neighbors in Luzon and southward than with the Chinese.

The Mongol and Manchu races have been considered as springing from the same stock, but during centuries of separation under different circumstances they have altered much. The Mongols are essentially a nomadic race, while the Manchus are an agricultural or a hunting people, according to the part of their country they inhabit. The Manchus are of a lighter complexion and somewhat larger than the Chinese, have the same conformation of the eyelids, but rather more beard, while their countenances indicate greater intellectual capacity. They seem to partake of both the Mongol and Chinese character, possessing more determination and largeness of plan than the latter, with much of the rudeness and haughtiness of the former. They have fair, if not florid, complexions, straight noses, and, in a few cases, brown hair and heavy beards. They are more allied to the Chinese, and when they ruled the northern provinces as the Kin dynasty, amalgamated with them. They may be regarded as the most improvable race in Central Asia, if not on the continent; and the skill with which they have governed the Chinese empire, and adopted a civilization higher than their own, gives promise of still further advances when they become familiar with the civilization of Christian lands.

Under the term Mongols or Moguls a great number of tribes occupying the steppes of Central Asia are comprised. They extend from the borders of the Khirgís steppe and Kokand eastward to the Sialkoi Mountains, and it is particularly to this race that the name *Tartars* or *Tatars* is applicable. No such word is now known among the people, except as an ignominious epithet, by the Chinese, who usually write it with two characters—*tah-tsz'*—meaning 'trodden-down people.' Klaproth confines the appellation of *Tartars* to the Mongols, Kalmucks, Kalkas, Eleuths, and Buriats, while the Kirghís, Usbecks, Cossacks, and Turks are of Kurdish and *Turkoman* origin.

The Mongol tribes generally are a stout, squat, swarthy, ill-favored race of men, having high and broad shoulders, short, broad noses, pointed and prominent chins, long teeth distant from each other, eyes black, elliptical, and unsteady, thick, short necks, extremities bony and nervous, muscular thighs, but short legs, with a stature nearly or quite equal to the European. They have a written language, but their literature is limited and mostly religious. The same language is spoken by all the tribes, with slight variations and only a small admixture of foreign words. Most of the accounts of their origin, their wars, and their habits, were written by foreigners living or travelling among them; but they themselves, as McCulloch remarks, know as little of these things as rats or marmots do of their descent. Yet it is not so easy to find the typical Mongol among the medley of nationalities in their towns. A crowd in a town like Yarkand exhibits all the varieties of the human race. The gaunt, almost beardless Manchu, with sunken eyes, high cheek-bones, and projecting jowl, contrasts with the smooth face, pinky yellow, oblique eye, flat cheeks, and rounded jowl of the Chinese. The bearded, sallow Toork, the angular, rosy Kirghís, the coarse, hard Dungani, and thick-lipped, square-faced Eleuth, all show poorly with the tall, handsome Cashmerian, the swarthy Badakshi, and robust, intelligent Uzbek. The fate of the vast swarms of this race which have descended from the table-land of Central Asia and overrun, in different ages, the plains of India, China, Syria, Egypt, and Eastern Europe, and the rise and fall of the gigantic empire they themselves erected under Genghis in the eleventh and twelfth centuries, are among the most remarkable episodes in the world's history. They have always maintained the same character in their native wilds, their conquests have been exterminations rather than subjugations, their history a record of continual quarrels between clans.

The last of the five races is the Tibetan, who partake of the physical characteristics of the Mongols and Hindus. They are short, squat, and broad-shouldered in body, with angular faces, wide, high cheek-bones, small black eyes, and scant beard. They are mild in disposition, have a stronger religious feeling than the Chinese, and have never left their own highlands either for emigration or conquest. Their civilization is fully equal to that of the Siamese and Burmese, and life and property are more secure with them than among their turbulent neighbors in Butan, Lahore, or Cabul.

It will be seen from this short survey that a full account of the geography, government, manners, literature, and civilization of so large a part of the world and its inhabitants requires the combined labors of many observers, all of them well acquainted with the languages and institutions of the people whom they describe. No one will look, therefore, for more than a brief outline of these subjects in the present work, minute enough, however, to enable readers to form a fair opinion of the people. It is the *industry* of the Chinese which has given them their high place among the nations of the earth. Not only has the indigenous vegetation been superseded wherever culture would remunerate toil, but lofty hills have been tilled and terraced almost to their tops, cities have been built upon them, and extensive ranges of wall erected along their summits. They practise all the industrial arts whose objects are to feed, clothe, educate or adorn mankind, and maintain the largest population ever united under one system of rule. Ten centuries ago they were the most civilized nation on earth, and the incredulity manifested in Europe, five hundred years ago, at the recitals of Marco Polo regarding their condition, is the counterpart of the sentiments now expressed by the Chinese when they hear of the power and grandeur of western nations.

Isolated by natural boundaries from other peoples, their civilization, developed under peculiar influences, must be compared to, rather than judged of, by European. A people from whom some of the most distinguishing inventions of modern Europe came (such as the compass, porcelain, gunpowder, and printing), and were known and practised many centuries earlier; who probably amount to more than three hundred millions, united in one system of manners, letters, and polity; whose cities and capitals rival in numbers the greatest metropoles of any age; who have not only covered the earth, but the waters, with towns and streets—such a nation must occupy a conspicuous place in the history of mankind, and the study of their character and condition commend itself to every well-wisher of his race.

It has been too much the custom of writers to overlook the influence of the Bible upon modern civilization; but when a comparison is to be drawn between European and Asiatic civilization, this element forces itself upon the attention as the main cause of the superiority of the former. It is not the civilization of luxury or of letters, of arts or of priestcraft; it is not the spirit of war, the passion for money, nor its exhibitions in trade and the application of machinery, that render a nation permanently great and prosperous. "Christianity is the summary of all civilization," says Chenevix; "it contains every argument which could be urged in its support, and every precept which explains its nature. Former systems of religion were in conformity with luxury, but this alone seems to have been conceived for the region of civilization. It has flourished in Europe, while it has decayed in Asia, and the most civilized nations are the most purely Christian." Christianity is essentially the religion of the people, and when it is covered over with forms and contracted into a priesthood, its vitality goes out; this is one reason why it has declined in Asia. The attainments of the Chinese in the arts of life are perhaps as great as they can be without this spring of action, without any other motives to industry, obedience, and morality, than the commands or demands of the present life.

A survey of the world and its various races in successive ages leads one to infer that God has some plan of national character, and that one nation exhibits the development of one trait, while another race gives prominence to another, and subordinates the first. Thus the Egyptian people were eminently a priestly race, devoted to science and occult lore; the Greeks developed the imaginative powers, excelling in the fine arts; the Romans were warlike, and the embodiment of force and law; the Babylonians and Persians magnificent, like the head of gold in Daniel's vision; the Arabs predacious, volatile, and imaginative; the Turks stolid, bigoted, and impassible; the Hindus are contemplative, religious, and metaphysical; the Chinese industrious, peaceful, literary, atheistic, and self-contained.[1] The same religion, and constant intercommunication among European nations, has assimilated them more than these other races ever could have become; but every one knows the national peculiarities of the Spaniards, Italians, French, English, etc., and how they are maintained, notwithstanding the motives to imitation and coalescence. The comparison of national character and civilization, with the view of ascertaining such a plan, is a subject worthy the profound study of any scholar, and one which would offer new views of the human race. The Chinese would be found to have attained, it is believed, a higher position in general security of life and property, and in the arts of domestic life and comfort among the mass, and a greater degree of general literary intelligence, than any other heathen or Mohammedan nation that ever existed—or indeed than some now calling themselves Christian, as Abyssinia. They have, however, probably done all they can do, reached as high a point as they can without the Gospel; and its introduction, with its attendant influences, will erelong change their political and social system. The rise and progress of this revolution among so mighty a mass of human beings will form one of the most interesting parts of the history of the world during the nineteenth century, and solve the problem whether it be possible to elevate a race without the intermediate steps of disorganization and reconstruction.

---

[1] For observations on the Chinese as compared with other nations, see Schlegel's *Philosophy of History*, p. 118, Bohn's edition.

CHAPTER II.

GEOGRAPHICAL DESCRIPTION OF THE EASTERN PROVINCES.

THE provinces of China Proper are politically subdivided in a scientific manner, but in the regions beyond them, these divisions are considerably modified. Manchuria is regarded as belonging to the reigning family, somewhat as Hanover once pertained to the kings of England, and its scanty population is ruled by a simple military organization, the higher officials being appointed by his majesty himself. The khans of the Mongols in Mongolia and Îlí, the Mohammedan begs in Turkestan, and the lamas in Tibet, are assisted in their rule by Chinese residents and generals who direct and uphold the government.

The geography of foreign countries has not been studied by the Chinese; and so few educated men have travelled even into the islands of the Indian Archipelago, or the kingdoms of Siam, Corea, or Burmah, that the people have had no opportunity to become acquainted with the countries lying on their borders, much less with those in remoter parts, whose names, even, they hardly know. A few native works exist on foreign geography, among which four may be here noticed. "1. *Researches in the East and West*, 6 vols. 8vo. It was written about two centuries ago; the first volume contains some rude charts intended to show the situation and form of foreign countries. 2. *Notices of the Seas*, 1 vol. Its author, Yang Ping-nan, obtained his information from a townsman, who, being wrecked at sea, was picked up by a foreign ship, and travelled abroad for fourteen years; on his return to China he became blind, and was engaged as an interpreter in Macao. 3. *Notices of Things heard and seen in Foreign Countries*, 2 vols. 12mo; written about a century ago, containing among other things a chart of the whole

Chinese coast. 4. *The Memoranda of Foreign Tribes*, 4 vols. 8vo, published in the reign of Kienlung."[1] A more methodical work is that of Lí Tsing-lai, called '*Plates Illustrative of the Heavens*,' being an astronomical and geographical work, much of whose contents were obtained from Europeans residing in the country. But even if the Chinese had better treatises on these subjects, the information contained in them would be of little use until it was taught in their schools. The high officers in the government begin now to see the importance of a better acquaintance with general geography. Commissioner Lin, in 1841, published a partial translation of Murray's *Cyclopædia of Geography*, in 20 volumes; Gov. Seu Ki-yu, in 1850, issued a compend of geographical notices with maps, and many others, more accurate and extensive, are now extant.

However scarce their geographical works upon foreign countries may be, those delineating the topography of their own are hardly equalled in number and minuteness in any language: every district and town of importance in the empire, as well as every department and province, has a local geography of its own. It may be said that the topographical and statistical works form, after the ethical, the most valuable portion of Chinese literature. It would not be difficult to collect a library of 10,000 volumes of such treatises alone; the topography of the city of Suchau, and of the province of Chehkiang, are each in 40 vols., while the *Kwangtung Tung Chí*, an 'Historical and Statistical Account of Kwangtung,' is in 182 volumes. None of these works, however, would bear to be translated entire, such is the amount of legendary and unimportant matter contained in them; but they contain many data not to be overlooked by one who undertakes to write a geography of China.

The *Climate* of the Eighteen Provinces has been represented in meteorological tables sufficiently well to ascertain its general salubrity. Pestilences do not frequently visit the land, nor, as in Southern India, is it deluged with rain during one monsoon, and parched with drought during the other. The average temperature of the whole empire is lower than that of any other

[1] Bridgman's *Chinese Chrestomathy*, p. 420. Macao, 1841.

country on the same latitude, and the coast is subject to the same extremes as that of the Atlantic States in America. The isothermal line of 70° F. as the average for the year, which passes south of Canton, runs by Cairo and New Orleans, eight degrees north of it; the line of 60° F. average passes from Shanghai to Marseilles, Raleigh, St. Louis, and north of San Francisco; and the line of 50° F. average goes near Peking, thence on to Vienna, Dublin, Philadelphia, and Puget's Sound, in lat. 52°. These various lines show that while Shanghai and Peking have temperatures similar to Raleigh and Philadelphia, nearly on their own parallels, Canton is the coldest place on the globe in its latitude, and the only place within the tropics where snow falls near the sea-shore. One result of this projection of the temperate zone into the tropical is seen in the greater vigor and size of the people of the three southern provinces over any races on the same parallel elsewhere; and the productions are not so strictly tropical. The isothermal lines for the year, as given above, are not so irregular as those for winter. The line of 60° F. runs by the south of Formosa and Hongkong, to Cairo and St. Augustine, a range of nine degrees; but the winter line of 40° F. passes from Shanghai to Constantinople, Milan, Dublin, and Raleigh, ending at Puget's Sound, a range of twenty degrees. A third line of 32° for winter passes through Shantung to N. Tibet and the Black Sea, Norway, New York, and Sitka—a range of twenty-five degrees.

Peking (lat. 39° 55′ N.) exhibits a fair average of the climate in that part of the Plain. The extremes range from 104° to zero F., but the mean annual temperature is 52.3° F., or more than 9° lower than Naples; the mean winter range is 12° below freezing, or about 18° lower than that of Paris (lat. 48° 50′), and 15° lower than Copenhagen. The rainfall seldom reaches sixteen inches in a year, most of it coming in July and August; the little snow that descends remains only two or three days on the ground, and is blown away rather than melted; no one associates white with winter, but snow is earnestly prayed for as a purifier of the air against diphtheria and fevers. The winds from the Plateau cause the barometer and thermometer to fall, but the sky is clear. In the spring, as the heat increases, the winds raise the dust and sand over the country; some of these sand-storms extend even to Shanghai, carrying millions of tons of soil from its original place. The dryness of the region has apparently increased during the last century, and constant droughts destroy the trees, which by their absence increase the desiccation now going on. Frost closes the rivers for three months, and ice is cheap. After the second crops fully start in August, the autumns become mild, and till the 10th of December are calm and genial.[1]

The climate of the Plain is generally good, but near the rivers and marshy grounds along the Grand Canal, agues and bowel complaints prevail. A resident speaks of the temperature of Nanking and the region around it: "This vast Plain being only a marsh half drained, the moisture is excessive, giving rise to many strange diseases, all of them serious, and not unfrequently mortal. The climate affects the natives from other provinces, and Europeans. I have not known one of the latter who was not sick for six months or a year after his arrival. Every one who comes here must prepare himself for a tertian or quotidian. For myself, after suffering two months from a malignant fever, I had ten attacks of a malady the Chinese here call the *sand*, from the skin being covered with little blackish pimples, resembling grains of dust. It is prompt and violent in its progress, and corrupts the blood so rapidly that in a few minutes it stagnates and coagulates in the veins. The best remedy the people have is to cicatrize the least fleshy parts of the body with a copper cash. The first attack I experienced rendered all my limbs insensible in two minutes, and I expected to die before I could receive extreme unction. After recovering a little, great lassitude succeeded."[2] The monsoons form an important element in the seaside climate as far north as latitude 31°. The dry and wet seasons correspond to the north-east and south-west monsoons, assuaging the heats of summer by their cooling showers, and making the winters

[1] Compare an article in the *China Review* for September–October, 1881, by H. Fritsche: *The Amount of Rain and Snow in Peking.*

[2] *Annales de la Foi*, Tome XVI., p. 293.

bracing and healthy. Above the Formosa Channel they are less regular in the summer than in winter.

The inhabitants of Shanghai suffer from rapid changes in the autumn and spring months, and pulmonary and rheumatic complaints are common. The maximum of heat is 100° F., and the minimum 24°, but ice is not common, nor does snow remain long on the ground. The average temperature of the summer is from 80° to 93° by day, and from 60° to 75° by night; the thermometer in winter ranges from 45° to 60° by day, and from 36° to 45° by night.

Owing in some degree to the hills, the extremes are rather greater at Ningpo than Shanghai. The thermometer ranges from 24° to 107° during the twelvemonth, and changes of 20° in the course of two hours are not unusual, rendering it the most unhealthy station along the coast. There is a hot and cold season of three months each at this place. The cold is very piercing when the north-east winds set in, and fires are needed, but natives content themselves with additional clothing. The large brick beds (*kang*) common in Chihlí are not often seen. Ice forms in pools, and is gathered to preserve fish. Snow frequently falls, but does not remain long. Occasionally it covers the hills in Chehkiang for several weeks to the depth of six inches. Fuhchau and Canton lie at the base of hills, within a hundred miles of the sea-coast, and their climates exhibit greater extremes than Amoy and Hongkong. Frost and ice are common every winter at each of the former, and fires are therefore pleasant in the house. The extremes at Fuhchau are from 38° to 95°, with an average of 56° during December and 82° for August. Along this whole coast the most refreshing monsoon makes the summers very agreeable. The climate of Amoy is delightful, but its insular position renders a residence somewhat less agreeable than on the main. Here the thermometer ranges from 40° to 96° during the year, without the rapid changes of Ningpo. The heat continues longer, though assuaged by breezes from the sea.

Meteorology at Canton and its vicinity has been carefully studied; on the whole, its climate, and especially that of Macao, may be considered more salubrious than in most other places situated between the tropics. The thermometer at Canton in July and August stands on an average at 80° to 88°, and in January and February at 50° to 60°. The highest recorded observation in 1831 was 94°, in July; and the lowest, 29° in January. Ice sometimes forms in shallow vessels a line or two in thickness, but no use is made of it. A fall of snow nearly two inches deep occurred there in February, 1835, which remained on the ground three hours. Having never seen any before, the citizens hardly knew what was its proper name, some calling it *falling cotton*, and every one endeavoring to preserve a little for a febrifuge. Another similar fall occurred in the winter of 1861. Fogs are common during February and March, and the heat sometimes renders them very disagreeable, it being necessary to keep up a little fire to dry the house. Most of the rain falls in May and June, but there is nothing like the rainy season at Calcutta and Manilla in July, August, and September. The regular monsoon comes from the south-west, with frequent showers to allay the heat. In the succeeding months, northerly winds commence, but from October to January the temperature is agreeable, the sky clear, and the air invigorating. Few large cities are more healthy than Canton; no epidemics nor malaria prevail, notwithstanding the fact that much of the town is built upon piles.

The climate of Macao and Hongkong has not so great a range as Canton, from their proximity to the sea. Few cities in Asia are more salutiferous than Macao, though it has been remarked that few of the natives there attain a great age. The maximum is 90°, with an average summer heat of 84°. The minimum is 50°, and average winter weather 68°, with almost uninterrupted sunshine. Fogs are not often seen here, but on the river they prevail, being frequent at Whampoa. North-easterly gales are common in the spring and autumn, and have a noticeable periodicity of three days. The vegetation does not change its general aspect during the winter, the trees cease to grow, and the grass becomes brownish; but the stimulus of the warm moisture in March soon makes a sensible difference in the appearance of the landscape, and bright green leaves rapidly replace the old. The reputed insalubrity of Hongkong, in early days, was owing to other causes than climate, and when it became a well-built and well-drained town, its unwholesomeness disappeared. The rain-fall is greater than in Macao, owing to the attraction of the high peaks. During the rainy weather the walls of houses become damp, and if newly plastered, drip with moisture.

The Chinese consider the provinces of Kwangtung, Kwangsí, and Yunnan to be the most unhealthy of the eighteen, and for this reason employ them as places of banishment for criminals from the north-eastern districts. The central portions of the country are on some accounts the most bracing, not so liable to sudden changes as the coast, nor so cold as the western and northern districts. Sz'chuen and Kweichau are cooler than Fuhkien and Chehkiang, owing to the mountains in and upon their borders.

The marked contrast between the Chinese and American coasts in regard to rain is doubtless owing, in a great degree, to the outlying islands from Formosa to Sagalien on the former, whose high mountains arrest the clouds in their progress inland. The *Kuro-siwo*, being outside of them, allows a far greater mass of cold water between it and the shore on the Chinese, than is the case on the Atlantic coast, and renders it the colder of the two by nearly eight degrees of latitude, if isothermal lines alone are regarded. This mass of cold water, having less evaporation, deprives the maritime provinces of rain in diminishing supply as one goes north along the skirts of the Plain, until the Chang-peh shan are reached. The rains which fall in the western provinces and the slopes of the Bayan kara Mountains, coming up from the Indian Ocean during the south-west monsoon, fall in decreasing quantities as the clouds are driven north-east across the basins of the Yangtsz' and Yellow rivers. In the western part of Kansuh the humidity covers the mountains with more vegetation than further east, toward the ocean. Snow falls as late as June, and frosts occur in every month of the year. The enormous elevation of the western side of China near Tibet, the absence of an expanse of water like the great lakes, and the bareness of the mountains north of the Mei ling, account for much of this difference between the United States and China; but more extended data are needed for accurate deductions.

The fall of rain at Canton is 70 inches annually, which is the mean of sixteen years' observation. Ninety inches was registered during one of these years. Nearly one-half of the whole falls during May, June, and September. The average at Shanghai for four years was 36 inches. No observations are recorded for the valley of the Yangtsz'. Near the edge of the Plateau the rainfall averages 16 inches in the province of Chihlí, and rather more in Shansí and Shantung, where moisture is attracted by the mountains. More than three-fourths of the rain falls during the ten weeks ending August 31st. Snow seldom remains on the level over a fortnight.

The increased temperature on the southern coast during the months of June and July operates, with other causes, to produce violent storms along the seaboard, called *tyfoons*, a word derived from the Chinese *ta-fung*, or 'great wind.' These destructive tornadoes occur from Hainan to Chusan, between July and October, gradually progressing northward as the season advances, and diminishing in fury in the higher latitudes. They annually occasion great losses to the native and foreign shipping in Chinese waters, more than half the sailing ships lost on that coast having suffered in them. Happily, their fury is oftenest spent at sea, but when they occur inland, the loss of life is fearful. In August, 1862, and September 21, 1874, the deaths reported in two such storms near Canton, Hongkong, and their vicinity, were upward of 30,000 each. In the latter instance the American steamer Alaska, of 3,500 tons, was lifted from her anchorage and quietly put down in five feet of water near the shore, from whence she was safely floated some months afterward.

Tyfoons exhaust their force within a narrow track, which, in such cases as have been registered, lies in no uniform direction, other than from south to north, at a greater or less angle, along the coast. The principal phenomena indicating their approach are the direction of the wind, which commences to blow in soft zephyrs from the north, without, however, assuaging the heat or disturbing the stifling calm, and the falling barometer. The glass usually begins to fall several hours before the storm commences, and the rarefaction of the air is further shown by the heavy swell rolling in upon the beach, though the sea remains unruffled. The wind increases as it veers to the north-east, and from that point to south-east blows with the greatest force in fitful gusts. The rain falls heaviest toward the close of the gale, when the glass begins to rise. The barometer not unfrequently falls below 28 *in.* Capt. Krusenstern in 1804 records his surprise at seeing the mercury sink out of sight.

The Chinese have erected temples in Hainan to the Tyfoon Mother, a goddess whom they supplicate for protection against these hurricanes. They say "that a few days before a tyfoon comes on, a slight noise is heard at intervals, whirling round and then stopping, sometimes impetuous and sometimes slow. This is a 'tyfoon brewing.' Then fiery clouds collect in thick masses; the thunder sounds deep and heavy. Rainbows appear, now forming an unbroken curve and again separating, and the ends of the bow dip into the sea. The sea sends back a bellowing sound, and boils with angry surges; the loose rocks dash against each other, and detached sea-weed covers the water; there is a thick, murky atmosphere; the water-fowl fly about affrighted; the trees and leaves bend to the south—the tyfoon has commenced. When to it is superadded a violent rain and a frightful surf, the force of the tempest is let loose, and away fly the houses up to the hills, and the ships and boats are removed to the dry land; horses and cattle are turned heels over head, trees are torn up by the roots, and the sea boils up twenty or thirty feet, inundating the fields and destroying vegetation. This is called *tieh kü*, or an *iron whirlwind*."[1] Those remarkable gusts which annually occur in the Atlantic States, called *tornadoes*, defined as local storms affecting a thread of surface a few miles long, are unknown in China. The healthy climate of China has had much to do with the civilization of its inhabitants. No similar area in the world exceeds it for general salubrity.

The Chinese are the only people who have, by means of a

---

[1] *Chinese Repository*, Vol. VIII., p. 230; Vol. IV., p. 197. See also Fritsche's paper in *Journal of N. C. Branch Royal Asiatic Society*, No. XII., 1878, pp. 127–335; also Appendix II. in No. X., containing observations taken at Zi-ka-wei.

term added to the name of a place, endeavored to designate its relative rank. Three of the words used for this purpose, viz., *fu*, *chau*, and *hien*, have been translated as 'first,' 'second,' and 'third' rank; but this gradation is not quite correct, for the terms do not apply to the city or town alone, but to the portions of country of which it is the capital. The nature of these and other terms, and the divisions intended by them, are thus explained:

"The Eighteen Provinces are divided into *fu*, *ting*, *chau*, and *hien*. A *fu* is a large portion or department of a province, under the general control of one civil officer immediately subordinate to the heads of the provincial government. A *ting* is a division of a province smaller than a *fu*, and either like it governed by an officer immediately subject to the heads of the provincial government, or else forming a subordinate part of a *fu*. In the former case it is called *chih-lí*, *i.e.* under the 'direct rule' of the provincial government; in the latter case it is simply called *ting*. A *chau* is a division similar to a *ting*, and like it either independent of any other division, or forming part of a *fu*. The difference between the two consists in the government of a *ting* resembling that of a *fu* more nearly than that of a *chau* does: that of the *chau* is less expensive. The *ting* and *chau* of the class to which the term *chih-lí* is attached, may be denominated in common with the *fu*, *departments* or *prefectures;* and the term *chih-lí* may be rendered by the word *independent*. The subordinate *ting* and *chau* may both be called *districts*. A *hien*, which is also a *district*, is a small division or subordinate part of a department, whether of a *fu*, or of an independent *chau* or *ting*.

"Each *fu*, *ting*, *chau*, and *hien*, possesses at least one walled town, the seat of its government, which bears the same name as the department or district to which it pertains. Thus Hiangshan is the chief town of the district Hiangshan hien; and Shauking, that of the department Shauking fu. By European writers, the chief towns of the *fu* or departments have been called cities of the first order; those of the *chau*, cities of the second order; and those of the *hien*, cities of the third order. The division called *ting*, being rarely met with, has been left out of the arrangement—an arrangement not recognized in China. It must be observed that the chief town of a *fu* is always also the chief town of a *hien* district; and sometimes, when of considerable size and importance, it and the country around are divided into two *hien* districts, both of which have the seat of their government within the same walls: but this is not the case with the *ting* and *chau* departments. A district is not always subdivided; instances may occur of a whole district possessing but one important town. But as there are often large and even walled towns not included in the number of chief or of district towns, consequently not the seat of a regular *chau* or *hien* magistracy, a subdivision of a district is therefore frequently rendered necessary; and for the better government of such towns and the towns surrounding them, magistrates are appointed to them, secondary to the magistrates of the departments or the districts in which they are comprised. Thus Fuhshan is a very large commercial town or mart called a *chin*, situated in the district of Nanhai, of the department of Kwangchau, about twelve miles distant from Canton. The chief officer of the department has therefore an assistant residing there, and the town is partly under his government and partly under that of the Nanhai magistrate, within whose district it is included, but who resides at Canton. There are several of these *chin* in the provinces, as Kingteh in Kiangsí, Siangtan in Hunan, etc.; they are not inclosed by walls. Macao affords another instance: being a place of some importance, both from its size and as the residence of foreigners, an assistant to the Hiangshan hien magistrate is placed over it, and it is also under the control of an assistant to the chief magistrate of the *fu*. Of these assistant magistrates, there are two ranks secondary to the chief magistrate of a *fu*, two secondary to the magistrate of a *chau*, and two also secondary to the magistrate of a *hien*. The places under the rule of these assistant magistrates are called by various names, most frequently *chin* and *so*, and sometimes also *chai* and *wei*. These names do not appear to have reference to any particular form of municipal government existing in them; but the *chai* and the *wei* are often military posts; and sometimes a place is, with respect to its civil government, the chief city of a *fu*, while with respect to its military position it is called *wei*. There are other towns of still smaller importance; these are under the government of inferior magistrates who are called *siun kien:* a division of country under such a magistrate is called a *sz'*, which is best represented by the term township or *commune*. The town of Whampoa and country around it form one such division, called Kiautang sz', belonging to the district of Pwanyu, in the department of Kwangchau.

"In the mountainous districts of Kwangsí, Yunnan, Kweichau, and Sz'-chuen, and in some other places, there are districts called *tu sz'*. Among these, the same distinctions of *fu*, *chau*, and *hien* exist, together with the minor division *sz'*. The magistrates of these departments and districts are hereditary in their succession, being the only hereditary local officers acknowledged by the supreme government.

"There is a larger division than any of the above, but as it does not prevail universally, it was not mentioned in the first instance. It is called *tau*, a *course* or *circuit*, and comprises two or more departments of a province, whether *fu*, or independent *ting* or *chau*. These circuits are subject to the government of officers called *tau-tai* or intendants of circuit, who often combine with political and judicial powers a military authority and various duties relating to the territory or to the revenue." [1]

The eighteen provinces received their present boundaries and divisions in the reign of Kienlung; and the little advance which has been made abroad in the geography of China is shown by the fact, that although these divisions were established a hundred years ago, the old demarkations, existing at

---

[1] *Chinese Repository*, Vol. IV., p. 54.

the time of the survey in 1710, are still found in many modern European geographies and maps. The following table shows their present divisions and government. The three columns under the head of *Departments* contain the *fu*, *chihlí ting*, and *chihlí chau*, all of which are properly prefectures; the three columns under the head of *Districts* contain the *ting*, *chau*, and *hien*.

The province of CHIHLÍ is the most important of the whole. On foreign maps it is sometimes written Pechele (*i.e.*, North Chihlí), a name formerly given it in order to distinguish it from Kiangnan, or *Nan-chihlí*, in which the seat of government was once located. This name is descriptive, rather than technical, and means 'Direct rule,' denoting that from this province the supreme power which governs the empire proceeds; any province, in which the Emperor and court should be fixed, would therefore be termed *Chihlí*, and its chief city *King*, 'capital,' or *King-tu* or *King-sz'*, 'court of the capital.' The surface of this province lying south of the Great Wall is level, excepting a few ridges of hills in the west and north, while the eastern parts, and those south to the Gulf, are among the flattest portions of the Great Plain.

It is bounded on the north-east by Liautung, where for a short distance the Great Wall is the frontier line; on the east by the Gulf of Pechele; on the south-east and south by Shantung; on the south-west by Honan; on the west by Shansí; and north by Inner Mongolia, where the river Liau forms the boundary. The extensive region beyond the Wall, occupied mostly by the Tsakhar Mongols, is now included within the jurisdiction, and placed under the administration of officers residing at one of the garrisoned gates of the Great Wall; the area of this part is about half that of the whole province. The chief department in the province, that of Shuntien, being both large and important, as containing the metropolis, is divided into four *lu* or circuits, each under the rule of a sub-prefect, who is subordinate to the prefect living at Peking.

Peking[1] (*i.e.*, Northern Capital) is situated upon a sandy

[1] This word should not be written Pekin; it is pronounced *Pei-ching* by the citizens, and by most of the people north of the Great River.

PROVINCES.	AREA IN ENGLISH SQ. MLS.	DEPARTMENTS.			DISTRICTS.			CAPITAL.	GOVERNMENT.
		Fu.	Ting.	Chau.	Ting.	Chau.	Hien.		
NORTHERN PROVINCES.									
Chihlí	58,949	11	..	6	3	17	124	Pauting fu.	Ruled by a governor-general or *tsungtuh.*
Shantung	65,104	10	..	2	..	9	96	Tsínan fu.	Each separately ruled by a lieutenant-governor or *fuyuen.*
Shansí	55,268	9	..	10	3	6	85	Taiyuen fu.	
Honan	65,104	9	..	4	..	6	97	Kaifung fu.	
EASTERN PROVINCES.									
Kiangsu	92,961	8	1	3	2	3	62	Kiangning fu.	Each under a lieutenant-governor, subordinate to one governor-general, called *Liang Kiang tsungtuh.*
Nganhwui		8	..	5	..	4	50	Nganking fu.	
Kiangsí	72,176	13	..	1	2	1	75	Nanchang fu.	
Chehkiang	39,150	11	..	..	1	1	76	Hangchau fu.	Each under a lieutenant-governor, subordinate to a governor-general, called *Min Cheh tsungtuh.*
Fuhkien	53,480	10	..	2	3	..	62	Fuhchau fu.	
CENTRAL PROVINCES.									
Hupeh	144,770	10	..	1	..	7	60	Wuchang fu.	Each under a lieutenant-governor, subordinate to a governor-general, called *Liang Hu tsungtuh.*
Hunan		9	3	4	..	3	64	Changsha fu.	
SOUTHERN PROVINCES.									
Kwangtung	79,456	9	2	4	3	7	79	Kwangchau fu, or Canton.	Two lieutenant-governors, subordinate to a governor-general, called *Liang Kwang tsungtuh.*
Kwangsí	78,250	11	..	1	3	16	47	Kweilin fu.	
Yunnan	107,969	14	3	4	5	27	39	Yunnan fu.	Two lieutenant-governors, subordinate to a governor-general, called *Yun Kwei tsungtuh.*
Kweichau	64,554	12	3	1	5	13	34	Kweiyang fu.	
WESTERN PROVINCES.									
Shensí	154,008	7	..	5	5	5	73	Singan fu.	Under a governor-general, called *Shen Kan tsungtuh,* and one lieutenant-governor over Shensí.
Kansuh		9	..	6	7	7	51	Lanchau fu.	
Sz'chuen	166,800	12	6	8	9	11	111	Chingtu fu.	Ruled by a governor-general.

plain, about twelve miles south-west of the Pei ho, and more than a hundred miles west-north-west of its mouth, in lat. 39° 54′ 36″ N., and long. 116° 27′ E., or nearly on the parallel of Samarkand, Naples, and Philadelphia. It is a city worthy of note on many accounts. Its ancient history as the capital of the *Yen Kwoh* (the 'Land of Swallows') during the feudal times, and its later position as the metropolis of the empire for many centuries, give it historical importance; while its imperial buildings, its broad avenues with their imposing gates and towers, its regular arrangement, extent, populousness, and diversity of costume and equipage, combine to render it to a traveller the most interesting and unique city in Asia. It is now ruinous and poor, but the remains of its former grandeur under Kienlung's prosperous reign indicate the justness of the comparisons made by the Catholic writers with western cities one hundred and eighty years ago. The entire circuit of the walls and suburbs is reckoned by Hyacinthe at twenty-five miles, and its area at twenty-seven square miles, but more accurate measurements of the walls alone give forty-one *li*, or 14.25 miles (or 23.55 kilometres) for the Manchu city, including the cross-wall, and twenty-eight *li*, or ten miles, for the Chinese city on its south; not counting the cross-wall, the circuit measures almost twenty-one miles. The suburbs near the thirteen outer gates altogether form a small proportion to the whole; the area within them is nearly twenty-six square miles. Those residents who have had the best opportunities estimate the entire population at a million or somewhat less; no census returns are available to prove this figure, nor can it be stated what is the proportion of Manchus, Mongols, and Chinese, except that the latter outnumber all others. Du Halde reckoned it to be about three millions, and Klaproth one million three hundred thousand; and each was probably true at some period, for the number has diminished with the poverty of the Government.

Peking is regarded by the Chinese as one of their ancient cities, but it was not made the capital of the whole empire until Kublai established his court at this spot in 1264. The Ming emperors who succeeded the Mongols held their court

THE AN-TING GATE, WALL OF PEKING.

at Nanking until Yungloh transferred the seat of government to Peking in 1411, where it has since remained. Under the Mongols, the city was called *Khan-baligh* (*i.e.*, city of the Khan), changed into Cambalu in the accounts of those times; on Chinese maps it is usually called *King-sz'*.

Peking has, during its history, existed under many different names; after each disaster her walls have been changed and her houses rebuilt, so that to-day she stands, like the capitals of the ancient Roman and Byzantine empires, upon the débris of centuries of buildings. The most important renovations have been those by the Liao dynasty, in 937 A.D., who entirely rebuilt the city, and by the Kin rulers in 1151.

It was at first surrounded by a single wall pierced by nine gates, whence it is sometimes called the City of Nine Gates. The southern suburbs were inclosed by Kiatsing in 1543, and the city now consists of two portions, the northern or inner city (*Nui ching*), containing about fifteen square miles, where are the palace, government buildings, and barracks for troops; and the southern or Outer city (*Wai ching*), where the Chinese live. The wall of the Manchu city averages fifty feet high, forty wide at top, and about sixty at bottom, most of the slope being on the inner face. That around the Outer city is no more than thirty in height, twenty-five thick at bottom, and about fifteen at top. The terre-plein throughout is paved with bricks weighing sixty pounds each; a crenellated parapet runs around the entire town, intended only for archers or musketeers, as no port-holes for cannon exist. It is undoubtedly the finest wall surrounding any city now extant. Near the gates, of which there are sixteen in all, the walls are faced with stone, but in other places with these large bricks, laid in a concrete of lime and clay, which in process of time becomes almost as durable as stone. The intermediate space between facings is filled up with the earth taken from the ditch which surrounds the city. Square buttresses occur at intervals of sixty yards on the outer face, each projecting fifty feet, and every sixth one being twice the size of the others; their tops furnish room for the troops posted there to resist side attacks. Each gate is surmounted with a brick tower of many stories, over a hundred feet high, built in galleries with port-holes, and giving a very imposing appearance to the city as one approaches it from the wide plain. The gates of the Manchu city have a double entrance formed by joining their supporting bastions with a circular wall in which are side entrances, thus making an enceinte of several acres, in which the yellow-tiled temple to the tutelary God of War is conspicuous. The arches of all the gates are built solidly of granite; the massive doors are closed and barred every night soon after dark.

At the sides of the gates, and also between them, are esplanades for mounting to the top; this is shut to the common people, and the guards are not allowed to bring their women upon the wall, which would be deemed an affront to Kwantí. The moat around the city is fed from the Tunghwui River, which also supplies all the other canals leading across or through the city. The approach to Peking from Tung chau is by an elevated stone road, but nothing of the buildings inside the walls is seen; and were it not for the lofty towers over the gates, it would more resemble an encampment inclosed by a massive wall than a large metropolis. No spires or towers of churches, no pillars or monuments, no domes or minarets, nor even many dwellings of superior elevation, break the dull uniformity of this or any Chinese city. In Peking, the different colored yellow or green tiles on official buildings,[1] mixed with the brown roofs of common houses, impart a variety to the scene, but the chief objects to relieve the monotony are the large clumps of trees, and the flag-staffs in pairs near the temples. The view from the walls impresses one with the grand ideas of the founders of the city; and the palaces in the Forbidden City, towering above everything else, worthily exhibit their notions of what was befitting the sovereigns of the Middle Kingdom. The Bell and Clock Towers, the Prospect Hill, the dagobas, pagodas, and gate towers, and lastly the Temple of

---

[1] "You would think them all made of, or at least covered with, pure gold enamelled in azure and green, so that the spectacle is at once majestic and charming." Magaillans, *Nouvelle Description de la Chine*, p. 353.

Heaven, are all likewise visible from this point, and render the scene picturesque and peculiar.[1]

The plan of the city here given is reduced from a large Chinese map, but is not very exact. The northern portion occupies for the most part the same area as the Cambaluc of Marco Polo, which, however, extended about two miles north, where the remains of the old north wall of the Mongols still exist. On their expulsion Hungwu erected the present northern wall, and his son Yungloh rebuilt the other three sides in 1419 on a rather larger scale; but the arrangement of the streets and gates is due to the Great Khan. When taken possession of by the Manchus in 1644, they found a magnificent city ready for them, uninjured and strong, which they apportioned among their officers and bannermen; but necessity soon obliged these men, less frugal and thrifty than the natives, to sell them, and content themselves with humbler abodes; consequently, the greater part of the northern city is now tenanted by Chinese. The innermost inclosure in the *Nui Ching* contains the palace and its surrounding buildings; the second is occupied by barracks and public offices, and by many private residences; the outer one, for the most part, consists of dwelling-houses, with shops in the large avenues. The inner inclosure measures 6.3 *li*, or 2.23 miles, in circuit, and is called *Tsz' Kin Ching*, or 'Carnation Prohibited City;' the wall is less solid and high than the city wall; it is covered with bright yellow tiles, guarded by numerous stations of bannermen and gendarmerie, and surrounded by a deep, wide moat. Two gates, the *Tung-hwa* and *Si-hwa*, on the east and west, afford access to the interior of this habitation of the Emperor, as well as the space and rooms appertaining, which furnish lodgment to the guard defending the approach to the Dragon's Throne; a tower at each corner, and one over each gateway, also give accommodation to other troops. The interior of this inclosure is divided

[1] See also *L'Univers Pittoresque, Chine Moderne*, par MM. Pauthier et Bazin, Paris, 1853, for a good map of Peking, with careful descriptions. Yule's *Marco Polo*, passim. De Guigues, *Voyages*, Tome I. Williamson, *Journeys in North China*, Vol. II. Dr. Rennie, *Peking and the Pekingese*. *Tour du Monde* for 1864, Tome II.

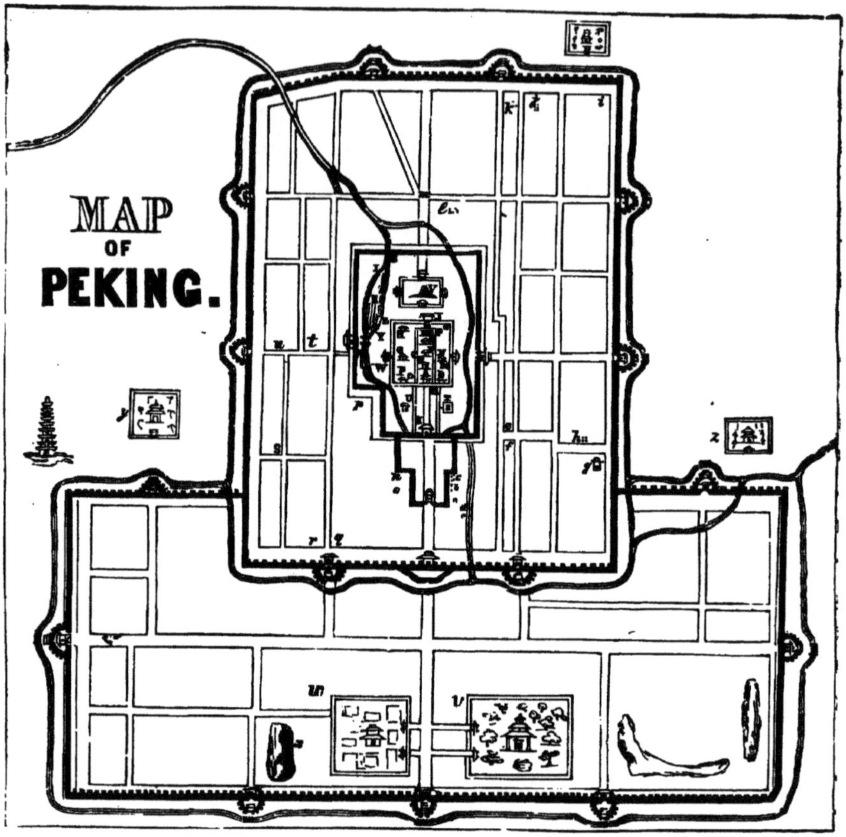

REFERENCES.

A. The Meridian Gate.
B. Gate of Extensive Peace.
C. Hall of Perfect Peace.
D. Hall of Secure Peace.
E. Palace of Heaven—the Emperor's.
F. Palace of Earth's Repose—the Empress'.
G. Gate to Earth's Repose, leads to a Garden.
H. Ching-hwang miao.
I. Temple of Great Happiness.
J. Northern gate of Forbidden City.
K. Nui Koh, or Privy Council Chamber, lies within the wall.
K. Gate of Heavenly Rest.
L. Hall of Intense Mental Exercises.
M. Library, or Hall of Literary Abyss.
N. Imperial Ancestral Hall.
O. Hall of National Portraits.
P. Printing Office.
Q. Court of Controllers of Imperial Clan.
R. Marble Isle; a marble bridge leads to it.
S Five Dragon Pavilion.
T. Great Ancestral Temple.
U. Altar to the Gods of Land and Grain.
V. Artificial Mountain. The Russian school lies just north of the Eastern gate near N.
W. A summer-house.
X. Military Examination Hall.
Y. Plantain Garden, or Conservatory.
Z. A Pavilion.

a. Medical College.
b. Astronomical Board.
c. Five of the Six Boards. The Hanlin Yuen lies just above them.
d. House of the Russian Mission.
e. Colonial Office.
f. Temple for Imperial worship.
g. Imperial Observatory, partly on the wall.
h. Hall of Literary Examination.
i. Russian Church of the Assumption.
j. Temple of Eternal Peace of the lamas.
k. Kwoh Tsz' Kien, a Manchu College.
l. Temple of the God of the North Star.
m. High Watch-tower and Police Office.
n. Board of Punishments.
o. Censorate.
p. Mohammedan Mosque.
q. Portuguese Church.
r. Elephant's Inclosure.
s. Principal Ching-hwang miau.
t. Temple of Deceased Emperors of all ages.
u. Obelisk covering a scab of Buddha.
v. Altar to Heaven.—Altar to Earth is on the north of the city.
w. Altar to Agriculture.
x. Black Dragon Pool, and Temple of God of Rain.
y. Altar to the Moon.
z. Altar to the Sun.

into three parts by two walls running from south to north, and the whole is occupied by a suite of court-yards and halls, which, in their arrangement and architecture, far exceed any other specimens of the kind in China. According to the notions of a common Chinese, all here is gold and silver; "he will tell you of gold and silver pillars, gold and silver roofs, and gold and silver vases, in which swim gold and silver fishes."

The southern gate, called the *Wu Măn*, or 'Meridian Gate,' is the fourth in going north from the entrance opposite the *Tsien Măn*, and this distance of nearly half a mile is occupied by troops. The *Wu Măn* leads into the middle division, in which are the imperial buildings; it is especially appropriated to the Emperor, and whenever he passes through it, a bell placed in the tower above is struck; when his troops return in triumph, a drum is beaten, and the prisoners are here presented to him; here, too, the presents he confers on vassals and ambassadors are pompously bestowed. Passing through this gate into a large court, over a small creek spanned by five marble bridges, ornamented with sculptures, the visitor is led through the *Tai-ho Măn* into a second court paved with marble, and terminated on the sides by gates, porticos, and pillared corridors. The next building, at the head of this court, called the *Tai-ho tien*, or 'Hall of Highest Peace,' is a superb marble structure, one hundred and ten feet high, standing on a terrace that raises it twenty feet above the ground; five flights of stairs, decorated with balustrades and sculptures, lead up to it, and five doors open through it into the next court-yard. It is a great hall of seventy-two pillars, measuring about two hundred feet by ninety broad, with a throne in the midst. Here the Emperor holds his levees on New Year's Day, his birthdays, and other state occasions; a cortége of about fifty household courtiers stand near him, while those of noble and inferior dignity and rank stand in the court below in regular grades, and, when called upon, fall prostrate as they all make the fixed obeisances. It was in this hall that Titsingh and Van Braam were banqueted by Kienlung, January 20, 1795, of which interesting ceremony the Dutch embassador gives an account, and since which event no European has entered the building. The three *Tien* in this inclosure are the audience halls, and the side buildings contain stores and treasures under the charge of the Household Board, with minor bureaus.

Beyond it are two halls; the first, the *Chung-ho tien*, or 'Hall of Central Peace,' having a circular roof, that rests on columns arranged nearly four-square. Here the Emperor comes to examine the written prayers provided to be offered at the state worship. The second is the *Pao-ho tien*, or 'Hall of Secure Peace,' elevated on a high marble terrace, and containing nine rows of pillars. The highest degrees for literary merit are here conferred triennially by the Emperor upon one hundred and fifty or more scholars; here, also, he banquets his foreign guests and other distinguished persons the day before New Year's Day. After ascending a stairway, and passing the *Kien Tsing Măn*, the visitor reaches the *Kien Tsing Kung*, or 'Palace of Heavenly Purity,' into which no one can enter without special license. In it is the council-chamber, where the Emperor usually sits at morning audience up to eight o'clock, to transact business with his ministers, and see those appointed to office. The building is the most important as it is described to be the loftiest and most magnificent of all the palaces. In the court before it is a small tower of gilt copper, adorned with a great number of figures, and on each side are large incense vases, the uses of which are no doubt religious. It was in this palace that Kanghí celebrated a singular and unique festival, in 1722, for all the men in the empire over sixty years of age, that being the sixtieth year of his reign. His grandson Kienlung, in 1785, in the fiftieth year of his reign, repeated the ceremony, on which occasion the number of guests was about three thousand.[1] Beyond it stands the 'Palace of Earth's Repose,' where 'Heaven's consort' rules her miniature court in the imperial harem; there are numerous buildings of lesser size in this part of the inclosure, and adjoining the northern wall of the Forbidden City is the imperial Flower Garden, designed for the use of its inmates. The gardens are adorned with elegant pavilions, temples, and

---

[1] *Chinese Repository*, Vol. IX., p. 259.

groves, and interspersed with canals, fountains, pools, and flower-beds. Two groves rising from the bosoms of small lakes, and another crowning the summit of an artificial mountain, add to the beauty of the scene, and afford the inmates of the palace an agreeable variety.

In the eastern division of the Prohibited City are the offices of the Cabinet, where its members hold their sessions, and the treasury of the palace. North of it lies the 'Hall of Intense Thought,' where sacrifices are presented to Confucius and other sages. Not far from this hall stands the *Wăn-yuen koh*, or the Library, the catalogue of whose contents is published from time to time, forming an admirable synopsis of Chinese literature. At the northern end of the eastern division are numerous palaces and buildings occupied by princes of the blood, and those connected with them; and in this quarter is placed the *Fung Sien tien*, a small temple where the Emperor comes to 'bless his ancestors.' Here the Emperor and his family perform their devotions before the tablets of their departed progenitors; whenever he leaves or returns to his palace, the first day of a season, and on other occasions, the monarch goes through his devotions in this hall.

The western division contains a great variety of edifices devoted to public and private purposes, among which may be mentioned the hall of distinguished sovereigns, statesmen, and literati, the printing-office, the Court of Controllers for the regulation of the receipts and disbursements of the court, and the *Ching-hwang Miao*, or 'Guardian Temple' of the city. The number of people residing within the Prohibited City cannot be stated, but probably is not large; most of them are Manchus.

The second inclosure, which surrounds the imperial palaces, is called *Hwang Ching*, or 'Imperial City,' and is an oblong rectangle about six miles in circuit, encompassed by a wall twenty feet high, and having a gate in each face. From the southern gate, called the *Tien-an Măn*, or 'Heavenly Rest,' a broad avenue leads up to the *Kin Ching;* and before it, outside of the wall, is an extensive space walled in, and having one entrance on the south, called the gate of Great Purity, which no one is allowed to enter except on foot, unless by special permission. On the right of the avenue within the wall is a gateway leading to the *Tai Miao*, or 'Great Temple' of the imperial ancestors, a large collection of buildings inclosed by a wall 3,000 feet in circuit. It is the most honored of religious structures next to the Temple of Heaven, and contains tablets to princes and meritorious officers. Here offerings are presented before the tablets of deceased emperors and empresses, and worship performed at the end of the year by the members of the imperial family and clan to their departed forefathers. Across the avenue from this temple is a gateway leading to the *Shié-Tsih tan*, or altar of the gods of Land and Grain. These were originally *Kau-lung*, a Minister of Works, B.C. 2500, and *Hau-tsih*, a remote ancestor of Chau Kung; here the Emperor sacrifices in spring and autumn. This altar consists of two stories, each five feet high, the upper one being fifty-eight feet square; no other altar of the kind is found in the empire, and it would be tantamount to high treason to erect one and worship upon it. The north, east, south, and west altar are respectively black, green, red, and white, and the top yellow; the ceremonies connected with the worship held here are among the most ancient practised among the Chinese.

On the north of the palace, separated by a moat, and surrounded by a wall more than a mile in circuit, is the *King Shan*, or 'Prospect Hill,' an artificial mound, nearly one hundred and fifty feet high, and having five summits, crowned with as many temples; many of these show the neglect in which public edifices soon fall. Trees of various kinds border its base, and line the paths leading to the tops. Its height allows the spectator to overlook the whole city, while, too, it is itself a conspicuous object from every direction. The earth and stone in it were taken from the ditches and pools dug in and around the city, and near its base are many tanks of picturesque shape and appearance; so that altogether it forms a great ornament to the city. Another name for it is *Mei Shan*, or 'Coal Hill,' from a tradition that a quantity of coal was placed there, as a supply in case of siege. The western part of this inclosure is chiefly occupied by the *Si Yuen*, or 'Western Park,' in and around which are found some of the most beautiful objects and spots in the metropolis. An artificial lake, more than a mile long, and averaging a furlong in breadth, occupies the centre; it is supplied from the Western Hills, and its waters are adorned with the splendid lotus. A marble bridge of nine arches crosses it, and its banks are shaded by groves of trees, under which are well-paved walks. On its south-eastern side is a large summer-house, consisting of several edifices partly in or over the water, and inclosing a number of gardens and walks, in and around which are artificial hills of rock-work beautifully alternating or supporting groves of trees and parterres of flowers.

On the western side is the hall for examining military candidates, where his majesty in person sees them exhibit their prowess in equestrian archery. At the north end of the lake is a bridge leading to an islet, which presents the aspect of a hill of gentle ascent covered with groves, temples, and summer-houses, and surmounted with a tower, from which an extensive view can be enjoyed. On the north of the bridge is a hill on an island called *Kiung-hwa tan*, capped by a white dagoba. Near by is an altar forty feet in circuit, and four feet high, inclosed by a wall, and a temple dedicated to Yuenfí, the reputed discoverer of the silk-worm, where the Empress annually offers sacrifices to her; in the vicinity a plantation of mulberry trees and a cocoonery are maintained. Near the temple of 'Great Happiness,' not far distant from the preceding, on the northern borders of the lake, is a gilded copper statue of *Maitreya*, or the coming Buddha, sixty feet high, with a hundred arms; the temple is one of the greatest ornaments of the Park. Across the lake on its western bank, and entered through the first gate on the south side of the street, is the *Tsz'-kwang Koh*, where foreign ministers are received by the Emperor; the inclosure is kept with great care, and numerous halls and temples are seen amidst groves of firs. The object kept in view in the arrangement of these gardens and grounds has been to make them an epitome of nature, and then furnish every part with commodious buildings. But however elegant the palaces and grounds may have appeared when new, it is to be feared that his majesty has no higher ideas of cleanliness and order than his subjects, and that the various public and private edifices and gardens in these two inclosures are despoiled of half their beauty by dirt and neglect. The number of the palaces in them both is estimated to be over two hundred, "each of which," says Attinet, in vague terms, "is sufficiently large to accommodate the greatest of European noblemen, with all his retinue."

Along the avenue leading south from the Imperial City to the division wall, are found the principal government offices. Five of the Six Boards have their bureaus on the east side, the Board of Punishments with its subordinate departments being situated with its courts on the west side; immediately south of this is the Censorate. The office attached to the Board of Rites, for the preparation of the Calendar, commonly called the Astronomical Board, stands directly east of this; and the Medical College has its hall not far off. The *Hanlin Yuen*, or National Academy, and the *Li-fan Yuen*, or Colonial Office, are also near the south-eastern corner of the Imperial City. Opposite to the Colonial Office is the *Tang Tsz'*, where the remote ancestors of the reigning family are worshipped by his majesty together with the princes of his family; when they come in procession to this temple in their state dresses, the Emperor, as high-priest of the family, performs the highest religious ceremony before his deified ancestors, viz., three kneelings and nine knockings. After he has completed his devotions, the attendant grandees go through the same ceremonies. The temple itself is pleasantly situated in the midst of a grove of fir and other trees, and the large inclosure around it is prettily laid out.

In the south-eastern part of the city, built partly upon the wall, is the Observatory, which was placed under the superintendence of the Romish missionaries by Kanghí, but is now confided to the care of Chinese astronomers. The instruments are arranged on a terrace higher than the city wall, and are beautiful pieces of bronze art, though now antiquated and useless for practical observations. Nearly opposite to the Observatory stands the Hall for Literary Examinations, where the candidates of the province assemble to write their essays. In the north-eastern corner of the city is the Russian Mission and

Astronomical Office, inclosed in a large compound; near it live the converts. About half a mile west is the *Yung-ho Kung*, or 'Lamasary of Eternal Peace,' wherein about 1,500 Mongol and Tibetan priests study the dogmas of Buddhism, or spend their days in idleness, under the control of a *Gegen* or living Buddha. Their course of study comprises instruction in metaphysics, ascetic duties, astrology, and medicine; their daily ritual is performed in several courts, and the rehearsal of prayers and chants by so many men strikes the hearer as very impressive. The rear building contains a wooden image, 70 feet in height, of Maitreya, the coming Buddha; the whole establishment exhibits in its buildings, pictures, images, cells, and internal arrangements for study, living, and worship, one of the most complete in the empire. Several smaller lamasaries occur in other parts of the city.

Directly west of the *Yung-ho Kung*, and presenting the greatest contrast to its life and activity, lies the Confucian Temple, where embowered in a grove of ancient cypresses stands the imposing *Wăn Miao*, or 'Literary Temple,' in which the Example and Teacher of all Ages and ten of his great disciples are worshipped. The hall is 84 feet in front, and the lofty roof is supported on wooden pillars over 40 feet high, covering the single room in which their tablets are placed in separate niches, he in the high seat of honor. All is simple, quiet, and cheerless; the scene here presents an impressive instance of merited honors paid to the moral teachers of the people. Opposite and across the court are ten granite stones shaped like drums, which are believed to have been made about the eighth century B.C., and contain stanzas recording King Süen's hunting expeditions. In another court are many stone tablets containing the lists of *Tsin-sz'* graduates since the Mongol dynasty, many thousands of names with places of residence. Contiguous to this temple is the *Pih-yung Kung*, or 'Classic Hall,' where the Emperor meets the graduates and literati. It is a beautiful specimen of Chinese architectural taste. Near it are 300 stone tablets on which the authorized texts of the classics are engraved.[1]

---

[1] Dr. Martin, *The Chinese* (New York, 1881), p. 85.

North of the Imperial City lies the extensive *yamun* of the *Ti-tuh*, who has the police and garrison of the city under his control, and exercises great authority in its civil administration. The Drum and Bell Towers stand north of the *Ti-ngan Măn* in the street leading to the city wall, each of them over a hundred feet high, and forming conspicuous objects; the drum and bell are sounded at night watches, and can be heard throughout the city; a clepsydra is still maintained to mark time—a good

Portal of Confucian Temple, Peking.

instance of Chinese conservatism, for clocks are now in general use, and correct the errors of the clepsydra itself.

Outside of the south-western angle of the Imperial City stands the Mohammedan mosque, and a large number of Turks whose ancestors were brought from Turkestan about a century ago live in its vicinity; this quarter is consequently the chief resort of Moslems who come to the capital. South-west of the mosque, near the cross-wall, stands the *Nan Tang*, or old Por tuguese church, and just west of the Forbidden City, inside of the *Hwang Ching*, is the *Peh Tang*, or Cathedral; both are imposing edifices, and near them are large schools and seminaries for the education of children and neophytes. There are religious edifices in the Chinese metropolis appropriated to many forms of religion, viz., the Greek, Latin, and Protestant churches, Islamism, Buddhism in its two principal forms, Rationalism, ancestral worship, state worship, and temples dedicated to Confucius and other deified mortals, besides a great number in which the popular idols of the country are adored. One of the most worthy of notice is the *Tí-Wang Miao*, lying on the avenue leading to the west gate, a large collection of halls wherein all the tablets of former monarchs of China from remote ages are worshipped. The rule for admission into this Walhalla is to accept all save the vicious and oppressive, those who were assassinated and those who lost their kingdoms. This memorial temple was opened in 1522; the Manchus have even admitted some of the Tartar rulers of the Kin and Liao dynasties, raising the total number of tablets to nearly three hundred. It is an impressive sight, these simple tablets of men who once ruled the Middle Kingdom, standing here side by side, worshipped by their successors that their spirits may bless the state. This selection of the good sovereigns alone recalls to mind the custom in ancient Jerusalem of allowing wicked princes no place in the sepulchres of the kings. Distinguished statesmen of all ages, called by the Chinese *kwoh chu*, or 'pillars of state,' are associated with their masters in this temple, as not unworthy to receive equal honors.

A little west of this remarkable temple is the *Peh-ta sz'*, or 'White Pagoda Temple,' so called from a costly dagoba near it erected about A.D. 1100, renovated by Kublai in the thirteenth century, and rebuilt in 1819. Its most conspicuous feature is the great copper umbrella on the top. When finished, the dagoba was described as covered with jasper, and the projecting parts of the roof with ornaments of exquisite workmanship tastefully arranged. Around this edifice, which contains twenty beads or relics of Buddha, two thousand clay pagodas and five books of charms, are also one hundred and eight small pillars on which lamps are burned. The portion of the city lying south of the cross-wall is inhabited mostly by Chinese, and contains hundreds of *hwui-kwan*, or club-houses, erected by the gentry of cities and districts in all parts of the empire to accommodate their citizens resorting to the capital. Its streets are narrow and the whole aspect of its buildings and markets indicates the life and industry of the people. Hundreds of inns accommodate travellers who find no lodging-places in the *Nui Ching*, and storehouses, theatres, granaries and markets attract or supply their customers from all parts. There is more dissipation and freedom from etiquette here, and the Chinese officials feel freer from their Manchu colleagues.

Three miles south of the Palace, in the Chinese City, is situated the *Tien Tan*, or 'Altar to Heaven,' so placed because it was anciently customary to perform sacrifices to Heaven in the outskirts of the Emperor's residence city. The compound is inclosed by more than three miles of wall, within which is planted a thick grove of locust (*Sophora*), pine and fir trees, interspaced with stretches of grass. Within a second wall, which surrounds the sacred buildings, rises a copse of splendid and thickly growing cypress trees, reminding one of the solemn shade in the vicinity of famous temples in Ancient Greece, or of those celebrated shrines described in Western Asia. The great South Altar, the most important of Chinese religious structures, is a beautiful triple circular terrace of white marble, whose base is 210, middle stage 150, and top 90 feet in width, each terrace encompassed by a richly carved balustrade. A curious symbolism of the number three and its multiples may be noticed in the measurements of this pile. The uppermost terrace, whose height above the ground is about eighteen feet, is paved with marble slabs, forming nine concentric circles—the inner of nine stones inclosing a central piece, and around this each receding layer consisting of a successive multiple of nine until the square of nine (a favorite number of Chinese philosophy) is reached in the outermost row. It is upon the single round stone in the centre of the upper plateau that the Emperor kneels when worshipping Heaven and his ancestors at the winter solstice.

Four flights of nine steps each lead from this elevation to the next lower stage, where are placed tablets to the spirits of the sun, the moon, the stars, and the Year God. On the ground at the end of the four stairways stand vessels of bronze in which are placed the bundles of cloth and sundry animals constituting part of the sacrificial offerings. But of vastly greater importance than these in the matter of burnt-offering is the great furnace, nine feet high, faced with green porcelain, and ascended on three of its sides by porcelain staircases. In this receptacle, erected some hundred feet to the south-east of the altar, is consumed a burnt-offering of a bullock—entire and without blemish—at the yearly ceremony. The slaughter-house of the sacrificial bullock stands east of the North Altar, at the end of an elaborate winding passage, or cloister of 72 compartments, each 10 feet in length.

Separated from the Altar to Heaven by a low wall, is a smaller though more conspicuous construction called *Ki-kuh Tan*, or 'Altar of Prayer for Grain.' Its proportions and arrangement are somewhat similar to those of the South Altar, but upon its upper terrace rises a magnificent triple-roofed, circular building known to foreigners as the 'Temple of Heaven.' This elaborate house of worship, whose surmounting gilded ball rests 100 feet above the platform, was originally roofed with blue, yellow and green tiles, but by Kienlung these colors were changed to blue. When, added to these brilliant hues, we consider the richly carved and painted eaves, the windows shaded by venetians of blue-glass rods strung together, and the rare symmetry of its proportions, it is no exaggeration to call this temple the most remarkable edifice in the capital—or indeed in the empire. The native name is *Ki-kien Tien*, or 'Temple of Prayer for the Year.' In the interior, the large shrines of carved wood for the tablets correspond to the movable blue wooden huts which on days of sacrifice are put up on the Southern Altar. Here, upon some day following the first of spring (Feb. 6), the Emperor offers his supplications to Heaven for a blessing upon the year. In times of drought, prayer for rain is also made at this altar, the Emperor being obliged to proceed on foot, as a repentant suppliant, to the 'Hall of Penitent Fasting,' a distance of three miles. A green furnace for burnt-offerings lies to the south-east of this, as of the North Altar; while in the open park not far from the two and seventy cloisters are seven great stones, said to have fallen from heaven and to secure good luck to the country.

Across the avenue upon which is situated this great inclosure of the *Tien Tan*, is the *Sien Nung Tan*, or 'Altar dedicated to Shinnung,' the supposed inventor of agriculture. These precincts are about two miles in circumference, and contain four separate altars: to the gods of the heavens, of the earth, of the planet Jupiter, and to Shinnung. The worship here is performed at the vernal equinox, at which time the ceremony of ploughing a part of the inclosed park is performed by the Emperor, assisted by various officials and members of the Board of Rites. The district magistrates and prefect also plough their plats; but no one touches the imperial portion save the monarch himself. The first two altars are rectangular; that to the gods of heaven, on the east, is 50 feet long and 4½ feet high: four marble tablets on it contain the names of the gods of the clouds, rain, wind, and thunder. That to the gods of earth is 100 feet long by 60 wide; here the five marble tablets contain the names of celebrated mountains, seas, and lakes in China. Sacrifices are offered to these divinities at various times, and, with the prayers presented, are burned in the furnaces, thus to come before them in the unseen world; the idea which runs through them partakes of the nature of homage, not of atonement.

Nearly one-half of the Chinese City is empty of dwellings, much of the open land being cultivated; a large pond for rearing gold-fish near the *Tien Tan* is an attractive place. West of this city wall is an old and conspicuous dagoba in the *Tienning sz'*, nearly 200 feet high, and a landmark for the city gate. This part of Peking was much the best built when the Liao and Kin dynasties occupied it. West of the main city is the Temple of the Moon, and on the east side, directly opposite, stands the Temple to the Sun; the *Ti Tan*, or 'Altar to Earth,' is on the north over against the Altar to Heaven, just described. At all these the Emperor performs religious rites during the twelve months.

MONUMENT, OR TOPE, OF A LAMA. HWANG SZ', PEKING.

The inclosure of the Altar to Earth is smaller, and everything connected with the sacrifices is on an inferior scale to those conducted in the Altar to Heaven. The main altar has two terraces, each 6 feet high, and respectively 106 feet and 60 feet square; the tablet to Imperial Earth is placed on the upper with those to the Imperial Ancestors, and all are adored at the summer solstice. The bullock for sacrifice is afterwards buried and not burned. Adjoining the terraced altar on the south is a small tank for water.

About two miles from the *Tĭ Tan*, in a northerly direction, passing through one of the ruined gates of the Peking of Marco Polo's time on the way, is found the *Ta-chung sz'*, or 'Bell Temple,' in which is hung the great bell of Peking. It was cast about 1406, in the reign of Yungloh, and was covered over in 1578 by a small temple. It is 14 feet high, including the umbones, 34 feet in circumference at the rim, and 9 inches thick; the weight is 120,000 lbs. av.; it is struck by a heavy beam swung on the outside. The Emperor cast five bells in all, but this one alone was hung. It is covered with myriads of Chinese characters, both inside and out, consisting of extracts from the *Fah-hwa King* and *Ling-yen King*, two Buddhist classics. In some respects this may be called the most remarkable work of art now in China; it is the largest suspended bell in the world. A square hole in the top prevents its fracture under the heaviest ringing.[1]

A short distance outside the northern gate, *Tah-shing Măn*, is an open ground for military reviews, and near it a Buddhist temple of some note, called *Hwang sz'*, containing in its enceinte a remarkable monument erected by Kienlung. In 1779 the Teshu Lama started for Peking with an escort of 1,500 men; he was met by the Emperor near the city of Sí-ning in Kansuh, conducted to Peking with great honor, and lodged in this temple for several months. He died here of small-pox, November 12, 1780, and this cenotaph of white marble was erected to his

[1] Compare Kircher, *China Illustrata*, where an engraving of it may be seen. A bell near Mandalay, mentioned by Dr. Anderson, is 12 feet high, 16 feet across the lips, and weighs 90 tons—evidently a heavier monster than this in Peking. (*Mandalay to Momien*, p. 18.)

memory; the body was inclosed in a gold coffin and sent to the Dalai Lama at Lhassa in 1781. The plinth of this beautiful work contains scenes in the prelate's life carved on the panels, one of which represents a lion rubbing his eyes with his paw as the tears fall for grief at the Lama's death.

The Summer Palace at *Yuen-ming Yuen* lies about seven miles from the north-west corner of Peking, and its entire circuit is reckoned to contain twelve square miles. The country in this direction rises into gentle hills, and advantage has been taken of the original surface in the arrangement of the different parts of the ground, so that the whole presents a great variety of hill and dale, woodlands and lawns, interspered with pools, lakes, caverns, and islets joined by bridges and walks, their banks thrown up or diversified like the free hand of nature. Some parts are tilled, groves or tangled thickets occur here and there, and places are purposely left wild to contrast the better with the cultivated precincts of a palace, or to form a rural pathway to a retired temple or arbor. Here were formerly no less than thirty distinct places of residence for various palace officials, around which were houses occupied by eunuchs and servants, each constituting a little village.

But all was swept away by the British and French troops in 1860, and their ruins still remain to irritate the officials and people of Peking against all foreigners. Near the Summer Palace is the great cantonment of Hai-tien, where the Manchu garrison is stationed to defend the capital, and whose troops did their best in the vain effort to stay the attack in 1860. As a contrast to the proceedings connected with this approach of the British, an extract from Sir John Davis's *Chinese* (chap. x.) will furnish an index of the changed condition of things.

"It was at a place called Hai-tien, in the immediate vicinity of these gardens, that the strange scene occurred which terminated in the dismissal of the embassy of 1816. On his arrival there, about daylight in the morning, with the commissioners and a few other gentlemen, the ambassador was drawn to one of the Emperor's temporary residences by an invitation from Duke Ho, as he was called, the imperial relative charged with the conduct of the negotiations. After passing through an open court, where were assembled a vast number of grandees in their dresses of ceremony, they were shown into a wretched room, and soon encompassed by a well-dressed crowd, among whom were princes of the blood by dozens, wearing yellow girdles. With a childish and unmannerly curiosity, consistent enough with the idle and disorderly life which many of them are said to lead, they examined the persons and dress of the gentlemen without ceremony; while these, tired with their sleepless journey, and disgusted at the behavior of the celestials, turned their backs upon them, and laid themselves down to rest. Duke Ho soon appeared, and surprised the ambassador by urging him to proceed directly to an audience of the Emperor, who was waiting for him. His lordship in vain remonstrated that to-morrow had been fixed for the first audience, and that tired and dusty as they all were at present, it would be worthy neither of the Emperor nor of himself to wait on his majesty in a manner so unprepared. He urged, too, that he was unwell, and required immediate rest. Duke Ho became more and more pressing, and at length forgot himself so far as to grasp the ambassador's arm violently, and one of the others stepped up at the same time. His lordship immediately shook them off, and the gentlemen crowded about him; while the highest indignation was expressed at such treatment, and a determined resolution to proceed to no audience this morning. The ambassador at length retired, with the appearance of satisfaction on the part of Duke Ho, that the audience should take place to-morrow. There is every reason, however, to suppose that this person had been largely bribed by the heads of the Canton local government to frustrate the views of the embassy, and prevent an audience of the Emperor. The mission, at least, was on its way back in the afternoon of the same day."

The principal part of the provisions required for the supply of this immense city comes from the southern provinces, and from flocks reared beyond the wall. It has no important manufactures, horn lanterns, wall papers, stone snuff-bottles, and pipe mouth-pieces, being the principal. Trade in silks, foreign fabrics, and food is limited to supplying the local demand, inasmuch as a heavy octroi duty at the gates restrains all enterprise. No foreign merchants are allowed to carry on business here. The government of Peking differs from that of other cities in the empire, the affairs of the department being separated from it, and administered by officers residing in the four circuits into which it is divided. "A minister of one of the Boards is appointed superintendent of the city, and subordinate to him is a *fuyin*, or mayor. Their duties consist in having charge of the metropolitan domain, for the purpose of extending good government to its four divisions. They have under them two district magistrates, each of whom rules half the city; none of these officers are subordinate to the provincial governor, but carry affairs which they cannot determine to the Emperor. They preside or assist at many of the festivals observed in the capital, superintend the military police, and hold the courts which take cognizance of the offences committed there."[1]

The thoroughfares leading across Peking, from one gate to the other, are broad, unpaved avenues, more than a hundred feet wide, which appear still wider owing to the lowness of the buildings; the centre is about two feet higher than the sides. The cross-streets in the main city are generally at right angles with them, not over forty feet wide, and for the most part occupied with dwellings. The inhabitants of the avenues are required to keep them well sprinkled in summer; but in rainy weather they are almost impassable from the mud and deep puddles, the level surface of the ground, and obstructed, neglected drains, preventing rapid drainage. The crowds which throng these avenues, some engaged in various callings, along the sides or in the middle of the way, and others busily passing and repassing, together with the gay appearance of the signboards, and an air of business in the shops, render the great streets of the Chinese metropolis very bustling, and to a foreigner a most interesting scene. Shop-fronts can be entirely opened when necessary; they are constructed of panels or shutters fitting into grooves, and secured to a row of strong posts which set into mortises. At night, when the shop is

---

[1] *Chinese Repository*, Vol. IV., p. 181.

closed, nothing of it is seen from without; but in the daytime, when the goods are exposed, the scene becomes more animated.

The sign-boards are often broad planks, fixed in stone bases on each side of the shop-front, and reaching to the eaves, or above them; the characters are large and of different colors, and in order to attract more notice, the signs are often hung with various colored flags, bearing inscriptions setting forth the excellence of the goods. The shops in the outer city are frequently constructed in this manner, others are made more compact for warmth in winter, but as a whole they are not brilliant in their fittings. Their signs are, when possible, images of the articles sold and always have a red pennon attached; the finer shop-fronts are covered with gold-leaf, brilliant when new, but shabby enough when faded, as it soon does. The appearance of the main streets exhibits therefore a curious mixture of decay and renovation, which is not lessened by the dilapidated temples and governmental buildings everywhere seen, all indicating the impoverished state of the exchequer. In many parts of the city are placed *pai-lau*, or honorary gateways, erected to mark the approach to the palace, and worthy, by their size and ornamental entablatures, to adorn the avenues and impress the traveller, if they were kept in good condition.

The police of the city is connected with the Bannermen, and is, on the whole, efficient and successful in preserving the peace. During the night the thoroughfares are quiet; they are lighted a little by lanterns hanging before the houses, but generally are dark and cheerless. In the metropolis, as in all Chinese cities, the air is constantly polluted by the stench arising from private vessels and public reservoirs for urine and every kind of offal, which is all carefully collected by scavengers. By this means, although the streets are kept clean, they are never sweet; but habit renders the people almost insensible to this as well as other nuisances. Carts, mules, donkeys and horses are to be hired in all the thoroughfares. The Manchu women ride astride; their number in the streets, both riding and walking, imparts a pleasant feature to the crowd, which is not seen in cities further south. The extraordinary length and elaborateness of marriage and funeral processions daily passing through the avenues, adds a pretty feature to them, which other cities with narrow streets cannot emulate.

The environs beyond the suburbs are occupied with mausolea, temples, private mansions, hamlets, and cultivated fields, in or near which are trees, so that the city, viewed from a distance, appears as if situated in a thick forest. Many interesting points for the antiquarian and scientist are to be found in and around this old city, which annually attracts more and more the attention of other nations. Its population has decreased regularly since the death of Kienlung in 1797, and is now probably rather less than one million, including the immediate suburbs. The climate is healthy, but subject to extremes from zero to 104°; the dryness during ten months of the year is, moreover, extremely irritating. The poor, who resort thither from other parts, form a needy and troublesome ingredient of the population, sometimes rising in large mobs and pillaging the granaries to supply themselves with food, but more commonly perishing in great numbers from cold and hunger. Its peace is always an object of considerable solicitude with the imperial government, not only as it may involve the personal safety of the Emperor, but still more from the disquieting effect it may have upon the administration of the empire. The possession of this capital by an invading force is more nearly equivalent to the control of the country than might be the case in most European kingdoms, but not as much as it might be in Siam, Burmah, or Japan. The good influences which may be exerted upon the nation from the metropolis are likewise correspondingly great, while the purification of this source of contamination, and the liberalizing of this centre of power, now well begun in various ways, will confer a vast benefit upon the Chinese people.[1]

Chihlí contains several other large cities, among which Pau-

[1] Compare the *Annales de la Foi*, Tome X., p. 100, for interesting details concerning the Romish missionaries in Peking. Also Pauthier's *Chine Moderne*, pp. 8–36 (Paris, 1852), containing an excellent map. Bretschneider's *Archeological and Historical Researches on Peking*, etc., published in the *Chinese Recorder*, Vol. VI. (1875, passim). *Mémoires concernant l'Histoire, les Sciences, les Arts, les Moeurs, les Usages, etc., des Chinois, par les Missionnaires de Pekin;* 16 vols., Paris, 1797–1814. N. B. Dennys, *Notes for Tourists in the North of China;* Hongkong, 1866.

ting, the former residence of the governor-general, and Tientsin, are the most important. The former lies about eighty miles south-west of the capital, on the Yungting River and the great road leading to Shansí. The whole department is described as a thoroughly cultivated, populous region; it is well watered, and possesses two or three small lakes.

Tientsin is the largest port on the coast above Shanghai. Owing, however, to the shallowness of the gulf and the bar at the mouth of the Pei ho, over which at neap tide only three or four feet of water flow, the port is rendered inaccessible to large foreign vessels. Its size and importance were formerly chiefly owing to its being the terminus of the Grand Canal, where the produce and taxes for the use of the capital were brought. Mr. Gutzlaff, who visited Tientsin in 1831, described it as a bustling place, comparing the stirring life and crowds on the water and shores outside of the walls of the city with those of Liverpool. The enormous fleet of grain junks carrying rice to the capital is supplemented by a still greater number of vessels which take the food up to Tung chau. Formerly the coast trade increased the shipping at Tientsin to thousands of junks, including all which lined the river for about sixty miles. This native trade has diminished since 1861, inasmuch as steamers are gradually ousting the native vessels, no one caring to risk insurance on freight in junks. The country is not very fertile between the city and the sea, owing to the soda and nitre in the soil; but scanty crops are brought forth, and these only after much labor; one is a species of grass (*Phragmites*) much used in making floor-mats. Sometimes the rains cause the Pei ho and its affluents to break over their banks, at which periods their waters deposit fertilizing matter over large areas.

The approach to Tientsin from the eastward indicates its importance, and the change from the sparsely populated country lying along the banks of the Pei ho, to the dense crowds on shore and the fleets of boats, adds greatly to the vivacity of its aspect. "If fine buildings and striking localities are required to give interest to a scene," remarks Mr. Ellis, "this has no claims; but, on the other hand, if the gradual crowding of junks till they become innumerable, a vast population, buildings, though not elegant, yet regular and peculiar, careful and successful cultivation, can supply these deficiencies, the entrance to Tientsin will not be without attractions to the traveller."[1] The stacks of salt along the river arrest the attention of the voyager; the immense quantity of this article collected at this city is only a small portion of the amount consumed in the interior. Tientsin will gradually increase in wealth, and now perhaps contains half a million of inhabitants. Its position renders it one of the most important cities in the empire, and the key of the capital.

Near the embouchure of the river is Ta-ku, with its forts and garrison, a small town noticeable as the spot where the first interview between the Chinese and English plenipotentiaries was held, in August, 1840; and for three engagements between the British and Chinese forces in 1858, 1859, and 1860. The general aspect of the province is flat and cheerless, the soil near the coast unproductive, but, as a whole, rich and well cultivated, though the harvests are jeopardized by frequent droughts.

The port of Peking is Tung chau on the Pei ho, twelve miles from the east gate, and joined to it by an elevated stone causeway. All boats here unload their passengers and freight, which are transported in carts, wheelbarrows, or on mules and donkeys. The city of Tung chau presents a dilapidated appearance amidst all its business and trade, and its population depends on the transit of goods for their chief support. The streets are paved, the largest of them having raised footpaths on their sides. The houses indicate a prosperous community. A single pagoda towers nearly 200 feet above them, and forms a waymark for miles across the country. Tung chau is only 100 feet above the sea, from which it is distant 120 miles in a direct line; consequently, its liability to floods is a serious drawback to its permanent prosperity.

Another city of note is Siuenhwa fu, finely situated between the branches of the Great Wall. Timkowski remarks, "the crenated wall which surrounds it is thirty feet high, and puts one in mind of that of the Kremlin, and resembles those of

---

[1] *Journal of Lord Amherst's Embassy to China*, 2d ed., p. 22. London, 1840

several towns in Russia; it consists of two thin parallel brick walls, the intermediate space being filled with clay and sand. The wall is flanked with towers. We passed through three gates to enter the city: the first is covered with iron nails; at the second is the guard-house; we thence proceeded along a broad street, bordered with shops of hardware; we went through several large and small streets, which are broad and clean; but, considering its extent, the city is thinly peopled."[1]

The department of Chahar, or Tsakhar, lies beyond the Great Wall, north and west of the province, a mountainous and thinly settled country, chiefly inhabited by Mongol shepherds who keep the flocks and herds of the Emperor.[2]

In the north-east of their grounds lies the thriving town of Dolon-nor (*i.e.*, Seven Lakes), or Lama-miao, of about 20,000 Chinese, founded by Kanghí. The Buddhist temples and manufactories of bells, idols, praying machines, and other religious articles found here, give it its name, and attract the Mongols, whose women array themselves in the jewelry made here. It is in latitude 42° 16′ N., about ten miles from the Shangtu River, a large branch of the river Liao, on a sandy plain, and is approached by a road winding among several lakes. North-west of Dolon-nor are the ruins of the ancient Mongolian capital of Shangtu, rendered more famous among English reading people by Coleridge's exquisite poem—

> In Xanadu did Kubla Khan
>   A stately pleasure-dome decree:
> Where Alph, the sacred river, ran
> Through caverns measureless to man
>   Down to a sunless sea.
> So twice five miles of fertile ground
> With walls and towers were girdled round—

than by Marco Polo's relation, which moved the poet to pen the lines. It was planned as Mukden now is, an outer and inner wall inclosing separate peoples, and its tumuli will probably furnish many tablets and relics of the Mongol emperors, when

---

[1] *Travels of the Russian Mission through Mongolia to China*, Vol. I., p. 293. London, 1827.

[2] Williamson, *Journeys in North China*, Vol. II., p. 90.

carefully dug over. It was too far from Peking for the Manchu monarchs to rebuild, and the Ming emperors had no power there. It was visited in 1872 by Messrs. Grosvenor and Bushell of the British Legation; Dr. Bushell's description corroborates Polo's account and Gerbillon's later notices of its size.[1]

There are several lakes, the largest of which, the Peh hu, in the south-western part, connects with the Pei ho through the river Hü-to. The various branches of the five rivers, whose united waters disembogue at Ta-ku, afford a precarious water communication through the southern half of Chihlí. Their head-waters rise in Shansí and beyond the Great Wall, bringing down much silt, which their lower currents only partially take out into the gulf; this sediment soon destroys the usefulness of the channels by raising them dangerously near the level of the banks. The utilization of their streams is a difficult problem in civil engineering, not only here but throughout the Great Plain.

Near the banks of the Lan ho, a large stream flowing south from the eastern slopes of the Chahar Hills, past Yungping fu into the gulf, and about one hundred and seventy-four miles north of Ta-ku, lies Chingpeh, or Jeh-ho, the Emperor's country palace. The approach to it is through a pass cut out of the rock, and resembles that leading to Damascus. The imperial grounds are embraced by a high range of hills forming a grand amphitheatre, which at this point is extremely fine. This descent to the city presents new and captivating views at every turn of the road. The hunting grounds are inclosed by a high wall stretching twenty miles over the hills, and stocked with deer, elks, and other game. The Buddhist temples form the chief attraction to a visitor. The largest one is square and castellated, eleven stories high, and about two hundred feet on each of its sides; the stories are painted red, yellow and green alternating. There are several similar but smaller structures below this one, and on each of the first two or three series is a row of small chinaware pagodas of a blue color; their tiles are

[1] *Journal of the Roy. Geog. Soc.*, 1874. Yule's *Marco Polo*, Vol. I., pp. 263–268. *Cathay and the Way Thither*, Vol. I., p. 134. Gerbillon, *Mémoires concernant les Chinois* (Astley's ed.), Vol. IV., pp. 701–716. *Journal Asiatique*, Ser. II., Tome XI., p. 345. Huc, *Tartary, etc.*, Vol. I., p 34, 2d ed., London

likewise blue. In the bright sunlight the effect of these brilliant bands is very good, and the general neatness adds to the pleasing result of the gay coloring. Nearly a thousand lamas live about these shrines. The town of Jeh-ho (*i.e.*, Hot River) consists mostly of one street coiling around the hills near the palace; its inhabitants are of a higher grade than usual in Chinese cities, the greater part being connected with the government. The road through Ku-peh kau in the Great Wall from Peking to Jeh-ho is one of the best in the province, and the journey presents a variety of charming scenery; its chief interest to foreigners is connected with the visit there of Lord Macartney, in 1793.[1] This fertile prefecture is rapidly settling by Chinese, whose numbers are now not far from two millions.

The principal productions of Chihlí are millet and wheat, sorghum, maize, oats, and many kinds of pulse and fruits, among which are pears, dried and fresh dates (*Rhamnus*), apples and grapes; all these are exported. Coal, both bituminous and anthracite, exists in great abundance; one mode of using hard coal is to mix its dust with powdered clay and work them into balls and cakes for cooking and fuel. The province also furnishes good marble, granite, lime, and iron, some kinds of precious stones, and clay for bricks and pottery.

The province of Shantung (*i.e.*, East of the Hills) has a long coast-line, its maritime border being more than half its whole circuit. It lies south of the Gulf of Pechele, south-east of Chihlí, north of Kiangsu, and borders on Honan, where the Yellow River divides the two. Most of its area is level, the hilly part is the peninsula portion, where the highest points rise too high to admit of cultivation. The Grand Canal enters the province on its course from Tientsin at Lintsing chau in the north-west, passing in a south-easterly direction to the old Yellow River, and adds greatly to its importance. The shores of the promontory are generally bold, and full of indentations, presenting several excellent harbors; no important river disembogues within the province, and on each side of the peninsula

---

[1] Sir G. L. Staunton, *Account of an Embassy from the King of Great Britain to the Emperor of China*. 2 vols. Lond., 1796.

the waters are shallow. Chifu, in the prefecture of Tăngchau, has the best harbor, and its trade will gradually draw toward it a large population. The hills along the shore have a remarkably uniform, conical shape, resembling the bonnets worn by officers. The hilly regions are arranged in a series of chains running across the promontory, the longest and highest of which runs with the general trend of the coast in Tai-ngan fu, some peaks reaching over five thousand feet, but most of them being under three thousand feet high. Their intervales are highly cultivated. The soil is generally productive, except near the shores of the gulf, where it is nitrous. Two crops are annually produced here as elsewhere in Northern China. The willow, aspen, ailantus, locust (*Sophora*), oak, mulberry, and conifera, are common trees; silk-worms fed on oak leaves furnish silk.

This province is one of the most celebrated in Chinese history, partly from its having been the scene of many remarkable events in the early history of the people up to B.C. 200, but more particularly from its containing the birthplaces of Confucius and Mencius, whose fame has gone over the earth. The inhabitants of the province are proud of their nativity on this score, much as the woman of Samaria was because Jacob's cattle had drunk water at the well of Sychar.

The high mountain called Tai shan, or 'Great mount,' is situated near Tai-ngan fu in this province. This peak is mentioned in the *Shu King* as that where Shun sacrificed to Heaven (B.C. 2254); it is accordingly celebrated for its historical as well as religious associations. It towers high above all other peaks in the range, as if keeping solitary watch over the country roundabout, and is the great rendezvous of devotees; every sect has there its temples and idols, scattered up and down its sides, in which priests chant their prayers, and practise a thousand superstitions to attract pilgrims to their shrines. During the spring, the roads leading to the Tai shan are obstructed with long caravans of people coming to accomplish their vows, to supplicate the deities for health or riches, or to solicit the joys of heaven in exchange for the woes of earth. A French missionary mentions having met with pilgrims going to it, one party of whom consisted of old dames, who had with infinite fatigue and discomfort come from the south of Honan, about three hundred miles, to "remind their god of the long abstinence from flesh and fish they had observed during the course of their lives, and solicit, as a recompense, a happy transmigration for their souls." The youngest of this party was 78, and the oldest 90 years.[1] Another traveller says that the pilgrims resort there during the spring, when there are fairs to attract them; high and low, official and commoner, men and women, old and young, all sorts gather to worship and traffic. A great temple lies outside the town, whose grounds furnish a large and secure area for the tents where the devotees amuse themselves, after they have finished their devotions. The road to the summit is about five miles, well paved and furnished with rest-houses, tea-stalls, and stairways for the convenience of the pilgrims, and shaded with cypresses. It is beset with beggars, men and women with all kinds of sores and diseases, crippled and injured, besieging travellers with cries and self-imposed sufferings, frequently lying across the path so as to be stepped upon. A vast number of them live on alms thus collected, and have scooped themselves holes in the side of the way, where they live; their numbers indicate the great crowds whose offerings support such a wretched throng on the hill.

The capital of the province is Tsínan, a well-built city of about 100,000 inhabitants. It was an important town in ancient times as the capital of Tsí, one of the influential feudal States, from B.C. 1100 to its conquest by Chí Hwangtí about 230; the present town lies not far east of the Ta-tsing ho, or new Yellow River, and is accessible by small steamers from sea. It has hills around it, and is protected by three lines of defence, composed of mud, granite, and brick. Three copious springs near the western gate furnish pure water, which is tepid and so abundant as to fill the city moat and form a lake for the solace of the citizens whether in boats upon its bosom or from temples around its shores. Its manufactures are strong fabrics of wild silk, and ornaments of *liu-lí*, a vitreous substance like strass, of

---

[1] *Annales de la Foi*, 1844, Tome XVI., p. 421.

which snuff-bottles, bangles, cups, etc., are made in great variety, to resemble serpentine, jade, ice, and other things. East of Tsí-nan is the prefect city of Tsing chau, once the provincial capital, and the centre of a populous and fertile region. Tsíning chau is an opulent and flourishing place, judging from the gilded and carved shops, temples, and public offices in the suburbs, which stretch along the eastern banks of the Canal; just beyond the town, the Canal is only a little raised above the level of the extensive marshes on each side, and further south the swamps increase rapidly: when Amherst's embassy passed, the whole country, as far as the eye could reach, displayed the effects of a most extensive recent inundation. Davis adds, "The waters were on a level with those of the Canal, and there was no need of dams, which were themselves nearly under water, and sluices for discharging the superfluous water were occasionally observed. Clumps of large trees, cottages, and towers, were to be seen on all sides, half under water, and deserted by the inhabitants; the number of the latter led to the inference that they were provided as places of refuge in case of inundation, which must be here very frequent. Wretched villages occurred frequently on the right-hand bank, along which the tracking path was in some places so completely undermined as to give way at every step, obliging them to lay down hurdles of reeds to afford a passage." [1]

Lin-tsing chau, on the Yu ho, at its junction with the Canal, lies in the midst of a beautiful country, full of gardens and cultivated grounds, interspersed with buildings. This place is the dépôt for produce brought on the Canal, and a rendezvous for large fleets of boats and barges. Near it is a pagoda in good repair, about 150 feet high, the basement of which is built of granite, and the other stories of glazed bricks.

The towns and villages of Shantung have been much visited during the past few years, and their inhabitants have become better acquainted with foreigners, with whom increased intercourse has developed its good and bad results. The productions of this fertile province comprise every kind of grain and vege-

---

[1] *Sketches of China*, Vol. I., p. 257.

table found in Northern China, and its trade by sea and along the Canal opens many outlets for enterprising capital. Among its mineral productions are gold, copper, asbestos, galena, antimony, silver, sulphur, fine agates, and saltpetre; the first occurs in the beds of streams. All these yield in real importance, however, to the coal and iron, which are abundant, and have been worked for ages. Its manufactures supply the common clothing and utensils of its people; silk fabrics, straw braid woven from a kind of wheat, glass, cheap earthenware, and rugs of every pattern.

Mr. Stevens, an American missionary who visited Wei-hai wei and Chifu in 1837, gives a description of the people, which is still applicable to most parts of the province: "These poor people know nothing, from youth to old age, but the same monotonous round of toil for a subsistence, and never see, never hear anything of the world around them. Improvements in the useful arts and sciences, and an increase of the conveniences of life, are never known among them. In the place where their fathers lived and died, do they live, and toil, and die, to be succeeded by another generation in the same manner. Few of the comforts of life can be found among them; their houses consisted in general of granite and thatched roofs, but neither table, chair, nor floor, nor any article of furniture could be seen in the houses of the poorest. Every man had his pipe, and tea was in most dwellings. They were industriously engaged, some in ploughing, others in reaping, some carrying out manure, and others bringing home produce; numbers were collected on the thrashing-floors, winnowing, sifting and packing wheat, rice, millet, peas, and in drying maize, all with the greatest diligence. Here, too, were their teams for ploughing, yoked together in all possible ludicrous combinatious; sometimes a cow and an ass; or a cow, an ox and an ass; or a cow and two asses; or four asses; and all yoked abreast. All the women had small feet, and wore a pale and sallow aspect, and their miserable, squalid appearance excited an indelible feeling of compassion for their helpless lot. They were not always shy, but were generally ill-clad and ugly, apparently laboring in the fields like the men. But on several occasions, young ladies clothed in gay silks and satins, riding astride upon bags on donkeys, were seen. No prospect of melioration for either men or women appears but in the liberalizing and happy influences of Christianity."[1]

The province of SHANSÍ (*i.e.*, West of the Hills) lies between Chihlí and Shensí, and north of Honan; the Yellow River bounds it on the west and partly on the south, and the Great Wall forms most of the northern frontier. It measures 55,268 square miles, nearly the same as England and Wales, or the State of Illinois. This province is the original seat of the Chinese people; and many of the places mentioned and the scenes recorded in their ancient annals occurred within its borders. Its rugged surface presents a striking contrast to the level tracts in Chihlí and Shantung. The southern portion of Shansí, including the region down to the Yellow River, in all an area of 30,000 square miles, presents a geological formation of great simplicity from Hwai king as far north as Ping ting. The plain around the first-named city is bounded on the north by a steep, castellated range of hills which varies from 1,000 to 1,500 feet in height; it has few roads or streams crossing it. On reaching the top, an undulating table-land stretches northward, varying from 2,500 to 3,000 feet above the Plain, consisting of coal formation, above the limestone of the lower steep hills. About forty miles from those hills, there is a second rise like the first, up which the road takes one to another plateau, nearly 6,000 feet above the sea. This plateau is built up of later rocks, sandstones, shales, and conglomerates of green, red, yellow, lilac, and brown colors, and is deeply eroded by branches of the Tsin River, which finally flow into the Yellow River. This plateau has its north-west border in the Wu ling pass, beyond which begins the descent to the basin of the Făn River. That basin is traversed near its eastern side by the Hoh shan nearly to Taiyuen; its peaks rise to 8,000 feet in some places; the rocks are granite and divide the coal measures, anthracite lying on its eastern side and bituminous on the west, as far as the Yellow

---

[1] *Chinese Repository*, Vol. IV., pp. 308–335. W. H. Medhurst's *China*, chaps. xv.–xix.

River, and north as far as Ta-tung. On top of both plateaus is spread the loess deposit, varying in depth from ten to five hundred feet, and deeply gullied by water-courses in every direction, which expose coal and iron mines.

On the eastern side of Shansí the rocks are made up of ancient formations or deposits of the Silurian age, presenting a series of peaks, passes and ranges that render travel very difficult down to the Plain. By these outlying ranges the province is isolated from Chihlí, as no useful water communication exists. This coal and iron formation is probably the largest in the world, and when railroads open it up to easy access it can be readily worked along the water-courses. The northern part of the province is drained through the rivers ending at Tientsin. This elevated region cannot be artificially irrigated, and when the rainfall is too small or too late, the people suffer from famine. The northern and southern prefectures exhibit great diversity in their animal, mineral, and vegetable productions. Some of the favorite imperial hunting-grounds are in the north; from the coal, iron, cinnabar, copper, marble, lapis-lazuli, jasper, salt, and other minerals which it affords, the inhabitants gain much of their wealth. The principal grains are wheat and millet, a large variety of vegetables and fruits, such as persimmons, pears, dates and grapes. The rivers are not large, and almost every one of them is a tributary of the Yellow River. The Făn ho, about 300 miles long, is the most important, and empties into it near the south-western corner of the province, after draining the central section. East of this stream, as far as the headwaters of those rivers flowing into Chihlí, extends an undulating table-land, having a general altitude of 3,000 feet above the Plain. South of it runs the river Kiang, also an affluent of the Yellow River, and near this, in Kiai chau, is a remarkable deposit of salt in a shallow lake (18 miles long and 3 broad), which is surrounded by a high wall. The salt is evaporated in the sun under government direction, the product bringing in a large revenue; the adjacent town of Lung-tsüen, containing 80,000 inhabitants, is devoted to the business. Salt has been obtained from this region for two thousand years; the water in some of the springs is only brackish, and used in culinary operations. There are two smaller lakes nearer the Yellow River.

The iron obtained in the lower plateau, in the south-east near Tsih chau, is from clay iron-ore and spathic ore with hematite, which occurs in limestone strata at the bottom of the coal formations. It is extracted in a rude manner, but the produce is equal to any iron in the world, while its price is only about two cents a pound. The working and transportation of coal and iron employ myriads of people, though they are miserably paid. The province barely supplies its own cotton, but woollen garments and sheepskins are produced to make up the demand for clothing.

Taiyuen fu, the capital, lies on the northern border of a fertile plain, 3,000 feet above the sea level; this plain extends about 2,000 square miles, and owes its existence to the gradual filling up of a lake there, the waters having cut their way out, and left the river Făn to drain the surplus. Across the Ho shan range lies another basin of equal fertility and mineral wealth, in Ping-ting chau, where coal, iron, clay and stone exist in unlimited quantities. In the northern part of this province the Buddhist temples at Wu-tai shan in Tai chau draw vast crowds of votaries to their shrines. The hills in which they are built rise prominently above the range, and each celebrated locality is memorialized by its own particular divinity, and the buildings where he is worshipped. The presence of a living Buddha, or *Gegen*, here attracts thousands of Mongols from the north to adore him; their toilsome journey adding to the worth of the visit. Most of the lamas are from the north and west. The region north of this seems to be gradually losing its fertility, owing to the sand which is drifted by north winds from the Ortous steppes; and as all the hills are bare of trees, the whole of Shansí seems destined to increasing poverty and barrenness. Its inhabitants are shrewd, enterprising traders as well as frugal agriculturists; many of the bankers in the Empire are from its cities.

The great roads from Peking to the south-west and west pass through all the chief towns of this province, and when new probably equalled in engineering and construction anything of the kind ever built by the Romans. The stones with which they are paved average 15 inches in thickness. Few regions can exceed in natural difficulties some of the passes over the loess-covered tracts of this province, where the road must wind

View over the Loess-clefts from the Han-sing ling Pass, Shansi. From Richthofen.

through miles of narrow cuts in the light and tenacious soil, to emerge before a landscape such as that seen in the illustration.[1]

The province of HONAN (*i.e.*, South of the River) comprises some of the most fertile parts of the Plain, and, on account of its abundance and central position, early received the name of

[1] Richthofen, *China.* Band I. S. 68. Rev. Arthur Smith, *Glimpses of Travel in the Middle Kingdom.* Shanghai, 1875.

Chung Hwa Tí, or the 'Middle Flowery Land,' afterwards enlarged into *Chung Kwoh*, or 'Middle Kingdom.' Its form is an irregular triangle, and its size nearly the same as Shantung; it has Shansí and Chihlí on the north, Nganhwui on the south-east, Hupeh on the south and south-west, and Shensí on the west, bordering also on Shantung and Kiangsu. This area is divided into three basins, that of the Yellow River in the north, of the Hwai River on the south, and the Han River on the south-west; the last two are separated by a marked range of mountains, the Fuh-niu shan, which is regarded as the eastern terminus of the Kwănlun Mountains; it is about 300 miles long, and its eastern end is near Jü-ning fu. This range maintains an elevation of 4,000 to 6,000 feet, and is crossed at Nanchau, where a remarkable natural pass about 30 miles long, rising to 1,200 or 1,500 feet, affords the needed facilities for trade and travel between the central and northern provinces. The Peh and Tan rivers drain its southern slopes into the Han, and the eastern sides are abundantly watered by the numerous branches of the Hwai River as they flow into Hungtsih Lake. The northern portion of Honan along the Yellow River is level, fertile and populous, forming one of the richest portions of the province.

For its climate, productions, literary reputation, historical associations, and variety of scenery, this province takes a prominent rank. The earliest records of the Black-haired race refer to this region, and the struggles for dominion among feudal and imperial armies occurred in its plains. Its present difficulty of access from the coast will ere long be overcome by railroads, when its capabilities may be further developed, and the cotton, hemp, iron, tutenag, silk and coal be increased for exportation. The people at present consume their own food and manufactures, and only require a good demand to increase the quality and amounts and exchange them for other things. The three prefectures north of the Yellow River are low-lying; through these the waters of that river have recently found their way into the River Wei and thence to the Gulf of Pechele, at Măng-tsin or east of it; the gradual rise of the bed renders their levels nearly the same, while it makes the main stream so broad and shallow that it is of little use for navigation. These plains are traversed by wheelbarrows and carts, whose drivers and trundlers form a vast body of stalwart men constantly going about in their employment from one city to another.

Kaifung fu, or Pien-liang, the capital, is situated about a league from the southern bank of the Yellow River, whose bed is here elevated above the adjacent country. It was the metropolis from A.D. 960 to 1129, and has often suffered from attacks of armies as well as from inundations. The dikes are mostly on the northern shore, and exhibit the industry and unavailing efforts of the people for scores of leagues. During the period of the Manchu conquest Kaifung was defended by a loyal general, who, seeing no other resource against the invaders, broke down the embankments to drown them, by which manœuvre upwards of 300,000 of the inhabitants perished. The city was rebuilt, but it has not attained to its ancient splendor, if credit can be given to the *Statistics of Kaifung*, in which work it is described as having been six leagues in circuit in the twelfth century, approached by five roads, and containing numerous palaces, gardens, and government houses. The valley of the River Loh lies between the Yellow River and the Fuh-niu Mountains, a fertile, populous region wherein many of the remarkable events of Chinese history were enacted. Loh-yang, near Honan, was the metropolis at three different intervals, and probably further researches here will bring to light many ancient relics; rock-cut temples and old inscriptions, with graceful bas-reliefs, near the natural gate of Lung-măn, where the road crosses Sung shan, have already been seen. Owing to the direction of the roads leading through this region from the south and east, and the passes for travel towards the north-west, it will form a very important centre of trade in the future of Central Asia and western China.

The province of KIANGSU is named from the first syllable of the capital, Kiangning, joined to Su, part of the name of the richest city, Suchau. It lies along the sea-coast, in a north-westerly direction, having Shantung on the north, Nganhwui on the west, and Chehkiang on the south. The area is about 45,000 square miles, equalling Pennsylvania or a little less than

England by itself. It consists, with little interruption, of level tracts interspersed with lakes and marshes, through which flow their two noble rivers, which as they are the source of the extraordinary fertility of this region, so also render it obnoxious to freshes, or cover the low portions with irreclaimable morasses. The region of Kiangnan is where the beauty and riches of China are most amply displayed; "and whether we consider," remarks Gutzlaff, speaking of this and the adjoining province, "their agricultural resources, their great manufactures, their various productions, their excellent situation on the banks of these two large streams, their many canals and tributary rivers, these two provinces doubtless constitute the best territory of China." The staple productions are grain, cotton, tea, silk, and rice, and most kinds of manufactures are here carried to the greatest perfection. The people have an exceptional reputation for intelligence and wit, and although the province has long ceased to possess a court, its cities still present a gayer aspect, and are adorned with better structures than any others in the empire. This province was the scene of the dreadful ravages of the Tai-ping rebellion, and large districts are still desolate, while their cities lie waste.

Probably no other country of equal extent is better watered than Kiangsu. The Great River, the Grand Canal, many smaller streams and canals, and a succession of lakes along the line of the canal, afford easy communication through every part. The sea-coast has not been surveyed north of the Yangtsz', where it is unapproachable in large vessels; dykes have been constructed in some portions to prevent the in-flow of the ocean. The largest lake is the Hungtsih, about two hundred miles in circumference. South of it lies Kauyu Lake, and on the eastern side of the canal opposite is Pauying Lake, both of them broad sheets of water. Numerous small lakes lie around them. Tai hu, or 'Great Lake,' lies partly in Kiangsu and partly in Chehkiang, and is the largest in the province. Its borders are skirted by romantic scenery, while its bosom is broken by numerous islets, affording convenient resort to the fishermen who get their subsistence from its waters.

Kiangning fu (better known abroad as Nanking), the capital

of the province, is situated on the south shore of the Yangtsz', 194 miles from Shanghai. It was the metropolis from A.D. 317 to 582, and again for 35 years during the Ming dynasty (1368–1403). This city is the natural location of an imperial court, accessible by land and water from all quarters, and susceptible of sure defence. When the Tai-pings were expelled in 1865, the city was nearly destroyed, and has since that date only slowly revived. When Hungwu made it his capital, he strengthened the wall around it, inclosing a great area, 35 miles in circuit, which was never fully covered with buildings, and at present has a most ruinous appearance. Davis remarks the striking resemblance between Rome and Nanking, the area within the walls of both being partially inhabited, and ruins of buildings lying here and there among the cultivated fields, the melancholy remains of departed glory. Both of them, however, have now brighter prospects for the future.

The part occupied by the Manchus is separated by a cross wall from the Chinese town. The great extent of the wall renders the defence of the city difficult, besides which it is overlooked from the hills on the east, from one of which, the Chung shan, a wide view of the surrounding country can be obtained. On this eastern face are three gates; the land near the two toward the river is marshy, and the gates are approached on stone causeys. A deep canal runs up from the river directly under the walls on the west, serving to strengthen the approaches on that side. Nanking is laid out in four rather wide and parallel avenues intersected by others of less width; and though not so broad as those of Peking, are on the whole clean, well-paved, and bordered with handsomely furnished shops.

The only remarkable monuments of royalty which remain are several guardian statues situated not far from the walls. These statues form an avenue leading up to the sepulchre where the Emperor Hungwu was buried about 1398. They consist of gigantic figures like warriors cased in armor, standing on either side of the road, across which at intervals large stone tablets are extended, supported by great blocks of stone instead of pillars. Situated at some distance are a number of rude colossal figures of horses, elephants, and other animals, all intended to represent the guardians of the mighty dead.[1]

Nothing made Nanking more celebrated abroad than the Porcelain Tower, called *Pao-ngăn tah*, or the 'Recompensing Favor Monastery,' which stood pre-eminent above all other similar buildings in China for its completeness and elegance, the material of which it was built, and the quantity of gilding with which its interior was embellished. It was erected by Yungloh to recompense the great favor of her majesty the Empress, and occupied 19 years (1411–1430) in its construction. It was maintained in good condition by the government, and three stories which had been thrown down by lightning in 1801 were rebuilt. The Tai-pings blew it up and carried off the bricks in 1856, fearing lest its geomantic influences should work against the success of their cause. As to its dimensions: Its form was octagonal, divided into nine equal stories, the circumference of the lower story being 120 feet, decreasing gradually to the top. Its base rested upon a solid foundation of brick-work ten feet high, up which a flight of twelve steps led into the tower, whence a spiral staircase of 190 steps carried the visitor to the summit, 261 feet from the ground. The outer face was covered with slabs of glazed porcelain of various colors, principally green, red, yellow, and white, the body of the edifice being brick. At every story was a projecting roof, covered with green tiles; from each corner and from the top of these roofs were suspended bells, numbering 150 in all.

This beautiful structure was visited in 1852 by Dr. Charles Taylor, an American missionary, who has left a full account of his observations.[2] It was to have been raised to an altitude of 329 feet and of thirteen stories, but only nine were built; careful measurement gave 261 feet as its height, 8½ feet its thickness at top, and 12 feet at the base, where it was 96 feet 10 inches

[1] The curious reader can consult the article by Mayer, in Vol. XII. of the *North China Branch Royal Asiatic Society's Journal*, 1878, for the meaning of these various objects.

[2] *Five Years in China*, Nashville, Tenn., 1860. See also *Voyages of the Nemesis*, pp. 450–452, for further details of this city in 1842; the *Chinese Repository*, Vols. I., p. 257, and XIII., p. 261, contain more details on the Pagoda

in diameter. The facing was of bricks made of fine porcelain clay; the prevailing color was green, owing to the predominance of the tiles on the numerous stories. The woodwork supporting these successive roofs was strong, curiously carved and richly painted. The many-colored tiles and bricks were highly glazed, giving the building a gay and beautiful appearance, that was greatly heightened when seen in the reflected sunlight. When new it had 140 lamps, most of them hanging outside; and a native writer says "that when lighted they illumine the 33 heavens, and detect the good and evil among men, as well as forever ward off human miseries." The destruction of a building like this, from mere fanciful ideas, goes far to explain the absence of all old or great edifices in China.

Nanking has extensive manufactories of fine satin and crape, Nankeen cotton cloth, paper and ink of fine quality, and beautiful artificial flowers of pith paper. In distant parts of the empire, any article which is superior to the common run of workmanship, is said to be from Nanking, though the speaker means only that it was made in that region. It is renowned, too, for its scholars and literary character, and in this particular stands among the first places of learning in the country. It is the residence of the governor-general of three provinces, and consequently the centre of a large concourse of officials, educated men, and students seeking for promotion; these, with its large libraries and bookstores, all indicating and assisting literary pursuits, combine to give it this distinguished position. In the monastery on Golden Island, near Chinkiang, a library was found by the English officers, but there was no haste in examining its contents, as they intended to have carried off the whole collection, had not peace prevented.

The city of Suchau now exceeds Nanking in size and riches. It is situated on islands lying in the Ta hu, and from this sheet of water many streams and canals connect the city with most parts of the department. The walls are about ten miles in circumference; outside of them are four suburbs, one of which is said to extend ten miles, besides which there is an immense floating population. The whole space includes many canals and pools connected with the Grand Canal and the lake, and presented in 1859 a scene of activity, industry, and riches which could not be surpassed elsewhere in China. The population probably then exceeded a million, including the suburbs. It lies north-west of Shanghai, the way passing through a continual range of villages and cities; the environs are highly cultivated, producing cotton, silk, rice, wheat, fruits, and vegetables. It was captured in 1860 by the rebels, and when retaken in 1865 was nearly reduced to a heap of ruins. It is, however, rapidly reviving, as the loss of life was comparatively small.

The Chinese regard this as one of their richest and most beautiful cities, and have a saying, "that to be happy on earth, one must be born in Suchau, live in Canton, and die in Liau-chau, for in the first are the handsomest people, in the second the most costly luxuries, and in the third the best coffins." It has a high reputation for its buildings, the elegance of its tombs, the picturesque scenery of its waters and gardens, the politeness and intelligence of its inhabitants, and the beauty of its women. Its manufactures of silk, linen, cotton, and works in iron, ivory, wood, horn, glass, lackered-ware, paper, and other articles, are the chief sources of its wealth and prosperity; the kinds of silk goods produced here surpass in variety and richness those woven in any other place. Vessels can proceed up to the city by several channels from the Yangtsz' kiang, but junks of large burden anchor at Shanghai, or Sungkiang; the whole country is so intersected by natural and artificial water-courses, that the people have hardly any need for roads and carts, but get about in barrows and sedans. Small steamers find their way to every large village at high tide.

Chinkiang, situated at the junction of the Grand Canal with the Yangtsz' kiang, was captured by the British in July, 1842, at a great loss of life to its defenders; the Manchu general Hai-ling, finding the city taken, seated himself in his office, and set fire to the house, making it his funeral pyre. Its position renders it the key of the country, in respect to the transport of produce, taxes and provisions for Peking, inasmuch as when the river and canal are both blockaded, the supplies for the north and south are to a great extent intercepted. In times of peace the scenes at the junction afford a good exhibition of the industry and trade of the people. Barrow describes, in 1794, "the multitude of ships of war, of burden and of pleasure, some gliding down the stream, others sailing against it; some moving by oars, and others lying at anchor; the banks on either side covered with towns and houses as far as the eye could reach; as presenting a prospect more varied and cheerful than any that had hitherto occurred. Nor was the canal, on the opposite side, less lively. For two whole days we were continually passing among fleets of vessels of different construction and dimensions."[1]

The country in the vicinity is well cultivated, moderately hilly, and presents a characteristic view of Chinese life and action. "On the south-east, the hills broke into an undulating country clothed with verdure, and firs bordering upon small lakes. Beyond, stretched the vast river we had just ascended. In the other direction, the land in the foreground continued a low and swampy flat, leaving it difficult at a little distance to determine which of the serpentine channels was the main branch; there were innumerable sheets of water, separated by narrow mounds, so that the whole resembled a vast lake, intersected by causeways. Willows grew along their sides, and dwellings were erected on small patches somewhat higher than the common surface."[2] This whole country was the scene of dreadful fighting for many years. Between the Imperialists and Tai-pings the city was totally destroyed, so that in 1861 hardly a house was left. It is now regaining its natural trade and prosperity.

Near the mouth of the Grand Canal is Kin shan, or Golden Island,[3] a beautiful spot, covered with temples and monastic establishments. A pagoda crowns the summit, and there are many pavilions and halls, of various sizes and degrees of elegance, on its sides and at the base, many of them showing their imperial ownership by the yellow or green tiling. Since the river has been open to traffic, and the devastations of the Tai-pings have ceased, the priests have returned in small num-

---

[1] *Travels in China.* [2] Capt. G. G. Loch, *Events in China*, p. 74.

[3] Mentioned by Marco Polo. Yule's edition, Vol. II., p. 137.

bers to their abodes, but the whole settlement is a poor mockery of its early splendor. A similar one, rather larger, is found at Siung shan, or Silver Island, below Chinkiang; it is, however, on a less extensive scale, though in a beautiful situation. Priests are the only occupants; temples and palaces the principal buildings, surrounded by gardens and bowers. Massive granite terraces, decorated with huge stone monsters, are reached from the water by broad flights of steps; fine temples, placed to be seen, and yet shaded by trees, open pavilions, and secluded summer-houses, give it a delightful air of retreat and comfort, which a nearer inspection sadly disappoints.

The banks of the Yangtsz' during the 250 miles of its course through this province, are uniformly low, and no towns of importance occur close to them, as they would be exposed to the floods. The vast body of water, with its freight of millions of tons of silt goes on its way in a quiet equable current into the Yellow Sea. The dense population of the prefectures on the south bank, contrasted with the sparseness of the region between the Canal and seashore on the north side, indicate the comparative barrenness of the latter, and the difficulty of cultivating marshy lands so nearly level with the sea.

The largest seaport in Kiangsu is Shanghai (*i.e.*, Approaching the Sea), now become one of the leading emporia in Asia. It lies on the north shore of the Wusung River, about fourteen miles from its mouth, in lat. 31° 10′ N., and long. 121° 30′ E., at the junction of the Hwang-pu with it, and by means of both streams communicates with Suchau, Sungkiang, and other large cities on the Grand Canal; while by the Yangtsz' it receives produce from Yunnan and Sz'chuen. In these respects its position resembles that of New Orleans.

The town of Wusung is at the mouth of that river, here about a mile wide; and two miles beyond lies the district town of Paushan. The wall of Shanghai is three miles in circuit, through which six gates open into extensive suburbs; around the ramparts flows a ditch twenty feet wide. The city stands in a wide plain of extraordinary fertility, intersected by numerous streamlets, and affording ample means of navigation and communication; its population is estimated to be at present over 500,-

000, but the data for this figure are rather imperfect. Since it was opened to foreign commerce in 1843, the growth of the town has been rapid in every element of prosperity, though subject to great vicissitudes by reason of the rebellion which devastated the adjoining country. Its capture by the insurgents in 1851, and their expulsion in February, 1853, with the destruction of the eastern and southern suburbs in 1860, have been its chief disasters since that date. The native trade has gradually passed from the unwieldy and unsafe junks which used to throng the Hwang-pu east of the city, into steamers and foreign craft, and is now confined, so far as the vessels are concerned, to the inland and coast traffic in coarse, cheap articles.

Shanghai city itself is a dirty place, and poorly built. The houses are mostly made of bluish square brick, imperfectly burned; and the walls are constructed in a cellular manner by placing bricks on their edges, and covering them with stucco. The streets are about eight feet wide, paved with stone slabs, and in the daytime crowded with people. Silk and embroidery, cotton, and cotton goods, porcelain, ready-made clothes, beautiful skins and furs, bamboo pipes of every size, bamboo ornaments, pictures, bronzes, specimens of old porcelain, and other curiosities, to which the Chinese attach great value, attract the stranger's notice. Articles of food form the most extensive trade of all; and it is sometimes a difficult matter to get through the streets, owing to the immense quantities of fish, pork, fruit, and vegetables, which crowd the stands in front of the shops. Dining-rooms, tea-houses, and bakers' shops, are met with at every step, from the poor man who carries around his kitchen or bakehouse, altogether hardly worth a dollar, to the most extensive tavern or tea-house, crowded with customers. For a few cash, a Chinese can dine upon rice, fish, vegetables, and tea; nor does it matter much to him, whether his table is set in the streets or on the ground, in a house or on a deck, he makes himself merry with his chopsticks, and eats what is before him.[1] The buildings composing the Ching-hwang miao, and the grounds attached to this establishment, present a good

[1] Fortune's *Wanderings in China*, p. 120.

instance of Chinese style and taste in architecture. Large warehouses for storing goods, granaries, and temples, are common; but neither these, nor the public buildings, present any distinguishing features peculiar to this city alone.

The contrast between the narrow, noisome and reeking parts of the native city, and the clean, spacious, well-shaded and well-paved streets and large houses of the foreign municipalities, is like that seen in many cities in India. The Chinese are ready enough to enjoy and support the higher style of living, but they are not yet prepared to adopt and maintain similar improvements among themselves. The difficulty of being sure of the co-operation of the rulers in municipal improvements deters intelligent natives from initiating even the commonest sanitary enterprise of their foreign neighbors.

The remaining cities and districts of Kiangsu present nothing worthy of special remark. The Grand Canal runs from north to south, and affords a safe and ample thoroughfare for multitudes of boats in its entire length. Tsing-kiang-pu and Hwai-ngan, near the old Yellow River, receive the traffic from the north and Hungtsih Lake, while Yangchau near the Yangtsz' River, takes that going north. In this part of the channel, constant dyking has resulted in raising the banks; the city of Hwai-ngan, for example, lies below the canal which brings trade to its doors, and may one day be drowned by its benefactor. Salt is manufactured in the districts south of the Yellow River, where the people cultivate but rare patches of arable land.

The island of Tsungming, at the mouth of the Yangtsz', is about sixty miles long, and sixteen wide, containing over nine hundred square miles, and is gradually enlarging by the constant deposits from the river; it is flat, but contains fresh water. It is highly cultivated and populous, though some places on the northern side are so impregnated with salt, and others so marshy, as to be useless for raising food. This island produces a variety of *kaoliang* or sorghum (*Holcus*), which is sweet enough to furnish syrup, and is grown for that purpose in the United States.

The province of NGANHWUI was so named by combining the

first words in its two large cities, Nganking and Hwuichau, and forms the south-western half of Kiangnan; it is both larger and more uneven than Kiangsu, ranges of hills stretching along the southern portions, and between the River Hwai and the Yangtsz'. It lies in the central and southern parts of the Plain, north of Kiangsí, west of Kiangsu and Chehkiang, and between them and Honan and Hupeh. Its productions and manufactures, the surface, cultivation of the country, and character of the people, are very similar to those of Kiangsu, but the cities are less celebrated. The terrible destruction of life in this province during the Tai-ping rule has only been partially rem edied by immigration from other provinces; it will require years of peace and industry to restore the prosperous days of Taokwang's reign.

The surface of the country is naturally divided into that portion which lies in the hilly regions around Hwaichau and Ningkwoh connected with the Tsientang River, the central plain of the Yangtsz' with its short affluents, and the northern portion which the River Hwai drains. The southern districts are superior for climate, fertility, and value of their products to most parts of the Empire; and the numerous rivulets which irrigate and open their beautiful valleys to traffic with other districts, render them attractive to settlers. No expense has been spared in erecting and preserving the embankments along the streams, whose waters are thereby placed at the service of the farmers.

The Great River passes through the south from south-west to north-east; several small tributaries flow into it on both banks, one of which connects with Chau hu, or Nest Lake, in Luchau fu, the principal sheet of water in the province. The largest section is drained by the River Hwai and its branches, which flow into Hungtsih Lake; most of these are navigable quite across to Honan. The productions comprise every kind of grain, vegetables, and fruit known in the Plain; most of the green tea districts lie in the south-eastern parts, particularly in the Sunglo range of hills in Hwuichau prefecture. Silk, cotton, and hemp are also extensively raised; but excepting iron, few metals are brought to market.

The provincial capital, Nganking or Anking, lies close to the northern shore of the Kiang. Davis describes the streets as very narrow, and the shops as unattractive; the courts and gateways of many good dwelling-houses presented themselves as he passed along the streets. "The palace of the governor we first took for a temple, but were soon undeceived by the inscriptions on the huge lanterns at the gateway. These official residences seldom display any magnificence. The pride of a Chinese officer of rank consists in his power and station, and as the display of mere wealth attracts little respect, it is neglected more than in any country of the world. The best shops that we saw were for the sale of horn lanterns and porcelain. They possess the art of softening horn by the application of a very high degree of moist heat, and extending it into thin laminæ of any shape. These lamps are about as transparent as ground-glass, and, when ornamented with silken hangings, have an elegant appearance." During the fifty years since his visit, this large city has been the sport of prosperous and adverse fortunes, and is now slowly recovering from its demolition during the Tai-ping rebellion. It is situated on rising ground near the base of a range of hills far in the north, the watershed of two basins.

The banks of the river, between Nanking and Nganking, a distance of 300 miles, are well cultivated, and contain towns and villages at short intervals. The climate, the scenery, the bustle on the river near the towns, and the general aspect of peaceful thrift along this reach, makes it on ordinary occasions one of the bright scenes in China. Wuhu hien, about sixty miles above Nanking, lies near the mouth of the Hwangchi, a stream connecting it with the back country, and making it the mart for much of that trade. It was next in importance to Chinkiang, but its sufferings between the rebels and imperialists nearly destroyed it. The revival in population and trade has been encouraging, and its former importance is sure to revive.

Hwuichau (or in Cantonese, Fychow) is celebrated, among other things, for its excellent ink and lackered-ware. Fung-yang (*i.e.*, the Rising Phœnix), a town lying north-west of Nanking, on the River Hwai, was intended, by Hungwu, the founder of the Ming dynasty, to have been the capital of the Empire instead of Nanking, and was thus named in anticipation of its future splendor.

The province of KIANGSÍ (*i.e.*, West of the River) lies south of Nganhwui and Hupeh, between Chehkiang and Fuhkien on the east, and Hunan on the west, reaching from the Yangtsz' to the Mei ling on the south. Its form is oblong, and its entire area is made up of the beautiful basin of the Kan kiang, including all the affluents and their minor valleys. The hilly portions form part of the remarkable series of mountainous ridges, which cover all south-eastern and southern China, an area of about 300,000 square miles, extending from Ningpo south-westerly to Annam. It is made up of ranges of short and moderate hills, cut up by a complicated net of water-courses, many of which present a succession of narrow defiles and gentle valleys with bottom lands from five to twelve miles wide. That part of this region in Kiangsí has an irregular watershed on the east, separating it from the Min basin, and a more definite divide on the west from Hunan and its higher mountains. The province entire is a little larger than all New England, or twice the size of Portugal, but, in population, vastly exceeds those countries. The surface of the land is rugged, and the character of the inhabitants partakes in some respects of the roughness of their native hills. It is well watered and drained by the River Kan and its tributaries, most of which rise within the province; the main trunk empties into Poyang Lake by numerous mouths, whose silt has gradually made the country around it swampy. For many miles on its eastern and southern banks extends an almost uninhabitable marsh, presenting a dreary appearance. The soil, generally, is productive, and large quantities of rice, wheat, silk, cotton, indigo, tea, and sugar, are grown and exported. It shares, in some degree, the manufactures of the neighboring provinces, especially in Nankeen cloth, vast quantities of which are woven here, but excels them all in the quality and amount of its porcelain. The mountains produce camphor, varnish, oak, banian, fir, pine, and other trees; those on the west are well wooded, but much of the timber has been carried away during the late rebellion, and left the hill-sides bare and profitless.

Nanchang, the provincial capital, lies near the southern shore of the Poyang Lake; the city walls are six miles in circuit, and accessible by water from all sides. The character of its population is not favorable among their countrymen, and owing to the difficulty of reaching it from the Yangtsz', it escaped the ruin and rapine which befel Kiukiang. Small steamers can come up to its jetties, but as the tea and porcelain are shipped on the south-east side of the lake, Nanchang is not likely to become a large mart; few of the cities above it can ever be reached by steamers. Barrow estimated that there were, independent of innumerable small craft, 100,000 tons of shipping lying before the place. The banks of the Kan kiang, near the lake, are flat, and not highly cultivated, but the scenery becomes more varied and agreeable the further one ascends the stream; towns and villages constantly come in sight, and the cultivation, though not universal, is more extended. Among other sights on this river are the bamboo water-wheels, which are so built on the steep banksides, that the buckets lift their freight 20 or 25 feet, and pour it out in a ceaseless stream over the fields. The flumes thrown out into the stream to turn a stronger current on the wheel, often seriously interfere with navigation. Many pagodas are seen on either bank of this water-course, some of them undoubtedly extremely old. As the voyager ascends the river, several large cities are passed, as Linkiang, Kih-ngan, Kanchau, and Nan-ngan (all capitals of departments), besides numerous towns and villages; so that if the extent of this river and the area of the valley it drains be considered, it will probably bear comparison with that of any valley in the world for populousness, amount and variety of productions, and diligence of cultivation.

Beyond Kihngan are the Shihpah tan, or 'Eighteen Rapids,' which are torrents formed by ledges of rocks running across the river, but not of such height or roughness as to seriously obstruct the navigation except at low water. The shores in their vicinage are exceedingly beautiful. The transparency of the stream, the bold rocks fringed with wood, and the varied forms of the mountains, call to mind those delightful streams that are discharged from the lakes and north counties of England. The hilly banks are in many places covered with the Camellia oleifera, whose white blossoms give them the appearance of snow, when the plant is in flower. Kanchau is the town where large boats are obliged to stop; but Nan-ngan is at the head of navigation, about three hundred miles from the lake, where all goods for the south are debarked to be carried across the Mei ling, or 'Plum Pass.'

Within the department of Jauchau in Fauliang hien, east of Poyang Lake, are the celebrated porcelain manufactories of Kingteh chin, named after an Emperor of the Sung dynasty, in whose reign, A.D. 1004, they were established. This mart still supplies all the fine porcelain used in the country, but was almost wholly destroyed during the rebellion, the kilns broken up, and the workmen dispersed to join the rebels or die from want. The million of workmen said to have been employed there thirty years ago are now only gradually resuming their operations, and slowly regaining their prosperity. The approach to the spot is announced by the smoke, and at night it appears like a town on fire, or a vast furnace emitting flames from numerous vents, there being, it is said, five hundred kilns constantly burning. Kingteh chin stands on the river Chang in a plain flanked by high mountains, about forty miles north-east from Jauchau, through which its ware is distributed over the empire.

Genius in China, as elsewhere, renders a place illustrious, and few spots are more celebrated than the vale of the White Deer in the Lü hills, near Nankang, on the west side of Lake Poyang, where Chu Hí, the great commentator of Confucius, lived and taught, in the twelfth century. It is a secluded valley about seven miles from the city, situated in a nook by the side of a rivulet. The unpretending buildings are comprised in a number of different courts, evidently intended for use rather than show. In one of the halls, the White Deer is represented, and near by a tree is pointed out, said to have been planted by the philosopher's own hand. This spot is a place of pilgrimage to Chinese literati at the present day, for his writings are prized by them next to their classics. The beauty and sublimity of this region are lauded by Davis, and its praises are frequent themes for poetical celebration among native scholars.[1]

The maritime province of CHEHKIANG, the smallest of the eighteen, lies estward of Kiangsí and Nganhwui, and between Kiangsu and Fuhkein north and south, and derives its name from the river Cheh or 'Crooked,' which runs across its southern part. Its area is 39,000 square miles, or nearly the same as Ohio; it lies south-east of the plain at the end of the Nan shan, and for fertility, numerous water-courses, rich and populous cities, variety of productions, and excellence of manufactures, is not at all inferior to the larger provinces. Baron Richthofen's letter to the Shanghai Chamber of Commerce, July 25, 1871, contains a good account of its topography. The whole province produces cotton, silk, tea, rice, ground nuts, wheat, indigo, vegetable tallow (*stillingia*), and pulse, in abundance. It possesses within its limits every requisite for the food and clothing of its inhabitants, while the excellence of its manufactures insures it in exchange a supply of the luxuries of other regions.

The rivers in Chehkiang rise in the province; and, as might be inferred from the position of the hills, their course is generally short and the currents rapid. Fourteen principal streams are enumerated, of which the Tsientang is the most important. The main branch of this river rises in the southern districts in two head-waters, which join at Küchau fu and run thence into Hangchau Bay. The bore which comes up into this river fifteen miles, as far as Hangchau, is the only one along the coast. As its wall of water approaches the city, the junks and boats prepare by turning their bows to meet it, and usually rise over its crest, 6 or 10 feet at times, without mishap. The basin of the Tsientang River measures nearly half of the province; by means of rafts and boats the people transport themselves and their produce for about 300 miles to its head-waters. The valley of Lanki is the largest of the bottom lands, 140 miles long and 5 to 15 wide, and passes north through a gorge 70 miles in length into the lower valley, where it receives

---

[1] Davis's *Sketches*, Vol. II., p. 55.

the Sin-ngan River from the west in Nganhwui, and thus communicates with Hwuichau at times of high water. It is just fitted for the rafting navigation of the region, and by means of its tortuous channels each one of the 29 districts in its entire basin can be reached by water.

The forest and fruit trees of Chehkiang comprise almost every valuable species known in the eastern provinces. The larch, elcococcus, camphor, tallow, fir, mulberry, varnish, and others, are common, and prove sources of wealth in their timber and products. The climate is most salubrious; the grains, vegetables, animals, and fishes, furnish food; while its beautiful manufactures of silk are unrivalled in the world, and have found their way to all lands. Hemp, lackered- and bamboo-wares, tea, crockery, paper, ink, and other articles, are also exported.

The inhabitants emulate those in the neighboring regions for wealth, learning, and refinements, with the exception of the hilly districts in the south bordering on Kiangsí and Fuhkien. The dwellers of these upland valleys are shut out by position and inclination, so that they form a singularly clannish race. Their dialects are peculiar and very limited in range, and each group of villagers suspects and shuns the others. They are sometimes rather turbulent, and in some parts the cultivation of the mountain lands is interdicted, and a line of military posts extends around them in the three provinces, in order to prevent the people from settling in their limits; though the interdiction does not forbid cutting the timber growing there.[1]

Hangchau, the capital of the province, lies in the northern part, less than a mile from the Tsientang. The velocity of this stream indicates a rapid descent of the country towards the ocean, but it discharges very little silt; the tide rises six or seven feet opposite the city, and nearly thirty at the mouth.

Only a moiety of the inhabitants reside within the walls of the city, the suburbs and the waters around them supporting a large population. A portion of the space in the north-western part is walled off for the accommodation of the Manchu garri-

---

[1] See *Chinese Repository*, Vol. IV., p. 488; *Journal of N. C. Br. R. A. Society*, Vol. VI., pp. 123–128; and *Chinese Recorder*, Vol. I., 1869, pp. 241–248. These people are relics of tribes of Miaotsz'.

son, which consists of 7,000 troops. The governor-general of Chehkiang and Fuhkien has an official house here, as well, also, as the governor of the province, but since the increased importance of Fuhchau, he seldom resides in this city; these, with their courts and troops, in addition to the great trade passing through, render it one of the richest and most important cities in the empire. The position is the most picturesque of any of the numerous localities selected by the Chinese for their capital. It lies in full view of the ocean, and from the hill-top in the centre a wide view of the plains south and east is obtained. The charming lake, Si Hu, and the numerous houses on its shores, with the varied scenery of the hills, copses, glades, and river banks, all highly cultivated, within a radius of ten miles, fully bear out the praises of the Chinese as to its singular beauty. Marco Polo lavishes all his admiration upon its size, riches, manufactures, and government, from which it is to be inferred that it suffered little in the Mongolian conquest. He visited the place when governor of Yangchau in 1286, and enthusiastically describes it as "beyond dispute the finest and the noblest in the world."[1] The Chinese have a proverb—*Shang yu tien tang: Hia yu Su Hang*—the purport of which is that Hangchau and Suchau are fully equal to paradise; but the comparison of the Venetian traveller gives one a poorer idêa of the European cities of his day, than it does of the magnificence of the Chinese, to those who have seen them. The streets are well-paved, ornamented with numerous honorary tablets erected to the memory of distinguished individuals, and agreeably interrupting the passage through them. The long main street extending along the Grand Canal into and through the city, thence out by the Tsientang, was, before its ruthless demolition by the Tai-pings in 1863, probably one of the finest streets in the whole Empire. The shops and warehouses, in point of size and stock of goods contained in them, might vie with the best in London. In population, luxury, wealth, and influence this city rivals Suchau, and for excellence of manufactures probably exceeds the latter place. Were Hangchau easily reached by

---

[1] Yule's *Marco Polo*, Vol. II., p. 145.

sea, and had it ample harbors, it would engross the trade of the eastern coast; but furious tides (running sometimes 11½ knots an hour); the bore jeoparding passage-boats and other small crafts; sand banks and quicksands;—these present insuperable difficulties to the commerce by the ocean.

This city was the metropolis of the country during the nine latter princes of the Sung dynasty (1129 to 1280), when the northern parts were under dominion of the tribe of Kin Tartars. One cause of celebrity is found in the beauty of its environs, especially those near the Si Hu, or West Lake, an irregular sheet of water about 12 miles in circuit. Barrow observes that "the natural and artificial beauties of this lake far exceeded anything we had hitherto had an opportunity of seeing in China. The mountains surrounding it were lofty, and broken into a variety of forms that were highly picturesque; and the valleys were richly clothed with trees of different kinds, among which three species were remarkably striking, not only by their intrinsic beauty, but also by the contrast they formed with themselves and the rest of the trees of the forest. These were the camphor and tallow trees, and the arbor vitæ. The bright, shining green foliage of the first, mingled with the purple leaves of the second, and over-topped by the stately tree of life, of the deepest green, produced a pleasing effect to the eye; and the landscape was rendered still more interesting to the mind by the very singular and diversified appearance of several thousand repositories of the dead upon the sloping sides of the inferior hills. Here, as well as elsewhere, the sombre and upright cypress was destined to be the melancholy companion of the tombs.

"Higher still, among the woods, avenues had been opened to admit of rows of small blue houses, exposed on white colonnades, which, on examination, were also found to be mansions of the dead. Naked coffins, of extraordinary thickness, were everywhere lying on the surface of the ground. The margins of the lake were studded with light aerial buildings, among which one of more solidity and greater extent than the rest was said to belong to the emperor. The grounds were inclosed with brick walls, and mostly planted with vegetables and fruit trees;

but in some there appeared to be collections of such shrubs and flowers as are most esteemed in the country." [1]

Staunton speaks of the lake as a beautiful sheet of water, perfectly pellucid, full of fish, in most places shallow, and ornamented with a great number of light and fanciful stone bridges, thrown across the arms of the lake as it runs up into the hills. A stone tower on the summit of a projecting headland attracted attention, from its presenting a different architecture from that usually seen in Chinese buildings. This tower, called the *Lui Fung tah*, *lit.* 'Tower of the Thunder Peak' (not Thundering Wind, as Staunton renders it), from the hill being at first owned by Mr. Lui, was built about A.D. 950, and is to-day a solid structure, though much ruined. It has now four stories, and is about 120 feet high; something like a regular order is still discernible in the moldering cornices. The legend of the White Snake is associated with this structure, and people constantly carry away pieces of its bricks as charms.

An interesting corroboration of this account is given by Polo, who says, "Inside the city there is a lake which has a compass of some 30 miles; and all around it are erected beautiful palaces and mansions, of the richest and most exquisite structure that you can imagine, belonging to the nobles of the city. There are also on its shores many abbeys and churches of the idolaters. In the middle of the lake are two islands, on each of which stands a rich, beautiful and spacious edifice, furnished in such a style as to seem fit for the palace of an emperor. And when any one of the citizens desired to hold a marriage feast, or to give any other entertainment, it used to be done at one of these palaces." [2]

The splendor and size of the numerous Buddhist temples in and around Hangchau attracted travellers to the city more even than did its position; these shrines have, however, all been destroyed, and their thousands of priests driven away; the Taipings left no building untouched. The Yoh Miao stands near the north-west corner of the Si Hu, and contains the tombs of the patriot general Yoh Fi of the Sung dynasty (A.D. 1125), and his son, who were unjustly executed as traitors. Two conical

[1] *Travels in China*, p. 522.

[2] Yule's *Marco Polo*, Vol. II., p. 146.

mounds mark their resting places, and separated by a wall, but inside the inclosure are four iron statues cast in a kneeling posture and loaded with chains,—on his right Tsin Kwei and his wife, on the left a judge and general, who subserved Tsin Kwei's hatred of Yoh Fi by their flagitious conduct. All four are here doing homage and penance to this just man whom they killed, and by the obloquy they receive serve as a warning to other traitors. In a temple, called *Ting-tsz' sz'*, not far from the city, the party of the Dutch embassy were well lodged, and attended by three hundred priests. The establishment was in good repair, and besides two guardian monsters more than thirty feet high, near the entrance, contained five hundred images of the Buddhist Arhans, with miniature pagodas of bronze, of beautiful workmanship.

Hangchau is better known abroad for manufactures of silk than for any other fabrics, but its position at the termination of the Canal may perhaps give its name to many articles which are not actually made there, for Huchau is now a greater dépôt for raw and woven silks. In the northern suburbs lies an irregular basin, forming the southern extremity of the Canal; but between the river and the basin there is no communication, so that all goods brought hither must be landed. The city contains, among other public buildings, a mosque, bearing an inscription in Arabic, stating that it is a "temple for Mussulmen, when travelling, who wish to consult the Koran."[1] It is higher than the adjacent buildings, and adorned with a cupola, pierced with holes at short intervals. It was spared in 1863, as not being an idolatrous temple. There are also several others in the city, it being a stronghold of Islamism in China. Water communication exists between Hangchau and Yüyau, south-east through Shauhing, and thence to Ningpo, by means of which goods find their way to and from the capital. A good road also runs between the two former cities; indeed, elsewhere in the province the thoroughfares are very creditable; they are laid with broad slabs of granite and limestone, and lead over plains and hills in numberless directions.

---

[1] De Guignes, *Voyages à Peking*, Vol. II., pp. 65–77.

Ningpo fu ('Peaceful Wave city') is the next important city in Chehkiang, in consequence of its foreign relations. It is admirably situated for trade and influence, at the junction of three streams, in lat. 29° 55′ N., and long. 121° 22′ E.; the united river flows on to the ocean, eleven and a half miles distant, under the name of the Tatsieh. Opposite the city itself, there are but two streams, but the southern branch again subdivides a few miles south-west of Ningpo. Its population has been variously estimated from one-fourth to one-third of a million, and even more, including the suburban and floating inhabitants. This place was called *King-yuen* by the Sung, and received its present name from the Mongols. It was captured in 1862 by the insurgents, who were deterred from destroying it by the presence of foreign men-of-war; the prosperity of the mart has since increased. When foreigners first resorted to China for trade, Ningpo soon became a centre of silk and other kinds of commodities; the Portuguese settled there, calling it *Liampo*, which is the same name. It is, moreover, an ancient city, and its Annals afford full information upon every point interesting to a Chinese antiquarian, though a foreigner soon tires of the many insignificant details mixed up with a few valuable statements.[1]

"The plain in which Ningpo lies is a magnificent amphitheatre, stretching away from twelve to eighteen miles on one side to the base of the distant hills, and on the other to the verge of the ocean. As the eye travels along, it catches many a pleasing object. Turn landward, it will see canals and water-courses, fields and snug farm-houses, smiling cottages, family residences, hamlets and villages, family tombs, monasteries and temples. Turn in the opposite direction, and you perceive a plain country descending toward the ocean; but the river alive with all kinds of boats, and the banks studded with ice-houses, most of all attract the attention. From without the city, and while still

[1] Compare R. M. Martin's *China* (Vol. II., p. 304), who gives considerable miscellaneous information about the open ports, previous to 1846; also Dennys' *Treaty Ports of China*, 1867, pp. 326–349; Richthofen's *Letters*, No. 5, 1871; Yule's *Marco Polo*, Vol. II., p. 181; *Missionary Recorder*, 1869, pp. 156, 177.

upon the ramparts, look within its walls, you will be no less gratified. Here there is nothing European, little to remind you of what you have seen in the west. The single-storied and the double-storied houses, the heavy prison-like family mansions, the family vaults and graveyards, the glittering roofs of the temples, the dilapidated official residences, the deserted literary and examination halls, and the prominent sombre Tower of Ningpo, are entirely Chinese. The attention is also arrested for a moment or two by ditches, canals, and reservoirs of water, with their wooden bridges and stone arches."[1] Two serious drawbacks to a residence here are the stifling heat of summer and the bad quality of the water.

The circumference of the walls is nearly five miles; they are about twenty-five feet high, fifteen feet wide at the top, and twenty-two at the base, built solidly, though somewhat dilapidated, and overgrown with grass. A deep moat partly surrounds them; commencing at the North gate, it runs on the west, south, and south-east side as far as Bridge gate, a distance of nearly three miles, and is in some places forty yards wide. Its constant use as a thoroughfare for boats insures its repair and proper depth; the other faces of the city are defended by the river. There are six gates, and two sally-ports near the south and west approaches intended for the passage of the boats that ply on the city canals.

On the east is Bridge gate, within which, and near the walls, the English factory was once situated. This opening leads out to the floating bridge; the latter structure is two hundred yards long and five broad, made of planks firmly lashed, and laid upon sixteen lighters closely linked and chained together, but which can be opened. A busy market is held on the bridge, and the visitor following the lively crowd finds his way to an extensive suburb on the opposite side. Ferry boats ply across both streams in vast numbers, adding greatly to the vivacity of the scene. The custom-house is situated beyond the bridge, and this eastern suburb contains several buildings of a religious

---

[1] Milne, in *Chinese Repository*, Vol. XIII., p. 22, and in his *Life in China*, part second. London, 1857.

and public character, lumber-yards, dock-yards, and rows of ice-houses, inviting the notice of the traveller. The environs beyond the north gate are not so thickly settled as those across the rivers; the well cultivated fields, divided and irrigated by numerous water-courses, with scattered hamlets, beguile the visitor in his rambles, and lead him onward.

There are numerous temples and monasteries, and a large variety of assembly-halls, governmental offices, and educational establishments, but none of these edifices are remarkable in an architectural point of view. The assembly-halls or club-houses are numerous, and in their internal arrangements form a curious feature of native society. It is the practice among residents or merchants from other provinces, to subscribe and erect on the spot where they are engaged in business, a temple, dedicated to the patron deity of their native province, in which a few priests are supported, and plays acted in its honor. Sometimes the building is put in charge of a layman, called a "master of ceremonies," and the current expenses defrayed by subscription. The club-houses are places of resort for travellers from the several provinces or districts, and answer, moreover, to European coffee-houses, in being points where news from abroad is heard and exchanged.

The streets are well paved, and interrupted here and there by honorary portals of considerable size and solidity, which also give variety to an otherwise dull succession of shops and sign-boards, or dead walls. Two small lagoons afford space for some aquatic amusements to the citizens. One called Sun Lake is only a thousand yards in circuit; the other, called Moon Lake, is near the West gate, and has three times its perimeter. Both are supplied by sluices passing through the city gates, while many canals are filled from them, which aid in irrigating the suburbs. Some of the pleasantest residences of the city are built on their banks.

Among interesting edifices is the *Tien-fung tah* (*i.e.*, Heaven-conferred pagoda), a hexagonal seven-storied tower upward of 160 feet high, which, according to the *Annals of Ningpo*, was first erected 1100 years ago, though during that period it has been destroyed and rebuilt several times. Upon the authority

TEMPLE OF THE GODDESS MA TSU-PU, NINGPO.

of this work, the tower was constructed before the city itself, and its preservation is considered as connected with the good luck of the place. The visitor mounts to the summit by a flight of narrow stone steps, ascending spirally within the walls.

The most elegant and solid building of the city lies on the water's edge outside the walls, between the East and Bridge gates; it is a temple dedicated to the marine goddess Ma Tsupu, and was founded by Fuhkien men in the 12th century, but the present structure was erected in 1680, and largely endowed. Its ornaments are elaborate and rich, and its appearance on festival days, gay and animated in an unusual degree. The lanterns and scrolls hanging from the ceiling attract attention by the curious devices and beautiful characters written and drawn on them in bright colors, while the walls are concealed by innumerable drawings.

Chinhai, at the mouth of the river, is so situated by nature and fortified by art, that it commands the passage. Its environs were the scene of a severe engagement between the Chinese and English in October, 1841, on which occasion great slaughter was committed upon the imperial troops. The town lies at the foot of a hill on a tongue of land on the northern bank of the river, and is partly sheltered from the sea on the north by a dyke about three miles long, composed of large blocks of hewn granite, and proving an admirable defence in severe weather. The walls are twenty feet high and three miles in circumference, but the suburbs extend along the water, attracted by, and for the convenience of, the shipping. Merchant ships report here when proceeding up the river, along whose banks the scenery is diversified, while the water, as usual in China, presents a lively scene. Numerous ice-houses are seen constructed of thick stone walls twelve feet high, each having a door on one side and an incline on the other for the removal and introduction of the ice, and protected by straw and a heavily thatched roof.

The Chusan archipelago forms a single district of which Tinghai is the capital; it is divided into thirty-four *chwang* or townships, whose officers are responsible to the district magistrate. The southern limit of the group is Quesan or the Kiu shan islands, in lat. 29° 21′ N., and long. 121° 10′ E., consisting of eleven islets, the northernmost of which is False Saddle Island; their total number is over a hundred. Tinghai city lies on the southern side of Chau shan or Boat Island, which gives its name on foreign maps to the whole group. It is twenty miles long, from six to ten wide, and fifty one and a half in circumference. The archipelago seems to be the highest portion of a vast submarine plain, geologically connected with the Nan shan range on the Continent and the mountains in Kiusiu and Nippon; it is a pivot for the changes in weather and temperature observed north and south of this point along the coast.

The general aspect of these islands and the mainland, is the same beautiful alternation of hills and narrow valleys, everywhere fertile and easily irrigated, with peaks, cascades, and woodlands interspersed. In Chusan itself the fertile and well-watered valleys usually reach to the sea, and are furnished with dykes along the beach, which convert them into plains of greater or less extent, through which run canals, used both for irrigation and navigation. Rice and barley, beans, yams, sweet potatoes, etc., are grown; every spot of arable soil being cultivated, and terraces constructed on most of the slopes. The view from the tops of the ridges, looking athwart them, or adown their valleys, or to seaward, is highly picturesque. The prevailing rocks belong to the ancient volcanic class, comprising many varieties, but principally clay-stone, trachyte, and compact and porphyritic felspar. The brief occupation of this island by the British forces in 1841 led to no permanent improvement in the condition of the people, and it has neither trade nor minerals sufficient to attract capital thither. Owing in part, perhaps, to this poverty, Tinghai escaped the ravages of the Tai-pings, and has now recovered from the damage sustained by its first capture.

Puto and a few smaller islands are independent of civil jurisdiction, being ruled by the abbot of the head monastery. This establishment, and that on Golden Island in the Yangtsz' are among the richest and best patronized of all the Buddhist monasteries in China; both of them have been largely favored by emperors at different periods.

Puto is a narrow islet, 3½ miles long, and lies 1½ miles from the eastern point of Chusan. Its surface is covered with sixty monasteries, pavilions, temples, and other religious buildings, besides grottos and sundry monuments of superstition, in which at least 2,000 idle priests chant the praises of their gods. One visitor describes his landing and ascending "a broad and well-beaten pathway which led to the top of one of the hills, at every crag and turn of which we encountered a temple or a grotto, an inscription or an image, with here and there a garden tastefully laid out, and walks lined with aromatic shrubs, which diffused a grateful fragrance through the air. The prospect from these heights was extremely delightful; numerous islands, far and near, bestudded the main, rocks and precipices above and below, here and there a mountain monastery rearing its head, and in the valley the great temple, with its yellow tiles indicative of imperial distinction, basked like a basilisk in the noonday-sun. All the aid that could be collected from nature and from Chinese art, was here concentrated to render the scene enchanting. But to the eye of the Christian philanthropist it presented a melancholy picture of moral and spiritual death. The only thing we heard out of the mouths of the priests was Ometo Fuh; to every observation that was made, re-echoed Ometo Fuh; and the reply to every inquiry was Ometo Fuh. Each priest was furnished with a rosary which he was constantly counting, and as he counted repeated the same senseless, monotonous exclamation. These characters met the eye at every turn of the road, at every corner of the temples, and on every scrap of paper; on the bells, on the gateways, and on the walls, the same words presented themselves; indeed the whole island seemed to be under the spell of this talismanic phrase, and devoted to recording and re-echoing Ometo Fuh."[1] The pristine glory of these temples has become sadly dimmed, many of the buildings present marks of decay, and some of the priesthood are obliged to resort to honest labor in order to gain a living. Deaths in their number are supplied by purchasing youths, who are taught nothing but re-

---

[1] Medhurst's *China, its State and Prospects*, p. 393.

ligious literature, a fit training to stunt their minds to pursue the dull mummery of singing Ometo Fuh. The two imperial temples present good specimens of Chinese architecture; but they as well as all other things to be seen at Puto are dilapidated and effete.

Temples were erected on this island as early as A.D. 550, and since it became a resort for priests it seems to have enjoyed the patronage of the government. The goddess of Mercy is said to have visited this spot, and her image is the principal object of worship. No females are allowed to live on the island, nor any persons other than the priests, unless in their employ. The revenues are derived from rent of the lands belonging to the temples, from the collection of those priests who go on begging excursions over the Empire, and from the alms of pilgrims who resort to this agreeable locality. It appears like one of the most beautiful spots on the earth when the traveller lands, just such a place as his imagination had pictured as exclusively belonging to the sunny East, and so far as nature and art can combine, it is really so: but here the illusion ends. Idleness and ignorance, celibacy and idolatry, vice, dirt, and dilapidation, in the inmates or in their habitations, form a poor back-ground for the well dressed community, and gay, variegated prospect seen when stepping ashore.

A town of considerable importance in this province is Chapu, about fifty miles north-west from Chinhai, across Hangchau Bay, and connected with that city through a luxuriant plain by a well-paved causeway about thirty miles long. Chapu was the port of Hangchau, and when it possessed the entire trade with Japan, boasted of being the largest mart on the seacoast of Chehkiang. The town lies at the bottom of a bay on the western face of some hills forming its eastern point; and at low tide the mud extends a long way from the lowland. The suburbs are situated near a small headland; the walled town stands about half a mile behind. When attacked by the British in May, 1842, the walls were found in poor condition, but the Manchu garrison stationed here upheld their ancient reputation for bravery. This body of troops occupies a separate division of the city, and their cantonment is planned on the model of a camp. The outer defences are numerous, but most of the old fortifications are considerably decayed. The country in the vicinity is highly cultivated, and possesses an unusual number of finely constructed, substantial houses.

South-west from Chapu lies the old town of Canfu (called Kanpu by the Chinese), which was once the port of Hangchau, but now deserted, since the stream on which it is situated has become choked with sand. This place is mentioned in the voyages of two Arabian travellers in the ninth century, as the chief port of China, where all shipping centred. The narrow entrance between Buffalo Island and Kitto Point is probably the Gates of China mentioned by them; and Marco Polo, in 1290, says, "The Ocean Sea comes within 25 miles of the city at a place called Ganfu, where there is a town and an excellent haven, with a vast amount of shipping which is engaged in the traffic to and from India and other foreign parts. . . . And a great river flows from the city of Kinsay to that sea-haven, by which vessels can come up to the city itself."[1] Marsden erroneously supposes Kanpu to be Ningpo. If this was in fact the *only* port allowed to be opened for foreign trade, it shows that, even in the Tang dynasty, the same system of exclusion was maintained that has so recently been broken up; though at that date the Emperors in Shansí had very little authority along the southern coasts. The changes in the Bay of Hangchau have been more potent causes for the loss of trade, and Yule reasonably concludes that the upper part of it is believed to cover now the old site in Polo's time.

The province of FUHKIEN (*i.e.* Happily Established) is bounded on the north by Chehkiang, north-west and west by Kiangsí, south-west by Kwangtung, and east by the channel of Formosa. Its western borders are determined, for the most part, by the watershed of the basins of the rivers Min and Kan; a rugged and fertile region of the Nan shan. The line of seacoast is bold, and bordered with a great number of islands, whose lofty granitic or trappean peaks extend in precipitous,

[1] Yule's *Marco Polo*, Vol. II., p. 149. *Cathay and the Way Thither*, p. cxciii. Reinaud, *Relations des Voyages faits par les Arabes dans l'Inde et à la Chine, etc.* (Paris, 1845), Tome I., p. 19.

barren headlands from Namoh as far as the Chusan archipelago. In the general features of its surface, the islands on its coasts, and its position with reference to the ocean, it resembles the region lying east of New Hampshire in the United States; including Formosa, it about equals Missouri in size.

The River Min is formed by the union of three large streams at Yenping fu; it drains all the country lying east of the Wu-í (Bohea) hills, or about three-fourths of the province. It is more than three hundred miles long, and owing to its regular depth, is one of the most useful streams in China; twenty-seven walled towns stand on its banks. The tide rises eighteen or twenty feet at the entrance, and this, with the many islands and reefs, renders the approach difficult. At Min-ngan hien, about fourteen miles from the mouth, the stream is contracted to less than half a mile for about three miles, the water being from twelve to twenty-five fathoms deep; the hills on each side rise from fifteen hundred to two thousand feet. One traveller speaks of the walls of its forts and batteries, in this part, as affording a sort of stairs for the more convenient ascent of the hills on which they are situated. From the top, "the view embraces a beautiful scene; nothing can be more picturesque than the little plats of wheat and barley intermixing their yellow crops on the acclivities with bristling pines and arid rocks, and crowned with garden spots, or surrounded with rice fields and orchards of oranges. The valley of the Min, viewed from the summit of the fortress, is truly a beautiful sight."[1] The scenery on this river, though of a different character, will bear comparison with that of the Hudson for sublimity and beauty; the hills are, however, much higher, and the country less fruitful, on the Min.

Beyond Pagoda Anchorage the passage is too shallow for large vessels, and this obstacle tends to prevent Fuhchau from becoming a place of commerce in keeping with its size and geographical advantages. From the city upwards the river is partially obstructed with rocks and banks, rendering the navigation troublesome as far as Mintsing hien, about thirty miles

---

[1] Borget, *La Chine Ouverte*, p. 126.

above it, beyond which the strong rapids render the passage to Yenping extremely tedious,—in high water impossible even with trackers. The banks are steep, and the tow-rope is sometimes taken 50 to 70 feet above the water.

Mr. Stevens says of this river, that "bold, high, and romantic hills give a uniform yet ever varying aspect to the country; but it partakes so much of the mountainous character, that it may be truly said that beyond the capital we saw not one plain even of small extent. Every hill was covered with verdure from the base to the summit. The less rugged were laid out in terraces, rising above each other sometimes to the number of thirty or forty. On these the yellow barley and wheat were waving over our heads. Here and there a laborer, with a bundle of grain which he had reaped, was bringing it down on his shoulder to thrash out. Orange, lemon, and mulberry, or other trees, sometimes shaded a narrow strip along the banks, half concealing the cottages of the inhabitants."[1]

Next in size is the Lung kiang, which flows by Changchau, and disembogues near Amoy after a course of two hundred miles. A large number of small islands lie on the coast of Fuhkien, the first of which, on the west, is Namoh or Nan-au, about thirteen miles long. Amoy and Quemoy are the largest islands of a group lying off the estuary of the Lung kiang. Chimmo Bay is north-east of Amoy, and is the entrance of the passage up to Chinchew, or Tsiuenchau fu, the *Zayton*[2] of Marco Polo, and still celebrated for the commercial enterprise of its inhabitants. Before the introduction of steamers into the coasting trade, the harbors and creeks along the provinces of Fuhkien and Kwangtung were infested with numerous fleets of pirates, which used to "sneak about like rats," and prey upon the peaceful traders.

The grain raised in Fuhkien is hardly enough to support its

---

[1] *Chinese Repository*, Vol. IV., p. 92.

[2] Yule's *Marco Po'o*, Vol. II., pp. 183–185, etc. A Turkish geography, printed at Constantinople, describes this port under the name of *Zeitoun*. Compare Klaproth, *Mémoires sur l'Asie*, Tome II., p. 208. See further, *Chinese Recorder*, Vol. III., p. 87; Vol. IV., p. 77; Vol. V., p. 327, and Vol. VI., p. 31, sqq.

population, especially on the sea-board, and large quantities of rice are brought from Siam, Formosa, and elsewhere. Black tea, camphor and other woods, sugar, chinaware, and grass-cloth, are the principal exports.

The city of Fuhchau (*i.e.*, Happy City), or Hokchiu, as it is called by the inhabitants, lies in lat. 26° 5′ north, and long. 119° 20′ east, on the northern side of the Min, thirty-four miles from its mouth, and nine from Pagoda Island. The city lies in a plain, surrounded by hills, forming a natural and most magnificent amphitheatre of vast dimensions, whose fertility emulates and adds to its beauty. Suburbs extend from the walls three miles to the banks, and stretch along on both sides the stream. They are connected with each other, and a small islet in the river, by a stone bridge built in the eleventh century. The scenery is bold, and such parts of the surrounding hills as are not cultivated or used for graves, are covered with pines; some of the hills north of the city are three thousand feet high. Opposite Fuhchau the land is lower, and the suburb is built upon an island formed by the division of the main channel, seven miles above the city; the branches reunite at Pagoda Island. This island, and the plain on each side, forms a large basin, about twenty miles long by fifteen wide. The river is crowded with floating habitations, ferry-boats, and trading craft, rendering its surface an animated and noisy scene. The flowers grown in pots on the boats, and those usually worn by the boatwomen in their hair, all assist in imparting a pleasing aspect to the lively sight.

The city walls are about thirty feet high and twelve wide at the top. The gates, seven in number, are overlooked by high towers; smaller guard-houses stand upon the walls at short intervals, in which a few soldiers lodge, and where two or three cannon indicate their object. The city is divided into wards and neighborhoods, each of which is under its own police and headmen, who are responsible for the peace of their respective districts.

From the Wu-shih shan, an eminence on the south of the city, the view is extensive, and presents a great diversity of charming objects. The square battlements of the wall are seen extending in a devious and irregular circuit for more than eight miles, and inclosing most of the buildings, except on the south. On the south-east, a hill rises abruptly more than two hundred feet, its sides built up with interspersed dwellings; and another on the extreme north of the city, surmounted by a watch-tower, closes the prospect in that direction. Two pagodas within, and fantastic looking watch-towers upon the walls, large, regular-built granaries, and a vast number of flag-staffs in pairs indicating temples and offices, contribute to relieve the otherwise dull monotony, which is still further diversified by many large trees. Several lookout houses are placed over the streets, or upon the roofs of buildings, for the accommodation of watchmen, one of which immediately attracts the attention of the visitor, from its height, and its clock-dial with Roman letters. Few vacant spaces occur within the walls of the city, which is everywhere equally well built.

Serpentine canals divide the country round about into plats of greater or less extent, of every form and hue; while they help drain the city and provide channels for boats coming from the river. These parts of the landscape are dotted with hamlets and cottages, or, where the ground is higher, with graves and tombstones. To one seated on this eminence, the confused hum of mingling cries ascending from the town below,—the beating of gongs, crackling of fireworks, reports of guns, vociferous cries of hucksters and coolies, combining with the barking of dogs and other domestic sounds, as well as those from the crows, fish-hawks, and magpies nearer by,—inform him in the liveliest manner that the beautiful panorama he is looking down upon is filled with teeming multitudes in all the tide of life. On the western side of the city is a sheet of water, called Si Hu, or West Lake, with a series of unpretending buildings and temples lying along its margin, a bridge crossing its expanse, and fishing-nets and boats floating upon its bosom. The watch-tower, on the hill in the northern part of the city, is upon the wall, which here runs near a precipice two hundred feet high; it is a most conspicuous object when approaching the place.

The Manchus occupy the eastern side of the city, and number altogether about 8,000 persons; the natives generally are not allowed to enter their precincts. They live under their own officers, in much the same style as the Chinese, and, not having any regular occupation, give no little trouble to the provincial authorities. Though vastly larger than Ningpo, the number of temples and substantial private residences in Fuhchau is much less, and as a whole it is not so well built. The streets are full of abominations, for which the people seem to care very little. Before foreign trade attained importance, paper money used to be issued by native mercantile firms in the city, varying in denomination from forty cents to a thousand dollars, and supplying all the advantages with few of the dangers of bank notes. The blue, red, and black colors, which are blended on these promissory bills, present a gay appearance of signatures and endorsings. The name of the issuing house, and a number of characters traced around the page, in bright blue ink, form the original impression. The date of issue, and some ingeniously wrought cyphers, for the reception of signatures and prevention of forgeries, are of a deep red; while the entry of the sum, and names of the partners and receiver, stand forth in large black characters. On the back are the endorsements of various individuals, through whose hands the bill has passed, in order to facilitate the detection of forgeries, but not rendering the writer at all liable. These bills have now nearly disappeared, and bank bills from Hongkong are gradually coming into use. The streets usually are thronged with craftsmen and hucksters, in the fashion of Chinese towns, where the shopmen, in their desire to attract buyers, seem to imagine, that the more they get in their customers' way, the more likely they are to sell them something. The shops are thrown open so widely, and display such a variety of articles, or expose the workmen so plainly, that the whole street seems to be rather the stalls of a market, or the aisle in a manufactory, than the town-thoroughfare.

The chief civil and military dignitaries of the province reside here, besides the prefect and the magistrates of Min and Haukwan districts. The *Ching-hwang miao* is one of the largest religious edifices in the place, and the temples of the goddess of Mercy, and god of War, the most frequented. The

Kiu Sien shan, or 'Hill of the Nine Genii,' on the southern side of the town, is a pretty object. The city wall runs over it, and on its sides little houses are built upon rocky steps; numerous inscriptions are carved in the face of the rocks. Near the eastern gate, called *Tang măn*, or 'Bath gate,' is a small suburb, where Chinese and Manchus live together, and take care of many hot wells filled from springs near by; the populace resort hither in large crowds to wash and amuse themselves.

The citizens of Fuhchau bear the character of a reserved, proud, rather turbulent people, unlike the polite, affable natives further north. They are better educated, however, and plume themselves on never having been conquered by foreigners. Their dialect is harsh, contrasting strongly with the nasal tones of the patois of Amoy, and the mellifluous sounds heard at Ningpo. There are few manufactures of importance in the city, its commerce and resources depending almost wholly on the trade with the interior by the River Min. Many culprits wearing the cangue are to be seen in the streets, and in passing none of the hilarious merriment which is heard elsewhere greets the ear. There is also a general lack of courtesy between acquaintances meeting in the highway, a circumstance quite unusual in China. Beggars crowd the thoroughfares, showing both the poverty and the callousness of the inhabitants. One half the male population is supposed to be addicted to the opium pipe, and annually expend millions of dollars for this noxious gratification. The population of the city and suburbs is reckoned at rather over than under a million souls, including the boat people; it is, no doubt, one of the chief cities in the Empire in size, trade, and influence.

The island in the river is settled by a trading population, a great part of whom consist of sailors and boatmen. The country women, who bring vegetables and poultry to market, are a robust race, and contrast strikingly with the sickly-looking, little-footed ladies of the city. Fishing-boats are numerous in the river, many of which are furnished with cormorants.[1]

Amoy is the best known port in the province, and 150 years

[1] *Chinese Repository*, Vol. XV., pp. 185, 225.

ago was the seat of a large foreign commerce. It lies in the district of Tung-ngan, within the prefecture of Tsiuenchau, in lat. 24° 40′ N., and long. 118° 20′ E., upon the south-western corner of the island of Amoy, at the mouth of the Lung Kiang. The island itself is about forty miles in circumference, and contains scores of large villages besides the city. The scenery within the bay is picturesque, caused partly by the numerous islands which define it, some of them surmounted by pagodas or temples, and partly by the high hills behind the city, and crowds of vessels in the harbor in the foreground.[1] There is an outer and inner city, as one approaches it seaward—or more properly a citadel and a city—divided by a ridge of rocky hills having a fortified wall along the top. A paved road connects the two, which is concealed from the view of the beholder as he comes in from sea, until he has entered the Inner harbor. The entire circuit of the city and suburbs is about eight miles, containing a population of 185,000, while that of the island is estimated at 100,000 more.

The harbor of Amoy is one of the best on the coast; the tide rises and falls from fourteen to sixteen feet. The western side of the harbor is formed by the island of Kulang su, the batteries upon it completely commanding the city. It is about a mile long and two and three-quarters around, and maintains a large rural population, scattered among four or five hamlets. The foreign residences scattered over its hills add measurably to the charm of its aspect when viewed from the harbor. Eastward of Amoy is the island of Quemoy (*i.e.*, Golden harbor), whose low, rice grounds on the south-west shore produce a very different effect as opposed to the high land on Amoy; its population is, moreover, much less.

The country in this part of Fuhkien is thickly settled and highly cultivated. Mr. Abeel, describing a trip toward Tung-ngan, says, "For a few miles up, the hills wore the same rugged, barren aspect which is so common on the southern coast of China, but fertility and cultivation grew upon us as we

---

[1] The *Boston Missionary Herald* for 1845 (p. 87) contains a notice of the "White Deer Cavern," in the neighborhood.

advanced; the mountains on the east became hills, and these were adorned with fields. The villages were numerous at intervals; many of them were indicated in the distance by large groves of trees, but generally the landscape looked naked. Well-sweeps were scattered over the cultivated hills, affording evidence of the need and the means of irrigation."[1]

In the other direction, toward Changchau, the traveller, beyond Pagoda Island, enters an oval bay ten or twelve miles long, bounded by numerous plains rising in the distance into steep barren mountains, and upon which numerous villages are found; twenty-three were counted at once by Mr. Abeel, and the boatmen said that all could not be seen. Several large towns, and "villages uncounted" are visible in every direction, as one proceeds up the river toward Changchau, thirty-five miles from Amoy. This city is well built, the streets paved with granite, some of them twelve feet wide, and intolerably offensive. A bridge, about eight hundred feet long, spans the river, consisting of beams stretching from one abutment to another, covered with cross pieces. From the hill-top behind a temple at the north-western corner of the city, the prospect is charming.

"Imagine an amphitheatre," says Mr. Lowrie, "thirty miles in length and twenty in breadth, hemmed in on all sides by bare pointed hills, a river running through it, an immense city at our feet, with fields of rice and sugar-cane, noble trees and numerous villages stretching away in every direction. It was grand and beautiful beyond every conception we had ever formed of Chinese scenery. Beneath us lay the city, its shape nearly square, curving a little on the river's banks, closely built, and having an amazing number of very large trees within and around. The guide said that in the last dynasty it had numbered 700,000 inhabitants, and now he thought it contained a million—probably a large allowance. The villages around also attracted our attention. I tried to enumerate them, but after counting thirty-nine of large size distinctly visible in less than half the field before us, I gave over the attempt. It is cer-

[1] *Chinese Repository*, Vol. XI., p. 506.

tainly within the mark to say that within the circuit of this immense plain there are at least one hundred villages, some of them small, but many numbering hundreds and even thousands of inhabitants." [1]

Changchau was the last city in the eastern provinces held by the Tai-pings, a small remnant of their forces having come across the country after the loss of Nanking. They were expelled in 1866, after the town had suffered much from the contending forces. Traces of this destruction have not yet entirely disappeared from the vicinity.

Shihma, or Chiohbé, is a place of some trade, extending a mile along the shore, and larger than Haitang hien, a district town between it and Amoy. Large numbers of people dwell in boats on this river, rendering a voyage up its channel somewhat like going through a street, for the noise and bustle.

The city of Chinchew (or Tsiuenchau), north of Amoy, was once the larger of the two. It is described by Marco Polo, who reached it after five days' journey from Fuhchau, meeting with a constant succession of flourishing cities, towns and villages. "At this city is the haven of Zayton, frequented by all the ships from India, . . . and by all the merchants of Manzi, for hither is imported the most astonishing quantity of goods and of precious stones and pearls. . . . For it is one of the two greatest havens in the world for commerce." [2] It was gradually forsaken for Amoy, which was more accessible to junks. From Zayton, Kublai Khan's expedition to Java and Japan sailed, and here the men from Egypt and Arabia traded for silks, sugar, and spices long after the Portuguese reached China.

The department of Hinghwa, situate on the coast between Tsiuenchau and Fuhchau, is exceedingly populous, and its dialect differs distinctly from both of the adjoining prefectures. Its people have a bad reputation, and female infanticide prevails here to a greater degree than elsewhere. At Yenping, on the Min River, the people speak the dialect of Nanking, showing their origin of not many scores of years past; there are

---

[1] *Chinese Repository*, Vol. XII., p. 530; Fortune's *Tea Districts*, chaps. xiv and xv.

[2] Yule's *Marco Polo*, Vol. II., p. 186.

many patois in these hilly parts of Fuhkien, and the province as a whole exhibits probably greater discrepancies in its dialects than any other. Its produce is exported north and west, as well as coastwise, and this intercourse tends to assimilate the speech of the inhabitants with their neighbors. The natural scenery in the ranges near the Bohea Hills in the borders of Kiangsí attracts visitors from afar. Fortune describes the picturesque grouping of steep rocks, lonely temples on jutting ledges and hidden adits, alternating with hamlets, along the banks of the stream which carries the boats and produce away to a market. The rocks and cliffs here have furnished Chinese artists with many subjects for pen and pencil, while the valley in addition to its natural beauty brings forth the best of teas.

The island of Formosa, lying 90 miles west of Amoy, together with the Pescadore group, forms a department called Taiwan. The former is a fertile, well-watered region, possessing a salubrious climate, and meriting in every respect its name *Formosa*—a descriptive term first given by the Portuguese to their settlement at Kilung in 1590, and extended afterward to the entire island. Its total length is about 235 miles, while the width at the centre is not far from 80 miles; the limits of Chinese jurisdiction do not, however, embrace more than the western or level portion, leaving to untamed aborigines the thickly wooded districts beyond the *Muh kan shan*, a lofty range of mountains running north and south and forming the backbone of the island. The western coast presents no good harbors, and vessels lying a long distance off shore are exposed to the double inconvenience of a dangerous anchorage and an inhospitable reception from the natives; the eastern side is still less inviting, owing to its possession by savage tribes. From recent reports it appears, moreover, that the whole coast line is rising with unusual persistence and regularity, and that the streams are being choked up at their mouths.

The aborigines of this island are, in those districts that remain uncontaminated by mixture with Chinese settlers, a remarkably well-built, handsome race, strong, large of eye, bold, and devoted to hunting and ardent spirits (when the latter is procurable), after the manner of wild people the world over;

no written language exists among them, nor do they employ any fixed method of reckoning time. They and the inhabitants of Lewchew and neighboring islands are probably of the same race with the Philippine Tagalas, though some have supposed them to be of Malay or Polynesian origin. Like the North American Indians they are divided into numerous clans, whose mutual feuds are likely to last until one party or another is exterminated; this turbulence restrains them from any united action against the Chinese, whose occupation of the island has always been irksome to the natives. Their social condition is extremely low; though free from the petty vices of thieving and deception, and friendly toward strangers, the principle of blood-requital holds among them with full force, and family revenge is usually the sole object of life among the men. No savage is esteemed who has not beheaded a Chinaman, while the greater the number of heads brought home from a fray, the higher the position of a brave in the community. The women are forced to attend both to house and field, but share the laziness of their masters, insomuch that they never cut from the growing rice or millet more than enough for the day's provision. "Although these people have men's forms," observes a Chinese writer in the peculiar antithetical style common to their literary productions, "they have not men's natures. To govern them is impossible; to exterminate them not to be thought of; and so nothing can be done with them. The only thing left is to establish troops with cannon at all the passes through which they issue on their raids, and so overawe them, by military display, from coming out of their fastnesses. The savage tracks lie only through the dense forests, thick with underbrush, where hiding is easy. When they cut off a head, they boil it to separate the flesh, adorn the skull with various ornaments, and hang it up in their huts as evidence of their valor." In addition to a few native clans who have submitted to the rulers from the mainland and dwell in the border region between the colonists and aborigines proper, a peculiarly situated race, called *Hakkas*, maintains a neutral position between the hill tribes and the Chinese. These people were formerly industrious but persecuted inhabitants of Kwangtung province, who, in order to better their lot, emigrated to Formosa and established close communication with the natives there, making themselves indispensable to them by procuring arms, powder, and manufactured goods, while owing to their industry they were able in time to monopolize the camphor trade. Though retaining the Chinese costume and shaving their heads, they practically ignore Chinese rule, paying tribute and intermarrying with the mountaineers, from whom they have also obtained large tracts of land.

Maize, potatoes, fruits, tobacco, indigo, sugar, rice, and tea, are all grown on this island, the three latter in rapidly increasing quantities for purposes of export. Of natural products salt, coal, sulphur, petroleum, and camphor are of the first importance. The vast coal basins have hardly been opened or even explored, the only mines now worked being those in the northern part, near Kilung. Native methods of mining are, however, the only ones employed thus far, and it is not surprising, considering their extreme simplicity, that they have not been able to extract coal from remote districts, where the natural difficulties encountered are greatest. Hand labor alone is used, and draining a pit unheard of—compelling a speedy abandoning of the mines when pierced to any great depth in the mountain side. The cost of the coal at the mouth of the pit is about 65 cents per ton for the first qualities, which price improved methods might reduce a third. The presence of volcanoes on this island will, nevertheless, present a serious obstacle to the employment of western mining machinery, especially along the coast, where the measures appear to be excessively dislocated and the work of draining is rendered more difficult. Petroleum is abundant in certain tracts of northern Formosa, flowing plentifully from crevices in the hills, and used to some extent for burning and medicinal purposes by the natives, but not exported. The possibilities of a large sulphur trade are much more important. It is brought from solfatarae and geysers at Tah-yu kang, near Kilung, where it is found in a nearly pure state, as well, too, as a great quantity of sulphurous acid which might with profit be used in the sugar refineries on the island. The manufacture of sulphur is, however, forbidden by treaty, though its exportation goes on in small quantities, the contractors taking on themselves all risk of seizure. Camphor, perhaps the greatest source of wealth to Formosa, is obtained here by saturating small sticks of the wood with steam, not by boiling as in Japan. The crystals of camphor condense in a receiver placed above the furnace; during the process of distillation an essential oil is produced, which when chemically treated with nitric acid becomes solid camphor. The trees from which the wood is cut grow in the most inaccessible tracts of the island, and are, according to all descriptions, of immense extent, though chopped down by the natives without discrimination or idea of encouraging a second growth.

Among the most interesting natural phenomena of this district are the so-called volcanoes, whose occasional eruptions have been noticed by many. Mr. Le Gendre, United States Consul at Amoy in 1869, upon a visit to Formosa took occasion to examine more closely into this subject. It appears from his report[1] that a gas is constantly issuing from the earth, and when a hole to the depth of a few inches is made it can be lighted. It is most likely, he continues, that from time to time gas jets break forth at points of the hills where they had not been observed before, rushing through its long grass and forests of huge trees, and the rock oil which as a general thing flows in their vicinity. As they are apt to spontaneously ignite in contact with the atmosphere, they must set fire to these materials and cause a local conflagration, that gives to the many peaks of the chain the appearance of volcanoes.

Previous to the first half of the fifteenth century the Chinese had little knowledge of Formosa, nor was their sway established over any part of it until 1683. It was never really colonized, and became a misgoverned and refractory region from the earliest attempts at subjection. A great emigration is constantly going on from the main, and lands are taken up by capitalists, who not only encourage the people in settling there, but actually purchase large numbers of poor people to occupy these districts. Taiwan fu, the seat of local government, is the

---

[1] *Commercial Relations between the U. S. and Foreign Nations.* 1869.

largest place on the island; other harbors or places of importance are Ku-sia and Takow, some miles south of Taiwan, the latter, with Tamsui, on the north-west coast, being one of the recently opened ports of trade. Kílung possesses a good harbor and is the entrepôt of goods for the northern end of the island. Since the opening (in 1861) of these three towns to foreign intercourse, and the more careful examination of the neutral territory at the foot of the mountains, the resources, peoples, and condition of this productive isle have become better known.

It may be of interest to refer, before leaving Formosa, to the extraordinary fabulous history of the island by one George Psalmanazar, the *nom de plume* of a remarkable impostor of the commencement of the eighteenth century, who pretended to be a Japanese convert to Christianity from Formosa, and who created a profound sensation in Europe by the publication in Latin of a fictitious notice of that country.[1]

About twenty-five miles west of Formosa, and attached to Taiwan fu, is the district of *Pănghu ting* or Pescadore Islands, consisting of a group of twenty-one inhabited islets, the largest of which, called Pănghu, is eighty-four miles in circumference; none of them rise three hundred feet above the sea. The two largest, called Pănghu and Fisher Islands, are situated near the centre of the cluster, and have an excellent harbor between them. The want of trees, and the absence of sheltered valleys, give these islands a barren appearance. Millet, ground-nuts, pine-apples, sweet potatoes, and vegetables are grown, but for most of their supplies they depend upon Formosa. The population of the group is estimated at 8000, of whom a large part are fishermen. The Dutch seized these islands in 1622, and attempted to fortify them by forced Chinese laborers, but removed to Formosa two years after at the instance of the governor of Fuhkien.

---

1 "*An Historical and Geographical Description of Formosa, an Island subject to the Emperor of Japan,*" etc. Klaproth (*Mémoires sur l'Asie*, Tome I., p. 321) translates an account of this island from Chinese sources. E. C. Taintor, *The Aborigines of Northern Formosa*—Shanghai, 1874—read before the North China branch of the Royal Asiatic Society. *Chinese Repository*, Vol. II., p 408, and Vol. V., p. 480.

CHAPTER III.

GEOGRAPHICAL DESCRIPTION OF THE WESTERN PROVINCES.

The central provinces of Hupeh and Hunan formerly constituted a single one under the name of Hukwang (*i.e.* Broad Lakes), and they are still commonly known by this appellation. Hupeh (*i.e.* North of the Lakes) is the smaller of the two, but contains the most arable land. It is bounded north by Honan, east by Nganhwui and Kiangsí, south by Hunan, and west by Sz'chuen and Shensí. Its area is about 70,000 square miles, or slightly above that of New England.

The Great River flows through the south, where it connects with all the lakes on both its shores, and nearly doubles its volume of water. The Han kiang, or Han shui rises in the southwest of Shensí, between the Fuh-niu shan and Tapa ling, and drains the south of that province and nearly the whole of Hupeh, joining the Yangtsz' at Wuchang. It is very tortuous in its course, flowing about 1,300 miles in all, and is navigable only a portion of the year, during the freshes, as far as Siang-yang, about 300 miles. Boats of small size come down, however, at all times from Sin-pu-wan, near its source in Shensí. The mouth is not over 200 feet broad, but the bed of the river as one ascends soon widens to 400 and 500 feet, and at Sha-yang, 168 miles from Hankow, it is half a mile wide. The area of its whole basin is about the same as the province.

The extraordinary effects of a large body of melted snow poured into a number of streams converging on the slopes of a range of hills, and then centring in a narrow valley, bringing their annual deposit of alluvial and silt are seen along the River Han. The rise of this stream is often fifty feet where it is narrowest, and the shores are high; at Íching the channel varies from 300 to 1,500 feet at different seasons, but the river-bed from 2,000 to 9,000 feet, the water rising 18 feet at the fresh. In these wide places, the river presents the aspect of a broad, winding belt of sand dunes, in which the stream meanders in one or many channels. Navigation, therefore, is difficult and dangerous, since moving sands shift the deep water from place to place, and boats are delayed or run aground. In high water the banks are covered, but the current is then almost as serious an obstacle as the shallows are in winter.

The southeastern part of Hupeh is occupied by an extensive depression filled with a succession of lakes. The length and breadth of this plain are not far from two hundred miles, and it is considered the most fertile part of China, not being subject to overflows like the shores of the Yellow River, while the descent of the land allows its abundance of water to be readily distributed. Every spot is cultivated, and the surplus of productions is easily transported wherever there is a demand. The portions nearest the Yangtsz' are too low for constant cultivation.

The Ax Lake, Millet Lake, Red Horse Lake, and Mienyang Lake, are the largest in the province. The remaining parts of both the Lake provinces are hilly and mountainous; the high range of the Ta-peh shan ('Great White Mountains'), commencing far into Shensí, extends to the west of Hupeh, and separates the basins of the Great River from its tributary, the Han kiang, some of its peaks rising to the snow line. The productions of Hupeh are bread-stuffs, silk, cotton, tea, fish, and timber; its manufactures are paper, wax, and cloth. The climate is temperate and healthy.

The favorable situation of Wuchang, the provincial capital, has drawn to it most of the trade, which has caused in the course of years the settlement of Hanyang and Hankow on the northern bank of the Yangtsz' and River Han. The number of vessels gathered here in former years from the other cities on these two streams was enormous, and gave rise to exaggerated ideas of the value of the trade. The introduction of steamers has destroyed much of this native commerce, and the cities themselves suffered dreadfully by the Tai-pings, from which they are rapidly recovering, and on a surer foundation. The cities lie in lat. 30° 33′ N. and long. 114° 20′ E., 582 geographical miles distant from Shanghai.

Wuchang is the residence of the provincial officers, the Manchu garrison, and a literary population of influence, while the working part depends mostly on Hankow for employment. Its walls are over twelve miles in circuit, inclosing more vacant than occupied surface, whose flatness is relieved by a range of low hills that extend beyond Hanyang on the other side of the river. The narrow streets are noisome from the offal, and in summer are sources of malaria, as the drainage is bad.

When Hankow was opened to foreign trade in 1861, it presented a most ruinous appearance, but the sense of security inspired by the presence of the men and vessels from far lands rapidly drew the scattered citizens and artisans to rebuild the ruins. The foreigners live near the river side, east of Hankow and west of the River Han, where the anchorage is very favorable, and out of the powerful current of the Yangtsz'. The difference in level of the great stream is about forty feet in the year. In the long years of its early and peaceful trade up to 1850, this region had gathered probably more people on a given area than could be found elsewhere in the world; and its repute for riches led foreigners to base great hopes on their share, which have been gradually dissipated. The appearance of the city as it was in 1845 is given by Abbé Huc in a few sentences:

"The night had already closed in when we reached the place where the river is entirely covered with vessels, of every size and form, congregated here from all parts. I hardly think there is another port in the world so frequented as this, which passes, too, as among the most commercial in the empire. We entered one of the open ways, a sort of a street having each side defined by floating shops, and after four hours' toilsome navigation through this difficult labyrinth, arrived at the place of debarkation. For the space of five leagues, one can only see houses along the shore, and an infinitude of beautiful and strange looking vessels in the river, some at anchor and others passing up and down at all hours."[1]

The coup d'œil of these three cities is beautiful, their environs being highly cultivated and interspersed with the mansions of the great; but he adds, "If you draw near, you will find on the margin of the river only a shapeless bank worn away with freshets, and in the streets stalls surmounted with palisades, and workshops undermined by the waters or tumbling to pieces from age. The open spots between these ruins are filled with abominations which diffuse around a suffocating odor. No regulations respecting the location of the dwellings, no sidewalks, no place to avoid the crowd which presses upon one, elbowing and disputing the passage, but all get along pell-mell, in the midst of cattle, hogs, and other domestic animals, each protecting himself as he best can from the filth in his way, which the Chinese collect with care for agricultural uses, and carry along in little open buckets through the crowd."

Above Hankow, the towns on the Yangtsz' lie nearer its banks, as they are not so exposed to the freshets. The largest trading places in this part of Hupeh on the river, are Shasí, opposite Kinchau fu, and Ĭchang near the borders of Sz'chuen, respectively 293 and 363 miles distance. From the first settlement there is a safe passage by canal across to Shayang, forty miles away on the River Han; the travel thence goes north to Shansí. The other has recently been opened to foreign trade. It is the terminus of navigation for the large vessels used from Shanghai upward, as the rapids commence a few miles beyond, necessitating smaller craft that can be hauled by trackers. These two marts are large centres of trade and travel, and were not made desolate by the Tai-pings, as were all other towns of importance on the lower Yangtsz'.

The portion of the Yangtsz' in this province, between Ĭchang and the Sz'chuen border, exhibits perhaps some of the most magnificent glimpses of scenery in the world. Breaking

[1] *Annales de la Foi*, 1845, Tome XVII., pp. 287, 290. See also Huc's *Travels in the Chinese Empire*, Harper's Ed., 1855, Vol. II., pp. 142–144. Pumpelly, pp. 224–226; Blakiston's *Yangtsze*, p. 65; *Treaty Ports of China*, 1867, Art. *Hankow*.

through the limestone foundations that dip on either side of the granite core of the rapids, the river first penetrates the Wu shan, Mitan, and Lukan gorges on the one side, then the long defile of Íchang on the other. At various points between and beyond these the stream is broken by more or less formidable rapids. Among these grand ravines the most impressive, though not the longest, is that of Lukan, whose vertical walls rise a thousand feet or more above the narrow river. Nothing can be more striking, observes Blakiston, than suddenly coming upon this huge split in the mountain mass "by which the river escapes as through a funnel."

The eastern portions of Hupeh are rougher than the southern, and were overrun during the rebellion by armed bands, so that their best towns were destroyed. Siangyang fu and Fanching, near the northern borders, are important places in the internal commerce of this region. Its many associations with leading events in Chinese early and feudal history render it an interesting region to native scholars. A large part of the southwestern prefecture of Shingan is hilly, and its mountainous portions are inhabited by a rude, illiterate population, many of whom are partly governed by local rulers.

The province of Hunan is bounded north by Hupeh, east by Kiangsí, south by Kwangtung and Kwangsí, west by Kweichau and Sz'chuen. Its area is reckoned at 84,000 square miles—equal to Great Britain or the State of Kansas. It is drained by four rivers, whose basins comprise nearly the whole province, and define its limits by their terminal watersheds. The largest is the Siang, which, rising in the hills on the south and east in numerous navigable streams, affords facilities for trade in small boats to the borders of Kiangsí and Kwangtung, the traffic concentring at Siangtan; this fertile and populous basin occupies well-nigh half of the province. Through the western part of Hunan runs the Yuen kiang, but the rapids and cascades occur so frequently as to render it far less useful than the Siang. Boats are towed up to the towns in the southwest with great labor, carrying only four or five tons cargo; these are exchanged for mere scows at Hangkia, 200 miles above Changteh, in order to reach Yuenchau. The contrast

'UKAN GORGE, YANGTSZ' RIVER.

between the two rivers as serviceable channels of intercourse is notable. Between these two main rivers runs the Tsz' kiang, navigable for only small batteaux, which must be pulled up so many rapids that the river itself has been called Tan ho, or 'Rapid River;' its basin is narrow and fertile, and the produce is carried to market over the hills both east and west. The fourth river, the Lí shui, empties, like all the others, into the Tungting Lake, and drains the northwestern portion of the province; it is navigable only in its lower course, and is almost useless for travel. These rivers all keep their own channels through the lake, which is rather a cesspool for the overflow of the Yangtsz' during its annual rise than a lake fed by its own springs and affluents. At Siangyin, on the River Siang, the banks are 35 feet above low water, and gradually slope down to its mouth at Yohchau, or near it. The variation of this lake from a large sheet of water at one season to a marsh at another, must of course affect the whole internal trade of the province, inasmuch as the rivers running through it are in a continual condition of flood or low water—either extreme cannot but seriously interfere with steam vessels.

The productions of Hunan do not represent a very high development of its soil or mines. Tea and coal are the main exports; tea-oil, ground-nut and *tung* oils, hemp, tobacco, and rice, with iron, copper, tin, and coarse paper make up the list. The coal-fields of southern Hunan contain deposits equal to those in Pennsylvania; anthracite occurs on the River Lui, and bituminous on the River Siang, both beds reaching over the border into Kwangtung. The timber trade in pine, fir, laurel, and other woods is also important. The population of Hunan was somewhat reduced during the Tai-ping rebellion; its inhabitants have in general a bad reputation among their countrymen for violence and rudeness. The hilly nature of the country tends to segregate them into small communities, which are imperfectly acquainted with each other, because travelling is difficult; nor is the soil fertile enough to support in many districts a considerable increase of population.

The capital of Hunan, Changsha, lies on the River Siang, and is one of the most influential, as it is historically one of the most interesting, cities in the central part of China; the festival of the Dragon Boats originated here. Siangtan, at the confluence of the Lien kí, more than 200 miles above Yohchau, is one of the greatest tea-marts in China. Its population is reckoned to be a million, and it is a centre of trade and banking for the products of this and other regions; it extends for three miles along the west bank, and nearly two miles inland, with thousands of boats lining the shores. Its return to prosperity since the rebellion has been marvellously rapid. The city of Changteh on the Yuen River is the next important town, as it is easily reached from Yohchau on the Yangtsz'; large amounts of rice are grown in the prefecture.

Hunan has a high position for letters, the people are well dressed, healthy, and usually peaceable. The boating population is, however, exceptionally lawless, and forms a difficult class for the local authorities to control. Aboriginal hill-tribes exist in the southwestern districts, which are still more unmanageable, probably through the unjust taxation and oppression of the imperial officers set over them. In addition to these ungovernable elements a large area is occupied by the *Yao-jin*, who have possessed themselves of the elevated territory lying between Yungchau and Kweiyang, in the southern point of the province, and there barricaded the mountain passes so that no one can ascend against their will.

The province of SHENSÍ (*i.e.*, Western Defiles) is bounded north by Inner Mongolia, from which it is divided by the Great Wall, east by Shansí and Honan, southeast by Hupeh, south by Sz'chuen, and west by Kansuh. Its area is not far from 70,000 square miles, which is geologically and politically most distinctly marked by the Tsingling shan, the watershed between the Wei and Han rivers. There is only one good road across it to Hanchung fu near its southern part; another, farther east, goes from Sí-ngan, by a natural pass between it and the Fuh-niu shan, to Shang, on the Tan ho, in the Han basin. This part comprises about one-third of Shensí. The other portion includes the basins of the Wei, Loh and Wu-ting, and some smaller tributaries of the Yellow River, of which the Wei is the most important. This river joins the Yellow at the lowest point of its basin, the Tung-kwan pass, where the larger stream breaks through into the lowlands of Honan, and divides eastern and southern China from the northwestern regions. The whole of this part presents a loess formation, and the beds of the streams are cut deep into it, the roads across them being few. The Wei basin is the most fertile part of the province; the history of the Chinese race has been more connected with its fortunes than with any other portion of their possessions. Its productiveness is shown in the rapid development and peopling of the districts along the banks and affluents.

On the north, the Great Wall separates Shensí from the Ordos Mongols, its western end reaching the Yellow River at Ninghia—the largest and only important city in that region. All the connections with this region are through Shensí and by Kwei-hwa-ching, but the configuration of the ranges of hills prevents direct travel. None of the rivers in this region are serviceable to any great degree for navigation, and but few of them for irrigation; the crops depend on the rainfall. The climate is more equable and mild than in Shansí, and not so wet as in many parts of Kansuh. The harvests of one good year here furnish food for three poor ones. The chief dependence of the people is on wheat, but rice is grown wherever water can be had; sorghum, millet, pulse, maize, barley, ground-nut, and fruits of many sorts fill up the list. Cotton, hemp, tobacco, rapeseed, and poppy are largely cultivated, but the surplus of any crop is not enough in average years to leave much for export. The ruthless civil war recently quenched in the destruction of the Mohammedans in the province has left it quite desolate in many parts, and its restoration to former prosperity and population must be slow.

The travel between Shensí and Sz'chuen is almost wholly confined to the great road reaching from Sí-ngan to Chingtu. It passes along the River Wei to Hienyang hien on the left bank, where the road north into Kansuh diverges, the other continuing west along the river through a populous region to Paokí hien, where it recrosses the Wei. During this portion, the Tai-peh Mountain, about eleven thousand feet high, with its white summit, adds a prominent feature to the scenery. At Paokí, the crossing at the Tsingling shan commences, and occupies seven days of difficult travel through a devious road of 163 miles to Fung hien on the confines of Kansuh. It crosses successive ridges from 6,000 to 9,000 feet high, and is carried along the sides of hills and down the gorges in a manner reflecting much credit on the engineers of the third century A.D. who made it. These mountainous regions are thinly settled all the way down to Paoching, near Hanchung; but upon gaining the River Han, one of the most beautiful and fertile valleys in China is reached. Its western watershed is the Kiu-tiao shan,[1] running southwesterly into Sz'chuen on the west side of the Kialing River.

The city of Sí-ngan is the capital of the northwest of China, and next to Peking in size, population, and importance. It surpasses that city in historical interest and records, and in the long centuries of its existence has upheld its earlier name of *Chang-an*, or 'Continuous Peace.' The approach to it from the east lies across a bluff, whose eastern face is filled with houses cut in the dry earth, and from whose summit the lofty towers and imposing walls are seen across the plain three miles away. These defences were too solid for the Mohammedan rebels, and protected the citizens while even their suburbs were burned. The population occupies the entire enciente, and presents a heterogeneous sprinkling of Tibetans, Mongols and Tartars, of whom many thousand Moslems are still spared because they were loyal. Sí-ngan has been taken and retaken, rebuilt and destroyed, since its establishment in the twelfth century B.C. by the Martial King, but its position has always assured for it the control of trade between the central and western provinces and Central Asia. The city itself is picturesquely situated, and contains some few remains of its ancient importance, while the

[1] Usually known as the Ta-pa ling; but Baron von Richthofen found that the natives of that region "call those mountains the Kiu-tiao shan, that is the 'nine mountain ridges,' designating therewith the fact that the range is made up of a number of parallel ridges. This name should be retained in preference to the other." *Letter on the Provinces of Chihli, Shansi, Shensi*, etc. Shanghai, 1872. See also his *China*, Band II. S. 563–576; Alex. Wylie, *Notes of a Journey from Chingtoo to Hankow*, *Journ. Roy. Geog. Soc.* Vol. XIV., p. 168.

neighborhood promises better returns to the sagacious antiquarian and explorer than any portion of China. The principal record of the Nestorian mission work in China, the famous tablet of A.D. 781, still remains in the yard of a temple. Some miles to the northwest lies the temple Ta-fu-sz', containing a notable colossus of Buddha, the largest in China, said to have been cut by one of the Emperors of the Tang in the ninth century. This statue is in a cave hewn out of the sandstone rock, being cut out of the same material and left in the construction of the grotto. Its height is 56 feet; the proportions of limbs and body of the sitting figure are, on the whole, good, the Buddha being represented with right hand upraised in blessing, and the figure as well as garments richly covered with color and gilt. Before the god stand two smaller colossi of the *Schang-hoa*, Buddha's favorite disciples; their inferior art and workmanship, however, testify to a later origin. The cave is lighted from above, after the manner of the Pantheon, by a single round opening in the vaulting. Sixty feet over the rock temple rises a tile roofing, and upon the hillside without the cavern are a number of minor temples and statues.[1]

Next to this city in importance is Hanchung, near the border of Sz'chuen; it was much injured by the Tai-pings, and is only slowly recovering, like all the towns in that valley which were exposed; none of these rebels crossed the Tsingling Mountains. Yu-lin ('Elm Forest') is an important city on the Great Wall in the north of Shensí, the station of a garrison which overawes the Mongols. Several marts carrying on considerable trade are on or near the Wei and Han Rivers.

Gold mines occur in Shensí, and gold is collected in some of the streams; other metals also are worked. The climate is too cold for rice and silk; wheat, millet, oats, maize, and cotton supply their places; rhubarb, musk, wax, red-lead, coal, and nephrite are exported. The trade of Sí-ngan is chiefly that of bartering the produce of the eastern provinces (reaching it by the great pass of Tung-kwan) and that from Tibet, Kansuh, and Ílí. Wild animals still inhabit the northern parts, and the num-

[1] See Kreitner, *Im fernen Osten*, p. 504. Wien, 1881.

ber of horses, sheep, goats, and cattle raised for food and service is large compared with eastern China.

The immense province of KANSUH (*i.e.*, Voluntary Reverence, made by uniting the names of Kanchau fu and Suh chau) belonged at one time to Shensí, and extended no farther west than Kiayü kwan; but since the division by Kienlung, its limits have been stretched across the desert to the confines of Songaria on the northwest, and to the borders of Tibet on the west. It is bounded north and northeast by Gobi and the Dsassaktu khanate, east by Shensí, south by Sz'chuen, southwest by Kokonor and the desert, and northwest by Cobdo and Îlí. Its entire area cannot be much under 400,000 square miles, the greater part of which is a barren waste; it extends across twelve degrees of latitude and twenty-one degrees of longitude, and comprises all the best part of the ancient kingdom of Tangut, which was destroyed by Genghis.

The topography of this vast region is naturally divided into two distinct areas by the Kiayü kwan at the end of the Great Wall; one a fertile, well-watered, populous country, differing *toto cœlo* from the sandy or mountainous wildernesses of the other. The eastern portion is further partitioned into two sections by the ranges of mountains which cross it nearly from south to north in parallel lines, dividing the basins of the Wei and Yellow Rivers near the latter. The passage between them is over the Făn-shui ling, not far from the Tao ho and by the town of Tihtao, leading thence up to Lanchau. This part of the province, watered by the Wei, resembles Shansí in fertility and productions, and its nearness to the elevated ranges of the Bayan-kara induces comparatively abundant rainfall. The streams in the extreme south flow into Sz'chuen, but furnish few facilities for navigation. The affluents of the Yellow River are on the whole less useful for irrigation and navigation, and the four or five which join it near Lanchau vary too much in their supply of water to be depended on.

The peculiar feature of Kansuh is the narrow strip projecting like a wedge into the Tibetan plateau, reaching from Lanchau northwesterly between the Ala shan and Kílien shan to the end of the Great Wall. This strip of territory commands the passage between the basin of the Tarim River and Central Asia and China Proper; its passage nearly controls trade and power throughout the northern provinces. The Ta-tung River flows on the south of the Kílien Mountains, but the travel goes near the Wall, where food and fuel are abundant, a long distance beyond its end—even to the desert. The roads from Sí-ngan to Lanchau pass up the King River to Pingliang and across several ranges, or else go farther up the River Wei to Tsin chau; the distances are between 500 and 600 miles. From Lanchau one road goes along the Yellow River down to Ninghia, a town inhabited chiefly by Mongols. Another leads 90 miles west to Sining, whither the tribes around Koko-nor repair for trade. The most important continues to Suhchau, this being an easier journey, while its trade furnishes employment to denizens of the region, whose crops are taken by travellers on passage; this road is about 500 miles in length. Its great importance from early days is indicated by the erection of the Great Wall, in order to prevent inroads along its sides, and by the fortress of Kiayü, which shuts the door upon enemies.

The climate of Kansuh exhibits a remarkable contrast to that of the eastern provinces. Prejevalsky says it is damp in three of the seasons; clear, cold winds blowing in winter, and alternating with calm, warm weather; out of 92 days up to September 30, he registered 72 rainy days, twelve of them snowy. The highest temperature was 88° F. in July. Snow and hail also fall in May. North of the Ala shan, which divides this moist region from the desert, everything is dry and sandy; their peaks attract the clouds, which sometimes discharge their contents in torrents, and leave the northern slopes dry; a marsh appears over against and only a few miles from a sandy waste.[1]

The country east of the Yellow River is fertile, and produces wheat, oats, barley, millet, and other edible plants. Wild animals are frequent, whose chase affords both food and peltry; large flocks and herds are also maintained by Tartars living within the province. The mountains contain metals and minerals, among which are copper, almagatholite, jade, gold, and

---

[1] Prejevalsky's *Travels in Mongolia*, Vol. II., pp. 256–266.

silver. The capital, Lanchau, lies on the south side of the Yellow River, where it turns northeast; the valley is narrow, and defended on the west by a pass, through which the road goes westward. At Síning fu, about a hundred miles east of Tsing hai, the superintendent of Koko-nor resides; its political importance has largely increased its trade within the last few years. Ninghia fu, in the northeast of the province, is the largest town on the borders of the desert. The destruction of life and all its resources during the recent Mohammedan rebellion, which was crushed out at Suhchau in October, 1873, is not likely to be repeated soon, as the rebels were all destroyed;[1] their Toorkish origin can even now be traced in their features.[2] No reliable description of the towns belonging to Kansuh in the districts around Barkul, since the pacification of the country by the Chinese, has been made.

The province of Sz'chuen ('Four Streams') was the largest of the old eighteen before Kansuh was extended across the desert, and is now one of the richest in its productions. It is bounded north by Kansuh and Shensí, east by Hupeh and Hunan, south by Kweichau and Yunnan, west and northwest by Tibet and Koko-nor; its area is 166,800 square miles, or double most of the other provinces, rather exceeding Sweden in superficies, as it falls below California, while it is superior to both in navigable rivers and productions. The emperors at Sí-ngan always depended upon it as the main prop of their power, and in the third century A.D. the After Hans ruled at its capital over the west of China.

Sz'chuen is naturally divided by the four great rivers which run from north to south into the Yangtsz', and thus form parallel basins; as a whole these comprise about half of the entire area, and all of the valuable portion. The western part beyond the Min River belongs to the high table lands of Central Asia, and is little else than a series of mountain ranges, sparsely populated and unfit for cultivation, except in small spaces and

---

[1] *Dip. Cor.*, 1874, p. 251.

[2] That this insurrection was not unprecedented we learn from a notice of a similar Mohammedan revolt here in 1784. *Nouvelles Lettres Edifiantes des Missions de la Chine*, Tome II., p. 23.

bottom lands. The eastern portion is a triangular shaped region surrounded with high mountains composed of Silurian and Devonian formations with intervening deposits, mostly of red clayey sandstone, imparting a peculiar brick color, which has led Baron von Richthofen to call it the Red Basin. The ranges of hills average about 3,500 feet high, but the rivers have cut their channels through the deposits from 1,500 to 2,500 feet deep, making the travel up and down their waters neither rapid nor easy. The towns which define this triangular red basin are Kweichau on the Yangtsz', from which a line running south of the river to Pingshan hien, not far from Süchau at its confluence with the Min, gives the southern border; thence taking a circuit as far west as Yachau fu on the Tsing-ï River, and turning northwesterly to Lung-ngan fu, the western side is roughly skirted, while the eastern side returns to Kweichau along the watershed of the River Han. Within this area, life, industry, wealth, prosperity, are all found; outside of it, as a rule, the rivers are unnavigable, the country uncultivable, and the people wild and insubordinate, especially on the south and west.

The four chief rivers in the province, flowing into the Yangtsz', are the Kialing, the Loh, the Min, and the Yalung, the last and westerly being regarded as the main stream of the Great River, which is called the Kin-sha kiang, west of the Min. The Kialing rises in Kansuh, and retains that name along one trunk stream to its mouth, receiving scores of tributaries from the ridges between its basin and the Han, until it develops into one of the most useful watercourses in China, coming perhaps next to the Pearl River in Kwangtung. Chungking, at its embouchure, is the largest depot for trade west of Ïchang, and like St. Louis, on the Mississippi, will grow in importance as the country beyond develops. The River Fo Loh (called *Fu-sung* by Blakiston) is the smallest of the four, its headwaters being connected with the Min above Chingtu; the town of Lu chau stands at its mouth; through its upper part it is called Chung kiang. The Min River has its fountains near those of the Kialing in Koko-nor, and like that stream it gathers contributions from the ranges defining and crossing its basin;

as it descends into the plain of Chingtu, its waters divide into a dozen channels below Hwan hien, and after running more than a hundred miles reunite above Mei hien, forming a deep and picturesque river down to Süchau, a thousand miles and more from the source. At its junction, the Min almost doubles the volume of water in summer, when the snows melt. The Yalung River is the only large affluent between the Min and the main trunk; it comes from the Bayan-kara Mountains, between the headwaters of the Yellow and Yangtsz' Rivers, and receives no important tributaries in its long, solitary, and unfructuous course. The Abbé Huc speaks of crossing its rapid channel near Makian-Dsung just before reaching Tatsienlu, the frontier town; it takes three names in its course.

From Chingtu as a centre, many roads radiate to the other large towns in the province, by which travel and trade find free course, and render the connections with other provinces safe and easy. The roads are paved with flagstones wide enough to allow passage for two pack-trains abreast; stairs are made on the inclines, up and down which mules and ponies travel without risk, though most of the goods and passengers are carried by coolies. In order to facilitate travel, footpaths are opened and paved, leading to every hamlet, and wherever the traffic will afford it, bridges of cut stone, iron chains or wire, span the torrent or chasm, according as the exigency requires; towns or hamlets near these structures take pride in keeping them in repair.

The products of this fertile region are varied and abundant. Rice and wheat alternate each other in summer and winter, but the amount of land producing food is barely sufficient for its dense population; pulse, barley, maize, ground-nuts, sorghum, sweet and common potatoes, buckwheat and tobacco, are each raised for home consumption. Sugar, hemp, oils of several kinds, cotton, and fruits complete the list of plants mostly grown for home use. The exports consist of raw and woven silk, of which more is sent abroad than from any province; salt, opium, musk, croton (*tung*) oil, gentian, rhubarb, tea, coal, spelter, copper, iron, and insect wax, are all grown or made for other regions. The peace which Sz'chuen enjoyed while other provinces were ravaged by rebels, has tended to develop all its products, and increase its abundance. The climate of this region favors the cultivation of the hillsides, which are composed of disintegrated sandstones, because the moist and mild winters bring forward the winter crops; snow remains only a few days, if it fall at all, and wheat is cut before May. The summer rains and freshets furnish water for the rice fields by filling the streams on a thousand hills. This climate is a great contrast to the dry regions further north, and it is subject to less extremes of temperature and moisture than Yunnan south of it. When this usual experience is altered by exceptional dry or wet seasons, the people are left without food, and their wants cannot be supplied by the abundance of other provinces, owing to the slowness of transit. Brigandage, rioting, cannibalism, and other violence then add to the misery of the poor, and to the difficulty of government.

Chingtu, the capital, lies on the River Min, in the largest plain in the province, roughly measuring a hundred miles one way, and fifty the other, conspicuous for its riches and populousness. The inhabitants are reckoned to number 3,500,000 souls. This city has been celebrated from the earliest days, but received its present name of the 'Perfect Capital' when Liu Pí made it his residence. Its population approaches a million, and its walls, shops, yamuns, streets, warehouses, and suburbs, all indicate its wealth and political importance. Marco Polo calls it Sindafu, and the province Acbalec Manzi, describing the fine stone bridge, half a mile long, with a roof resting on marble pillars, under which "trade and industry is carried on,"[1] which spans the Kian-suy, *i.e.*, the Yangtsz', as the Min is still often termed. The remarkable cave houses of the old inhabitants still attract the traveller's notice as he journeys up to Chingtu, along its banks.

M. David, who lived at this city several months, declares it to be one of the most beautiful towns in China, placed in the midst of a fertile plain watered by many canals, which form a network of great solidity and usefulness. The number of hon-

[1] Yule's *Marco Polo*, Vol. II., p. 23.

orary gateways in and near it attract the voyager's eye, and their variety, size, inscriptions, and age furnish an interesting field of inquiry. Many statues cut in fine stone are scattered about the city or used to adorn the cemeteries.

The city of Chungking, on the Yangtsz', at the mouth of the Kialing River, 725 miles from Hankow, is the next important city in Sz'chuen, and the centre of a great trade on both rivers. The other marts on the Great River are also at the mouths of its affluents, and from Kwaichau to Süchau and Pingshan hien, a distance of 496 miles, there is easy and safe communication within the province for all kinds of boats; steam vessels will also here find admirable opportunities for their employment.

In the western half of Sz'chuen, the people are scattered over intervales and slopes between the numberless hills and mountains that make this one of the roughest parts of China; they are governed by their own local rulers, under Chinese superintendence. They belong to the Lolos race, and have been inimical and insubordinate to Chinese rule from earliest times, preventing their own progress and destroying all desire on the part of their rulers to benefit them. Yachau fu, Tatsienlu, and Batang are the largest towns west of Chingtu, on the road to Tibet. On the other side of the province, at Fungtu hien, occur the fire-wells, where great supplies of petroleum gas are used to evaporate the salt dug out near by. The many topics of interest in all parts of Sz'chuen, can only be referred to in a brief sketch, for it is of itself a kingdom.[1]

The province of Kwangtung (*i.e.*, Broad East), from its having been for a long time the only one of the eighteen to which foreigners have had access, has almost become synonymous with China, although but little more is really known of it than of the others—except in the vicinage of Canton, and along the course of the Peh kiang, from Nanhiung down to that city. It is bounded north by Kiangsí and Hunan, northeast by Fuh-

---

[1] *Chinese Repository*, Vol. XIX., pp. 317 and 394. *Annales de la Foi*, Tome III., pp. 369–381, and Tome IV., pp. 409–415. *Letter* by Baron Richthofen *on the Provinces of Chihli*, *Shansi*, *Shensi*, *Sz'chuen*, etc. Shanghai, 1872. Kreitner, *Im fernen Osten*, pp. 780–829.

kien, south by the ocean, and west and northwest by Kwangsí; with an area about the same as that of the United Kingdom. The natural facilities for internal navigation and an extensive coasting trade, are unusually great; for while its long line of coast, nearly a thousand miles in length, affords many excellent harbors, the rivers communicate with the regions on the west, north, and east beyond its borders.

The Nan shan runs along the north, between it and Kiangsí and Hunan, in a northeasterly and southwesterly direction. presenting the same succession of short ridges, with bottom lands and clear streams between them, which are seen in Fuhkien. These ridges take scores of names as they follow one another from Kwangsí to Fuhkien, but no part is so well known as the road, twenty-four miles in length, which crosses the Mei ling (*i.e.* Plum ridge), between Nan-ngan and Nanhiung. The elevation here is about a thousand feet, none of the peaks in this part exceeding two thousand, but rising higher to the west. Their summits are limestone, with granite underlying; granite is also the prevailing rock along the coast. Lí-mu ridge in Hainan has some peaks reaching nearly to the snow-line. The bottoms of the rivers are wide, and their fertility amply repays the husbandman. Fruits, rice, silk, sugar, tobacco, and vegetables, constitute the greater part of the productions. Lead, iron, and coal, are abundant.

The Chu kiang, or Pearl River, which flows past Canton, takes this name only in that short portion of its course; it is however preferable to employ this as a distinctive name, comprehending the whole stream, rather than to confuse the reader by naming the numerous branches. It is formed by the union of three rivers, the West, North, and East, the two first of which unite at Sanshwui, west of the city, while the East River joins them at Whampoa. The Sí kiang, or West River, by far the largest, rises in the eastern part of Yunnan, and receives tributaries throughout the whole of Kwangsí, along the southern acclivities of the Nan shan, and after a course of 500 miles, passes out to sea through numerous mouths, the best known of which is the Bocca Tigris. The Peh kiang, or North River, joins it after a course of 200 miles, and the East River is nearly the same length; these two streams discharge the surplus waters of all the northern parts of Kwangtung. The country drained by the three cannot be much less than 150,000 square miles, and most of their channels are navigable for boats to all the large towns in this and the province of Kwangsí. The Han kiang is the only river of importance in the eastern end of Kwangtung; the large town of Chauchau lies near its mouth. There can hardly be less than three hundred islands scattered along the deeply indented coast line of this province between Namoh Island and Annam, of which nearly one-third belong to the department of Kwangchau.

Canton, or Kwangchau fu (*i.e.* Broad City), the provincial capital, lies on the north bank of the Pearl River, in lat. 23° 7′ 10″ N., and long. 113° 14′ 30″ E., nearly parallel with Havana, Muskat, and Calcutta; its climate is, however, colder than any of those cities. The name *Canton* is a corruption of Kwangtung, derived in English from *Kamtom*, the Portuguese mode of writing it; the citizens themselves usually call it *Kwangtung săng ching*, *i.e.* the provincial capital of Kwangtung or simply *săng ching*. Another name is *Yang-ching*, or the 'City of Rams,' and a third the City of Genii, both derived from ancient legends. It lies at the foot of the White Cloud hills, along the banks of the river, about seventy miles north of Macao in a direct line, and ninety northwest of Hongkong; these distances are greater by the river.

The delta into which the West, North, and East Rivers fall might be called a gulf, if the islands in it did not occupy so much of the area. The whole forms one of the most fertile parts of the province, and one of the most extensive estuaries of any river in the world,—being a rough triangle about a hundred miles long on each side. The bay of Lintin—so called from the islet of that name, where opium and other store ships formerly anchored—is the largest sheet of water, and lies below the principal embouchure of the river, called *Fu Mun*, *i.e.* Bocca Tigris, or Bogue. Few rivers can be more completely protected by nature than this; their defences of walls and guns at this spot, however, have availed the Chinese but little against the skill and power of their enemies. Ships pass through it up to the anchorage at Whampoa, about thirty miles, from whence Canton lies twelve miles nearly due west. The approach to it is indicated by two lofty pagodas within the walls, and the multitude of boats and junks thronging the river, amidst which the most pleasing object to the "far-travelled stranger" is the glimpse he gets through their masts of the foreign houses on Sha-meen, and the flagstaffs bearing their national ensigns.

The part of Canton inclosed by walls is about six miles in circumference; having a partition wall running east and west, which divides it into two unequal parts. The entire circuit, including the suburbs, is nearly ten miles. The population on land and water, so far as the best data enable one to judge, cannot be less than a million of inhabitants. This estimate has been doubted; and certainty upon the subject is not to be attained, for the census affords no aid in determining this point, owing to the fact that it is set down by districts, and Canton lies partly in two districts, Nanhai and Pwanyü, which extend beyond the walls many miles. Davis says, "the whole circuit of the city has been compassed within two hours by persons on foot, and cannot exceed six or seven miles;"—which is true, but he means only that portion contained within the walls; and there are at least as many houses without the walls as within them, besides the boats. The city is constantly increasing, the western suburbs present many new streets entirely built up within the last ten years. The houses stretch along the river from opposite the Fa tí or Flower grounds to French Folly, a distance of four miles, and the banks are everywhere nearly concealed by the boats and rafts.

The situation of Canton is one which would naturally soon attract settlers. The earliest notices of the city date back two centuries before Christ, but traders were doubtless located here prior to that time. It grew in importance as the country became better settled, and in A.D. 700, a regular market was opened, and a collector of customs appointed. When the Manchus overran the country in 1650, this city resisted their utmost efforts to reduce it for the space of eleven months, and was finally carried by treachery. Martini states that a hundred thousand *men* were killed at its sack; and the whole number who lost their lives at the final assault and during the siege was 700,000—if the native accounts are trustworthy.[1] Since then, it has been rebuilt, and has increased in prosperity until it is regarded as the second city in the empire for numbers, and is probably at present the first in wealth.

The foundations of the city walls are of sandstone, their upper part being brick; they are about twenty feet thick, and from twenty-five to forty feet high, having an esplanade on the inside, and pathways leading to the rampart, on three sides. The houses are built near the wall on both sides of it, so that except on the north, one hardly sees it when walking around the city. There are twelve outer gates, four in the partition wall, and two water gates, through which boats pass, into the moat, from east to west. A ditch once encompassed the walls, now dry on the northern side; on the other three, and within the city, it and most of the canals are filled by the tide, which as it runs out does much to cleanse the city from its sewage. The gates are all shut at night, and a guard is stationed near them to preserve order, but the idle soldiers themselves cause at times no little disturbance. Among the names of the gates are *Great-Peace* gate, *Eternal-Rest* gate, *Five-Genii* gate, *Bamboo-Wicket* gate, etc.

The appearance of the city when viewed from the hills on the north is insipid and uninviting, compared with western cities, being an expanse of reddish roofs, often concealed by frames for drying or dyeing clothes, or shaded and relieved by a few large trees, and interspersed with high, red poles used for flagstaffs. Two pagodas shoot up within the walls, far above the watch towers on them, and with the five-storied tower on Kwanyin shan near the northern gate, form the most conspicuous objects in the prospect.

To a spectator at this elevation, the river is a prominent feature in the landscape, as it shines out covered with a great diversity of boats of different colors and sizes, some stationary others moving, and all resounding with the mingled hum of

[1] The French bishop Palafox gives still another account of the capture of Canton; his statement contains, however, one or two glaring errors. Vid. *Histoire de la Conquête de la Chine par les Tartares*, pp. 150 ff.

laborers, sailors, musicians, hucksters, children, and boatwomen, pursuing their several sports and occupations. On a low sandstone ledge, in the channel off the city, once stood the Sea Pearl (*Hai Chu*) Fort, called Dutch Folly by foreigners, the quietude reigning within which contrasted agreeably with the liveliness of the waters around. Beyond, on its southern shore, lie the suburb and island of Honam, and green fields and low hills are seen still farther in the distance; at the western angle of this island the Pearl River divides, at the *Peh-ngo tan* or Macao Passage, the greatest body of water flowing south, and leaving a comparatively narrow channel before the city. The hills on the north rise twelve hundred feet, their acclivities for miles being covered with graves and tombs, the necropolis of this vast city.

The streets are too narrow to be seen from such a spot. Among their names, amounting in all to more than six hundred, are *Dragon* street, *Martial Dragon* street, *Pearl* street, *Golden Flower* street, *New Green Pea* street, *Physic* street, *Spectacle* street, *Old Clothes* street, etc. They are not as dirty as those of some other cities in the empire, and on the whole, considering the habits of the people and surveillance of the government, which prevents almost everything like public spirit, Canton has been a well governed, cleanly city. In these respects it is not now as well kept, perhaps, as it was before the war, nor was it ever comparable to modern cities in the West, nor should it be likened to them: without a corporation to attend to its condition, or having power to levy taxes to defray its unavoidable expenses, it cannot be expected that it should be as wholesome. It is more surprising, rather, that it is no worse than it is. The houses along the waterside are built upon piles and those portions of the city are subject to inundations. On the edge of the stream, the water percolates the soil, and spoils all the wells.

The temples and public buildings of Canton are numerous. There are two pagodas near the west gate of the old city, and one hundred and twenty-four temples, pavilions, halls, and other religious edifices within the circuit of the city. The *Kwang tah* or 'Plain pagoda,' was erected by the Mohammedans (who still reside near it), about ten centuries ago, and is rather a minaret than a pagoda, though quite unlike those structures of

Turkey in its style of architecture; it shoots up in an angular, tapering tower, to the height of one hundred and sixty feet. The other is an octagonal pagoda, of nine stories, one hundred and seventy feet high, first erected more than thirteen hundred years ago. The geomancers say that the whole city is like a junk, these two pagodas are her masts, and the five-storied tower on the northern wall, her stern sheets.

Among the best known monuments to foreigners visiting this city was the monastery of *Chong-show sz'*, 'Temple of Longevity,' founded in 1573, and occupying spacious grounds. "In the first pavilion are three Buddhas; in the second a seven-story, gilt pagoda, in which are 79 images of Buddha. In the third pavilion is an image of Buddha reclining, and in a merry mood. A garden in the rear is an attractive place of resort, and another, on one side of the entrance, has a number of tanks in which gold fish are reared. In the space in front of the temple a fair is held every morning for the sale of jade ornaments and other articles."[1] This temple was destroyed in November, 1881, by a mob who were incensed at the alleged misbehaviour of some of the priests toward the female devotees—an instance of the existence in China of a lively popular sentiment regarding certain matters. Near this compound stands the 'Temple of the Five Hundred Genii,' containing 500 statues of various sizes in honor of Buddha and his disciples.

The *Hai-chwang sz'*, a Buddhist temple at Honam usually known as the Honam Joss-house, is one of the largest in Canton. Its grounds cover about seven acres, surrounded by a wall, and divided into courts, garden-spots, and a burial-ground, where are deposited the ashes of priests after cremation. The buildings consist mostly of cloisters or apartments surrounding a court, within which is a temple, a pavilion, or a hall; these courts are overshadowed by bastard-banian trees, the resort of thousands of birds. The outer gateway leads up a gravelled walk to a high portico guarded by two huge demoniac figures, through which the visitor enters a small inclosure, separated from the largest one by another spacious porch, in which are

---

[1] Dr. Kerr, *Canton Guide*.

four colossal statues. This conducts him to the main temple, a low building one hundred feet square, and surrounded by pillars; it contains three wooden gilded images, in a sitting posture, called *San Pao Fuh*, or the Past, Present, and Future Buddha, each of them about twenty-five feet high, and surrounded by numerous altars and attendant images. Daily prayers are chanted before them by a large chapter of priests, all of whom, dressed in yellow canonicals, go through the liturgy. Beyond this a smaller building contains a marble carving somewhat resembling a pagoda, under which is preserved a relic of Buddha, said to be one of his toe-nails. This court has other shrines, and many rooms for the accommodation of the priests, among which are the printing-office and library, both of them respectable for size, and containing the blocks of books issued by them, and sold to devotees.

There are about one hundred and seventy-five priests connected with the establishment, only a portion of whom can read. Among the buildings are several small temples dedicated to national deities whom the Buddhists have adopted into their mythology. One of the houses adjoining holds the hogs (not *bugs*, as was stated in one work) offered by worshippers who feed them as long as they live.

Two other shrines belonging to the Buddhists, are both of them, like the Honam temple, well endowed. One called *Kwang-hiao sz'*, or 'Temple of Glorious Filial Duty,' contains two hundred priests, who are supported from glebe lands, estimated at three thousand five hundred acres. The number of priests and nuns in Canton is not exactly known, but probably exceeds two thousand, nine-tenths of whom are Buddhists. There are only three temples of the Rationalists, their numbers and influence being far less in this city than those of the Buddhists.

The *Ching-hwang miao* is an important religious institution in every Chinese city, the temple, being a sort of palladium, in which both rulers and people offer their devotions for the welfare of the city. The superintendent of that in Canton pays $4,000 for his situation, which sum, with a large profit, is obtained again in a few years, by the sale of candles, incense, etc., to the worshippers. The temples in China are generally cheerless and gloomy abodes, well enough fitted, however, for the residence of inanimate idols and the performance of unsatisfying ceremonies. The entrance courts are usually occupied by hucksters, beggars, and idlers, who are occasionally driven off to give room for the mat-sheds in which theatrical performances got up by priests are acted. The principal hall, where the idol sits enshrined, is lighted only in front, and the altar, drums, bells, and other furniture of the temple, are little calculated to enliven it; the cells and cloisters are inhabited by men almost as senseless as the idols they serve, miserable beings, whose droning, useless life is too often only a cloak for vice, indolence, and crime, which make the class an opprobrium in the eyes of their countrymen.

Canton is the most influential city in Southern China, and its reputation for riches and luxury is established throughout the central and northern provinces, owing to its formerly engrossing the entire foreign trade up to 1843, for a period of about one hundred years. At that time the residence of the governor-general was at Shao-king fu, west of Canton, and his official guard of 5,000 troops is still quartered there, as the Manchu garrison is deemed enough for the defence of Canton. He and the Hoppo, or collector of customs, once had their yamuns in the New City, but a Romish Cathedral has been built on the site of the former's office since its capture in 1857. The governor, treasurer, Manchu commandant, chancellor, and the lower local magistrates (ten in all), live in the Old City, and with their official retinues compose a large body of underlings. Some of these establishments occupy four or five acres.

The *Kung Yuen* or Examination Hall, lies in the southeastern corner of the Old City, similar in size and arrangement to these edifices in other cities. It is 1,330 feet long, 583 wide, and covers over sixteen acres. The wall surrounding it is entered at the east and west corners of the south end, where door-keepers are stationed to prevent a crowd of idlers. The cells are arranged in two sets on each side of the main passage, which is paved and lined with trees; they are further disposed in rows of 57 and 63 cells each—all reached through one side door. The total is 8,653; each cell is 5 feet 9 inches deep, by 3 feet

8 inches wide; grooves are made in the wall to admit a plank, serving as a table by day and a bed by night. Once within, the students are confined to their several stalls, and the outer gate is sealed. A single roof covers the cells of one range, the ranges being 3 feet 8 inches apart. The northern portion includes about one-third of the whole, and is built over with the halls, courts, lodging-rooms, and guard or eating-houses of the highest examiners, their assistants and copyists, with thousands of waiters, printers, underlings, and soldiers. At the biennial examination the total number of students and others in the Hall reaches nearly twelve thousand men.

There are four prisons in the city, all of them large establishments; all the capital offenders in the province are brought to Canton for trial before the provincial officers, and this regulation makes it necessary to provide spacious accommodations for them. The execution-ground is a small yard near a pottery manufacture between the southern gate and the river side, and unless the ground is newly stained with blood, or cages containing the heads of the criminals are hung around, has nothing about it to attract the attention. Another public building, situated near the governor's palace, is the *Wan-shao kung*, or 'Imperial Presence hall,' where three days before and after his majesty's birthday, the officers and citizens assemble to pay him adoration. The various guilds among the people, and the clubs of scholars and merchants from other provinces, have, each of them, public halls which are usually called *consoo houses* by foreigners, from a corruption of a native term *kung-sz'*, *i.e.*, public hall; but the usual designation is *kwui kwan* or 'Assembly Hall.' Their total number must be quite one hundred and fifty, and some of them are not destitute of elegance.[1]

The former residences of foreigners in the western suburbs were known as *Shih-san Hang*, or 'Thirteen Hongs,'[2] and for

---

[1] *Chinese Repository*, Vol. II., pp. 145, 191, &c.

[2] This word is derived from the Chinese *hong* or *hang*, meaning a row or series, and is applied to warehouses because these consist of a succession of rooms. The foreign factories were built in this manner, and therefore the Chinese called each block a hong; the old security-merchants were dubbed *hong-merchants*, because they lived in such establishments.

nearly two centuries furnished almost the only exhibition to the Chinese people of the *yang jin* or 'ocean-men.' Here the fears and the greed of the rulers, landlords, and traders combined to restrain foreigners of all nations within an area of about fifteen acres, a large part of this space being the Garden or *Respondentia* Walk on the bank of the river. All these houses and out-houses covered a space scarcely as great as the base of the Great Pyramid; its total population, including native and foreign servants, was upwards of a thousand souls. The shops and markets of the Chinese were separated from them only a few feet, and this greatly increased the danger from fire, as may be inferred from the sketch of the street next on the west side. In 1856, the number of hongs was reckoned to be 16, and the local calendar for that year contained 317 names, not including women and children. Besides the 16 hongs, four native streets, bordered with shops for the sale of fancy and silk goods to their foreign customers, ran between the factories. This latter name was given to them from their being the residences of *factors*, for no handicraft was carried on here, nor were many goods stored in them. Fires were not unusual, which demolished portions of them; in 1822 they were completely consumed; another conflagration in 1843 destroyed two hongs and a street of shops; and in 1842, owing to a sudden riot, connected with paying the English indemnity, the British Consulate was set on fire. Finally, as if to inaugurate a new era, they were all simultaneously burned by the local authorities to drive out the British forces, in December, 1856, and every trace of this interesting spot as it existed for so long a time in the annals of foreign intercourse obliterated. Since the return of trade, a new and better site has been formed at Shameen, west of the old spot, by building a solid stone wall and filling in a long, marshy low-tide bank, formerly occupied by boats, to a height of 8 or 10 feet, on which there is room for gardens as well as houses. This is surrounded by water, and thereby secure from fire and mobs to which the old hongs were exposed. Residences are obtainable anywhere in the city by foreigners, and the common sight in the olden times of their standing outside of the *Great Peace Gate* to see the crowd pass in and out while

VIEW OF A STREET IN CANTON.

they themselves could not enter, is no longer seen. A very good map of the enciente was made by an American missionary, Daniel Vrooman, by taking the angles of all the conspicuous buildings therein, with the highest points in the suburbs; he then taught a native to pace the streets between them, compass in hand (noting courses and distances, which he fixed by the principal gates), until a complete plan was filled out. When the city was opened four years afterwards this map was found to need no important corrections.

The trades and manufactories at Canton are mainly connected with the foreign commerce. Many silk fabrics are woven at Fatshan, a large town situated about ten miles west of the city; fire-crackers, paper, mat-sails, cotton cloth, and other articles, are also made there for exportation. The number of persons engaged in weaving cloth in Canton is about 50,000, including embroiderers; nearly 7,000 barbers and 4,200 shoemakers are stated as the number licensed to shave the crowns and shoe the soles of their fellow-citizens.

The opposite suburb of Honam offers pleasant walks for recreation, and the citizens are in the habit of going over the river to saunter in its fields, or in the cool grounds of the great temple; a race-course and many enjoyable rides on horseback also tempt foreigners into the country. A couple of miles up the river are the Fa tí or Flower gardens which once supplied the plants carried out of the country, and are resorted to by pleasure parties; but to one accustomed to the squares, gardens, and esplanades of western cities, these grounds appear mean in the extreme. Foreigners ramble into the country, but rowing upon the river is their favorite recreation. Like Europeans in all parts of the East, they retain their own costume and modes of living, and do not espouse native styles; though if it were not for the shaven crown, it is not unlikely that many of them would adopt the Chinese dress.

The Cantonese enumerate eight remarkable localities, called *pah king*, which they consider worthy the attention of the stranger. The first is the peak of Yuehsiu, just within the walls on the north of the city, and commanding a fine view of the surrounding country. The *Pi-pa Tah*, or Lyre pagoda at

Whampoa, and the 'Eastern Sea Fish-pearl,' a rock in the Pearl River off the city, on which the fort already referred to as the 'Dutch Folly' was formerly situated, are two more; the pavilion of the Five Genii, with the five stone rams, and print of a man's foot in the rock, "always filled with water," near by; the rocks of Yu-shan; the lucky wells of Faukiu in the western suburbs; cascade of Sí-tsiau, forty miles west of the city; and a famous red building in the city, complete the eight "lions."

The foreign shipping all anchored, in the early days, at Whampoa, but this once important anchorage has been nearly deserted since the river steamers began their trips to the outer waters. There are two islands on the south side of the anchorage, called French and Danes' islands, on which foreigners are buried, some of the gravestones marking a century past. The prospect from the summit of the hills hereabouts is picturesque and charming, giving the spectator a high idea of the fertility and industry of the land and its people. The town of Whampoa and its pagoda lie north of the anchorage; between this and Canton is another, called Lob creek pagoda, both of them uninhabited and decaying.

Macao (pronounced *Makow*) is a Portuguese settlement on a small peninsula projecting from the south-eastern end of the large island of Hiangshan. Its Chinese inhabitants have been governed since 1849 by the Portuguese authorities somewhat differently from their own people, but the mixed government has succeeded very well. The circuit of this settlement is about eight miles; its position is beautiful and very agreeable; nearly surrounded with water, and open to the sea breezes, having a good variety of hill and plain even in its little territory, and a large island on the west called *Tui-mien shan* or Lapa Island, on which are pleasant rambles, to be reached by equally pleasant boat excursions, it offers, moreover, one of the healthiest residences in south-eastern Asia. The population is not far from 80,000, of whom more than 7,000 are Portuguese and other foreigners, living under the control of the Portuguese authorities. The Portuguese have refused to pay the former annual ground-rent of 600 taels to the Chinese Government, since the assassination of their governor in 1849, and now control all the inhabitants living within the Barrier wall, most of whom have been born therein. The houses occupied by the foreign population are solidly built of brick or adobie, large, roomy, and open, and from the rising nature of the ground on which they stand, present an imposing appearance to the visitor coming in from the sea.

There are a few notable buildings in the settlement; the most imposing edifice, St. Paul's church, was burned in 1835. Three forts on commanding eminences protect the town, and others outside of the walls defend its waters; the governor takes the oaths of office in the Monte fort; but the government offices are mostly in the Senate house, situated in the middle of the town. Macao was, up to 1843, the only residence for the families of merchants trading at Canton. Of late the authorities are doing much to revive the prosperity of the place, by making it a free port. The Typa anchorage lies between the islands Mackerara and Typa, about three miles off the southern end of the peninsula; all small vessels go into the Inner harbor on the west side of the town. Ships anchoring in the Roads are obliged to lie about three miles off in consequence of shallow water, and large ones cannot come nearer than six or seven miles.[1] Since the ascendancy of Hongkong, this once celebrated port has fallen away in trade and importance, and for many years had an infamous reputation for the protection its rulers afforded the coolie trade.

Eastward from Macao, about forty miles, lies the English colony of Hongkong, an island in lat. 22° 16½′ N., and long. 114° 8½′ E., on the eastern side of the estuary of the Pearl River. The island of Hongkong, or Hiangkiang (*i.e.*, the Fragrant Streams), is nine miles long, eight broad, and twenty-six in circumference, presenting an exceedingly uneven, barren surface, consisting for the most part of ranges of hills, with narrow intervales, and a little level beach land. Victoria Peak is 1,825 feet. Probably not one-twentieth of the surface is availa-

[1] *Chinese Repository*, passim. *An Historical Sketch of the Portuguese Settlements in China.* By Sir A. Ljungstedt. Boston, 1836.

ble for agricultural purposes. The island and harbor were first ceded to the Crown of England by the treaty made between Captain Elliot and Kíshen, in January, 1841, and again by the treaty of Nanking, in August, 1842; lastly, by the Convention of Peking, October 24, 1860, the opposite peninsula of Kowlung was added, in order to furnish space for quartering troops and storehouse room for naval and military supplies. The town of Victoria lies on the north side, and extends more than three miles along the shore. The secure and convenient harbor has attracted the settlement here, though the uneven nature of the ground compels the inhabitants to stretch their warehouses and dwellings along the beach.

The architecture of most of the buildings erected in Victoria is superior to anything heretofore seen in China. Its population is now estimated at 130,000, of whom five-sixths are Chinese tradesmen, craftsmen, laborers, and boatmen, few of whom have their families. The government of the colony is vested in a governor, chief-justice, and a legislative council of five, assisted by various subordinate officers and secretaries, the whole forming a cumbrous and expensive machinery, compared with the needs and resources of the colony The Bishop of Victoria has an advisory control over the missions of the establishment in the southern provinces of China, and supervises the schools in the colony, where many youths are trained in English and Chinese literature.

The supplies of the island are chiefly brought from the mainland where an increasing population of Chinese, under the control of the magistrate of Kowlung, find ample demand for all the provisions they can furnish.

Three newspapers are published in English, and two in Chinese. The Seaman's and Military hospitals, the chapels and schools of the London and Church Missionary Society, St. John's Cathedral, Roman Catholic establishment, the government house, the magistracy, jail, the ordnance and engineer departments, Exchange, and the Club house, are among the principal edifices. The amount of money expended in buildings in this colony is enormous, and most of them are substantial stone or brick houses. The view of the city as seen from the harbor is only excelled in beauty by the wider panorama spread out before the spectator on Victoria Peak. During the forty-odd years of its occupation, this colony has slowly advanced in commercial importance, and become an entrepôt for foreign goods designed for native markets in Southern China. Every facility has been given to the Chinese who resort to its shops to carry away their purchases, by making the port free of every impost, and preventing the imperial revenue cutters from interfering with their junks while in sight of the island. The arrangements of this contested point so that the Chinese revenue shall not suffer have not satisfied either party, and as it is in the similar case of Gibraltar, is not likely to soon be settled. Smugglers must run their own risks with the imperial officers. The most valuable article leaving Hongkong is opium, but the greatest portion of its exports pay the duties on entering China at the five open ports in the province of Kwangtung. As the focus of postal lines of passenger steamers, and the port where mercantile vessels come to learn markets, Hongkong exerts a greater influence on the southeast of Asia than her trade and size indicate. The island of Shangchuen or Sançian, where Xavier died, lies southwest of Macao about thirty miles, and is sometimes visited by devout persons from that place to reverence his tomb, which they keep in repair.

The city of Shauchau in the northern part of the province lies at the fork of the river, which compels a change of boats for passengers and goods; it is one of the largest cities after Canton, and a pontoon bridge furnishes the needed facilities for stopping and taxing the boats and goods passing through. Shauking, west of Canton, is another important town, which held out a long time against the Manchus;[1] it was formerly the seat of the provincial authorities, till they removed to Canton in 1630 to keep the foreigners under control. It stretches along six miles of the river bank, a well-built city for China, in a beautiful position. Some of its districts furnish green teas and matting for the Canton market, and this trade has opened the way for a large emigration to foreign countries. Among

---

[1] Palafox, *Conquête de la Chine*, p. 172.

other towns of note is Nanhiung, situated at the head of navigation on the North River, where goods cross the Mei ling. Before the coast was opened to trade, fifty thousand porters obtained a livelihood by transporting packages, passengers, and merchandise to and from this town and Nan-ngan in Kiangsí. It is a thriving place, and the restless habits of these industrious carriers give its population somewhat of a turbulent character. Many of them are women, who usually pair off by themselves and carry as heavy burdens as the men.

Not far from Yangshan hien is a fine cavern, the *Niu Yen* or 'Ox Cave,' on a hillside near the North River. Its entrance is like a grand hall, with pillars 70 feet high and 8 or 10 feet thick. The finest part is exposed to the sun, but many pretty rooms and niches are revealed by torches; echoes resound through their recesses. The stalactites and stalagmites present a vast variety of shapes—some like immense folds of drapery, between which are lamps, thrones and windows of all shapes and sizes, while others hang from the roof in fanciful forms.

The scenery along the river, between Nanhiung and Shauchau, is described as wild, rugged, and barren in the extreme; the summits of the mountains seem to touch each other across the river, and massive fragments fallen from their sides, in and along the river, indicate that the passage is not altogether free from danger. In this mountainous region coal is procured by opening horizontal shafts to the mines. Ellis[1] says, it was brought some distance to the place where he saw it, to be used in the manufacture of green vitriol. Many pagodas are passed in the stretch of 330 miles between Nanhiung and Canton, calculated to attract notice, and assure the native boatmen which swarm on its waters, of the protection of the two elements he has to deal with—wind and water. One of the most conspicuous objects in this part of the river are five rocks, which rise abruptly from the banks, and are fancifully called *Wu-ma-tao*, or 'Five-horses' heads.' The formation of this part of the province consists of compact, dark-colored limestone, overlying

[1] *Embassy* (of Lord Amherst) *to China*, Moxon's ed., 1840, p. 98.

sandstone and breccia. Nearly halfway between Shauchau and Canton is a celebrated mountain and cavern temple, dedicated to Kwanyin, the goddess of Mercy, and most charmingly situated amid waterfalls, groves, and fine scenery, near a hill about 1,850 feet high. The cliff has a sheer descent of five hundred feet; the temple is in a fissure a hundred feet above the water, and consists of two stories; the steps leading up to them, the rooms, walls, and cells, are all cut out of the rock. Inscriptions and scrolls hide the naked walls, and a few inane priests inhabit this somewhat gloomy abode. Mr. Barrow draws a proper comparison between these men and the inmates of the Cork Convent in Portugal, or the Franciscan Convent in Madeira, who had likewise "chained themselves to a rock, to be gnawed by the vultures of superstition and fanaticism," but these last have less excuse.

The island of Hainan constitutes a single department, Kiungchau, but its prefect has no power over the central and mountainous parts. In early European travels it is named Aynao, Kainan and Aniam. It is about one hundred and fifty miles long and one hundred broad, being in extent nearly twice the size of Sicily. It is separated from the main by Luichau Strait, sixteen miles wide, whose shoals and reefs render its passage uncertain. The interior of the island is mountainous, and well wooded, and the inhabitants give a partial submission to the Chinese; they are identical in race with the mountaineers in Kweichau. This ridge is called Lí-mu ling; a remarkable peak in the centre of the southern half, *Wu-chi shan* or 'Five-finger Mountain,' probably rises 10,000 feet. The Chinese inhabitants are mostly descendants of emigrants from Fuhkien, and are either trading, agricultural, marine, or piratical in their vocation, as they can make most money. The lands along the coast are fertile, producing areca-nuts, cocoa-nuts, and other tropical fruits, which are not found on the main. Kiungchau fu lies at the mouth of the Lí-mu River, opposite Luichau. The port is Hoihau, nineteen miles distant, but the entrance is too shallow for most vessels, and the trade consequently seeks a better market at Pakhoi, a town which has recently risen to importance as a treaty port on the mainland. All the thirteen district towns are situated on the coast, and within their circuit, on Chinese maps, a line is drawn, inclosing the centre of the island, within which the *Lí min*, or Lí people live, *some* of whom are acknowledged to be independent. They are therefore known as wild and civilized Lí, and are usually in a state of chronic irritation from the harsh treatment of the rulers. It is probable that they originally came from the Malayan Peninsula (as their features, dress, and habits indicate their affinity with those tribes), and have gradually withdrawn themselves into their recesses to avoid oppression. In 1292, the Emperor Kublai gave twenty thousand of them lands free for a time in the eastern parts, but the Ming sovereigns found them all intractable and belligerent. The population of the island is about a million. Its productions are rice, sweet potatoes, sugar, tobacco, fruits, timber, and insect wax.[1]

The province of KWANGSÍ (*i.e.*, Broad West) extends westward of Kwangtung to the borders of Annam, occupying the region on the southwest of the Nan ling, and has been seldom visited by foreigners, whose journeys have been up the Kwai kiang or 'Cassia River' into Hunan. The banks of the rivers sometimes spread out into plains, more in the eastern parts than elsewhere, on which an abundance of rice is grown. There are mines of gold, silver, and other metals, in this province, most of which are worked under the superintendence of government, but no data are accessible from which to ascertain the produce. Among the commercial productions of Kwangsí, are cassia, cassia-oil, ink-stones, and cabinet-woods; its natural resources supply the principal articles of trade, for there are no manufactures of importance. Many partially subdued tribes are found within the limits of this province, who are ruled by their own hereditary governors, under the supervision of the Chinese authorities; there are twenty-four *chau* districts occupied by these people, the names of whose head-men are given in the Red

[1] E. C. Taintor, *Geographical Sketch of the Island of Hainan*, with map. Canton, 1868. *Journal N. C. Br. R. A. S.*, No. VII., Arts. I., II., and III. *China Review*, Vols. I., p. 124, and II., p. 332. N. B. Dennys, *Report on the newly-opened ports of Kiungchow (Hoihau) in Hainan, and Haiphong in Tonquin.* Hongkong, 1878.

Book, and their position marked in the statistical maps of the empire, but no information is furnished in either, concerning the numbers, language, or occupations, of the inhabitants. Kwangsí is well watered by the West River and its branches, which enable traders to convey timber and surplus produce to Canton, and receive from thence salt and other articles. The mountains on the northwest are occasionally covered with snow; many of the western districts furnish little besides wood for buildings and boats. The basin of the West River is subdivided by ranges of hills into three large valleys, through which flow many tributaries of the leading streams, and as they each usually drop the old name on receiving a new affluent, it is a confusing study to follow them all. On the south the river Yuh rises near Yunnan, and deflects south to Nan-ning near the borders of Kwangtung, joining the central trunk at Sinchau, after a course of five hundred miles. On the north the river Lung and the Hung-shui receive the surplus drainage of the northern districts and of Kweichau, a region where the Miaotsz' have long kept watch and ward over their hilly abodes. The waters are then poured into the central trench a few miles west of Sinchau. This main artery of the province rises in Yunnan and would connect it by batteaux with Canton City if the channel were improved; it is called Sz' ho, and ranks as the largest tributary of the Pearl River.

The capital, Kweilin (*i.e.*, Cassia Forest), lies on the Cassia River, a branch of the West River, in the northeast part of the province; it is a poorly built city, surrounded by canals and branches of the river, destitute of any edifices worthy of notice, and having no great amount of trade. During the Tai-ping rebellion, this and the next town were nearly destroyed between the insurgents and imperialists.

Wuchau fu, on the same river, at its junction with the Lung kiang, or 'Dragon River,' where they unite and form the West River, is the largest trading town in the province. The independent *chau* districts are scattered over the southwest near the frontiers of Annam, and if anything can be inferred from their position, it may be concluded that they were settled by Laos tribes, who had been induced, by the comparative security of life and property within the frontiers, to acknowledge the Chinese sway.[1]

The province of KWEICHAU (*i.e.*, Noble Region) is on the whole the poorest of the eighteen in the character of its inhabitants, amount of its products, and development of its resources. A range of mountains passes from the northeast side in a southwesterly course to Yunnan, forming the watershed between the valleys of the Yangtsz' and Siang Rivers, a rough but fertile region. The western slopes are peopled by Chinese tillers of the soil, a rude and ignorant race, and rather turbulent; the eastern districts are largely in the hands of the Miaotsz', who are considered by the officials and their troops to be lawful objects of oppression and destruction. The climate of the province is regarded as malarious, owing to the quantity of stagnant water and the impurity of that drawn from wells. Its productions consist of rice, wheat, musk, insect wax, tobacco, timber, and cassia, with lead, copper, silver, quicksilver, and iron. The quicksilver mines are in Kai chau, north of the provincial capital, and apparently exceed in extent and richness all other known deposits of this metal; they have been worked for centuries. Cinnabar occurs at various places, about lat. 27°, in a belt extending quite across the province, and terminating near the borders of Yunnan. Two kinds of silk obtained from the worms which feed on the mulberry and oak, furnish material for clothing so cheaply that cotton is imported from other provinces. Horses and other domestic animals are reared in larger quantities than in the eastern provinces.

The largest river is the Wu, which drains the central and northern parts of the province, and empties into the Yangtsz', through the river Kien near Chungking. Other tributaries of that river and West River, also have their sources in this province, and by means of batteaux and rafts are all more or less available for traffic. The natural outlet for the products of Kweichau is the river Yuen in Hunan, whose various branches flow into it from the eastern prefectures, but their unsettled condition prevents regular or successful intercourse.

---

[1] *Chinese Repository*, Vol. XIV., pp. 171 ff.

The capital, Kweiyang, is situated among the mountains; it is the smallest provincial capital of the eighteen, its walls not being more than two miles in circumference. The other chief towns or departments are of inferior note. There are many military stations in the southern prefectures at the foot of the mountains, intended to restrain the unsubdued tribes of Miaotsz' who inhabit them.

Miaotsz' Types.

This name Miaotsz' is used among the Chinese as a general term for all the dwellers upon these mountains, but is not applied to every clan by the people themselves. They consist of eighty-two tribes in all (found scattered over the mountains in Kwangtung, Hunan, and Kwangsí, as well as in Kweichau), speaking several dialects, and differing among themselves in their customs, government, and dress. The Chinese have often described and pictured these people, but the notices are confined to a list of their divisions, and an account of their most striking peculiarities. Their language differs entirely from the Chinese, but too little is known of it to ascertain its analogies to other tongues; its affinities are most likely with the Laos, and those tribes between Burmah, Siam, and China. One clan, inhabiting Lípo hien in the extreme south, is called *Yau-jin*, and although they occasionally come down to Canton to trade, the citizens of that place firmly believe them to be furnished with short tails like monkeys. They carry arms, are inclined to live at peace with the lowlanders, but resist every attempt to penetrate into their fastnesses. The Yau-jin first settled in Kwangsí, and thence passed over into Lien chau about the twelfth century, where they have since maintained their footing. Both sexes wear their hair braided in a tuft on the top of the head—but never shaven and tressed as the Chinese—and dress in loose garments of cotton and linen; earrings are in universal use among them. They live at strife among themselves, which becomes a source of safety to the Chinese, who are willing enough to harass and oppress, but are ill able to resist, these hardy mountaineers. In 1832, they broke out in active hostilities, and destroyed numerous parties of troops sent to subdue them, but were finally induced to return to their retreats by offers of pardon and largesses granted to those who submitted.

A Chinese traveller among the Miaotsz' says that some of them live in huts constructed upon the branches of trees, others in mud hovels; and one tribe in cliff houses dug out of the hillsides, sometimes six hundred feet up. Their agriculture is rude, and their garments are obtained by barter from the lowlanders in exchange for metals and grain, or woven by themselves. The religious observances of these tribes are carefully noted, and whatever is connected with marriages and funerals. In one tribe, it is the custom for the father of a new-born child, as soon as its mother has become strong enough to leave her couch, to get into bed himself and there receive the congratulations of his acquaintances, as he exhibits his offspring—a custom which has been found among the Tibetan tribes and elsewhere. Another class has the counterpart of the may-pole and its jocund dance, which, like its corresponding game, is availed of by young men to select their mates.[1]

The province of YUNNAN (*i.e.*, Cloudy South—south of the *Yun ling*, or 'Cloudy Mountains'[2]) is in the southwest of the empire, bounded by north Sz'chuen, east by Kweichau and Kwangsí, south by Annam, Laos, and Siam, and west by Burmah. Its distance from the central authority of the Empire since its partial conquest under the Han dynasty has always made it a weak point, and the uneducated, mixed character of the inhabitants has given an advantage to enterprising leaders to resist Chinese rule. It was recovered from the aborigines by the Tang Emperors, who called it Jung chau, or the region of the Jung tribes, from which the name *Karajang*, *i.e.*, Black Jung, which Marco Polo calls it, is derived; Kublai Khan himself led an army in 1253 thither before he conquered China, and sent the Venetians on a mission there about the year 1278, after his establishment at Peking. A son of the Emperor was his Viceroy over this outlying province at that time. The recent travels of Margary, Baber, and Anderson, of the British service, with Monhot and Garnier of the French, have done much to render this secluded province better known. The central portion is occupied by an extensive plateau, ramifying in various directions and intersected with valley-plains at altitudes of 5,000 to 6,000 feet, in which lie several large lakes and the seven principal cities in the province. These plains are overtopped by the ridges separating them, which, seen from the lower levels, appear, as in Shansí, like horizontal, connected summit-lines. All are built up of red sandstone, like the basin in Sz'chuen, through which rivers, small and large, have furrowed their beds hundreds and thousands of feet, rendering communication almost impossible in certain directions as soon as one leaves the plateau. In the east and northwest, the defiles

---

[1] *Chinese Repository*, Vol. I., p. 29; Vol. XIV., pp. 105–117; G. T. Lay, *Chinese as They Are*, p. 316; *Journal of N. C. Branch of Royal Asiatic Society*, No. III., 1859, and No. VI., 1869. *Chinese Recorder*, Vols. II., p. 265, and III., pp. 33, 74, 96, 134 and 147. *Peking Gazette* for 1872. *China Review*, Vol. V., p. 92.

[2] Known as *Widiharit* in Pali records. *Chinese Recorder*, Vol. III., pp. 33, 74, sqq.; see also pp. 62, 93, 126, for the record of a visit.

are less troublesome, and in this latter portion of the province are some peaks rising far above the snow line. These are called on Col. Yule's map the *Goolan Sigon* range. The climate is cooler than in Sz'chuen, owing to this elevation, and not very healthy; snow lies for weeks at Yunnan fu, and the summers are charming.

The Yangtsz' enters the province on the northwest for a short distance. The greatest river in it is the Lantsan, which rises in Tibet, and runs for a long distance parallel with and between the Yangtsz' and Nu Rivers till the three break through the mountains not far from each other, and take different courses,—the largest turning to the eastward across China, the Lantsan southeast through Yunnan to the gulf of Siam, under the name of the Meikon or river of Cambodia, and the third, or Salween, westerly through Burmah. The Meikon receives many large tributaries in its course across the province, and its entire length is not less than 1,500 miles. The Lungchuen, a large affluent of the Irrawadi, runs a little west of the Salween. The Meinam rises in Yunnan, and flows south into Siam under the name of the Nanting, and after a course of nearly eight hundred miles, empties into the sea below Bangkok. East of the Lantsan are several important streams, of which three that unite in Annam to form the Sangkoi, are the largest. The general course of these rivers is southeasterly, and their upper waters are separated by mountain ridges, between which the valleys are often reduced to very narrow limits. There are two lakes in the eastern part of the province, south of the capital, called Sien and Tien; the latter is about seventy miles long by twenty wide, and the Sien hu (*i.e.*, 'Fairy Lake') about two-thirds as large. Another sheet of water in the northwest, near Talí fu, communicating with the Yangtsz' kiang, is called Urh hai or Uhr sea, which is more than a hundred miles long, and about twenty in width.

The capital, Yunnan, lies upon the north shore of Lake Tien, and is a town of note, having, moreover, considerable political importance from its trade with other parts of the country through the Yangtsz', and with Burmah. The city was seriously injured in 1834, by an earthquake, which is said to have lasted three entire days, forcing the inhabitants into tents or the open fields, and overthrowing every important building.[1] The traffic between this province and Burmah centres at the fortified post of Tsantah, in the district of Tăngyueh, both of them situated on a branch of the Irrawadi. The principal part of the commodities is transported upon animals from these dépôts to Bhamo, upon the Irrawadi, the largest market-town in this part of Chin-India. The Chinese participate largely in this trade, which consists of raw and manufactured silk to the amount of $400,000 annually, tea, copper, carpets, orpiment, quicksilver, vermilion, drugs, fruits, and other things, carried from their country in exchange for raw cotton to the amount of $1,140,000 annually, ivory, wax, rhinoceros and deer's horns, precious stones, birds' nests, peacocks' feathers, and foreign articles. The entire traffic is probably $2,500,000 annually, and for a few years past has been regularly increasing.

There is considerable intercourse and trade on the southern frontiers with the Lolos, or Laos and Annamese,[2] partly by means of the head-waters of the Meinam and Meikon—which are supposed to communicate with each other by a natural canal—and partly by caravans over the mountains. Yunnan fu was the capital of a Chinese prince about the time of the decadence of the Ming dynasty, who had rendered himself independent in this part of their empire by the overthrow of the rebel Lí, but having linked his fortunes with an imbecile scion of that house, he displeased his officers, and his territories gradually fell under the sway of the conquering Manchus. The southern and western districts of the province are inhabited by half-subdued tribes who are governed by their own rulers, under the nominal sway of the Chinese, and pass and repass across the frontiers in pursuit of trade or occupation.

The extension of British trade from Rangoon toward this part of China, has brought those hill tribes more into notice, and proved in their present low and barbarous condition the accuracy of the ancient description by Marco Polo and the Roman Catholic missionaries. Colonel Yule aptly terms this wide re-

---

[1] *Annales de la Foi*, Tome VIII., p. 87.

[2] Two thousand Chinese families live in Amerapura.

gion an "Ethnological Garden of tribes of various race and in every stage of uncivilization." The unifying influence of the Chinese written language and literary institutions has been neutralized among these races by their tribal dissensions and inaptitude for study of any kind. Anderson gives short vocabularies of the Kakhyen, Shan, Hotha Shan, Le-sau and Poloung languages, all indicating radical differences of origin, the existence of which would keep them from mingling with each other as well as from the Chinese.[1]

The mineral wealth of Yunnan is greater and more varied than that of any other province, certain of the mines having been worked since the Sung dynasty. Coal occurs in many places on the borders of the central plateau; some of it is anthracite of remarkable solidity and uniformity. Salt occurs in hills, not in wells as in Sz'chuen; the brine is sometimes obtained by diving tunnels into the hillsides. Metalliferous ores reach from this province into the three neighboring ones. Copper is the most abundant, and the mines in Ningyuen fu, in the southwestern part of Sz'chuen, have supplied both copper and zinc ores during the troubles in Yunnan. The copper at Hwuilí chau in that prefecture is worked by companies which pay a royalty of two taels a pecul to the government, and furnish the metal to the mine owners for $8 per pecul. The *peh-tung* or argentan ores are mixed with copper, tin, or lead, by the manufacturers according to the uses the alloys are put to. Silver exists in several places in the north, and the exploitation of the mines was successful until within 30 years past; now they cannot be safely or profitably worked, in consequence of political disturbances. Gold is obtained in the sand of some rivers but not to a large extent; lead, iron, tin, and zinc occur in such plenty that they can be exported, but no data are accessible as to the entire product or export.[2]

---

[1] Yule's *Marco Polo*, Vol. II. Anderson, *Mandalay to Momien.*

[2] *Proced. Roy. Geog. Soc.*, Vols. XIII., p. 392, XIV., p. 335, XV., pp. 163 and 343. Col. Yule, *Trade Routes to Western China—The Geographical Magazine*, April, 1875. Richthofen, *Recent Attempts to find a direct Trade-Road to Southwestern China—Shanghai Budget*, March 26, 1874. *Journey of A. R. Margary from Shanghae to Bhamo.* London, 1875. Col. H. Browne in *Blue Books*, Nos. 1, 2, 3, and 4 (1876–77).

CHAPTER IV.

GEOGRAPHICAL DESCRIPTION OF MANCHURIA, MONGOLIA, ÍLÍ, AND TIBET.

THE portions of the Chinese Empire beyond the limits of the Eighteen Provinces, though of far greater extent than China Proper, are comparatively of minor importance. Their vast regions are peopled by different races, whose languages are mutually unintelligible, and whose tribes are held together under the Chinese sway rather by interest and reciprocal hostilities or dislike, than by force. European geographers have vaguely termed all that space lying north of Tibet to Siberia, and east of the Tsung ling to the Pacific, *Chinese Tartary;* while the countries west of the Tsung ling or Belur tag, to the Aral Sea, have been collectively called *Independent Tartary.* Both these names have already become nearly obsolete on good maps of those regions; the more accurate knowledge brought home by recent travellers having ascertained that their inhabitants are neither all Tartars (or Mongols) nor Turks, and further that the native names and divisions are preferable to a single comprehensive one. Such names as Manchuria, Mongolia, Songaria, and Turkestan, derived from the leading tribes dwelling in those countries, are more definite, though these are not permanent, owing to the migratory, changeable habits of the people. From their ignorance of scientific geography, the Chinese have no general designations for extensive countries, long chains of mountains, or devious rivers, but apply many names where, if they were better informed, they would be content with one.

The following table presents a general view of these countries, giving their leading divisions and forms of government.

GENERAL VIEW OF THE COLONIES AND THEIR SUBDIVISIONS.

COLONIES.	PROVINCES.	DIVISIONS.	CAPITALS.	FORMS OF GOVERNMENT.
MANCHURIA	Shingking	Two fu departments and 15 districts; and 13 garrisons	Mukden or Fungtien	Manchuria is ruled by military boards, and generals at the garrisons.
	Kirin	Three ting departments, or 8 garrisoned posts	Kirin ula hotun	Under three generals at the prefectures.
	Tsitsihar	Six commanderies	Tsitsihar hotun	Under six generals.
MONGOLIA	Inner Mongolia	Six corps, subdivided into 24 tribes and 49 standards	No common capital	Each tribe has its own chieftain or general, and is governed by the Lí-fan Yuen in Peking.
	Outer Mongolia	Four khanates, viz.: Tuchétu, Sainnoin, Tsetsen, and Dsassaktu	Urga or Kurun	Four khans under the Kutuktu.
	Koko-nor	One residency, having 29 standards	Síning in Kansuh.	Under a Manchu residency.
	Uliasutai	Cobdo, having 11 tribes and 31 standards. Ulianghai tribes under 21 tso-ling	Uliasutai	By an amban over the chieftains.
ÍLÍ	Northern Circuit or Songaria	Ílí	Kuldja	Ruled by a military governor, 2 councillors, and 34 residents in the cities.
		Kur-kara usu	Kur-kara usu	Under resident subordinate to the governor.
		Tarbagatai	Sui-tsing ching	
	Southern Circuit or Eastern Turkestan	Ten cities, viz.: Harashar, Kuché, Sairim, Bai, Ushi, Aksu, Khoten, Kashgar, Yangi Hissar, and Yarkand	Yarkand	Each city under a resident amenable to the governor at Ílí, and native begs.
TIBET	Anterior Tibet	Wei and Kham, divided into eight cantons and 39 feudal townships	H'lassa	Ruled by the Dalai-lama and his hierarchy, overseen by Chinese residents.
	Ulterior Tibet	Tsang and Nari, divided into six cantons	Shigatsé	Ruled by the Teshu-lama, assisted by a resident from Peking.

They cannot be classed, however, in the same manner as the provinces, nor are the divisions and capitals here given to be regarded as definitely settled. Their united area is 3,951,130 square miles, or a little more than all Europe; their separate areas cannot be precisely given. Manchuria contains about 400,000 square miles; Mongolia between 1,300,000 and 1,500,-000 square miles; Ílí about 1,070,000 square miles; and Tibet from 500,000 to 700,000 square miles.

MANCHURIA is so termed from the leading race who dwell there, the *Mandjurs* or *Manchus;* it is a word of foreign origin, the Chinese having no general appellation for the vice-royalty ruled from Mukden. It comprises the eastern portion of the high table land of Central Asia, and lies between latitudes 39° and 52° N., and longitudes 120° to 134° E. These points include the limits in both directions, giving the region a rectangular shape lying in a north-east and south-west direction; roughly speaking, its dimensions are 800 by 500 miles. It is bounded on the south by the Gulf of Pechele, and the highlands of Corea on the north bank of the Yaluh River; on the east by a line running from the Russian town of Possiet northerly to the River Usuri, so as to include Hinka Lake; thence from its headwaters to its junction with the Amur. This river forms the northern frontier; its tributary, the River Argun, together with the large lakes Hurun and Puyur, lie on the west; from the latter lake an artificial line stretching nearly due east for six degrees in lat. 47° strikes the town of Tsitsihar on the River Nonni. The rest of the western border follows the rivers Nonni and Songari to the Palisade. This obsolete boundary commences at Shan-hai kwan on the Gulf of Liatung and runs north-easterly; it nominally separates the Mongols from the Manchus for nearly 300 miles, and really exists only at the passes where the roads are guarded by military.

But a portion of this region has yet been traversed by Europeans, and most of it is a wilderness. The entire population is not stated in the census of 1812, and from the nature of the country and wandering habits of the people, many tribes of whom render no allegiance to the Emperor, it would be impossible to take a regular census. Parts of Manchuria, as here defined, have been known under many names at different periods. *Liautung* ('East of the River Liau') has been applied to the country between that river, Corea, and the Sea of Japan; *Tungking* ('Eastern Capital') referred to the chief town of that region, under the Ming dynasty; and *Kwantung* ('East of the Pass'), denoting the same country, is still a common designation for the whole territory.

Manchuria is now chiefly comprised in the valleys between the Usuri and Nonni Rivers, up to the Amur on the north, while the basin of the Liau on the south embraces the rest. There are three principal mountain chains. Beginning nearly a hundred miles east of Mukden, in lat. 43°, are the Long White Mountains[1] (*Chang-peh shan* of the Chinese, or *Kolmin-shang-uin alin* of the Manchus), which form the watershed between the Songari and Yaluh Rivers and serve for the northern frontier of Corea as far as Russian territory. There it divides and takes the name of Sih-hih-teh, or Sihoti Mountains, for the eastern spur which runs near the ocean, east of the River Usuri; and the name of Hurkar Mountains for the western and lower spurs between that river and the Hurkar. One noted peak, called Mount Chakoran, rising over 10,000 feet, lies south-east of San-săng on the Amur. On the plain, north of Kirin, numerous buttes occur, sometimes isolated, and often in lines fifteen or twenty miles apart; most of them are wooded.

In the western part of Tsitsihar lies the third great range of mountains in Manchuria, called the Sialkoi Mountains, a continuation of the Inner Hing-an range of Mongolia, and separating the Argun and Nonni basins. The Sialkoi range extends over a great part of Mongolia, commencing near the bend of the Yellow River, and reaching in a north-easterly direction, it forms in Manchuria three sides of the extensive valley of the Nonni, ending between the Amur and Songari Rivers at their junction. These regions are more arid than the eastern portions, and the mountains are rather lower; but our information is vague and scanty. As a whole, Manchuria should be called hilly

[1] Klaproth (*Mémoires Relatifs à l'Asie*, Tome I., Paris, 1824) has translated from the Manchu a narrative of a visit made in 1677 by one of the grandees of Kanghi's court to a summit in this range. *Chinese Repository*, Vol. XX., p. 296.

rather than mountainous, its intervales alone repaying cultivation.

The country north of the Chang-peh shan as far as the Stanovoi Mountains is drained by one river, viz., the Sagalien, Amur, Kwăntung, or Hehlung kiang (for it is known by all these names), and its affluents; *Sagalien ula* in Manchu and *Hehlung kiang* in Chinese, each mean 'Black' or 'Black Dragon River.' The Amur drains the north-eastern slope of Central Asia by a circuitous course, aided by many large tributaries. Its source is in lat. 50° N. and long. 111° E., in a spur of the Daourian Mountains, called Kenteh, where it is called the Onon. After an east and north-east course of nearly five hundred miles, the Onon is joined in long. 115° E. by the Ingoda, a stream coming from the east of Lake Baikal, where it takes its rise by a peak called Tshokondo, the highest of the Yablonsi Khrebet Mountains. Beyond this junction, under the Russian name of Shilka, it flows about two hundred and sixty miles north-east till it meets the Argun. The Argun rises about three degrees south of the Onon, on the south side of the Kenteh, and under the name of Kerlon runs a solitary north-east course for four hundred and thirty miles to Lake Hurun, Kerlon, or Dalai-nur; the Kalka here comes in from Lake Puyur or Pir, and their waters leave Lake Hurun at Ust-Strelotchnoi (the Arrow's Mouth) under the name of the Argun, flowing north nearly four hundred miles to the union with the Shilka in lat. 53°; from its exit as the Argun and onward to the entrance of the Usuri, it forms the boundary between China and Russia for 1,593 versts, or 1,062 miles.

Beyond this town the united stream takes the name of the Amur (*i.e.*, Great River) or Sagalien of the Manchus, running nearly east about 550 miles beyond Albazin, when its course is south-east till it joins the Songari. Most of the affluents are on the north bank; the main channel grows wider as its size increases, having so many islands and banks as seriously to interfere with navigation. The valley thus watered possesses great natural advantages in soil, climate, and productions, which are now gradually attracting Russian settlers. In lat. 47½° the Songari River (*Sung-hwa kiang* of the Chinese) unites with the

Amur on the right bank, 950 miles from Ust-Strelotchnoi, bringing the drainings of the greater portion of Manchuria, and doubling the main volume of water. The headwaters of this stream issue from the northern slopes of the Chang-peh shan; quickly combined in a single channel, these waters flow past the town of Kirin, scarcely a hundred miles from the mountains, in a river twelve feet deep and 900 wide. Near Petuné the River Nonni joins it from Tsitsihar, and their united stream takes the Chinese name of Kwantung ('Mingled Union'); it is a mile and a half wide here and only three or four feet deep, a sluggish river full of islands. Then going east by north, growing deeper by its affluents, the Hurka, Mayen, Tunni, Hulan, and other smaller ones, it unites with the Amur at at Changchu, a hundred miles west from the Usuri. All accounts agree in giving the Songari the superiority. At Sansing, it is a deep and rapid river, but further down islands and banks interfere with the navigation. The Hurka drains the original country of the Manchus.[1]

The district south-east of the desert, and north of the Great Wall, is drained and fertilized by the Sira-muren, or Liau River, which is nearly valueless for navigation. Its main and western branch divides near the Ín shan Mountains into the Hwang ho and Lahar; the former rises near the Pecha peak, a noted point in those mountains. The Sira-muren runs through a dry region for nearly 400 miles before it turns south, and in a zigzag channel reaches the Gulf of Liautung, a powerful stream carrying its quota of deposit into the ocean; the width at Yingtsz' is 650 feet. The depth is 16 feet on the bar at high tide. The Yaluh kiang, nearly three hundred miles long, runs in a very crooked channel along the northern frontiers of Corea. But little is known about the two lakes, Hurun and Pir, except that their waters are fresh and full of fish; the River Urshun unites them, and several smaller streams run into the latter.

---

[1] *Voyage Down the Amur*, by Perry McD. Collins, in 1857. New York, 1860, chaps. xxxii.–lx., passim. Ravenstein's *Amur*. *Chinese Repository*, Vol. XIX., p. 289. Rev. A. Williamson, *Journeys in North China*, Vol. II., chaps. x.–xiii.

The larger part of Manchuria is covered by forests, the abode of wild animals, whose capture affords employment, clothing, and food to their hunters. The rivers and coasts abound in fish; among which carp, sturgeon, salmon, pike, and other species, as well as shell-fish, are plenty; the pearl-fishery is sufficiently remunerative to employ many fishermen; the Chinese Government used to take cognizance of their success, and collect a revenue in kind. The argali and jiggetai are found here as well as in Mongolia; bears, wolves, tigers, deer, and numerous fur-bearing animals are hunted for their skins. The troops are required to furnish 2,400 stags annually to the Emperor, who reserves for his own use only the fleshy part of the tail as a delicacy. Larks, pheasants, and crows of various species, with pigeons, thrushes, and grouse, abound. The condor is the largest bird of prey, and for its size and fierceness rivals its congener of the Andes.

The greater half of Shingking and the south of Kirin is cultivated; maize, Setaria wheat, barley, pulse, millet, and buckwheat are the principal crops. Ginseng and rhubarb are collected by troops sent out in detachments under the charge of their proper officers. These sections support, moreover, large herds of various domestic animals. The timber which covers the mountains will prove a source of wealth as soon as a remunerative market stimulates the skill and enterprise of settlers; even now, logs over three feet in diameter find their way up to Peking, brought from the Liau valley.

Manchuria is divided into three provinces, *Shingking*, *Kirin*, and *Tsitsihar*. The province of SHINGKING includes the ancient Liautung, and is bounded north by Mongolia; north-east and east by Kirin; south by the Gulf of Liautung and Corea, from which latter it is separated by the Yaluh River; and west by Chahar in Chihlí. It contains two departments, viz., Fungtien and Kinchau, subdivided into fifteen districts; there are also twelve garrisoned posts at the twelve gates in the Palisade, whose inmates collect a small tax on travellers and goods. Manchuria is under a strictly military government, every male above eighteen being liable for military service, and being, in fact, enrolled under that one of the eight standards to which by birth he belongs. The administration of Shingking is partly civil and partly military; that of Kirin and Tsitsihar is entirely military.

The population of the province has been estimated by T. T. Meadows [1] at twelve millions, consisting of Manchus and Chinese. The coast districts are now mostly occupied and cultivated by emigrants from Shantung, who are pushing the Manchus toward the Amur, or compelling them to leave their hunting and take to farming if they wish to stay where they were born. The conquerors are being civilized and developed by their subjects, losing the use of their own meagre language, and becoming more comfortable as they learn to be industrious. But few aboriginal settlements now remain who still resist these influences. The inhabitants collect near the river, or along the great roads, where food or a market are easiest found.

The capital of Shingking is usually known on the spot as Shin-yang, an older name than the Manchu Mukden, or the Chinese name Fungtien. As the metropolis of Manchuria, it is also known as Shingking (the 'Affluent Capital'), distinguished from the name of the province by the addition of *pun-ching*, or 'head-garrison.' It lies in lat. 41° 50½′ N. and long. 123° 30′ E., on the banks of the Shin, a small branch of the Liau, and is reckoned to be five hundred miles north-east from Peking. The town is surrounded by a low mud wall about ten miles in circuit, at least half a mile distant from the main city wall, whose eight gates have double archways so that the crowd may not interfere in passing; this wall is about three miles around, and its towers and bastions are in good condition. It is 35 or 40 feet high, and 15 feet wide at the top, of brick throughout; a crenulated parapet protects the guard. But for its smaller scale, the walls and buildings here are precisely similar to those at Peking. The streets are wide, clean, and the main business avenues lined with large, well built shops, their counters, windows, and other arrangements indicating a great trade. This capital contains a large proportion of governmental establishments, *yamuns*, and nearly all the officials belong to the ruling race. Main

[1] *The Chinese and their Rebellions.* London, 1856.

streets run across the city from gate to gate, with narrow roads or *hu-tung* intersecting them. The palace of the early Manchu sovereigns occupies the centre; while the large warehouses are outside of the inner city. Everywhere marks of prosperity and security indicate an enterprising population, and for its tidy look, industrious and courteous population, Mukden takes high rank among Chinese cities. Its population is estimated to be under 200,000, mostly Chinese. The Manchu monarchs made it the seat of their government in 1631, and the Emperors have since done everything in their power to enlarge and beautify it. The Emperor Kienlung rendered himself celebrated among his subjects, and made the city of Mukden better known abroad, by a poetical eulogy upon the city and province, which was printed in sixty-four different forms of Chinese writing. This curious piece of imperial vanity and literary effort was translated into French by Amyot.

The town of Hingking,[1] sixty miles east of it, is one of the favored places in Shingking, from its being the family residence of the Manchu monarchs, and the burial-ground of their ancestors. It is pleasantly situated in an elevated valley, the tombs being three miles north of it upon a mountain called *Tsz'yun shan*. The circuit of the walls is about three miles. Hingking lies near the Palisade which separates the province from Kirin, and its officers have the rule over the surrounding country, and the entrances into that province. It has now dwindled to a small hamlet, and the guards connected with the tombs comprise most of the inhabitants.

Kinchau, fifteen leagues from Mukden, carries on considerable trade in cattle, pulse, and drugs. Gutzlaff[2] describes the harbor as shallow, and exposed to southern gales; the houses in the town are built of stone, the environs well cultivated and settled by Chinese from Shantung, while natives of Fuhkien conduct the trade. The Manchus lead an idle life, but keep on good terms with the Chinese. When he was there in 1832,

---

[1] Also called *Yenden;* Klaproth, *Mémoires*, Tome I., p. 446. Rémusat informs us that this name formerly included all of Kirin, or that which was placed under it.

[2] *Voyages Along the Coast of China.* New York, 1833.

the authorities had ordered all the females to seclude themselves in order to put a stop to debauchery among the native sailors. Horses and camels are numerous and cheap, but the carriages are clumsy. Kaichau, another port lying on the east side of the gulf, possesses a better harbor, but is not so much frequented.

Since the treaty of 1858 opened the port of Niuchwang or Yingtsz', on the River Liau, to foreign trade, the development of Shingking has rapidly increased. The trade in pulse and bean-cake and oil employs many vessels annually. Opium, silk, and paper are prepared for export through this mart, besides foreign goods. Fung-hwang ting, lying near the Yaluh River, commands all the trade with Corea, which must pass through it. There are many restrictions upon this intercourse by both governments, and the Chinese forbid their subjects passing the frontiers. The trade is conducted at fairs, under the supervision of officers and soldiers; the short time allowed for concluding the bargains, and the great numbers resorting to them, render these bazaars more like the frays of opposing clans than the scenes of peaceable trade. There is a market-town in Corea itself, called Kí-iu wăn, about four leagues from the frontier, where the Chinese "supply the Coreans with dogs, cats, pipes, leather, stags' horns, copper, horses, mules, and asses; and receive in exchange, baskets, kitchen utensils, rice, corn, swine, paper, mats, oxen, furs, and small horses." Merchants are allowed not more than four or five hours in which to conduct this fair, and the Corean officers under whose charge it is placed, drive all strangers back to the frontier as soon as the day closes.[1]

The borders of the sea consist of alluvial soil, efflorescing a nitrous white salt near the beach, but very fertile inland, well cultivated and populous. Beyond, the hill-country is extremely picturesque. Ever-changing views, torrents and fountains, varied and abounding vegetation, flocks of black cattle grazing on the hillsides, goats perched on the overhanging crags, horses, asses, and sheep lower down in the intervales, numerous

---

[1] *Annales de la Foi,* Tome XVIII., 1846, p. 302.

well-built hamlets, everywhere enliven the scene. The department of Kinchau lies along the Gulf of Liautung, between the Palisade and the sea, and contains four small district towns, with forts, around whose garrisons of agricultural troops have collected a few settlers. On the south, toward Chihlí and the Wall, the country is better cultivated.

The climate of Manchuria, as a whole, is healthy and moderate, far removed from the rigor of the plateau on its west, and not so moist as the outlying islands on the east. In summer the ranges are 70° to 90° F., thence down to 10° or 20° below zero. The rivers remain frozen from December nearly to April, and the fall of snow is less than in Eastern America. The seasons are really six weeks of spring, five months of summer, six weeks of autumn and four months of winter; the last is in some respects the enjoyable period, and is used by the farmers to bring produce to market. If the houses were tighter, their inmates would suffer little during the cold season. Huc speaks of hail storms which killed flocks of sheep in Mongolia, near Chahar. Darwin (*Naturalist's Voyage*, 2d ed., 1845, p. 115) corroborates the possibility of his statement by a somewhat similar experience near Buenos Ayres. He here saw many deer and other wild animals killed by "hail as large as small apples and extremely hard." Of the denuded country, near the Liau River, Abbé Huc says: "Although it is uncertain where God placed paradise, we may be sure that he chose some other country than Liautung; for of all savage regions, this takes a distinguished rank for the aridity of the soil and rigor of the climate. On his entrance, the traveller remarks the barren aspect of most of the hills, and the nakedness of the plains, where not a tree nor a thicket, and hardly a slip of a herb is to be seen. The natives are superior to any Europeans I have ever seen for their powers of eating; beef and pork abound on their tables, and I think dogs and horses, too, under some other name; rich people eat rice, the poor are content with boiled millet, or with another grain called *hac-bam*, about thrice the size of millet and tasting like wheat, which I never saw elsewhere. The vine is cultivated, but must be covered from October to April; the grapes are so watery that a hundred litres of juice produce by distillation only forty of poor spirit. The leaves of an oak are used to rear wild silkworms, and this is a considerable branch of industry. The people relish the worms as food after the cocoons have been boiled, drawing them out with a pin, and sucking the whole until nothing but the pellicle is left."[1] Another says, the ground freezes seven feet in Kirin, and about three in Shingking; the thermometer in winter is thirty degrees below zero. The snow is raised into the air by the north-east winds, and becomes so fine that it penetrates the clothes, houses, and enters even the lungs. When travelling, the eyebrows become a mass of ice, the beard a large flake, and the eyelashes are frozen together; the wind cuts and pierces the skin like razors or needles. The earth is frozen during eight months, but vegetation in summer is rapid, and the streams are swollen by the thawing drifts of snow.

The province of Kirin, or Girin, comprises the country north-east of Shingking, as far as the Amur and Usuri, which bound it on the north and east, while Corea and Shingking lie on the south-east (better separated by the Chang-peh shan than any political confine) and Mongolia on the west. All signs of the line of palisades have disappeared (save at the Passes) in the entire *trajet* between the Songari and Shan-hai kwan. The region is mountainous, except in the link of that river after the Nonni joins it till the Usuri comes in, measuring about one-fourth of the whole. This extensive region is thinly inhabited by Manchus settled in garrisons along the bottoms of the rivers, by Goldies, Mangoons, Ghiliaks, and tribes having affinity with them, who subsist principally by hunting and fishing, and acknowledge their fealty by a tribute of peltry, but who have no officers of government placed over them. Du Halde calls them *Kiching Tatse*, *Yupi Tatse*, and other names, which seem, indeed, to have been their ancient designations. The *Yu-pi Tahtsi*, or 'Fish-skin Tartars,'[2] are said to inhabit the extensive valley of the Usuri, and do not allow the subjects of the Emperor to

---

[1] *Annales de la Foi*, Tome XVI., p. 359.

[2] The inhabitants of ancient Gedrosia, now Beloochistan, are said to have clothed themselves in fish-skins. Heeren, *Historical Researches among Asiatic Nations*, Vol. I., p. 175.

live among them. In winter they nestle together in kraals like the Bushmen, and subsist upon the products of their summer's fishing, having cut down fuel enough to last them till warm weather. Shut out, as they have been during the past, from all elevating influences, these people are likely to be ere long amalgamated and lost, as well among Russian and other settlers coming in from the north, as amid the Chinese immigrants who occupy their land in the south. The entire population of this province cannot be reckoned, from present information, as high as three millions, the greater part of which live along the Songari valley.

Kirin is divided into three ruling *ting* departments or commanderies, viz., Kirin ula, or the garrison of Kirin, Petuné or Pedné, and Changchun ting. Kirin, the largest of the three, is subdivided into eight garrison districts. The town, called *Chuen Chwang*, or 'Navy Yard,' in Chinese, is finely situated on the Songari, in lat. 43° 45′ N., and long. 127° 25′ E., at the foot of encircling hills, where the river is a thousand feet wide. The streets are narrow and irregular, the shops low and small, and much ground in the city is unoccupied. Two great streets cross each other at right angles, one of them running far into the river on the west supported by piles. The highways are paved with wooden blocks, and adorned with flowers, gold fish, and squares; its population is about 50,000.

The four other important places in Kirin are Petuné, Larin, Altchuku, or A-shi-ho, and Sansing, the latter at the confluent of the Songari and Hurka. Altchuku is the largest, and Petuné next in size, each town having not far from 35,000 inhabitants; Larin is perhaps half as large, and like the others steadily increasing in numbers and importance. Ninguta on the river Hurka has wide regions under its sway where ginseng is gathered; near the stockaded town is a subterranean body of water that furnishes large fish. A great and influential portion of the Chinese population is Moslem, but no Manchus reside in the place. The former control trade and travel in every town.

Petuné, in lat. 45° 20′ N., and long. 125° 10′ E., is inhabited by troops and many persons banished from China for their crimes. Its favorable position renders it a place of considerable trade, and during the summer months it is a busy mart for these thinly peopled regions. It consists of two main streets, with the chief market at their crossing. A large mosque attracts attention. The third commandery of Changchun, west of Kirin and south of Petuné, just beyond the Palisade, is a mere post for overseeing the Manchus and Mongols passing to and fro on the edge of the steppe.

The resources of this wide domain in timber, minerals, metals, cattle and grain have not yet been explored or developed. The hills are wooded to the top, the bottoms bring forth two crops annually, and the rivers take down timber and grain to the Russian settlers. Sorghum, millet, barley, maize, pulse, indigo, and tobacco are the chief crops; and latterly opium, which has rapidly extended, because it pays well. Oil and whiskey are extensively manufactured, packed in wicker baskets lined with paper and transported on wheelbarrows. The wild and domestic animals are numerous. Among the latter the hogs and mules, more than any other kind, furnish food and transportation; while tigers, panthers, and leopards, bears, wolves, and foxes reward the hunters for their pains in killing them.

The province of TSI-TSI-HAR, or Hehlung kiang, comprises the northwest of Manchuria, extending four hundred miles from east to west, and about five hundred from north to south. It is bounded north by the Amur, from Shilka to its junction with the Songari; east and southeast by Kirin, from which the Songari partly separates it; southwest by Mongolia, and west by the River Argun, dividing it from Russia. The greatest part of it is occupied by the valley of the Nonni, Noun or Nún; its area of about two hundred thousand square miles is mostly an uninhabited, mountainous wilderness. It is divided into six commanderies, viz.: Tsitsihar, Hulan, Putek, Merguen, Sagalien ula, and Hurun-pir, whose officers have control over the tribes within their limits; of these, Sagalien or Igoon is the chief town in the northeast districts, and is used by the government of Peking as a penal settlement. The town stands on a plain but a rood or so above the river, which sweeps off to the mountains in the distance. Here is posted a large force of officers and men, their extensive barracks indicating the importance attached to the place. The garrison has gradually attracted a population of natives and Chinese from the south, who live by fishing and hunting, as well as farming.

Tsitsihar, the capital of the province, lies on the River Nonni, in lat. 47° 20′ N., and long. 124° E., and is a place of some trade, resorted to by the tribes near the river. Merguen, Hurunpir, and Hulan are situated upon rivers, and accessible when the waters are free from ice. Tsitsihar was built in 1692 by Kanghí to owerawe the neighboring tribes. It is inclosed by a stockade and a ditch. The one-storied houses are constructed of logs, or of brick stuccoed, where timber is dear, and warmed by the brick beds; the tall chimneys outside the main buildings give a peculiar appearance to villages. Pulse, maize, tobacco, millet, and wheat, and latterly poppy are common crops. The valley of the Nonni is cultivated by the Taguri Manchus, among whom six thousand six hundred families of Yakutes settled in 1687, when they emigrated from Siberia. The Korchin Mongols occupy the country south and west of this valley. Some of its streams produce large pearls. The region lying between the Sialkoi Mountains and the River Argun is rough and sterile, presenting few inducements to agriculturalists. Fish abound in all the rivers, and furs are sought in the hills. Pasturage is excellent in the bottoms. Fairs, between the natives and Cossacks, are constantly held at convenient places on the Argun and other rivers. The racial distinction between the Mongols and Manchus is here seen in the agricultural labors of the latter, so opposed to the nomadic habits of the former. This region has, within the last half century, attracted Chinese settlers from Shantung and Chihlí. These colonists are fast filling up the vacant lands along the rivers, dispossessing the Manchus by their thrift and industry, and making the country far more valuable. They will in this way secure its possession to the Peking Government, and bring it, by degrees, under Chinese control, greatly to the benefit of all. In early days the policy of the Manchus, like that of the E. I. Company in India towards British immigration, discountenanced the entrance of Chinese settlers, and in both cases to the disadvantage of the ruling power.

The administration of Manchuria consists of a supreme civil

government at Mukden, and three provincial military ones, though Shingking is under both civil and military. There are five Boards, each under a president, whose duties are analogous to those at Peking. The oversight of the city itself is under a *fuyin* or mayor, superior to the prefect. The three provinces are under as many marshals, whose subordinates rule the commanderies, and these last have garrison officers subject to them, whose rank and power correspond to the size and importance of their districts. These delegate part of their power to "assistant directors," or residents, who are stationed in every town; on the frontier posts, the officers have a higher grade, and report directly to the marshals or their lieutenants. All the officers, both civil and military, are Manchus, and a great portion of them belong to the imperial clan, or are intimately connected with it. By this arrangement, the Manchus are in a measure disconnected with the general government of the provinces, furnished with offices and titles, and induced to recommend themselves for promotion in the Empire by their zeal and fidelity in their distant posts.[1]

MONGOLIA is the first in order of the colonies, by which are meant those parts of the Empire under the control of the *Lí-fan Yuen*, or Foreign Office.[2] According to the statistics of the Empire, it comprises the region lying between lats. 35° and 52° N., and from long. 82° to 123° E.; bounded north by the Russian governments of Trans-Baikalia, Irkutsk, Yeniseisk, Tomsk, and Semipolatinsk; northeast and east by Manchuria; south by the provinces of Chihlí and Shansí, and the Yellow River; southwest by Kansuh; and west by Cobdo and Ílí. These limits are not very strictly marked at all points, but the length from east to west is about seventeen hundred miles, and one thousand in its greatest breadth, inclosing an area of

---

[1] Rev. Alex. Williamson, *Travels in Northern China*. London, 1870. Vol. II., Chaps. I. to XIV.; *Chinese Repository*, Vols. IV., p. 57; XV., p. 454; *Chinese Recorder*, Vol. VII., 1876, "The Rise and Progress of the Manjows," by J. Ross, pp. 155, 235, and 315.

[2] Compare Niebuhr's *History of Rome*, Vol. II., Sect. "Of the Colonies," where can be observed the essential differences between Roman settlements abroad and those of the Chinese; and still greater differences will be found in contrasting these with the offsets of Grecian States.

1,400,000 square miles, supporting an estimated population of two millions. This elevated plain is almost destitute of wood or water, inclosed southward by the mountains of Tibet, and northward by offsets from the Altai range. The central part is occupied by the desert of Gobi, a barren steppe having an average height of 4,000 feet above the sea level, and destitute of all running water. Owing to its elevation, extremely variable climate, and the absence of oases, it may be considered quite as terrible as Sahara, although the sand-waste here is, perhaps, hardly as unmitigated.

The climate of Mongolia is excessively cold for the latitude, arising partly from its elevation and dry atmosphere, and, on the steppes, to the want of shelter from the winds. But this has its compensation in an unclouded sky and the genial rays of the sun, which support and cheer the people to exertion when the thermometer is far below zero. The air has been drained of its moisture by the ridges on every side; day after day the sun's heat reaches the earth with smaller loss than obtains in moister regions in the same latitudes. Otherwise these wastes would support no life at all at such an elevation. In the districts bordering on Chihlí, the people make their houses partly under ground, in order to avoid the inclemency of the season. The soil in and upon the confines of this high land is unfit for agricultural purposes, neither snow nor rain falling in sufficient quantities, except on the acclivities of the mountain ranges; but millet, barley, and wheat might be raised north and south of it. The nomads rejoice in their freedom from tillage, however, and move about with their herds and possessions within the limits marked out by the Chinese for each tribe to occupy.

The space on the north of Gobi to the confines of Russia, about one hundred and fifty miles wide, is warmer than the desert, and supports a greater population than the southern sides. Cattle are numerous on the hilly tracts, but none are found in the desert, where wild animals and birds hold undisputed possession. The thermometer in winter sinks to thirty and forty degrees below zero (Fr.), and sudden and great changes are frequent. No month in the year is free from snow or frost; but on the steppes, the heat in summer is almost intolerable, owing to the radiation from the sandy or stony surface. The snow does not fall very deep, and even in cold weather the cattle find food under it; the flocks and herds are not, however, large.

The principal divisions of Mongolia are four, viz.: 1, Inner Mongolia, lying between the Wall and south of the desert; 2, Outer Mongolia, between the desert and the Altai Mountains, and reaching from the Inner Hing-an to the Tien shan; 3, the country about Koko-nor, between Kansuh, Sz'chuen, and Tibet; and, 4, the dependencies of Uliasutai, lying northwestward of the Kalkas khanates. The whole of this region has been included under the comprehensive name of Tartary, and if the limits of Inner and Outer Mongolia had been the bounds of Tartary, the appellation would have been somewhat appropriate. But when Genghis arose to power, he called his own tribe *Kukai Mongöl*, 'Celestial People,' and designated all the other tribes *Tatars*, that is 'tributaries.'[1] The three tribes of Kalkas, Tsakhars, and Sunnites, now constitute the great body of Mongols under Chinese rule.

INNER MONGOLIA, or *Nui Mungku*, is bounded north by Tsitsihar, the Tsetsen khanate, and Gobi, their frontiers being

[1] Abulgasi-Bayadur-chan (*Histoire Genéalogique des Tatars, traduite du Manuscript Tartare;* Leyde: 1726), gives another derivation for these two names. "Alänzä-chan eut deux fils jumeaux l'un appelle Tatar and l'autre Mogull ou pour bien dire Mung'l, entre les quels il partagea ses Estates lorsqu'il se vit sur la fin de sa vie." It is the first prince, he adds, from whom came the name *Tartar*—not from a river called Tata, as some have stated—while of the second: "Le terme Mung'l a esté changé par une corruption generale en Mogull; *Mung veut dire triste ou un homme triste*, et parceque ce prince estoit naturellement d'une humeur fort triste, il porta ce nom dans la verité"—(pp. 27–29). But Visdelon (D'Herbelot, ed. 1778, Tome IV., p. 327) shows more acquaintance with their history in producing proofs that the name *Tatar* was applied in the eighth century by the Chinese to certain tribes living north of the În shan, Ala shan, and River Liau. In the dissensions following upon the ruin of the Tang dynasty, some of them migrated eastwards beyond the Songari, and there in time rallied to subdue the northern provinces, under the name of *Nu-chih*. These are the ancestors of the Manchus. Another fraction went north to the marshy banks of Lakes Hurun and Puyur, where they received the name of *Moungul Tahtsz'*, *i.e.*, Marsh Tatars. This tribe and name it was that the warlike Genghis afterwards made conspicuous. The sound *Mogul* used in India is a dialectal variation.

almost undefinable; east by Kirin and Shingking; south by Chihlí and Shansí; and west by Kansuh. Wherever it runs the Wall is popularly regarded as the boundary between China and Mongolia. The country is divided into six *ming* or *chalkans*, like our corps, and twenty-four *aimaks* [1] (tribes), which are again placed under forty-nine standards or *khochoun*, each of which generally includes about two thousand families, commanded by hereditary princes, or dsassaks. The principal tribes are the Kortchin and Ortous. The large tribe of the Tsakhars, which occupies the region north of the Wall, is governed by a *tutung*, or general, residing at Kalgan, and their pasture grounds are now nominally included in the province of Chihlí. The province of Shansí in like manner includes the lands occupied by the Toumets, who are under the control of a general stationed at Suiyuen, beyond the Yellow River. In the pastures northwest from Kalgan, in the vicinity of Lakes Chazau and Ichí, and reaching more than a hundred miles from the Great Wall, lie the tracts appropriated to raising horses for the "Yellow Banner Corps." Excepting such grazing lands or the vast hunting grounds near Jeh-ho, reserved in like manner by the government, small settlements of Chinese are continually squatting over the plains of Inner Mongolia, from whence they have already succeeded in driving many of the aboriginal Mongol tribes off to the north. Those natives who will not retire are fain to save themselves from starvation or absorption by cultivating the soil after the fashion of their neighbors, the Chinese immigrants. It was, indeed, this influx of settlers which led Kanghí to erect the southern portion of Inner Mongolia into prefectures and districts like China Proper. This alteration of habits among its population seems destined, ere long, to modify the aspect of the country.

Most of the smaller tribes, except the Ortous, live between the western frontiers of Manchuria, and the steppes reaching north to the Sialkoi range, and south to Chahar. These tribes are peculiarly favored by the Manchus, from their having joined them in their conquest of China, and their leading men are

---

[1] *Abulgasi* (p. 83) furnishes a notice of these *aimaks* and their origin.

often promoted to high stations in the government of the country.

OUTER MONGOLIA, or *Wai Mungku*, is the wild tract lying north of the last as far as Russia. It is bounded north by Russia, east by Tsitsihar, southeast and south by Inner Mongolia, southwest by Barkul in Kansuh, west by Tarbagatai, and northwest by Cobdo and Uliasutai. The desert of Gobi occupies the southern half of the region. It is divided into four *lu*, or circuits, each of which is governed by a khan or prince, claiming direct descent from Genghis, and superintending the internal management of his own khanate. The Tsetsen khanate lies west of Hurun-pir in Tsitsihar, extending from Russia south to Inner Mongolia. West of it, reaching from Siberia across the desert to Inner Mongolia, lies the Tuchétu (or *Tusiétu* of Klaproth[1]) khanate, the most considerable of the four; the road from Kiakhta to Kalgan lies within its borders. West of the last, and bounded south by Gobi and northeast by Uliasutai, lies the region of the Kalkas of Sainnoin; and on its northwest lies the Dsassaktu khanate, south of Uliasutai, and reaching to Barkul and Cobdo on the south and west. All of them are politically under the control of two Manchu residents stationed at Urga, who direct the mutual interests of the Mongols, Chinese, and Russians.

Urga, or Kuren, the capital, is situated in the Tuchétu khanate, in lat. 48° 20′ N., and long. 107½° E., on the Tola River, a branch of the Selenga. It is the largest and most important place in Mongolia, and is divided into *Maimai chin*, the Chinese quarter, and *Bogdo-Kuren*, the Mongol settlement, nearly three miles from the other. Its total population is estimated at 30,000, the Chinese inhabitants of which are forbidden by law to live with their families; of the Mongols here, by far the larger part is composed of lamas. In the estimation of these people Urga stands next to H'lassa in degree of sanctity, being the seat of the third person in the Tibetan patriarchate. According to the Lama doctrine this dignitary—the *Kutuktu*—is the terrestrial impersonation of the Godhead and never dies, but passes,

---

[1] *Mémoires*, Tome I., p. 2.

after his apparent decease, into the body of some newly born boy, who is sought for afterwards according to the prophetic indications of the Dalai-lama in Tibet. This holy potentate, though of limited education and entirely under the control of the attendant lamas, exercises an unbounded influence over the Kalkas. It is, indeed, by means of him that the Chinese officials control the native races of Mongolia. His wealth, owing to contributions of enthusiastic devotees, is enormous; in and about Urga he owns 150,000 slaves, an abundance of worldly goods, and the most pretentious palace in Mongolia. Outside of its religious buildings, Urga is disgustingly dirty; the filth is thrown into the streets, and the habits of the people are loathsome. Decrepid beggars and starving dogs infest the ways; dead bodies, instead of being interred, are flung to birds and beasts of prey; huts and hovels afford shelter for both rich and poor.[1]

The four khanates constitute one *aimak* or tribe, subdivided into eighty-six standards, each of which is restricted to a certain territory, within which it wanders about at pleasure. There are altogether one hundred and thirty-five standards of the Mongols. The Kalkas chiefly live between the Altai Mountains and Gobi, but do not cultivate the soil to much effect. They are devoted to Buddhism, and the lamas hold most of the power in their hands through the *Kutuktu*. They render an annual tribute to the Emperor of horses, camels, sheep, and other animals or their skins, and receive presents in return of many times its value, so that they are kept in subjection by constant bribing; the least restiveness on their part is visited by a reduction of presents and other penalties. An energetic government, however, is not wanting in addition. The supreme tribunal is at Urga; it is the *yamun*, par excellence, and has both civil and military jurisdiction. The decisions are subject to the revision of the two Chinese residents, and sentences are usually carried into execution after their confirmation. The punishments are horribly severe; but only a decided

---

[1] Prejevalsky, *Mongolia*, Vol. I.; Pumpelly, *Across America*, pp. 382–385; Michie, *Across Siberia*.

and cruel hand over these wild tribes can keep them from constant strife.

Letters are encouraged among them by the Manchus, but with little success. Many Buddhist books have been translated into Mongolian by order of the Emperors; nor can we wonder at the indifference to literature when this stuff is the aliment provided them. Their tents, or *yurts*, are made of wooden laths fastened together so as to form a coarse lattice-work; the framework consists of several lengths secured with ropes, leaving a door about three feet square. The average size is twelve feet across and ten feet high; its shape is round and the conical roof admits light where it emits smoke. The poles or rafters are looped to the sides, and fastened to a hoop at the top. Upon this framework sheets of heavy felt are secured according to the season. A hearth in the centre holds the fire which heats the kettle hanging over it, and warms the inmates squatted round, who usually place only felt and sheepskins under them. The felt protects from cold, rain, snow, and heat in a wonderful manner. A first-class *yurt* is by no means an uncomfortable dwelling, with its furniture, lining, shrine, and hot kettle in the centre. A carpet for sleeping and sitting on is sometimes seen in *yurts* of the wealthier classes; in these, too, the walls are lined with cotton or silk, and the floors are of wood. The lodges of the rich Kalkas have several apartments, and are elegantly furnished, but destitute of cleanliness, comfort, or airiness. Most of their cloths, utensils, and arms are procured from the Chinese. The Sunnites are fewer than the Kalkas, and roam the wide wastes of Gobi. Both derive some revenue from conducting caravans across their country, but depend for their livelihood chiefly upon the produce of their herds and hunting. Their princes are obliged to reside in Urga, or keep hostages there, in order that the residents may direct and restrain their conduct; but their devotion to the *Kutuktu*, and the easy life they lead, are the strongest inducements to remain.

The trade with Russia formerly all passed through Kiakhta, a town near the frontier, and was carried on by special agents and officials appointed by each nation. The whole business was managed in the interest of the government, and its ramifications furnished employment, position, and support to so many persons as to form a bond of union and guaranty of peace between them and their subjects. Timkowski's journey with the decennial mission to Peking in 1820-21 furnishes one of the best accounts of this trade and intercourse now accessible, and with Klaproth's notes, given in the English translation published in 1827, has long been the chief reliable authority for the divisions and organization of the Mongol tribes. Since the opening of the Suez Canal, through which Russian steamers carry goods to and fro between Odessa and China, the largest portion of the Chinese produce no longer goes to Kiakhta. That which is required for Siberia is sent from Hankow by way of Shansí, or from Kalgan and Tientsin, under the direction of Russian merchants at those places. Furs, which once formed the richest part of this produce, are gradually diminishing in quality and quantity with the increase of settlers. In 1843 the export of black tea for Russian consumption was only eight millions of pounds, besides the brick tea taken by the Mongols. Cottrell states the total value of the trade, annually, at that period, at a hundred millions of rubles, reckoned then to be equal to $20,830,000, on which the Russians paid, in 1836, about $2,500,000 as import duty. The data respecting this trade of forty years ago are not very accurate, probably; the monopoly was upheld mostly for the benefit of the officials, as private traders found it too much burdened.

Kiakhta is a hamlet of no importance apart from the trade. The frontier here is marked by a row of granite columns; a stockade separates it from Maimai chin. Pumpelly says: "One can hardly imagine a sharper line than is here drawn. On the one side of the stockade wall, the houses, churches, and people are European, on the other, Chinese. With one step the traveller passes really from Asia and Asiatic customs and language, into a refined European society." The goods pay duty at the Russian *douane* in a suburb of fifty houses, near Kiakhta. The Chinese town is also a small place, numbering between twelve and fifteen hundred men (no women being allowed in the settlement) who lived in idleness most of the year. This curious hamlet has two principal streets crossing at right angles, and gates at the four ends, in the wooden wall which surrounds it. These streets are badly paved, while their narrowness barely allows the passage of two camels abreast. The one-storied houses are constructed of wood, roofed with turf or boards, and consist of two small rooms, one used as a shop and the other as a bedroom. The windows in the rear apartment are made of oiled paper or mica, but the door is the only opening in the shop. The dwellings are kept clean, the furniture is of a superior description, and considerable taste and show are seen in displaying the goods. The traders live luxuriously, and attract a great crowd there during the fair in February, when the goods are exchanged. They are under the control of a Manchu, called the *dzarguchi*, who is appointed for three years, and superintends the police of the settlement as well as the commercial proceedings. There are two Buddhist temples here served by lamas, and containing five colossal images sitting cross-legged, and numerous smaller idols.[1]

The western portion of Mongolia, between the meridians of 84° and 96° E., extending from near the western extremity of Kansuh province to the confines of Russia, comprising Uliasutai and its dependencies, Cobdo, and the Kalkas and Tourgouths of the Tangnu Mountains, is less known than any other part of it. The residence of the superintending officer of this province is at Uliasutai (*i.e.*, 'Poplar Grove'), a town lying northwest of the Selenga, in the khanate of Sainnoin, in a well cultivated and pleasant valley.

Cobdo, according to the Chinese maps, lies in the northwest of Mongolia; it is bounded north and west by the government Yeniseisk, northeast by Ulianghai, and southeast by the Dsassaktu khanate, south by Kansuh, and west by Tarbagatai. The part occupied by the Ulianghai or Uriyangkit tribes of the Tangnu Mountains lies northeast of Cobdo, and north of the Sainnoin and Dsassaktu khanates, and separated from Russia by the Altai. These tribes are allied to the Samoyeds, and the rule over them is

[1] Cottrell's *Recollections of Siberia*, Chap. IX., p. 314; Timkowski's *Travels*, Vol. I., pp. 4–91, 1821; Pumpelly, *Across America and Asia*, p. 387, 1871; Klaproth, *Mémoires*, Tome I., p. 63; Ritter, *Die Erdkunde von Asien*, Bd. II., pp. 198–226.

administered by twenty-five subordinate military officers, subject to the resident at Uliasutai. This city is said to contain about two thousand houses, is regularly built, and carries on some trade with Urga; it lies on the Iro, a tributary of the Jabkan. Cobdo comprises eleven tribes of Kalkas divided into thirty-one standards, whose princes obey an amban at Cobdo City, himself subordinate to the resident at Uliasutai. The Chinese rule over these tribes is conducted on the same principles as that over the other Mongols, and they all render fealty to the Emperor through the chief resident at Uliasutai, but how much obedience is really paid his orders is not known. The Kalkas submitted to the Emperor in 1688 to avoid extinction in their war with the Eleuths, by whom they had been defeated.

Cobdo contains several lakes, many of which receive rivers without having any outlet. The largest is Upsa-nor, which receives from the east the River Tes, and the Íkí-aral-nor into which the Jabkan runs. The River Irtysh falls into Lake Dzaisang. The existence of so many rivers indicates a more fertile country north of the Altai or Ektag Mountains, but no bounties of nature would avail to induce the inhabitants to adopt settled modes of living and cultivate the soil, if such a clannish state of society exists among them as is described by M. Lévchine to be the case among their neighbors, the Kirghís. The tribes in Cobdo resemble the American Indians in their habits, disputes, and modes of life, more than the eastern Kalkas, who approximate in their migratory character to the Arabs.

The province of Tsing hai, or KOKO-NOR (called Tsok-gumbam by the Tanguts), is not included in Mongolia by European geographers, nor in the Chinese statistical works is it comprised within its borders; the inhabitants are, however, mostly Mongols, both Buddhist and Moslem, and the government is conducted on the same plan as that over the Kalkas tribes further north. This region is known in the histories of Central Asia under the names of Tangout, Sifan, Turfan, etc. On Chinese maps it is politically called Tsing hai ('Azure Sea'), but in their books is named *Sí Yu* or *Sí Yih*, 'Western Limits.' The borders are now limited on the north by Kansuh, southeast by Sz'chuen, south by Anterior Tibet, and west by the desert, comprising about four degrees of latitude and eleven of longitude.

It includes within its limits several large lakes, which receive rivers into their bosoms, and many of them having no outlets. The Azure Sea is the largest, lying at an altitude of 10,500 feet and overlooked by high mountains, which in winter are covered with snow, and in summer form an emerald frame that deepens the blueness of the water. It is over 200 miles in circuit, and its evaporation is replaced by the inflowing waters of eight large streams; one small islet contains a monastery, whose inmates are freed from their solitude only when the ice makes a bridge, as no boat is known to have floated on its salt water. The wide, moist plains on the east and west furnish pasturage for domestic and wild animals, and constant collisions occur between the tribes resorting there for food. The travels of Abbé Huc and Col. Prejevalsky furnish nearly all that is known concerning the productions and inhabitants of Koko-nor. The country is nominally divided into thirty-four banners, and its Chinese rulers reside at Síning, east of the lake; but they have more to do in defending themselves than in protecting their subjects. The whole country is occupied by the Tanguts of Tibetan origin, who are brigands by profession, and roam over the mountains around the headwaters of the Yangtsz' and Yellow Rivers; by the Mohammedan Dunganis, who have latterly been nearly destroyed in their recent rebellion; and by tribes of Mongols under the various names of Eleuths, Kolos, Kalkas, Surgouths, and Koits. The Chinese maps are filled with names of various tribes, but their statistical accounts are as meagre of information as the maps are deficient in accurate and satisfactory delineations.

The topographical features of this region are still imperfectly known, and its inhospitable climate is rendered more dangerous by man's barbarity. High mountain masses alternate with narrow valleys and a few large depressions containing lakes; the country lying south of the Azure Sea, as far as Burmah, is exceedingly mountainous. West and southwest of the lake extends the plain of Tsaidam, which at a recent geological age has been the bed of a huge lake; it is now covered with morasses, shaking bogs, small rivers, and sheets of water—the most considerable of the latter being Lake Kara, in the extreme western portion. The saline argillaceous soil of this region is not adapted to vegetation. Large animals are scarce, due in part to the plague of insects which compels even the natives to retreat to the mountains with their herds during certain seasons. Its inhabitants are the same as those of Eastern Koko-nor; they are divided into five banners, and number about 1,000 *yurts*, or 5,000 souls.

The Burkhan-buddha range forms the southern boundary of this plain, and the northernmost limit of the lofty plateau of Tibet. Its length from east to west is not far from 130 miles, its eastern extremity being near the Yegrai-ula (the near sources of the Yellow River) and Toso-nor. The range has no lofty peaks, and stretches in an unbroken chain at a height of 15,000 to 16,000 feet; it is terribly barren, but does not attain the line of perpetual snow. The southern range, which separates the headwaters of the Yellow and Yangtsz' Rivers, is called the Bayan-kara Mountains; that northwest of this is called on Chinese maps, Kílien shan and Nan shan, and bounds the desert on the south. On the northern declivities of the Nan shan range are several towns lying on or near the road leading across Central Asia, which leaves the valley of the Yellow River at Lanchau, in Kansuh, and runs N.N.W. over a rough country to Liangchau, a town of some importance situated in a fertile and populous district. From this place it goes northwest to Kanchau, noted for its manufactures of felted cloths which are in demand among the Mongol tribes of Koko-nor, and where large quantities of rhubarb, horses, sheep, and other commodities are procured. Going still northwest, the traveller reaches Suhchau, the last large place before passing the Great Wall, which renders it a mart for provisions and all articles brought from the west in exchange for the manufactures of China. This city was the last stronghold of the Dungani Moslems, and when they were destroyed in 1873 it began to revive out of its ruins. About fifty miles from this town is the pass of Kiayü, beyond which the road to Hami, Urumtsi, and Ílí leads directly across the desert, here about three hundred miles wide. This route has been for ages the line of internal communication between the west of China and the regions lying around and in the basins of the Tarim River and the Caspian.[1] A better idea of the security of traffic and caravans within the Empire, and consequently of the goodness of the Chinese rule, is obtained by comparing the usually safe travel on this route with the hazards, robberies, and poverty formerly met with on the great roads in Bokhara, and the regions south and west of the Belur tag.

The productions of Koko-nor consist of grain and other vegetables raised along the bottoms of the rivers and margins of the lakes; sheep, cattle, horses, camels, and other animals. Alpine hares, wild asses,[2] wild yaks, vultures, lammergeiers, pheasants, antelopes, wolves, mountain sheep, and wild camels are among the denizens of the wilds. The Chinese have settled among the tribes, and Mohammedans of Turkish origin are found in the large towns. There are eight corps between Koko-nor and Uliasutai, comprising all the tribes and banners, and over which are placed as many supreme generals or commanders appointed from Peking. The leading tribes in Koko-nor are Eleuths, Tanguts, and Tourbeths, the former of whom are the remnants of one of the most powerful tribes in Central Asia. Tangout submitted to the Emperor in 1690, and its population since the incorporation has greatly increased. They inhabit the hilly region of Kansuh, Koko-nor, Eastern Tsaidam, and the basin of the Upper Yellow River. They resemble gipsies, being above the average in height, with thick-set features, broad shoulders, hair and whiskers, black, dark eyes, nose straight, lips thick and protruding, face long and never flat, skin tawny. Unlike the Mongols and Chinese they have a strong growth of beard and whiskers which, however, they always shave. They wear no tail, but shave their heads; their dress consists of furs and cloths made into long coats that reach to the knees. Shirts or trowsers are not made use of; their upper legs are generally left bare. Women dress like the men. Their habitations are wooden huts or black cloth tents. The Tangut is cunning,

---

[1] Compare Richthofen, *China*, Band I., 2er Theil.; Yule, *Cathay and the Way Thither*, passim.

[2] The wild ass is called by Prejevalsky the most remarkable animal of these steppes. Compare Yule's *Marco Polo*, Vol. I., p. 220 (2d edition).

stingy, lazy, and shiftless. His sole occupation that of tending cattle (yaks). He is even more zealous a Buddhist than are the Mongols, and extremely superstitious.[1] The trade at Síning is large, but not equal to that between Yunnan and Burmah at Talí and Bhamo; dates, rhubarb, chowries, precious stones, felts, cloths, etc., are among the commodities seen in the bazaar. It lies about a hundred miles from the sea, at an elevation of 7,800 feet, and near it is the famous lamasary of Kumbum, where MM. Huc and Gabet lived in 1845. The town is well situated upon the Síning ho, and though constructed for the most part of wood, presents a fine appearance owing to the number of official buildings therein. The population numbers some 60,000 souls.[2]

The towns lying between the Great Wall and Ílí, though politically belonging to Kansuh, are more connected with the colonies in their form of government than with the Eighteen Provinces. The first town beyond the Kiayü Pass is Yuhmun, distant about ninety miles, and is the residence of officers, who attend to the caravans going to and from the pass. It is represented as lying near the junction of two streams, which flow northerly into the Purunkí. The other district town of Tunhwang lies across a mountainous country, upwards of two hundred miles distant. The city of Ngansí chau has been built to facilitate the communication across the desert to Hami or Kamil, the first town in Songaria, and the dépôt of troops, arms, and munitions of war. "With the town of Hami," says an Austrian visitor in these regions, "the traveller comes upon the southern foot-hills of the Tien shan, and the first traces of Siberian civilization. Magnificent mountain scenery accompanies him on his way toward the west to the Russian line. In the government of Semipolatinsk are the ex-

---

[1] For a notice of the *Ouigours*, who formerly ruled Tangout, consult Klaproth, *Mémoires*, Tome II., p. 301, ff. See also Rémusat, *Nouveaux Mélanges Asiatiques*, Tome II., p. 61, for a notice of the *Ta-ta-tung'o*, who applied their letters to write Mongolian.

[2] *Chinese Repository*, Vol. IX., p. 113; Vol. I., p. 118. *Penny Cyclopædia*, Arts. BAYAN KARA, TANGUT. Kreitner, *Im fernen Osten*, p. 702. Huc, *Travels*, passim.

press mail-wagons which stand ready at his order to carry him at furious speed to the town of the same name, then to the right bank of the River Irtysh, and so to Omsk."[1] This route and that stretching towards the southwest bring an important trade to Hami; the country around it is cultivated by poor Mongols.[2] Barkul, or Chinsí fu, in lat. 43° 40′ N., and long. 93° 30′ E., is the most important place in the department; the district is called Îho hien. A thousand Manchus, and three thousand Chinese, guard the post. The town is situated on the south of Lake Barkul, and its vicinity receives some cultivation. Hami and Turfan each form a *ting* district in the southeast and west of the department. The trade at all these places consists mostly of articles of food and clothing.

Urumtsi, or Tih-hwa chau (the *Bich-balik* of the Ouigours in 1100[3]), in lat. 43° 45′ N., and long. 89° E., is the westernmost department of Kansuh, divided into three districts, and containing many posts and settlements. In the war with the Eleuths in 1770, the inhabitants around this place were exterminated, and the country afterwards repeopled by upwards of ten thousand troops, with their families, and by exiles; emigrants from Kansuh were also induced to settle there. The Chinese accounts speak of a high mountain near the city, always covered with ice and snow, whose base is wooded, and abounding with pheasants; coal is also obtained in this region. The cold is great, and snow falls as late as July. Many parts produce grain and vegetables. All this department formerly constituted a portion of Songaria. The policy of the Chinese government is to induce the tribes to settle, by placing large bodies of troops with their families at all important points, and sending their exiled criminals to till the soil; the Mongols then find an increasing demand for their cattle and other products, and are induced to become stationary to meet it. So far as is known, this policy had succeeded well in the regions beyond the Wall, and those around Koko-nor; but the rebellion of the Dunganis,

---

[1] Lieut. Kreitner, *Im fernen Osten.*

[2] In Rémusat's *Histoire de la Ville de Khotan* (p. 76) there is an account of a journey made in the 10th century between Kanchan and Khoten.

[3] Rémusat calls it *Pentalope.* *Nouveaux Mélanges,* Tome I., p. 5.

who arose in these outlying regions at the moment when the energies of the Peking government were all directed to suppressing the Tai-ping insurrection, destroyed these improvements, and frustrated, for an indefinite period, the promising development of civilization among the inhabitants.

That part of the Empire called ÍLÍ is a vast region lying on each side of the Tien shan, and including a tract nearly as large as Mongolia, and not much more susceptible of cultivation. Its limits may be stated as extending from lat. 36° to 49° N., and from long. 71° to 96° E., and its entire area, although difficult to estimate from its irregularity, can hardly be less than 900,000 square miles, of which Songaria occupies rather more than one-third. It is divided into two *Lu*, or 'Circuits,' viz., the Tien shan Peh Lu, and Tien shan Nan Lu, or the circuits north and south of the Celestial Mountains. The former is commonly designated Songaria, or Dzungaria, from the Songares or Eleuths, who ruled it till a few scores of years past, and the latter used to be known as Little Bokhara, or Eastern Turkestan.

Ílí is bounded north by the Altai range, separating it from the Kirghís; northeast by the Irtysh River and Outer Mongolia; east and southeast by Urumtsi and Barkul in Kansuh; south by the desert and the Kwănlun range; and west by the Belur-tag, dividing it from Badakshan and Russian territory.[1]

---

[1] The recent treaty between Russia and China (ratified in 1881), marks the boundaries between Ílí and Russian territory in the following sections:

Art. VII. A tract of country in the west of Ílí is ceded to Russia, where those who go over to Russia and are thereby dispossessed of their land in Ílí may settle. The boundary line of Chinese Ílí and Russian territory will stretch from the Pieh-chên-tao [Bedschin-tau] Mountains along the course of the Ho-êrh-kwo-ssŭ [Yehorsos] River, to its junction with the Ílí River, thence across the Ílí River, and south to the east of the village of Kwo-li-cha-tê [Kaldschat] on the Wu-tsung-tau range, and from this point south along the old boundary line fixed by the agreement of Ta-Chêng [Tashkend] in the year 1864.

Art. VIII. The boundary line to the east of the Chi-sang lake, fixed in the year 1864 by the agreement of Ta-Chêng [Tashkend], having proved unsatisfactory, high officers will be specially deputed by both countries jointly to examine and alter it so that a satisfactory result may be attained. That there may be no doubt what part of the Khassak country belongs to China and what to Russia, the boundary will consist of a straight line drawn from the Kwei Tung Mountains across the Hei-i-êrh-te-shih River to the Sa-wu-êrh range, and

In length, the Northern Circuit extends about nine hundred miles, and the width, on an average, is three hundred miles. The Southern Circuit reaches nearly twelve hundred and fifty miles from west to east, and varies from three hundred to five hundred in breadth, as it extends to the Kwănlun range on the south. There is probably most arable land in the Northern Circuit.

Ílí, taken north of the Tarim basin, may be regarded as an inland isthmus, extending southwest from the south of Siberia, off between the Gobi and Caspian deserts, till it reaches the Hindu Kush, leading down to the valley of the Indus. The former of these deserts incloses it on the east and south, the other on the west and northwest, separated from each other by the Belur and Muz-tag ranges, which join with the Tien shan, that divide the isthmus itself into two parts. These deserts united are equal in extent to that of Sahara, but are not as arid and tenantless.

This region has some peculiar features, among which its great elevation, its isolation in respect to its water-courses, and the character of its vegetation, are the most remarkable. Songaria is especially noticeable for the many closed river-basins which occur between the Altai and Tien shan, among the various minor ranges of hills, each of which is entirely isolated, and containing a lake, the receptacle of its drainage. The largest of these singular basins is that of the River Ílí, which runs about three hundred miles westward, from its rise in the Tien shan (lat. 85°) till it falls into Lake Balkash, which also receives some other streams; the superficies of the whole basin is about forty thousand square miles. The other lakes lie northeastward of Balkash; the largest of them are the Dzaisang, which receives the Irtysh, the Kisilbash, into which the Urungu

---

the high officers deputed to settle the boundary will fix the new boundary along such straight line which is within the old boundary.

Art. IX. As to the boundary on the west, between the Province of Fei-ěrh-kan [Ferghana], which is subject to Russia, and Chinese Kashgar, officials will be deputed by both countries to examine it, and they will fix the boundary line between the territories at present actually under the jurisdiction of either country, and they will erect boundary stones thereon.

flows, and four or five smaller ones between them, lying north of the city of Ílí. Lake Temurtu, or Issik-kul, lies now just beyond the southwestern part of this Circuit, and was until recently contained therein. This sheet of water is deep and never freezes; it is brackish, but full of fish; the dimensions are about one hundred miles long, and thirty-five wide; its superabundant waters flow off through the Chu ho into the Kirghís steppe.

The Ala-tau range defines the lake on the north shore. Says a Russian traveller in describing this region, "It would be difficult to imagine anything more splendid than the view of the Tien shan from this spot. The dark blue surface of the Issik-kul, like sapphire, may well bear comparison with the equally blue surface of Geneva Lake, but its expanse—five times as great—seeming almost unlimited, and the matchless splendor of its background, gives it a grandeur which the Swiss lake does not possess. The unbroken, snowy chain here stretches away for at least 200 miles of the length of the Issik-kul; the sharp outlines of the spurs and dark valleys in the front range are softened by a thin mist, which hangs over the water and heightens the clear, sharp outlines of the white heads of the Tien shan giants, as they rise and glisten on the azure canopy of a central Asian sky. The line of perpetual snow commences at three-fifths of their slope up, but as one looks, their snowless base seems to sink the deeper in the far east, till the waves of the lake seem to wash the snowy crests of Khan-Tengsè." Forty small rivers flow into it, but its size is gradually lessening.[1]

Little is known concerning the topography, the productions, or the civilization of the tribes who inhabit a large part of Songaria, but the efforts of the Chinese government have been systematically directed to developing its agricultural resources, by stationing bodies of troops, who cultivate the soil, there, and by banishing criminals thither, who are obliged to work for and assist the troops. It gives one a higher idea of the rulers of China, themselves wandering nomads originally, when they are seen carrying on such a plan for extending the capabilities of

---

[1] Compare also Schuyler, *Turkistan*, Vol. II., pp. 127 *ff*

these remote parts of their Empire, and teaching, partly by force, partly by bribes, and partly by example, the Mongol tribes under them the advantages of a settled life.

The productions of Songaria are numerous. Wheat, barley, rice and millet, are the chief corn stuffs; tobacco, cotton, melons, and some fruits, are grown; herds of horses, camels, cattle, and sheep, afford means of locomotion and food to the people, while the mountains and lakes supply game and fish. The inhabitants are composed mostly of Eleuths, with a tribe of Tourgouths, and remnants of the Songares, together with Mongols, Manchus, and Chinese troops, settlers and criminals.

TIEN-SHAN PEH LU is divided by the Chinese into three commanderies, *Ílí* on the west, *Tarbagatai* on the north, and *Kurkara usu* on the east, between Ílí and the west end of Kansuh. The government of the North and South Circuits is under the control of Manchu military officers residing at Ílí. This city, called by the Chinese Hwuiyuen ching, and Gouldja (or Kuldja) and Kuren by the natives, lies on the north bank of the Ílí River, in lat. 43° 55′ N., and long. 81½° E.; it contains about fifty thousand inhabitants, and carries on considerable trade with China through the towns in Kansuh. The city was defended by six strong fortresses in its neighborhood, and the solidity of the stone walls enabled it to resist a vigorous assault in the Dungani rebellion. Its circuit is nearly four miles, and two wide avenues cross its centre, dividing it into four equal parts, through each of which run many lanes. Its houses indicate the Turkish origin of its builders in their clay or adobe walls and flat roofs, and this impression is increased by the Jumma mosque of the Taranchis, and the Dungan mosque, outside of the walls. The last has a wonderful minaret built of small-roofed pavilions one over another; both of them affect the Chinese architecture in their roofs, and their walls are faced with diamond-shaped tiles. The Buddhist temple has hardly been rebuilt since the city has returned to Chinese rule. The supply of meats and vegetables is constant, and the variety and quality exceed that of most other towns in the region. The population is gradually increasing with the return of peace and trade, but is still under twenty thousand, of which not one-fifth are Chinese and Manchus: the Taranchis constitute half of the whole, and Dunganis are the next in number. The province is the richest and best cultivated of all this region of Ílí; its coal, metals, and fruits are sources of prosperity, and with its return to Chinese sway under new relations in respect to Russian trade, its future is promising.

The destruction of life was dreadful at the capture of Kuldja and other towns, which were then left a heap of ruins.[1] Schuyler estimates that not more than a hundred thousand people remained in the province, out of a third of a million in 1860. It is stated in Chinese works that when Amursana, the discontented chief of the Songares, applied, in 1775, to Kienlung for assistance against his rival Tawats or Davatsi, and was sent back with a Chinese army, in the engagements which ensued, more than a million of people were destroyed, and the whole country depopulated. At that time, Kuldja was built by Kienlung, and soon became a place of note. Outside of the town are the barracks for the troops, which consist of Eleuths and Mohammedans, as well as Manchus and Chinese. Coal is found in this region, and most of the inland rivers produce abundance of fish, while wild animals and birds are numerous. The resources of the country are, however, insufficient to meet the expenses of the military establishment, and the presents made to the begs, and the deficit is supplied from China.[2]

---

[1] 175,000 perished in Kuldja alone.

[2] The question of the existence of volcanoes in Central Asia, especially on the Kuldja frontier, has always been a matter of doubt and discussion among geologists and Russian explorers. The Governor of Semiretchinsk, General Kolpakofsky, was, in 1881, able to report the discovery of the perpetual fires in the Tien shan range of mountains. The mountain Bai shan was found twelve miles northeast of Kuldja, in a basin surrounded by the massive Ailak mountains; its fires are not volcanic, but proceed from burning coal. On the sides of the mountain there are caves emitting smoke and sulphurous gas. Mr. Schuyler, in his *Turkistan*, mentions that these perpetual fires in the mountains, referred to by Chinese historians, were considered by Severtzoff, a Russian, who explored the region, as being caused by the ignition of the seams of coal, or the carburetted hydrogen gas in the seams. The same author further mentions that Captain Tosnofskey, another Russian explorer, was told of a place in the neighborhood from which steam constantly rose, and that near this crevice there had existed, from ancient times, three pits, where persons afflicted with rheumatism or skin diseases were in the habit of bathing.

Subordinate to the control of the commandant at Kuldja are nine garrisoned places situated in the same valley, at each of which are bodies of Chinese convicts. The two remaining districts of Tarbagatai and Kur-kara usu are small compared with Ílí; the first lies between Cobdo and the Kirghís steppe, and is inhabited mostly by emigrants from the steppes of the latter, who render merely a nominal subjection to the garrisons placed over them, but are easily governed through their tribal rulers. The Tourgouths, who emigrated from Russia in 1772, into China, are located in this district and Cobdo, as well as in the valleys of the Tekes and Kunges rivers. They have become more or less assimilated with other tribes since they were placed here. In the war with the Songares, many of the people fled from the valley of Ílí to this region, and after that country was settled, they submitted to the Emperor, and partly returned to Ílí. The chief town, called Tuguchuk by the Kirghís, and Suitsing ching by the Chinese, is situated not far from the southern base of the Tarbagatai Mountains, and contains about six hundred houses, half of which belong to the garrison. It is one of the nine fortified towns under the control of the commandant at Kuldja, and a place of some trade with the Kirghís. There are two residents stationed here, with high powers to oversee the trade across the frontier, but their duties are inferior in importance to those of the officials at Urga. 2,500 Manchu and Chinese troops remain at this post, and since the conquest of the country in 1772 by Kienlung, its agricultural products have gradually increased under the industry of the Chinese. The tribes dwelling in this distant province are restricted within certain limits, and their obedience secured by presents. The climate of Tarbagatai is changeable, and the cold weather comprises more than half the year. The basin of Lake Ala-kul, or Alaktu-kul, occupies the southwest, and part of the Irtysh and Lake Dzaisang the northeast, so that it is well watered. The trade consists chiefly of domestic animals and cloths.

The town of Kur-kara usu lies on the River Kur, northeast from Kuldja and on the road between it and Urumtsi; it is called Kingsui ching by the Chinese. The number of troops stationed at all these posts is estimated at sixty thousand, and the total population of Songaria under two millions.

The Tien-shan Nan Lu, or Southern Circuit of Îlí, the territory of 'the eight Mohammedan cities,' was named *Sin Kiang* ('New Frontier') by Kienlung. It is less fertile than the Northern Circuit, the greatest part of its area consisting of rugged mountains or barren wastes, barely affording subsistence for herds of cattle and goats. The principal boundaries are the Kwănlun Mountains, and the desert, separating it from Tibet on the south; Cashmere lies on the southwest, and Badakshan and Kokand are separated from it on the west and northwest by the Belur-tag, all of them defined and partitioned by the mountain ranges over which the passes 12,000 to 16,000 feet high furnish both defence and travel according to the season.

The greater part of this Circuit is occupied with the basin of the Tarim or Ergu, which flows from the Belur range in four principal branches[1] (called from the towns lying upon their banks the Yarkand, Kashgar, Aksu, and Khoten Rivers), and running eastward, receives several affluents from the north and south, and falls into Lake Lob in long. 89° E., after a course, including windings, of between 1,100 and 1,300 miles. Of the river system from which this stream flows Baron Richthofen says, "the region which gives birth to this river is on a scale of grandeur such as no other river in the world can boast. It is girt round by a wide semicircular collar of mountains of the loftiest and grandest character, often rising in ridges of 18,000 to 20,000 feet in height, while the peaks shoot up to 25,000 and even 28,000 feet. The basin which fills in the horse-shoe shaped space encompassed by these gigantic elevations, though deeply depressed below them, stands at a height above the sea varying from 6,000 feet at the margin to about 2,000 in the middle, and formed the bed of an ancient sea. From its wall-like sides on the south, west, and north, the waters rush headlong down, and though the winds blowing from all directions deposit most of their moisture on the remoter sides of the surrounding

[1] Wood, *Journey to the Source of the River Oxus*, p. 356. From the hills that encircle Lake Sir-i-kol rise some of the principal rivers in Asia: the Yarkand, Kashgar, Sirr, Kuner, and Oxus.

ranges, viz., the southern foot of the Himalayas, the west side of the Pamir, and the northern slope of the Tien shan, the streams formed thereby winding through the cloud-capped lofty cradle-land, and breaking through the mountain chains, reach the old ocean bed only partly well watered. The smallest of them disappear in the sand, others flow some distance before expanding into a level salt basin and are there absorbed. Only the largest, whose number the Chinese estimate at sixty, unite with the Tarim, a river 1,150 miles long, and therefore in length between the Rhine and Danube, but far surpassing both in the massiveness of surrounding mountains, just as it exceeds the Danube in the extent of its basin. Its tributaries form along the foot of the mountains a number of fruitful oases, and these by means of artificial irrigation have been converted into flourishing, cultivated states, and have played an important part in the history of these regions."[1] Col. Prejevalsky's explorations in this totally unknown country have brought out a multitude of facts pregnant with interest both for historical and geographical study. Among the most important results of his discoveries is the location of Lob more than a degree to the south of its position on Chinese maps, and a consequent bend of the Tarim from its due eastern course before it reaches its outlet. This lake, consisting of two sheets of water, the Kara-buran and Kara-kurchin (or Chon-kul), lies on the edge of the desert, in an uninhabited region, and surrounded by great swamps, which extend also northwest along the Tarim to its junction with the Kaidu. It is shallow, overgrown with weeds, and is for the most part a morass, the water being fresh, despite the salt marshes in the vicinity. The people living near it speak a language most like that of Khoten; they are Moslems. Lake Lob is elliptical, 90 to 100 versts long and 20 wide, 2,200 feet above the sea. Enormous flocks of birds come from Khoten on the southwest, as they go north, and make Lob-nor their stopping-place. The desert in this region is poor and desolate in the extreme. Its southern side is formed by the Altyn-tag range, a spur of the Kwănlun Mountains that rises about 14,000 feet in a sheer

[1] *Richthofen's Remarks* in Prejevalsky's *Lob-nor*, p. 138. London, 1879.

wall. Wild camels are found in its ravines, whose sight, hearing, and smell are marvellously acute. No other river basins of any size are found within the Circuit, except a large tributary called the Kaidu, which, draining a parallel valley north of Lob-nor, two hundred miles long, runs into a lake nearly as large, called Bostang-nor, from which an outlet on the south continues it into the Tarim, about eighty miles from its mouth. The tributaries of this river are represented as much more serviceable for agricultural purposes than the main trunk is for navigation. The plain through which the Tarim flows is about two hundred miles broad and not far from nine hundred miles long, most of it unfit for cultivation or pasturage. The desert extends considerably west of the two lakes. The climate of this region is exceedingly dry, and its barrenness is owing, apparently, more to the want of moisture than to the nature of the soil. The western parts are colder than those toward Kansuh, the river being passable on ice at Yarkand, in lat. 38°, for three months, while frost is hardly known at Hami, in lat. 43°.

The productions of the valley of the Tarim comprise most of the grains and fruits found in Southern Europe; the sesamum is cultivated for oil instead of the olive. Few trees or shrubs cover the mountain acclivities or plains. All the domestic animals abound, except the hog, which is reared in small numbers by the Chinese. The camel and yak are hunted and raised for food and service, their coats affording both skins and hair for garments. The horse, camel, black cattle, ass, and sheep, are found wild on the edge of the desert, where they find a precarious subsistence. The mountains and marshes contain jackals, tigers, bears, wolves, lynxes, and deer, together with some large species of birds of prey. Gold, copper, and iron are brought from this region, but the amount is not large, and as articles of trade they are less important than the sal-ammoniac, saltpetre, sulphur, and asbestos obtained from the volcanic region in the east of the Celestial Mountains. The best specimens of the *yuh* or nephrite, so highly prized by the Chinese, are obtained in the Southern Circuit.

The present divisions of this Circuit are regulated by the

position of the eight Mohammedan cities. The western depart ments of Kansuh naturally belong to the same region, and the cities now pertaining to that province are inhabited by entirely similar races, and governed in the same feudal manner, with some advantages in consideration of their early submission to Kienlung. The first town on the road, of note, is Hami; Turfan and Pidshan are less important as trading posts than as garrisons. The eight cities are named in the *Statistics of the Empire* in the following order, beginning at the east: Harashar, Kuché, Ushí (including Sairim and Bai), Aksu, Khoten, Yarkand, Kashgar, and Yingkeshar or Yangi Hissar. The superior officers live at Yarkand, but the Southern Circuit is divided into four minor governments at Harashar, Ushí, Yarkand, and Khoten, each of whose residents reports both to Kuldja and Peking. There is constant restiveness on the part of the subject races, who are all Moslems, arising from their clannish habits and feuds; they have not the elements of substantial progress and national growth, either under their own rulers or Chinese. They have lately thrown off the Peking Government, but they have generally regretted the rapines and waste caused by the strifes and change, and would probably receive the *Kitai* (so they term the Chinese) back again. The latter are not hard masters, and bring trade and wealth the longer they remain. One of the Usbek chiefs under Yakub khan gave the pith of the situation between the two, when he replied to Dr. Bellew's remark that he talked like a Chinese himself, "No, I hate them. But they were not bad rulers. We had everything then; we have nothing now. We never see any signs of the Kitai trade, nor of the wealth they brought here."

Harashar (or Karashar) lies on the Kaidu River, not far from Lake Bagarash or Bostang, about two hundred and ninety miles west of Turfan, in lat. 42° 15′ N., and long. 87° E. It is a large district, and has two towns of some note within the jurisdiction of its officers—namely, Korla and Bukur. Harashar is fortified, and from its being a secure position, and the seat of the chief resident, attracts considerable trade. The embroidery is superior; but the tribes living in the district are more addicted to hunting than disposed to sedentary trades. Korla lies southwest of Harashar on the Kaidu, between lakes Bostang and Lob, and the productions of the town and its vicinity indicate a fertile soil; the Chinese say the Mohammedans who live here are fond of singing, but have no ideas of ceremony or urbanity. Bukur lies two hundred miles west of Korla and "might be a rich and delicious country," says the Chinese account, "but those idle, vagrant Mohammedans only use their strength in theft and plunder; the women blush at nothing." The town formerly contained upward of ten thousand inhabitants, but Kienlung nearly destroyed it; the district has been since resettled by Hoshoits, Tourbeths, and Turks, and the people carry on some trade in the produce of their herds, skins, copper, and agates.

Kuché, about eighty miles west from Bukur, lat. 41° 37′ N., and long. 83° 20′ E., is a larger and more important city than that of Harashar, for the road which crosses the Tien shan by the pass Muz-daban to Îlí, here joins that coming from Aksu on the west and Hami on the east. It is three miles in circuit, and is defended by ten forts and three hundred troops. The bazaars contain grain, fruits, and vegetables, raised in the vicinity by great labor, for the land requires to be irrigated by hand from wells, pools, and streams. Copper, sulphur, and saltpetre are carried across to Îlí, for use of government as well as traffic, being partly levied from the inhabitants as taxes; linen is manufactured in the town, and sal ammoniac, cinnabar, and quicksilver are procured from the mountains. Kuché is considered the gate of Turkestan, and is the chief town, politically speaking, between Hami and Yarkand. The district and town of Shayar lie south of Kuché, in a marshy valley producing abundance of rice, melons, and fruit; the pears are particularly good. Two small lakes, Baba-kul and Sary-kamysch, lie to the east of this town, and are the only bodies of water between Bostang-nor and Issik-kul. The population is about four thousand, ruled by *begs* subordinate to the general at Kuché.

The valley of the Aksu contains two large towns, Aksu and Ushí or Ush-turfan, besides several posts and villages. Between the former and Kuché, lie the small garrisons and districts of Bai and Sairim. The first contains from four to five hundred families, ruled by their own chiefs. Sairim or Hanlemuh is subordinate to Ushí in some degree, but its productions, climate, and inhabitants are like those of Kuché. "Their manners are simple," remarks a Chinese writer, speaking of the people; "they are neither cowards nor rogues like the other Mohammedans; they are fond of singing, drinking, and dancing, like those of Kuché." Aksu is a large commercial and manufacturing town, containing twenty thousand inhabitants, situated, like Kuché, at the termination of a road leading across the Tien shan to Īlí, and attracting to its market traders from Siberia, Bokhara, and Kokand, as well as along the great road. Its manufactures of cotton, silk, leather, harnesses, crockery, precious stones, and metals are good, and sent abroad in great numbers. The country produces grain, fruits, vegetables, and cattle in perfection, and the people are more civilized than those on the east and north; "they are generous and noble, and both sing and ridicule the oddities and niggardliness of the other Mohammedans." The Chinese garrison consists of three thousand soldiers, and the officers are accountable to those at Ushí.

Ushí lies about 70 miles due west of Aksu, in lat. 41° 15′ N. and long. 79° 40′ E., and is stated to contain ten thousand inhabitants. The Chinese name is Yung-ning ching (*i.e.* 'City of Eternal Tranquillity'). The officers stationed here report to the commandant at Īlí, but they communicate directly with Peking, and receive the Emperor's sanction to their choice of begs, and to the envoys forwarded to the capital with tribute. Copper money is cast here in ingots, somewhat like the ingots of sycee in the provinces. There are six forts attached to Ushí, to keep in order the wandering tribes of the Kirghís, called Pruth Kirghís,[1] which roam over the frontier regions between Ushí and Yarkand. They pay homage to the officers at Ushí, but give no tribute. Those who do pay tribute are taxed a tenth, but the Kirghís on this frontier are usually allowed to roam where they like, provided they keep the peace. This region was nearly depopulated by Kienlung's generals, and at present sup-

[1] Called also *Pourouts.* Compare Klaproth (*Mémoires*, Tome III., p. 332), who has a notice of these tribes.

ports a sparse population compared with its fertility and resources.

The government of Kashgar, known, at the time of the Arab conquest, as *Kichik Bukhara*, presents a vast, undulating plain, of which the slope is very gradual toward the east, and of which the general elevation may be reckoned at from three to four thousand feet above the sea. The aspect of its surface is mostly one of unmitigated waste—a vast spread of bare sand and gloomy salts, traversed in all directions by dunes and banks of gravel, with the scantiest vegetation, and all but absence of animal life. Such is the view that meets the eye and joins the horizon everywhere on the plain immediately beyond the river courses and the settlements planted on their banks.[1] The population of this whole district is considerably less than a million and a half. The natural mineral productions here are of great value, and it is a knowledge of this fact which has induced the Chinese to persevere in retaining so expensive and turbulent a frontier province. The gold and jade of Khoten, silver and lead of Cosharab, and copper of Khalistan, have given abundant employment to Chinese settlers; while coal, iron, sulphur, alum, sal ammoniac, and zinc, though worked in unimportant quantities before the insurrection of Yakub khan (Atalik Ghazi), furnished the inhabitants with supplies for domestic use. An important hinderance to building villages in many sections of this territory is the prevalence of sand dunes here. Solitary houses and even whole settlements lying in the path of these moving hills are suddenly overwhelmed and oftentimes totally effaced.

The town of Kashgar is situated at the northwestern angle of the Southern Circuit, on the Kashgar River, a branch of the Tarim, in lat. 39° 25′ N., and long. 76° 5′ E., at the extreme west of the Empire. Several roads meet here. Going in a northwest direction, one leads over the Tien shan to Kokand; a second passes south, through Yarkand and Khoten, to Leh and Cashmere; a third, the great caravan route, from China through

---

[1] H. W. Bellew, *Kashmir and Kashgar. A Narrative of the Journey of the Embassy to Kashgar in* 1873–4, p. 2.

Ushí, may be said to end here; and the fourth and most frequented, leads off northwest over the Tien shan through the Rowat Pass, and along the western banks of Lake Issik-kul to Ílí. Kashgar was the capital of the Oigours for a long time, and its ruler forced his people, as far east as Hami, to accept Islamism about the year 1000. They then came under Genghis' sway, and this city increased its importance, but when Abubahr Miza took Yarkand, he razed Kashgar to the ground. Under Chinese rule it became one of the richest marts in Central Asia, and its future importance is secured by its position. The city is enclosed with high and massive walls, supported by buttress bastions, and protected by a deep ditch on three sides, the river flowing under the fourth. There are but two gates; the area within is about fifty acres. Around it are populous suburbs.

In the middle of the town is a large square, and four bazaars branch from it through to the gates; the garrison is placed without the walls. The manufactures of Kashgar excel those of any other town in the two Circuits, especially in jade, gold, silk, cotton, gold and silver cloths, and carpets. The country around produces fruit and grain in abundance; "the manners of the people have an appearance of elegance and politeness," says the Chinese geographer; "the women dance and sing in family parties; they fear and respect the officers, and have not the wild, uncultivated aspect of those in Ushí." This judgment is in a measure confirmed by Bellew, who credits the people with being singularly free from prejudice against the foreigners, quite indifferent on any score of his nationality or religion, and content so long as he pays his way and does not offend the customs of the natives. Several towns are subordinate to Kashgar, because of its oversight of their rulers, and consumption of their products. Southwest lies Tashbalig, and on the road leading to Yarkand is Yangi Hissar, both of them towns of some importance; the whole distance from Kashgar presents a succession of sandy or saline tracts, alternating with fertile bottoms wherever water runs. Small villages and post houses serve to connect the larger towns, but the soil does not reward the cultivators with much produce.

Yarkand, or Yerkiang, is the political capital of the Southern Circuit, as the highest military officers and strongest force are stationed here. It is situated on the Yarkand River, in lat. 36° 30′ N., and long. 77° 15′ E., in the midst of a sand-girt oasis of great fertility. The environs are abundantly supplied with water by canals. The stone walls are three miles in circumference, but its suburbs are much larger; the houses are built of dried bricks, and the town has a more substantial appearance than others in Îlí. There are many mosques and colleges, which, with the public buildings occupied by the government and troops, add to its consideration. Yarkand is one of the ancient cities of Tartary, and was, in remote times, a royal residence of Turk princes of the Afrasyab dynasty. In modern times it owes its rank as a well-built city chiefly to Abubahr Miza, whose short-lived sway from Aksu to Wakhan left its chief results in the mosques and bazaars erected or enlarged by him. By means of quarrying jade in the Karakash valley, and working the bangles, ear-rings and other articles in the city, thousands of families found employment under Chinese rule.

With the overthrow of that sway and then of Yakub khan in its restoration, all this industry disappeared. In the destruction ensuing on these long struggles for supremacy, one learns the explanation of the barbarism which has succeeded the downfall of mighty empires all over Western Asia. The city has no important manufactures; it enjoys a local reputation for its leather, and boots and shoes made here are esteemed all over the province. Among other articles of trade are horses, silk, and wool, and fabrics made from them; but everything found at Kashgar is sold also at this market. In a Chinese notice of the city, the customs at Yarkand are stated to have yielded over $45,000 annually; the taxes are 35,400 sacks of grain, 57,569 pieces of linen, 15,000 lbs. of copper, besides gold, silk, varnish, and hemp, part of which are carried to Îlí. Jade is obtained from the river in large pieces, yellow, white, black, and reddish, and the articles made from it are carried to China. The Chinese authorities have no objection to the resorting thither of natives of Kokand, Badakshan, and other neighboring states, many of whom settle and marry.

Khoten is situated on the southern side of the desert, and the district embraces all the country south of Aksu and Yarkand, along the northern base of the Kwănlun Mountains, for more than three hundred miles from east to west. The capital is called Ílchí on Chinese maps, and lies in an extensive plain on the Khoten River in lat. 37° N., and long. 80° E. The town of Karakash (meaning 'Black Jade')[1] lies in lat. 37° 10′, long. 80° 13′ 30″, a few miles northwest in the same valley, and is said by traders to be the capital rather than Ílchí; it is located on the road to Yarkand, distant twelve days' journey. On this road the town of Gummí is also placed, whose chief had in his possession a stone supposed to have the power of causing rain. Kirrea lies five days' journey east of Ílchí, near the pass across the mountains into Tibet and Ladak; a gold mine is worked near this place, the produce of which is monopolized by the Chinese. The three towns of Karakash, Ílchí, and Kirrea, are the only places of importance between the valley of the Tarim and Tibet, but none of them have been visited for a long time by Europeans.[2] The population of the town or district is unknown; one notice[3] gives it a very large number, approaching three millions and even more, which at any rate indicates a more fertile soil and genial climate than the regions north and south of it. Dr. Morrison, in his *View of China*, puts it at 44,630 inhabitants; and although the former includes the whole district, and is probably too large, the second seems to be much too small.

Khoten is known, in Chinese books, by the names of *Yu-tien*, *Hwan-na*, *Kieu-tan*, and *Kiu-sa-tan-na*—the last meaning, in Sanscrit, "Breast of the Earth."[4] Its eastern part is marshy, but that the country must have a considerable elevation is manifest from the fact that the river which drains and connects it with the Tarim runs quite across the desert in its course. The country is governed by two high officers and a

---

[1] But Rémusat says that Karakash is a river and no town.

[2] Wood (*Journey to the Oxus*, p. 279) refers to a frontier town by the name of Ecla.

[3] *Penny Cyclopædia*, *Art.* THIAN SHAN NAN LU.

[4] Rémusat, *Histoire de Khotan*, p. 35.

detachment of troops; there are six towns under their jurisdiction, the inhabitants of which are ruled in the same manner as the other Mohammedan cities. The people, however, are said to be mostly of the Buddhist faith, and the Chinese give a good account of their peacefulness and industry. The trade with Leh and H'lassa is carried on by a road crossing the Kwănlun over the Kirrea Pass, beyond which it divides. The productions of Khoten are fine linen and cotton stuffs, jade ornaments, amber, copper, grain, fruits, and vegetables; the former for exportation, the latter for use. It was in this region that Col. Prejevalsky discovered (in 1879) a new variety of wild horse, a specimen of which has been stuffed and exhibited in St. Petersburg. The animal in question, though belonging undoubtedly to the genus *Equus*, presents, in many respects, an intermediate form between the domestic horse and the wild ass.

Rémusat published, in 1820, an account of this country, drawn from Chinese books, in which the principal events in its history are stated, commencing with the Han dynasty, before the Christian era, down to the Manchu conquest. In the early part of its history, Khoten was the resort of many priests from India, and the Buddhist faith was early established there. It was an independent kingdom most of the time, from its earliest mention to the era of Genghis khan, the princes sometimes extending their sway from the Kiayü pass and Koko-nor to the Tsung ling, and then being obliged to contract to the valley now designated as Khoten. After the expulsion of the Mongols from China, Khoten asserted its independence, but afterward fell under the sway of the Songares and Eleuths, and lost many of its inhabitants. The Manchus conquered it in 1770, when the rest of the region between the Tien shan and Kwănlun fell under their sway, but neither have they settled in it to the same extent, nor made thereof a penal settlement, as in other parts of Ĭlí.[1]

The government of Ĭlí differs in some respects from that of Mongolia, where religion is partly called in to aid the state. In

[1] Concerning the nomenclature of this region compare Rémusat, *Histoire de Khotan*, p. 66. See, moreover, *ib.*, p. 47 ff., the legend of a drove of desert rats assisting the king of this land against the army of his enemies.

the Northern Circuit, the authority is strictly military, exercised by means of residents and generals, with bodies of troops under their control. The supreme command of all Îlí is intrusted by the colonial office to a Manchu *tsiangkiun*, or military governor-general at Kuldja, who has under him two councillors to take cognizance of civil cases, and thirty-four residents scattered about in both Circuits. This governor has also the control of the troops stationed in the three western departments of Kansuh, but has nothing to do with the civil jurisdiction of those towns. The entire number of soldiers under his hand is stated at 60,000, most of whom have families, and add agricultural, mechanical, or other labors to the profession of arms. The councillors are not altogether subordinate to the general, but report to the Colonial Office.

In the Northern Circuit, there is a deputy appointed for every village and town, invested with military powers over the troops and convicts, and civil supervision over the native *píko* or chieftains, who are the real rulers acknowledged by the clans. The character of the inhabitants north of the Tien shan is rendered unlike that of those dwelling in the Southern Circuit, not more by the diversity in their language and nomadic habits, than by the sway religious rites and allegiance have over them. Through this latter motive, the government of Mongolia and the Northern Circuit is rendered far easier and more effectual for the distant court of Peking than it otherwise would be. The appointment of the native chieftains is first announced to the general at Kuldja and the Colonial Office, and they succeed to their post when confirmed, which, as the station is in a measure hereditary, usually follows in course.

The inhabitants of the Southern Circuit are Mohammedans and acknowledge a less willing subjection to the Emperor than those in the Northern, the differences in race, religion, and language being probably the leading reasons. The government of the whole region is divided among the Manchu residents or *ambans* at the eight cities, who are nominally responsible to the general at Îlí, and independent of each other, but there is a gradation in rank and power, the one at Yarkand having the priority. The begs are chosen by the tribes themselves, and exercise authority in all petty cases arising among the people, without the interference of the Chinese. The troops are all Manchu or Chinese, none of the Turks being enrolled in separate bodies, though individuals are employed with safety. There is considerable difference in the rank and influence of the begs, which is upheld and respected by the *ambans*. The allowances and style granted them are regulated in a measure by their feudal importance. The revenue is derived from a monthly capitation tax on each man of about half a dollar, and tithes on the produce; there are no transit duties as in China, but custom-houses are established at the frontier trading towns. The language generally used in the Southern Circuit is the Jaghatai Turki of the Kalmucks; the Usbecks constitute the majority of the people, but Eleuths and Kalmucks are everywhere intermixed. The Tibetans have settled in Khoten, or more probably, remnants still exist there of the former inhabitants.

The history of the vast region constituting the present government of Îlí early attracted the attention of oriental scholars, and few portions of the world have had a more exciting history. After the expulsion of the Mongols from China by Hungwu, A.D. 1366, they found that they, as a tribe, were inferior in power to the western tribes, but it was not till about 1680 that the Eleuths, north of the Tien shan under the Galdan,[1] began to attack the Kalkas, and drive them eastward. The Sunnites, Tsakhars, and Solons, portions of the Eastern Mongols, had already joined the Manchus; and the Kalkas, to avoid extermination, submitted to them also, and besought their assistance against the Eleuths. Kanghí received their allegiance, and tried to settle the difficulties peaceably, but was obliged to send his troops against the Galdan, and drive him from the territory of the Kalkas to the westward of Lob-nor and Barkul. The Emperor was materially aided in this enterprise by the secession from the Eleuths of the Songares, whose khan had taken offence, and drawn his hordes off to the south. The khans of the Kalkas and their vast territory thus

[1] "Galdan, better known by his title of Contaïsch"—Rémusat, *Nouveaux Mélanges*, Tome II., p. 29. See also Schuyler's *Turkistan*, Vol. II., p. 168.

became subject to the Chinese. The Galdan lost all his forces, and expired by poison, in 1697, his power dying with him, and his tribe having already become too weak to resist.

Upon the ruins of his power arose that of Arabdan, the khan of the Songares. He subjugated the Northern Circuit, passed over into Turkestan, Tangout, and Khoten, and gradually reduced to his sway nearly all the elevated region of Central Asia west of Kansuh. He expelled the Tourgouths from their possessions in Cobdo, and compelled them to retreat to the banks of the Volga. Kanghí expelled the Songares from the districts about Koko-nor, but made no impression upon their authority in Songaria. After the death of Arabdan, about 1720, his throne was disputed, and the power weakened by dissensions among his sons, so that it was seized by two usurpers, Amursana and Tawats, who also fell out after their object was gained. Amursana repaired to Peking for assistance, and with the aid of a Chinese army expelled Tawats, and took possession of the throne of Arabdan. But he had no intention of becoming a vassal to Kienlung, and was no sooner reinstated than he resisted him; he defeated two Chinese armies sent against him, but succumbed on the third attack, and fled to Tobolsk, where he died in 1757.

The territory of Arabdan then fell to Kienlung, and he pursued his successes with such cruelty that the Northern Circuit was nearly depopulated, and the Songares and Eleuths became almost extinct as distinct tribes. The banished tribe of Tourgouths was then invited by the Emperor to return from Russian sway to their ancient possessions, which they accepted in 1772; the history of the Chinese embassy to them, and their disastrous journey back to Cobdo over the Kirghís steppe and through the midst of their enemies, is one of the most remarkable instances of nomadic wanderings and unexampled suffering in modern times.[1] Chinese troops, emigrants, exiles, and nomadic tribes and families, were sent and encouraged to come

---

[1] Compare Rémusat (*Nouveaux Mélanges*, Tome II., p. 102), who has compiled a brief life of their leader Ubusha. De Quincey's essay, *The Flight of a Tartar Tribe*. Ritter, *Asien*, Bd. V. pp. 531–583: *Welthistorischer Einfluss des chinesichen Reichs auf Central- und West-Asien.*

into the vacant territory, so that erelong it began to resume its former importance. In the period which has since elapsed, the Manchus have been enabled to prevent any combination among the clans, and maintain their own authority by a mixed system of coercion and coaxing which they well know how to practise. The agricultural and mineral resources of the country have been developed, many of the nomads induced to attend to agriculture by making their chieftains emulous of each other's prosperity, and by exciting a spirit of traffic among all.

There have been some disturbances from time to time, but no master spirit has arisen who has been able to unite the tribes against the Chinese. In 1825, there was an attempt made from Kokand by Jehangír, grandson of the *kojeh* or prince of Kashgar, to regain possession of Turkestan; the khan of Kokand assisted him with a small army, and such was their dislike of the Chinese, that as soon as Jehangír appeared, the Mohammedans arose and drove the Chinese troops away or put them to death, opening the gates to the invader. He took possession of Yarkand and Kashgar, and advanced to Aksu, where the winter put a stop to the campaign. In the next year, the khan of Kokand, seeing the disposition of the people, thought he would embark himself in the same cause, and made an incursion as far as Aksu and Khoten, reducing more than half the Southern Circuit to himself, but ostensibly in aid of Jehangír. The kojeh, beginning to fear his aid, withdrew; and the khan, having suffered some reverses from the Chinese troops, made his peace on very favorable terms, and returned to his own country. Jehangír went to Khoten from Yarkand, but his conduct there displeasing the people, the Chinese troops, about 60,000 in number, had no difficulty in dispersing his force, and resuming their sway. The adherents of the kojeh fled toward Badakshan, while he himself repaired to Isaac, the newly appointed kojeh of Kashgar, by whom he was delivered up to the Chinese with his family, and all of them most barbarously destroyed.

The kojeh was rewarded with the office of prince of Kashgar, but having been accused of treasonable designs he was ordered to come to Peking for trial; the charges were all disproved, and he returned to Kashgar after several years' residence at the capital of the Empire. The country was gradually reduced by Changling, the general at Ílí, but Kashgar suffered so much by the war and removal of the chief authority to Yarkand, that it has not since regained its importance. During this war, the dislike of the Mohammedans to the Chinese sway was exhibited in the large forces Jehangír brought into the field; and if he had been a popular spirited leader, there is reason for supposing he might have finally wrested these cities from the Chinese. The joy of Taukwang at the successful termination of the expedition and capture of the rebel, was so extravagant as to appear childish; and when Jehangír was executed at Peking, he ordered the sons of two officers who had been reported killed, "to witness his execution, in order to give expansion to the indignation which had accumulated in their breasts; and let the rebel's heart be torn out and given to them to sacrifice it at the tombs of their fathers, and thus console their faithful spirits." Honors were heaped upon Changling at his return to Peking, and rewards and titles showered upon all the troops engaged in the war.

Since this insurrection, the frontiers of Kashgar and Kokand have been passed and repassed by the Pruth Kirghís; in 1830, they excited so much trouble because their trade was restricted, that a large force was called out to restrain them, and many lives were lost before the rising was subdued. The causes of the dispute were then examined, and the trade allowed to go on as before. The oppressions of the residents sometimes goad on the Mohammedans to rise against the Chinese, but the policy of the Emperor is conciliatory, and the complaints of the people are in general listened to. The visits of the begs and princes to Peking with tribute affords them an opportunity to state their grievances, while it also prevents them from caballing among themselves. In 1871 the Russians took possession of nearly the whole of Tien-Shan Peh Lu during an insurrection of the Dunganis against Chinese control. The Tarantchis having attacked a Russian outpost, and Yakub Beg being on suspiciously good terms with the rebels, it was determined to occupy Kuldja—which was effected after a campaign of less than a month, led by Gen. Kolpakofsky. The Chinese government was immediately informed that the place should be restored whenever a sufficient force could be brought there to hold it against attacks, and preserve order. After the final conquest of the Dungan tribes in 1879–80, this territory was returned by the Russians upon conclusion of their last treaty with China, exactly ten years from the date of possession. The old manner of government is now resumed and the country slowly recovering from the frightful devastation of the insurrection. The salaries of the governor-general and his councillors, and the residents, are small, and they are all obliged to resort to illegal means to reimburse their outlays. The highest officer receives about $5,200 annually, and his councillors about $2,000 ; the residents from $2,300 down to $500 and less. These sums do not, probably, constitute one-tenth of the receipts of their situations.[1]

The third great division of the colonial part of the Chinese empire, that of TIBET, is less known than Ílí, though its area is hardly less extensive. It constitutes the most southern of the three great table lands of Central Asia, and is surrounded with high mountains which separate it from all the contiguous regions. The word Tibet or Tubet is unknown among the inhabitants as the name of their country; it is a corruption by the Mongols of *Tu po*,[2] the country of the Tu, a race which overran it in the sixth century ; Turner gives another name, *Pue-koa-chim*, signifying the 'snowy country of the north,' doubtless a local or ancient term. The general appellation by the people is *Pot* or *Bod*, or *Bod yul*—" the land of Bod." [3] It is roughly bounded northeast by Koko-nor ; east by Sz'chuen and Yunnan ; south by Assam, Butan, Nipal, and Gurhwal ; west by Cashmere ; and north by the unknown ranges of the Kwănlun Mountains. The southern frontier curves considerably in its course,

[1] *Chinese Repository*, Vol. V., pp. 267, 316, 351, etc. ; Vol. IX., p. 113. *Penny Cyclopædia*, *Art.* SONGARIA. Boulger, *Russia and England in Central Asia*, 2 Vols., London, 1879. Schuyler, *Turkistan*, 2 vols., N. Y., 1877. Petermann's *Mittheilungen*, Appendices XLII. and XLIII., 1875.

[2] This derivation is explained somewhat differently in Rémusat, *Nouveaux Mélanges*, Tome I., p. 190.

[3] To these Ritter adds the names of Wei, Dzang, Nga-ri, Kham, Bhodi, Peu-u-Tsang, Si-Dzang, Thupho, Tobbat, Töböt, Tübet, Tibet, and Barantola, as all applying to this country. *Asien*, Bd. III., S. 174–183.

but is not less than 1,500 miles from the western extremity of Nípal to the province of Yunnan ; the northern border is about 1,300 miles ; the western frontiers cannot be accurately defined, and depend more upon the possession of the passes through which trade is carried on than any political separation. Beltistan, Little Tibet, and Ladak, although included in its limits on Chinese maps, have too little subjection or connection with the court of Peking, to be reckoned among its dependencies.

Tibet, in its largest limits, is a table land, the highest plains of which have a mean elevation of 11,510 feet, or about 1,300 feet lower than the plateau of Bolivia, near Lake Titicaca. The snow-line on the north side of the Himalaya is at an altitude of 16,630 feet ; on the southern slope it is at 12,982 feet. Several striking analogies may be traced between this country and Peru : the tripartite divisions caused by lofty ranges ; their common staples of wool, from alpacas and vicunas in one, and sheep and goats in the other ; the abundance of precious metals, and many specific customs. The entire province of Tibet is divided by mountain chains into three distinct parts ; its western portion consists of the basin of the Indus, until it breaks through into Cashmere at Makpon-i-Shagaron. It begins near Mount Kailasa, and stretches northwest between the Hindu Kush and Himalaya, comprising the whole of Beltistan and Ladak ; the Kara-korum, Mus-tag, or Tsung ling range defines it on the northeast. The second part consists of an extensive desert land, commencing at Mount Kailasa, and having the Tsung ling on the west, the Kwănlun on the north (which separates it from Khoten, and the high watershed of the Yangtsz', Salween, and other rivers), and Lake Tengkiri, on the east ; the Himalaya constitutes its southern boundary. This high region, called Katshe or Kor-kache, has not been traversed by intelligent travellers and is one of the few yet unknown regions of the earth, and is nearly uninhabitable, owing to the extreme rigor of its climate.[1]

---

[1] See Rémusat, *Nouveaux Mélanges*, I., p. 190, for notices of tribes anciently inhabiting this district and Bokhara. Compare also Heeren (*Historical Researches*, Vol. I., pp. 180–186), who gives in brief the accounts of Herodotus and Ctesias.

The eastern part, consisting of the basin of the Yaru-tsangbu, contains, in its plains, most of the towns in Tibet, until it reaches the Alpine region which lies between the River Yaru and the Yangtsz', a space extending from long. 95° to 99° E. This district is described as a succession of ridges and gorges, over which the road takes the traveller on narrow and steep paths, crossing the valleys by ropes and bridges enveloped in the clouds. Mount Kailasa, a notable peak lying in the north-eastern part of Nari, is not far from 26,000 feet high. The number of summits covered with perpetual snow exceeds that of any other part of the world of the same extent.

The road from Sz'chuen to H'lassa strikes the Yalung kiang, in the district of Ta tsien lu, and then goes southwesterly to Batang on the Yangtsz' kiang; crossing the river it proceeds up the narrow valley a short distance, and then crosses the mountains northwest to the Lantsan kiang or River Meikon, by a series of pathways leading over the gorges, till it reaches Tsiamdo; from this point the road turns gradually south-west, following the valleys when practicable, till it ends at H'lassa.

The largest river in Tibet is the Erechumbu, or Yaru-tsangbu; *tsangbu* means river, and is often alone used for this whole name. It rises in the Tamchuk range, at the Mariam-la pass in Nari, 60 miles east of Lake Manasarowa, the source of the Sutlej; it flows a little south of east for about seven hundred miles, through the whole of Southern Tibet, between the first and second ranges of the Himalayas, as far as long. 90° E. Its tributaries on the north are numerous, and among them the Nauk-tsangbu and Dzangtsu are the largest. The volume of water which flows through the mountains into Assam by this river, is equal to that by the Indus into Scinde. The disputed question, whether the Yaru-tsangbu joins the Brahmaputra or Irrawadi, has been settled by presumptive evidence in favor of the former, but a distance of about 400 miles is still unexplored;[1] the fall in this part is about 11,000 feet, to where the river Dihong has been traced in Assam. This makes the Brah-

[1] Introduction by Col. Yule, in Gill's *River of Golden Sand.*

maputra the largest and longest river in Southern Asia; its passage into Assam is near 95° E. longitude.

The eastern part of Tibet, beyond this meridian, is traversed by numerous ranges of lofty mountains, having no separate names, the direction of which is from west to east, and from northwest to southeast. From these ranges, lateral branches run out in different directions, containing deep valleys between them. In proportion as the principal chains advance towards the southeast they converge towards one another, and thus the valleys between them gradually become narrower, until at last, on the frontiers of Yunnan and Burmah, they are mere mountain passes, whose entire breadth does not much exceed a hundred miles, having four streams flowing through them. In fact, Tibet incloses the fountain heads of all the large rivers of Southern and Eastern Asia. The names and courses of those in Eastern Tibet are known only imperfectly from Chinese maps, but others have described them after their entrance into the lowlands.

Tibet, especially the central part, is a country of lakes, in this respect resembling Cobdo. The largest, Tengkiri-nor, situated in the midst of stupendous mountains, about one hundred and ten miles northwest of H'lassa, is over a hundred miles long and about thirty wide. The region north of it contains many isolated lakes, most of them salt. Two of the largest, the Bouka and Kara, are represented as connected with the River Nu. Lake Khamba-la, Yamoruk or Yarbrokyu, sometimes called Palti, from a town on its northern shore, is a large lake south of H'lassa, remarkable for its ring shape, the centre being filled by a large island, around which its waters flow in a channel thirty miles or more in width. On the island is a nunnery, called the Palace of the Holy Sow, said to be the finest in the country. In Balti or Little Tibet are many sheets of water, the largest of which, the Yik and Paha, are connected by a river flowing through a marshy country. A long succession of lakes fill one of the basins in Katsche, suggesting the former existence of another Aral Sea. The sacred lakes of Manasarowa and Ravan-hrad (Mapam-dalai and Langga-nor, of the Chinese) form the headwaters of the Sutlej.

The climate of Tibet is characterized by its purity and excessive dryness. The valleys are hot, notwithstanding their proximity to snow-capped mountains; from May to October the sky is clear in the table-lands, and in the valleys the moisture and temperature are favorable to vegetation, the harvest being gathered before the gales and snows set in, after October. The effects of the air resemble or are worse than those of the kamsín in Egypt. The trees wither, and their leaves may be ground to powder between the fingers; planks and beams break, and the inhabitants cover the timbers and wood-work of their houses with coarse cotton, in order to preserve them against the destructive saccidity. The timber neither rots nor is worm-eaten. Mutton, exposed to the open air, becomes so dry that it may be powdered like bread; when once dried it is preserved during years. This flesh-bread is a common food in Tibet. The carcass of the animal, divested of its skin and viscera, is placed where the frosty air will have free access to it, until all the juices of the body dry up, and the whole becomes one stiffened mass. No salt is used, nor does it ever become tainted, and is eaten without any further dressing or cooking; the natives eat it at all periods after it is frozen, and prefer the fresh to that which has been kept some months. The food called *jamba* is prepared by cooking brick tea during several hours, then adding butter and salt, and stirring the mixture until it becomes a thick broth. When eaten the stuff is served in wooden bowls, and a plentiful supply of roasted barley-meal poured in, the whole being kneaded by the hands and devoured in the shape of dough pellets.

The productions of Tibet consist of domestic animals, cattle, horses, pigs; some wild animals, such as the white-breasted argali, orongo-antelope, ata-dzeren, wolf, and steppe-fox; and few plants or forests, presenting a strong contrast with Nípal and Butan, where vegetable life flourishes more luxuriantly. Sheep and goats are reared in immense flocks, for beasts of burden over the passes, and for their flesh, hair, and coats. Chiefest among the animals of this mountain land is the yak.[1] The

---

[1] Called by Wood *Kash-gow* (*Journey to the Oxus*, p. 319). *Chauri gau*, *sarlyk*, and *sarlac*, are other names.

domesticated variety, or long-haired yak, is the inseparable companion and most trusty servant not only of the Tibetans, but of tribes in Cashmere, Ladak, Tangout, and Mongolia, even as far north as Urga. It is a cross-breed, or mule from the yak bull and native cow, which alone is hardy enough for these elevated regions.[1] These creatures are of the same size as our cattle, strong, sure-footed and possessed of extraordinary endurance; they retain, however, something of their wild nature, even after long domestication, and must be carefully treated,

Domesticated Yak.

especially when being loaded and unloaded. They thrive best in hilly countries, well watered and covered with grass—the two last being indispensable. The hair is black or black and white, seldom entirely white. One sort is without horns, and when crossed with the cow bears sterile males, or females which are fertile for one generation. As to the wild yak of Tibet, a traveller says: "This handsome animal is of extraordinary size and beauty, measuring, when grown, eleven feet in length, exclusive of its bushy tail, which is three feet long; its height at the hump is six feet; girth around the body eleven feet, and its

[1] This cross is mentioned by Marco Polo, *Yule's ed.*, Vol. I., p. 241.

weight ten or eleven hundred weight. The head is adorned with ponderous horns, two feet nine inches long, and one foot four inches in circumference at the root. The body is covered with thick, black hair, which in the old males assumes a chestnut color on the back and upper parts of the sides, and a deep fringe of black hair hangs down from the flanks. The muzzle is partly gray, and the younger males have marks of the same color on the upper part of the body, whilst a narrow, silvery-gray stripe runs down the centre of the back. The hair of young yaks is much softer than that of older ones; they are also distinguishable by their smaller size, and by handsomer horns, with the points turned up. The females are much smaller than the males, and not nearly so striking in appearance; their horns are shorter and lighter, the hump smaller, and the tail and flanks not nearly as hairy."[1] This animal is useful for its milk, flesh, and wool, as well as for agricultural purposes and travel.

There is comparatively little agriculture. The variety of wild animals, birds, and fishes, is very great; among them the musk deer, feline animals, eagles, and wild sheep, are objects of the chase. The brute creation are generally clothed with an abundance of fine hair or wool; even the horses have a shaggier coat than is granted to bears in more genial climes. The Tibetan mastiff is one of the largest and fiercest of its race, almost untamable, and unknown out of its native country. The musk deer is clothed with a thick covering of hair two or three inches long, standing erect over the whole body; the animal resembles a hog in size and form, having, however, slender legs. The Tibetan goat affords the shawl wool, so highly prized for the manufacture of garments.[2]

---

[1] Prejevalsky, *Travels in Mongolia*, etc., Vol. I., p. 187.

[2] B. H. Hodgson, Notice of the Mammals of Tibet, *Journal As. Soc. of Bengal*, Vol. XI., pp. 275 ff.; also *ib.* Vols. XVI., p. 763, XIX., p. 466, and XXVI., No. 3, 1857. Abbé Armand David, Notes sur quelques oiseaux de Thibet, *Nouv. Arch. du Museum, Bull.*, V. 1869, p. 33; *ib. Bull*, VI., pp. 19 and 33. *Bull*, VIII., 1872, pp. 3–128, IX., pp. 15–48, X., pp. 3–82. *Recherches pour servir à l'histoire naturelle des mammifères comprennant des considérations sur la classification de ces animaux, etc., des études sur la faune de la Chine et du Tibet oriental*, par MM. Milne-Edwards, etc., 2 vols. Paris, 1868–74.

Fruits are common; small peaches, grapes, apples, and nuts, constitute the limited variety. Barley is raised more than any other grain the principal part of agricultural labors being performed by the women. Pulse and wheat are cultivated, but no rice west of H'lassa. Rhubarb, asafœtida, ginger, madder, and safflower are collected or prepared, but most of the medicines come from China and Butan. Turnips, rape, garlic, onions, and melons are raised in small quantities. The mineral productions are exceedingly rich. Gold occurs in mines and placer diggings, and forms a constant article of export; lead, silver, copper, and cinnabar are also dug out of the ground, but iron has not been found to much extent. The great difficulty in the way of the inhabitants availing themselves of their metallic wealth, apart from their ignorance of the best modes of mining, is the want of fuel with which to smelt the ore. Tincal, or crude borax, is gathered on the borders of a small lake in the neighborhood of Tengkiri-nor, where also any quantity of rock salt can be obtained. Precious stones are met with, most of which find their way to China.

The present divisions of Tibet, by the Chinese, are *Tsien Tsang*, or Anterior Tibet, and *Hau Tsang*, or Ulterior Tibet. Anterior Tibet is also called U (Wei) and U-tsang, and includes the central part of Bod-yur where H'lassa is; east of this lies Kham (Kăng) or Khamyul, and northeast toward Koko-nor is Khamsok, *i.e.*, Kham on the River Sok. Near the bend of the Brahmaputra is the district of Kongbo, where rice can be raised; going westward are Takpo, doUs and gTsang on the borders of Nari, ending in a line nearly continuous with the eastern border of Nípal. The Chinese books mention eight cantons in Anterior Tibet, five of them lying east of H'lassa, added to which are thirty-nine feudal townships in Khamsok called *tu-sz'*, all of them chiefly nominal or at present antiquated. Csoma de Körös speaks of several small principalities in Kham, and describes the inhabitants as differing from the rest of the Tibetans in appearance and language; they assimilate probably with the tribes on the Burman and Chinese frontiers. Nari (A-li in Chinese) is divided into Mangyul, Khorsum, and Maryul. The first of these districts lies nearly conterminous with Nípal, and its area is probably about the same, but its cold, dry, and elevated regions, support only a few shepherds; Khorsum and Maryul lie north and northwest in a still more inhospitable clime; the latter adjoins Ladak and Balti and is the reservoir of hundreds of lakes situated from 12,000 to 15,000 feet above the sea. A ridge separates the valley of the Indus from the Sutlej, crossed at the Bogola Pass, 19,220 feet high, and then over the Gugtila Pass, 19,500 feet into Gartok. The people throughout this elevated region are forced to live in tents, wood being almost unknown for building.

H'lassa, the *gyalsa* or capital of Tibet, is situated on the Ki-chu River, about twelve leagues from its junction with the Yaru, in lat. 29° 39′ N., and long. 91° 05′ E.; the name signifies *God's ground*, and it is the largest town in this part of Asia. It is famous for the convents near it, composing the ecclesiastical establishments of the Dalai (or 'Ocean')-lama, whose residence is in the monastery of Pobrang-marbu (*i.e.*, 'Red town') on Mount Putala. The principal building of this establishment is three hundred and sixty-seven feet high, and it contains, as the Chinese expression is, "a myriad of rooms." This city is the head-quarters of Buddhism, and the hierarchy of lamas, who, by means of the Dalai-lama, and his subordinate the Kutuktu, exercise priestly control over wellnigh all Mongolia as well as Tibet. The city lies in a fertile plain nearly 12,000 feet high, about twelve miles wide, and one hundred and twenty-five from north to south, producing harvests of barley and millet, with abundant pasturage and some fruit trees. Mountains and hills encircle it; of these the westernmost is Putala, the river running so near its base that a wall has been built to preserve the buildings from the rise of the waters. The Chinese garrison is quartered about two miles north of this mount, and two large temples, called *H'lassa tso-kang* and *Ramotsie tso-kang*, resplendent with gold and precious stones, stand very near it. The four monasteries, Séra, Brebung, Samyé, and Galdan, constitute as many separate establishments.[1] During the sway of the Songares in

[1] Klaproth, *Description du Tubet*, p. 246.

Ilí, their prince Arabdan made a descent upon H'lassa, and the Lama was killed. Kanghí placed a new one upon the see, in 1720, appointing six leading officers of the old Lama to assist him in the government. Three of these joined in an insurrection, and in the conflicts which succeeded, H'lassa suffered considerably. The population of the town is conjectured to be 24,000; that of the province is reckoned by Csoma at about 650,000.

The town was visited in the year 1811 by Mr. Manning, whose description of its dirty and miserable streets swarming with dogs and beggars, and the meanness of its buildings, corresponds with what Huc and Gabet found in 1846. Mr. Manning remained there nearly five months, and had several interviews with the Dalai-lama; he was much impeded in his observations by a Cantonese *munshí* or teacher, and exposed to danger of illness from insufficient shelter and clothing. His reception by the chief of the Buddhist faith on the 17th of December, was equally remarkable with that by the Teshu-lama of Bogle in 1774, and of Turner in 1783. Mr. Manning was alone and unprotected and had very few presents, but his offering was accepted; it consisted of a piece of fine broadcloth, two brass candlesticks, twenty new dollars, and two vials of lavender water. He rode to the foot of the mountain Putala, and dismounted on the first platform to ascend by a long stairway of four hundred steps, part of them cut in the rock, and the rest ladder steps from story to story in the palace, till he reached a large platform roof off which was the reception hall. Upon entering this he found that the *Ti-mu-fu* or *Gesub Rimboché*, the highest civil functionary in Tibet, was also present, which caused him some confusion: "I did not know how much ceremony to go through with one before I began with the other. I made the due obeisance, touching the ground three times with my head to the Grand Lama, and once to the *Ti-mu-fu.* I presented my gifts, delivering the coins with a handsome silk scarf with my own hands to them both. While I was *kotowing*, the awkward servants let one of the bottles of lavender water fall and break. Having delivered the scarf to the Grand Lama, I took off my hat, and humbly gave him my clean shaven head to lay his hands upon. . . . The Lama's beautiful and interesting face and manner engrossed all my attention. He was about seven years old; had the simple manners of a well educated princely child. His face was, I thought, poetically and affectingly beautiful. He was of a cheerful disposition, his beautiful mouth perpetually unbending into a graceful smile, which illuminated his whole countenance. No doubt my grim beard and spectacles excited his risibility. We had not been seated long before he put questions which we rose to receive and answer. He inquired whether I had met with difficulties on the road; to which I replied that I had had troubles, but now that I had the happiness of being in his presence they were amply compensated. I could see that this answer pleased both him and his people, for they found that I was not a mere rustic, but had some tincture of civility in me."[1]

The capital of Tsang or Ulterior Tibet is Shigatsé, situated 126 miles west of H'lassa, and under its control. The monastery where the Teshu-lama and his court resides is a few miles distant, and constitutes a town of about 4,000 priests, named Teshu-Lumbo. He is styled Panchen Rimboché, and is the incarnation of Amitabha Buddha. His palace is built of dark brick and has a roof of gilded copper; the houses rise one above another and the gilt ornaments on the temples combine to give a princely appearance to the town. The fortress of Shigatsé stands so as to command both places. The plain between this town and H'lassa is a fertile tract, and judging from the number of towns in the valleys of the basin of the Yaru, its productive powers are comparatively great. Ulterior Tibet is divided into six other cantons, besides the territory under the jurisdiction of the chief town, most of their fortified capitals lying westward of Shigatsé.

The degree of skill the Tibetans have attained in manufactures, mechanical arts, and general civilization, is less than that of the Chinese, but superior to the Mongols. They appear to be a mild and humane people, possessing a religious sense

---

[1] *Mission of George Bogle to Tibet and Journey of Thomas Manning to Lhasa.* Edited by C. R. Markham. London, 1876, p. 265.

and enjoying an easy life compared with their southern neighbors. They are well-bred and affable, fond of gossiping and festivities, which soften the heart and cheer the temper. Women are treated with care and are not often compelled to work out of doors. No two people or countries widely separated present a stronger contrast than do the stout, tall, muscular, and florid Butías, upon their fertile fields and wooded hills, with the squat, puny, sluggish, and swarthy Tibetans in their rugged, barren mountains. They distinguish five sorts of people among themselves, the last of whom are the Butías; the others are the inhabitants of Kham, or Anterior Tibet, those in Tsang, the nomads of Kor-kache, and the people of Little Tibet. All of them speak Tibetan with some variations. The Tibetans are clad with woollens and furs to such a degree that they appear to emulate the animals they derive them from in their weight and warmth; and with this clothing is found no small quantity of dirt. The dress of the sexes varies slightly in its shape; yellow and red are the predominant colors. Large bulgar boots of hide are worn by all persons; the remainder of the dress consists of woollen robes and furs like those of the Chinese. The women wear many jewels, and adorn their hair as do the Mongols with pearls, coral, and turquoises. Girls braid their hair in three tresses, married women in two. The head is protected by high velvet caps; the men wear broad-brimmed coverings of various materials.

The two religious sects are distinguished by yellow and red caps; the latter are comparatively few, allow marriage to the lamas, but do not differ materially in their ritual or tenets. There is no country where so large a proportion of the people are devoted to religious service as in Tibet, nor one where the secular part of the inhabitants pays such implicit deference to the clergy. The food of the Tibetans is taken at all hours, mutton, barley, and tea constituting the staple articles. On all visits tea is presented, and the cup replenished as often as it is drained. Spirits and beer, both made from barley, are common beverages. On every visit of ceremony, and whenever a letter is sent from one person to another, it is necessary to connect a silk scarf with it, the size and texture being proportioned to the rank and condition of the parties. The sentence *Om mani padmí hum* is woven upon each end.

The following note by Col. Yule, condensed from Koeppen's *Lamaische Hierarchie und Kirche*, contains the most satisfactory explanation of this puzzling mystic formula: "Om mani padmí hûm!—the primeval six syllables, as the lamas say, among all prayers on earth form that which is most abundantly recited, written, printed, and even spun by machines for the good of the faithful. These syllables form the only prayer known to the ordinary Tibetans and Mongols; they are the first words that the child learns to stammer, and the last gasping utterance of the dying. The wanderer murmurs them on his way, the herdsman beside his cattle, the matron at her household tasks, the monk in all the stages of contemplation (*i.e.*, of *far niente*); they form at once a cry of battle and a shout of victory! They are to be read wherever the Lama church hath spread, upon banners, upon rocks, upon trees, upon walls, upon monuments of stone, upon household utensils, upon strips of paper, upon human skulls and skeletons! They form, according to the idea of the believers, the utmost conception of all religion, of all wisdom, of all revelation, the path of rescue and the gate of salvation! . . . . . . Properly and literally these four words, a single utterance of which is sufficient of itself to purchase an inestimable salvation, signify nothing more than: "O the Jewel in the Lotus! Amen!" In this interpretation, most probably, the *Jewel* stands for the Bodhisatva Avalokiteçvara, so often born from the bud of a lotus flower. According to this the whole formula is simply a salutation to the mighty saint who has taken under his especial charge the conversion of the North, and with him who first employed it the mystic formula meant no more than *Ave Avalokiteçvara!* But this simple explanation of course does not satisfy the Lama schoolmen, who revel in glorifications and multitudinous glossifications of this formula. The six syllables are the heart of hearts, the root of all knowledge, the ladder to re-birth in higher forms of being, the conquerors of the five evils, the flame that burns up sin, the hammer that breaks up torment, and so on. *Om* saves the gods, *ma* the Asuras, *ni* the men, *pad* the animals, *mí* the spectre world of *pretâs*, *hûm* the inhabitants of hell! *Om* is 'the blessing of self-renunciation, *ma* of mercy, *ni* of chastity, etc.' 'Truly monstrous,' says Koeppen, 'is the number of *padmís* which in the great festivals hum and buzz through the air like flies.' In some places each worshipper reports to the highest Lama how many *om manis* he has uttered, and the total number emitted by the congregation is counted by the billion."

Grueber and Dorville describe *Manipe* as an idol, before which *stulta gens insolitis gesticulationibus sacra sua facit, identiden verba haec repetens*:—'O Manipe, mi hum, O Manipe, mi hum; *id est* Manipe, salva nos!'" Rémusat (*Mélanges Posthumes*, Paris, 1843, p. 99) translates this phrase by: "Adoration, O thou precious stone who art in the lotus!" and observes that it illustrates the fundamental dogma of Buddhism, viz.: the production of the material universe by an absolute being; all things which exist are shut up in the breast of the divine substance; the 'precious stone' signifying that *the world is in God.* Mr. Jameson says that the sentence *Om mani padmí hung* is formed of the initial letters of various deities, all of whom are supposed to be implored in the prayer.[1]

In reverential salutations, the cap is removed by the inferior, and the arms hang by the side. The bodies of the dead are placed in an open inclosure, in the same manner as practised by the Parsees, where birds and beasts of prey devour them, or they are dismembered in an exposed place. Lamas are burned, and their ashes collected into urns. As soon as the breath has departed, the body is seated in the same attitude as Buddha is represented, with the legs bent before, and the soles of the feet turned upwards. The right hand rests upon the thigh, the left turns up near the body, the thumb touching the shoulder. In this attitude of contemplation, the corpse is burned.

In Tibet, as in Butan, the custom of polyandry prevails. The choice of a wife lies with the eldest son, who having made known his intentions to his parents sends a matchmaker to pro-

---

[1] Compare, for further discussion of this subject, Timkowski's *Mission to Peking*, London, 1827, Vol. II., p. 349. Wilson's *Abode of Snow*, p. 329.

pose the matter to the parents of the girl. The consent of the parents being obtained, the matchmaker places an ornament of a jewel set in gold, called *sedzia* upon the head of the damsel, and gives her presents of jewels, dresses, cattle, etc., according to the means of the young man. The guests invited on the day of the marriage bring presents of such things as they choose, which augments the dowry. A tent is set up before the bride's house, in which are placed three or four square cushions, and the ground around sprinkled with wheat; the bride is seated on the highest cushion, her parents and friends standing near her according to their rank, and the assembled party there partake of a feast. The bride is then conducted to the house of her lover by the friends present, her person being sprinkled with wheat or barley as she goes along, and there placed by his side, and both of them served with tea and spirits. Soon after, the groom seats himself apart, and every one present gives a scarf, those of superior rank binding them around their necks, equals and inferiors laying them by their sides. The next day, a procession is formed of the relatives of the newly married pair, which visits all the friends, and the marriage is completed. The girl thus becomes the wife of all the brothers, and manages the domestic concerns of their household. The number of her husbands is sometimes indicated by as many points in her cap. This custom is strengthened by the desire, on the part of the family, to keep the property intact among its members; but it does not prevent one of the husbands leaving the roof and marrying another woman, nor is the usage universal. Rémusat speaks of a novel in Tibetan, in which the author admirably portrays the love of his heroine, Triharticha, for her four lovers, and brings their marriage in at the end in the happiest manner.

The dwellings of the poor are built of unhewn stones, rudely piled upon each other without cement, two stories high, and resembling brick-kilns in shape and size; the windows are small, in order not to weaken the structure; the roof is flat, defended by a brushwood parapet, and protected from the molestation of evil spirits by flags, strips of paper tied to strings, or branches of trees. Timber is costly and little used; the floors are of marble or tiles, and the furniture consists of little else than mats and cushions. The temples and convents are more imposing and commodious structures; some of those at H'lassa are among the noblest specimens of architecture in Central Asia.

The mausoleum of the Teshu-lama at Teshu Lumbu resembles a plain square watch-tower surmounted by a double Chinese canopy roof, the eaves of which are hung with bells, on which the breeze plays a ceaseless dirge. The body of the lama reposes in a coffin of gold, and his effigy, also of gold, is placed within the concavity of a large shell upon the top of the pyramidal structure which contains it. The sides of the pyramid are silver plates, and on the steps are deposited the jewels and other costly articles which once appertained to him. An altar in front receives the oblations and incense daily presented before the tomb, and near by is a second statue of the deceased as large as life in the attitude of reading. Scrolls and pennons of silk hang from the ceiling, and the walls are adorned with paintings of priests engaged in prayer. The whole structure is substantially built, and its rich ornaments are placed there not less for security than to do honor to the revered person deposited beneath. The windows are closed with mohair curtains, and a skylight in the upper story serves for lighting the room, and for passing out upon the roof. The roof or parapet is ornamented with cylinders of copper or other materials, which imparts a brilliant appearance to the edifices.

The manufactures of Tibet consist of woollens, cloth, blankets, yarn, goat-hair shawls, musk, paper, metals, and jewelry. Their lapidaries cut every kind of ornament in superior style, and gold and silverware forms a considerable article of trade to China. These and other crafts must necessarily languish, however, from the immense proportion of men who are withdrawn from labor into monasteries, compelling the residue to devote most of their strength to tillage. The most important exports to China consist of gold dust, precious stones, bezoars, asafœtida, musk, woollens, and skins; for which the people receive silks, teas, chinaware, tobacco, musical instruments, and metals. The trade is carried on through Síning fu in Kansuh, and

Batang in Sz'chuen. Tincal, rock-salt, and shawl wool, are additional articles sent to Ladak, Butan, and India.

Music is studied by the priesthood for their ceremonies, and with much better effect than among the Chinese priests. Their amusements consist in archery, dancing, and observance of many festivals connected with the worship of the dead or of the living. Dram-drinking is common, but the people cannot be called a drunken race, nor does the habit of opium eating or smoking, so fatally general in Assam, prevail, inasmuch as the poppy cannot well be cultivated among the mountains.

Education is confined to the priesthood, but the women, who conduct much of the traffic, also learn arithmetic and writing. The language is alphabetical, and reads from left to right; there are two forms of the character, the *uchen* used for books, and the *umin* employed in writing, which do not differ more than the Roman and the running-hand in English. The form of the characters shows their Sanscrit origin, but there are many consonants in the language not found in that tongue, and silent letters are not unfrequent in the written words. There are thirty consonants in the alphabet, distributed into eight classes, with four additional vowel signs; each of them ends in a short *a*, as *ka*, *nga*, *cha*, which can be lengthened by a diacritical mark placed underneath. The syllables are separated from each other by a point; the accented consonant is that which follows the vowel, and the others, whether before or after it, are pronounced as rapidly as possible, and not unfrequently omitted altogether in speaking. The variations in this respect constitute the chief features of the patois found in different parts where Tibetan is spoken. A dictionary and grammar[1] of this language were printed in 1834 in Calcutta by Csoma de Körös, a Hungarian who resided among the priests near Ladak. The literature is almost wholly theological, as far as it has been examined, and such works as are not of this character, have probably been introduced from China. Their divisions of time, numeration, chronology, and weights, have also been adopted

---

[1] *Essay towards a Dictionary, Tibetan and English. A Grammar of the Tibetan Language in English.* Calcutta, 1834.

from that country with a few alterations. An Englishman, Mr. Brian Hodgson, who lived in Nípal from 1820 to 1843, has added more than any one else to our knowledge of the literature of this country. This gentleman procured complete copies of the original documents of the Buddhist canon preserved in Sanscrit in Nípalese monasteries, as well as (by a present from the Dalai-lama) the whole of the existing literary remains of the once flourishing Christian mission at H'lassa. His more important essays on these lands have now been brought together in a single volume.[1]

The history of Tibet has been made partially known to Europe through the Mongol author, Sanang Setsen,[2] but if free access could be had to their annals, it is probable that a methodical history could be extracted, reaching back at least three centuries before Christ. Tibet was ruled by its own princes till the rise of Genghis; the first monarch, who united the various tribes under his sway B. C. 313, was Seger-Sandilutu-Kagan-Tül-Esen,[3] and from the fact that Buddhism was introduced during his reign, it might be inferred that he came from the south. H'lassa was founded by Srongzan-Gambo, or Srongbdzan sgambouo,[4] about A.D. 630, after which time Tibetan history becomes more authentic, inasmuch as this king introduced the alphabet. The Tang dynasty carried their arms into Tibet from Khoten, but the people threw off their yoke during the decline of that family. Mohammedanism also disturbed the supremacy of the Buddhist faith, and severe persecutions followed about the beginning of the tenth century by an Islam prince Darma, but it was repelled at his death, and has never since made the least impression upon the people. Genghis reduced Tangout, one of the principalities, northeast of Koko-nor, and soon after brought the whole country under his sway; this

---

[1] *Essays on the Language, Literature, and Religion of Nepal and Tibet*, etc. London, 1874.

[2] Rémusat, *Observations sur l'Histoire des Mongols orienteaux de Sanang Setsen*, Paris, l'an 8. *Ssanang Ssetsen, Geschichte der Mongolen*, Uebers., von. J. J. Schmidt, Petersb., 1829.

[3] Rémusat relates the story of his origin, *Mélanges Posthumes*, p. 400.

[4] Klaproth, *Description du Tubet.*

Kublai still further settled as a dependency of his empire. The people recovered their independence on the expulsion of the Mongols, and under the Ming dynasty formed several small kingdoms, among which were Ladak and Rodok, both of them still existing.

From a short résumé of letters written from Tibet in 1626, by Romish missionaries living there, it appears that the kingdom of Sopo was the most powerful in the north, and Cogué, U-tsang, and Maryul were three southern principalities. The king of Cogué allowed these missionaries to reside in his territories, and took pleasure in hearing them converse and dispute with the lamas. The Dalai-lama at this time was the king's brother, and possessed subordinate influence in the state, but the priests were numerous and influential. The conquest of Mongolia and Tangout opened the way for Kanghí to enter Tibet, but the intercourse between the Emperor and Dalai-lama was chiefly connected with religion and carrying tribute. An index of the freedom of communication between Tibet and the west is found in the passports issued to the traders visiting H'lassa in 1688. The lamas held the supreme power until towards the end of his reign, when Chinese influence became paramount. The country had already been conquered by the Songar chieftain, so that on his defeat it could offer little resistance. Kanghí appointed six of the highest princes or *gialbo* over the provinces; but soon after his death, in 1727, three of them conspired against Yungching, and were not subdued without considerable resistance. The Emperor then appointed the loyal prince or *gialbo* as governor-general, and he remained in his vice-regal office till his death, about 1750. Kienlung, finding that his son was endeavoring to make himself fully independent, executed him as a rebel, suppressed the office, and appointed two Chinese generals to be associated with the Dalai-lama and his coadjutor, in the administration of the country. The troops were increased and forts erected in all parts of the country to awe the people and facilitate trade.

The present government of Tibet is superintended by two *ta chin*, 'or great ministers,' residing at H'lassa, who act conjointly, while they serve as checks upon each other; they do not hold their office for a long time. They have absolute control over all the troops in the country, and the military are generally confined to the garrisons, and do not cultivate the soil. The collection of revenue, transmission of tribute to Peking, and direction of the persons who carry it, and those who conduct the trade at Batang and Síning fu, are all under their control. The Dalai-lama, and the Teshu-lama are the high religious officers of the country, each of them independent in his own province, but the former holding the highest place in the hierarchy. The Chinese residents confer with each concerning the direction of his own province. All their appointments to office or nobility must be sanctioned by the residents before they are valid, but merely religious officers are not under this surveillance. In the villages, the authority is administered by secular deputy lamas called *deba*, and by commandants called *karpon*, who are sent from the capital. Each *deba* is assisted by a native *vazir* of the place, who, with the chief lama, form the local government, amenable to the supreme magistracy. The western province of Nari is peopled by nomads, who wander over the regions north of Ravan-hrad, and are under the authority of *karpons* sent from H'lassa, without the assistance of lamas. The two high-priests themselves are likewise assisted by councillors. One of these, called Soopoon Choomboo, who held the office of *sadeek* or adviser when Turner visited Teshu-Lumbo, was a Manchu by birth, but had long lived in Tibet.

The nomadic clans of Dam Mongols and other tribes occupying the thirty-nine feudal townships or *tu-sz'* in Anterior Tibet, are governed by the residents without the intervention of the lamas. The disturbances in Ulterior Tibet in 1792, resulting from the irruption of the Nípalese and sack of Teshu-Lumbo, were speedily quelled by the energy of Kienlung's government, and the invaders forced to sue for mercy. The southern frontier was, in consequence of this inroad, strongly fortified by a chain of posts, and the communication with the states between Tibet and India strictly forbidden and watched. It gave the Chinese an opportunity to strengthen their rule and extend their influence north to Khoten and into Ladak. The natural mildness of character of the Tibetans, and similarity of religion renders them much easier under the Chinese yoke, than the Mohammedans.[1]

---

[1] Authorities on Tibet besides those already referred to: *Journal Asiatique*, Tomes IV., p. 281; VIII., p. 117; IX., p. 31; XIV., pp. 177, ff. 277, 406, etc. Du Halde, *Description of China*, Vol. II., pp. 384–388. Capt. Samuel Turner, *Account of an Embassy to the Court of Teshoo Lama in Tibet*, London, 1800. *Histoire de ce qui s'est passé au Royaume du Tibet, en l'année* 1626; trad. de l'Italien. Paris, 1829. P. Kircher, *China Illustrata.* MM. Péron et Billecocq, *Recueil de Voyages du Thibet*, Paris, 1796. *Journal of the Asiatic Society of Bengal*, passim. *Chinese Repository*, Vols. VI., pp. 28, 494, IX., p. 26, and XIII., p. 505. Ritter, *Asien*, Bd. II., 4er Abschnitt, and Bd. III., S. 137–424. Richthofen, *China*, Bd. I., S. 228, 247, 466, 670, 683, etc. C. H. Desgodin, *La mission du Tibet de* 1855 *à* 1870, *comprennant l'exposé des affaires religieuses*, etc. *D'après les lettres de M. l'abbé Desgodins, missionaire apostolique*, Verdun, 1872. Lieut. Kreitner, *Im fernen Osten*, pp. 829 ff., and in *The Popular Science Monthly*, for August, 1882. Emil Schlagintweit, *Tibetan Buddhism, Illustrated by Literary Documents and Objects of Religious Worship*, London, 1863. Abbé Huc, *Travels through Tartary, Tibet and China*, 2 vols.

CHAPTER V.

POPULATION AND STATISTICS.

Much of the interest appertaining to the country and people here treated of, in the minds of philanthropic and intelligent men, has arisen from the impression they have received of its vast population. A country twice the size of the Chinese empire would present few attractions to the Christian, the merchant, or the ethnologist, if it were no better inhabited than Sahara, or Arizona: a people might possess most admirable institutions, and a matchless form of government, yet these excellencies would lose their interest, did we hear that it is the republic of San Marino or the kingdom of Muscat, where they are found. The population of few countries in the world has been accurately ascertained, and probably that of China is less satisfactory than any European or American state of the present day. It is far easier to take a census among a people who understand its object, and will honestly assist in its execution, than in a despotic, half-civilized country, where the mass of the inhabitants are afraid of contact or intercourse with their rulers; in most of such states, as Abyssinia, Turkey, Persia, etc., there is either no regular enumeration at all, or merely a general estimate for the purposes of revenue or conscription.

The subject of the population of China has engaged the attention of the monarchs of the present dynasty, and their censuses have been the best sources of information in making up an intelligent opinion upon the matter. Whatever may be our views of the actual population, it is plain that these censuses, with all their discrepancies and inaccuracies, are the only reliable sources of information. The conflicting opinions and conclusions of foreign writers neither give any additional weight to them, nor detract at all from their credibility. As the question stands at present, they can be doubted, but cannot be denied; it is impossible to prove them, while there are many grounds for believing them; the enormous total which they exhibit can be declared to be improbable, but not shown to be impossible.

No one who has been in China can hesitate to acknowledge that there are some strong grounds for giving credit to them, but the total goes so far beyond his calculations, that entire belief must, indeed, be deferred till some new data have been furnished. There are, perhaps, more peculiar encouragements to the increase of population there than in any other country, mostly arising from a salubrious climate, semi-annual crops, unceasing industry, early marriages, and an equable taxation, involving reasonable security of life and property. Turning to other countries of Asia, we soon observe that in Japan and Persia these causes have less influence; in Siam and Burmah they are weak; in Tibet they are almost powerless.

At this point every one must rest, as the result of an examination into the population of the Chinese Empire; though, from the survey of its principal divisions, made in the preceding chapters, its capability of maintaining a dense population needs no additional evidence. The mind, however, is bewildered in some degree by the contemplation of millions upon millions of human beings thus collected under one government; and it almost wishes there might be grounds for disbelieving the enormous total, from the dreadful results that might follow the tyrannical caprice or unrestrained fury of their rulers, or the still more shocking scenes of rapine and the hideous extremities of want which a bad harvest would necessarily cause.

Chinese literature contains many documents describing classes of society comprised in censuses in the various dynasties. The results of those enumerations have been digested by Ma Twan-lin in a judicious and intelligent manner in the chapters treating on population, from which M. Ed. Biot has elaborated many important data.[1] The early records show that the census was designed to contain only the number of taxable people, excluding all persons bound to give personal service, who were under the control of others. Moreover, all officials and slaves, all persons over 60 or 66 years of age, the weak or sick, those needing help, and sometimes such as were newly placed on state lands, were likewise omitted. Deducting these classes, Ma Twan-lin gives one census taken in the ninth century, B.C., as 13,704,923 persons, between the ages of 15 and 65, living within the frontiers north of the Yangtsz' River. This figure would be worth, according to the tables of modern statistics, about 65 per cent. of the entire population, or as representing 21,753,528 inhabitants.

The mighty conqueror, Tsin Chí Hwangtí, changed the personal corvée to scutage, and introduced a kind of poll-tax, by accepting the money from many who could not be forced to do the work required. This practice was followed in the Han dynasty, and in B.C. 194, the poll-tax was legalized, to include all men between 15 and 66, while a lighter impost was levied on those between 7 and 14. During the four centuries of this family's régime, the object and modes of a census were well understood. Ma Twan-lin gives the results of ten taken between A.D. 2 and 155. His details show that it was done simply for revenue, and was omitted in bad years, when drought or freshets destroyed the harvests; they show, too, an increase in the number of slaves, that women were now enumerated, and that girls between 15 and 30 paid a poll-tax. In B.C. 30, the limits of age were placed between 7 and 56. The average of these ten censuses is 63,500,600, the first one being as high as 83,640,000, while the next and lowest, taken fifty-five years afterwards, is only 29,180,000, and the third is 47,396,000. These great variations are explained by the disturbances arising in consequence of the usurpation of Wangmang, A.D. 9–27, and subsequent change of the capital, and the impossibility, during this troubled period, of canvassing all parts of the Empire.

[1] This careful digest is contained in the *Journal Asiatique* for 1836 (April and May), and will repay perusal.

The inference from these data, that the real population of the Chinese Empire north of the Nan ling at the time of Christ was at least eighty millions, is as well grounded as almost any fact in its history.[1]

After the downfall of the Han dynasty, a long period of civil war ensued, in which the destruction of life and property was so enormous that the population was reduced to one-sixth of the amount set down in A.D. 230, when disease, epidemics, and earthquakes increased the losses caused by war and the cessation of agriculture, according to Ma Twan-lin; and it is not till A.D. 280, when the Tsin dynasty had subjected all to its sway, that the country began to revive. In that year an enumeration was made which stated the free people between 12 and 66 years in the land at 14,163,863, or 23,180,000 in all. From this period till the Sui dynasty came into power, in 589, China was torn by dissensions and rival monarchs, and the recorded censuses covered only a portion of the land, the figures including even fewer of the people, owing to the great number of serfs or bondmen who had sought safety under the protection of landowners. At this time a new mode of taking the census was ordered, in which the people were classified into those from 1 to 3 years, then 3 to 10, then 10 to 17, and 17 to 60, after which age they were not taxed; the ratio of the land tax was also fixed. A census taken in 606 in this way gives an estimated population of 46,019,956 in all China; the frontiers, at this period, hardly reached to the Nan ling Mountains, and the author's explanation of the manner of carrying on some public works shows that even this sum did not include persons who were liable to be called on for personal service, while all officials, slaves, and beggars were omitted. Troubles arose again from these enforced works, and it was not till the advent to power of the Tang dynasty, in 618, that a regular enumeration was possible.

---

[1] The population of the Roman Empire at the same period is estimated at 85,000,000 by Merivale (Vol. IV., pp. 336–343), but the data are less complete than in China; he reckons the European provinces at 45,000,000, and the Asiatic and African colonies at the remainder, giving 27,000,000 to Asia Minor and Syria. The area of China, at this time, was less than Rome by about one-fourth.

This family reigned 287 years, and Ma Twan-lin gives fifteen returns of the population up to 841. They show great variations, some of them difficult to explain even by omitting or supplying large classes of the inhabitants. The one most carefully taken was in A.D. 754, and gives an estimated total of about seventy millions for the whole Empire, which, though nearly the same as that in the Han dynasty in A.D. 2, extended over a far greater area, even to the whole southern seaboard. In addition to former enumerated classes, many thousands of priests were passed by in this census.

The years of anarchy following the Tang, till A.D. 976, when the Sung dynasty obtained possession, caused their usual effect. Its first census gives only about sixteen millions of taxable population that year, when its authority was not firmly assured; but in 1021 the returns rise to 43,388,380, and thence gradually increase to 100,095,250 in 1102, just before the provinces north of the Yellow River, by far the most fertile and loyal, were lost. The last enumeration, in 1223, while Ma Twan-lin was living, places the returns in the southern provinces at 63,304,000; this was fifty years before Kublai khan conquered the Empire. Our author gives some details concerning the classes included in the census during his own lifetime, which prove to a reasonable mind that the real number of mouths living on the land was, if anything, higher than the estimates. In 1290, the Mongol Emperor published his enumeration, placing the taxable population at 58,834,711, "not counting those who had fled to the mountains and lakes, or who had joined the rebels." This was not long after his ruthless hand had almost depopulated vast regions in the northern provinces, before he could quiet them.

In the continuation of Ma Twan-lin's *Researches*, there are sixteen censuses given for the Ming dynasty between 1381 and 1580; the lowest figure is 46,800,000, in 1506, and the highest, 66,590,000, in 1412, the average for the two centuries being 56,715,360 inhabitants. One of its compilers declares that he cannot reconcile their great discrepancies, and throws doubts on their totals from his inability to learn the mode of enumeration. Three are given for three consecutive years (1402–1404), the difference between the extremes of which amounts to sixteen millions, but they were all taken when Yungloh was fighting Kienwăn, his nephew, at Nanking, and settling himself at Peking as Emperor, during which years large districts could not possibly have been counted.

Before entering upon a careful examination of this question, it will be well to bring together the various estimates taken of the population during the present dynasty. The details given in the table on page 264 have been taken from the best sources, and are as good as the people themselves possess.

Besides these detailed accounts, there have been several aggregates of the whole country given by other native writers than Ma Twan-lin, and some by foreigners, professedly drawn from original sources, but who have not stated their authorities. The most trustworthy, together with those given in the other table, are here placed in chronological order.

	Reign of Monarch.		A.D.	Population.	Authorities.
1.	Hungwu,	13th year,	1381	59,850,000	Continuation of Ma Twan-lin. Ed. Biot, *Journal Asiatique*, 1836.
2.	Yungloh,	9th year,	1412	65,377,000	
3.	Wanleih,	7th year,	1580	60,692,000	
4.	Shunchí,	18th year,	1662	21,068,600	*General Statistics of the Empire;* Medhurst's *China*, p. 53.
5.	Kanghí,	6th year,	1668	25,386,209	
6.	"	49th year,	1710 ?	23,312,200	
7.	"	49th year,	1710 ?	27,241,129	*Yih Tung Chí*, a statistical work; Morrison's *View of China*.
8.	"	50th year,	1711	28,605,716	*General Statistics; Chinese Repository*, Vol. I., p. 359.
9.	Kienlung,	1st year,	1736	125,046,245	*Mémoires sur les Chinois*, Tome VI., p. 277 ff.
10.	"	8th year,	1743	157,343,975	
11.	"	8th year,	1743	149,332,730	
12.	"	8th year,	1743	150,265,475	*Les Missionaires*, De Guignes, Tome III., p. 67.
13.	"	18th year,	1753	103,050,060	*General Statistics; Chinese Repository*, Vol. I., p. 359.
14.	"	25th year,	1760 ?	143,125,225	*Yih Tung Chi*, a statistical work; Morrison's *View of China*.
15.	"	25th year,	1760 ?	203,916,477	*Mémoires sur les Chinois*, Tome VI.
16.	"	26th year,	1761	205,293,053	De Guignes, Tome III., p. 72.
17.	"	27th year,	1762	198,214,553	Allerstein; Grosier; De Guignes, Tome III., p. 67.
18.	"	55th year.	1790	155,249,897	"Z." of Berlin, in *Chinese Repository*, Vol. I., p. 361.
19.	"	57th year,	1792	307,467,200	*General Statistics;* Dr. Morrison, Anglo-Chinese Coll. Report, 1829.
20.	"	57th year,	1792	333,000,000	Statement made to Lord Macartney.
21.	Kiaking,	17th year,	1812	362,467,183	*General Statistics; Chinese Repository*, Vol. I., p. 359.
22.	Tungchí,	8th year,	1868	404,946,514	Vassilivitch.
23.	Kwangsü,	7th year,	1881	380,000,000	*Chinese Custom's Reports.*

Seven of these censuses, viz., the 7th, 8th, 12th, 13th, 17th, 20th, 21st and 23d, are given in detail in the following table.

TABLE OF THE DIFFERENT CENSUSES OF THE EIGHTEEN PROVINCES.

PROVINCES.	Area in English square miles.	Aver. population to a sq. m. in 1812.	Census in 1710, or before.	Census of 1711.	Census of 1753.	Last Census of 1812.	Estimate in 1792, given Macartney.	Census in 1762 by Allerstein.	Census of 1743, from De Guignes.	*Almanac de Gotha*, 1882, taken from Chinese Customs' Reports.	Revenue in taels of $1.33 each.
Chihli	58,949	475	3,260,075	3,274,870	9,374,217	27,990,871	38,000,000	15,222,940	16,702,765	28,000,000	3,942,000
Shantung	65,104	444	....	2,278,595	12,769,872	28,958,764	24,000,000	25,180,734	12,159,680	29,000,000	6,344,000
Shansi	55,268	252	1,792,329	1,727,144	5,162,351	14,004,210	27,000,000	9,768,189	8,969,475	17,056,925	6,313,000
Honan	65,104	420	2,005,088	3,094,150	7,114,346	23,037,171	25,000,000	16,332,507	12,637,280	29,069,771	5,651,008
Kiangsu.........	44,500	850	3,917,707	2,656,465	12,618,987	37,843,501	32,000,000	23,161,409	26,766,365	37,800,000	11,738,000
Nganhwui.......	48,461	705	1,350,131	1,357,829	12,435,361	34,168,059		22,761,030		34,200,000	
Kiangsi	72,176	320	5,528,499	2,172,587	5,055,251	23,046,999	19,000,000	11,006,640	6,681,350	23,000,000	3,744,000
Chehkiang	39,150	671	2,710,649	2,710,312	8,662,808	26,256,784	21,000,000	15,429,690	15,623,990	26,300,000	5,856,000
Fuhkien.........	53,480	276	1,468,145	706,311	4,710,399	14,777,410	15,000,000	8,063,671	7,643,035	14,800,000	2,344,000
Hupeh	70,450	389	469,927	433,943	4,568,860	27,370,098	14,000,000	8,080,603	4,264,850	27,400,000	2,091,000
Hunan	74,320	251	375,782	335,034	4,336,332	18,652,507	13,000,000	8,829,320		20,048,969	1,905,000
Shensi...........	67,400	153	240,809	2,150,696	3,851,043	10,207,256	18,000,000	7,287,443	14,804,035	10,309,769	3,042,000
Kansuh	86,608	175	311,972	368,525	2,133,222	15,193,125	12,000,000	7,812,014		9,285,377	563.000
Sz'chuen	166,800	128	144,154	3,802,689	1,368,496	21,435,678	27,000,000	2,782,976	15,181,710	35,000,000	2,968,000
Kwangtung......	79,456	241	1,148,918	1,142,747	3,969,248	19,174,030	21,000,000	6,797,597	6,006,600	19,200,000	193,000
Kwangsi	78,250	93	205,995	210,674	1,975,619	7,313,895	10,000.000	3,947,414	1,143,450	8,121,327	794,000
Kweichau	64,554	82	51,089	37,731	1,718,848	5,288,219	9,000,000	3,402,722	255,445	5,679,128	185,000
Yunnan	107,969	51	2,255,666	145,414	1,003,058	5,561,320	8.000,000	2,078,802	1,189,825	5,823,670	432,000
Shingking.......	......	..	· 4,194	....	221,742	2,167,286	....	668,852	235,620	....	....
	1,297,999	268	27,241,129	28,605,716	103,050,060	362,447,183	333,000,000	198,214,553	150,265,475	380,000,000	58,097,000

The first three belong to the Ming dynasty, and are taken from a continuation of Ma Twan-lin's *Researches*, whence they were quoted in the *Mirror of History*, without their details. During the Ming dynasty, a portion of the country now called the Eighteen Provinces, was not under the control of Hungwu and his descendants. The wars with the Japanese, and with tribes on the north and west, together with the civil wars and struggles between the Chinese themselves, and with the Nü-chí in Manchuria, must have somewhat decreased the population.

The first census of 1662 (No. 4), is incidentally mentioned by Kienlung in 1791, as having been taken at that time, from his making some observations upon the increase of the population and comparing the early censuses with the one he had recently ordered. This sum of 21,068,600 does not, however, include all the inhabitants of China at that date; for the Manchus commenced their sway in 1644, and did not exercise full authority over all the provinces much before 1700; Canton was taken in 1650, Formosa in 1683.

The census of 1668 (No. 5), shows a little increase over that of 1662, but is likewise confined to the conquered portions; and in those provinces which had been subdued, there were extensive tracts which had been almost depopulated at the conquest. Any one who reads the recitals of Semedo, Martini, Trigautius, and others, concerning the massacres and destruction of life both by the Manchus and by Chinese bandits, between 1630 and 1650, will feel no loss in accounting for the diminution of numbers, down to 1710. But the chief explanation of the decrease from sixty to twenty-seven millions is to be found in the object of taking the census, viz., to levy a poll-tax, and get at the number of men fit for the army—two reasons for most men to avoid the registration.

The census of 1711 (No. 8), is the first one on record which bears the appearance of credibility, when its several parts are compared with each other. The dates of the preceding (Nos. 6 and 7), are rather uncertain; the last was extracted by Dr. Morrison from a book published in 1790, and he thought it was probably taken as early as 1650, though that is unlikely. The other is given by Dr. Medhurst without any explanation, and their great disparity leads us to think that both are dated wrongly. The census of 1711 is much more consistent in itself, though there are some reasons for supposing that neither did it include all the population then in China. The census was still taken for enrolment in the army, and to levy a capitation tax upon all males between the ages of sixteen and sixty. But this tax and registration were evaded and resisted by the indignant Chinese, who had never been chronicled in this fashion by their own princes; the Emperor Kanghí, therefore, abolished the capitation tax. It was not till about this time that the Manchus had subdued and pacified the southern provinces, and it is not improbable that this census, and the survey taken by the Jesuits, were among their acts of sovereignty. Finding the people unwilling to be registered, the poll tax was merged in the land tax, and no census ordered during the reign of Yungching, till Kienlung revived it in order to have some guide in apportioning relief during seasons of distress and scarcity, establishing granaries, and aiding the police in their duties. Many, therefore, who would do all in their power to prevent their names being taken, when they were liable to be taxed or called on to do military service, could have no objection to come forward, when the design of the census was to benefit themselves. It matters very little, however, for what object the census was taken, if there is reason to believe it to have been accurate. It might indeed act as a stimulus to multiply names and figures whom there were no people to represent, as the principle of paying the marshals a percentage on the numbers they reported did in some parts of New York State in 1840.

The three next numbers (9, 10, and 11), are taken from De Guignes, who quotes Amiot, but gives no Chinese authorities. The last is given in full by De Guignes, and both this and that of Allerstein, dated twenty years after, are introduced into the table. There are some discrepancies between these two and the census of 1753, taken from the *General Statistics*, which cannot easily be reconciled. The internal evidence is in favor of the latter, over the census of 1743; it is taken from a new edition of the *Ta Tsing Hwui Tien*, or 'General Statistics of the Empire,' and the increase during the forty-two years which had elapsed since the last census is regular in all the provinces, with the exception of Shantung and Kiangnan. The extraordinary fertility of these provinces would easily induce immigration, while in the war of conquest, their populousness and wealth attracted the armies of the Manchus, and the destruction of life was disproportionably great. The smaller numbers given to the western and southern provinces correspond moreover to the opposition experienced in those regions. On the whole, the census taken in 1753 compares very well with that of 1711, and both of them bear an aspect of verity, which does not belong to the table of 1743 quoted by De Guignes.

From 1711 to 1753, the population doubled itself in about twenty-two years, premising that the whole country was faithfully registered at the first census. For instance, the province of Kweichau, in 1711, presents on the average a mere fraction of a little more than a single person to two square miles; while in 1753 it had increased in the unexampled ratio of three to a square mile, which is doubling its population every seven years; Kwangtung, Kwangsí, and Kansuh (all of them containing to this day, partially subdued tribes), had also multiplied their numbers in nearly the same proportion, owing in great measure, probably, to the more extended census than to the mere increase of population.

The amounts for 1736, three of 1743, and those of 1760, 1761, and 1762 (Nos. 9, 10, 11, 12, 15, 16, and 17), are all extracted from De Guignes, who took them from the *Mémoires sur les Chinois.* The last, that of 1762, is given in detail in the table. The discrepancy of sixty millions between that given by Amiot for 1760, and that by Dr. Morrison for the same year, is owing, there can be little doubt, to foreigners, and not to an error of the Chinese. The work from which Dr. Morrison extracted his estimate for that year was published in 1790, but the census was taken between 1760 and 1765. The same work contains the census of 1711 (No. 8), quoted by him, and there is good cause for believing that Amiot's or Grosier's estimate of 157,343,975 for 1743, is the very same census, he having multiplied the number 28,605,716 by five, supposing them to have been families and not individuals. The three ascribed to the year 1743, are probably all derived from the same native authorities by different individuals.

The three dated in 1760, 1761, and 1762, are harmonious with each other; but if they are taken, those of 1753 and 1760, extracted from the *Yih Tung Chí* by Dr. Morrison, must be rejected, which are far more reasonable, and correspond better with the preceding one of 1711. It may be remarked, that by reckoning five persons to a family in calculating the census of 1753, as Amiot does for 1743, the population would be 189,223,820 instead of 103,050,060, as given in the table. This explains the apparent decrease of fifty millions. All the discrepancies between these various tables and censuses must not be charged upon the Chinese, since it is by no means easy to ascertain their modes of taking the census and their use of terms. In the tables, for example, they employ the phrase *jin-ting*, for a male over 15 years of age, as the integer; this has, then, to be multiplied by some factor of increase to get at the total population; and this last figure must be obtained elsewhere. It must not be overlooked that the object in taking a census being to calculate the probable revenue by enumerating the taxable persons, the margin of error and deficiency depends on the peace of the state at the time, and not chiefly on the estimate of five or more to a household.

The amount for 1736 corresponds sufficiently closely with that for 1743; and reckoning the same number of persons in a family in 1753, that tallies well enough with those for 1760, 1761, and 1762, the whole showing a gradual increase for twenty-five years. But all of them, except that of 1753, are probably rated too high. That for 1762 (No. 17), has been justly considered as one of the most authentic.

The amount given by "Z." of Berlin (No. 18), of 155⅛ millions for 1790 is quoted in the *Chinese Repository*, but the writer states no authorities, was probably never in China, and as it appears at present, is undeserving the least notice. That given by Dr. Morrison for 1792 (No. 19), the year before Lord Macartney's embassy, is quoted from an edition of that date, but probably was really taken in 1765 or thereabouts, but he did not publish it in detail.[1] It is probably much nearer the truth than the amount of 333 millions by the commissioner Chau to the English ambassador. This estimate has had much more respect paid to it as an authentic document than it deserved. The Chinese commissioner would naturally wish to exalt his country in the eyes of its far-travelled visitors, and not having the official returns to refer to, would not be likely to state them less than they were. He gave the population of the provinces in round numbers, perhaps altogether from his own memory, aided by those of his attendant clerks, with the impression that his hearers would never be able to refer to the original native authorities.

The next one quoted (No. 21) is the most satisfactory of all the censuses in Chinese works, and was considered by both the Morrisons and by Dr. Bridgman, editor of the *Chinese Repository*, as "the most accurate that has yet been given of the population."

In questions of this nature, one well authenticated table is worth a score of doubtful origin. It has been shown how apocryphal are many of the statements given in foreign books, but with the census of 1812, the source of error which is chiefly to be guarded against is the average given to a family. This is done by the Chinese themselves on no uniform plan, and it may be the case that the estimate of individuals from the number of families is made in separate towns, from an intimate acquaintance with the particular district, which would be less liable to error than a general average. The number of families given in the census of 1753, is 37,785,552, which is more than one-third of the population.

The four censuses which deserve the most credit, so far as the sources are considered, are those of 1711, 1753, 1792, and 1812 (*i.e.*, Nos. 8, 13, 19, and 21); these, when compared, show the following rate of increase:

From 1711 to 1753, the population increased 74,222,602, which was an annual advance of 1,764,824 inhabitants, or a

---

[1] Sir G. Staunton, *Embassy to China*, Vol. II., Appendix, p. 615: "Table of the Population and Extent of China proper, within the Great Wall. Taken in round numbers from the Statements of Chow ta-zhin."

little more than six per cent. per annum for forty-two years. This high rate, it must be remembered, does not take into account the more thorough subjugation of the south and west at the later date, when the Manchus could safely enrol large districts, where in 1711 they would have found so much difficulty that they would not have attempted it.

From 1753 to 1792, the increase was 104,636,882, or an annual advance of 2,682,997 inhabitants, or about 2½ per cent. per annum for thirty-nine years. During this period, the country enjoyed almost uninterrupted peace under the vigorous sway of Kienlung, and the unsettled regions of the south and west rapidly filled up.

From 1792 to 1812, the increase was 54,126,679, or an annual advance of 2,706,333—not quite one per cent. per annum —for twenty years. At the same rate of progress the present population would amount to over 450,000,000, and this might have been the case had not the Tai-ping rebellion reduced the numbers. An enumeration (No. 22), was published by the Russian Professor of Chinese Vassilivitch in 1868 as a translation from official documents. Foreigners have had greater opportunities for travel through the country, between the years 1840 to 1880, and have ascertained the enormous depopulation in some places caused by wars, short supplies of food in consequence of scarcity of laborers, famines, or brigandage, each adding its own power of destruction at different places and times. The conclusion will not completely satisfy any inquirer, but the population of the Empire cannot now reasonably be estimated as high as the census of 1812, by at least twenty-five millions. The last in the list of these censuses (No. 23), is added as an example of the efforts of intelligent persons residing in China to come to a definite and independent conclusion on this point from such data as they can obtain. The Imperial Customs' Service has been able to command the best native assistance in their researches, and the table of population given above from the *Gotha Almanac* is the summary of what has been ascertained. The population of extra-provincial China is really unknown at present. Manchuria is put down at twelve millions by one author, and three or four millions, by another, without any official authority for either; and all those vast regions in Ílí and Tibet may easily be set down at from twelve to fifteen millions. To sum up, one must confess that if the Chinese censuses are worth but little, compared with those taken in European states, they are better than the guesses of foreigners who have never been in the country, or who have travelled only partially in it.

The Chinese are doubtless one of the most conceited nations on the earth, but with all their vanity, they have never bethought themselves of rating their population twenty-five or thirty per cent. higher than they suppose it to be, for the purpose of exalting themselves in the eyes of foreigners or in their own. Except in one case none of the estimates were presented to, or intended to be known by foreigners. The distances in *li* between places given in Chinese itineraries correspond very well with the real distances; the number of districts, towns, and villages in the departments and provinces, as stated in their local and general topographical works, agree with the actual examination, so far as it can be made: why should their censuses be charged with gross error, when, however much we may doubt them, we cannot disprove them, and the weight of evidence derived from actual observation rather confirms them than otherwise; and while their account of towns, villages, distances, etc., are unhesitatingly adopted until better can be obtained? Some discrepancies in the various tables are ascribable to foreigners, and some of the censuses are incomplete, or the year cannot be precisely fixed, both of which vitiate the deductions made from them as to the rate of increase. Some reasons for believing that the highest population ascribed to the Chinese Empire is not greater than the country can support, will first be stated, and the objections against receiving the censuses then considered.[1]

[1] This interesting subject can then be left with the reader, who will find further remarks in Medhurst's *China*, De Guignes' *Voyages à Peking*, The Missionaries, in Tomes VI. and VIII. of *Mémoires*, Ed. Biot, in *Journal Asiatique* for 1836. *The Numerical Relations of the Population of China during the* 4,000 *Years of its Historical Existence; or the Rise and Fall of the Chinese Population*, by T. Sacharoff. Translated into English by the Rev. W. Lobscheid, Hongkong, 1862. *Notes and Queries on China and Japan*, Vol. II., pp. 88, 103, and 117.

The area of the Eighteen Provinces is rather imperfectly given at 1,348,870 square miles, and the average population, therefore, for the whole, in 1812, was 268 persons on every square mile; that of the nine eastern provinces in and near the Great Plain, comprising 502,192 square miles, or two-fifths of the whole, is 458 persons, and the nine southern and western provinces, constituting the other three-fifths, is 154 to a square mile. The surface and fertility of the country in these two portions differ so greatly, as to lead one to look for results like these. The areas of some European states and their population, are added to assist in making a comparison with China, and coming to a clearer idea about their relative density.

States.	Area.	Population.	Average to sq. m.	Census of
France	204,092	36,905,788	182	December, 1876.
Germany	212,091	45,194,172	213	December, 1880.
Great Britain	121,608	35,246,562	289	April, 1881.
Italy	114,296	28,437,091	249	December, 1879.
Holland	20,497	4,060,580	198	December, 1880.
Spain	190,625	16,053,961	84	December, 1877.
Japan	160,474	34,338,479	213	1877.
Bengal	156,200	68,750,747	440	1881.

All these are regarded as well settled countries, but England and Bengal are the only ones which exceed that of China, taken as a whole, while none of them come up to the average of the eastern provinces. All of them, China included, fall far short, however, of the average population on a square mile of the kingdoms of Judah and Israel, in the reigns of Abijah and Jeroboam, if the 1,200,000 men brought into the field by them can be taken as a ratio of the whole number of inhabitants; or if the accounts given by Josephus of the density in his day are trustworthy. In estimating the capabilities of these European countries to support a dense population, allowances must be made for roads, pasture-lands, and parks of noblemen, all of which afford little or no food.

In England and Wales, there are nearly twenty-nine millions of acres under cultivation, seventeen millions of which are pasture-lands, and only ten millions devoted to grain and vegetables; the other two millions consist of fallow-ground, hop-beds, etc. One author estimates that in England 42 acres in a hundred, and in Ireland 64, are pastures—a little more than half of the whole. There are, then, on the average about two acres of land for the support of each individual, or rather less than this, if the land required for the food of horses be subtracted. It has been calculated that eight men can be fed on the same amount of land that one horse requires; and that four acres of pasture-land will furnish no more food for man than one of ploughed land. The introduction of railroads has superseded the use of horses to such an extent that it is estimated there are only 200,000 horses now in England, instead of a million in 1830. If, therefore, one-half the land appropriated to pasture should be devoted to grain, and no more horses and dogs raised than a million of acres could support, England and Wales could easily maintain a population of more than four hundred to a square mile, supposing them to be willing to live on what the land and water can furnish.

The Irish consume a greater proportion of vegetables than the English, even since the improvement by emigration after 1851; many of these live a beggarly life upon half an acre, and even less, and seldom taste animal food. The quantity of land under cultivation in Belgium is about fifteen-seventeenths of the whole, which gives an average of about two acres to each person, or the same as in England. In these two countries, the people consume more meat than in Ireland, and the amount of land occupied for pasturage is in nearly equal proportions in Belgium and England. In France, the average of cultivated land is $1\frac{2}{3}$ acre; in Holland, $1\frac{4}{5}$ acre to each person.

If the same proportion between the arable and uncultivated land exists in China as in England, namely one-fourth, there are about six hundred and fifty millions of acres under cultivation in China; and we are not left altogether to conjecture, for by a report made to Kienlung in 1745, it appears that the area of the land under cultivation was 595,598,221 acres; a subsequent calculation places it at 640,579,381 acres, which is almost the same proportion as in England. Estimating it at six hundred and fifty millions—for it has since increased rather than diminished—it gives one acre and four-fifths to every person, which is by no means a small supply for the Chinese, considering that there are no cultivated pastures or meadows.

In comparing the population of different countries, the manner of living and the articles of food in use, form such important elements of the calculation, in ascertaining whether the country be overstocked or not, that a mere tabular view of the number of persons on a square mile is an imperfect criterion of the amount of inhabitants the land would maintain if they consumed the same food, and lived in the same manner in all of them. Living as the Chinese, Hindus, Japanese, and other Asiatics do, chiefly upon vegetables, the country can hardly be said to maintain more than one-half or one-third as many people on a square mile as it might do, if their energies were developed to the same extent with those of the English or Belgians. The population of these eastern regions has been repressed by the combined influences of ignorance, insecurity of life and property, religious prejudices, vice, and wars, so that the land has never maintained as many inhabitants as one would have otherwise reasonably expected therefrom.

Nearly all the cultivated soil in China is employed in raising food for man. Woollen garments and leather are little used, while cotton and mulberry cultivation take up only a small proportion of the soil. There is not, so far as is known, a single acre of land sown with grass-seed, and therefore almost no human labor is devoted to raising food for animals, which will not also serve to sustain man. Horses are seldom used for pomp or war, for travelling or carrying burdens, but mules, camels, asses, and goats are employed for transportation and other purposes north of the Yangtsz' River. Horses are fed on cooked rice, bran, sorghum seed, pulse, oats, and grass cut along the banks of streams, or on hillsides. In the southern and eastern provinces, all animals are rare, the transport of goods and passengers being done by boats or by men. The natives make no use of butter, cheese, or milk, and the few cattle employed in agriculture easily gather a living on the waste ground around the villages. In the south, the buffalo is applied more than the ox to plough the rice fields, and the habits of this animal make it cheaper to keep him in good condition, while he can also do more work. The winter stock is grass cut upon the hills, straw, bean stalks, and vegetables. No wool being wanted for making cloth, flocks of sheep and goats are seldom seen—it may almost be said are unknown in the east and south.

No animal is reared cheaper than the hog; hatching and raising ducks affords employment to thousands of people; hundreds of these fowl gather their own food along the river shore, being easily attended by a single keeper. Geese and poultry are also cheaply reared. In fishing, which is carried on to an enormous extent, no pasture-grounds, no manuring, no barns, are needed, nor are taxes paid by the cultivator and consumer.

While the people get their animal food in these ways, its preparation takes away the least possible amount of cultivated soil. The space occupied for roads and pleasure-grounds is insignificant, but there is perhaps an amount appropriated for burial places quite equal to the area used for those purposes in European countries; it is, however, less valuable land, and much of it would be useless for culture, even if otherwise unoccupied. Graves are dug on hills, in ravines and copses, and wherever they will be retired and dry; or if in the ancestral field, they do not hinder the crop growing close around them. Moreover, it is very common to preserve the coffin in temples and cemeteries until it is decayed, partly in order to save the expense of a grave, and partly to worship the remains, or preserve them until gathered to their fathers, in their distant native places. They are often placed in the corners of the fields, or under precipices where they remain till dust returns to dust, and bones and wood both moulder away. These and other customs limit the consumption of land for graves much more than would be supposed, when one sees, as at Macao, almost as much space taken up by the dead for a grave as by the living for a hut. The necropolis of Canton occupies the hills north of the city, of which not one-fiftieth part could ever have been used for agriculture, but where cattle are allowed to graze, as much as if there were no tombs.

Under its genial and equable climate, more than three-fourths of the area of China Proper produces two crops annually. In Kwangtung, Kwangsí, and Fuhkien, two crops of rice are taken year after year from the low lands; while in the loess regions of the northwest, a three-fold return from the grain fields is annually looked for, if the rain-fall is not withheld. In the winter season, in the neighborhood of towns, a third crop of sweet potatoes, cabbages, turnips, or some other vegetable is grown. De Guignes estimates the returns of a rice crop at ten for one, which, with the vegetables, will give full twenty-five fold from an acre in a year; few parts, however, yield this increase. Little or no land lies fallow, for constant manuring and turning of the soil prevents the necessity of repose. The diligence exhibited in collecting and applying manure is well known, and if all this industry result in the production of two crops instead of one, it really doubles the area under cultivation, when its superficies are compared with those of other countries. If the amount of land which produces two crops be estimated at one-fourth of the whole (and it is perhaps as near one-third), the area of arable land in the provinces may be considered as representing a total of 812 millions of acres, or $2\frac{3}{4}$ acres to an individual. The land is not, however, cut up into such small farms as to prevent its being managed as well as the people know how to stock and cultivate it; manual labor is the chief dependence of the farmer, fewer cattle, carts, ploughs, and machines being employed than in other countries. In rice fields no animals are used after the wet land has received the shoots, transplanting, weeding, and reaping being done by men.

In no other country besides Japan is so much food derived from the water. Not only are the coasts, estuaries, rivers, and lakes, covered with fishing-boats of various sizes, which are provided with everything fitted for the capture of whatever lives in the waters, but the spawn of fish is collected and reared. Rice fields are often converted into pools in the winter season, and stocked with fish; and the tanks dug for irrigation usually contain fish. By all these means, an immense supply of food is obtained at a cheap rate, which is eaten fresh or preserved with or without salt, and sent over the Empire, at a cost which places it within the reach of all above beggary. Other articles of food, both animal and vegetable, such as dogs, game, worms, spring greens, tripang, leaves, etc., do indeed compose part of their meals, but it is comparatively an inconsiderable fraction, and need not enter into the calculation. Enough has been stated to show that the land is abundantly able to support the population ascribed to it, even with all the drawbacks known to exist; and that, taking the highest estimate to be true, and considering the mode of living, the average population on a square mile in China is less than in several European countries.

The political and social causes which tend to multiply the inhabitants are numerous and powerful. The failure of male posterity to continue the succession of the family, and worship at the tombs of parents, is considered by all classes as one of the most afflictive misfortunes of life; the laws allow unlimited facilities of adoption, and secure the rights of those taken into the family in this way. The custom of betrothing children, and the obligation society imposes upon the youth when arrived at maturity, to fulfil the contracts entered into by their parents, acts favorably to the establishment of families and the nurture of children, and restricts polygamy. Parents desire children for a support in old age, as there is no legal or benevolent provision for aged poverty, and public opinion stigmatizes the man who allows his aged or infirm parents to suffer when he can help them. The law requires the owners of domestic slaves to provide husbands for their females, and prohibits the involuntary or forcible separation of husband and wife, or parents and children, when the latter are of tender age. All these causes and influences tend to increase population, and equalize the consumption and use of property more, perhaps, than in any other land.

The custom of families remaining together tends to the same result. The local importance of a large family in the country is weakened by its male members removing to town, or emigrating; consequently, the patriarch of three or four generations endeavors to retain his sons and grandsons around him, their houses joining his, and they and their families forming a social, united company. Such cases as those mentioned in the

Sacred Commands are of course rare, where nine generations of the family of Chang Kung-i inhabited one house, or of Chin, at whose table seven hundred mouths were daily fed,[1] but it is the tendency of society. This remark does not indicate that great landed proprietors exist, whose hereditary estates are secured by entail to the great injury of the state, as in Great Britain, for the farms are generally small and cultivated by the owner or on the metayer system. Families are supported on a more economical plan, the claims of kindred are better enforced, the land is cultivated with more care, and the local importance of the family perpetuated. This is, however, a very different system from that advocated by Fourier in France, or Greeley in America, for these little communities are placed under one natural head, whose authority is acknowledged and upheld, and his indignation feared. Workmen of the same profession form unions, each person contributing a certain sum on the promise of assistance when sick or disabled, and this custom prevents and alleviates a vast amount of poverty.

The obstacles put in the way of emigrating beyond sea, both in law and prejudice, operate to deter respectable persons from leaving their native land. Necessity has made the law a dead letter, and thousands annually leave their homes. No better evidence of the dense population can be offered to those acquainted with Chinese feelings and character, than the extent of emigration. "What stronger proof," observes Medhurst, "of the dense population of China could be afforded than the fact, that emigration is going on in spite of restrictions and disabilities, from a country where learning and civilization reign, and where all the dearest interests and prejudices of the emigrants are found, to lands like Burmah, Siam, Cambodia, Tibet, Manchuria, and the Indian Archipelago, where comparative ignorance and barbarity prevail, and where the extremes of a tropical or frozen region are to be exchanged for a mild and temperate climate? Added to this consideration, that not a single female is permitted or ventures to leave the country, when consequently, all the tender attachments that

[1] *Sacred Edict*, pp. 51, 60.

bind heart to heart must be burst asunder, and, perhaps, forever."[1]

Moreover, if they return with wealth enough to live upon, they are liable to the vexatious extortions of needy relatives, sharpers, and police, who have a handle for their fleecing whip in the law against leaving the country;[2] although this clause has been neutralized by subsequent acts, and is not in force, the power of public opinion is against going. A case occurred in 1832, at Canton, where the son of a Chinese living in Calcutta, who had been sent home by his parent with his mother, to perform the usual ceremonies in the ancestral hall, was seized by his uncle as he was about to be married, on the pretext that his father had unequally divided the paternal inheritance; he was obliged to pay a thousand dollars to free himself. Soon after his marriage, a few sharpers laid hold of him and bore him away in a sedan, as he was walking near his house, but his cries attracted the police, who carried them all to the magistrates, where he was liberated—after being obliged to fee his deliverers.[3] Another case occurred in Macao in 1838. A man had been living several years in Singapore as a merchant, and when he settled in Macao still kept up an interest in the trade with that place. Accounts of his great wealth became rumored abroad, and he was seriously annoyed by relatives. One night, a number of thieves, dressed like police-runners, came to his house to search for opium, and their boisterous manner terrified him to such a degree, that in order to escape them he jumped from the terrace upon the hard gravelled court-yard, and broke his leg, of which he shortly afterward died. A third case is mentioned, where the returned emigrants, consisting of a man and his wife, who was a Malay, and two children, were rescued from extortion, when before the magistrate, by the kindness of his wife and mother, who wished to see the foreign woman.[4] Such instances are now unknown,

---

[1] *China: Its State and Prospects*, p. 42.

[2] *Ta Tsing Leu Lee; being the Fundamental Laws, etc., of the Penal Code of China*, by Sir G. T. Staunton, Bart, London, 1810. Section CCXXV.

[3] *Chinese Repository*, Vol. I., p. 332.

[4] *Ibid.*, Vol. VII., p. 503; Vol. II., p. 161.

owing to the increase of emigration; they were, indeed, never numerically great, on account of the small number of those who came back.

The anxiety of the government to provide stores of food for times of scarcity, shows rather its fear of the disastrous results following a short crop—such as the gathering of clamorous crowds of starving poor, the increase of bandits and disorganization of society—than any peculiar care of the rulers, or that these storehouses really supply deficiencies. The evil consequences resulting from an overgrown population are experienced in one or another part of the provinces almost every year; and drought, inundations, locusts, mildew, or other natural causes, often give rise to insurrections and disturbances. There can be no doubt, however, that, without adding a single acre to the area of arable land, these evils would be materially alleviated, if the intercommunication of traders and their goods, between distant parts of the country, were more frequent, speedy, and safe; but this is not likely to be the case until both rulers and ruled make greater advances in just government, science, obedience, and regard for each other's right.

It would be a satisfaction if foreigners could verify any part of the census. But this is, at present, impossible. They cannot examine the records in the office of the Board of Revenue, nor can they ascertain the population in a given district from the archives in the hands of the local authorities, or the mode of taking it. Neither can they go through a village or town to count the number of houses and their inhabitants, and calculate from actual examination of a few parts what the whole would be. Wherever foreigners have journeyed, there has appeared much the same succession of waste land, hilly regions, cultivated plains, and wooded heights, as in other countries, with an abundance of people, but not more than the land could support, if properly tilled.

The people are grouped into hamlets and villages, under the control of village elders and officers. In the district of Nanhai, which forms the western part of the city of Canton, and the surrounding country for more than a hundred square miles, there are one hundred and eighty *hiang* or villages; the population of each *hiang* varies from two hundred and upwards to one hundred thousand, but ordinarily ranges between three hundred and thirty-five hundred. If each of the eighty-eight districts in the province of Kwangtung contains the same number of *hiang*, there will be, including the district towns, 15,928 villages, towns, and cities in all, with an average population of twelve hundred inhabitants to each. From the top of the hills on Dane's Island, at Whampoa, thirty-six towns and villages can be counted, of which Canton is one; and four of these contain from twelve to fifteen hundred houses. The whole district of Hiangshan, in which Macao lies, is also well covered with villages, though their exact number is not known. The island of Amoy contains more than fourscore villages and towns, and this island forms only a part of the district of Tung-ngan. The banks of the river leading from Amoy up to Changchau fu, are likewise well peopled. The environs of Ningpo and Shanghai are closely settled, though that is no more than one always expects near large cities, where the demand for food in the city itself causes the vicinity to be well peopled and tilled. In a notice of an irruption of the sea in 1819, along the coast of Shantung, it was reported that a hundred and forty villages were laid under water.

Marco Polo describes the mode followed in the days of Kublai khan: "It is the custom for every burgess of the city, and in fact for every description of person in it, to write over his door his own name, the name of his wife, and those of his children, his slaves, and all the inmates of his house, and also the number of animals that he keeps. And if any one dies in the house, then the name of that person is erased, and if a child is born its name is added. So in this way the sovereign is able to know exactly the population of the city. And this is the practice throughout all Manzi and Cathay."[1] This custom was observed long before the Mongol conquest, and is followed at present; so that it is perhaps easier to take a census in China than in most European countries.

The law upon this subject is contained in Secs. LXXV. and

[1] Yule's *Marco Polo*, Vol. II., p. 152.

LXXVI. of the statutes.[1] It enacts various penalties for not registering the members of a family, and its provisions all go to show that the people are desirous rather of evading the census than of exaggerating it. When a family has omitted to make any entry, the head of it is liable to be punished with one hundred blows if he is a freeholder, and with eighty if he is not. If the master of a family has among his household another distinct family whom he omits to register, the punishment is the same as in the last clause, with a modification, according as the unregistered persons and family are relatives or strangers. Persons in government employ omitting to register their families, are less severely punished. A master of family failing to register all the males in his household who are liable to public service, shall be punished with from sixty to one hundred blows, according to the demerits of the offence; this clause was in effect repealed, when the land tax was substituted for the capitation tax. Omissions, from neglect or inadvertency to register all the individuals and families in a village or town, on the part of the headmen or government clerks, are punishable with different degrees of severity. All persons whatsoever are to be registered according to their accustomed occupations or professions, whether civil or military, whether couriers, artisans, physicians, astrologers, laborers, musicians, or of any other denomination whatever; and subterfuges in representing one's self as belonging to a profession not liable to public service, are visited as usual with the bamboo; persons falsely describing themselves as belonging to the army, in order to evade public service, are banished as well as beaten. From these clauses it is seen that the Manchus have extended the enumeration to classes which were exempted in the Han, Tang, and other dynasties, and thus come nearer to the actual population.

"In the Chinese government," observes Dr. Morrison, "there appears great regularity and system. Every district has its appropriate officers, every street its constable, and every ten houses their tything man. Thus they have all the requisite means of ascertaining the population with considerable accu-

---

[1] *Penal Code*, p. 79, Staunton's translation.

racy. Every family is required to have a board always hanging up in the house, and ready for the inspection of authorized officers, on which the names of all persons, men, women, and children, in the house are inscribed. This board is called *mun-pai* or 'door-tablet,' because when there are women and children within, the officers are expected to take the account from the board at the door. Were all the inmates of a family faithfully inserted, the amount of the population would, of course, be ascertained with great accuracy. But it is said that names are sometimes omitted through neglect or design; others think that the account of persons given in is generally correct." The door-tablets are sometimes pasted on the door, thus serving as a kind of door-plate; in these cases correctness of enumeration is readily secured, for the neighbors are likely to know if the record is below the truth, and the householder is not likely to exaggerate the taxable inmates under his roof. I have read these *mun-pai* on the doors of a long row of houses; they were printed blanks filled in, and then pasted outside for the *pao-kiah* or tithing man to examine. Both Dr. Morrison and his son, than whom no one has had better opportunities to know the true state of the case, or been more desirous of dealing fairly with the Chinese, regarded the censuses given in the *General Statistics* as more trustworthy than any other documents available.

In conclusion, it may be asked, are the results of the enumeration of the people, as contained in the statistical works published by the government, to be rejected or doubted, therefore, because the Chinese officers do not wish to ascertain the exact population; or because they are not capable of doing it; or, lastly, because they wish to impose upon foreign powers by an arithmetical array of millions they do not possess? The question seems to hang upon this trilemma. It is acknowledged that they falsify or garble statements in a manner calculated to throw doubt upon everything they write, as in the reports of victories and battles sent to the Emperor, in the memorials upon the opium trade, in their descriptions of natural objects in books of medicine, and in many other things. But the question is as applicable to China as to France: is the estimated population of France in 1801 to be called in question, because the *Moniteur* gave false accounts of Napoleon's battles in 1813? It would be a strange combination of conceit and folly, for a ministry composed of men able to carry on all the details of a complicated government like that of China, to systematically exaggerate the population, and then proceed, for more than a century, with taxation, disbursements, and official appointments, founded upon these censuses. Somebody at least must know them to be worthless, and the proof that they were so, must, one would think, ere long be apparent. The provinces and departments have been divided and subdivided since the Jesuits made their survey, because they were becoming too densely settled for the same officers to rule over them.

Still less will any one assert that the Chinese are not capable of taking as accurate a census as they are of measuring distances, or laying out districts and townships. Errors may be found in the former as well as in the latter, and doubtless are so; for it is not contended that the four censuses of 1711, 1753, 1792, and 1812 are as accurate as those now taken in England, France, or the United States, but that they are the best data extant, and that if they are rejected we leave tolerable evidence and take up with that which is doubtful and suppositive. The censuses taken in China since the Christian era are, on the whole, more satisfactory than those of all other nations put together up to the Reformation, and further careful research will no doubt increase our respect for them.

Ere long we may be able to traverse a census in its details of record and deduction, and thus satisfy a reasonable curiosity, especially as to the last reported total after the carnage of the rebellion. On the other hand, it may be stated that in the last census, the entire population of Manchuria, Koko-nor, Îlí, and Mongolia, is estimated at only 2,167,286 persons, and nearly all the inhabitants of those vast regions are subject to the Emperor. The population of Tibet is not included in any census, its people not being taxable. It is doubtful if an enumeration of any part of the extra provincial territory has ever been taken, inasmuch as the Mongol tribes, and still less the Usbeck or other Moslem races, are unused to such a thing, and would not be numbered. Yet, the Chinese cannot be charged with exaggeration, when good judges, as Klaproth and others, reckon the whole at between six and seven millions; and Khoten alone, one author states, has three and a half millions. No writer of importance estimates the inhabitants of these regions as high as thirty millions—as does R. Mont. Martin—which would be more than ten to a square mile, excluding Gobi; while Siberia (though not so well peopled) has only 3,611,300 persons on an area of 2,649,600 square miles, or $1\frac{1}{3}$ to each square mile.

The reasons just given why the Chinese desire posterity are not all those which have favored national increase. The uninterrupted peace which the country enjoyed between the years 1700 and 1850 operated to greatly develop its resources. Every encouragement has been given to all classes to multiply and fill the land. Polygamy, slavery, and prostitution, three social evils which check increase, have been circumscribed in their effects. Early betrothment and poverty do much to prevent the first; female slaves can be and are usually married; while public prostitution is reduced by a separation of the sexes and early marriages. No fears of overpassing the supply of food restrain the people from rearing families, though the Emperor Kienlung issued a proclamation in 1793, calling upon all ranks of his subjects to economize the gifts of heaven, lest, erelong, the people exceed the means of subsistence.

It is difficult to see what this or that reason or objection has to do with the subject, except where the laws of population are set at defiance, which is not the case in China. Food and work, peace and security, climate and fertile soil, not universities or steamboats, are the encouragements needed for the multiplication of mankind; though they do not have that effect in all countries (as in Mexico and Brazil), it is no reason why they should not in others. There are grounds for believing that not more than two-thirds of the whole population of China were included in the census of 1711, but that allowance cannot be made for Ireland in 1785; and consequently, her annual percentage of increase, up to 1841, would then be greater than China, during the forty-two years ending with 1753. McCulloch quotes De Guignes approvingly, but the Frenchman takes the rough estimate of 333,000,000 given to Macartney, which is less trustworthy than that of 307,467,200, and compares it with Grosier's of 157,343,975, which is certainly wrong through his misinterpretation. De Guignes proceeds from the data in his possession in 1802 (which were less than those now available), and from his own observations in travelling through the country in 1796, to show the improbability of the estimated population. But the observations made in journeys, taken as were those of the English and Dutch embassies, though they passed through some of the best provinces, cannot be regarded as good evidence against official statistics.

Would any one suppose, in travelling from Boston to Chatham, and then from Albany to Buffalo, along the railroad, that Massachusetts contained, in 1870, exactly double the population on a square mile of New York? So, in going from Peking to Canton, the judgment which six intelligent travellers might form of the population of China could easily be found to differ by one-half. De Guignes says, after comparing China with Holland and France, "All these reasons clearly demonstrate that the population of China does not exceed that of other countries;" and such is in truth the case, if the kind of food, number of crops, and materials of dress be taken into account. His remarks on the population and productiveness of the country are, like his whole work, replete with good sense and candor; but some of his deductions would have been different, had he been in possession of all the data since obtained.[1] The discrepancies between the different censuses have been usually considered a strong internal evidence against them, and they should receive due consideration. The really difficult point is to fix the percentage that must be allowed for the classes not included as taxable, and the power of the government to enumerate those who wished to avoid a census and the subsequent taxation.

After all these reasons for receiving the total of 1812 as the best one, there are, on the other hand, two principal objections against taking the Chinese census as altogether trustworthy. The first is the enormous averages of 850, 705, and 671 inhab-

---

[1] *Voyages à Peking*, Tome III., pp. 55–86.

itants on a square mile, severally apportioned to Kiangsu, Nganhwui, and Chehkiang, or, what is perhaps a fairer calculation, of 458 persons to the nine eastern provinces. Whatever amount of circumstantial evidence may be brought forward in confirmation of the census as a whole, and explanation of the mode of taking it, a more positive proof seems to be necessary before giving implicit credence to this result. Such a population on such an extensive area is marvellous, notwithstanding the fertility of the soil, facilities of navigation, and salubrity of the climate of these regions, although acknowledged to be almost unequalled. While we admit the full force of all that has been urged in support of the census, and are willing to take it as the best document on the subject extant, it is desirable to have proofs derived from personal observation, and to defer the settlement of this question until better opportunities are afforded. So high an average is, indeed, not without example. Captain Wilkes ascertained, in 1840, that one of the islands of the Fiji group supported a population of over a thousand on a square mile. On Lord North's Island, in the Pelew group, the crew of the American whaler Mentor ascertained there were four hundred inhabitants living on half a square mile. These, and many other islands in that genial clime, contain a population far exceeding that of any large country, and each separate community is obliged to depend wholly on its own labor. They cannot, however, be cited as altogether parallel cases, though if it be true, as Barrow says, "that an acre of cotton will clothe two or three hundred persons," not much more land need be occupied with cotton or mulberry plants, for clothing in China, than in the South Sea Islands.

The second objection against receiving the result of the census is, that we are not well informed as to the mode of enumerating the people by families, and the manner of taking the account, when the patriarch of two or three generations lives in a hamlet, with all his children and domestics around him. Two of the provisions in Sec. XXV. of the *Code*, seem to be designed for some such state of society; and the liability to underrate the males fit for public service, when a capitation tax was ordered, and to overrate the inmates of such a house, when the head of it might suppose he would thereby receive increased aid from government when calamity overtook him, are equally apparent. The door-tablet is also liable to mistake, and in shops and workhouses, where the clerks and workmen live and sleep on the premises, it is not known what kind of report of families the assessors make. On these important points our present information is imperfect, while the evident liability to serious error in the ultimate results makes one hesitate. The Chinese may have taken a census satisfactory for their purposes, showing the number of families, and the average in each; but the point of this objection is, that we do not know how the families are enumerated, and therefore are at fault in reckoning the individuals. The average of persons in a household is set down at five by the Chinese, and in England, in 1831, it was 4.7, but it is probably less than that in a thickly settled country, if every married couple and their children be taken as a family, whether living by themselves, or grouped in patriarchal hamlets.

No one doubts that the population is enormous, constituting by far the greatest assemblage of human beings using one speech ever congregated under one monarch. To the merchants and manufacturers of the West, the determination of this question is of some importance, and through them to their governments. The political economist and philologist, the naturalist and geographer, have also greater or less degrees of interest in the contemplation of such a people, inhabiting so beautiful and fertile a country. But the Christian philanthropist turns to the consideration of this subject with the liveliest solicitude; for if the weight of evidence is in favor of the highest estimate, he feels his responsibility increase to a painful degree. The danger to this people is furthermore greatly enhanced by the opium traffic—a trade which, as if the Rivers Phlegethon and Lethe were united in it, carries fire and destruction wherever it flows, and leaves a deadly forgetfulness wherever it has passed. Let these facts appeal to all calling themselves Christians, to send the antidote to this baleful drug, and diffuse a knowledge of the principles of the Gospel among them, thereby placing life as well as death before them.

If the population of the Empire is not easily ascertained, a satisfactory account of the public revenue and expenditures is still more difficult to obtain; it possesses far less interest, of course, in itself, and in such a country as China is subject to many variations. The market value of the grain, silk, and other products in which a large proportion of the taxes are paid, varies from year to year; and although this does not materially affect the government which receives these articles, it complicates the subject very much when attempting to ascertain the real taxation. Statistics on these subjects are only of recent date in Europe, and should not yet be looked for in China, drawn up with much regard to truth. The central government requires each province to support itself, and furnish a certain surplusage for the maintenance of the Emperor and his court; but it is well known that his Majesty is continually embarrassed for the want of funds, and that the provinces do not all supply enough revenue to meet their own outlays.

The amounts given by various authors as the revenue of China at different times, are so discordant, that a single glance shows that they were obtained from partial or incomplete returns, or else refer only to the surplusage sent to the capital. De Guignes remarks very truly, that the Chinese are so fully persuaded of the riches, power, and resources of their country, that a foreigner is likely to receive different accounts from every native he asks; but there appears to be no good reason why the government should falsify or abridge their fiscal accounts. In 1587, Trigault, one of the French missionaries, stated the revenue at only tls. 20,000,000. In 1655, Nieuhoff reckoned it at tls. 108,000,000. About twelve years after, Magalhaens gave the treasures of the Emperor at $20,423,962; and Le Comte, about the same time, placed the revenue at $22,000,000, and both of them estimated the receipts from rice, silk, etc., at $30,000,000, making the whole revenue previous to Kanghí's death, in 1721, between fifty and seventy millions of dollars. Barrow reckoned the receipts from all sources in 1796 at tls. 198,000,000, derived from a rough estimate given by the commissioner who accompanied the embassy. Sir George Staunton places the total sum at $330,000,000; of which $60,000,000 only were transmitted to Peking. Medhurst, drawing his information from original sources, thus states the principal items of the receipts:

Land taxes in money,	sent to Peking,	Tls.	31,745,966	valued at	$42,327,954
Land taxes in grain,		Shih	4,230,957	"	12,692,871
Custom and transit duties,		Tls.	1,480,997	"	1,974,662
Land taxes in money,	kept in provinces	Tls.	28,705,125	"	38,273,500
Grain,		Shih	31,596,569	"	105,689,707
					$200,958,694

The *shih* of rice is estimated at $3, but this does not include the cost of transportation to the capital.[1] At $200,000,000, the tax received by government from each person on an average is about sixty cents; Barrow estimates the capitation at about ninety cents. The account of the revenue in taels from each province given in the table of population on page 264, is extracted from the *Red Book* for 1840;[2] the account of the revenue in rice, as stated in the official documents for that year, is 4,114,000 shih, or about five hundred and fifty millions of pounds, calling each *shih* a pecul. The manner in which the various items of the revenue are divided is thus stated for Kwangtung, in the *Red Book* for 1842:

	Taels.
Land tax in money	1,264,304
Pawnbrokers' taxes	5,990
Taxes at the frontier and on transportation	719,307
Retained	339,143
Miscellaneous sources	59,530
Salt department (gabel)	47,510
Revenue from customs at Canton	43,750
Other stations in the province	53,670
	2,533,204

This is evidently only the sum sent to the capital from this province, ostensibly as the revenue, and which the provincial treasury must collect. The real receipts from this province or any other cannot well be ascertained by foreigners; it is, however, known, that in former years, the collector of customs at Canton was obliged to remit annually from eight hundred thousand to one million three hundred thousand taels, and

[1] The *shih*, says Medhurst, is a measure of grain containing 3,460 English cubic inches. *China: Its State and Prospects*, p. 68. London, 1838.

[2] *Annales de la Foi*, Tome XVI., p. 440.

the gross receipts of his office were not far from three millions of taels.[1] This was then the richest collectorate in the Empire; but since the foreign trade at the open ports has been placed under foreign supervision, the resources of the Empire have been better reported. A recent analysis of the sources of revenue in the Eighteen Provinces has been furnished by the customs service; it places them under different headings from the preceding list, though the total does not materially differ. Out of this whole amount the sum derived from the trade in foreign shipping goes most directly to the central exchequer.

	Taels.
Land tax in money	18,000,000
Li-kin or internal excise on goods	20,000,000
Import and export duties collected by foreigners	12,000,000
Import and export duties on native commerce	3,000,000
Salt gabel	5,000,000
Sales of offices and degrees	7,000,000
Sundries	1,400,000
Amount paid in silver	66,400,000
Land tax paid in produce	13,100,000
	79,500,000

De Guignes has examined the subject of the revenue with his usual caution, and bases his calculations on a proclamation of Kienlung in 1777, in which it was stated that the total income in bullion at that period was tls. 27,967,000.

	Taels.
Income in money as above	27,967,000
Equal revenue in kind from grain	27,967,000
Tax on the second crop in the southern provinces	21,800,000
Gabel, coal, transit duties, etc	6,479,400
Customs at Canton	800,000
Revenue from silk, porcelain, varnish, and other manufactures	7,000,000
Adding house and shop taxes, licenses, tonnage duties, etc	4,000,000
Total revenue	89,713,400

The difference of about eighty millions of dollars between this amount and that given by Medhurst, will not surprise one who has looked into this perplexing matter. All these calculations are based on approximations, which, although easily made

[1] *Chinese Commercial Guide*, 2d edition, 1842, p. 143.

up, cannot be verified to our satisfaction; but all agree in placing the total amount of revenue below that of any European government in proportion to the population. In 1823, a paper was published by a graduate upon the fiscal condition of the country, in which he gave a careful analysis of the receipts and disbursements. P. P. Thoms translated it in detail, and summarized the former under three heads of taxes reckoned at tls. 33,327,056, rice sent to Peking 6,346,438, and supplies to army 7,227,360—in all tls. 46,900,854. Out of the first sum tls. 24,507,933 went to civilians and the army, leaving tls. 5,819,-123 for the Peking government, and tls. 3,000,000 for the Yellow River repairs and Yuen-ming Palace. The resources of the Empire this writer foots up at tls. 74,461,633, or just one-half of what Medhurst gives. The extraordinary sources of revenue which are resorted to in time of war or bad harvests, are sale of office and honors, temporary increase of duties, and demands for contributions from wealthy merchants and landholders. The first is the most fruitful source, and may be regarded rather as a permanent than a temporary expediency employed to make up deficiencies. The mines of gold and silver, pearl fisheries in Manchuria and elsewhere, precious stones brought from Ílí and Khoten, and other localities, furnish several millions.

The expenditures, almost every year, exceed the revenue, but how the deficit is supplied does not clearly appear; it has been sometimes drawn from the rich by force, at other times made good by paltering with the currency, as in 1852–55, and again by reducing rations and salaries. In 1832, the Emperor said the excess of disbursements was tls. 28,000,000;[1] and, in 1836, the defalcation was still greater, and offices and titles to the amount of tls. 10,000,000 were put up for sale to supply it. This deficiency has become more and more alarming since the drain of specie annually sent abroad in payment for opium has been increased by military exactions for suppressing the rebellion up to 1867. At that date the Empire began to recuperate. The principal items of the expenditure are thus stated by De Guignes:

[1] *Chinese Repository*, Vol. I., p. 159.

	Taels.
Salary of civil and military officers, a tithe of the impost on lands.	7,773,500
Pay of 600,000 infantry, three taels per month, half in money and half in rations	21,600,000
Pay of 242,000 cavalry, at four taels per month	11,616,000
Mounting the cavalry, twenty taels each	4,840,000
Uniforms for both arms of the service, four taels	3,368,000
Arms and ammunition	842,000
Navy, revenue cutters, etc.	13,500,000
Canals and transportation of revenue	4,000,000
Forts, artillery, and munitions of war	3,800,000
	71,339,500

This, according to his calculation, shows a surplus of nearly twenty millions of taels every year. But the outlays for quelling insurrections and transporting troops, deficiency from bad harvests, defalcation of officers, payments to the tribes and princes in Mongolia and Íli, and other unusual demands, more than exceed this surplus. In 1833, the *Peking Gazette* contained an elaborate paper on the revenue, proposing various ways and means for increasing it. The author, named Na, says the income from land tax, the gabel, customs and transit duty, does not in all exceed forty millions of taels, while the expenditures should not much transcend thirty in years of peace.[1] This places the budget much lower than other authorities, but the censor perhaps includes only the imperial resources, though the estimate would then be too high. The pay and equipment of the troops is the largest item of expenditure, and it is probable that here the apparent force and pay are far too great, and that reductions are constantly made in this department by compelling the soldiers to depend more and more for support upon the plats of land belonging to them. It is considered the best evidence of good government on the part of an officer to render his account of the revenue satisfactorily, but from the injudicious system which exists of combining fiscal, legislative, and judicial functions and control in the same person, the temptations to defraud are strong, and the peculations proportionably great.

The salaries of officers, for some reasons, are placed so low as

[1] *Chinese Repository*, Vol. II., p. 431.

to prove that the legal allowances were really the nominal incomes, and the sums set against their names in the *Red Book* as *yang tien*, or anti-extortion perquisites (lit., 'nourishing frugality'), are the salaries. That of a governor-general is from 15,000 to 25,000 taels for the latter, and only 180 or 200 taels for the legal salary; a governor gets 15,000 when he is alone, and 10,000 or 12,000 when under a governor-general; a treasurer from 4,500 to 10,000; a judge from 3,000 to 8,000; a prefect from 2,000 to 4,500; district magistrates from 700 to 1,000, according to the onerousness of the post; an intendant from 3,000 to 4,500; a literary chancellor from 2,000 to 5,000; and military men from 4,000 taels down to 100 or 150 per annum. The perquisites of the highest and lowest officers are disproportionate, for the people prefer to lay their important cases before the highest courts at once, in order to avoid the expense of passing through those of a lower grade. The personal disposition of the functionary modifies the exactions he makes upon the people so much, that no guess can be made as to the amount.

The land tax is the principal resource for the revenue in rural districts, and this is well understood by all parties, so that there is less room for exactions. The land tax is from 1½ to 10 cents a *mao* (or from 10 to 66 cents an acre), according to the quality of the land, and difficulty of tillage; taking the average at 25 cents an acre, the income from this source would be upward of 150 millions of dollars. The clerks, constables, lictors, and underlings of the courts and prisons, are the "claws" of their superiors, as the Chinese aptly call them, and perform most of their extortions, and are correspondingly odious to the people. In towns and trading places, it is easier for the officers to exact in various ways from wealthy people, than in the country, where rich people often hire bodies of retainers to defy the police, and practise extortion and robbery themselves. Like other Asiatic governments, China suffers from the consequences of bribery, peculation, extortion, and poorly paid officers, but she has no powerful aristocracy to retain the money thus squeezed out of the people, and ere long it finds its way out of the hands of emperors and ministers back into the mass of the people.

The Chinese believe, however, that the Emperor annually remits such amounts as he is able to collect into Mukden, in time of extremity; but latterly he has not been able to do so at all, and probably never sent as much to that city as the popular ideas imagine. The sum applied to filling the granaries is much larger, but this popular provision in case of need is really a light draft upon the resources of the country, as it is usually managed. In Canton, there are only fourteen buildings appropriated to this purpose, few of them more than thirty feet square, and none of them full.

CHAPTER VI.

NATURAL HISTORY OF CHINA.

THE succinct account of the natural history of China given by Sir John Davis in 1836, contained nearly all the popular notices of much value then known, and need not be repeated, while summarizing the items derived from other and later sources. Malte-Brun observed long ago, "That of even the more general, and, according to the usual estimate, the more important features of that vast sovereignty, we owe whatever knowledge we have obtained to some ambassadors who have seen the courts and the great roads—to certain merchants who have inhabited a suburb of a frontier town—and to several missionaries who, generally more credulous than discriminating, have contrived to penetrate in various directions into the interior." The volumes upon China in the Edinburgh Cabinet Library contain the best digest of what was known forty years since on this subject. The botanical collections of Robert Fortune in 1844–1849, and those of Col. Champion at Hongkong, have been studied by Bentham, while the later researches of Hance, Bunge and Maximowitch have brought many new forms to notice. In geology, Pumpelly, Kingsmill, Bickmore, and Baron Richthofen have greatly enlarged and certified our knowledge by their travels and memoirs; while Père David, Col. Prejevalsky, Swinhoe, Stimpson, and Sir John Richardson have added hundreds of new species to the scientific fauna of the Empire.

Personal investigation is particularly necessary in all that relates to the geology and fossils of a country, and the knowledge possessed on these heads is, it must be conceded, still meagre, though now sufficient to convey a general idea of the formations, deposits, and contents of the mountains and mines, as well as the agencies at work in modifying the surface of this land. The descriptions and observed facts recorded in native books may furnish valuable hints when they can be compared with the places and productions, for at present the difficulty of explaining terms used, and understanding the processes described, render these treatises hard to translate. The empirical character of Chinese science compels a careful sifting of all its facts and speculations by comparisons with nature, while the amount of real information contained in medical, topographical, and itinerant works render them always worth examining. Large regions still await careful examination in every part of the Empire; and it will be well for the Chinese Government if no tempting metallic deposits are found to test its strength to protect and work them for its own benefit. But in mere science it cannot be doubted that so peculiar a part of the world as the plateau of Central Asia will, when thoroughly examined, solve many problems relating to geology, and disclose many important facts to illustrate the obscure phenomena of other parts of the world.

A few notices of geological formations furnished in the writings of travellers, have already been given in the geographical account of the provinces. The summary published by Davis is a well digested survey of the observations collected by the gentlemen attached to the embassies.[1]

The loess-beds, covering a great portion of Northern China, are among the most peculiar natural phenomena and interesting fields for geological investigation on the world's surface. Since attention was first directed to this deposit by Pumpelly, in 1864, its formation and extent have been more carefully examined by other geologists, whose hypotheses are now pretty generally discarded for that of Baron von Richthofen. The loess territory begins, at its eastern limit, with the foot hills of the great alluvial plane. From this rises a terrace of from 90 to 250 feet in height, consisting entirely of loess, and westward of it, in

---

[1] *The Chinese*, Vol. II., pp. 333–343.

a nearly north and south line, stretches the Tai-hang shan or dividing range between the alluvial land and the hill country of Shansí. An almost uninterrupted loess-covered country extends west of this line to the Koko-nor and head-waters of the Yellow River. On the north the formation can be traced from the vicinity of Kalgan, along the water-shed of the Mongolian steppes, and into the desert beyond the Ala shan. Toward the south its limits are less sharply defined; though covering all the country of the Wei basin (in Shensí), none is found in Sz'chuen, due south of this valley, but it appears in parts of Honan and Eastern Shantung. Excepting occasional spurs and isolated spots—as at Nanking and the Lakes Poyang and Tungting—loess may be considered as ending everywhere on the north side of the Yangtsz' valley, and, roughly speaking, to cover the parallelogram between longs. 99° and 115°, and lats. 33° and 41°. The district within China Proper represents a territory half as large again as that of the German Empire, while outside of the Provinces there is reason to believe that loess spreads far toward the east and north. In the Wu-tai shan (Shansí), Richthofen observed this deposit to a height of 7,200 feet above the sea, and supposes that it may occur at higher levels.

The term *loess*, now generally accepted, has been used to designate a tertiary deposit appearing in the Rhine valley and several isolated sections of Europe; its formation has heretofore been ascribed to glaciers, but its enormous extent and thickness in China demand some other origin. The substance is a brownish colored earth, extremely porous, and when dry easily powdered between the fingers, when it becomes an impalpable dust that may be rubbed into the pores of the skin. Its particles are somewhat angular in shape, the lumps varying from the size of a peanut to a foot in length, whose appearance warrants the peculiarly appropriate Chinese name meaning 'ginger stones.' After washing, the stuff is readily disintegrated, and spread far and wide by rivers during their freshets; Kingsmill[1] states that a number of specimens which crumbled in the moist

[1] *Journal of the Geolog. Soc.*, London, for 1871, p. 379.

air of a Shanghai summer, rearranged themselves afterward in the bottom of a drawer in which they had been placed. Every atom of loess is perforated by small tubes, usually very minute, circulating after the manner of root-fibres, and lined with a thin coating of carbonate of lime. The direction of these little canals being always from above downward, cleavage in the loess mass, irrespective of its size, is invariably vertical, while from the same cause surface water never collects in the form of rain puddles or lakes, but sinks at once to the local water level.

One of the most striking, as well as important phenomena of this formation is the perpendicular splitting of its mass into sudden and multitudinous clefts that cut up the country in every direction, and render observation, as well as travel, often exceedingly difficult. The cliffs, caused by erosion, vary from cracks measured by inches to cañons half a mile wide and hundreds of feet deep; they branch out in every direction, ramifying through the country after the manner of tree-roots in the soil—from each root a rootlet, and from these other small fibres—until the system of passages develops into a labyrinth of far-reaching and intermingling lanes. Were the loess throughout of the uniform structure seen in single clefts, such a region would indeed be absolutely impassable, the vertical banks becoming precipices of often more than a thousand feet. The fact, however, that loess exhibits all over a terrace formation, renders its surface not only habitable, but highly convenient for agricultural purposes; it has given rise, moreover, to the theory advanced by Kingsmill and some others, of its stratification, and from this a proof of its origin as a marine deposit. Richthofen argues that these apparent layers of loess are due to external conditions, as of rocks and débris sliding from surrounding hillsides upon the loess as it sifted into the basin or valley, thus interrupting the homogeneity of the gradually rising deposit. In the sides of gorges near the mountains are seen layers of coarse débris which, in going toward the valley, become finer, while the layers themselves are thinner and separated by an increasing vertical distance; along these rubble beds are numerous calcareous concretions which stand upright. These are then the terrace-forming layers which, by their resistance to the action of water, cause the broken chasms and step-like contour of the loess regions. Each bank does indeed cleave vertically, sometimes—since the erosion works from below—leaving an overhanging bank; but meeting with this horizontal layer of marl stones, the abrasion is interrupted, and a ledge is made. Falling clods upon such spaces are gradually spread over their surfaces by natural action, converting them into rich fields. When seen from a height in good seasons, these systems of terraces present an endless succession of green fields and growing crops; viewed from the deep cut of a road below, the traveller sees nothing but yellow walls of loam and dusty tiers of loess ridges. As may be readily imagined, a country of this nature exhibits many landscapes of unrivalled picturesqueness, especially when lofty crags, which some variation in the water-course has left as giant guardsmen in fertile river valleys, stand out in bold relief against the green background of neighboring hills and a fruitful alluvial bottom, or when an opening of some ascending pass allows the eye to range over leagues of sharp-cut ridges and teaming crops, the work of the careful cultivator.

The extreme ease with which loess is cut away tends at times to seriously embarrass traffic. Dust made by the cart-wheels on a highway is taken up by strong winds during the dry season and blown over the surrounding lands, much after the manner in which it was originally deposited here. This action continued over centuries, and assisted by occasional deluges of rain, which find a ready channel in the road-bed, has hollowed the country routes into depressions of often 50 or 100 feet, where the passenger may ride for miles without obtaining a glimpse of the surrounding scenery. Lieutenant Kreitner, of the Széchenyí exploring expedition, illustrates,[1] in a personal experience in Shansí, the difficulty and danger of leaving these deep cuts; after scrambling for miles along the broken loess above the road, he only regained it when a further passage was cut off by a precipice on the one side, while a jump of some 30 feet into the beaten track below awaited him on the other. Difficult as

[1] *Im fernen Osten*, p. 462.

may be such a territory for roads and the purposes of trade, the advantages to a farmer are manifold. Wherever this deposit extends, there the husbandman has an assured harvest, two and even three times in a year. It is easily worked, exceedingly fertile, and submits to constant tillage, with no other manure than a sprinkling of its own loam dug from the nearest bank.

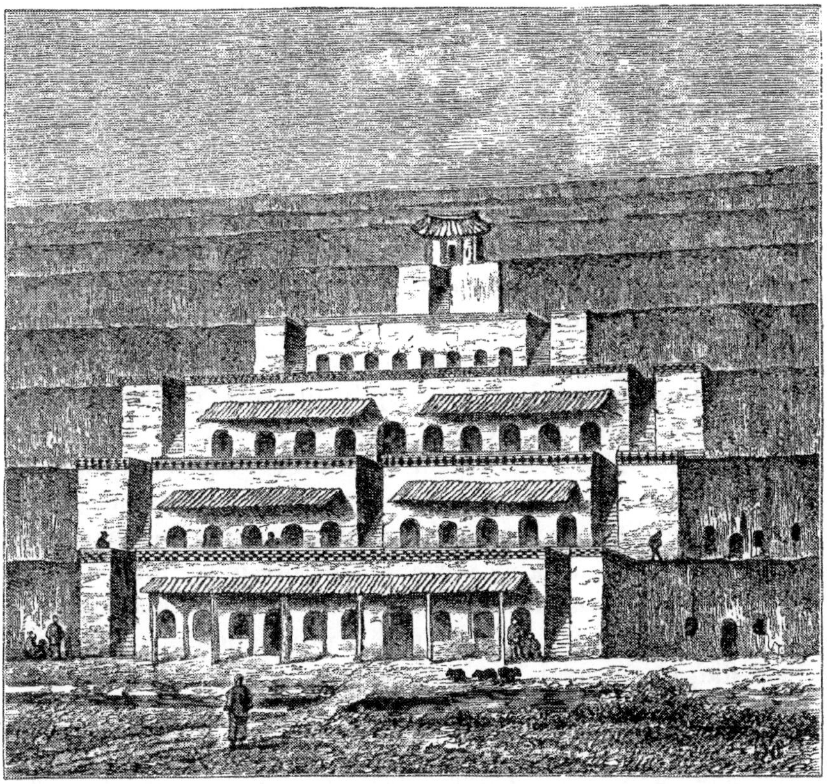

Facade of Dwelling in Loess Cliffs, Ling-shï hien. (From Richthofen.)

But loess performs still another service to its inhabitants. Caves made at the base of its straight clefts afford homes to millions of people in the northern provinces. Choosing an escarpment where the consistency of the earth is greatest, the natives cut for themselves rooms and houses, whose partition walls, cement, bed and furniture are made from the same loess. Whole villages cluster together in a series of adjoining or superimposed chambers, some of which pierce the soil to a depth of often more than 200 feet. In more costly dwellings the terrace or succession of terraces thus perforated are faced with brick, as well as the arching of rooms within. The advantages of such habitations consist as well in imperviousness to changes of temperature without, as in their durability when constructed in properly selected places, many loess dwellings outlasting six or seven generations. The capabilities of defence in a country such as this, where an invading army must inevitably become lost in the tangle of interlacing ways, and where the defenders may always remain concealed, is very suggestive.

There remains, lastly, a peculiar property of loess which is perhaps more important than all other features when measured by its man-serving efficiency. This is the manner in which it brings forth crops without the aid of manure. From a period more than 2,000 years before Christ, to the present day, the province of Shansí has borne the name of Grainery of the Empire, while its fertile soil, *hwang-tu*, or 'yellow earth,' is the origin of the imperial color. Spite of this productiveness, which, in the fourteenth century, caused the Friar Odoric to class it as the second country in the world, its present capacity for raising crops seems to be as great as ever. In the nature of this substance lies the reason for this apparently inexhaustible fecundity. Its remarkably porous structure must indeed cause it to absorb the gases necessary to plant life to a much greater degree than other soils, but the stable production of those mineral substances needful to the yearly succession of crops is in the ground itself. The salts contained more or less in solution at the water level of the region are freed by the capillary action of the loess when rain-water sinks through the spongy mass from above. Surface moisture following the downward direction of the tiny loess tubes establishes a connection with the waters compressed below, when, owing to the law of diffusion, the ingredients, being released, mix with the moisture of the little canals, and are taken from the lowest to the topmost levels, permeating the ground and furnishing nourishment to the plant roots at the surface. It is on account of this curious action of loess that a copious rain-fall is more necessary in North

China than elsewhere, for with a dearth of rain the capillary communication from above, below, and *vice versa*, is interrupted, and vegetation loses both its manure and moisture. Drought and famine are consequently synonymous terms here.

As to the formation and origin of loess, Richthofen's theory is substantially as follows:[1] The uniform composition of this material over extended areas, coupled with the absence of stratification and of marine or fresh-water organic remains, renders impossible the hypothesis that it is a water deposit. On the other hand, it contains vast quantities of land-shells and the vestiges of animals (mammalia) at every level, both in remarkably perfect condition. Concluding, also, that from the conformation of the neighboring mountain chains and their peculiar weathering, the glacial theory is inadmissible, he advances the supposition that loess is a sub-aërial deposit, and that its fields are the drained analogues of the steppe-basins of Central Asia. They date from a geological era of great dryness, before the existence of the Yellow and other rivers of the northern provinces. As the rocks and hills of the highlands disintegrated, the sand was removed, not by water-courses seaward, but by the high winds ranging over a treeless desert landward, until the dust settled in the grass-covered districts of what is at present China Proper. New vegetation was at once nourished, while its roots were raised by the constantly arriving deposit; the decay of old roots produced the lime-lined canals which impart to this material its peculiar characteristics. Any one who has observed the terrible dust-storms of North China, when the air is filled with an impalpable yellow powder, which leaves its coating upon everything, and often extends, in a fog-like cloud, hundreds of miles to sea, will understand the power of this action during many thousand years. This deposition received the shells and bones of innumerable animals, while the dissolved solutions contained in its bulk stayed therein, or saturated the water of small lakes. By the sinking of mountain chains in the south, rain-clouds emptied themselves over this region with much greater frequency, and gradually the system became

[1] *China: Ergebnisse eigener Reisen.* Band I., S. 74. Berlin, 1877.

drained, the erosion working backward from the coast, slowly cutting into one basin after another. With the sinking of its salts to lower levels, unexampled richness was added to the wonderful topography of this peculiar formation.[1]

Pumpelly, while accepting this ingenious theory in place of his own (that of a fresh-water lake deposit), adds that the supply of loess might have been materially increased by the vast *mers-de-glace* of High Asia and the Tien shan, whose streams have for ages transported the products of glacial attrition into Central Asia and Northwest China. Again, he insists that Richthofen has not given importance enough to the parting planes, wrongly considered by his predecessors as planes of stratification. "These," he says, "account for the marginal layers of débris brought down from the mountains. And the continuous and more abundant growth of grasses *at one plane* would produce a modification of the soil structurally and chemically, which superincumbent accumulations could never efface. It should seem probable that we have herein, also, the explanation of the calcareous concretions which abound along these planes; for the greater amount of carbonic acid generated by the slow decay of this vegetation would, by forming a bicarbonate, give to the lime the mobility necessary to produce the concretions."

The metallic and mineral productions used in the arts comprise nearly everything found in other countries, and the common ones are furnished in such abundance, and at such rates, as conclusively prove them to be plenty and easily worked. The careful digest of observations published by Pumpelly through the Smithsonian Institution, carries out this remark, and indicates the vast field still to be explored. Coal exists in every province in China, and Pumpelly enumerates seventy-four localities which have been ascertained. Marco Polo's well-known notice of its use shows that the people had long employed it: "It is a fact that all over the country of Cathay there is a kind of black stone existing in beds in the mountains, which they dig out and burn like firewood. It is true that they have plenty of

[1] Compare Kingsmill, in the *Quar. Journal of the Geol. Soc. of London*, 1868, pp. 119 ff., and in the *North China Herald*, Vol. IX., 85, 86.

wood also, but they do not burn it, because those stones burn better and cost less.[1] This mineral seems to have been unknown in Europe till after the return of the Venetian to his native land, while it was employed before the Christian era in China, and probably in very ancient times, if the accessible deposits in Shensí then cropped out in its eroded gorges, as represented by Richthofen. The few fossil plants hitherto examined indicate that the mass of these deposits are of the Mesozoic age. The mode of working the coal mines is described by Pumpelly,[2] and was probably no worse two thousand five hundred years ago. Want of machinery for draining them prevents the miners from going much below the water-level, and a rain-storm will sometimes flood and ruin a shaft. An inclined plane seldom takes the workmen more than a hundred feet below the level of the mouth, and then a horizontal gallery conducts him to the end of the mine. Some water is bailed out by buckets handed from one level up to another at the top, and the coal is carried out in baskets on the miners' backs, or dragged in sleds over smooth, round sticks along passages too low for the coolies to do better than crawl as they work. Mr. Pumpelly found the gallery of one mine near Peking so low that he had to crawl the whole distance (six thousand feet) to see its construction, and when he emerged into daylight, with his knees nearly skinned, ascertained that the workmen padded theirs. The timbering is very expensive, yet, with all drawbacks, the coal sells, at the pit's mouth, for $2.00 down to 50 cents a ton. The mines, lying on the slopes of the plateau reaching from near Corea to the Yellow River, supply the plain with cheap and excellent fuel.

Blakiston gives an account of the manner in which coal is worked on the Upper Yangtsz', near the town of Süchau: "Having to be got out at a great height up in the cliff, very thick hawsers, made of plaited bamboo, are tightly stretched from the mouth, or near the mouth, of the working gallery, to a space near the water where the coal can be deposited. These

---

[1] Yule's *Marco Polo*, Vol. I., p. 395.

[2] *Across America and Asia*, pp. 291 ff.

ropes are in pairs, and large pannier-shaped baskets are made to traverse on them, a rope passing from one over a large wheel at the upper landing, and down again to the other, so that the full basket going down pulls the empty one up, the velocity being regulated by a kind of brake on the wheel at the top. At some places the height at which the coal is worked is so great that two or more of these contrivances are used, one taking to a landing half way down, and another from thence to the river. The hawsers are kept taut by a windlass for that purpose at the bottom."[1] This useful mineral appears to be abundant throughout Sz'chuen Province, and is used here much less sparingly than in the east. With such inexpensive methods of getting coal to the water-courses, foreign machinery can hardly be expected to reduce its price very materially.

The economical use of coal in the household and the arts has been carried to great perfection. Anthracite is powdered and mixed with wet clay, earth, sawdust or dung, according to the exigencies of the case, in the proportion of about seven to one; the balls thus made are dried in the sun. The brick-beds (*kang*) are effective means of warming the house, and the hand furnaces enable the poor to cook with these balls—aided by a little charcoal or kindlings—at a trifling expense. This form of consumption is common north of the Yellow River, and brings coal within reach of multitudes who otherwise would suffer and starve. Bituminous, brown, and other varieties of coal occur in the same abundance and extent as in other great areas, giving promise of adequate supplies for future ages. The coal worked on the Peh kiang, in Kwangtung, contains sulphur, and is employed in the manufacture of copperas.[2]

Crystallized gypsum is brought from the northwest of the province to Canton, and is ground to powder in mills; plaster

[1] *Five Months on the Yang-tsze*, p. 265. *Annales de la Foi*, Tome IX., p. 457.

[2] *N. C. Br. R. A. Soc. Journal*, New Series, No. III., pp. 94–106, and No. IV., pp. 243 ff. Notes by Mr. Hollingworth of a Visit to the Coal Mines in the Neighborhood of Loh-Ping. *Blue Book, China*, No. 2, 1870, p. 11. *Notes and Queries on China and Japan*, Vol. II., pp. 74–76. *North China Herald*, passim. Richthofen's *Letters*, and in *Ocean Highways*, Nov., 1873. *Chinese Repository*, Vol. XIX., pp. 385 ff.

COAL GORGE ON THE YANGTSZ'. (FROM BLAKISTON.)

of Paris and other forms of this sulphate are common all over China. It is not used as a manure, but the flour is mixed with wood-oil to form a cement for paying the seams of boats after they have been caulked. The powder is employed as a dentifrice, a cosmetic, and a medicine, and sometimes, also, is boiled to make a gruel in fevers, under the idea that it is cooling. The bakers who supplied the English troops at Amoy, in 1843, occasionally put it into the bread to make it heavier, but not, as was erroneously charged upon them, with any design of poisoning their customers, for they do not think it noxious; its employment in coloring green tea, and adulterating powdered sugar, is also explainable by other motives than a wish to injure the consumers.

Limestone is abundant at Canton, both common clouded marble and blue limestone; the last is extensively used in the artificial rockwork of gardens. Even if the Cantonese knew of the existence of lime in limestone, which they generally do not, the expense of fuel for calcining it would prevent their burning it while oyster-shells are so abundant in that region. In other provinces stone-lime is burned, by the aid of coal, in small kilns. The fine marble quarried near Peking is regarded as fit alone for imperial uses, and is seen only in such places as the Altar of Heaven and palace grounds. The marble used for floors is a fissile crystallized limestone, unsusceptible of polish; no statues or ornaments are sculptured from this mineral, but slabs are sometimes wrought out, and the surfaces curiously stained and corroded with acids, forming rude representations of animals or other figures, so as to convey the appearance of natural markings. Some of these simulated petrifactions are exceedingly well done. Slabs of argillaceous slate are also chosen with reference to their layers, and treated in the same manner. An excellent granite is used about Canton and Amoy for building, and no people exceed the Chinese in cutting it. Large slabs are split out by wooden wedges, cut for basements and foundations, and laid in a beautiful manner; pillars are also hewn from single stones of different shapes, though of no extraordinary dimensions, and their shafts embellished with inscriptions. Ornamental walls are frequently formed of large slabs set in posts, like panels, the outer faces of which are beautifully carved with figures representing a landscape or procession. Red and gray sandstone, gneiss, mica slate, and other species of rock, are also worked for pavements and walls.

Nitre is cheap and common enough in the northern provinces to obviate any fear of its being smuggled into the country from abroad; it is obtained in Chihlí by lixiviating the soil, and furnishes material for the manufacture of gunpowder. A lye is obtained from ashes, which partially serves the purposes of soap; but the people are still ignorant of the processes necessary for manufacturing it. Fourteen localities of alum are given in Pumpelly's list, but the greatest supply for the eastern provinces comes from deposits of shale, in Ping-yang hien, in Chehkiang, which produces about six thousand tons annually. It is used mostly by the dyers, also to purify turbid water, and whiten paper. Other earthy salts are known and used, as borax, sal-ammoniac (which is collected in Mongolia and Îlí from lakes and the vicinity of extinct volcanoes), and blue and white vitriol, obtained by roasting pyrites. Common salt is procured along the eastern and southern coasts by evaporating sea-water, rock-salt not having been noticed; in the western provinces and Shansí, it is obtained from artesian wells and lakes as cheaply as from the ocean; in Tsing-yen hien, in Central Sz'chuen, two hundred and thirty-seven wells are worked. At Chusan the sea-water is so turbid that the inhabitants filter it through clay, afterward evaporating the water.

The minerals heretofore found in China have, for the most part, been such as have attracted the attention of the natives, and collected by them for curiosity or sale. The skilful manner in which their lapidaries cut crystal, agate, and other quartzose minerals, is well known.[1] The corundum used for polishing and finishing these carvings occurs in China, but a good deal of emery in powder is obtained from Borneo. A composition of granular corundum and gum-lac is usually employed by workmen in order to produce the highest lustre of

---

[1] Compare Rémusat, *Histoire de Khotan*, pp. 163 ff., where there is an extended list of Chinese precious stones drawn from native sources.

which the stones are capable. The three varieties of the silicate of alumina, called jade, nephrite, and jadeite by mineralogists, are all named *yuh* by the Chinese, a word which is applied to a vast variety of stones—white marble, ruby, and cornelian all coming under it—and therefore not easy to define. Jade has long been known in Europe as a variety of jasper, its separation from that stone into a species by itself being of comparatively recent origin. Since the third edition of Boetius, in 1647, the two minerals have been regarded as entirely distinct. Its value in the eyes of the Chinese depends chiefly upon its sonorousness and color. The costliest specimens are brought from Yunnan and Khoten; a greenish-white color is the most highly prized, a plain color of any shade being of less value. A cargo of this mineral was once imported into Canton from New Holland, but the Chinese would not purchase it, owing to a fancy taken against its origin and color. The patient toil of the workers in this hard mineral is only equalled by the prodigious admiration with which it is regarded; both fairly exhibit the singular taste and skill of the Chinese. Its color is usually a greenish-white, or grayish-green and dark grass-green; internally it is scarcely glimmering. Its fracture is splintery; splinters white; mass semi-transparent and cloudy; it scratches glass strongly, and can itself generally be scratched by flint or quartz, but while not excessively hard it is remarkable for toughness. The stone when freshly broken is less hard than after a short exposure. Specific gravity from 2.9 to 3.1.[1] Fischer (pp. 314–318) gives some one hundred and fifty names as occurring in various authors—ancient and modern—for jade or nephrite.[2] An interesting testimony to the esteem

---

[1] Murray's *China*, Edinburgh, 1843, Vol. III., p. 276; compare also an article on this stone by M. Blondel, of Paris, published in the *Smithsonian Report* for 1876. *Mémoires concernant les Chinois*, Tome XIII., p. 389. Rémusat in the *Journal des Savans*, Dec., 1818, pp. 748 ff. *Notes and Queries on C. and J.*, Vol. II., pp. 173, 174, and 187; Vol. III., p. 63; Vol. IV., pp. 13 and 33. *Macmillan's Magazine*, October, 1871. Yule, *Cathay and the Way Thither*, Vol. II., p. 564.

[2] *Nephrit und Jadeit, nach ihren mineralogischen Eigenschaften sowie nach ihrer urgeschichtlichen und ethnographischen Bedeutung*. Heinrich Fischer, Stuttgart, 1880. An exhaustive treatise on every phrase and variety of the mineral.

in which this stone was held in China during the middle ages comes from Benedict Goës (1602), who says: "There is no article of traffic more valuable than lumps of a certain transparent kind of marble, which we, from poverty of language, usually call jasper. . . . Out of this marble they fashion a variety of articles, such as vases, brooches for mantles and girdles, which, when artistically sculptured in flowers and foliage, certainly have an effect of no small magnificence. These marbles (with which the Empire is now overflowing) are called by the Chinese Iusce. There are two kinds of it; the first and more valuable is got out of the river at Cotan, almost in the same way in which divers fish for gems, and this is usually extracted in pieces about as big as large flints. The other and inferior kind is excavated from the mountains." The ruby, diamond, amethyst, sapphire, topaz, pink tourmaline, lapis-lazuli,[1] turquoises, beryl, garnet, opal, agate, and other stones, are known and most of them used in jewelry. A ruby brought from Peking is noticed by Bell as having been valued in Europe at $50,000. The seals of the Boards are in many instances cut on valuable stones, and private persons take great pride in quartz or jade seals, with their names carved on them; lignite and jet are likewise employed for cheaper ornaments, of which all classes are fond.

All the common metals, except platina, are found in China, and the supply would be sufficient for all the purposes of the inhabitants, if they could avail themselves of the improvements adopted in other countries in blasting, mining, etc. The importations of iron, lead, tin, and quicksilver, are gradually increasing, but they form only a small proportion of the amount used throughout the Empire, especially of the two first named; iron finds its way in because of its convenient forms more than its cheapness. The careful examination of Chinese topographical works by Pumpelly,[2] records the leading localities of iron in every province, and where copper, tin, lead, silver, and quicksilver have been observed; he also mentions fifty-two places pro-

---

[1] Obtained from Badakshan. Wood, *Journey to the Oxus*, p. 263.

[2] *Geological Researches in China*, Chap. X.

ducing gold in various forms, most of them in Sz'chuen. The rumor of gold-washings occurring not far from Chifu, in Shantung, caused much excitement in 1868, but they were soon found to be not worth the labor. Gold has never been used as coin in China, but is wrought into jewelry; most of it is consumed in gilding and exported to India as bullion, in the shape of small bars or coarse leaves.

Silver is mentioned in sixty-three localities by the same author; large amounts are brought from Yunnan, and the mines in that region must be both extensive and easily worked to afford such large quantities as have been exported. The working of both gold and silver mines has been said to be prohibited, but this interdiction is rather a government monopoly of the mines than an injunction upon working those which are known. The importation of gold into China during the two centuries the trade has been opened, does not probably equal the exportation which has taken place since the commencement of the opium trade. It is altogether improbable that the Chinese are acquainted with the properties of quicksilver in separating these two metals from their ores, though its consumption in making vermilion and looking-glasses calls for over two thousand flasks yearly at Canton. Cinnabar occurs in Kweichau and Shensí and furnishes most of the "water silver," as the Chinese call it, by a rude process of burning brushwood in the wells, and collecting the metal after condensation.

Copper is used for manufacturing coin, bells, bronze articles, domestic and cooking utensils, cannon, gongs, and brass-foil. It is found pure in some instances, and the sulphuret, the blue and green carbonates, pyrities, and other ores are worked; malachite is ground for a paint. It occurs in every province, and is specially rich in Shansí and Kweichau. The ores of zinc and copper in Yunnan and Sz'chuen furnish spelter, and the peculiar alloy known as white copper or argentan, containing in addition tin, iron, nickel, and lead. So much use indicates large deposits of the ores. Tin is rather abundant, but lead is more common; thirty-nine localities of the first are mentioned, some of which are probably zinc ores, as the Chinese confound tin and zinc under one generic name. Lead occurs with silver in many places; twenty-four mines are mentioned in Pumpelly's list, and those in Fuhkien are rich; but the extensive importations prove that its reduction is too expensive to compete with the foreign.

Realgar is quite common, this and orpiment being used as paints; statuettes and other articles are carved from the former, while arsenic is used in agriculture to quicken grain and preserve it from insects. Amber and fossilized copal are collected in several localities; the first is much employed in the making of court necklaces and hair ornaments. The *fei-tsui* or jadeite is the most prized of the semi-precious stones; it is cut into ear-rings, finger-rings, necklaces, etc. Pumpelly mentions pieces of this mineral set in relics obtained from tombs in Mexico, though no locality where it abounds has yet been found in America. Lapis-lazuli is employed in painting upon copper and porcelain ware; this mineral is obtained in Chehkiang and Kansuh; jadeite, topaz, and other fine stones are most plenty in Yunnan. A few minerals and fossils have been noticed in the vicinity and shops at Canton, but China thus far has furnished very few petrifactions in any strata. Coarse epidote occurs at Macao, and tungstate of iron has been noticed in the quartz rocks at Hongkong. Petrified crabs (*macrophthalmus*) have been brought to Canton from Hainan, which are prized by the natives for their supposed medicinal qualities. Scientists have hitherto described a score or more species of Devonian shells, and recognized fragments of the hyena, tapir, rhinoceros, and stegedon, among some other doubtful vertebratæ in the "dragon's bones" sold in medicine shops; but further examinations will doubtless increase the list. Orthoceratites and bivalve shells of various kinds are noticed in Chinese books as being found in rocks, and fossil bones of huge size in caves and river banks.

There are many hot springs and other indications of volcanic action along the southern acclivities of the table land in the provinces of Shensí and Sz'chuen; and at Jeh-ho, in Chihlí, there are thermal springs to which invalids resort. The *Ho tsing*, or Fire wells, in Sz'chuen are apertures resembling artesian springs, sunk in the rock to a depth of one thousand five hundred or one thousand eight hundred feet, whilst their breadth does not exceed five or six inches. This is a work of great difficulty, and requires in some cases the labor of two or three years. The water procured from them contains a fifth part of salt, which is very acrid, and mixed with much nitre. When a lighted torch is applied to the mouth of some of those which have no water, fire is produced with great violence and a noise like thunder, bursting out into a flame twenty or thirty feet high, and which cannot be extinguished without great danger and expense. The gas has a bituminous smell, and burns with a bluish flame and a quantity of thick, black smoke. It is conducted under boilers in bamboos, and employed in evaporating the salt-water from the other springs.[1] Besides the gaseous and aqueous springs in these provinces, there are others possessing different qualities, some sulphurous and others chalybeate, found in Shansí and along the banks of the Yellow River. Sulphur occurs, as has been noted, in great abundance in Formosa, and is purified for powder manufacturers.

The animal and vegetable productions of the extensive regions under the sway of the Emperor of China include a great variety of types of different families. On the south the islands of Hainan and Formosa, and parts of the adjacent coasts, slightly partake of a tropical character, exhibiting in the cocoanuts, plantains, and peppers, the parrots, lemurs, and monkeys, decided indications of an equatorial climate. From the eastern coast across through the country to the northwest provinces occur mountain ranges of gradually increasing elevation, interspersed with intervales and alluvial plateaus and bottoms, lakes and rivers, plains and hills, each presenting its peculiar productions, both wild and cultivated, in great variety and abundance. The southern ascent of the high land of Mongolia, the uncultivated wilds of Manchuria, the barren wastes of the desert of Gobi, with its salt lakes, glaciers, extinct volcanoes, and isolated mountain ranges; and lastly the stupendous

---

[1] Humboldt, *Fragmens Asiatiques*, Tome I., p. 196. *Annales de la Foi*, Janvr., 1829, pp. 416 ff.

chains and valleys of Tibet, Koko-nor, and Kwănlun all differ from each other in the character of their productions. In one or the other division, every variety of soil, position, and temperature occur which are known on the globe; and what has been ascertained within the past fifteen years by enterprising naturalists is an earnest of future greater discoveries.

Of the quadrumanous order of animals, there are several species. The Chinese are skilful in teaching the smaller kinds of monkeys various tricks, but M. Breton's picture of their adroitness and usefulness in picking tea in Shantung from plants growing on otherwise inaccessible acclivities, is a fair instance of one of the odd stories furnished by travellers about China, inasmuch as no tea grows in Shantung, and monkeys are taught more profitable tricks.[1] One of the most remarkable animals of this tribe is the *douc*, or Cochinchinese monkey (*Semnopithecus nemœus*). It is a large species of great rarity, and remarkable for the variety of colors with which it is adorned. Its body is about two feet long, and when standing in an upright position its height is considerably greater. The face is of an orange color, and flattened in its form. A dark band runs across the front of the forehead, and the sides of the countenance are bounded by long spreading yellowish tufts of hair. The body and upper parts of the forearms are brownish gray, the lower portions of the arms, from the elbows to the wrists, being white; its hands and thighs are black, and the legs of a bright red color, while the tail and a large triangular spot above it are pure white. Such a creature matches well, for its grotesque and variegated appearance, with the mandarin duck and gold fish, also peculiar to China.

Chinese books speak of several species of this family, and small kinds occur in all the provinces. M. David has recently added two novelties to the list from his acquisitions in Eastern Koko-nor, well fitted for that cold region by their abundant hair. The *Rhinopithecus roxellanœ* inhabits the alpine forests, nearly two miles high, where it subsists on the buds of plants and bamboo shoots laid up for winter supply; its face is green-

[1] Breton, *China, its Costumes, Arts*, etc., Vol. II.

ish, the nose remarkably *rétroussé*, and its strong, brawny limbs well fitted for the arboreal life it leads; the hair is thick and like a mane on the back, shaded with yellow and white tints. In this respect it is like the Gelada monkey of Abyssinia, and a few others protected in this part of the body from cold. This is no doubt the kind called *fí-fí* in native books, and once found in flocks along many portions of western China, as these authors declare. Their notices are rather tantalizing, but, now that we have found the animal, are worth quoting: "The *fí-fí* resembles a man; it is clothed with its hair, runs quick and eats men; it has a human face, long lips, black, hairy body, and turns its heels. It laughs on seeing a man and covers its eyes with its lips; it can talk and its voice resembles a bird. It occurs in Sz'chuen, where it is called *jin hiung*, or 'human bear;' its palms are good eating, and its skin is used; its habit is to turn over stones, seeking for crabs as its food. Its form is like that of the men who live in the Kwănlun Mountains."

Another large simia (*Macacus thibetanus*) comes from the same region; it lives in bands like the preceding, but lower down the mountains. A third species of great size was reported to occur in the southwestern part of Sz'chuen, and described as greenish like the *Macacus tcheliensis* from the hills northwest of Peking—the most northern species of monkey known. The former of these two may possibly be the *sing-sing* of the Chinese books, though its characteristics involve some confusion of the Macacus and baboon on the part of those writers. Two other species of Macacus, and as many of the gibbons, have been noticed in Hainan, Formosa, and elsewhere in the south.

The singular proboscis monkey (*Nasalis laivalus*), called *khi-doc* in Cochinchina and *hai-tuh* by the Chinese, exhibits a strange profile, part man and part beast, reminding one of the combinations in Da Vinci's caricatures. It is a large animal, covered with soft yellowish hair tinted with red; the long nose projects in the form of a sloping spatula. The Chinese account says: "Its nose is turned upward, and the tail very long and forked at the end, and that whenever it rains, the animal thrusts the forks into its nose. It goes in herds, and lives in friendship; when one dies, the rest accompany it to burial. Its activity is so great that it runs its head against the trees; its fur is soft and gray, and the face black."[1]

The *Chinese Herbal*, from which the preceding extract is taken, describes the bat under various names, such as 'heavenly rat,' 'fairy rat,' 'flying rat,' 'night swallow,' and 'belly wings;'

Fí-fí and Hai-tuh. (From a Chinese cut.)

it also details the various uses made of the animal in medicine, and the extraordinary longevity attained by some of the white species. The bat is in form like a mouse; its body is of an ashy black color; and it has thin fleshy wings, which join the four legs and tail into one. It appears in the summer, but becomes torpid in the winter; on which account, as it eats nothing during that season, and because it has a habit of swallowing its breath, it attains a great age. It has the character of a night

[1] Bridgman's *Chinese Chrestomathy*, p. 469.

rover, not on account of any inability to fly in the day, but it dares not go abroad at that time because it fears a kind of hawk. It subsists on mosquitoes and gnats. It flies with its head downward, because the brain is heavy.[1] This quotation is among the best Chinese descriptions of animals, and shows how little there is to depend upon in them, though not without interest in their notices of habits. Bats are common everywhere, and seem to be regarded with less aversion than in certain other countries. Twenty species belonging to nine genera are given in one list, most of them found in southern China; the wings of some of these measure two feet across; a large sort in Sz'chuen is eaten.

The brown bear is known, and its paws are regarded as a delicacy; trained animals are frequently brought into cities by showmen, who have taught them tricks. The discovery by David of a large species (*Ailuropus melanoleurus*) allied to the Himalayan panda (*Ailurus fulgens*), also found on the Sz'chuen Mountains, adds another instance of the strange markings common in Tibetan fauna. This beast feeds on flesh and vegetables; its body is white, but the ears, eyes, legs, and tip of the tail are quite black; the fur is thick and coarse. It is called *peh hiung*, or white bear, by the hunters, but is no doubt the animal called *pi* in the classics, common in early times over western China, and now rare even in Koko-nor. The Tibetan black bear occurs in Formosa, Shantung, and Hainan, showing a wide range. The badger is quite as widespread, and the two species have the same general appearance as their European congeners.

Carnivorous animals still exist, even in thickly settled districts. The lion may once have roamed over the southwestern Manji kingdom, but the name and drawings both indicate a foreign origin. It has much connection with Buddhism, and grotesque sculptures of rampant lions stand in pairs in front of temples, palaces, and graves, as a mark of honor and symbol of protection. The last instance of a live lion brought as tribute was to Hientsung in A.D. 1470, from India or Ceylon.

---

[1] *Chinese Repository*, Vol. VII., p. 90.

Many other species of *felis* are known, some of them peculiar to particular regions. The royal tiger has been killed near Amoy, and in Manchuria the panther, leopard, and tiger-cat all occur in the northern and southern provinces, making altogether a list of twelve species ranging from Formosa to Sagalien. Mr. Swinhoe's[1] account of his rencounter with a tiger near Amoy in 1858 explains how such large animals still remain in thickly settled regions where food is abundant and the people are timid and unarmed. In thinly peopled parts they become a terror to the peasants. M. David enumerates six kinds, including a lynx, in Monpin alone, one of which (*Felis scripta*) is among the most prettily marked of the whole family. Hunting-leopards and tigers were used in the days of Marco Polo by Kublai, but the manly pastime of the chase, on the magnificent scale then practised, has fallen into disuse with the present princes. A small and fierce species of wild-cat (*Felis chinensis*), two feet long, of a brownish-gray color, and handsomely marked with chestnut spots and black streaks, is still common in the southwestern portions of Fuhkien. Civet cats of two or three kinds, tree-civets (*Helictes*), and a fine species of marten (*Martes*), with yellow neck and purplish-brown body, from Formosa, are among the smaller carnivora in the southern provinces.

The domestic animals offer few peculiarities. The cat, *kia li*, or 'household fox,' is a favorite inmate of families, and the ladies of Peking are fond of a variety of the Angora cat, having long silky hair and hanging ears. The common species is variously marked, and in the south often destitute of a tail; when reared for food it is fed on rice and vegetables, but is not much eaten. Popular superstition has clustered many omens of good and bad luck about cats; it is considered, for example, the prognostic of certain misfortune when a cat is stolen from a house—much as, in some countries of the western world, it is unlucky when a black cat crosses one's pathway.

The dog differs but little from that reared among the Esquimaux, and is perhaps the original of the species. There is

---

[1] *Zoöl. Soc. Proc.*, 1870, p. 626.

little variation in their size, which is about a foot high and two feet in length; the color is a pale yellow or black, and always uniform, with coarse bristling hair, and tails curling up high over the back, and rising so abruptly from the insertion that it has been humorously remarked they almost assist in lifting the legs from the ground. The hind legs are unusually straight, which gives them an awkward look, and perhaps prevents them running very rapidly. The black eyes are small and piercing, and the insides of the lips and mouths, and the tongue, are of the same color, or a blue black. The bitch has a dew-claw on each hind leg, but the dog has none. The ears are sharp and upright, the head peaked, and the bark a short, thick snap, very unlike the deep, sonorous baying of our mastiffs. In Nganhwui a peculiar variety has pendant ears of great length, and thin, wirey tails. One item in the Chinese description of the dog is that it 'can go on three legs'—a gait that is often exhibited by them. They are used to watch houses and flocks; the Mongolian breed is fierce and powerful. The dogs of Peking are very clannish, and each set jealously guards its own street or yard; they are fed by the butchers in the streets, and serve as scavengers there and in all large towns. They are often mangey, presenting hideous spectacles, and instances of *plica polonica* are not uncommon, but, as among the celebrated street dogs of Constantinople, hydrophobia is almost unheard of among them. Dog markets are seen in every city where this meat is sold; the animals are reared expressly for the table, but their flesh is expensive.

One writer remarks on their habits, when describing the worship offered at the tombs: "Hardly had the hillock been abandoned by the worshippers, when packs of hungry dogs came running up to devour the part of the offerings left for the dead, or to lick up the grease on the ground. Those who came first held up their heads, bristled their hair, and showed a proud and satisfied demeanor, curling and wagging their tails with selfish delight; while the late-comers, tails between their legs, held their heads and ears down. There was one of them, however, which, grudging the fare, held his nose to the wind as if sniffing for better luck; but one lean, old, and ugly beast, with a flayed back and hairless tail, was seen gradually separating himself from the band, though without seeming to hurry himself, making a thousand doublings and windings, all the while looking back to see if he was noticed. But the old sharper knew what he was about, and as soon as he thought himself at a safe distance, away he went like an arrow, the whole pack after him, to some other feast and some other tomb."[1]

Wolves, raccoon-dogs, and foxes are everywhere common, in some places proving to be real pests in the sheepfold and farmyard. In the vicinity of Peking, it is customary to draw large white rings on the plastered walls, in order to terrify the wolves, as these beasts, it is thought, will flee on observing such traps. The Chinese regard the fox as the animal into which human spirits enter in preference to any other, and are therefore afraid to destroy or displease it. The elevated steppes are the abodes of three or four kinds, which find food without difficulty. The Tibetan wolf (*Canis chanco*) has a warm, yellowish-white covering, and ranges the wilds of Tsaidam and Koko-nor in packs. The fox (*Canis cossac*) spreads over a wide range, and is famed for its sagacity in avoiding enemies.

The breed of cattle and horses is dwarfish, and nothing is done to improve them. The oxen are sometimes not larger than an ass; some of them have a small hump, showing their affinity to the zebu; the dewlap is large, and the contour neat and symmetrical. The forehead is round, the horns small and irregularly curved, and the general color dun red. The buffalo (*shui niu*), or 'water ox,' is the largest beast used in agriculture. It is very docile and unwieldy, larger than an English ox, and its hairless hide is a light black color; it seeks coolness and refuge from the gnat in muddy pools dug for its convenience, where it wallows with its nose just above the surface. Each horn is nearly semi-circular, and bends downward, while the head is turned back so as almost to bring the nose horizontal. The herd-boys usually ride it, and the metaphor of a lad astride a buffalo's back, blowing the flute, frequently enters into Chinese

---

[1] Borget, *La Chine Ouverte*, p. 147.

descriptions of rural life. The yak of Tibet is employed as a beast of burden, and to furnish food and raiment. It is covered with a mantle of hair reaching nearly to the ground, and the soft pelage is used for making standards among the Persians, and its tail as fly-flaps or chowries in India; the hair is woven into carpets. The wild yak (*Poephagus grunniens*) has already been described. Great herds of these huge bovines roam over the wastes of Koko-nor, where their dried droppings furnish the only fuel for the nomads crossing those barren wilds.

The domestic sheep is the broad-tailed species, and furnishes excellent mutton. The tail is sometimes ten inches long and three or four thick; and the size of this fatty member is not affected by the temperature. The sheep are reared in the north by Mohammedans, who prepare the fleeces for garments by careful tanning; the animal is white, with a black head. Goats are raised in all parts, but not in large numbers. The argali and wild sheep of the Ala shan Mountains (*Ovis Burrhel*) furnish exciting sport in chasing them over their native cliffs, which they clamber with wonderful agility. Another denizen of those dreary wilds is the *Antilope picticauda*, a small and tiny species, weighing about forty pounds, of a dusky gray color, with a narrow yellow stripe on the flanks. Its range is about the head-waters of the Yangtsz' River; its swiftness is amazing; it seems absolutely to fly. It scrapes for itself trenches in which to lie secure from the cold.

Many genera of ruminants are represented in China and the outlying regions; twenty-seven rare species are enumerated in Swinhoe's and David's lists, of which eleven are antelopes and deer. The range of some of them is limited to a narrow region, and most of them are peculiar to the country. The wealthy often keep deer in their grounds, especially the spotted deer (*Cervus pseudaxis*), from Formosa, whose coat is found to vary greatly according to sex and age; its name, *kin-tsien luh*, or 'money deer,' indicates its markings. Mouse-deer are also reared as pets in the southern provinces.

One common species is the *dzeren* or *hwang yang* (*Antilope gutturosa*), which roams over the Mongolian wilds in large herds, and furnishes excellent venison. It is heavy in comparison to the gazelle; horns thick, about nine inches long, annulated to the tips, lyrated, and their points turned inward. The goitre, which gives it its name, is a movable protuberance occasioned by the dilatation of the larnyx; in the old males it is much enlarged. The animal takes surprising bounds when running. Great numbers are killed in the autumn, and their flesh, skins, and horns are all of service for food, leather, and medicine.

Several kinds of hornless (or nearly hornless) deer, allied to the musk-deer, exist. One is the river-deer (*Hydropotes*), common near the Yangtsz' River, which resembles the pudu of Chili; it is very prolific on the bottoms and in the islands. Another sort in the northwest (*Elaphodus*) is intermediary between the muntjacs and deer, having long, trenchant, canine upper teeth, and a deep chocolate-colored fur. Three varieties of the musk-deer (*Moschus*) have been observed, differing a little in their colors, all called *shié* or *hiang chang* by the Chinese, and all eagerly hunted for their musk. This perfume was once deemed to be useful in medicine, and is cited in a Greek prescription of the sixth century; the abundance of the animal in the Himalayan regions may be inferred from Tavernier's statement that he bought 7673 bags or pods at Patna in one of his journeys over two hundred years ago. This animal roams over a vast extent of alpine territory, from Tibet and Shensí to Lake Baikal, and inhabits the loftiest cliffs and defiles, and makes its way over rugged mountains with great rapidity. It is not unlike the roe in general appearance, though the projecting teeth makes the upper lip to look broad. Its color is grayish-brown and its limbs slight; the hair is coarse and brittle, almost like spines. The musk is contained in a pouch beneath the tail on the male, and is most abundant during the rutting season. He is taken in nets or shot, and the hunters are said to allure him to destruction by secreting themselves and playing the flute, though some would say the animal showed very little taste in listening to such sounds as Chinese flutes usually produce. The musk is often adulterated with clay or mixed with other substances to moderate its powerful odor. A singular and interesting member of this family is reared in the great park south of Peking--a kind of elk with short horns. This large animal (*Elaphurus Davidianus*), of a gentle disposition, equals in size the largest deer; its native name, *sz'-puh siang*, indicates that it is neither a horse, a deer, a camel, nor an ox, but partakes in some respects of the characteristics of each of them. Its gentle croaking voice seems to be unworthy of so huge a body; the color is a uniform fawn or light gray.

The horse is not much larger than the Shetland pony; it is bony and strong, but kept with little care, and presents the worst possible appearance in its usual condition of untrimmed coat and mane, bedraggled fetlocks, and twisted tail. The Chinese language possesses a great variety of terms to designate the horse; the difference of age, sex, color, and disposition, all being denoted by particular characters. Piebald and mottled, white and bay horses are common; but the improvement of this noble animal is neglected, and he looks sorry enough compared with the coursers of India. He is principally used for carrying the post, or for military services; asses and mules being more employed for draught. He is hardy, feeds on coarse food, and admirably serves his owners. The mule is well-shaped, and those raised for the gentry are among the very best in the world for endurance and strength; dignitaries are usually drawn by sumpter mules. Donkeys are also carefully raised. Chinese books speak of a mule of a cow and horse, as well as from the ass and horse, though, of course, no such hybrid as the former ever existed.

The wild ass, or onager (under the several names by which it is known in different lands, *kyang*, *djang*, *kulan*, *djiggetai*, *ghor-khar*, and *yé-lu*), still roams free and untameable. It is abundant in Koko-nor, gathering in troops of ten to fifty, each under the lead of a stallion to defend the mares. The flesh is highly prized, and the difficulty of procuring it adds to the delicacy of the dish; the color is light chestnut, with white belly.

Elephants are kept at Peking for show, and are used to draw the state chariot when the Emperor goes to worship at the Altars of Heaven and Earth, but the sixty animals seen in the days of Kienlung, by Bell, have since dwindled to one or two. Van Braam met six going into Peking, sent thither from Yunnan. The deep forests of that province also harbor the rhinoceros and tapir. The horn of the former is sought after as medicine, and the best pieces are carved most beautifully into ornaments or into drinking cups, which are supposed to sweat whenever any poisonous liquid is put into them. The tapir is the white and brown animal found in the Malacca peninsula, and strange stories are recorded of its eating stones and copper. The wild boar grows to weigh over four hundred pounds and nearly six feet long. In cold weather its frozen carcass is brought to Peking, and sold at a high price. A new species of

The Chinese Pig.

hog has been found in Formosa, about three feet long, twenty-one inches high, and showing a dorsal row of large bristles; a third variety occurs among the novelties discovered in Sz'chuen (*Sus moupinensis*), having short ears. Wild boars are met with even in the hills of Chehkiang, and seriously annoy the husbandmen in the lowlands by their depredations. Deep pits are dug near the base of the hills, and covered with a bait of fresh grass, and many are annually captured or drowned in them. They are fond of the bamboo shoots, and persons are stationed near the groves to frighten them away by striking pieces of wood together.

The Chinese hollow-backed pig is known for its short legs,

round body, crooked back, and abundance of fat; the flesh is the common meat of the people south of the Yangtsz' River. The black Chinese breed, as it is called in England, is considered the best pork raised in that country. The hog in the northern provinces is a gaunt animal, uniformly black, and not so well cared for as its southern rival. Piebald pigs are common in Formosa, resulting from crossing; sometimes animals of this kind are quite woolly. The Chinese in the south, well aware of the perverse disposition of the hog, find it much more expeditious to carry instead of drive him through their narrow

Mode of Carrying Pigs.

streets. For this purpose cylindrical baskets, open at both ends, are made; and in order to capture the obstinate brute, it is secured just outside the half-opened gate of the pen. The men seize him by the tail and pull it lustily; his rage is roused by the pain, and he struggles; they let go their hold, whereupon he darts out of the gate to escape, and finds himself snugly caught. He is lifted up and unresistingly carried off.

The camel is employed in the trade carried on across the desert, and throughout Mongolia, Manchuria, and northern China near the plateau; without his aid those regions would be impassible; the passes across the ranges near Koko-nor, sixteen thousand feet high, are traversed by his help, though amid suffering and danger. In the summer season it sheds all its hair, which is gathered for weaving into ropes and rugs; at this period, large herds pasture on the plateau to recuperate. The humps at this season hang down the back like empty bags, and the poor animal presents a distressed appearance during the hot weather. In its prime condition it carries about six hundred pounds weight, but is not used to ride upon as is the Arabian species. The two kinds serve man in one continuous *kafilah* from the Sea of Tartary across two continents to Timbuctoo. The Chinese have employed the camel in war, and trained it to carry small gingalls so that the riders could fire them while resting on its head, but this antique kind of cavalry has disappeared with the introduction of better weapons.

Among the various tribes of smaller animals, the Chinese Empire furnishes many interesting peculiarities, and few families are unrepresented. No marsupials have yet been met, and the order of edentata is still restricted to one instance. Several families in other orders are rare or wanting, as baboons, spider-monkeys, skunks, and ichneumons. In the weasel tribe, some new species have been added to the already long list of valuable fur-bearing animals found in the mountains—the sable ermine, marten, pole-cat, stoat, etc., whose skins still repay the hunters. The weasel is common, but not troublesome. The otter is trained in Sz'chuen to catch fish in the mountain streams with the docility of a spaniel; another species (*Lutia swinhosi*) occurs along the islands on the southern coast, while in Hainan Island appears a kind of clawless otter of a rich brown color above and white beneath; each of these is about twenty inches long. The furs of all these, and also the sea-otter, are prepared for garments, especially collars and neck-wraps.

A kind of mole exists in Sz'chuen, having a muzzle of extreme length, while the scent of another variety near Peking is so musky as to suggest its name (*Scaptochirus moschatus*). Musk-rats and shrew-mice are found both north and south; and one western species has only a rudimentary tail; while another, the

Scaptonyx, forms an intermediate species between a mole and a shrew, having a blunt muzzle, strong fore feet and a long tail; and lastly, a sort fitted for aquatic habits, with broad hind feet and flattened tail. Tiny hedgehogs are common even in the streets and by-lanes of Peking, where they find food and refuge in the alluvial earth. Two or three kinds of marmots and mole-rats are found in the north and west (*Siphucus Arctomys*), all specifically unlike their congeners elsewhere. The Chinese have a curious fancy in respect to one beast, one bird, and one fish, each of which, they say, requires that two come together to make one complete animal, viz., the jerboa, the spoonbill and sole-fish; the first (*Dipus annulatus*) occurs in the sands of northern China, the second in Formosa, and the third along the coasts.

Many kinds of rodents have been described. The alpine hare (*Lagomys ogotona*) resembles a marmot in its habits and is met with throughout the grassy parts of the steppes; its burrows riddle the earth wherever the little thing gathers, and endangers the hunters riding over it. It is about the size of a rat, and by its wonderful fecundity furnishes food to a great number of its enemies—man, beasts, and birds; it is not dormant, but gathers dry grass for food and warmth during cold weather; this winter store is, however, often consumed by cattle before it is stored away. Hares and rabbits are well known. Two species of the former are plenty on the Mongolian grass-lands, one of which has very long feet; in winter their frozen bodies are brought to market. One species is restricted to Hainan Island. Ten or twelve kinds of squirrels have been described, red, gray, striped, and buff; one with fringed ears. Their skins are prepared for the furriers, and women wear winter robes lined with them. Two genera of flying-squirrel (*Pteromys* and *Sciuropterus*) have been noticed, the latter in Formosa and the former mostly in the western provinces. Chinese writers have been puzzled to class the flying-squirrel; they place it among birds, and assure their readers that it is the only kind which suckles its young when it flies, and that "the skin held in the hand during parturition renders delivery easier, because the animal has a remarkably lively disposition." The long, dense fur of the *P. alborufous* makes beautiful dresses, the white tips of the hair contrasting prettily with the red ground.

Of the proper rats and mice, more than twenty-five species have been already described. Some of them are partially arboreal, others have remarkably long tails, and all but three are peculiar to the country. A Formosan species, called by Swinhoe the spinous county rat, had been dedicated to Koxinga, the conqueror of that island; while another common in Sz'chuen bears the name of *Mus Confucianus*. The extent to which the Chinese eat rats has been greatly exaggerated by travellers, for the flesh is too expensive for general use.

One species of porcupine (*Hystrix subcristata*) inhabits the southern provinces, wearing on its head a purplish-black crest of stout spines one to five inches long; the bristles are short, but increase in size and length to eight or nine inches toward the rump; the entire length is thirty-three inches. The popular notion that the porcupine darts its quills at its enemies as an effectual weapon is common among the Chinese.

No animal has puzzled the Chinese more than the scaly anteater or pangolin (*Manis dalmanni*), which is logically considered as a certain and useful remedy by them, simply because of its oddity. It is regarded as a fish out of water, and therefore named *ling-lí*, or 'hill carp,' also dragon carp, but the most common designation is *chuen shan kiah*, or the 'scaly hill borer.' One author says: "Its shape resembles a crocodile; it can go in dry paths as well as in the water; it has four legs. In the daytime it ascends the banks of streams, and lying down opens its scales wide, putting on the appearance of death, which induces the ants to enter between them. As soon as they are in, the animal closes its scales and returns to the water to open them; the ants float out dead, and he devours them at leisure." A more accurate observer says: "It continually protrudes its tongue to entice the ants on which it feeds;" and true to Chinese physiological deductions, *similia similibus curantur*, he recommends the scales as a cure for all antish swellings. He also remarks that the scales are not bony, and consist of the agglutinated hairs of the body. The adult specimens measure thirty-three inches. It walks on the sides of the hind feet and tips of the claws of the fore feet, and can stand upright for a minute or two. The large scales are held to the skin by a fleshy nipple-like pimple, which adheres to the base.

Among the cetaceous inhabitants of the Chinese waters, one of the most noticeable is the great white porpoise (*Delphinus chinensis*), whose uncouth tumbles attract the traveller's notice as he sails into the estuary of the Pearl River on his way to Hongkong, and again as he steams up the Yangtsz' to Hankow. The Chinese fishermen are shy of even holding it in their nets, setting it free at once, and never pursuing it; they call it *peh-kí* and deem its presence favorable to their success. A species of fin-whale (*Balænoptera*) has been described by Swinhoe, which ranges the southern coast from the shores of Formosa to Hainan. Its presence between Hongkong and Amoy induced some foreigners to attempt a fishery in those waters, but the yield of oil and bone was too small for their outlay. The native fishermen join their efforts in the winter, when it resorts to the seas near Hainan, going out in fleets of small boats from three to twenty-five tons burden each, fifty boats going together. The line is about three hundred and fifty feet long, made of native hemp, and fastened to the mast, the end leading over the bow. The harpoon has one barb, and is attached to a wooden handle; through an eye near the socket, the line is so fastened along the handle, that when the whale begins to strain upon it, the handle draws out upon the line, leaving only the barb buried in the skin. The boat is sailed directly upon the fish, and the harpooner strikes from the bow just behind the blow-hole. As soon as the fish is struck the sail is lowered, the rudder unshipped, and the boat allowed to drag stern foremost until the prey is exhausted. Other boats come up to assist, and half a dozen harpoons soon dispatch it. The species most common there yield about fifty barrels each; the oil, flesh, and bone are all used for food or in manufactures. The fish resort to the shallow waters in those seas for food, and to roll and rub on the banks and reefs, thus ridding themselves of the barnacles and insects which torment them; they are often seen leaping entirely out of water, and falling back perpendicularly against the hard bottom.[1]

The Yellow Sea affords a species of cow-fish, or round headed cachalot (*Globicephalus Rissii*), which the Japanese capture.[2] Seals have been observed on the coast of Liautung, but nothing is known of their species or habits; the skins are common and cheap in the Peking market. Native books speak of a marine animal in Koko-nor, from which a rare medicine is obtained, that probably belongs to this family.

This imperfect account of the mammalia known to exist in China has been drawn from the lists and descriptions inserted in the zoölogical periodicals of Europe, and may serve to indicate the extent and richness of the field yet to be investigated. The lists of Swinhoe and David alone contain nearly two hundred species, and within the past ten years scores more have been added, but have not exhausted the new and unexplored zoölogical regions. The emperors of the Mongol dynasty were very fond of the chase, and famous for their love of the noble amusement of falconry; Marco Polo says that Kublai employed no less than seventy thousand attendants in his hawking excursions. Falcons, kites, and other birds were taught to pursue their quarry, and the Venetian speaks of eagles trained to stoop at wolves, and of such size and strength that none could escape their talons.[3] Ranking has collected[4] a number of notices of the mode and sumptuousness of the field sports of the Mongols in China and India, but they convey little more information to the naturalist, than that the game was abundant and comprised a vast variety. Many species of accipitrine birds are described in Chinese books, but they are spoken of so vaguely that nothing definite can be learned from the notices. Few of them are now trained for sport by the Chinese, except a kind of sparrow-hawk to amuse dilettanti hunters in showing their skill in catching small birds. The fondness for sport in the wilds of Manchuria which the old emperors

---

1 *Chinese Repository*, Vol. XII., p. 608.

2 Ibid., Vol. VI., p. 411.

3 Yule's *Marco Polo*, Vol. I., p. 353.

4 *Wars and Sports of the Mongols and Romans.*

encouraged two centuries ago has all died out among their descendants.

Within the last fifteen years a greater advance has been made in the knowledge of the birds of China than in any other branch of its natural history, perhaps owing somewhat to their presenting themselves for capture to the careful observer. The list of described species already numbers over seven hundred, of which the careful paper of the lamented Swinhoe, in the *Proceedings of the Zoölogical Society* for May, 1871, gives the names of six hundred and seventy-five species, and M. David's list, in the *Nouvelles Archives* for 1871, gives four hundred and seventy as the number observed north of the River Yangtsz'. The present sketch must confine itself to selecting a few of the characteristic birds of the country, for this part of its fauna is as interesting and peculiar as the mammalia.

Among birds of prey are vultures, eagles, and ernes, all of them widespread and well known. One of the fishing-eagles (*Haliætus macei*) lives along the banks of the bend of the Yellow River in the Ortous country. The golden eagle is still trained for the chase by Mongols; Atkinson accompanied a party on a hunt. "We had not gone far," he says, "when several large deer rushed past, bounding over the plain about three hundred yards from us. In an instant the barkut was unhooded and his shackles removed, when he sprung from his perch and soared on high. He rose to a considerable height, and seemed to poise for a minute, gave two or three flaps with his wings, and swooped off in a straight line for the prey. I could not see his wings move, but he went at a fearful rate, and all of us after the deer; when we were about two hundred yards off, the bird struck the deer, and it gave one bound and fell. The barkut had struck one talon in his neck, the other into his back, and was tearing out his liver. The Kirghis sprung from his horse, slipped the hood over the eagle's head and the shackles on his legs, and easily took him off, remounting and getting ready for another flight."[1] Other smaller species are trained to capture or worry hares, foxes, and lesser game.

---

[1] *Oriental and Western Siberia*, p. 416.

The falcons which inhabit the gate-towers and trees in Peking form a peculiar feature of the place, from their impudence in foraging in the streets and markets, snatching things out of the hands of people, and startling one by their responsive screams. Much quarrelling goes on between them and the crows and magpies for the possession of old nests as the spring comes on. Their services as scavengers insures them a quiet residence in their eyries on the gate-towers. Six sorts of harriers (*Circus*), with various species of falcons, bustards, gledes, and sparrow-hawks, are enumerated. The family of owls is well represented, and live ones are often exposed for sale in the markets; its native name of 'cat-headed hawk' (*mao-'rh-tao ying*) suggests the likeness of the two. Out of the fifty-six species of accipitrine birds, the hawks are much the most numerous.

The great order of Passerinæ has its full share of beautiful and peculiar representatives, and over four hundred species have been catalogued. The night-hawks have only three members, but the swallows count up to fifteen species. Around Peking they gather in vast numbers, year after year, in the gate-towers, and that whole region was early known by the name of *Yen Kwoh*, or 'Land of Swallows.' The immunity granted by the natives to this twittering, bustling inmate of their houses has made it a synonym for domestic life; the phrase *yin yen* (*lit.* to 'drink swallows') means to give a feast. The family of king-fishers contains several most exquisitely colored birds, and multitudes of the handsome ones, like the turquoise king-fisher (*Halcyon smyrnensis*), are killed by the Chinese for the sake of the plumage. Beautiful feather-work ornaments are made from this at Canton. The hoopoe, bee-eater, and cuckoo are not uncommon; the first goes by the name of the *shan ho-shang*, or 'country priest,' from its color. Six species of the last have been recognized, and its peculiar habits of driving other birds from their nests has made it well known to the people, who call it *ku-ku* for the same reason as do the English. On the upper Yangtsz' the short-tailed species makes its noisy agitated flight in order to draw off attention from its nest. The Chinese say it weeps blood as it bewails its mate all night long. The *Cucutus striatus* varies so greatly in different provinces that it has much perplexed naturalists; all of them are only summer visitants.

The habit of the shrike of impaling its prey on thorns and elsewhere before devouring it has been noticed by native writers; no less than eleven species have been observed to cross the country in their migrations from Siberia to the Archipelago. Of the nuthatches, tree and wall creepers, wrens, and chats, there is a large variety, and one species of willow-wren (*Sylvia borealis*) has been detected over the entire eastern hemisphere; six sorts of redstarts (*Ruticilla*) are spread over the provinces.

Among the common song birds reared for the household, the thrush and lark take precedence; their fondness for birds and flowers is one of the pleasant features of Chinese national character. A kind of grayish-yellow thrush (*Garrulax perspicilatus*), called *hwa-mí*, or 'painted eyebrows,' is common about Canton, where a well-trained bird is worth several dollars. This genus furnishes six species, but they are not all equally musical; another kind (*Suthoria webbiana*) is kept for its fighting qualities, as it will die before it yields. These and other allied birds furnish the people with much amusement, by teaching them to catch seeds thrown into the air, jump from perches held in the hand, and perform tricks of various kinds. A party of gentlemen will often be seen on the outskirts of a town in mild weather, each one holding his pet bird, and all busily engaged in catching grasshoppers to feed them. The spectacle thrush (*Leucodioptrum*) has its eyes surrounded by a black circle bearing a fancied resemblance to a pair of spectacles; it is not a very sweet songster, but a graceful, lively fellow. The species of wagtail and lark known amount to about a score altogether, but not all of them are equally good singers. The southern Chinese prefer the lark which comes from Chihlí, and large numbers are annually carried south. The shrill notes of the field lark (*Alauda cœlivox* and *arvensis*) are heard in the shops and streets in emulous concert with other kinds—these larks becoming at times well-nigh frantic with excitement in their struggles for victory. The Chinese name of *peh-ling*, or 'hundred spirits,' given to the Mongolian lark, indicates the reputation it has earned as an active songster; and twenty-five dollars is not an uncommon price for a good one.[1]

The tits (*Parus*) and reedlings (*Emberiza*), together with kindred genera, are among the most common small birds, fifteen or twenty species of each having been noticed. In the proper season the latter are killed for market in such numbers as to excite surprise that they do not become extinct. In taking many of the warblers, orioles, and jays, for rearing or sale as fancy birds, the Chinese are very expert in the use of birdlime. In all parts of the land, the pie family are deemed so useful as scavengers that they are never molested, and in consequence become very common. The magpie is a favorite bird, as its name, *hí tsioh*, or 'joyous bird,' indicates, and occurs all over the land. Ravens, choughs, crows, and blackbirds keep down the insects and vermin and consume offal. The palace grounds and inclosures of the nobility in Peking are common resorts for these crows, where they are safe from harm in the great trees. Every morning myriads of them leave town with the dawn, returning at evening with increased cawing and clamor, at times actually darkening the sky with their flocks. A pretty sight is occasionally seen when two or three thousand young crows assemble just at sunset in mid-air to chase and play with each other. The crow is regarded as somewhat of a sacred bird, either from a service said to have been rendered by one of his race to an ancestor of the present dynasty, or because he is an emblem of filial duty, from a notion that the young assist their parents when disabled. The owl, on the other hand, has an odious name because it is stigmatized as the bird which eats its dam. One member of the pie family deserving mention is the long-tailed blue jay of Formosa (*Urocissa*), remarkable for its brilliant plumage. Another, akin to the sun birds (*Æthopyga dabryi*), comes from Sz'chuen, a recent discovery. The body is red, the head, throat, and each side of the neck a brilliant violet, belly yellow, wings black with the primaries tinted green along the edge, and the feathers long, tapering, of a black or steel blue.

[1] *Journal of the North China Branch of the Royal Asiatic Society*, **May, 1859**, p. 289.

The *Mainah*, or Indian mino (*Acridotheus*), known by its yellow carbuncles, which extend like ears from behind the eye, is reared, as are also three species of *Munia*, at Canton. Sparrows abound in every province around houses, driving away other birds, and entertaining the observer by their quarrels and activity. Robins, ouzels, and tailor-birds are not abundant. None of the humming-birds or birds of paradise occur, and only one species has hitherto been seen of the parrot group. Woodpeckers (*Picus*) are of a dozen species, and the wryneck occasionally attracts the eye of a sportsman. The canary is reared in great numbers, being known under the names of 'white swallow' and 'time sparrow;' the chattering Java sparrow and tiny avedavat are also taught little tricks by their fanciers, in compensation for their lack of song. The two or three proper parrots are natives of Formosa.

The family of pigeons (*Columbidæ*) is abundantly represented in fourteen species, and doves form a common household bird; their eggs are regarded as proper food to prevent small-pox, and sold in the markets, being also cooked in birdnest and other kinds of soups. The Chinese regard the dove as eminently stupid and lascivious, but grant it the qualities of faithfulness, impartiality, and filial duty. The cock is said to send away its mate on the approach of rain, and let her return to the nest with fine weather. They have an idea that it undergoes periodic metamorphoses, but disagree as to the form it takes, though the sparrow-hawk has the preference.[1] The bird is most famed, however, for its filial duty, arising very probably from imperfect observations of the custom of feeding its young with the macerated contents of its crop; the wood pigeon is said to feed her seven young ones in one order in the morning, and reversing it in the evening. Its note tells the husbandman when to begin his labors, and the decorum observed in the nests and cotes of all the species teach men how to govern a family and a state. The visitor to Peking is soon attracted by the æolian notes proceeding from doves which circle around their homes for a short time (forty or fifty or less in a flock), and

[1] *Journal N. C. Br. R. A. Soc.*, Vol. IV., 1867, Art. XI., by T. Watters.

then settle. These birds are called *pan-tien kiao-jin*, or 'mid-sky houris,' and their weird music is caused by ingenious wooden whistles tied on the rumps of two or three of the flock, which lead the others and delight themselves. Carrier pigeons are used to some extent, and training them is a special mystery. One of the prettiest sort is the rose pigeon, and half a dozen kinds of turtles enliven the village groves with their gentle notes and peculiar plumage.

No tribe of birds in China, however, equals the Gallinaceous for its beauty, size, and novelty, furnishing some of the most elegant and graceful birds in the world, and yet none of them have become domesticated for food. As a connecting link between this tribe and the last is the sand-grouse of the desert (*Syrrhaptis paradoxus*), whose singular combination attracted Marco Polo's eye. "This bird, the *barguerlac*, on which the falcons feed," says he, "is as big as a partridge, has feet like a parrot's, tail like a swallow's, and is strong in flight."[1] Abbé Huc speaks of the immense flocks which scour the plateau.

The gold and silver pheasants are reared without trouble in all the provinces, and have so long been identified with the ornithology of China as to be regarded as typical of its grotesque and brilliant fauna. Among other pheasants may be mentioned the Impeyan, Reeves, Argus, Medallion, Amherst, l'Huys, and Pallas, each one vieing with the other for some peculiarly graceful feature of color and shape, so that it is hard to decide which is the finest. The Amherst pheasant has the bearing, the elegance, and the details of form like the gold pheasant, but the neck, shoulders, back and wing covers are of a sparkling metallic green, and each feather ends in a belt of velvet black. A little red crest allies it to the gold pheasant, and a pretty silvery ruff with a black band, a white breast and belly, and a tail barred with brown, green, white, and red bands, complete the picturesque dress. Hidden away in these Tibetan wilds are other pheasants that dispute the palm for beauty, among which four species of the eared pheasant (*Crossoptilon*) attract notice. One is of a pure white, with a black tail curled up and spread

---

[1] Yule's *Marco Polo*, Vol. I., p. 237.

out like a plume, and is well called the snow pheasant. Another is the better known Pallas pheasant, nearly as large as a turkey, distinguished by ear-like appendages or wattles behind the head, and a red neck above a white body, whence its native name of *ho-ki*, or 'fire hen.' Another genus (*Lophophorus*) contains some elegant kinds, of which the l'Huys pheasant is new, and noted for a coppery-green tail bespangled with white. The longer known Reeves pheasant is sought for by the natives for the sake of its white and yellow-barred tail feathers, which are used by play actors to complete a warrior's dress; Col. Yule proves a reference to it in Marco Polo from this part of its plumage, which the Venetian states to be ten palms in length—not far beyond the truth, as they have been seen seven feet long.[1] It is a long time for a bird of so much beauty to have been unknown, from 1350 to 1808, when Mr. Thomas Beale procured a specimen in Canton, and sent others to England in 1832; Mr. Reeves took it thither, and science has recorded it in her annals. As New Guinea is the home of the birds of paradise, so do the Himalayas contain most of these superb pheasants and francolins, each tribe serving as a foil and comparison with the Creator's handiwork in the other.

The island of Formosa has furnished a second species, Swinhoe's pheasant, of the same genus as the silver pheasant (*Euplocamus*), and another smaller kind (*Phasianus formosanus*); the list is also increased by fresh acquisitions from Yunnan and Cochinchina through Dr. Anderson. This is not, however, the place where we may indulge in details respecting all of these gorgeous birds; we conclude, then, with the Medallion, or horned pheasant. It has a "beautiful membrane of resplendent colors on the neck, which is displayed or contracted according as the cock is more or less roused. The hues are chiefly purple, with bright red and green spots, which vary in intensity according to the degree of excitement."

The peacock, though not a native, is reared in all parts; it bears the name of *kung tsioh*, sometimes rendered 'Confucius'

---

[1] Yule's *Marco Polo*, Vol. I., p. 246—where there is an admirable wood-cut of one from Wood.

bird,' though it is more probable that the name means the great or magnificent bird. The use of the tail feathers to designate official rank, which probably causes a large consumption of them, does not date previous to the present dynasty. Poultry is reared in immense quantities, but the assortment in China does not equal in beauty, excellence, and variety the products of Japanese culture. The silken cock, the vane of whose plume is so minutely divided as to resemble curly hair, is probably the same sort with that described by some writers as having wool like sheep. The Mongols succeed very well in rearing the tall, Shanghai breed, and their uniform cold winter enables them to preserve frozen flesh without much difficulty. The smaller gallinaceous birds already described, grouse, quails, francolins, partridges, sand-snipe, etc., amount to a score or more species, ranging all over the Empire. The red partridge is sometimes tamed to keep as a house bird with the fowls. The Chinese quail (*Coturnix*) has a brown back, sprinkled with black spots and white lines, blackish throat and chestnut breast. It is reared for fighting in south China, and, like its bigger Gallic rival, is soon eaten if it allows itself to be beaten.

The widespread family of waders sends a few of its representatives from Europe to China, but most of the members are Oriental. The marshes and salt lakes of Mongolia attract enormous numbers of migratory birds in summer to rear their young in safety, in the midst of abundant food. Col. Prejevalsky watched the arrival of vast flocks early in February, and thus describes their appearance: "For days together they sped onward, always from the W.S.W., going further east in search of open water, and at last settling down among the open pools; their favorite haunts were the flat mud banks overgrown with low saline bushes. Here every day vast flocks would congregate toward evening, crowding among the ice; the noise they made on rising was like a hurricane, and at a distance they resembled a thick cloud. Flocks of one, two, three, and even five thousand, followed one another in quick succession, hardly a minute apart. Tens and hundreds of thousands, even millions of birds appeared at Lob-nor during the fortnight ending the 21st of February, when the flight was at its height. What prodigious quantities of food must be necessary for such numbers!"[1] Wading and web-footed birds all harmlessly mix in these countless hosts, but hawks, eagles, and animals gather too, to prey on them.

Among the noticeable waders of China, the white Manchurian or Montigny crane is one of the finest and largest; it is the official insigna of the highest rank of civilians. Five species of crane (*Grus*) are recognized, and seven of plovers, together with as many more allied genera, including an avocet, bustard, and oyster-catcher. Curlews abound along the flat shores of the Gulf of Pechele, and are so tame that they race up and down with the naked children at low tide, hunting for shell-fish; as the boy runs his arm into the ooze the curlew pokes his long bill up to the eyes in the same hole, each of them grasping a crab. Godwits and sandpipers enliven the coasts with their cries, and seven species of gambets (*Totanus*) give them them the largest variety of their family group, next to the snipes (*Tringa*), of which nine are recorded. Herons, egrets, ibis, and night-herons occur, and none of them are discarded for food. At Canton, a pure white egret is often exposed for sale in the market, standing on a shelf the livelong day, with its eyelids sewed together—a pitiable sight. Its slender, elegant shape is imitated by artists in making bronze candlesticks. The singular spoonbill (*Platalea*) is found in Formosa, and the jacana in southwestern China. The latter is described by Gould as "distinguished not less by the grace of its form than its adaptation to the localities which nature has allotted it. Formed for traversing the morass and lotus-covered surface of the water, it supports itself upon the floating weeds and leaves by the extraordinary span of the toes, aided by the unusual lightness of the body."[2] Gallinules, crakes, and rails add to this list, but the flamingo has not been recorded.

In the last order, sixty-five species of web-footed birds are enumerated by naturalists as occurring in China. The fenny

---

[1] *From Kulja to Lob-nor*, p. 116.

[2] John Gould, *Century of Birds*. London, 1831–32.

margins of lakes and rivers, and the seacoast marshes, afford food and shelter to flocks of water-fowl. Ten separate species of duck are known, of which four or five are peculiar. The whole coast from Hainan to Manchuria swarms with gulls, terns, and grebes, while geese, swans, and mallards resort to the inland waters and pools to rear their young. Ducks are sometimes caught by persons who first cover their heads with a gourd pierced with holes, and then wade into the water where the birds are feeding; these, previously accustomed to empty calabashes floating about on the water, allow the fowler to approach, and are pulled under without difficulty. The wild goose is a favorite bird with native poets. The reputation for conjugal fidelity has made its name and that of the mandarin duck emblems of that virtue, and a pair of one or the other usually forms part of wedding processions. The epithet *mandarin* is applied to this beautiful fowl, and also to a species of orange, simply because of their excellence over other varieties of the same genus, and not, as some writers have inferred, because they are appropriated to officers of government.

The *yuen-yang*, as the Chinese call this duck, is a native of the central provinces. It is one of the most variegated birds known, vieing with the humming-birds and parrots in the diversified tints of its plumage, if it does not equal them for brilliancy. The drake is the object of admiration, his partner being remarkably plain, but during the summer season he also loses much of his gay vesture. Mr. Bennet tells a pleasant story in proof of the conjugal fidelity of these birds, the incidents of which occurred in Mr. Beale's aviary at Macao. A drake was stolen one night, and the duck displayed the strongest marks of despair at her loss, retiring into a corner and refusing all nourishment, as if determined to starve herself to death from grief. Another drake undertook to comfort the disconsolate widow, but she declined his attentions, and was fast becoming a martyr to her attachment, when her mate was recovered and restored to her. Their reunion was celebrated by the noisiest demonstrations of joy, and the duck soon informed her lord of the gallant proposals made to her during his absence; in high dudgeon, he instantly attacked the luckless bird which would have supplanted him, and so maltreated him as to cause his death.

The aviary here mentioned was for many years, up to 1838, one of the principal attractions of Macao. Its owner, Mr. Thomas Beale, had erected a wire cage on one side of his house, having two apartments, each of them about fifty feet high, and containing several large trees; small cages and roosts were placed on the side of the house under shelter, and in one corner a pool afforded bathing conveniences to the water-fowl. The genial climate obviated the necessity of any covering, and only those species which would agree to live quietly together were allowed the free range of the two apartments. The great attraction of the collection was a living bird of paradise, which, at the period of the owner's death, in 1840, had been in his possession eighteen years, and enjoyed good health at that time. The collection during one season contained nearly thirty specimens of pheasants, and besides these splendid birds, there were upward of one hundred and fifty others, of different sorts, some in cages, some on perches, and others going loose in the aviary. In one corner a large cat had a hole, where she reared her young; her business was to guard the whole from the depredations of rats. A magnificent peacock from Damaun, a large assortment of macaws and cockatoos, a pair of magpies, another of the superb crowned pigeons (*Goura coronata*), one of whom moaned itself to death on the decease of its mate, and several Nicobar ground pigeons, were also among the attractions of this curious and valuable collection.

Four or five kinds of grebe and loon frequent the coast, of which the *Podiceps cristatus*, called *shui nu*, or 'water slave,' is common around Macao. The same region affords sustenance to the pelican, which is seen standing motionless for hours on the rocks, or sailing on easy wing over the shallows in search of food. Its plumage is nearly a pure white, except the black tips of the wings; its height is about four feet, and the expanse of the wings more than eight feet. The bill is flexible like whalebone, and the pouch susceptible of great dilatation. Gulls abound on the northeast coasts, and no one who has seen it can forget the beautiful sight on the marshes at the entrance of the Pei ho, where myriads of white gulls assemble to feed, to preen, and to quarrel or scream—the bright sun rendering their plumage like snow. The albatross, black tern, petrel, and noddy increase the list of denizens in Chinese waters, but offer nothing of particular interest.[1]

There are four fabulous animals which are so often referred to by the Chinese as to demand a notice. The *kí-lin* is one of these, and is placed at the head of all hairy animals; as the *fung-hwang* is pre-eminent among feathered races; the dragon and tortoise among the scaly and shelly tribes; and *man* among naked animals! The naked, hairy, feathered, shelly, and scaly tribes constitute the quinary system of ancient Chinese naturalists. The *kí-lin* is pictured as resembling a stag in its body and a horse in its hoofs, but possessing the tail of an ox and a parti-colored or scaly skin. A single horn having a fleshy tip proceeds out of the forehead. Besides these external marks to identify it, the *kí-lin* exhibits great benevolence of

The Kí-lin, or Unicorn.

[1] On the birds of China, see in general *Les Oiseaux de la Chine*, par M. l'Abbé Armand David, avec un Atlas de 124 Planches dessinées et lith. par M. Arnoul. Paris, 1877. R. Swinhoe, in the *Proceedings of the Scientific Meetings of the Zoölogical Soc. of London*, and in *The Ibis, a Magazine of General Ornithology*, passim. *Journ. N. C. Br. R. A. Soc.*, Nos. II., p. 225, and III., p. 287.

disposition toward other living animals, and appears only when wise and just kings, like Yau and Shun, or sages like Confucius, are born, to govern and teach mankind. The Chinese description presents many resemblances to the popular notices of the unicorn, and the independent origin of their account adds something to the probability that a single-horned equine or cervine animal has once existed.[1]

Cuvier expresses the opinion that Pliny's description of the

The Fung-hwang, or Phœnix.

Arabian phœnix was derived from the golden pheasant, though others think the Egyptian plover is the original type. From his likening it to an eagle for size, having a yellow neck with purple, a blue tail varied with red feathers, and a richly feathered tufted head, it is more probable that the Impeyan pheasant was Pliny's

[1] *Chinese Repository*, Vol. VII., p. 213. Compare Yule's note, *Marco Polo*, Vol. I., p. 232. Huc, *Travels in Tartary*, etc., Vol. II., p. 246. Bell, *Journey from St. Petersburgh in Russia to Ispahan in Persia*, Vol. I., p. 216. Also Heeren, *Asiatic Nations*, Vol. I., p. 98, where there is a *résumé* of Ctesias' account of the unicorn.

type. The Chinese *fung-hwang*, or phœnix, is probably based on the Argus pheasant. It is described as adorned with every color, and combines in its form and motions whatever is elegant and graceful, while it possesses such a benevolent disposition that it will not peck or injure living insects, nor tread on growing herbs. Like the *kí-lin*, it has not been seen since the halcyon days of Confucius, and, from the account given of it, seems to have been entirely fabulous. The etymology of the characters implies that it is the emperor of all birds. One Chinese author describes it "as resembling a wild swan before and a unicorn behind; it has the throat of a swallow, the bill of a cock, the neck of a snake, the tail of a fish, the forehead of a crane, the crown of a mandarin drake, the stripes of a dragon, and the vaulted back of a tortoise. The feathers have five colors, which are named after the five cardinal virtues, and it is five cubits in height; the tail is graduated like Pandean pipes, and its song resembles the music of that instrument, having five modulations." A beautiful ornament for a lady's head-dress is sometimes made in the shape of the *fung-hwang*, and somewhat resembles a similar ornament, imitating the vulture, worn by the ladies of ancient Egypt.

The *lung*, or dragon, is a familiar object on articles from China. It furnishes a comparison among them for everything terrible, imposing, and powerful; and being taken as the imperial coat of arms, consequently imparts these ideas to his person and state. The type of the dragon is probably the boa-constrictor or sea-serpent, or other similar monster, though the researches of geology have brought to light such a near counterpart of the *lung* in the iguanadon as to tempt one to believe that this has been the prototype. There are three dragons, the *lung* in the sky, the *lí* in the sea, and the *kiao* in the marshes. The first is the only *authentic* species, according to the Chinese; it has the head of a camel, the horns of a deer, eyes of a rabbit, ears of a cow, neck of a snake, belly of a frog, scales of a carp, claws of a hawk, and palm of a tiger. On each side of the mouth are whiskers, and its beard contains a bright pearl; the breath is sometimes changed into water and sometimes into fire, and its voice is like the jingling of copper pans. The dragon of the sea occasionally ascends to heaven in water-spouts, and is the ruler of all oceanic phenomena.[1] The dragon is worshipped and feared by Chinese fishermen, and their *lung-wang*, or 'dragon king,' answers to Neptune in western mythology; perhaps the ideas of all classes toward it is a modified relic of the widespread serpent worship of ancient times. The Chinese suppose that elfs, demons, and other supernatural beings often transform themselves into snakes; and M. Julien has translated a fairy story of this sort, called *Blanche et Bleue.* The *kwei*, or tortoise, has so few fabulous qualities attributed to it that it hardly comes into the list; it was, according to the story, an attendant on Pwanku when he chiselled out the world. A semi-classical work, the *Shan-hai King*, or 'Memoirs upon the Mountains and Seas,' contains pictures and descriptions of these and kindred monsters, from which the people now derive strange notions respecting them, the book having served to embody and fix for the whole nation what the writer anciently found floating about in the popular legends of particular localities.

A species of alligator (*A. sinensis*) has been described by Dr. A. Fauvel in the *N. C. Br. R. A. Soc. Journal*, No. XIII., 1879, in which he gives many historical and other notices of its existence. Crocodiles are recorded as having been seen in the rivers of Kwangtung and Kwangsi, but none of this family attain a large size.

Marco Polo's account of the huge serpent of Yunnan,[2] having two forelegs near the head, and one claw like that of a lion or hawk on each, and a mouth big enough to swallow a man whole, referring no doubt to the crocodile, is a good instance of the way in which truth and fable were mingled in the accounts of those times. The flesh is still eaten by the Anamese, as he says it was in his day. A gigantic salamander, analogous to the one found in Japan (the *Sieboldia*), has suggested it as the

---

[1] *Chinese Repository*, Vol. VII., p. 250. For a careful analysis of this relic of ancient lore, see the *Nouveau Journal Asiatique*, Tome XII., pp. 232–243, 1833; also Tome VIII., 3d Series, pp. 337–382, 1839, for M. Bazin's estimate of its value.

[2] Yule's *Marco Polo*, Vol. II., p. 46.

type of the dragon which figures on the Chinese national flag. Small lizards abound in the southern parts, and the variety and numbers of serpents, both land and water, found in the maritime provinces, are hardly exceeded in any country in the world; they are seldom poisonous. A species of naja is the only venomous snake yet observed at Chusan, and the hooded cobra is one of the few yet found around Canton. Another species frequents the banks, and is driven out of the drains and creeks by high water into the houses. A case is mentioned by Bennet of a Chinese who was bitten, and to whose wound the mashed head of the reptile had been applied as a poultice, a mode of treatment which probably accelerated his death by mixing more of the poison diluted in the animal's blood with the man's own blood. It is, however, rare to hear of casualties from this source. This snake is called 'black and white,' from being marked in alternate bands of those two colors. A species of acrochordon, remarkable for its abrupt, short tail, has been noticed near Macao.

It is considered felicitous by the Buddhist priests to harbor snakes around their temples; and though the natives do not play with poisonous serpents like the Hindoos, they often handle or teach them simple tricks. The common frog is taken in great numbers for food. Tortoises and turtles from fresh and salt water are plenty along the coast, while both the emys and trionyx are kept in tubs in the streets, where they grow to a large size. An enormous carnivorous tortoise inhabits the waters of Chehkiang near the ocean. The natives have strange ideas concerning the hairy turtle of Sz'chuen, and regard it as excellent medicine; it is now known that the supposed hair consists of confervæ, whose spores, lodged on the shell, have grown far beyond the animal's body.

The ichthyology of China is one of the richest in the world, though it may be so more from the greater proportion of food furnished by the waters than from any real superabundance of the finny tribes. The offal thrown from boats near cities attracts some kinds to those places, and gives food and employment to multitudes. Several large collections of fishes have been made in Canton, and Mr. Reeves deposited one of the richest in the British Museum, together with a series of drawings made by native artists from living specimens; they have been described by Sir John Richardson in the *Report of the British Association for the Advancement of Science, for* 1845. In this paper he enumerates one hundred and ninety genera and six hundred and seventy-one species, nearly all of which are marine or come out to sea at certain times. Since it was prepared great accessions to this branch have been made from the inland waters, so that probably a thousand sorts in all have been observed. The salmon and cod families are comparatively scarce, but the mackerel, goby, and herring families are very abundant. The variety of fish is so great in Macao, that if one is willing to eat all that are brought to market, as the Chinese do (including the sharks, torpedoes, gudgeons, etc.), one can have a different species every day in the year. It may with truth be said that the Chinese eat nearly every living thing found in the water, some of the hideous fishing frogs or gurnards alone excepted.

The cartilaginous fishes, sharks, rays, and saw-fish, are abundant on the sea-coast. The sturgeon is not common at the south, but in the winter it is brought from the Songari and other rivers to Peking for the imperial table, being highly prized by Chinese epicures. There is found in the Yangtsz' a singular species of sturgeon, the *yiu yü*, which lies under the banks in still water and sucks its prey into a sac-like mouth projecting like a cusp under the long snout; it has no scales, and is four feet long. Common sturgeon, weighing a thousand pounds, are caught in this river. The hammer-headed and zebra shark (*Cestracion zebra*) are seen in the markets at Macao; also huge skates, some of them measuring five feet across; the young of all these species are regarded as particularly good eating. A kind of torpedo (*Narcine lingula*) is not uncommon on the southern coast, but the natives do not seem to be aware of any electrical properties. It is said that the fishermen sometimes destroy the shark by boiling a melon and throwing it out as a bait; when swallowed, the heat kills the fish. The true cod has not been observed on the Chinese coast, but several species of serrani (as *Plectropoma susuki*, *Serranus shihpan*, *Megachir*, etc.), generally called *shih-pan* by the natives, and garoupa by foreigners, are common off Canton, and considered to be most delicate fare. Another fine fish is the *Polynemus tetradactylus*, or bynni-carp, often called salmon by foreigners; isinglass is prepared from its skin. The pomfret, or *tsang yü* (*Stromateus argenteus*), is a good pan-fish, but hardly so delicate as the sole, many fine species of which abound along the whole coast. Besides these, two or three species of mackerel, the *Sciæna lucida*, an ophicephalus, the mullet, and the 'white rice fish' occur. The shad is abundant off the Yangtsz', and is superior to the American species; Chinese epicures will sometimes pay fifty dollars for the first one of the season.

The carp family (*Cyprinidæ*) is very abundant in the rivers and lakes of China, and some species are reared in fish-pools and tubs to a monstrous size; fifty-two species are mentioned in Richardson's list. The gold-fish is the most celebrated, and has been introduced into Europe, where it was first seen toward the end of the seventeenth century. The Chinese say that its native place is Lake Tsau, in the province of Nganhwui. The effects of domestication in changing the natural form of this fish are great; specimens are often seen without any dorsal fin, and the tail and other fins tufted and lobed to such a degree as to resemble artificial appendages or wings rather than natural organs. The eyes are developed till the globe projects beyond the socket like goggles, presenting an extraordinary appearance. Some of them are so fantastic, indeed, that they would be regarded as lusus naturæ were they not so common. The usual color is a ruddy golden hue, but both sexes exhibit a silvery or blackish tint at certain stages of their growth; and one variety, called the silver-fish, retains this shade all its life. The Chinese keep it in their garden ponds, or in earthern jars, in which are placed rocks covered with moss, and overgrown with tufts of ferns, to afford them a retreat from the light. When the females spawn, the eggs must be removed to a shallow vessel, lest the males devour them, where the heat of the sun hatches them; the young are nearly black, but gradually become whitish or reddish, and at last assume a golden or silvery hue. Specimens upward of two feet long have been noticed, and those who rear them emulate each other in producing new varieties.

The rearing of fish is an important pursuit, the spawn being collected with the greatest care and placed in favorable positions for hatching. The *Bulletin Universel* for 1829 asserts that in some part of China the spawn so taken is carefully placed in an empty egg-shell and the hole closed; the egg is then replaced in the nest, and, after the hen has sat a few days upon it, reopened, and the spawn placed in vessels of water warmed by the sun, where it soon hatches.

The immense fleets of fishing boats on the Yangtsz' and its tributaries indicate the finny supplies its waters afford. A species of pipe-fish (*Fistularia immaculata*), of a red color, and the gar-pike, with green bones, are found about Canton; as are also numerous beautiful parrot-fish and sun-fish (*Chætodon*). An ingenious mode of taking its prey is practised by a sort of chætodon, or chelmon; it darts a drop of water at the flies or other insects lighting on the bank near the edge, in such a manner as to knock them off, when they are devoured. All the species of ophicephalus, or *săng yü*, so remarkable for their tenacity of life, are reared in tanks and pools, and are hawked alive through the streets.

Eels, mullets, alewives or file-fish, breams, gudgeons, and many other kinds, are seen in the markets. Few things eaten by the Chinese look more repulsive than the gobies as they lie wriggling in the slime which keeps them alive; one species (*Trypauchen vagina*), called *chu pih yü*, or 'vermilion pencil-fish,' is a cylindrical fish, six or eight inches long, of a dark red color; its eyes protrude so that it can see behind, like a giraffe. Some kinds of gobies construct little hillocks in the ooze, with a depression on the top, in which their spawn is hatched by the sun; at low tide they skip about on the banks like young frogs, and are easily captured with the hand. A delicious species of Saurus (*Leucosoma Chinensis*), called *pih fan yü*, or 'white rice fish,' and *yin yü*, or silver-fish, ranges from Hakodate to Canton. It is six or eight inches long, the body scaleless and transparent, so that the muscles, intestines, and spinal column can be seen without dissection; the bones of the head are thin, flexible, and diaphanous. Many species of file-fish, sole-fish, anchovy, and eels, are captured on the coast. Vast quantities of dried fish, like the stock fish in Sweden, are sent inland to sell in regions where fish are rare. The most common sorts are the perch, sun-fish, gurnard, and hair-tail (*Trichinrus*).

Shell-fish and mollusks, both fresh and salt, are abundant in the market. Oysters of a good quality are common along the coast, and a species of mactra, or sand-clam, is fished up near Macao. The Pearl River affords two or three kinds of fresh-water shell-fish (*Mytilus*), and snails (*Voluta*) are plenty in all pools. The crangons, prawns, shrimps, crabs, and other kinds of crustacea met with, are not less abundant than palatable; one species of craw-fish, as large as (but not taking the place of) the lobster, called *lung hai*, or 'dragon crab,' together with cuttle-fish of three or four kinds, and the king-crab (*Polyphemus*), are all eaten. The inland waters produce many species of shells, and the new genus theliderma, allied to the unio, was formed by Mr. Benson, of Calcutta, from specimens obtained of a shopkeeper at Canton. The land shells are abundant, especially various kinds of snails (*Helix*, *Lymnea*, etc.); twenty-two species of helix alone were contained in a small collection sent from Peking, in which region all this kind of food is well known. A catalogue of nearly sixty shells obtained in Canton is given in Murray's *China*,[1] but it is doubtful whether even half of them are found in the country, as the shops there are supplied in a great degree from the Archipelago. Dr. Cantor[2] mentions eighty-eight genera of shells occurring between Canton and Chusan. Pearls are found in China, and Marco Polo speaks of a salt lake, supposed now to be in Yunnan, which produced them in such quantity that the fishery in his day was farmed out and restricted lest they should become too cheap and common. In Chehkiang the natives take a large kind of clam (*Alasmodonta*) and gently attach leaden images

---

[1] Vol. III., p. 445.

[2] Conspectus of collections made by Dr. Cantor, *Chinese Repository*, Vol. X., p. 434. General features of Chusan, with remarks on the Flora and Fauna of that Island, by T. E. Cantor, *Annal. Nat. Hist.*, Vol. IX. (1842), pp. 265, 361, and 481. *Journal As. Soc. of Bengal*, Vol. XXIV., 1855.

of Buddha under the fish, after which it is thrown back into the water. Nacre is deposited over the lead, and after a few months the shells are retaken, cleaned, and then sent abroad to sell as proofs of the power and presence of Buddha. The *Quarterly Review* speaks of a mode practised by the Chinese of making pearls by dropping a string of small mother-of-pearl beads into the shell, which in a year are covered with the pearly crust. Leeches are much used by native physicians; the hammer-headed leech has been noticed at Chusan.

The insects of China are almost unknown to the naturalist. In Dr. Cantor's collection, from Chusan, there are fifty-nine genera mentioned, among which tropical forms prevail; there are also six genera of arachnidæ, and the list of spiders could easily be multiplied to hundreds; among them are many showing most splendid coloring. One large and strong species is affirmed to capture small birds on the trees. Locusts sometimes commit extensive ravages, and no part of the land is free from their presence, though their depredations do not usually reach over a great extent of country, or often for two successive years. They are, however, sufficiently troublesome to attract the notice of the government, as the edict against them, inserted in another chapter, proves. Centipedes, scorpions, and some other species in the same order are known, the former being most abundant in the central and western regions, where scorpions are rare.

The most valuable insect is the silkworm, which is reared in nearly every province, and the silk from other wild worms found on the oak and ailantus in Shantung, Sz'chuen, and elsewhere also gathered; the proper silkworm itself has been met with to some extent in northern Shansí and Mongolia. Many other insects of the same order (*Lepidopteræ*) exist, but those sent abroad have been mostly from the province of Kwangtung. Eastward of the city of Canton, on a range of hills called Lofau shan, large butterflies and night moths of immense size and brilliant coloring are captured. One of these insects (*Bombyx atlas*) measures about nine inches across; the ground color is a rich and varied orange brown, and in the centre of each wing there is a triangular transparent spot, resembling a piece of mica. Sphinxes of great beauty and size are common, and in their splendid coloring, rapid noiseless flight from flower to flower, at the close of the day, remind one of the humming-bird. Some families are more abundant than others; the coleopterous exceed the lepidopterous, and the range of particular tribes in each of these is often very limited. The humid regions of Sz'chuen furnished a great harvest of beautiful butterflies to M. David, while the lamellicorn beetles and cerambycidæ are the most common in the north and central parts.

Many tribes of coleopterous insects are abundant, but the number of species yet identified is trifling. Several water beetles, and others included under the same general designation, have been found in collections sold at Canton, but owing to the careless manner in which those boxes are filled, very few specimens are perfect, the antennæ or tarsi being broken. The mole-cricket occurs everywhere. The common cricket is caught and sold in the markets for gambling; persons of all ranks amuse themselves by irritating two of these insects in a bowl, and betting upon the prowess of their favorites. The cicada, or broad locust, is abundant, and its stridulous sound is heard from trees and groves with deafening loudness. Boys tie a straw around the abdomen of the male, so as to irritate the sounding apparatus, and carry it through the streets in this predicament, to the great annoyance of every one. This insect was well known to the Greeks; the ancient distich—

> "Happy the cicadas' lives,
> For they all have voiceless wives,"

hints at their knowledge of this sexual difference, as well as intimates their opinion of domestic quiet. Again it forms the subject of Meleager's invocation:

> "O shrill-voiced insect! that with dew-drops meet,
> Inebriate, dost in desert woodlands sing;
> Perch'd on the spray top with indented feet,
> Thy dusky body's echoings harp-like ring."

The lantern-fly (*Fulgora*) is less common than the cicada. It is easily recognized by its long cylindrical snout, arched in an upward direction, its greenish reticulated elytra, and orange-yellow wings with black extremities; but its appearance in the evening is far from being as luminous as are the fire-fly and glow-worm of South America. The *Peh lah shu*, or 'white wax tree' (*Fraxinus chinensis*), affords nourishment to an insect of this order called *Coccus pela*. The larvæ alone furnish the wax, the secretion being the result of disease. Sir Geo. L. Staunton first described the fly from specimens seen in Annam in 1795, where the natives collected a white powder from the bark of the tree on which it occurs. Daniel Hanbury figured the insect and tree with the deposit of crude wax on the limbs, all obtained in Chekhiang province.[1] Baron Richthofen speaks of this industry in Sz'chuen as one furnishing employment to great multitudes. The department of Kia-ting furnishes the best wax, as its climate is warmer than Chingtu. The eggs of the insect are gathered in Kien-chang and Ning-yuen, where the tree flourishes on which it deposits them, and its culture is carefully attended to. The insect lives and breeds on this evergreen, and in April the eggs are collected and carried up to Kia-ting by porters. This journey is mostly performed by night so as to avoid the risk of hatching their loads; 300 eggs weigh one tael. They are instantly placed on the same kind of tree, six or seven balls of eggs done up in palm-leaf bags and hung on the twigs. In a few days the larvæ begin to spread over the branches, but do not touch the leaves; the bark soon becomes incrusted with a white powder, and is not disturbed till August. The loaded branches are then cut off and boiled, when the wax collects on the surface of the water, is skimmed off, and melted again to be poured into pans for sale. A tael's weight of eggs will produce two or three catties of the translucent, highly crystalline wax; it sells there for five mace a tael and upward. The annual income is reckoned at Tls. 2,000,000.[2] The purposes to which this singular product are applied include all those of beeswax. Pills are ingeniously enclosed in small

[1] Hanbury's notes on *Chinese Materia Medica*, 1862; *Pharmaceutical Journal*, Feb., 1862.

[2] Baron Richthofen's *Letters*, No. VII., to Shanghai Chamber of Commerce, May, 1872, p. 52.

globes of it, and candles of every size made. Wax is also gathered from wild and domestic bees, but honey is not much used; a casing of wax, colored with vermilion, is used to inclose the tallow of great painted candles set before the idols and tablets.

The *Chinese Herbal* contains a singular notion, prevalent also in India, concerning the generation of the sphex, or solitary wasp. When the female lays her eggs in the clayey nidus she makes in houses, she encloses the dead body of a caterpillar in it for the subsistence of the worms when they hatch. Those who observed her entombing the caterpillar did not look for the eggs, and immediately concluded that the sphex took the worm for her progeny, and say that as she plastered up the hole of the nest, she hummed a constant song over it, saying, "*Class with me! Class with me!*"—and the transformation gradually took place, and was perfected in its silent grave by the next spring, when a winged wasp emerged to continue its posterity in the same mysterious way.[1]

White ants are troublesome in the warmer parts, and annoy the people there by eating up the coffins in the graves. They form passages under ground, and penetrate upward into the woodwork of houses, and the whole building may become infested with them almost before their existence is suspected. They will even eat their way into fruit trees, cabbages, and other plants, destroying them while in full vigor. Many of the internal arrangements of the nests of bees and ants, and their peculiar instincts, have been described by Chinese writers with considerable accuracy. The composition of the characters for the bee, ant, and mosquito, respectively, denote the *awl* insect, the *righteous* insect, and the *lettered* insect; referring thereby to the sting of the first, the orderly working and subordination of the second, and the letter-like markings on the wings of the latter. Mosquitoes are plenty, and gauze curtains are considered to be a more necessary part of bed furniture than a mattress.

The botany of China is rather better known than its zoölogy,

[1] Darwin, *Naturalist's Voyage*, p. 35, notices a similar habit of the sphex in the vicinity of Rio Janeiro. The insect partially kills the spider or caterpillar by stinging, when they are stored in a rotting state with her eggs.

though vast and unexplored fields, like that reaching from Canton to Silhet and Assam, still invite the diligent collector to gather, examine, and make known their treasures. One of the earliest authors in this branch was Père Loureiro, a Portuguese for thirty-six years missionary in Cochinchina, and professor of mathematics and physic in the royal palace. He gathered a large herbarium there and in southern Kwangtung, and published his *Flora Cochinchinensis* in 1790, in which he described one hundred and eighty-four genera and more than three hundred new species. The only other work specially devoted to Chinese botany is Bentham's *Flora Hongkongensis*, published in 1861. The materials for it were collected by Drs. Hinds, Hance and Harland, Col. Champion, and others, during the previous twenty years, and amounted in all to upward of five thousand specimens, gathered exclusively on the island. Since its publication, Dr. Hance has added to our accurate knowledge of the Chinese flora many new specimens growing in other parts of the Empire, whose descriptions are scattered through various publications. Père David, during his extensive travels in northern China, gathered thousands of specimens which have yet to be carefully described. The Russian naturalists Maximowitch, Bunge, Tatarinov, Bretschneider, Prejevalsky, and others have largely increased our knowledge of the plants of Mongolia, the Amur basin, and the region about Peking. The first named has issued a separate work on the Amur flora, but most of the papers of these scientists are to be found in periodicals. In very early days, China was celebrated for the camphor, varnish, tallow, oil, tea, cassia, dyes, etc., obtained from its plants; and the later monographs of professed botanists, issued since Linneus looked over the two hundred and sixty-four species brought by his pupil Osbeck in 1750, down to the present day, have altogether given immense assistance to a thorough understanding of their nature and value.

Mr. Bentham's observations on the range of the plants collected in the island of Hongkong represent its flora, in general character, as most like that of tropical Asia, of which it offers, in numerous instances, the northern limit. The damp, wooded ravines on the north and west furnish plants closely allied to those of Assam and Sikkim; while other species, in considerable numbers, have a much more tropical character, extending with little variation over the Archipelago, Malaysia, Ceylon, and even to tropical Africa, but not into India. Within two degrees north of the island these tropical features (so far as is known) almost entirely cease, and out of the one thousand and fifty-six species described in the *Flora Hongkongensis*, only about eighty have been found in Japan; thus indicating that very few of the plants known to range across from the Himalaya to Japan grow south of Amoy. On the twenty-nine square miles forming the area of Hongkong there exists, Mr. Bentham says, a greater number of monotypic genera than in any other flora from an equal area in the world; he gives a comparative table of the floras of Hongkong, Aden and Ischia islands, about equal in extent, showing one thousand and three species growing on the first, ninety-five on the second, and seven hundred and ninety-two on the third. The proportion of woody to herbaceous species in Hongkong is nearly one-half, while in Ischia it is one to eleven; yet Hongkong has actually fewer trees than Ischia. Out of the one thousand and three species of wild plants there, three hundred and ninety-eight also occur in the tropical Asiatic flora, while one hundred and eighty-seven others have been found as well on the mainland; one hundred and fifty-nine are peculiar to the island.

Many species of coniferæ are floated down to Canton, taken from the Mei ling, or brought from Kwangsí; the timber is used for fuel, but more for rafters and pillars in buildings. The wood of the pride of India is employed for cabinet work; there are also many kinds of fancy wood, some of which are imported, and more are indigenous. The *nan muh*, or southern wood, a magnificent species of laurus common in Sz'chuen, which resists time and insects, is peculiarly valuable, and reserved for imperial use. The cœsalpinia, rose wood, aigle wood, and the camphor, elm, willow, and aspen, are also serviceable in carpentry.

The people collect seaweed to a great extent, using it in the arts and also for food; among these the *Gigartina tenax* affords an excellent material for glues and varnishes. It is boiled, and the transparent glue obtained is brushed upon very coarse silk or mulberry paper, filling up their substance, and making a transparent covering for lanterns; it is also used as a size for stiffening silks and gauze. This and other kinds of fuci are boiled to a jelly and used for food; it is known in commerce under the name of agar-agar. The thick fronds of the laminaria are gathered on the northern coasts and imported from Japan. Among other cryptogams, the Tartarian lamb (*Aspidium barometz*), so graphically described by Darwin in his *Botanic Garden*, has long been celebrated; it is partly an artificial production of the ingenuity of Chinese gardeners taking advantage of the natural habits of the plant to form it into a shape resembling a sheep or other object.

Among remarkable grasses the zak or saxaul (*Haloxylon*) and the *sulhir* (*Agriophyllum*), which grow in the sandy parts of the desert of Gobi, should be mentioned. The first is found across the whole length of this arid region, growing on the bare sand, furnishing to the traveller a dry and ready fuel in its brittle twigs, while his camels greedily browse on its leafless but juicy and prickly branches. The Mongols pitch their tents be-beath its shelter, seeking for some covert from the wintry winds, and encouraged to dig at its roots for water which has been detained by their succulent nature, a wonderful provision furnished by God in the bleakest desert. The *sulhir* is even more important, and is the "gift of the desert." It grows on bare sand, is about two feet high, a prickly saline plant, producing many seeds in September, of a nutritious, agreeable nature, food for man and beast.

The list of gramineous plants cultivated for food is large; the common sorts include rice, wheat, barley, oats, maize, sugar-cane, panic, sorghum, spiked and panicled millet, of each kind several varieties. The grass (*Phragmites*) raised along the river banks is carefully cut and dried, to be woven into floor-matting; a coarser sort, called *atap*, is made of bamboo splints for roofs of huts, awnings, and sheds. In the milder climes of the southern coasts, cheap houses are constructed of these materials. The coarse grass and shrubbery on the hills is cut in the autumn for fuel by the poor; and when the hills are well sheared of their grassy covering, the stubble is set on fire, in order to supply ashes for manuring the next crop—an operation which tends to keep the hills bare of all shrubbery and trees.

Few persons who have not seen the bamboo growing in its native climes get a full idea from pictures of its grace and beauty. A clump of this magnificent grass will gradually develop by new shoots into a grove, if care be taken to cut down the older stems as they reach full maturity, and not let them flower and go to seed; for as soon as they have perfected the seed, they die down to the root, like other grasses. The stalks usually attain the height of fifty feet, and in the Indian islands often reach seventy feet and upward, with a diameter of ten or twelve inches at the bottom. A road lined with them, with their feathery sprays meeting overhead, presents one of the most beautiful avenues possible to a warm climate.

In China the industry and skill of the people have multiplied and perpetuated a number of varieties (one author contents himself with describing sixty of them), among which are the yellow, the black, the green, the slender sort for pipes, and a slenderer one for writing-pencils, the big-leaved, etc. Its uses are so various that it is not easy to enumerate them all. The shoots come out of the ground nearly full-sized, four to six inches in diameter, and are cut like asparagus to eat as a pickle or a comfit, or by boiling or stewing. Sedentary Buddhist priests raise this lenten fare for themselves or to sell, and extract the tabasheer from the joints of the old culms, to sell as a precious medicine for almost anything which ails you. The roots are carved into fantastic and ingenious images and stands, or divided into egg-shaped divining-blocks to ascertain the will of the gods, or trimmed into lantern handles, canes, and umbrella-sticks.

The tapering culms are used for all purposes that poles can be applied to in carrying, propelling, supporting, and measuring, for which their light, elastic, tubular structure, guarded by a coating of silicious skin, and strengthened by a thick septum at each joint, most admirably fits them. The pillars and props of houses, the framework of awnings, the ribs of mat-sails, and the shafts of rakes are each furnished by these culms. So, also, are fences and all kinds of frames, coops, and cages, the wattles of abatis, and the ribs of umbrellas and fans. The leaves are sewed into rain-cloaks for farmers and sailors, and thatches for covering their huts and boats, pinned into linings for tea-boxes, plaited into immense umbrellas to screen the huckster and his stall from the sun and rain, or into coverings for theatres and sheds. Even the whole lot where a two-story house is building is usually covered in by a framework of bamboo-poles and *attap*—as this leaf covering is called, from its Malay name—all tied together by rattan, and protecting the workmen and their work from sun and rain.

The wood, cut into splints of proper sizes and forms, is woven into baskets of every shape and fancy, sewed into window-curtains and door-screens, plaited into awnings and coverings for tea-chests or sugar-cones, and twisted into cables. The shavings and curled threads aid softer things in stuffing pillows; while other parts supply the bed for sleeping, the chopsticks for eating, the pipe for smoking, and the broom for sweeping. The mattress to lie upon, the chair to sit upon, the table to eat on, the food to eat, and the fuel to cook it with, are also derivable from bamboo. The master makes his ferule from it, the carpenter his foot-measure, the farmer his water-pipes, irrigating wheels, and straw-rakes, the grocer his gill and pint cups, and the mandarin his dreaded instrument of punishment. This last use is so common that the name of the plant itself has come in our language to denote this application, and the poor wretch who is *bambooed* for his crimes is thus taught that laws cannot be violated with impunity.

The paper to write on, the book to study from, the pencil to write with, the cup to hold the pencils, and the covering of the lattice-window instead of glass are all indebted to this grass in their manufacture. The shaft of the soldier's spear, and oftentimes the spear altogether, the plectrum for playing the lute, the reed in the native organ, the skewer to fasten the hair, the undershirt to protect the body, the hat to screen the head, the bucket to draw the water, and the easy-chair to lounge on, besides cages for birds, fish, bees, grasshoppers, shrimps, and cockroaches, crab-nets, fishing-poles, sumpitans or shooting-tubes, flutes, fifes, fire-holders, etc., etc., are among the things furnished from this plant, whose beauty when growing is commensurate to its usefulness when cut down. A score or two of bamboo-poles for joists and rafters, fifty fathoms of rattan ropes, with plenty of palm-leaves and bamboo-matting for roof and sides, supply material for a common dwelling in the south of China. Its cost is about five dollars. Those houses built over creeks, or along the low banks of rivers and sea-beaches, are elevated a few feet, and their floors are neatly made of split bamboos, which allow the water to be seen through. The decks, masts, yards, and framework of the mat-sails of the small boats of the islanders in the Archipelago are all more or less made of this useful plant. Throughout the south of Asia it enters into the daily life of the people in their domestic economy more than anything else, or than any other one thing does in any part of the world. The Japanese supply us with fans neatly formed, ribs and handle, from a single branch of bamboo, and covered with paper made from mulberry bark, while their skill is shown also in the exquisite covering of fine bamboo threads woven around cups and saucers.[1]

In ancient times the date palm was cultivated in China, but is now unknown. The cocoanut flourishes in Hainan and the adjacent coasts, where its fruit, leaves, and timber are much used. A great variety of utensils are carved from the nut-case, and ropes spun from the coir, while the cultivators drink the toddy made from the juice. The fan palm (*Chamærops*) is the common palm of the country, two species being cultivated for the wiry fibres in the leaf-sheaths, and for their broad leaves. This fibre is far more useful than that from cocoanut husks, as it is longer and smoother, and is woven into ropes, mats, cloaks, and brushes. The tree is spread over the greater part of the provinces, one of their most ornamental and useful trees. Another sort (*Caryota*) also furnishes a fibre employed in the same way, but its timber is more valuable; sedan thills are made of its wood. Still another is the talipot palm (*Borassus*), from

[1] Compare Yule's *Marco Polo*, Vol. I., p. 271; A. R. Wallace, *The Malay Archipelago*, pp. 87–91, American Ed.

whose leaves a material for writing books upon was once produced, as is the case now in Siam.[1]

Several species of Aroideæ are cultivated, among which the *Caladium cuculatum*, *Arum esculentum*, and *Indicum* are common. The tuberous farinaceous roots of the *Sagittaria sinensis* are esteemed; the roots of these plants, and of the water-chestnut, are manufactured into a powder resembling arrow-root. The sweet-flag (*Calamus*) is used in medicine for its spicy warmth. The stems of a species of Juncus are collected and the pith carefully taken out and dried for the wicks of water-lamps, and the inner layers of the pith hats so generally worn in southern China.

The extensive group of lillies contains many splendid ornaments of the conservatory and garden, natives of China; some are articles of food. The *Agapanthus*, or blue African lily, four species of *Hemerocallis*, or day lily, and the fragrant tuberose, are all common about Canton; the latter is widely cultivated for its blossoms to scent fancy teas. Eight or ten species of Lilium (among which the speckled tiger lily and the unsullied white are conspicuous) also add their gay beauties to the gardens; while the modest Commelina, with its delicate blue blossoms, ornaments the hedges and walks. Many alliaceous plants, the onion, cives, garlic, etc., belong to this group; and the Chinese relish them for the table as much as they admire the flowers of their beauteous and fragrant congeners for bouquets. The singular red-leaved iron-wood (*Dracæna*) forms a common ornament of gardens.

The yam, or *ta-shu* (*i.e.*, 'great tuber'), is not much raised, though its wholesome qualities as an article of food are well understood. The same group (*Musales*) to which the yam belongs furnishes the custard-apple, one of the few fruits which have been introduced from abroad. The Amaryllidæ are represented by many pretty species of Crinum, Nerine, and Amaryllis. Their unprofitable beauty is compensated by the plain but useful plantain, said to stand before the potato and sago palm as producing the greatest amount of wholesome food, in propor-

[1] See also in *Notes and Queries on C. and J.*, Vol. III., pp. 115, 129, 139, 147, 150, 170.

tion to its size, of any cultivated plant.[1] There are many varieties of this fruit, some of them so acid as to require cooking before eating.

That pleasant stomachic, ginger, is cultivated through all the country, and exposed for sale as a green vegetable, to spice dishes, and largely made into a preserve. The Alpinia and Canna, or Indian shot, are common garden flowers. The large group of Orchideæ has nineteen genera known to be natives of China, among which the air plants (*Vanda* and *Ærides*) are great favorites. They are suspended in baskets under the trees, and continue to unfold their blossoms in gradual succession for many weeks, all the care necessary being to sprinkle them daily. The true species of Ærides are among the most beautiful productions of the vegetable world, their flowers being arrayed in long racemes of delicate colors and delicious fragrance. The beautiful Bletia, Arundina, Spathoglottis, and Cymbidium are common in damp and elevated places about the islands near Macao and Hongkong.

Many species of the pine, cypress, and yew, forming the three subdivisions of cone-bearing plants, furnish a large proportion of the timber and fuel. The larch is not rare, and the *Pinus massoniana* and *Cunninghamia* furnish most of the common pine timber. The finest member of this order in China is the white pine (*Pinus bungiana*), peculiar to Chihlí; its trunk is a clear white, and as it annually sheds the bark it always looks as if whitewashed. Some specimens near Peking are said to be a thousand years old. Two members of the genus *Sequoia*, of a moderate size, occur near Tibet. The juniper and thuja are often selected by gardeners to try their skill in forcing them to grow into rude representations of birds and animals, the price of these curiosities being proportioned to their grotesqueness and difficulty. The nuts of the maiden-hair tree (*Salisburia adiantifolia*) are eaten, and the leaves are sometimes put into books as a preservative against insects.

The willow is a favorite plant and grows to a great size, Staunton mentioning some which were fifteen feet in girth;

---

[1] From calculations of Humboldt it was estimated that the productiveness of this plant as compared with wheat is as 133 to 1, and as against potatoes, 44 to 1.

they shade the roads near the capital, and one of them is the true Babylonian willow; the trees are grown for timber and for burning into charcoal. Their leaves, shape, and habits afford many metaphors to poets and writers, much more use being made of the tree in this way, it might almost be said, than any other. The oak is less patronized by fine writers, but the value of its wood and bark is well understood; the country affords several species, one of which, the chestnut oak, is cultivated for the cupules, to be used in dyeing. The galls are used for dyeing and in medicine, and the acorns of some kinds are ground in mills, and the flour soaked in water and made into a farinaceous paste. Some of the missionaries speak of oaks a hundred feet high, but such giants in this family are rare. "One of the largest and most interesting of these trees, which," writes Abel, "I have called *Quercus densifolia*, resembled a laurel in its shining green foliage. It bore branches and leaves in a thick head, crowning a naked and straight stem; its fruit grew along upright spikes terminating the branches. Another species, growing to the height of fifty feet, bore them in long, pendulous spikes."

The chestnut, walnut, and hazelnut together furnish a large supply of food. The queer-shaped ovens fashioned in imitation of a raging lion, in which chestnuts are roasted in the streets of Peking, attract the eye of the visitor. The Jack-fruit (*Artocarpus*) is not unknown in Canton, but it is not much used. There are many species of the banian, but none of them produce fruit worth plucking; the Portuguese have introduced the common fig, but it does not flourish. The bastard banian is a magnificent shade tree, its branches sometimes overspreading an area a hundred or more feet across. The walls of cities and dwellings are soon covered with the *Ficus repens*, and if left unmolested its roots gradually demolish them. The paper mulberry (*Broussonetia*) is largely cultivated in the northern provinces, and serves the poor with their chief material for windows. The leaf of the common mulberry is the principal object of its culture, but the fruit is eaten and the wood burned for lampblack to make India-ink.

Hemp (*Cannabis*) is cultivated for its fibres, and the seeds furnish an oil used for household purposes and medicinal preparations; the intoxicating substance called *bang*, made in India, is unknown in China. The family Proteaceæ contains the *Eleococca cordata*, or *wu-tung*, a favorite tree of the Chinese for its beauty, the hard wood it furnishes, and the oil extracted from its seeds. The *Stillingia* belongs to the same family; this symmetrical tree is a native of all the eastern provinces, where it is raised for its tallow; it resembles the aspen in the form and color of the leaf and in its general contour. The castor-oil is cultivated as a hedge plant, and the seeds are used both in the kitchen and apothecaries' shop.

The order Hippurinæ furnishes the water caltrops (*Trapa*), the seeds of which are vended in the streets as a fruit after boiling; one native name is 'buffalo-head fruit,' which the unopened nuts strikingly resemble. Black pepper is imported, not so much as a spice as for its infusion, to be administered in fevers. The betel pepper is cultivated for its leaves, which are chewed with the betel-nut. The pitcher plant (*Nepenthes*), called pig-basket plant, is not unfrequent near Canton; the leaves, or ascidia, bear no small resemblance to the open baskets employed for carrying hogs.

Many species of the tribe *Rumicinæ* are cultivated as esculent vegetables, among which may be enumerated spinach, green basil, beet, amaranthus, cockscomb, broom-weed (*Kochia*), buckwheat, etc. Two species of Polygonum are raised for the blue dye furnished by the leaves, which is extracted, like indigo, by maceration. Buckwheat is prepared for food by boiling it like millet; one native name means 'triangular wheat.' The flour is also employed in pastry. The cockscomb is much admired by the Chinese, whose gardens furnish several splendid varieties. The rhubarb is a member of this useful tribe, and large quantities are brought from Kansuh and Koko-nor, where its habits have lately been observed by Prejevalsky. The root is dug by Chinese and Tanguts during September and October, dried in the shade, and transported by the Yellow River to the coast towns, where Europeans pay from six to ten times its rate among the mountain markets.[1] The Chinese consider the rest

---

[1] Compare Yule's *Marco Polo*, Vol. I., p. 197.

of the world dependent on them for tea and rhubarb, whose inhabitants are therefore forced to resort thither to procure means to relieve themselves of an otherwise irremediable costiveness. This argument was made use of by Commissioner Lin in 1840, when recommending certain restrictive regulations to be imposed upon foreign trade, because he supposed merchants from abroad would be compelled to purchase them at any price.

The order *Ilicinæ*, or holly, furnishes several genera of Rhamneæ, whose fruits are often seen on tables. The Zizyphus furnishes the so-called Chinese dates[1] in immense quantities throughout the northern provinces. The fleshy peduncles of the Hovenia are eaten; they are common in the southeastern provinces. The leaves of the *Rhamnus theezans* are among the many plants collected by the poor as a make-shift for the true tea. The fruit called the Chinese olive, obtained from the Pimela, is totally different from and is a poor substitute for the rich olive of the Mediterranean countries.[2]

The Leguminosæ hold an important place in Chinese botany, affording many esculent vegetables and valuable products. Peas and beans are probably eaten more in China than any other country, and soy is prepared chiefly from the Soja or Dolichos. One of the modes of making this condiment is to skin the beans and grind them to flour, which is mixed with water and powdered gypsum, or turmeric. It is eaten as a jelly or curd, or in cakes, and a meal is seldom spread without it in some form. One genus of this tribe affords indigo, and from the buds and leaves of a species of Colutea a kind of green dye is said to be obtained. Liquorice is esteemed in medicine; and the red seeds of the *Abrus precatorius* are gathered for ornaments. The Poinciana and Bauhinia are cultivated for their flowers, and the Erythrina and Cassia are among the most magnificent flowering trees in the south.

---

[1] The application of this name to the jujube plum by foreigners, because the kind cured in honey resembled Arabian dates in color, size, and taste when brought on the table, is a good instance of the manner in which errors arise and are perpetuated from mere carelessness.

[2] Compare Dr. H. F. Hance, in *Journal of Botany*, Vol. IX., p. 38.

The fruits are, on the whole, inferior in flavor and size to those of the same names at the west. Several varieties of pears, plums, peaches, and apricots are known; it is probable that China is the native country of each of these fruits, and some of the varieties equal those found anywhere. Erman[1] mentions an apple or haw which grows in "long bunches and is round, about the size of a cherry, of a red color, and very sweet taste," found in abundance near Kiakhta. There are numerous species of Amygdalus cultivated for their flowers; and at new year the budding stems of the flowering almond, narcissus, plum, peach, and bell-flower (*Enkianthus reticulatus*) are forced into blossom for exhibition, as indicating good luck the coming year. The apples and quinces are generally destitute of that flavor looked for in them elsewhere, but the *lu-kuh*, or *loquat*, is a pleasant acid spring fruit. The pomegranate is chiefly cultivated for its beauty as a flowering plant; but the guava and Eugenia, or rose-apple, are sold in the market or made into jellies. The rose is a favorite among the Chinese and extensively cultivated; twenty species are mentioned, together with many varieties, as natives of the country; the Banks rose is developed and trained with great skill. The Spiræa or privet, myrtle, Quisqualis, Lawsonia or henna, white, purple, and red varieties of crape-myrtle or Lagerstrœmia, Hydrangea, the passion-flower, and the house-leek are also among the ornamental plants found in gardens. Few trees in any country present a more elegant appearance, when in full flower, than the Lagerstrœmias. The Pride of India and Chinese tamarix are also beautiful flowering trees. Specimens of the Cactus and Cereus, containing fifty or more splendid flowers in full bloom, are not unusual at Macao in August.

The watermelon, cucumber, squash, tomato, brinjal or egg-plant, and other garden vegetables are abundant; the tallow-gourd (*Benincasa cerifera*) is remarkable for having its surface covered with a waxy exudation which smells like rosin. The dried bottle-gourd (*Cucurbita lagenaria*) is tied to the backs of children on the boats to assist them in floating if they should

[1] *Travels in Siberia*, Vol. II., p. 151.

unluckily fall overboard. The fruit and leaves of the papaw, or *muh kwa*, 'tree melon,' are eaten after being cooked; the Chinese are aware of the intenerating property of the exhalations from the leaves of this tree, and make use of them sometimes to soften the flesh of ancient hens and cocks, by hanging the newly killed birds in the tree or by feeding them upon the fruit beforehand. The carambola (*Averrhoa*) or tree gooseberry is much eaten by the Chinese, but is not relished by foreigners; the tree itself is also an ornament to any pleasure grounds.

Ginseng is found wild in the forests of Manchuria, where it is collected by detachments of soldiers detailed for this purpose; these regions are regarded as imperial preserves, and the medicine is held as a governmental monopoly. The importation of the American root does not interfere to a very serious degree with the imperial sales, as the Chinese are fully convinced that their own plant is far superior. Among numerous plants of the malvaceous and pink tribes (*Dianthaceæ*) remarkable for their beauty or use, the *Lychnis coronata*, five sorts of pink, the *Althæa Chinensis*, eight species of Hibiscus, and other malvaceous flowers may be mentioned; the cotton tree (*Salmalia*) is common at Canton; the fleshy petals are sometimes prepared as food, and the silky stamens dried to stuff cushions. The *Gossypium herbaceum* and *Pachyrrhizus* afford the materials for cotton and grasscloth; both of them are cultivated in most parts of China. The latter is a twining, leguminous plant, cultivated from remote antiquity, and still grown for its fibres, which are woven into linen. The petals of the *Hibiscus rosa-sinensis* furnish a black liquid to dye the eyebrows, and at Batavia they are employed to polish shoes. The fruits of the *Hibiscus ochra*, or okers, are prepared for the table in a variety of ways.

The *Camellia Japonica* is allied to the same great tribe as the Hibiscus, and its elegant flowers are as much admired by the people of its native country as by florists abroad; thirty or forty varieties are enumerated, many of them unknown out of China, while Chinese gardeners are likewise ignorant of a large proportion of those found in our conservatories. This flower is cultivated solely for its beauty, but other species of Camellia are raised for their seeds, the oil expressed from them being serviceable for many household and mechanical purposes. From the fibres of a species of Waltheria, a plant of the same tribe, a fine cloth is made; and the *Pentapetes Phœnicia*, or 'noon flower,' is a common ornament of gardens.

The widely diffused tribe Ranunculiaceæ has many representatives, some of them profitable for their timber, others sought after for their fruit or admired for their beauty, and a few prized for their healing properties. There are eight species of Magnolia, all of them splendid flowering plants; the bark of the *Magnolia yulan* is employed as a febrifuge. The seed vessels of the *Ilicium anisatum*, or star-aniseed, are gathered on account of their spicy warmth and fragrance. The *Artabotrys odoratissimus* and *Unona odorata* are cultivated for their perfume. Another favorite is the *mowtan*, or tree pæony, reared for its large and variegated flowers; its name of *hwa wáng*, or 'king of flowers,' indicates the estimation in which it is held. The skill of native gardeners has made many varieties, and their patience is rewarded by the high prices which fine specimens command. Good imitations of full-grown plants in flower are sometimes made of pith paper. The Clematis, the foxglove, the *Berberis Chinensis*, and the magnificent lotus, all belong to this tribe; the latter, one of the most celebrated plants in Asia, is more esteemed by the Chinese for its edible roots than reverenced for its religious associations. The *Actæa aspera* is sometimes collected, as is the scouring rush, for cleaning pewter vessels, for which its hispid leaves are well fitted.

The groups which include the poppy, mustard, cabbage, cress, and many ornamental species, form an important portion of native agriculture. The poppy has become a common crop in all the provinces, driving out the useful cereals by its greater value and profit. The leaves of many cruciferous plants are eaten, whether cultivated or wild; and one kind (*Isates*) yields a fine blue dye in the eastern provinces; the variety and amount of such food consumed by the Chinese probably exceeds that of any other people. Another tribe, Rutaceæ, contains the oranges and shaddocks, and some very fragrant shrubs, as the

Murraya exotica and *paniculata*, and the *Aglaia odorata;* while the bladder-tree (*Koelreuteria*) is a great attraction when its whole surface is brilliant with golden flowers. The *whampe*, *i.e.*, yellow skin (*Cookia punctata*), is a common and superior fruit. The seeds of the Gleditschia, besides their value in cleansing, are worn as beads, "because," say the Buddhists, "all demons are afraid of the wood;" one name means 'preventive of evil.' Two native fruits, the *lìchí* and *lungan*, are allied to the Sapindus in their affinities; while the *fung shu*, or Liquidambar, and many sorts of maple, with the *Pittosporum tobira*, an ornamental shrub, may be mentioned among plants used for food or sought after for timber.

These brief notices of Chinese plants may be concluded by mentioning some of the most ornamental not before spoken of; but all the beautiful sorts are soon introduced into western conservatories by enterprising florists. In the extensive tribe of Rubiacinæ are several species of honeysuckle, and a fragrant Viburnum resembling the snowball. The Serissa is cultivated around beds like the box; the *Ixora coccinea*, and other species of that genus, are among common garden shrubs. The seeds of two or three species of Artemisia are collected, dried, and reduced to a down, to be burned as an actual cautery. The dried twigs are frequently woven into a rope to slowly consume as a means of driving away mosquitoes. From the *Carthamus tinctoirus* a fine red dye is prepared. The succory, lettuce, dandelion, and other cichoraceous plants, either wild or cultivated, furnish food; while innumerable varieties of Chrysanthemums and Asters are reared for their beauty.

The Labiatæ afford many genera, some of them cultivated; and the Solanaceæ, or nightshades, contain the tomato, potato, tobacco, stramony, and several species of Capsicum, or red pepper. It has been disputed whether tobacco is native or foreign, but the philological argument and historical notices prove that both this plant and maize were introduced within half a century after the discovery of America, or about the year 1530. The Chinese dry the leaves and cut them into shreds for smoking; the snuff is coarser and less pungent than the Scotch; it is said that powdered cinnabar is sometimes mixed with it.

Among the Convolvulaceæ are many beautiful species of Ipomea, especially the cypress vine, or *quamoclit*, trained about the houses even of the poorest. The *Ipomea maritima* occurs, trailing over the sandy beaches along the coast from Hainan to Chusan and Lewchew. The *Convolvulus reptans* is planted around the edges of pools on the confines of villages and fields, for the sake of its succulent leaves. The narcotic family of Apocyneæ contains the oleander and Plumeria, prized for their fragrance; while the yellow milkweed (*Asclepias curassavica*) and the *Vinca rosea*, or red periwinkle, are less conspicuous, but not unattractive, members of the same group. The jasmine is a deserved favorite, its clusters of flowers being often wound by women in their hair, and planted in pots in their houses. The *Olea fragrans*, or *kwei hwa*, is cultivated for scenting tea.

In the eastern provinces the hills are adorned with yellow and red azaleas of gorgeous hue, especially around Ningpo and in Chusan. "Few," says Mr. Fortune, "can form any idea of the gorgeous beauty of these azalea-clad hills, where, on every side, the eye rests on masses of flowers of dazzling brightness and surpassing beauty. Nor is it the azalea alone which claims our admiration; clematises, wild roses, honeysuckles, and a hundred others, mingle their flowers with them, and make us confess that China is indeed the 'central flowery land.'"[1]

A few notices of the advance made by the Chinese themselves in the study of natural history, taken from their great work on materia medica, the *Pun tsao*, or 'Herbal,' will form an appropriate conclusion to this chapter. This work is usually bound in forty octavo volumes, divided into fifty-two chapters, and contains many observations of value mixed up with a deal of incorrect and useless matter; and as those who read the book have not sufficient knowledge to discriminate between what is true and what is partly or wholly wrong, its reputation tends greatly to perpetuate the errors. The compiler of the *Pun tsao*, Lí Shí-chin, spent thirty years in collecting all the information on these subjects extant in his time, arranged it in a methodical manner for popular use, adding his own observations, and pub-

---

[1] *Wanderings in China.*

lished it about 1590. He consulted some eight hundred preceding authors, from whom he selected one thousand five hundred and eighteen prescriptions, and added three hundred and seventy-four new ones, arranging his materials in fifty-two books in a methodical and (for his day) scientific manner. But how far behind the writings of Pliny and Dioscorides! The nucleus of Lí's production is a small work which tradition ascribes to Shinnung, the God of Agriculture, and is doubtless anterior to the Han dynasty. His composition was well received, and attracted the notice of the Emperor, who ordered several succeeding editions to be published at the expense of the state. It was, in fact, so great an advance on all previous books, that it checked future writers in that branch, and Lí is likely now to be the first and last purely native critical writer on natural science in his mother tongue.

The first two volumes contain a collection of prefaces and indices, together with many notices of the theory of anatomy and medicine, and three books of pictorial illustrations of the rudest sort. Chapters I. and II. consist of introductory observations upon the practice of medicine, and an index of the recipes contained in the work, called the *Sure Guide to a Myriad of Recipes;* the whole filling the first seven volumes. Chapters III. and IV. contain lists of medicines for the cure of all diseases, occupying three volumes and a half, and comprising the therapeutical portion of the work, except a treatise on the pulse in the last volume.

In the subsequent chapters the author carefully goes over the entire range of nature, first giving the correct name and its explanation; then comes descriptive remarks, solutions of doubts and corrections of errors being interspersed, closing with notes on the savor, taste, and application of the recipes in which it is used. Chapters V. and VI. treat of inorganic substances under water and fire, and minerals under Chapters VII. to XI., as earth, metals, gems, and stones. Water is divided into aerial and terrestrial, *i.e.*, from the clouds, and from springs, the ocean, etc. Fire is considered under eleven species, among which are the flames of coal, bamboo, moxa, etc. The chapter on earth comprises the secretions from various animals, as well as soot, ink, etc.; that on metals includes metallic substances and their common oxides; and gems are spoken of in the next division. The eleventh chapter, in true Chinese style, groups together what could not be placed in the preceding sections, including salts, minerals, etc. In looking at this arrangement one detects the similarity between it and the classification of characters in the language itself, showing the influence this has had upon it; thus *ho*, *shui*, *tu*, *kin*, *yuh*, *shih*, and *lu*, or fire, water, earth, metals, gems, stones, and salts, are the seven radicals under which the names of inorganic substances are classified in the imperial dictionary. A like similarity runs through other parts of the *Herbal*.

Chapters XII. to XXXVII., inclusive, treat of the vegetable kingdom, under five *pu*, or 'divisions,' viz.: herbs, grains, vegetables, fruits, and trees; which are again subdivided into *lui*, or 'families,' though the members of these families have no more relationship to each other than the heterogeneous family of an Egyptian slave dealer. The lowest term in the Chinese scientific scale is *chung*, which sometimes includes a genus, but quite as often corresponds to a species or even a variety, as Linneus understood those terms.

The first division of herbs contains nine families, viz.: hill plants, odoriferous, marshy, noxious, scandent or climbing, aquatic, stony, and mossy plants, and a ninth of one hundred and sixty-two miscellaneous plants not used in medicine, making six hundred and seventy-eight species in all. In this classification the habitat is the most influential principle of arrangement for the families, while the term *tsao*, or 'herb,' denotes whatever is not eaten or used in the arts, or which does not attain to the magnitude of a tree.

The second division of grains contains four families, viz.: 1, that of hemp, sesamum, buckwheat, wheat, rice, etc.; 2, the family of millet, maize, opium, etc.; 3, leguminous plants, pulse, peas, vetches, etc.; and 4, fermentable things, as bean curd, boiled rice, wine, yeast, congee, bread, etc., which, as they are used in medicine, and produced from vegetables, seem most naturally to come in this place. The first three families embrace thirty-nine species, and the last tweny-nine articles.

The third division of kitchen herbs contains five families: 1, offensive pungent plants, as leeks, mustard, ginger; 2, soft and mucilaginous plants, as dandelions, lilies, bamboo sprouts; 3, vegetables producing fruit on the ground, as tomatoes, egg-plants, melons; 4, aquatic vegetables; and 5, mushrooms and fungi. The number of species is one hundred and thirty-three, and some part of each of them is eaten.

The fourth division of fruits contains seven families: 1, the five fruits, the plum, peach, apricot, chestnut, and date (Rhamnus); 2, hill fruits, as the orange, pear, citron, persimmon; 3, foreign fruits, as the cocoanut, líchí, carambola; 4, aromatic fruits, as pepper, cubebs, tea; 5, trailing fruits, as melons, grape, sugar-cane; 6, aquatic fruits, as water caltrops, water lily, water chestnuts, etc.; and 7, fruits not used in medicine, as whampe. In all, one hundred and forty-seven species.

The fifth division of trees has six families: 1, odoriferous trees, as pine, cassia, aloes, camphor; 2, stately trees, as the willow, tamarix, elm, soapberry, palm, poplar, julibrissin or silk tree; 3, luxuriant growing trees, as mulberry, cotton, Cercis, Gardenia, Bombax, Hibiscus; 4, parasites or things attached to trees, as the mistletoe, pachyma, and amber; 5, flexible plants, as bamboo; this family has only four species; 6, includes what the other five exclude, though it might have been thought that the second and third families were sufficiently comprehensive to contain almost all miscellaneous plants. The number of species is one hundred and ninety-eight. All botanical subjects are classified in this manner under five divisions, thirty-one families, and one thousand one hundred and ninety-five species, excluding all fermentable things.

The arrangement of the botanical characters in the language does not correspond so well to this as does that of inorganic substances. The largest group in the language system is *tsao*, which comprises in general such herbaceous plants as are not used for food. The second, *muh*, includes all trees or shrubs; and the bamboo, on account of its great usefulness, stands by itself, though the characters mostly denote names of articles made of bamboo. No less than four radicals, viz., rice, wheat, millet, and grain, serve as the heads under which the esculent grasses are arranged; there are consequently many synonymes and superfluous distinctions. One family includes beans, and another legumes; one comprises cucurbitaceous plants, another the alliaceous, and a fourth the hempen; the importance of these plants as articles of food or manufacture no doubt suggested their adoption. Thus all vegetable substances are distributed in the language under eleven different heads.

The zoölogical grouping in the *Pun tsao* is as rude and unscientific as that of plants. There are five *pu*, or divisions, namely: insect, scaly, shelly, feathered, and hairy animals. The first division contains four families: 1 and 2, insects born from eggs, as bees and silkworms, butterflies and spiders; 3, insects produced by metamorphosis, as glow-worms, mole-crickets, bugs; and 4, water insects, as toads, centipedes, etc. The second division has four families: 1, the dragons, including the manis, "the only fish that has legs;" 2, snakes; 3, fishes having scales; and 4, scaleless fishes, as the eel, cuttle-fish, prawn. The third division is classified under the two heads of tortoises or turtles and mollusks, including the star-fish, echinus, hermit-crab, etc. The fourth division contains birds arranged under four families: 1, water-fowl, as herons, king-fishers, etc.; 2, heath-fowl, sparrows, and pheasants; 3, forest birds, as magpies, crows; and 4, wild birds, as eagles and hawks. Beasts form the fifth division, which likewise contains four families: 1, the nine domesticated animals and their products; 2, wild animals, as lions, deers, otters; 3, rodentia, as the squirrel, hedgehog, rat; and 4, monkeys and fairies. The number of species in these five divisions is three hundred and ninety-one, but there are only three hundred and twenty different objects described, as the roe, fat, hair, exuviæ, etc., of animals are separately noticed.

The sixteen zoölogical characters in the language are not quite so far astray from being types of classes as the eleven botanical ones. Nine of them are mammiferous, viz.: the tiger, dog, and leopard, which stand for the carnivora; the rat for rodentia; the ox, sheep, and deer for ruminants; and the horse and hog for pachydermatous. Birds are chiefly comprised under one radical *niao*, but there is a sub-family of short-tailed gallinaceous fowls, though much confusion exists in the division. Fishes form one group, and improperly include crabs, lizards, whales, and snakes, though most of the latter are placed along with insects, or else under the dragons. The tortoise, toad, and dragon are the types of three small collections, and insects are comprised in the sixteenth and last. These groups, although they contain many anomalies, as might be expected, are still sufficiently natural to teach those who write the language something of the world around them. Thus, when one sees that a new character contains the radical *dog* in composition, he will be sure that it is neither fowl, fish, nor bug, nor any animal of the pachydermatous, cervine, or ruminant tribes, although he may have never seen the animal nor heard its name. This peculiarity runs through the whole language, indeed, but in other groups, as for instance those under the radicals man, woman, and child, or heart, hand, leg, etc., the characters include mental and passionate emotions, as well as actions and names, so that the type is not sufficiently indicative to convey a definite idea of the words included under it; the names of natural objects being most easily arranged in this manner.

Between the account of plants and animals the *Herbal* has one chapter on garments and domestic utensils, for such things "are used in medicine and are made out of plants." The remaining chapters, XXXIX.–LII., treat of animals, as noticed above. The properties of the objects spoken of are discussed in a very methodical manner, so that a student can immediately turn to a plant or mineral and ascertain its virtue. For instance, the information relative to the history and uses of the horse is contained in twenty-four sections. The first explains the character, *ma*, which was originally intended to represent the outline of the animal. The second describes the varieties of horses, the best kinds for medical use, and gives brief descriptions of them, for the guidance of the practitioner. "The pure white are the best for medicine. Those found in the south and east are small and weak. The age is known by the teeth. The eye reflects the full image of a man. If he eats rice his feet will become heavy; if rat's dung, his belly will grow long; if his teeth be rubbed with dead silkworms, or black plums, he will not eat, nor if the skin of a rat or wolf be hung in his manger. He should not be allowed to eat from a hog's trough, lest he contract disease; and if a monkey is kept in the stable he will not fall sick."

The third section goes on to speak of the flesh, which is an article of food; that of a pure white stallion is the most wholesome. One author recommends "eating almonds, and taking a rush broth, if the person feel uncomfortable after a meal of horse-flesh. It should be roasted and eaten with ginger and pork; and to eat the flesh of a black horse, and not drink wine with it, will surely produce death." The fourth describes the crown of the horse, the "fat of which is sweet, and good to make the hair grow and the face to shine." The fifth and succeeding sections to the twenty-fourth treat of the sanative properties and mode of exhibiting the milk, heart, lungs, liver, kidneys, placenta, teeth, bones, skin, mane, tail, brains, blood, perspiration, and excrements.

Some of the directions are dietetic, and others are prescriptive. "When eating horse-flesh do not eat the liver," is one of the former, given because of the absence of a gall-bladder in the liver, which imports its poisonous qualities. "The heart of a white horse, or that of a hog, cow, or hen, when dried and rasped into spirit and so taken, cures forgetfulness; if the patient hears one thing he knows ten." "Above the knees the horse has *night-eyes* (warts), which enable him to go in the night; they are useful in the toothache;" these sections partake both of the descriptive and prescriptive. Another medical one is: "If a man be restless and hysterical when he wishes to sleep, and it is requisite to put him to rest, let the ashes of a skull be mingled with water and given him, and let him have a skull for a pillow, and it will cure him." The same preservative virtues appear to be ascribed to a horse's hoof hung in a house as are supposed, by some who should know better, to belong to a horseshoe when nailed upon the door.[1] The whole of this extensive work is liberally sprinkled with such whimsies, but the practice of medicine among the Chinese is vastly

[1] *Chinese Repository*, Vol. VII., p. 393.

better than their theories; for as Rémusat justly observes, "To see well and reason falsely are not wholly incompatible, and the naturalists of China, as well as the chemists and physicians of our ancient schools, have sometimes tried to reconcile them."

Another work on botany besides the *Herbal*, issued in 1848, deserves notice for its research and the excellence of its drawings. It is the *Chih Wuh Ming-shih Tu-kao*, or *Researches into the Names and Virtues of Plants*, with plates, in sixty volumes. There are one thousand seven hundred and fifteen drawings of plants, with descriptions of each, arranged in eleven books, followed by medical and agricultural observations on the most important in four books. One of its valuable points to the foreigner is the terminology furnished by the two authors for describing the parts and uses of plants. Rémusat read a paper in 1828, 'On the State of the Natural Sciences among the Orientals,' in which he indicates the position attained by Chinese in their researches into the nature and uses of objects around them. After speaking of the adaptation the language possesses, from its construction, to impart some general notions of animated and vegetable nature, he goes on to remark upon the theorizing propensities of their writers, instead of contenting themselves with examining and recording facts. "In place of studying the organization of bodies, they undertake to determine by reasoning how it should be, an aim which has not seldom led them far from the end they proposed. One of the strangest errors among them relates to the transformation of beings into each other, which has arisen from popular stories or badly conducted observations on the metamorphoses of insects. Learned absurdities have been added to puerile prejudices; that which the vulgar have believed the philosophers have attempted to explain, and nothing can be easier, according to the oriental systems of cosmogony, in which a simple matter, infinitely diversified, shows itself in all beings. Changes affect only the apparent properties of bodies, or rather the bodies themselves have only appearances; according to these principles, they are not astonished at seeing the electric fluid or even the stars converted into stones, as happens when aerolites fall. That animated beings become inanimate is proven by fossils and petrifactions. Ice enclosed in the earth for a millennium becomes rock crystal; and it is only necessary that lead, the *father* of all metals (as Saturn, its alchemistic type, was of gods), pass through four periods of two centuries each to become successively cinnabar, tin, and silver. In spring the rat changes into a quail, and quails into rats again during the eighth month.

"The style in which these marvels is related is now and then a little equivocal; but if they believe part of them proved, they can see nothing really impossible in the others. One naturalist, less credulous than his fellows, rather smiles at another author who reported the metamorphosis of an oriole into a mole, and of rice into a carp; 'it is a ridiculous story,' says he; 'there is proof only of the change of rats into quails, which is reported in the almanac, and which I have often seen myself, for there is an unvaried progression, as well of transformations as of generations.' Animals, according to the Chinese, are viviparous as quadrupeds, or oviparous as birds; they grow by transformations, as insects, or by the effect of humidity, as snails, slugs, and centipedes. . . . . . The success of such systems is almost always sure, not in China alone either, because it is easier to put words in place of things, to stop at nothing, and to have formulas ready for solving all questions. It is thus that they have formed a scientific jargon, which one might almost think had been borrowed from our dark ages, and which has powerfully contributed to retain knowledge in China in the swaddling-clothes we now find it. Experience teaches that when the human mind is once drawn into a false way, the lapse of ages and the help of a man of genius are necessary to draw it out. Ages have not been wanting in China, but the man whose superior enlightenment might dissipate these deceitful glimmerings, would find it very difficult to exercise this happy influence as long as their political institutions attract all their inquiring minds or vigorous intellects far away from scientific researches into the literary examinations, or put before them the honors and employments which the functions and details of magisterial appointments bring with them." [1]

[1] *Mélanges Orientales, Posthumes*, p. 215.

This last observation indicates the reason, to a great degree, for the fixedness of the Chinese in all departments of learned inquiry; hard labor employs the energy and time of the ignorant mass, and emulation in the strife to reach official dignities consumes and perverts the talents of the learned. Then their language itself disheartens the most enthusiastic students in this branch of study, on account of its vagueness and want of established terms. When the vivifying and strengthening truths of revelation shall be taught to the Chinese, and its principles acted upon among them, we may expect more vigor in their minds and more profit in their investigations into the wonders of nature.

CHAPTER VII.

LAWS OF CHINA, AND PLAN OF ITS GOVERNMENT.

The consideration of the theory and practice of the Chinese government recommends itself to the attention of the intelligent student of man by several peculiar reasons, among which are its acknowledged antiquity, the multitudes of people it rules, and the comparative quiet enjoyed by its subjects. The government of a heathen nation is so greatly modified by the personal character of the executive, and the people are so liable to confound institutions with men, either from imperfect acquaintance with the nature of those institutions, or from being, through necessity or habit, easily guided and swayed by designing and powerful men, that the long continuance of the Chinese polity is a proof both of its adaptation to the habits and condition of the people, and of its general good management. The antiquity and excellence of such a government, and its orderly administration, might, however, be far greater than it is in China, without being invested with the interest which at present attaches to it in that Empire in consequence of the immense population, whose lives and property, food and well-being, depend to so great a degree upon it. What was at first rather a feeling of curiosity, gradually becomes one of awe, when the evil results of misgovernment, or the beneficent effects of equitable rule, are seen to be so momentous.

The theory of the Chinese government is undoubtedly the patriarchal; the Emperor is the sire, his officers are the responsible elders of its provinces, departments, and districts, as every father of a household is of its inmates. This may, perhaps, be the theory of other governments, but nowhere has it been systematized so thoroughly, and acted upon so consistently and for so long a period, as in China. Two causes, mutually acting upon each other, have, more than anything else, combined to give efficiency to this theory. The ancient rule of Yau and Shun [1] was strictly, so far as the details are known, a patriarchal chieftainship, conferred upon them on account of their excellent character; and their successors under Yu of the Hia dynasty were considered as deriving their power from heaven, to whom they were amenable for its good use. When Chingtang, founder of the Shang dynasty, B.C. 1766, and Wu Wang, of the Chau, B.C. 1122, took up arms against the Emperors, the excuse given was that they had not fulfilled the decrees of heaven, and had thereby forfeited their claim to the throne.

Confucius, in teaching his principles of political ethics, referred to the conduct of those ancient kings both for proof of the correctness of his instructions and for arguments to enforce them. The large number of those who followed him during his lifetime furnishes some evidence that his countrymen assented to the propriety of his teachings. This may account for their reception, illustrated as they were by the high character the sage bore; but it was not till the lapse of two or three centuries that the rulers of China perceived the great security the adoption and diffusion of these doctrines would give their sway. They therefore turned their attention toward the embodiment of these precepts into laws, and toward basing the institutions of government upon them; through all the convulsions and wars which have disturbed the country and changed the reigning families, these writings have done more than any one thing else to uphold the institutions of the Chinese and give them their character and permanence. Education being founded on them, those who as students had been taught to receive and reverence them as the oracles of political wisdom, would, when they entered upon the duties of office, endeavor to carry out, in some degree at least, their principles. Thus the precept and the practice have mutually modified, supported, and enforced each other.

---

[1] 2357 and 2255 before Christ.

But this civilization is Asiatic and not European, pagan and not Christian. The institutions of China are despotic and defective, and founded on wrong principles. They may have the element of stability, but not of improvement. The patriarchal theory does not make men honorable, truthful, or kind; it does not place woman in her right position, nor teach all classes their obligations to their Maker; the wonder is, to those who know the strength of evil passions in the human breast, that this huge mass of mankind is no worse. We must, indeed, look into its structure in order to discover the causes of this stability, inasmuch as here we have neither a standing army to enforce nor the machinery of a state religion to compel obedience toward a sovereign. A short inspection will show that the great leading principles by which the present administration preserves its power over the people, consist in a system of *strict surveillance* and *mutual responsibility* among all classes. These are aided in their efficiency by the geographical isolation of the country, a remarkable spirit of loyal pride in their own history, and a general system of political education and official examinations.

These two principles are enforced by such a minute gradation of rank and subordination of offices as to give the government more of a military character than at first appears, and the whole system is such as to make it one of the most unmixed oligarchies now existing. It is like a network extending over the whole face of society, each individual being isolated in his own mesh but responsibly connected with all around him. The man who knows that it is almost impossible, except by entire seclusion, to escape from the company of secret or acknowledged emissaries of government, will be cautious of offending the laws of the country, knowing, as he must, that though he should himself escape, yet his family, his kindred, or his neighbors will suffer for his offence; that if unable to recompense the sufferers, it will probably be dangerous for him to return home; or if he does, it will be most likely to find his property in the possession of neighbors or officials, who feel conscious of security in plundering one whose offences have forever placed him under a ban.

The effect of these two causes upon the mass of the people is to imbue them with a great fear of the government, both of its officers and its operations; each man considers that safety is best to be found in keeping aloof from both. This mutual surveillance and responsibility, though only partially extended throughout the multitude, necessarily undermines confidence and infuses universal distrust; while this object of complete isolation, though at the expense of justice, truth, honesty, and natural affection, is what the government strives to accomplish and actually does to a wonderful degree. The idea of government in the minds of the uneducated people is that of some ever-present terror, like a sword of Damocles; and so far has this undefined fear of some untoward result when connected with it counteracted the real vigor of the Chinese, that to it may be referred much of their indifference to improvement, contentment with what is already known and possessed, and submission to petty injustice and spoliation.

Men are deterred, too, as much by distrust of each other as by fear of the police, from combining in an intelligent manner to resist governmental exactions because opposed to principles of equity, or joining with their rulers to uphold good order; no such men, and no such instances, as John Hampden going to prison for refusing to subscribe to a forced loan, or Thomas Williams and his companions throwing the tea overboard in Boston harbor, ever occurred in China or any other Asiatic country. They dread illegal societies quite as much from the cruelties this same distrust induces the leaders to exercise over recreant or suspected members, as from apprehensien of arrest and punishment by the regular authorities. Thus, with a state of society at times on the verge of insurrection, this mass of people is kept in check by the threefold cord of responsibility, fear, and isolation, each of them strengthening the other, and all depending upon the character of the people for much of their efficiency. Since all the officers of government received their intellectual training when commoners under these influences, it is easy to understand why the supreme powers are so averse to improvement and to foreign intercourse—from both of which causes, in truth, the monarch has the greatest reason to dread lest the charm of his power be weakened and his sceptre pass away.

There is, however, a further explanation for the general peace which prevails to be found back of this. It is owing partly to the diffusion of a political education among the people—teaching them the principles on which all government is founded, and the reasons for those principles flowing from the patriarchal theory—and partly to their plodding, industrious character. A brief exposition of the construction and divisions of the central and provincial governments and their mutual relations, and the various duties devolving upon the departments and officers, will exhibit more of the operation of these principles.

Although the Emperor is regarded as the head of this great organization, as the fly-wheel which sets other wheels of the machine in motion, he is still considered as bound to rule according to the code of the land; and when there is a well-known law, though the source of law, he is expected to follow it in his decrees. The statutes of China form an edifice, the foundations of which were laid by Lí Kwei twenty centuries ago. Successive dynasties have been building thereon ever since, adding, altering, pulling down, and putting together as circumstances seemed to require. The people have a high regard for the code, "and all they seem to desire is its just and impartial execution, independent of caprice and uninfluenced by corruption. That the laws of China are, on the contrary, very frequently violated by those who are their administrators and constitutional guardians, there can, unfortunately, be no question; but to what extent, comparatively with the laws of other countries, must at present be very much a matter of conjecture: at the same time it may be observed, as something in favor of the Chinese system, that there are substantial grounds for believing that neither flagrant nor repeated acts of injustice do, in point of fact, often, in any rank or station, ultimately escape with impunity."[1] Sir George Staunton is well qualified to speak on this point, and his opinion has been corroborated

[1] *Penal Code*, Introduction, p. xxviii.

by most of those who have had similar opportunities of judging; while his translation of the *Code* has given all persons interested in the question the means of ascertaining the principles on which the government ostensibly acts.

This body of laws is called *Ta Tsing Liuh Lí*, *i.e.*, 'Statutes and Rescripts of the Great Pure Dynasty,' and contains all the laws of the Empire. They are arranged under seven leading heads, viz.: General, Civil, Fiscal, Ritual, Military, and Criminal laws, and those relating to Public Works; and subdivided into four hundred and thirty-six sections, called *liuh*, or 'statutes,' to which the *lí*, or modern clauses, to limit, explain or alter them, are added; these are now much more numerous than the original statutes. A new edition is published by authority every five years; in the reprint of 1830 the Emperor ordered that the Supreme Court should make but few alterations, lest wily litigants might take advantage of the discrepancies between the new and old law to suit their own purposes. This edition is in twenty-eight volumes, and is one of the most frequently seen books in the shops of any city. The clauses are attached to each statute, and have the same force. No authorized reports of cases and decisions, either of the provincial or supreme courts, are published for general use, though their record is kept in the court where they are decided; the publication of such adjudged cases, as a guide to officers, is not unknown. An extensive collection of notes, comments, and cases, illustrating the practice and theory of the laws, was appended to the edition of 1799.

A short extract from the original preface of the *Code*, published in 1647, only three years after the Manchu Emperors took the throne, will explain the principles on which it was drawn up. After remarking upon the inconveniences arising from the necessity of aggravating or mitigating the sentences of the magistrates, who, previous to the re-establishment of an authentic code of penal laws, were not in possession of any fixed rules upon which they could build a just decision, the Emperor Shunchí goes on to describe the manner of revising the code:

"A numerous body of magistrates was assembled at the capital, at our command, for the purpose of revising the penal code formerly in force under the late dynasty of Ming, and of digesting the same into a new code, by the exclusion of such parts as were exceptionable and the introduction of others which were likely to contribute to the attainment of justice and the general perfection of the work. The result of their labors having been submitted to our examination, we maturely weighed and considered the various matters it contained, and then instructed a select number of our great officers of state carefully to revise the whole, for the purpose of making such alterations and emendations as might still be found requisite. Wherefore, it being now published, let it be your great care, officers and magistrates of the interior and exterior departments of our Empire, diligently to observe the same, and to forbear in future to give any decision, or to pass any sentence, according to your private sentiments, or upon your unsupported authority. Thus shall the magistrates and people look up with awe and submission to the justice of these institutions, as they find themselves respectively concerned in them; the transgressor will not fail to suffer a strict expiation of his crimes, and will be the instrument of deterring others from similar misconduct; and finally both officers and people will be equally secured for endless generations in the enjoyment of the happy effects of the great and noble virtues of our illustrious progenitors."

Under the head of General Laws are forty-seven sections, comprising principles and definitions applicable to the whole, and containing some singular notions on equity and criminality. The description of the five ordinary punishments, definition of the ten treasonable offences, regulations for the eight privileged classes, and general directions regarding the conduct of officers of government, are the matters treated of under this head. The title of Section XLIV. is "On the decision of cases not provided for by law;" and the rule is that "such cases may then be determined by an accurate comparison with others which are already provided for, and which approach most nearly to those under investigation, in order to ascertain afterward to what extent an aggravation or mitigation of the punishment would be equitable. A provisional sentence conformable thereto shall be laid before the superior magistrates, and, after receiving their approbation, be submitted to the Emperor's final decision. Any erroneous judgment which may be pronounced, in consequence of adopting a more summary mode of proceeding in cases of a doubtful nature, shall be punished as wilful deviation from justice." This, of course, gives great latitude to the magistrate, and as he is thus allowed to decide and act before the new law can be confirmed or annulled, the chief restraints to his injustice in such cases (which, however, are not numerous) lie in the fear of an appeal and its consequences, or of summary reprisals from the suffering parties.

The six remaining divisions pertain to the six administrative boards of the government. The second contains Civil Laws, under twenty-eight sections, divided into two books, one of them referring to the system of government, and the other to the conduct of magistrates, etc. The hereditary succession of rank and titles is regulated, and punishments laid down for those who illegally assume these honors. Most of the nobility of China are Manchus, and none of the hereditary dignities existing previous to the conquest were recognized, except those attached to the family of Confucius. Improperly recommending unfit persons as deserving high honors, appointing and removing officers without the Emperor's sanction, and leaving stations without due permission, are the principal subjects regulated in the first book. The second book contains rules regarding the interference of superior magistrates with the proceedings of the lower courts, and prohibitions against cabals and treasonable combinations among officers, which are of course capital crimes; all persons in the employ of the state are required to make themselves acquainted with the laws, and even private individuals "who are found capable of explaining the nature and comprehending the objects of the laws, shall receive pardon in all offences resulting purely from accident, or imputable to them only from the guilt of others, provided it be the first offence."

The third division, of Fiscal Laws, under eighty-two sections, contains rules for enrolling the people, and of succession and inheritance; also laws for regulating marriages between various classes of society, for guarding granaries and treasuries, for preventing and punishing smuggling, for restraining usury, and for overseeing shops. Section LXXVI. orders that persons and families truly represent their profession in life, and restrains them from indulging in a change of occupation; "generation after generation they must not vary or alter it." This rule is, however, constantly violated. Section XC. exempts the buildings of literary and religious institutions from taxation. The general aim of the laws relating to holding real estate is to secure the cultivation of all the land taken up, and the regular payment of the tax. The proprietor, in some cases, can be deprived of his lands because he does not till them, and though in fact owner in fee simple, he is restricted in the disposition of them by will in many ways, and forfeits them if the taxes are not paid.

The fourth division, of Ritual Laws, under twenty-six sections, contains the regulations for state sacrifices and ceremonies, those appertaining to the worship of ancestors, and whatever belongs to heterodox and magical sects or teachers. The heavy penalties threatened in some of these sections against all illegal combinations under the guise of a new form of worship presents an interesting likeness to the restrictions issued by the English, French, and German princes during and after the Reformation. The Chinese authorities had the same dread lest the people should meet and consult how to resist them. Even processions in honor of the gods may be forbidden for good reason, and are not allowed at all at Peking; while, still more, the rites observed by the Emperor cannot be imitated by any unauthorized person; women are not allowed to congregate in the temples, nor magicians to perform any strange incantations. Few of these laws are really necessary, and those against illegal sects are in fact levelled against political associations, which usually take on a religious guise.

The fifth division, of Military Laws, in seventy-one sections, provides for the protection of the palace and government of the army, for guarding frontier passes, management of the imperial cattle, and forwarding despatches by couriers. Some of these ordinances lay down rules for the protection of the Emperor's person, and the disposition of his body-guard and troops in the palace, the capital, and over the Empire. The sections relating to the government of the army include the rules for the police of cities; and those designed to secure the protection of the frontier comprise all the enactments against foreign intercourse, some of which have already been referred to in passing. The supply of horses and cattle for the army is a matter of some importance, and is minutely regulated; one law orders all persons who possess vicious and dangerous animals to restrain them, and if through neglect any person is killed or wounded, the owner of the animal shall be obliged to redeem himself from the punishment of manslaughter by paying a fine. This provision to compel the owners of unruly beasts to exercise proper restraint over them is like that laid down by Moses in Exodus XXI., 29, 30. There is as yet no general post-office establishment, but governmental couriers often take private letters; local mails are safely carried by express companies. The required rate of travel for the official post is one hundred miles a day, but it does not ordinarily go more than half that distance. Officers of government are allowed ninety days to make the journey from Peking to Canton, a distance of twelve hundred miles, but couriers frequently travel it in twelve days.

The sixth division, on Criminal Laws, is arranged in eleven books, containing in all one hundred and seventy sections, and is the most important of the whole. The clauses under some of the sections are numerous, and show that it is not for want of proper laws or insufficient threatenings that crimes go unpunished. The books of this division relate to robbery, in which is included high treason and renunciation of allegiance; to homicide and murder; quarrelling and fighting; abusive language; indictments, disobedience to parents, and false accusations; bribery and corruption; forging and frauds; incest and adultery; arrests and escapes of criminals, their imprisonment and execution; and, lastly, miscellaneous offences.

Under Section CCCXXIX. it is ordered that any one who is guilty of addressing abusive language to his or her father or mother, or father's parents, or a wife who rails at her husband's parents or grandparents, shall be strangled; provided always that the persons so abused themselves complain to the magistrate, and had personally heard the language addressed to them. This law is the same in regard to children as that contained in Leviticus XX., 9, and the power here given the parent does not seem to be productive of evil. Section CCCLXXXI. has reference to "privately hushing up public crimes," but its penalties are for the most part a dead letter, and a full account of the various modes adopted in the courts of withdrawing cases from the cognizance of superiors, would form a singular chapter in Chinese jurisprudence. Consequently those who refuse every offer to suppress cases are highly lauded by the people. Another section (CCCLXXXVI.) ordains that whoever is guilty of improper conduct, contrary to the spirit of the laws, but not a breach of any specific article, shall be punished at least with forty blows, and with eighty when of a serious nature. Some of the provisions of this part of the code are praiseworthy, but no part of Chinese legislation is so cruel and irregular as criminal jurisprudence. The permission accorded to the judge to torture the criminal opens the door for much inhumanity.

The seventh division contains thirteen sections relating to Public Works and Ways, such as the weaving of interdicted patterns of silk, repairing dikes, and constructing edifices for government. All public residences, granaries, treasuries and manufactories, embankments and dikes of rivers and canals, forts, walls, and mausolea, must be frequently examined, and kept in repair. Poverty or peculation render many of these laws void, and many subterfuges are often practised by the superintending officer to pocket as much of the funds as he can. One officer, when ordered to repair a wall, made the workmen go over it and chip off the faces of the stones still remaining, then plastering up the holes.

Besides these laws and their numerous clauses, every high provincial officer has the right to issue edicts upon such public matters as require regulation, some of them even affecting life and death, either reviving some old law or giving it an application to the case before him, with such modifications as seem to be necessary. He must report these acts to the proper board at Peking. No such order, which for the time has the force of law, is formally repealed, but gradually falls into oblivion, until circumstances again require its reiteration. This mode of publishing statutes gives rise to a sort of common and unwritten law in villages, to which a council of elders sometimes compels individuals to submit; long usage is also another ground for enforcing them.

Still, with all the tortures and punishments allowed by the law, and all the cruelties superadded upon the criminals by irritated officers or rapacious underlings and jailors, a broad survey of Chinese legislation, judged by its results and the general appearance of society, gives the impression of an administration far superior to other Asiatic countries. A favorable comparison has been made in the *Edinburgh Review:*[1] "By far the most remarkable thing in this code is its great reasonableness, clearness, and consistency, the business-like brevity and directness of the various provisions, and the plainness and moderation in which they are expressed. There is nothing here of the monstrous *verbiage* of most other Asiatic productions, none of the superstitious deliration, the miserable incoherence, the tremendous *non-sequiturs* and eternal repetitions of those oracular performances—nothing even of the turgid adulation, accumulated epithets, and fatiguing self-praise of other Eastern despotisms—but a calm, concise, and distinct series of enactments, savoring throughout of practical judgment and European good sense, and if not always conformable to our improved notions of expediency, in general approaching to them more nearly than the codes of most other nations. When we pass, indeed, from the ravings of the Zendavesta or the Puranas to the tone of sense and business in this Chinese collection, we seem to be passing from darkness to light, from the drivellings of dotage to the exercise of an improved understanding; and redundant and absurdly minute as these laws are in many particulars, we scarcely know any European code that is at once so copious and so consistent, or that is so nearly free from intricacy, bigotry, and fiction. In everything relating to political freedom or individual independence it is indeed wofully defective; but for the repression of disorder and the gentle coer-

---

[1] Vol. XVI., 1810.

cion of a vast population, it appears to be equally mild and efficacious. The state of society for which it was formed appears incidentally to be a low and wretched one; but how could its framers have devised a wiser means of maintaining it in peace and tranquillity?"

This encomium is to a certain extent just, but the practice of legislation in China has probably not been materially improved by the mere possession of a reasonable code of laws, though some melioration in jurisprudence has been effected.[1] The infliction of barbarous punishments, such as blinding, cutting off noses, ears, or other parts of the body, still not uncommon in Persia and Turkey, is not allowed or practised in China; and the government, in minor crimes, contents itself with but little more than opprobrious exposure in the pillory, or castigation, which carry with them no degradation.

The defects in this remarkable body of laws arise from several sources. The degree of liberty that can safely be awarded to the subject is not defined in it, and his rights are unknown in law. The government is despotic, but having no efficient military power in their hands, the lawgivers resort to a minuteness of legislation upon the practice of social and relative virtues and duties which interferes with their observance; though it must be remembered that no pulpit or Sabbath-school exists there to expound and enforce them from a higher code, and the laws must be the chief guide in most cases. The code also exhibits a minute attention to trifles, and an effort to legislate for every possible contingency, which must perplex the judge when dealing with the infinite shades of difference occurring in human actions. There are now many vague and obsolete statutes, ready to serve as a handle to prosecute offenders for the gratification of private pique; and although usage and precedent both combine to prove their disuse, malice and bribery can easily effect their reviviscence and application to the case.

Sheer cruelty, except in cases of treason against the Emperor, cannot be charged against this code as a whole, though many of the laws seem designed to operate chiefly *in terrorem*,

[1] *Chinese Repository*, Vol. IV., pp. 24–29.

and the penalty is placed higher than the punishment really intended to be inflicted, to the end that the Emperor may have scope for mercy, or, as he says, "for leniency beyond the bounds of the law." The principle on which this is done is evident, and the commonness of the practice proves that such an exercise of mercy has its effect. The laws of China are not altogether unmeaning words, though the degree of efficiency in their execution is subject to endless variations; some officers are clement, others severe; the people in certain provinces are industrious and peaceable, in others turbulent and averse to quiet occupations, so that one is likely to form a juster idea of their administration by looking at the results as seen in the general aspect of society, and judging of the tree by its fruits, than by drawing inferences applicable to the whole machine of state from particular instances of oppression and insubordination, as has been so often the case with travellers and writers.

The general examination of the Chinese government here proposed may be conveniently considered under the heads of the Emperor and his court, classes of society, the different branches of the supreme administration, the provincial authorities, and the execution of the laws.

The Emperor is at the head of the whole; and if the possession of great power, and being the object of almost unbounded reverence, can impart happiness, he may safely be considered as the happiest mortal living; though to his power there are many checks, and the reverence paid him is proportioned somewhat to the fidelity with which he administers the decrees of heaven. "The Emperor is the sole head of the Chinese constitution and government; he is regarded as the vice-gerent of heaven, especially chosen to govern all nations; and is supreme in everything, holding at once the highest legislative and executive powers, without limit or control." Both he and the Pope claim to be the vice-gerent of heaven and interpreter of its decrees to the whole world, and these two rulers have emulated each other in their assumption of arrogant titles. The most common appellation employed to denote the Emperor in state papers and among the people is *hwangtí*, or 'august sovereign;' it is defined as "the appellation of one possessing complete virtues, and able to act on heavenly principles."[1] This title is further defined as meaning heaven: "Heaven speaks not, yet the four seasons follow in regular succession, and all things spring forth. So the three august ones (Fuhhí, Shinnung, and Hwangtí) descended in state, and without even uttering a word the people bowed to their sway; their virtue was inscrutable and boundless like august heaven, and therefore were they called *august* ones."

Among the numerous titles given the monarch may be mentioned *hwang shang*, the 'august lofty one;' *tien hwang*, 'celestial august one;' *shing hwang*, the 'wise and august,' *i.e.*, infinite in knowledge and complete in virtue; *tien tí*, 'celestial sovereign;' and *shing tí*, 'sacred sovereign,' because he is able to act on heavenly principles. He is also called *tien tsz'*, 'son of heaven,' because heaven is his father and earth is his mother, and *shing tien tsz'*, 'wise son of heaven,' as being born of heaven and having infinite knowledge; terms which are given him as the ruler of the world by the gift of heaven. He is even addressed, and sometimes refers to himself, under designations which pertain exclusively to heaven. *Wan sui yé*, 'sire of ten thousand years,' is a term used when speaking of him or approaching him, like the words, *O king, live forever!* addressed to the ancient kings of Persia. *Pí hia*, 'beneath the footstool,' is a sycophantic compellation used by his courtiers, as if they were only worthy of being at the edge of his footstool.

The Emperor usually designates himself by the terms *chin*, 'ourself;' *kwa jin*, the 'solitary man,' or the one man; and *kwa kiun*, the 'solitary prince.' He has been loaded with many ridiculous titles by foreign writers, as Brother of the Sun and Moon, Grandson of the Stars, King of Kings, etc., but no such epithets are known among his subjects. His palace has various appellations, such as hall of audience, golden palace, the ninth entrance, vermilion avenue, vermilion hall, rosy hall, forbidden pavilion, the crimson and forbidden palace, gemmeous steps, golden steps, meridian portal, gemmeous avenue, celestial steps,

[1] *Chinese Repository*, Vol. IV., p. 12; *Chinese Chrestomathy*, p. 558.

celestial court, great interior, the maple pavilion, royal house, etc. To see him is to see the dragon's face; the throne is called the "dragon's throne," and also the "divine utensil," *i.e.*, the thing given him by heaven to sit in when executing his divine mission; his person is styled the dragon's body, and a five-clawed dragon is emblazoned, like a coat of arms, on his robes, which no one can use or imitate. Thus the Old Dragon, it might be almost said, has coiled himself around the Emperor of China, one of the greatest upholders of his power in this world, and contrived to get himself worshipped, through him, by one-third of mankind.

The Emperor is the fountain of power, rank, honor, and privilege to all within his dominions, which are termed *tien hia*, meaning all under heaven, and were till recently, even by his highest officers, ignorantly supposed to comprise all mankind. As there can be but one sun in the heavens, so there can be but one *hwangti* on earth, the source and dispenser of benefits to the whole world.[1] The same absolute executive power held by him is placed in the hands of his deputies and governor-generals, to be by them exercised within the limits of their jurisdiction. He is the head of religion and the only one qualified to adore heaven; he is the source of law and dispenser of mercy; no right can be held in opposition to his pleasure, no claim maintained against him, no privilege protect from his wrath. All the forces and revenues of the Empire are his, and he has a right to claim the services of all males between sixteen and sixty. In short, the whole Empire is his property, and the only checks upon his despotism are public opinion, the want of an efficient standing army, poverty and the venality of the agents of his power.

When the Manchus found themselves in possession of Peking, they regarded this position as fully entitling them to assume all imperial rights. Their sovereign thus announced his elevation in November, 1644: "I, the Son of Heaven, of the Ta-tsing

---

[1] The attributes ascribed to a *chakrawartti* in the Buddhist mythology have many points of resemblance to the *hwangti*, and Hardy's *Manual of Buddhism* (p. 126) furnishes an instructive comparison between the two characters, one fanciful and the other real.

dynasty, humbly as a subject dare to announce to Imperial Heaven and Sovereign Earth. Though the world is vast, Shangtí looks on all without partiality. My Imperial Grandfather received the gracious decree of Heaven and founded a kingdom in the East, which became firmly established. My Imperial Father succeeding to the kingdom, extended it; and I, Heaven's servant, in my poor person became the inheritor of the dominion they transmitted. When the Ming dynasty was coming to its end, traitors and men of violence appeared in crowds, involving the people in misery. China was without a ruler. It fell to me reverentially to accept the responsibility of continuing the meritorious work of my ancestors. I saved the people, destroyed their oppressors; and now, in accordance with the desires of all, I fix the urns of Empire at Yen-king. . . . I, receiving Heaven's favor, and in accordance with their wishes, announce to Heaven that I have ascended the throne of the Empire, that the name I have chosen for it is the Great Pure, and that the style of my reign is *Shun-chí* ('Obedient Rule'). I beg reverentially Heaven and Earth to protect and assist the Empire, so that calamity and disturbance may soon come to an end, and the land enjoy universal peace. For this I humbly pray, and for the acceptance of this sacrifice."

The present Emperor is the ninth of the Tsing dynasty who has reigned in China. *Tsing* means Pure, and was taken by the Manchus as a distinctive term for their new dynasty, alluding to the purity of justice they intended to maintain in their sway. Some of the founders of the ancient dynasties derived their dynastic name from their patrimonial estates, as *Sung*, *Han*, *Chau*, etc., but the later ones have adopted names like *Yuen*, or 'Original,' *Ming*, or 'Illustrious,' etc., which indicate their vanity.

The present monarch is still a minor, and the affairs of government are nominally under the direction of the Empress-dowager, who held the same office during the minority of his predecessor, Tungchí. The surname of the reigning family is *Gioro*, or 'Golden,' derived from their ancestral chief, Aisin Gioro, whom they feign to have been the son of a divine virgin. They are the lineal descendants of the Kin, a rude race which drove out the Chinese rulers and occupied the northern provinces about 1130, making Peking their capital for many years. On the approach of the Mongols they were chased away to the east, and retained only a nominal independence; changing their name from Nüchih to Manjurs, they gradually increased in numbers, but did not assume any real importance until they became masters of China. The acknowledged founder of the reigning house was the chief Hien-tsu (1583–1615), whose actual descendants are collectively designated *Tsung-shih*, or 'Imperial Clan.' The second Emperor further limited the Clan by giving to each of his twenty-four sons a personal name of two characters, the first of which, Yun, was the same for all of them. For the succeeding generations he ordered a series of characters to be used by all the members of each, so that through all their ramifications the first name would show their position. Kanghí's own name was *Hiuen*, then followed *Yun*, *Hung*, *Yung*, *Mien*, *Yih*, and *Tsai*, the last and present sovereigns being both named *Tsai*. All who bear this name are direct descendants of Kanghí. Since the application of these seven generation names, eight more have been selected for future use by imperial scions.

In order still further to distinguish those most nearly allied in blood, as sons, nephews, etc., it is required that the second names of each family always consist of characters under the same radical. Thus Kiaking and his brothers wrote their first names *Yung*, and under the radical *gun* for the second; Taukwang and his brothers and cousins *Mien*, and under the radical *heart*. For some unexplained reason the radicals *silk* and *gold*, chosen for the second names of the next two generations, were altered to *words* and *water*. This peculiarity is easily represented in the Chinese characters; a comparison can be made in English with the supposed names of a family of sons, as Louis Edward, Louis Edwin, Louis Edwy, Louis Edgar, etc., the word *Louis* answering to *Mien*, and the syllable *Ed* to the radical *heart*.

The present Emperor's personal name is Tsai-tien, and, like those of his predecessors, is deemed to be too sacred to be spoken, or the characters to be written in the common form

The same reverence is observed for the names after death, so that twelve characters have been altered since the Manchu monarchs began to reign; Hiuen-wa, which was the personal name of Kanghí, has become permanently altered in its formation. The present sovereign was born August 15, 1871, and on January 12, 1875, succeeded his cousin Tsaishun, who died without issue—the first instance in the Gioro family for nearly three centuries. At this time there was some delay as to which of his cousins should succeed to the dragon throne, when the united council of the princes was led by the mother of the deceased Emperor to adopt her nephew, the son of Prince Chun. The little fellow was sent for at night to be immediately saluted as *hwangtí*, and ere long brought in before them, cross and sleepy as he was, to begin his reign under the style of Kwangsü, or 'Illustrious Succession.'

This title is called a *kwoh hao*, or national designation, and answers more nearly to the name that a new Pope takes with the tiara than to anything else in western lands. It is the expression of the idea which the monarch wishes to associate with his reign, and is the name by which he is known to his subjects during his life. It has been called a *period* by some writers, but while it is not strictly his name, yet period is not so correct as *reign*. Usage has made it equivalent in foreign books to the personal name, and it is plainer to say the Emperor Taukwang than the period Taukwang or the reign Taukwang, or still more than to write, as Wade has done, "the Emperor Mien-Ning, the style of whose reign was Tau Kwang;" or than Legge has done, to say, "the Emperor Pattern, of the period Yungching." In such cases it is not worth the trouble to attempt strict accuracy in a matter so entirely unlike western usages.

The use of the *kwoh hao* began with Wăn-tí, of the Han dynasty,[1] B.C. 179, and has continued ever since. Some of

[1] The remark of Heeren (*Asiatic Nations*, Vol. I., p. 57), that the names by which the early Persian monarchs, Darius, Xerxes, and others, were called, were really titles or surnames, and not their own personal names, suggests the further comparison whether those renowned names were not like the *kwoh hao* of the Chinese emperors, whose adoption of the custom was after the ex-

the early monarchs changed their *kwoh hao* many times during their reigns; Kao-tsung (A.D. 650–684), for example, had thirteen in a régime of thirty-four years, which induced historians to employ the *miao hao,* or ancestral name, as more suitable and less liable to confusion. The reason for thus investing the sovereign with a title different from his real name is not fully apparent, but arose probably out of the vanity of the monarch, who wished thus to glorify himself by a high-sounding title, and make his own name somewhat ineffable at the same time. The custom was adopted in Japan about A.D. 645, and is practised in Corea and Annam.

When a monarch ascends the throne, or as it is expressed in Chinese, "when he receives from Heaven and revolving nature the government of the world," he issues an inaugural proclamation. There is not much change in the wording of these papers, and an extract from the one issued in 1821 will exhibit the practice on such occasions:

"Our Ta Tsing dynasty has received the most substantial indication of Heaven's kind care. Our ancestors, Taitsu and Taitsung, began to lay the vast foundation [of our Empire]; and Shítsu became the sole monarch of China. Our sacred ancestor Kanghí, the Emperor Yungching, the glory of his age, and Kienlung, the eminent in honor, all abounded in virtue, were divine in martial prowess, consolidated the glory of the Empire, and moulded the whole to peaceful harmony.

"His late Majesty, who has now gone the great journey, governed all under Heaven's canopy twenty-five years, exercising the utmost caution and industry. Nor evening nor morning was he ever idle. He assiduously aimed at the best possible rule, and hence his government was excellent and illustrious; the court and the country felt the deepest reverence and the stillness of profound awe. A benevolent heart and a benevolent

tinction of the Persian monarchy. Herodotus (Book VI., 98) seems to have been familiar with these names, not so much as being arbitrary and meaningless terms as epithets whose significations were associated with the kings. The new names given to the last two sons of Josiah, who became kings of Judah by their conquerors (2 Kings, 23: 34, and 24: 17), indicate even an earlier adoption of this custom.

administration were universally diffused: in China Proper, as well as beyond it, order and tranquillity prevailed, and the tens of thousands of common people were all happy. But in the midst of a hope that this glorious reign would be long protracted, and the help of Heaven would be received many days, unexpectedly, on descending to bless, by his Majesty's presence, Lwanyang, the dragon charioteer (the holy Emperor) became a guest on high.

"My sacred and indulgent Father had, in the year that he began to rule alone, silently settled that the divine utensil should devolve on my contemptible person. I, knowing the feebleness of my virtue, at first felt much afraid I should not be competent to the office; but on reflecting that the sages, my ancestors, have left to posterity their plans; that his late Majesty has laid the duty on me—and Heaven's throne should not be long vacant—I have done violence to my feelings and forced myself to intermit awhile my heartfelt grief, that I may with reverence obey the unalterable decree; and on the 27th of the 8th moon (October 3d) I purpose devoutly to announce the event to Heaven, to earth, to my ancestors, and to the gods of the land and of the grain, and shall then sit down on the imperial throne. Let the next year be the first of Taukwang.

"I look upward and hope to be able to continue former excellences. I lay my hand on my heart with feelings of respect and cautious awe.—When a new monarch addresses himself to the Empire, he ought to confer benefits on his kindred, and extensively bestow gracious favors: what is proper to be done on this occasion is stated below."

(Here follow twenty-two paragraphs, detailing the gifts to be conferred and promotions made of noblemen and officers; ordering the restoration of suspended dignitaries to their full pay and honors, and sacrifices to Confucius and the Emperors of former dynasties; pardons to be extended to criminals, and banished convicts recalled; governmental debts and arrearages to be forgiven, and donations to be bestowed upon the aged.)

"Lo! now, on succeeding to the throne, I shall exercise myself to give repose to the millions of my people. Assist me to sustain the burden laid on my shoulders! With veneration I receive charge of Heaven's great concerns.—Ye kings and statesmen, great and small, civil and military, let every one be faithful and devoted, and aid in supporting the vast affairs, that our family dominion may be preserved hundreds and tens of thousands of years in never-ending tranquillity and glory! Promulgate this to all under Heaven—cause every one to hear it!"

The programme of ceremonies to be observed when the Emperor "ascends the summit," and seats himself on the dragon's throne, was published for the Emperor Taukwang by the Board of Rites a few days after. It details a long series of prostrations and bowings, leading out and marshalling the various officers of the court and members of the imperial family. After they are all arranged in proper precedence before the throne, "at the appointed hour the president of the Board of Rites shall go and entreat his Majesty to put on his mourning, and come forth by the gate of the eastern palace, and enter at the left door of the middle palace, where his Majesty, before the altar of his deceased imperial father, will respectfully announce that he receives the decree—kneel thrice and bow nine times."

He then retires, and soon after a large deputation of palace officers "go and solicit his Majesty to put on his imperial robes and proceed to the palace of his mother, the Empress-dowager, to pay his respects. The Empress-dowager will put on her court robes and ascend her throne, before which his Majesty shall kneel thrice and bow nine times." After this filial ceremony is over the golden chariot is made ready, the officer of the Astronomical Board—whose business is to *observe times*—is stationed at the palace gate, and when he announces the arrival of the chosen and felicitous moment, his Majesty comes forth and mounts the golden chariot, and the procession advances to the Palace of Protection and Peace. Here the great officers of the Empire are marshalled according to their rank, and when the Emperor sits down in the palace they all kneel and bow nine times.

"This ceremony over, the President of the Board of Rites, stepping forward, shall kneel down and beseech his Majesty, saying, 'Ascend the imperial throne.' The Emperor shall then rise from his seat, and the procession moving on in the same order to the Palace of Peace, his Majesty shall ascend the seat of gems and sit down on the imperial throne, with his face to the south." All present come forward and again make the nine prostrations, after which the proclamation of coronation, as it would be called in Europe, is formally sealed, and then announced to the Empire with similar ceremonies. There are many other lesser rites observed on these occasions, some of them appropriate to such an occasion, and others, according to our notions, bordering on the ludicrous; the whole presenting a strange mixture of religion, splendor, and farce, though as a whole calculated to impress all with a sentiment of awe toward one who gives to heaven, and receives from man, such homage and worship.[1]

Nothing is omitted which can add to the dignity and sacredness of the Emperor's person or character. Almost everything used by him, or in his personal service, is tabued to the common people, and distinguished by some peculiar mark or color, so as to keep up the impression of awe with which he is regarded, and which is so powerful an auxiliary to his throne. The outer gate of the palace must always be passed on foot, and the paved entrance walk leading up to it can only be used by him. The vacant throne, or even a screen of yellow silk thrown over a chair, is worshipped equally with his actual presence, and an imperial dispatch is received in the provinces with incense and prostrations; the vessels on the canal bearing articles for his special use always have the right of way. His birthday is celebrated by his officers, and the account of the opening ceremony, as witnessed by Lord Macartney, shows how skilfully every act tends to maintain his assumed character as the son of heaven.

"The first day was consecrated to the purpose of rendering a solemn, sacred, and devout homage to the supreme majesty of the Emperor. The ceremony was no longer performed in a tent, nor did it partake of the nature of a banquet. The princes,

---

[1] *Chinese Repository*, Vol. X., pp. 87–98. *Indo-Chinese Gleaner*, February, 1821.

tributaries, ambassadors, and great officers of state were assembled in a vast hall; and upon particular notice were introduced into an inner building, bearing at least the semblance of a temple. It was chiefly furnished with great instruments of music, among which were sets of cylindrical bells suspended in a line from ornamental frames of wood, and gradually diminishing in size from one extremity to the other, and also triangular pieces of metal, arranged in the same order as the bells. To the sound of these instruments a slow and solemn hymn was sung by eunuchs, who had such a command over their voices as to resemble the effect of musical glasses at a distance. The performers were directed, in the gliding from one tone to the other, by the striking of a shrill and sonorous cymbal; and the judges of music among the gentlemen of the embassy were much pleased with their execution. The whole had, indeed, a grand effect. During the performance, and at particular signals, nine times repeated, all present prostrated themselves nine times, except the ambassador and his suite, who made a profound obeisance. But he whom it was meant to honor continued, as if in imitation of the Deity, invisible the whole time. The awful impression intended to be made upon the minds of men by this apparent worship of a fellow-mortal was not to be effaced by any immediate scenes of sport or gaiety, which were postponed to the following day."[1] The mass of the people are not admitted to participate in these ceremonies; they are kept at a distance, and care, in fact, very little about them. In every provincial capital there is a hall, called *Wan-shao kung*, dedicated solely to the honor of the Emperor, and where, three days before and after his birthday, all the civil and military officers and the most distinguished citizens assemble to do him the same homage as if he were present. The walls and furniture are yellow.

The right of succession is hereditary in the male line, but it is always in the power of the sovereign to nominate his successor from among his own children. The heir-apparent is not commonly known during the lifetime of the incumbent, though

---

[1] Staunton's *Embassy*, 8vo edition, London, 1797, Vol. III., p. 63.

there is a titular office of guardian of the heir-apparent. During the Tsing dynasty the succession has varied, but the bloody scenes enacted in Turkey, Egypt, and India to remove competitors are not known at Peking, and the people have no fear that they will be enacted. Of the eight preceding sovereigns, Shunchí was the ninth son, Kanghí the third, Yungching the fourth, Kienlung the fourth, Kiaking the fifteenth, Taukwang the second, Hienfung the fourth, and Tungchí the only son. When Kwangsü was chosen this regular line failed, and thus was terminated an unbroken succession during two hundred and fifty-nine years (1616 to 1875), when ten rulers (including two in Manchuria) occupied the throne. It can be paralleled only in Judah, where the line of David down to Jehoiachin (B.C. 1055 to 599) continued regularly in the same manner—twenty kings in four hundred and fifty-six years.

In the reign of Kienlung, one of the censors memorialized him upon the desirableness of announcing his sucsessor, in order to quiet men's minds and repress intrigue, but the suggestion cost the man his place. The Emperor said that the name of his successor, in case of his own sudden death, would be found in a designated place, and that it was highly inexpedient to mention him, lest intriguing men buzzed about him, forming factions and trying to elevate themselves. The soundness of this policy cannot be doubted, and it is not unlikely that Kienlung knew the evils of an opposite course from an acquaintance with the history of some of the princes of Central Asia or India. One good result of not indicating the heir-apparent is that not only are no intrigues formed by the crown-prince, but when he begins to reign he is seldom compelled, from fear of his own safety, to kill or imprison his brothers or uncles; for, as they possess no power or party to render them formidable, their ambition finds full scope for its exercise in peaceful ways. In 1861, when the heir was a child of five years, a palace intrigue was started to remove his custody out of the hands of his mother into those of a cabal who had held sway for some years, but the promoters were all executed.

The management of the imperial clan appertains entirely to the Emperor, and has been conducted with considerable sagacity. All its members are under the control of the *Tsung-jin fu*, a sort of clansmen's court, consisting of a presiding controller, two assistant directors, and two deputies of the family. Their duties are to regulate whatever belongs to the government of the Emperor's kindred, which is divided into two branches, the direct and collateral, or the *tsung-shih* and *Gioro*. The *Tsung-shih*, or 'Imperial House,' comprise only the lineal descendants of Tienming's father, named Hien-tsu, or 'Illustrious Sire,' who first assumed the title of Emperor A.D. 1616. The collateral branches, including the children of his uncles and brothers, are collectively called Gioro. Their united number is unknown, but a genealogical record is kept in the national archives at Peking and Mukden. The *Tsung-shih* are distinguished by a yellow girdle, and the *Gioro* by a red one; when degraded, the former take a red, the latter a carnation girdle. There are altogether twelve degrees of rank in the *Tsung-shih*, and consequently some of the distant kindred are reduced to straitened circumstances. They are shut out from useful careers, and generally exhibit the evils ensuent upon the system of education and surveillance adopted toward them, in their low, vicious pursuits, and cringing imbecility of character. The sum of $133 is allowed when they marry, and $150 to defray funeral expenses, which induces some of them to maltreat their wives to death, in order to receive the allowance and dowry as often as possible.

The titular nobility of the Empire, as a whole, is a body whose members are without power, land, wealth, office, or influence, in virtue of their honors; some of them are more or less hereditary, but the whole system has been so devised, and the designations so conferred, as to tickle the vanity of those who receive them, without granting them any real power. The titles are not derived from landed estates, but the rank is simply designated in addition to the name, and it has been a question of some difficulty how to translate them. For instance, the title *Kung tsin-wang* literally means the 'Reverent Kindred Prince,' and should be translated Prince Kung, not Prince of Kung, which conveys the impression to a foreign reader that *Kung* is an appanage instead of an epithet.

The twelve orders of nobility are conferred solely on the members of the imperial house and clan: 1. *Tsin wang*, 'kindred prince,' *i.e.*, prince of the blood, conferred usually on his Majesty's brothers or sons. 2. *Kiun wang*, or 'prince of a princedom;' the eldest sons of the princes of these two degrees take a definite rank during their father's lifetime, but the collateral branches descend in precedence as the generations are more and more remote from the direct imperial line, until at last the person is simply a member of the imperial clan. These two ranks were termed *regulus* by the Jesuit writers, and each son of an Emperor enters one or other as he becomes of age. The highest princes receive a stipend of about $13,300, some rations, and a retinue of three hundred and sixty servants, altogether making an annual tax on the state of $75,000 to $90,000. The second receive half that sum, and inferior grades in a decreasing ratio, down to the simple members, who each get four dollars a month and rations. 3 and 4. *Beile* and *Beitse*, or princes of and in collateral branches. The 5th to 8th are dukes, called Guardian and Sustaining, with two subordinate grades not entitled to enter the court on state occasions. The 9th to 12th ranks are nobles, or rather generals, in line of descent. The number of persons in the lower ranks is very great. Few of these men hold offices at the capital, and still more rarely are they placed in responsible situations in the provinces, but the government of Manchuria is chiefly in their hands.

Besides these are the five ancient orders of nobility, *kung*, *hao*, *peh*, *tsz'*, and *nan*, usually rendered duke, count, viscount, baron, and baronet, which are conferred without distinction on Manchus, Mongols, and Chinese, both civil and military, and as such are highly prized by their recipients as marks of honor. The three first take precedence of the highest untitled civilians, but an appointment to most of the high offices in the country carries with it an honorary title. The direct descendant of Confucius is called *Yen-shing kung*, 'the Ever-sacred duke,' and of Koxinga *Hai-ching kung*, or 'Sea-quelling duke;' these two are the only perpetual titles among the Chinese, but among the Manchus, the chiefs of eight families which aided in settling the crown in the Gioro line were made hereditary princes, who are collectively called princes of the iron crown. Besides the above-mentioned, there are others, which are deemed even more honorable, either from their rarity or peculiar privileges, and answer to membership of the various orders of the Garter, Golden Fleece, Bath, etc., in Europe.

The internal arrangements of the court are modelled somewhat after those of the Boards, the general supervision being under the direction of the *Nui-wu fu*, composed of a president and six assessors, under whom are seven subordinate departments. It is the duty of these officers to attend upon the Emperor and Empress at sacrifices, and conduct the ladies of the harem to and from the palace; they oversee the households of the sons of the Emperor, and direct, under his Majesty, everything belonging to the palace and whatever appertains to its supplies and the care of the imperial guard. The seven departments are arranged so as to bear no little resemblance to a miniature state: one supplies food and raiment; a second is for defence, to regulate the body-guard when the Emperor travels; the third attends to the etiquette the members of this great family must observe toward each other, and brings forward the inmates of the harem when the Emperor, seated in the inner hall of audience, receives their homage, led by the Empress herself; a fourth department selects ladies to fill the harem, and collects the revenue from crown lands; a fifth superintends all repairs necessary in the palace, and sees that the streets of the city be cleared whenever the Emperor, Empress, or any of the women or children in the palace wish to go out; a sixth department has in charge the herds and flocks of the Emperor; and the last is a court for punishing the crimes of soldiers, eunuchs, and others attached to the palace.

The Emperor ought to have three thousand eunuchs, but the actual number is rather less than two thousand, who perform the work of the household. His sons and grandsons are allowed from thirty down to four, while the iron-crown princes and imperial sons-in-law have twenty or thirty; all these nobles are constrained to employ some eunuchs in their establishments, if not able to maintain the full quota, for show. Most of this class are compelled to submit to mutilation by their parents before the age of eight (and not always from poverty), as it usually insures a livelihood. Some take to this condition from motives of laziness and the high duties falling to their share if they behave themselves. From very ancient times certain criminals have been punished by castration. There is a separate control for the due efficiency of these servants of the court, who are divided into forty-eight classes; during the present dynasty they have never caused trouble. The highest pay any of them receive is twelve taels a month.

The number of females attached to the harem is not accurately known; all of them are under the nominal direction of the Empress. Every third year his Majesty reviews the daughters of the Manchu officers over twelve years of age, and chooses such as he pleases for concubines; there are only seven legal concubines, but an unlimited number of illegal. The latter are restored to liberty when they reach the age of twenty-five, unless they have borne children to his Majesty. It is generally considered an advantage to a family to have a daughter in the harem, especially by the Manchus, who endeavor to rise by this backstairs influence.[1] To the poor women themselves it is a monotonous, weary life of intriguing unrest. As soon as one enters the palace she bids final adieu to all her male relatives, and rarely sees her female friends; the eunuchs who take care of her are her chief channels of communication with the outer world. It may be added, however, that the comforts and influence of her condition are vastly superior to those of Hindu females.

In the forty-eighth volume of the *Hwui Tien*, from which work most of the details in this chapter are obtained, is an account of the supplies furnished his Majesty and the court. There should daily be placed before the Emperor thirty pounds of meat in a basin and seven pounds boiled into soup; hog's fat and butter, of each one and one-third pound; two sheep, two fowls, and two ducks, the milk of eighty cows, and seventy-

[1] *Chinese Repository*, Vol. XIV., p. 521; *N. C. Br. R. As. Soc. Journal*, No. XI.

five parcels of tea. Her Majesty receives twenty-one pounds of meat in platters and thirteen pounds boiled with vegetables; one fowl, one duck, twelve pitchers of water, the milk of twenty-five cows, and ten parcels of tea. Her maids and the concubines receive their rations according to a regular fare.

The Empress-dowager is the most important subject within the palace, and his Majesty does homage at frequent intervals, by making the highest ceremony of nine prostrations before her. When the widow of Kiaking reached the age of sixty in 1836, many honors were conferred by the Emperor. An extract from the ordinance issued on this festival will exhibit the regard paid her by the sovereign:

"Our extensive dominions have enjoyed the utmost prosperity under the shelter of a glorious and enduring state of felicity. Our exalted race has become most illustrious under the protection of that honored relative to whom the whole court looks up. To her happiness, already unalloyed, the highest degree of felicity has been superadded, causing joy and gladness to every inmate of the Six Palaces. The grand ceremonies of the occasion shall exceed in splendor the utmost requirements of the ancients in regard to the human relations, calling forth the gratulation of the whole Empire. It is indispensable that the observances of the occasion should be of an exceedingly unusual nature, in order that our reverence for our august parent and care of her may both be equally and gloriously displayed. . . . . . . In the first month of the present winter occurs the sixtieth anniversary of her Majesty's sacred natal day. At the opening of the happy period, the sun and moon shed their united genial influences on it. When commencing anew the revolution of the sexagenary cycle, the honor thereof adds increase to her felicity. Looking upward and beholding her glory, we repeat our gratulations, and announce the event to Heaven, to Earth, to our ancestors, and to the patron gods of the Empire. On the nineteenth day of the tenth moon in the fifteenth year of Taukwang, we will conduct the princes, the nobles, and all the high officers, both civil and military, into the presence of the great Empress, benign and dignified, universally placid, thoroughly virtuous, tranquil and self-collected, in favors unbounded; and we will then present our congratulations on the glad occasion, the anniversary of her natal day. The occasion yields a happiness equal to what is enjoyed by goddesses in heaven; and while announcing it to the gods and to our people, we will tender to her blessings unbounded."

Besides the usual tokens of favor, such as rations to soldiers, pardons, promotions, advances in official rank, etc., it was ordered in the eleventh article, "That every perfectly filial son or obedient grandson, every upright husband or chaste wife, upon proofs being brought forward, shall have a monument erected, with an inscription in his or her honor." Soldiers who had reached the age of ninety or one hundred received money to erect an honorary portal, and tombs, temples, bridges, and roads were ordered to be repaired; but how many of these "exceedingly great and special favors" were actually carried into effect cannot be stated.[1]

For the defence and escort of the Emperor and his palaces there are select bodies of troops, which are stationed within the *Hwang-ching* and the capital and at the various cantonments near the city. The Bannermen form three separate corps, each containing the hereditary troops of Manchu, Mongol, and enrolled Chinese, organized at the beginning of the dynasty under eight standards. Their flags are triangular, a plain yellow, white, red, and blue for troops in the left wing, and the same bordered with a narrow stripe of another color for troops in the right wing. All the families of these soldiers remain in the corps into which they were born.

Two special forces are selected, one named the Vanguard Division, the other the Flank Division, from the Manchu and Mongol Bannermen; these guard the Forbidden City, form his Majesty's escort when he goes out, and number respectively about one thousand five hundred and fifteen thousand men. For the preservation of the peace of the capital a force of upward of twenty thousand, called the Infantry Division, or Gendarmerie, is stationed in and around the walls, in addition to the palace forces. Besides these a cadet corps of five hundred

---

[1] *Chinese Repository*, Vol. IV., p. 576.

young men armed with bows and spears, two battalions with firearms, and four larger battalions of eight hundred and seventy-five men each, drilled in rifle-practice, are relied on to aid the Gendarmerie and Vanguard in case of danger. Whenever the One Man goes out of the palace gate to cross the city, the streets through which he passes are screened with matting, to keep off the crowds as well as diminish the risks of his person. The result has been that few of the citizens have ever seen their sovereign's face during the last two hundred years. The young Emperor Tungchí obtained great favor among them on one occasion of his return from the Temple of Heaven by ordering the screen of mats to be removed so that he and his people could see each other.

Under the Emperor is the whole body of the people, a great family bound implicitly to obey his will as being that of heaven, and possessing no right or property *per se;* in fact, having nothing but what has been derived from or may at any time be reclaimed by him. The greatness of this family, and the absence of an entailed aristocracy to hold its members or their lands in serfdom, have been partial safeguards against excess of oppression. Liberty is unknown among the people; there is not even a word for it in the language. No acknowledgment on the part of the sovereign of certain well-understood rights belonging to the people has ever been required, and is not likely to be demanded or given by either party until the Gospel shall teach them their respective rights and duties. Emigration abroad, and even removal from one part of the Empire to another, are prohibited or restrained by old laws, but at present no real obstacle exists to changing one's place of residence or occupation. Notwithstanding the fact that Chinese society is so homogeneous when considered as distinct from the sovereign, inequalities of many kinds are constantly met with, some growing out of birth or property, others out of occupation or merit, but most of them derived from official rank. There is no caste as in India, though the attempt to introduce the miserable system was vainly made by Wăn-tí about A.D. 590. The ancient distinctions of the Chinese into scholars, agriculturists, artisans, and traders is far superior to that of Zoroaster into priests, warriors, agriculturists, and artisans; a significant index of the different polities of eastern and western Asiatic nations is contained in this early quaternary division, and the superiority of the Chinese in its democratic element is also noticeable. There are local prejudices against associating with some portions of the community, though the people thus shut out are not remnants of old castes. The *tankia*, or boat-people, at Canton form a class in some respects beneath the other portions of the community, and have many customs peculiar to themselves. At Ningpo there is a degraded set called *to min*, amounting to nearly three thousand persons, with whom the people will not associate. The men are not allowed to enter the examinations or follow an honorable calling, but are play-actors, musicians, or sedan-bearers; the women are match-makers or female barbers and are obliged to wear a peculiar dress, and usually go abroad carrying a bundle wrapped in a checkered handkerchief. The *tankia* at Canton also wear a similar handkerchief on their head, and do not cramp their feet. The *to min* are supposed to be descendants of the Kin, who held northern China in A.D. 1100, or of native traitors who aided the Japanese, in 1555–1563, in their descent upon Chehkiang. The *tankia* came from some of the Miaotsz' tribes so early that their origin is unknown.[1]

The modern classifications of the people, recognized, however, more by law than custom, are various and comprehensive. First, natives and aliens; the latter include the unsubdued mountaineers and aboriginal tribes living in various parts, races of boat-people on the coasts, and all foreigners residing within the Empire, each of whom are subject to particular laws. Second, conquerors and conquered; having reference almost entirely to a prohibition of intermarriages between Manchus and Chinese. Third, freemen and slaves; every native is allowed to purchase slaves and retain their children in servitude, and free persons sometimes forfeit their freedom on account of their crimes, or mortgage themselves into bondage. Fourth, the

---

[1] *Missionary Chronicle*, Vol. XIV., p. 324; Hardy, *Manual of Buddhism*, p 69; Heeren, *Asiatic Nations*, Vol. I., p. 246.

honorable and the mean, who cannot intermarry without the former forfeiting their privileges; the latter comprise, besides aliens and slaves, criminals, executioners, police-runners, actors, jugglers, beggars, and all other vagrant or vile persons, who are in general required to pursue for three generations some honorable and useful employment before they are eligible to enter the literary examinations. These four divisions extend over the whole body of the people, but really affect only a small minority.

It is worthy of note how few have been the slaves in China, and how easy has been their condition in comparison with what it was in Greece and Rome. Owing chiefly to the prevalence of education in the liberal principles of the Four Books, China has been saved from this disintegrating element. The proportion of slaves to freemen cannot be stated, but the former have never attracted notice by their numbers nor excited dread by their restiveness. Girls are more readily sold than boys; at Peking a healthy girl under twelve years brings from thirty to fifty taels, rising to two hundred and fifty or three hundred for one of seventeen to eighteen years old. In times of famine orphans or needy children are exposed for sale at the price of a few cash.[1]

There are also eight privileged classes, of which the privileges of imperial blood and connections and that of nobility are the only ones really available; this privilege affects merely the punishment of offenders belonging to either of the eight classes. The privilege of imperial blood is extended to all the blood relations of the Emperor, all those of the Empress-mother and grandmother within four degrees, of the Empress within three, and of the consort of the crown prince within two. Privileged noblemen comprise all officers of the first rank, all of the second holding office, and all of the third whose office confers a command. These ranks are distinct from titles of nobility, and are much thought of by officers as honorary distinctions. There are nine, each distinguished by a different colored ball placed on the apex of the cap, by a peculiar emblazonry of a bird for

[1] M. Ed. Biot furnished a good account to the *Journal Asiatique* (3d series, Vol. III.) of the legal condition of slaves in China; see also *Chinese Repository*, Vol. XVIII., pp. 347–363, and passim; Archdeacon Gray's *China*.

civilians and a beast for military officers on the breast, and a different clasp to the girdle.

Civilians of the first rank wear a precious ruby or transparent red stone; a Manchurian crane is embroidered on the back and breast of the robe, while the girdle clasp is jade set in rubies; military men have a unicorn, their buttons and clasps being the same as civilians.

Civilians of the second rank wear a red coral button, a robe embroidered with a golden pheasant, and a girdle clasp of gold set in rubies; the lion of India is emblazoned on the military.

Civilians of the third rank carry a sapphire and one-eyed peacock's feather, a robe with a peacock worked on the breast, and a clasp of worked gold; military officers have a leopard.

Different Styles of Official Caps.

Civilians of the fourth rank are distinguished by a blue opaque stone, a wild goose on the breast, and a clasp of worked gold with a silver button; military officers carry a tiger in place of the embroidered wild goose.

Civilians of the fifth rank are denoted by a crystal button, a silver pheasant on the breast, and a clasp of plain gold with a silver button; the bear is the escutcheon of military men.

Civilians of the sixth rank wear an opaque white shell button, a blue plume, an egret worked on the breast, and a mother-of-pearl clasp; military men wear a tiger-cat.

Civilians of the seventh rank have a plain gold button, a mandarin duck on the breast, and a clasp of silver; a mottled bear designates the military, as it also does in the last rank.

The eighth rank wear a worked gold button, a quail on the breast, and a clasp of clear horn; military men have a seal.

The ninth rank are distinguished by a worked silver button, a long-tailed jay on the breast, and a clasp of buffalo's horn; military men are marked by a rhinoceros embroidered on the robe. All under the ninth can embroider the oriole on their breasts, and unofficial Hanlin take the egret.

The mass of people show their democratic tendencies in many ways, some of them conservative and others disorganizing. They form themselves into clans, guilds, societies, professions, and communities, all of which assist them in maintaining their rights, and give a power to public opinion it would not otherwise possess. Legally, every subject is allowed access to the magistrates, secured protection from oppression, and can appeal to the higher courts, but these privileges are of little avail if he is poor or unknown. He is too deeply imbued with fear and too ignorant of his rights to think of organized resistance; his mental independence has been destroyed, his search after truth paralyzed, his enterprise checked, and his whole efforts directed into two channels, viz., labor for bread and study for office. The people of a village, for instance, will not be quietly robbed of the fruits of their industry; but every individual in it may suffer multiplied insults, oppressions, and cruelties, without thinking of combining with his fellows to resist. Property is held by a tolerably secure tenure, but almost every other right and privilege is shamefully trampled on.

Although there is nominally no deliberative or advisatory body in the Chinese government, and nothing really analogous to a congress, parliament, or *tiers état*, still necessity and law compel the Emperor to consult and advise with the heads of tribunals. There are two imperial councils, which are the organs of communication between the head and the body politic; these are the Cabinet, or Imperial Chancery, and the Council of State; both of them partake of a deliberative character, but the first has the least power. Subordinate to these two councils are the administrative parts of the supreme government, consisting of the six Boards, the Colonial Office, Censorate, Courts of Representation and Appeal, and the Imperial Academy;

making in all thirteen principal departments, each of which will require a short description. It need hardly be added that there is nothing like an elective body in any part of the system; such a feature would be almost as incongruous to a Chinese as the election of a father by his family.

1. The Nui Koh, or Cabinet, sometimes called the Grand Secretariat, consists of four *ta hioh-sz'*, or principal, and two *hiehpan ta hioh-sz'*, or 'joint assistant chancellors,' half of them Manchus and half Chinese. Their duties, according to the Imperial Statutes, are to "deliberate on the government of the Empire, proclaim abroad the imperial pleasure, regulate the canons of state, together with the whole administration of the great balance of power, thus aiding the Emperor in directing the affairs of state." Subordinate to these six chancellors are six grades of officers, amounting in all to upward of two hundred persons, of whom more than half are Manchus. Under the six chancellors are ten assistants, called *hioh-sz'*, 'learned scholars;' some of the sixteen are constantly absent in the provinces or colonies, when their places are supplied by substitutes. What in other countries is performed by one person as prime minister, is in China performed by the four chancellors, of whom the first in the list is usually considered to be the premier, though perhaps the most influential man and the real leader of government holds another station.

The most prominent daily business of the Cabinet is to receive imperial edicts and rescripts, present memorials, lay before his Majesty the affairs of the Empire, procure his instructions thereon, and forward them to the appropriate office to be copied and promulgated. In order to expedite business in court, it is the custom, after the ministers have read and formed an opinion upon each document, to fasten a slip of paper at the foot—or more than one if elective answers are to be given—and thus present the document to his Majesty, in the presence-chamber, who, with a stroke of his pencil on the answer he chooses, decides its fate. The papers, having been examined and arranged, are submitted to the sovereign at daylight on the following morning; one of the six Manchu *hioh-sz'* first reads each document and hands it over to one of the four Chinese *hioh-sz'*, who inscribes the answer dictated by the sovereign, or hands it to him to perform that duty with the vermilion pencil. By this arrangement a large amount of business can be summarily despatched; but it is also evident that much depends upon the manner in which the answer written upon the slip is drawn up, as to the reception or rejection of the paper, though care has been taken in this particular by requiring that codicils be prepared showing the reasons for each answer. The appointment, removal, and degradation of all officers throughout his vast dominions, orders respecting the apportionment or remittal of the revenue and taxes, disposition of the army, regulation of the nomadic tribes—in short, all concerns, from the highest appointments and changes down to petty police cases of crime, are in this way brought to the notice and action of the Emperor.

Besides these daily duties there are additional functions devolving upon the members of the Cabinet, who are likewise all attached to other bureaus, such as presiding on all state occasions and sacrifices, coronations, reception of embassies, etc.; these duties are fulfilled by the ten assistant *hioh-sz'*, who are all vice-presidents of the Board of Rites. They are the keepers of the twenty-five seals of government, each of which is of a different form and used for different and special purposes, according to the custom of orientals, who place so much dependence upon the seal for vouching for the authenticity of a document.[1] Attached to the Cabinet are ten subordinate offices, one of which is for translating documents into the various languages found in the Empire. The higher members of the Cabinet are familiarly called *koh lao*, *i.e.*, elders of the council-room, from which the word *colao*, often met with in old books upon China, is derived.[2]

---

[1] *Chinese Chrestomathy*, Chap. XVII., Sec. 4, p. 570.

[2] A still more common designation for officers of every rank in the employ of the Chinese government has not so good a parentage; this is the word *mandarin*, derived from the Portuguese *mandar*, to command, and indiscriminately applied by foreigners to every grade, from a premier to a tide-waiter; it is not needed in English as a general term for officers, and ought to be disused, moreover, from its tendency to convey the impression that they are in some way unlike similar officials in other lands. Compare *Notes and Queries on China and Japan*, Vol. III., p. 12.

2. The Kiun-kí Chu, Council of State or General Council, was organized about 1730, but has now become the most influential body in the government; and, though quite unlike in its construction, corresponds to the *ministry* of western nations more than does any other branch of the Chinese system. It can be composed of any grandees, as princes of the blood, chancellors, presidents and vice-presidents of the Six Boards, and chief officers of all the other metropolitan courts. They are selected at the Emperor's pleasure, and unitedly called "great ministers directing the machinery of the army"—the army being here taken to signify the nation. Its duties are "to write imperial edicts and decisions, and determine such things as are of importance to the army and nation, in order to aid the sovereign in regulating the machinery of affairs." The number of members of the General Council probably varies according to his Majesty's pleasure, for no list of them is given in the *Red Book;* but latterly their number has been four, two of each nationality, and Prince Kung as the president. This body is one of the mainsprings of the government, and its composition shows the tendency of the national councils and polity.

The members of the General Council assemble daily in the Forbidden Palace, between five and six in the morning; when summoned by his Majesty into the council-chamber they sit upon mats or low cushions, no person being permitted to sit on chairs in the real or supposed presence of the Emperor. His Majesty's commands being written down by them, are, if public, transmitted to the Inner Council to be promulgated; but on any matter requiring secrecy or expedition, a despatch is forthwith made up and sent under cover to the Board of War, to be forwarded. In all important consultations or trials this Council, either alone or in connection with the appropriate court, is called in; and in time of war it is formed into a committee of ways and means. Lists of officers entitled to promotion are kept by it, and the names of proper persons to supply vacancies furnished the Emperor. Many of the residents in the colonies are members of the Council, and communicate directly with his Majesty through it, and receive allowances and gifts with great formality from the throne—a device of statecraft designed to maintain an awe of the imperial character and name as much as possible among the mixed races under them.

The General Council fills an important station in the system, and tends greatly to consolidate the various branches of government, facilitating their harmonious action as well as supplying the deficiencies of an imbecile, or restraining the acts of a tyrannical monarch. The statutes speak of various record-books, both public and secret, kept by the members for noting down the opinions of his Majesty, and add that there are no fixed times for audiences, one or more sessions being held daily, according to the exigencies of the state. Besides these functions, its members are further charged with certain literary matters, and three subordinate offices are attached to the Council for their preparation. One is for drawing up narratives of important transactions—a few of those relating to the wars and negotiations with foreigners since 1839 would be of much interest now; a second is for translating documents; and the third, entitled "an office for observing that imperial edicts are carried into effect," must be at times rather an arduous task, though probably its responsibility ends when the despatch goes forward. An office with this title shows that the Chinese government, with all its business-like arrangements, is still an Asiatic one.[1]

The duties of these supreme councils are general, comprising matters relating to all departments of the government, and serving to connect the head of the state with the subordinate bodies, not only at the capital, but throughout the provinces, so that he can, and probably does to a very great degree, thereby maintain a general acquaintance with what is done in all parts, and sooner rectify disorders and malpractices. The rivalry between their members, and the dislike entertained by the Chinese and Manchus composing them, cause, no doubt, some trouble to the Emperor; but this has some effect in thwarting conspiracies and intrigues. It must not be supposed, however, that every high officer in the Chinese government is wholly unprincipled, venal, and intriguing; most of them desire to serve and maintain their country. The personal character and knowledge of

[1] *Chinese Repository*, Vol. IV., p. 138. *Chinese Chrestomathy*, p. 573.

the monarch has much to do with the efficiency of his government, and the guidance of its affairs demands constant oversight. If he allows his ministers to conduct their trusts without restraint, they soon engross and misuse this power for selfish ends. In natural sequence every branch feels the fatal laxity, while its functionaries lose no time in imitating their superiors. This was the case during the reign of Hienfung, but matters have much improved under the regency since 1861. In ordinary times, the daily intercourse between the Emperor of China and his ministers presents very similar features of confidence, courtesy, and esteem between them as those seen in western lands.

The *King Pao*, *i.e.*, '*Metropolitan Reporter*,' usually called the *Peking Gazette*, is compiled from the papers presented before the General Council, and constitutes the principal source of information available to the people for ascertaining what is going on in the Empire. Every morning ample extracts from the papers decided upon or examined by the Emperor, including his own orders and rescripts, are placarded upon boards in a court of the palace, and form the materials for the annals of government and the history of the Empire. Couriers are despatched to all parts of the land, carrying copies of these papers to the high provincial officers; certain persons are also permitted to print these documents, but always without note or change, and circulate them at their own charges to their customers. This is the *Peking Gazette*, and such the mode of its compilation. It is simply a record of official acts, promotions, decrees, and sentences, without any editorial comments or explanations; and as such of great value in understanding the policy of government. It is very generally read and discussed by educated people in cities, and tends to keep them more acquainted with the character and proceedings of their rulers than ever the Romans were of their sovereigns and Senate. In the provinces thousands of persons find employment by copying and abridging the *Gazette* for readers who cannot afford to purchase the complete edition.[1]

[1] *Fraser's Magazine*, February, 1873. *China Review*, Vol. III., p. 13. *Note on the Condition and Government of the Chinese Empire in* 1849. By T F. Wade. Hongkong, 1850. Translations of several years of the *Gazette* have appeared since 1872, reprinted from the columns of the *North China Herald*.

The principal executive bodies under these two Councils are the *Luh Pu*, or 'Six Boards,' which were modelled on much the same plan during the ancient dynasties. At the head of each Board are two presidents, called *shang-shu*, and four vice-presidents, called *shĭlang*, alternately a Manchu and a Chinese; and over three of them—those of Revenue, War, and Punishment—are placed superintendents, who are frequently members of the Cabinet; sometimes the president of one Board is superintendent of another. There are three subordinate grades of officers in each Board, who may be called directors, under-secretaries, and controllers, with a great number of minor clerks, and their appropriate departments for conducting the details of the general and peculiar business coming under the cognizance of the Board, the whole being arranged and subordinated in the most business-like style. The detail of all the departments in the general and provincial governments is regulated in the same manner. For instance, each Board has a different style of envelope for its despatches, and the papers in the offices are filed away in them.

3. The Lí Pu, or Board of Civil Office, "has the government and direction of all the various officers in the civil service of the Empire, and thereby it assists the Emperor to rule all people;" these duties are further defined as including "whatever appertains to the plans of selecting rank and gradation, to the rules of determining degradation and promotion, to the ordinances of granting investitures and rewards, and the laws for fixing schedules and furloughs, that the civil service may be supplied." Civilians are presented to the Emperor, and all civil and literary officers throughout the Empire distributed by this Board. The great power apparently thus entrusted is shared by the two preceding, whose members are made advisory overseers of the highest appointments, while the provincial authorities put men in vacant posts as fast as they are needed. The danger arising from the arrangement is noticed by Biot[1] as having early attracted criticism.

This Board is subdivided into four bureaus. The first at-

[1] *Essai sur l'Instruction en Chine*, pp. 540–589.

tends to the distinctions, precedence, promotion, exchanging, etc., of officers. The second investigates their merits and worthiness to be recorded and advanced, or contrariwise; ascertains the character each officer bears and the manner in which he fulfils his duties, and prescribes his furloughs. The third regulates retirement from office on account of mourning or filial duties, and supervises the registration of official names; it is through this bureau that Hwang Ngăn-tung, the Governor of Kwangtung, was degraded in 1846 for not resigning his office on the death of his mother. The fourth regulates the distribution of titles, patents, and posthumous honors. The Chinese is the only government that ennobles ancestors for the merits of their descendants; the custom arose out of the worship paid them, in which the rites are proportionate to the rank of the deceased, not of the survivor; and if the deceased parent or grandparent were commoners, they receive proper titles in consequence of the elevation of their son or grandson. This custom is not a trick of state to get money, for commoners cannot buy these posthumous titles; they can only buy nominal titles for themselves. The usage, however, offers an unexpected illustration of the remark of Job, "His sons come to honor, and he knoweth it not."

4. The Hu Pu, or Board of Revenue, "directs the territorial government of the Empire, and keeps the lists of population in order to aid the Emperor in nourishing all people; whatever appertains to the regulations for levying and collecting duties and taxes, to the plans for distributing salaries and allowances, to the rates for receipts and disbursements at the granaries and treasuries, and to the rights for transporting by land and water are reported to this Board, that sufficient supplies for the country may be provided." Besides these duties, it obtains the admeasurement of all lands in the Empire, and proportions taxes and conscriptions, according to the divisions, population, etc., regulates the expenditure, and ascertains the latitude and longitude of places. One minor office prepares lists of all the Manchu girls fit to be introduced into the palace for selection as inmates of the harem, a duty which is enjoined on it because the allowances, outfits, and positions of these women

come within its control. The injudicious mode of collecting revenue common under the Persian and Syrian kings, by which the sums obtained from single cities and provinces were apportioned among the royal family and favorites, and carried directly to them, has never been practised by the Chinese.

There are fourteen subordinate departments to attend to the receipt of the revenue from each of the provinces, each of which corresponds with the treasury department in its respective province. The revenue being paid in sundry ways and articles, as money, grain, manufactures, etc., the receipt and distribution of the various articles require a large force of assistants. This Board is moreover a court of appeal on disputes respecting property, and superintends the mint in each province; one bureau is called the "great ministers of the Three Treasuries," viz., of metals, silks and dye-stuffs, and stationery.

5. The Lí Pu, or Board of Rites, "examines and directs concerning the performance of the five kinds of ritual observances, and makes proclamation thereof to the whole Empire, thus aiding the Emperor in guiding all people. Whatever appertains to the ordinances for regulating precedence and literary distinctions, to the canons for maintaining religious honor and fidelity, to the orders respecting intercourse and tribute, and to the forms of giving banquets and granting bounties, are reported to this Board in order to promote national education." The five classes of rites are defined to be those of a propitious and those of a felicitous nature, military and hospitable rites, and those of an infelicitous nature. Among the subordinate departments is that of ceremonial forms, which "has the regulation of the etiquette to be observed at court on all occasions, on congratulatory attendances, in the performance of official duties, etc.; also the regulation of dresses, caps, etc.; as to the figure, size, color, and nature of their fabrics and ornaments, of carriages and riding accoutrements, their form, etc., with the number of followers and insignia of rank. It has also the direction of the entire ceremonial of personal intercourse between the various ranks or peers, minutely defining the number of bows and degree of attention which each is to pay to the other when meeting in official capacities, according as they are

on terms of equality or otherwise. It has also to direct the forms of their written official intercourse, including those to be observed in addresses to and from foreign states. The regulation of the literary examinations, the number of the graduates, the distinction of their classes, the forms of their selection, and the privileges of successful candidates, with the establishment of governmental schools and academies, are all under this department."

Another office superintends the rites to be observed in worshipping deities and spirits of departed monarchs, sages, and worthies, and in "saving the sun and moon" when eclipsed. The third, called "host and guest office," looks after tribute and tribute-bearers, and takes the whole management of foreign embassies, supplying not only provisions, but translators, and ordering the mode of intercourse between China and other states. The fourth oversees the supplial of food for banquets and sacrifices. The details of all the multifarious ritual duties of this Board occupy fourteen volumes of the Statutes. "Truly nothing is without its ceremonies," as Confucius taught, and no nation has paid so much attention to them in the ordering of its government as the Chinese. The *Book of Rites* is the foundation of ceremonies and the infallible standard as to their meaning; the importance attached to them has elevated etiquette and ritualism into a kind of crystallizing force which has molded Chinese character in many ways.

Connected with the Board of Rites is a Board of Music, containing an indefinite number of officers whose duties "are to study the principles of harmony and melody, to compose musical pieces and form instruments proper to play them, and then suit both to the various occasions on which they are required." Nor are the graces of posture-making neglected by these ceremony-mongers; but it may with truth be said, that if no other nation ever had a Board of Music, and required so much official music as the Chinese, certainly none ever had less real melody.

6. The Ping Pu, or Board of War, "has the duty of aiding the sovereign to protect the people by the direction of all military affairs in the metropolis and the provinces, and to

regulate the hinge of the state upon the reports received from the various departments regarding deprivation of, or appointment to, office; succession to, or creation of, hereditary military rank; postal or courier arrangements; examination and selection of the deserving, and accuracy of returns." The navy is also under the control of this Board. The management of the post is confided to a special department, and the transmission of official despatches is performed with great efficiency and regularity. A minor bureau of the courier office is called "the office for the announcement of victories," which, from a recital of its duties, appears to be rather a *grande vitesse*, whose couriers should hasten as if they announced a victory.

To enable this Board of War to discharge its duties, they are apportioned under four *sz'*, or bureaus, severally attending to promotion for various reasons; to the regulation of the distribution of rewards and punishments, inspection of troops and issue of general orders, answering to an adjutant-general's department; to the supply and distribution of horses for the cavalry; and, lastly, to the examination of candidates, preparation of estimates and rosters, with all the details connected with equipments and ammunition. The conception of all government with the Manchus being military and not civil, they have developed this Board more than was the case during the last dynasty, the possessions in Central Asia having drawn greatly on their resources and prowess.

The Household troops and city Gendarmerie have already been noticed; their control is vested in the *Nui-wu Fu*, and the oversight of all the Bannermen in the Empire vests in the metropolitan office of the *Tu-tung*, or Captains-general, of whom there are twenty-four, one to every banner of each race. The Board of War has no control directly over this large portion of the Chinese army, and as the direction of the land and sea forces in each province is entrusted in a great degree to the local authorities, its duties are really more circumscribed than one would at first imagine. The singular subordination of military to civil power, which has ever distinguished the Chinese polity, makes the study of the army, as at present constituted, a very interesting feature of the national history; for while it has often proved inefficient to repress insurrection and defend the people against brigandage, it has never been used to destroy their institutions. In times of internal commotion the national soldiers have usually been loyal to their flag, though it must be confessed that discipline within the ranks is not so perfect as to prevent the soldiers from occasionally harassing and robbing those whom they are set to protect.[1]

7. The HING PU, or Board of Punishments, "has the government and direction of punishments throughout the Empire, for the purpose of aiding the sovereign in correcting all people. Whatever appertains to measures of applying the laws with leniency or severity, to the task of hearing evidence and giving decisions, to the rights of granting pardons, reprieves, or otherwise, and to the rate of fines and interest, are all reported to this Board, to aid in giving dignity to national manners." The *Hing Pu* partakes of the nature of both a criminal and civil court; its officers usually meet with those of the Censorate and Talí Sz', the three forming the *San Fah Sz'*, or 'Three Law Chambers,' which decide on capital cases brought before them. In the autumn these three unite with members from six other courts, forming collectively a Court of Errors, to revise the decisions of the provincial judges before reporting them to his Majesty. These precautions are taken to prevent injustice when life is involved, and the system shows an endeavor to secure a full and impartial consideration for all capital cases, which, although it may signally fail of its full effect, does the rulers high credit, when the small value set upon life generally by Asiatic governments is considered. These bodies are expected to conform their decisions to the law, nor are they permitted to cite the Emperor's own decisions as precedents, without the law on these decisions has been expressly entered as a supplementary clause in the code.

It also belongs to sub-officers in the Board of Punishments to record all his Majesty's decisions upon appeals from the provinces at the autumnal assizes, when the entire list is presented

[1] *Chinese Repository*, Vol. IV., pp. 188, 276–287; Vol. V., pp. 165–178; Vol. XX., pp. 250, 300, and 363. *Mémoires concernant les Chinois, par les Missionaires à Pekin*, Tomes VII. and VIII., passim.

for his examination and ultimate decision, and see that these sentences are transmitted to the provincial judges. Another office superintends the publication of the code, with all the changes and additions; a third oversees jails and jailers; a fourth receives the fines levied by commutation of punishments, and a fifth registers the receipts and expenditures. If the administration of the law in China at all corresponded with the equity of most of its enactments, or the caution taken to prevent collusion, malversation, and haste on the part of the judges, it would be incomparably the best governed country out of Christendom; but the painful contrast between good laws and wicked rulers is such as to show the utter impossibility of securing the due administration of justice without higher moral principles than heathenism can teach.

The *yamun* of the *Hing Pu* in the capital is the most active of all the Boards, but little is known of what goes on within its walls. Its prisoners are mostly brought from the provinces, officers of high rank arrested for malfeasance or failure, and criminals convicted or condemned there who have appealed to the highest tribunals. Few of those who enter its gates ever return through them, and their sufferings seldom end as long as they have any property left. The narrative of the horrible treatment endured by Loch and his comrades in 1860, while confined within this *yamun*, gives a vivid picture of their sufferings, but native prisoners are not usually kept bound and pinioned. In the rear wall of the establishment is an iron door, through which dead bodies are thrust to be carried away to burial.

8. The KUNG PU, or Board of Works, "has the government and direction of the public works thoughout the Empire, together with the current expenses of the same, for the purpose of aiding the Emperor to keep all people in a state of repose. Whatever appertains to plans for buildings of wood or earth, to the forms of useful instruments, to the laws for stopping up or opening channels, and to the ordinances for constructing the mausolea and temples, are reported to this Board in order to perfect national works." Its duties are of a miscellaneous nature, and are performed in other countries by no one department, though

the plan adopted by the Chinese is not without its advantages One bureau takes cognizance of the condition of all city walls, palaces, temples, altars, and other public structures; sits as a prize-office, and furnishes tents for his Majesty's journeys; supplies timber for ships, and pottery and glassware for the court. A second attends to the manufacture of military stores and utensils employed in the army; sorts the pearls from the fisheries according to their value; regulates weights and measures, furnishes "death-warrants" to governors and generals; and, lastly, takes charge of arsenals, stores, camp-equipage, and other things appertaining to the army. A third department has charge of all water-ways and dikes; it also repairs and digs canals, erects bridges, oversees the banks of rivers by means of deputies stationed at posts along their course, builds vessels of war, collects tolls, mends roads, digs the sewers in Peking and cleans out its gutters, preserves ice, makes book-cases for public records, and, lastly, looks after the silks sent as taxes. The fourth of these offices confines its attention chiefly to the condition of the imperial mausolea, the erection of the sepulchres and tablets of meritorious officers buried at public expense, and the adornment of temples and palaces, as well as superintending all workmen employed by the Board.

The mint is under the direction of two vice-presidents, and the manufacture of gunpowder is specially intrusted to two great ministers. One would think, from this recital, that the functions of the Board of Works were so diverse that it would be one of the most efficient parts of government; but if the condition of forts, ports, dikes, etc., in other parts of the country corresponds to those along the coast, there is, as the Emperor once said of the army, "the appearance of going to war, but not the reality"—most of the works being on record, and suffered to remain there, except when danger threatens, or his Majesty specially orders a public work, and, what is more important, furnishes the money.

9. The Lí Fan Yuen, or Court for the Government of Foreigners, commonly called the Colonial Office, "has the government and direction of the external foreigners, orders their emoluments and honors, appoints their visits to court, and

regulates their punishments, in order to display the majesty and goodness of the state." This is an important branch of the government, and has the superintendence of all the wandering and settled tribes in Mongolia, Cobdo, Îlí, and Koko-nor. All these are called *wai fan*, or 'external foreigners,' in distinction from the tributary tribes in Sz'chuen and Formosa, who are termed *nui fan*, or 'internal foreigners.' There are also *nui í* and *wai í*, or 'internal and external barbarians,' the former comprising the unsubdued mountaineers of Kweichau, and the latter the inhabitants of all foreign countries who do not choose to range themselves under the renovating influences of the Celestial Empire. The Colonial Office regulates the government of the nomads and restricts their wanderings, lest they trespass on each other's pasture-grounds. Its officers are all Manchus and Mongols, having over them one president and two vice-presidents, Manchus, and one Mongolian vice-president appointed for life.

Besides the usual secretaries for conducting its general business, there are six departments, whose combined powers include every branch necessary for the management of these clans. The first two have jurisdiction over the numerous tribes and corps of the Inner Mongols, who are under more complete subjection than the others, and part have been placed under the control of officers in Chihlí and Shansí. The appointment of local officers, collecting taxes, allotting land to Chinese settlers, opening roads, paying salaries, arranging the marriages, retinues, visits to courts, and presents made by the princes and the review of the troops, all appertain to these two departments. The third and fourth have a similar, but less effectual control over the princes, lamas, and tribes of Outer Mongolia. At Urga reside two high ministers, organs of communication with Russia, and general overseers of the frontier. The oversight of the lama hierarchy in Mongolia is now completely under the control of this office; and in Tibet their power has been considerably abridged. The fifth department directs the actions, restrains the powers, levies the taxes, and orders the tributary visits of the Mohammedan begs in the Tien shan Nan Lu, who are quiet pretty much as they are paid by presents and flattered by honors. The sixth department regulates the penal discipline of the tributary tribes. The salaries paid the Mongolian princes are distributed according to an economical scale. A *tsin wang* annually receives $2,600 and twenty-five pieces of silk; a *kiun wang* receives about $1,666 and fifteen pieces of silk; and so on through the ranks of Beile, Beitse, Duke, etc., the last of whom gets a stipend of only $133 and four pieces of silk. The internal organization of these tribes is probably the same now as it was at first among the Scythians and Huns, and partakes of the features of the feudal and tribal system, modified by the nomadic lives they are obliged to lead. The Chinese government is endeavoring to reduce the influence and retinues of the khans and begs and elevate the people to positions of independent owners and cultivators of the soil.

10. The Tu-chah Yuen, or Censorate, *i.e.*, 'All-examining Court,' is entrusted with the "care of manners and customs, the investigation of all public offices within and without the capital, the discrimination between the good and bad performance of their business, and between the depravity and uprightness of the officers employed in them; taking the lead of other censors, and uttering each his sentiments and reproofs, in order to cause officers to be diligent in attention to their daily duties, and to render the government of the Empire stable." The Censorate, when joined with the Board of Punishments and Court of Appeal, forms a high court for the revision of criminal cases and hearing appeals from the provinces; and, in connection with the Six Boards and the Court of Representation and Appeal, makes one of the *Kiu King*, or 'Nine Courts,' which deliberate on important affairs of government.

The officers are two censors and four deputy censors, besides whom the governors, lieutenant-governors, and the governors of rivers and inland navigation are *ex-officio* deputy censors. A class of censors is placed over each of the Six Boards, whose duties are to supervise all their acts, to receive all public documents from the Cabinet, and after classifying them transmit them to the several courts to which they belong, and to make a semi-monthly examination of the papers entered on the archives of each court. All criminal cases in the provinces come under the oversight of the censors at the capital, and the department which superintends the affairs of the metropolis revises its municipal acts, settles the quarrels, and represses the crimes of its inhabitants. These are the duties of the Censorate, than which no part of the Chinese government has attracted more attention. The privilege of reproof given by the law to the office of censor has sometimes been exercised with remarkable candor and plainness, and many cases are recorded in history of these officers suffering for their fidelity, but such instances must be few indeed in proportion to the failures.

The celebrated Sung, who was appointed commissioner to accompany Lord Macartney, once remonstrated with the Emperor Kiaking upon his attachment to play-actors and strong drink, which degraded him in the eyes of his people and incapacitated him from performing his duties. The Emperor, highly irritated, called him to his presence, and on his confessing to the authorship of the memorial, asked him what punishment he deserved. He answered, "Quartering." He was told to select some other; "Let me be beheaded;" and on a third command, he chose to be strangled. He was then ordered to retire, and the next day the Emperor appointed him governor in Îlí, thus acknowledging his rectitude, though unable to bear his censure.

History records the reply of another censor in the reign of an Emperor of the Tang dynasty, who, when his Majesty once desired to inspect the archives of the historiographer's office, in order to learn what had been recorded concerning himself, under the excuse that he must know his faults before he could well correct them, was answered: "It is true your Majesty has committed a number of errors, and it has been the painful duty of our employment to take notice of them; a duty which further obliges us to inform posterity of the conversation which your Majesty has this day, very improperly, held with us."

The censors usually attend on all state occasions by the side of his Majesty, and are frequently allowed to express their opinions openly, but in a despotic government this is little else than a fiction of state, for the fear of offending the imperial ear, and consequent disgrace, will usually prove stronger than the consciousness of right or the desires of a public fame and martyrdom for the sake of principle. The usual mode of advising is to send in a remonstrance against a proposed act, as when one of the body in 1832 remonstrated against the Emperor paying attention to anonymous accusations; or to suggest a different procedure, as the memorials of Chu Tsun against legalizing opium. The number of these papers inserted in the *Peking Gazette* for the information of the Empire, in many of which the acts of officers are severely reprehended, shows that the censors are not altogether idle. In 1833 a censor named Sü requested the Emperor to interdict official persons at court from writing private letters concerning public persons and affairs in the provinces. He stated that when candidates left the capital for their provincial stations, private letters were sent by them from their friends to the provincial authorities, "sounding the voice of influence and interest," by which means justice was perverted. The Emperor ordered the Cabinet to examine the censor and get his facts in proof of these statements, but on inquiry he either would not or could not bring forward any cases, and he himself consequently received a reprimand. "These censors are allowed," says the Emperor, "to tell me the reports they hear, to inform me concerning courtiers and governors who pervert the laws, and to speak plainly about any defect or impropriety which they may observe in the monarch himself; but they are not permitted to employ their pencils in writing memorials which are filled with vague surmises and mere probabilities or suppositions. This would only fill my mind with doubts and uncertainty, and I would not know what men to employ; were this spirit indulged, the detriment of government would be most serious. Let Sü be subjected to a court of inquiry."

The suspension or disgrace of censors for their freedom of speech is a common occurrence, and among the forty or fifty persons who have this privilege a few are to be found who do not hesitate to lift up their voice against what they deem to be wrong; and there is reason for supposing that only a small portion of their remonstrances appears in the *Gazette*. With regard to this department of government, it is to be observed that although it may tend only in a partial degree to check oppression and reform abuses, and while a close examination of its real operations and influence and the character of its members may excite more contempt than respect, still the existence of such a body, and the publication of its memorials, can hardly fail to rectify misconduct to some degree, and check maladministration before it results in widespread evil. The Censorate is, however, only one of a number of checks upon the conduct of officers, and perhaps by no means the strongest.[1]

11. The TUNG-CHING Sz', which may be called a Court of Transmission, consists of a small body of six officers, whose duty is to receive memorials from the provincial authorities and appeals from their judgment by the people and present them to the Cabinet. Attached to this Court is an office for attending at the palace-gate to await the beating of a drum, which, in conformity with an ancient custom, is placed there that applicants may by striking it obtain a hearing. It is also the channel through which the people can directly appeal to his Majesty, and cases occur of individuals, even women and girls, travelling to the capital from remote places to present their petitions for redress before the throne. The feeling of blood revenge prevails among the Chinese, and impels many of these weak and unprotected persons to undergo great hardships to obtain legal redress, when the lives of their parents have been unjustly taken by powerful and rich enemies.

12. The TA-LÍ Sz', or Court of Judicature and Revision, has the duty of adjusting all the criminal courts in the Empire, and forms the nearest approach to a Supreme Court in the government, though the cases brought before it are mostly criminal. When the crimes involve life, this and the preceding unite with the Censorate to form one court, and if the judges are not unanimous in their decisions they must report their reasons to the Emperor, who will pass judgment upon them. In a despotic government no one can expect that the executive officers of courts will exercise their functions with that caution and

---

[1] Compare an article by E. C. Taintor, in *Notes and Queries on China and Japan*. *Chinese Repository*, Vols. IV., pp. 148, 164, and 177, and XII., pp. 32 and 67.

equity required in Christian countries, but considerable care has been taken to obtain as great a degree of justice as possible.

14. The HANLIN YUEN, or Imperial Academy, is entrusted "with the duty of drawing up governmental documents, histories, and other works; its chief officers take the lead of the various classes, and excite their exertions to advance in learning in order to prepare them for employments and fit them for attending upon the sovereign." This body has, it is highly probable, some similarity to the collection of learned men to whom the King of Babylon entrusted the education of promising young men, for although the members of the Hanlin Yuen do not, to any great degree, educate persons, they are constantly referred to as the Chaldeans were by Belshazzar. Sir John Davis likens it to the Sorbonne, inasmuch as it expounds the sacred books of the Chinese. Its chief officers are two presidents or senior members, called *chwang yuen hioh-sz'*, who are usually appointed for life; they attend upon the Emperor, superintend the studies of graduates, and furnish semi-annual lists of persons to be "speakers" at the "classical feasts," where the literary essays of his Majesty are translated from and into Manchu and read before him.

Subordinate to the two senior members are four grades of officers, five in each grade, together with an unlimited number of senior graduates, each forming a sort of college, whose duties are to prepare all works published under governmental sanction; these persons are subject from time to time to fresh examination, and are liable to lose their degrees or be altogether dismissed from office if found faulty or deficient. Subordinate to the Hanlin Yuen is an office consisting of twenty-two selected members, who in rotation attend on the Emperor and make a record of his words and actions. There is also an additional office for the preparation of national histories.

The situation of a member of the Hanlin is one of considerable honor and literary ease, and scholars look forward to a station in it as one which confers dignity in a government where all officers are appointed according to their literary merit, but much more from its being the body from which the Emperor selects his most responsible officers. A graduate of this rank is most likely to be nominated to a vacant office, though the possession of the title does not of itself warrant a place.[1]

Before proceeding to consider the provincial governments, notices of some of the other departments not connected with the general machinery of the state are here in place. The municipality of Peking has already been mentioned when describing the capital; it is intimately connected with the general government and forms an integral part of the machine. Among the courts not connected with the municipal rule of the metropolis, nor forming one of the great departments of state, is *Tai-chang Sz'*, or 'Sacrificial Court,' whose officers "direct the sacrificial observances and distinguish the various instruments and the quality of the sacrifices." Their duties are of importance in connection with the state religion, and they rank high among the court dignitaries of the Empire, but as members of this, possess no power. The *Tai-puh Sz'*, or Superintendent of H. I. M.'s Stud, is an office for "rearing horses, taking account of their increase, and regulating their training;" large tracts of land beyond the Great Wall are appropriated to this purpose, and the clerks of this office, under the direction of the Board of War, oversee the herdsmen and grooms.

The *Kwangluh Sz'*, or 'Banqueting House,' has the charge of "feasting the meritorious and banqueting the deserving;" it is somewhat subordinate to the Board of Rites, and provides whatever is necessary for banquets given to literary graduates, foreign ambassadors, etc. The *Hunglu Sz'*, or 'Ceremonial Court,' regulates the forms to be observed at these banquets, which consist in little else than marshalling the guests according to their proper ranks and directing them when to make the *kotow*, called also *san kwei kiu kao*, "three kneelings and nine knockings." The *Kwoh-tsz' Kien*, or 'National College,' is a different institution from the Hanlin Yuen, and intended for teaching graduates of the lower degrees; the departments of study are the Chinese language, the classics and mathematics, each branch having its appropriate teachers, with some higher officers, both Chinese and Manchu.

---

[1] Dr. W. A. P. Martin, *The Chinese.*

The *Kin Tien Kien*, or 'Imperial Astronomical College,' as might be expected, is much more astrological than astronomical; its duties are defined to be "to direct the ascertainment of times and the movements of the heavenly bodies, in order to attain conformity with the celestial periods and to regulate the notation of time among men; all things relating to divination and the selection of days are under its charge." The preparation of the almanac, in which, among other things, lucky and unlucky days are marked for the performance of all the important acts of life, and astrological and chiromantic absurdities inserted for the amusement of fortune-tellers and others, the instruction of a few pupils, and care of the observatory, occupy most of the time of its officers. It is now of no practical use, and as the *Tung-wăn Kwan* develops into a learned and efficient college, including astronomy and medicine and their kindred branches, these native Boards will gradually pass away.

The other local courts of the capital seem to have been subdivided and multiplied to a great degree for the purpose of affording employment to a larger number of persons, especially Manchus and graduates, so that the Emperor can attach them to himself and be surer of their support in case of any insurrection on the part of the people, and also that he may have them more under his control. The number of clerks and minor offices in all the general departments of state is doubtless more numerous than it would be in a European government. In the mutual relations of the great departments of the Chinese government the principles of responsibility and surveillance among the officers are plainly exhibited, while regard has been paid to such a division and apportionment of labor as would secure great efficiency and care, if every member of the machine faithfully did his duty. Two presidents are stationed over each Board to assist and watch each other, while the two presidents oversee the four vice-presidents; the president of one Board is sometimes the vice-president of another; and by means of the Censorate and the General Council every portion is brought under the cognizance of several independent officers, whose mutual jealousy and regard for individual advancement, or a partial desire for the well-being of the state, affords the Emperor some guarantee of fidelity. The seclusion in which he lives makes it difficult for any conspirator to approach his person, but his own fears regarding the management of such an immense Empire compel him to inform himself respecting the actions of ministers, generals, and proconsular governors. The conduct and devotion of hundreds of officers, both civil and military, during the wars with Great Britain and the suppression of rebellions within the last thirty years, afford proof enough that he has attached his subordinates to his service by some other principle than fear. The total number of civilians holding office is estimated at about fourteen thousand persons, but those dependent on the government are many times this amount.

The rulers of China have contrived the system of provincial governments in an admirable manner, considering the character of the people and the materials they had to work with; no better proof of their sagacity in this respect can be required than the general degree of good order which has been maintained for nearly two centuries, and the great progress the people have made in wealth, numbers, and power. By a well-arranged plan of checks and changes in the provincial authorities, the chances of their abusing position and power and combining to overthrow the supreme government have been reduced almost to an impossibility; the influence of mutual responsibility among them does something to prevent outrageous oppression of the people, by leading one to accuse another of high crimes in order to exonerate himself or obtain his place. The sons and relatives of the Emperor being excluded from civil office in the provinces, the high-spirited and talented native Chinese do not feel inclined to cabal against the government because every avenue to emolument and power is filled and closed against them by creatures and connections of the sovereign; nor when in office are they disposed to attempt the overthrow of the reigning family, lest they lose what has cost them many years of toilsome study and the wealth and influence of friends to attain. The examination of these pashaliks is furthermore entitled to notice from the degree of power delegated to their highest officers, and the shrewd manner in which its exercise has been circumscribed and rendered amenable to its imperial source.

The highest officers in the provinces are a *tsungtuh*, lit. 'general director,' or governor-general, and the *futai* or *fuyuen*, 'soother' or governor. The former is often called a viceroy, but that term seems to be quite inapplicable when used to denote an officer within the limits of the state; governor-general, or proconsul, is more analogous to his duties. A translation of these and many other Chinese titles does not convey their exact functions, but in some cases an equivalent is more intelligible than a translation.[1] The *tsungtuh* has rule over two provinces, or else fills two high offices in one province, while the *futai* is placed over one province, either independent of or in subordination to a *tsungtuh*, as enumerated in the table on page 61.

An examination of the *Red Book* for 1852 showed that out of a total of 20,327 names in it, 16,474 were Chinese, 3,295 were Manchus and Mongols, and 558 enrolled Chinese; in the copy for 1844, out of 12,758 names, 10,463 were Chinese, 1,768 Manchus, and 527 enrolled Chinese; these figures include only civilians and the employees in Peking. The Eighteen Provinces have altogether less than two thousand persons in office above the rank of assistant district magistrate, viz.: 8 governor-generals, 15 governors, 19 treasurers, 18 judges, 17 chancellors, 15 commanders of the forces, including 2 admirals and 1,740 prefects and magistrates. All those filling the high grades in this series report themselves to the Emperor twice every month, by sending him a salutatory card upon yellow paper, enclosed in a silken envelope; stating, for instance, that 'Lin Tseh-sü, governor-general of Liang Kwang, humbly presents his duty to the throne, wishing his Majesty repose.' The Emperor replies with the vermilion pencil, *Chin ngan*, *i.e.*, 'Ourself is well.'

The duties of the governor-general consist in the collective control of all affairs, civil and military, in the region under his jurisdiction; he occupies, in his sphere, under correction, the same authority that the Emperor does over the whole Empire.

---

[1] Mayers' *Manual of Chinese Titles* furnishes the best compend for learning their duties and names.

The *futai* has a similar control, but in an inferior degree when there is a *tsungtuh*, in the more special supervision of the administrative part of the civil government, as distinguished from the revenue, gabel, or literary branches.

The departments of the civil government are five, viz.: administrative, literary, gabel, commissariat, and excise; the first being also divided into the territorial and financial and the judicial branches. At the head of the first branch is the *puching sz'* (*i.e.*, regulating-government commissioner), who is usually called the treasurer; the *ngan-chah sz'*, or 'criminal judge,' presides over the second. These two officers often unite their deliberations in the direction of any territorial or financial business, or the trial of important cases. The literary department is placed under the direction of an officer selected from among the members of the Hanlin Academy, called a *hioh-ching*, director of learning, or literary chancellor; there are seventeen of them altogether. The gabel and commissariat are usually supervised by certain intermediate officers called *tao*, or *taotai*, sometimes termed intendants of circuit, who have other functions in addition. The excise, or commercial department, is under *kientuh*, or superintendents, but the details of these three branches vary considerably in different provinces. The officers of the excise, either in the interior or on the coast, are made amenable to their superiors in the province, but their functions are exercised in an irregular manner; for the collection of the revenue is a difficult affair, and mostly entrusted to the local magistrates.

The military government of a province includes both the land and sea forces. It is under a *títuh*, or commander-in-chief, of which rank there are in all sixteen, twelve of them commanding one arm alone, and four controlling both land and sea forces. In five provinces the *futai* is commander-in-chief, and in Kansuh there are two. Above the *títuh*, in point of rank but not of power, are placed garrisons of Manchu Bannermen under a *tsiang-kiun*, or general, whose office is conferred, and his actions directly controlled, by the captains-general in Peking; he has jurisdiction, usually, only in the city itself, the principal object of the appointment, apparently, being to check any treasonable designs of the civil authorities.

The duties and relations of these various grades with one another require some further explanation, however, to be understood. The three officers, *tsungtuh*, *futai*, and *tsiangkiun* (if there be one), form a supreme council, and unite in deliberating upon a measure, calling in the subordinate officer to whose department it particularly belongs, and to whom its execution is to be committed, the whole forming a deliberative board, though the responsibility of the act rests with the two highest officers. By this means the various members of the provincial government become better acquainted with each other's character and plans, though their intercourse is much restricted by precedence and rivalry. In the provincial courts civilians always take precedence of military officers; the governor-general and Banner commander, governor and major-general, the literary chancellor and collector of customs, rank with each other; then follow the treasurer, the judge, and other civilians. The authority of the governor-general extends to life and death, to the temporary appointment to all vacant offices in the province, to ordering the troops to any part of it, issuing such laws and taking such measures as are necessary for the security and peace of the region committed to his care, or any other steps he sees necessary. The *futai* also has the power of life and death, and attends to appeals of criminal cases; he oversees, moreover, the conduct of the lower civilians.

Next in rank to the *pu-ching sz'* and *ngan-chah sz'*, who always reside in the provincial capital, are the intendants of circuit, who are located in the circuits consisting of two or three prefectures united for this purpose. They are deputies of the two highest functionaries, and their delegated power often includes military as well as civil authority, the chief object of their appointment being to relieve and assist those high functionaries in the discharge of their extensive duties. Some of the intendants are appointed to supervise the proceedings of the prefects and district magistrates; others are stationed at important posts to protect them, and those connected with foreign trade at the open ports have no territorial jurisdiction.

Subordinate to the governors, through the intendants of circuits, are the prefects or head magistrates of departments, called *chífu*, *chíchau*, and *ting tungchí*, *i.e.*, 'knowers' of them, according as they are placed over *fu*, *chau*, or *ting* departments. It is the duty of these persons to make themselves acquainted with everything that takes place within their jurisdiction, and they are held responsible for the full execution of whatever orders are transmitted to them, all presenting their reports and receiving their orders through the intendants.

The practical efficiency of the Chinese government in promoting the welfare of the people and preserving the peace depends chiefly upon these officers. The people themselves are prone to quarrel and oppress each other; beggars, robbers, tramps, and shysters stir up disorders in various ways, and need wise and vigorous hands to repress and punish them; while all classes avoid and resist the tax-gatherer as much as is safe. The proverb, "A *chífu* can exterminate a family, a *chíhien* can confiscate a patrimony," indicates the popular fear of their power.

The subdivisional parts of departments, called *ting*, *chau*, and *hien*, have each their separate officers, who report to the *chífu* and *chíchau* above them; these are called *tungchí*, *chíchau*, and *chíhien*, and may all be denominated district magistrates. The parts of districts called *sz'* are placed under the control of *siun-kien*, circuit-restrainers, or hundreders, who form the last in the regular series of descending rank—the last of the "commissioned officers," as they might not improperly be called. The prefects sometimes have deputies directly under them, as the governor has his intendants, when their jurisdiction is very large or important, who are called *kiunmin fu* and *tungchí*, *i.e.*, 'joint-knowers.' The deputies of district magistrates are termed *chautung* and *chaupwan* for the *chíchau*, and *hienching* and *chufu* for the *chíhien*; the last also have others called *tso-tang* and *yu-tang*, *i.e.*, left-tenants and right-tenants.

Besides these assistants there are others, both in the departments and districts, having the oversight of the police, collection of the taxes and management of the revenue, care of waterways, and many other subdivisions of legislative duties, which it is unnecessary to particularize. They are appointed whenever and wherever the territory is so large and the duties so onerous that one man cannot attend to all, or it is not safe to entrust him with them. They have nearly as much power as their superiors in the department entrusted to them, but none of them have judicial or legislative functions, and the routine of their offices affords them less scope for oppression. Nor is it worth while to notice the great number of clerks, registrars, and secretaries found in connection with the various ranks of dignitaries here mentioned, or the multitude of petty subordinates found in the provinces and placed over particular places or duties as necessity may require. Their number is very large, and the responsibility of their proceedings devolves upon the higher officers who receive their reports and direct their actions.

The common people suffer more from these "rats under the altar," as a Chinese proverb calls them, than from their superiors, because, unlike them, they are usually natives of the place and better acquainted with the condition of the inhabitants, and are not so often removed. The fear of getting into their clutches restrains from evil doings perhaps more than all punishments, though the people soon complain of high-handed acts in a way not to be disregarded. One saying, "Underlings see money as a fly sees blood," indicates their penchant, as another, "Cash drops into an underling's paw as a sheep falls into a tiger's jaw," does the popular notion how to please them. Each intendant, prefect, and district magistrate has special secretaries in his office for filing papers, writing and transmitting despatches, investigating cases, recording evidence, keeping accounts, and performing other functions. All above the *chí-hien* are allowed to keep private secretaries, called *sz' ye*, who are usually personal friends, and accompany the officers whereever they go for the purpose of advising them and preparing their official documents. The *ngan-chah sz'* have jailers under their control, as have also the more important prefects.

The appointment of officers being theoretically founded on literary merit, those to whom is committed the supervision of students and conferment of degrees would naturally be of a high grade. The *hioh-ching*, or literary chancellor, of the province, therefore ranks next to the governor, more, however, because he is specially appointed by his Majesty and oversees this branch of the government, than from the power committed to his hands. Under him are head-teachers of different degrees of authority, residing in the chief towns of departments and districts, the whole forming a similar series of functionaries to what exists in the civil department. These subordinates have merely a greater or less degree of supervision over the studies of students, and the colleges established for the promotion of learning in the chief towns of departments. The business of conferring the lower degrees appertains exclusively to the chancellor, who makes an annual circuit through the province for that purpose, and holds examinations in the chief town of each department, to which all students residing within its limits can come.

The gabel, or salt department, is under the control of a special officer, called a "commissioner for the transport of salt," and forming in the five maritime provinces one of the *san sz'*, or three commissioners, of which the *pu-ching sz'* and *ngan-chah sz'* are the other two. There are, above these commissioners, eight directors of the salt monopoly, stationed at the dépôts in Chihlí and Shantung, who, however, also fill other offices, and have rather a nominal responsibility over the lower commissioners. The number and rank of the officers connected with the salt monopoly show its importance, and is proof of how large a revenue is derived from an article which will bear such an expensive establishment. At present its administration costs about as much as its receipts.

The commissariat and revenue department is unusually large in China compared with other countries, for the plan of collecting any part of the revenue in kind necessarily requires numerous vehicles for transporting and buildings for storing it, which still further multiplies the number of clerks and hands employed. The transportation of grain along the Yangtsz' River is under the control of a *tsungtuh*, who also oversees the disposal and directs the collectors of it in eight of the provinces adjacent to this river. The office of *liang-chu tao*, or commissioner to collect grain, is found in twelve provinces, the *pu-ching sz'* attending to this duty in six; the supervision of the subordinate agents of this department in the several districts is in the hands of the prefects and district magistrates. That feature of the

Chinese system which makes officers mutually responsible, seems to lead the superior powers to confer such various duties upon one functionary, in order that he may thus have a general knowledge of what is going on about and under him, and report what he deems amiss. It is not, indeed, likely that such was the original arrangement, for the Chinese government has come to its present composition by slow degrees; but such is, so far as can be seen, the effect of it, and it serves in no little degree to accomplish the designs of the rulers to bind the main and lesser wheels of the huge machine to themselves and to one another.

The customs and excise are under the management of different grades of officers according to the importance of their posts. The transit duties levied at the excise stations placed in every town are collected by officers acting under the local authorities, and have nothing to do with the collection of maritime duties. This tax, called *li-kin*, or 'a cash a catty,' has lately been greatly increased, and the natural result has been to destroy the trade it preyed on, or divert it to other channels. The foreign merchants and officers have, too, protested against its imposition, seeing that their trade was checked.

Recapitulating in tabular form, we may say that outside of the Cabinet, Council, Boards, and Courts at the capital, the government (in the Eighteen Provinces) is in the hands of:

8 Governors-General (6 governing two provinces each).	64 Intendants of Circuit.
15 Governors.	182 Prefects.
19 Commissioners of Finance (2 for Kiangsu).	68 Prefects of Inferior Departments.
18 Commissioners of Justice.	18 Independent Subprefects.
4 Directors of the Salt Gabel.	180 Dependent Subprefects.
9 Collectors (independent of these).	139 Deputy Subprefects.
13 Commissioners of Grain, or Commissaries.	141 District Magistrates of the Fifth Class.
	1,232 District Magistrates of the Seventh Class.

The military section of the provincial governments is under the control of a *títuh*, or major-general, who resides at a central post, and, in conjunction with the governor-general and governor, directs the movements of the forces, while these last have also an independent control over a certain body of troops belonging to them officially. The various grades of officers in the native army, and the portion of troops under each of them, stationed in the garrisons and forts in different parts of the provinces, are all arranged in a methodical manner, which will bear examination and comparison with the army of any country in the world. The native force in each province is distinct from the Manchu troops, and is divided somewhat according to the Roman plan of legion, cohort, maniple, and century, over each of which are officers, from colonel down to sergeant. Nothing is wanting to the Chinese army to make it fully adequate to the defence of the country but discipline and confidence in itself; for lack of practice and systematic drilling have made it an army of paper warriors against a resolute enemy. Nevertheless, the recent campaigns against the rebels in the extreme western colonies indicate the fact that its regeneration is already of some weight. On the other hand, it has no doubt been for the good of the Chinese people and government—the advance of the first in wealth, numbers, and security, and the consolidation and efficiency of the latter—that they have cultivated letters rather than arms, peace more than war.

All the general officers in the army have fixed places of residence, at which the larger portion of their respective brigades remain, while detachments are stationed at various points within their command. The governor, major-general, and Banner commandant have commands independent of each other, but the *títuh*, or major-general, exercises the principal military sway. The naval officers have the same names as those in the army, and the two are interchanged and promoted from one service to the other. Admirals and vice-admirals usually reside on shore, and despatch their subordinates in squadrons or single vessels wherever occasion requires. This system must, ere long, give place to a better division of the two arms with the building of steam vessels and management of arsenals, when junks are superseded.

The system of mutually checking the provincial officers is also exhibited in their location. For example, in the city of Canton the governor-general is stationed in the New city near the collector of customs, while the lieutenant-governor and Manchu general are so located in the Old city that should circumstances require they can act against the two first. The governor has the general command of all the provincial troops, estimated to be one hundred thousand men, but the particular command of only five thousand, and they are stationed fifty miles off, at Shauking fu. The *tsiang kiun* has five thousand men under him in the Old city, which, in an extreme case, would make him master of the capital, while his own allegiance is secured by the antipathy between the Manchus and Chinese preventing him from combining with the latter. Again, the governor-general has the power of condemning certain criminals to death, but the *wang-ming*, or death-warrant, is lodged with the *futai*, and the order for execution must be countersigned by him; his despatches to court must be also countersigned by his coadjutor. The general absence of resistance to the imperial sway on the part of these high officers during the two centuries of Manchu rule, when compared with the multiplied intrigues and rebellions of the pashas in the Turkish Empire, proves how well the system is concocted.

In order to enable the superior officers to exercise greater vigilance over their inferiors, they have the privilege of sending special messengers, invested with full power, to every part of their jurisdiction. The Emperor himself never visits the provinces judicially, nor has an Emperor been south of the capital during the present century; he therefore constantly sends commissioners or legates, called *kinchai*, to all parts of the Empire, ostensibly entrusted with the management of a particular business, but required also to take a general surveillance of what is going on. The ancient Persians had a similar system of commissioners, who were called the eyes and ears of the prince, and made the circuit of the empire to oversee all that was done. There are many points of resemblance between the structure of these two ancient monarchies, the body of councillors who assisted the prince in his deliberations, the presidents over the provinces, the satraps, etc.; but the Persians had not the elements of perpetuity which the system of common schools and official examinations give to the Chinese government.[1]

---

[1] Rollin's *Ancient History*, Chap. IV. *Manners of the Assyrians.* Heeren's *Asiatic Researches*, Vol. I., Chap. II.

Governors in like manner send their deputies and agents, called *weiyuen*, over the province; and even the prefects and intendants despatch their messengers. All these functionaries, during the time of their mission, take rank with the highest officers according to the quality of their employers; but the imperial commissioners, who for one object or another are constantly passing and repassing through the Empire in every direction, exercise great influence in the government, and are powerful agents in the hands of the Emperor for keeping his proconsuls at their duty.

CHAPTER VIII.

ADMINISTRATION OF THE LAWS.

The preceding chapter contains a general view of the plan upon which the central and provincial governments of the Empire are constructed; and if an examination of the conduct of officers in every department shows their extortion, cruelty, and venality, it will not, in the opinion of the liberal-minded reader, detract from the general excellence of the theory of the government, and the sagacity exhibited in the system of checks designed to restrain the various parts from interfering with the well-being of the whole. In addition to the division of power and the restrictions upon Chinese officers already mentioned, there are other means adopted in their location and alternation to prevent combination and resistance against the head of the state. One of them is the law forbidding a man to hold any civil office in his native province, which, besides stopping all intrigue where it would best succeed, has the further effect of congregating aspirants for office at Peking, where they come in hope of obtaining some post, or of succeeding in the examination for the highest literary degrees. The central government could not contrive a better plan for bringing all the ambitious and talented men in the country under its observation before appointing them to clerkships in the capital, or scattering them in the provinces.

Moreover, no officer is allowed to marry in the jurisdiction under his control, nor own land in it, nor have a son, brother, or near relative holding office under him; and he is seldom continued in the same station or province for more than three or four years. Manchus and Chinese are mingled together in high stations, and obligations are imposed on certain grandees to inform the Emperor of each other's acts. Members of the imperial clan are required to attend the meetings of the Boards at the capital, and observe and report what they deem amiss or of interest to the Emperor and his council; while in all the upper departments of the general and provincial governments, a system of espionage is carried out, detrimental to all principles of honorable fidelity, such as we look for in officials, but not without some good effects in a weak despotism like China. There is, besides this constant surveillance, a triennial catalogue made out of the merits and demerits of all officers in the Empire, which is submitted to imperial inspection by the Board of Civil Office. In order to collect the details for this catalogue, it is incumbent upon every provincial officer to report upon the character and qualifications of those under him, and the list, when made out, is forwarded by the governor to the capital. The points of character are arranged under six different heads, viz.: those who are not diligent, the inefficient, the superficial, the untalented, superannuated, and diseased. According to the opinion given in this report, officers are elevated or degraded so many steps in the scale of merit, like school-boys in a class, and whenever they issue an edict are required to state how many steps they have been advanced or degraded, and how many times recorded. Officers are required to accuse themselves, when guilty of crime, either in their own conduct or that of their subordinates, and request punishment. The results of this peculiar and patriarchal mode of teaching officers their duty will be best exhibited by quoting from a rescript of Taukwang's, issued in February, 1837, after one of the catalogues had been submitted to his Majesty.

"The cabinet minister Changling has strenuously exerted himself during a long lapse of years; he has reached the eightieth year of his age, yet his energies are still in full force. His colleagues Pwan Shí-ngăn and Muchangah, as well as the assistant cabinet minister Wang Ting, have invariably displayed diligence and attention, and have not failed in yielding us assistance. Tang Kin-chau, president of the Board of Office, has knowledge and attainments of a respectable and sterling character, and has shown himself public-spirited and intelligent in the performance of special duties assigned to him. Shí Chí-yen, president of the Board of Punishments, retains his usual strength and energies, and in the performance of his judicial duties has displayed perspicacity and circumspection. The assistant cabinet minister and governor of Chihlí province, Kishen, transacts the affairs of his government with faithfulness, and the military force under his control is well disciplined. Husungé, the governor of Shensí and Kansuh provinces, is cautious and prudent, and performs his duties with careful exactness. Ílípu, governor of Yunnan and Kweichau, is well versed in the affairs of his frontier government, and has fully succeeded in preserving it free from disturbance. Linking, who is entrusted with the general charge of the rivers in Kiangnan, has not failed in his care of the embankments, and has preserved the surrounding districts from all disquietude. To show our favor unto all these, let the Board of Office determine on appropriate marks of distinction for them.

"Kweisan, subordinate minister of the Cabinet, is hasty and deficient, both in precision and capacity; he is incapable of moving and acting for himself; let him take an inferior station, and receive an appointment in the second class of the guards. Yihtsih, vice-president of the Board of Works for Mukden, possesses but ordinary talents, and is incompetent to the duties of his present office; let him also take an inferior station, and be appointed to a place in the first class of guards. Narkingé, the governor-general of Hukwang, though having under him the whole civil and military bodies of two provinces, has yet been unable, these many days, to seize a few beggarly impish vagabonds: after having in the first instance failed in prevention, he has followed up that failure by idleness and remissness, and has fully proved himself inefficient. Let him take the lower station of governor in Hunan, and within one year let him, by the apprehension of Lan Ching-tsun, show that he is aroused to greater exertions.

"Let all our other servants retain their present appointments. Among them Tau Shu, the governor of Kiangnan and Kiangsí, is bold and determined in the transaction of affairs, but has not yet attained enlarged views in regard to the salt department; Chung Tsiang, the governor of Fuhkien and Chehkiang, finds his energies failing; Tăng Ting-ching, the governor of Kwangtung and Kwangsí, possesses barely an adequate degree of talent and knowledge; and Shin Kí-hien, though faithful and earnest in the performance of his duties, has, in common with these others, been not very long in office.

"That all ministers will act with purity and devotedness of purpose, with public spirit and diligence, is our most fervent hope. A special edict."[1]

The effect of such confessions and examination of character is to restrain the commission of outrageous acts of oppression; it is still further enforced by the privilege, common alike to censors and private subjects, of complaining to the Emperor of misdeeds done to them by persons in authority. Fear for their own security has suggested this multiplicity of checks, but the Emperor and his ministry have no doubt thereby impeded the

---

[1] *Chinese Repository*, Vol. VI., p. 48.

efficiency of their subordinates, and compelled them to attend so much to their own standing that they care far less than they otherwise would for the prosperity of the people.

The position of an officer in the Chinese government can hardly be ascertained from the enumeration of his duties, nor can we easily appreciate, from a general account of the system, his temptations to oppress inferiors and deceive superiors. His duties, as indicated in the code, are so minute, and often so contradictory, as to make it impossible to fulfil them strictly; it is found, accordingly, that few or none have ascended the slippery heights of promotion without frequent relapses. Degradation, when to a step or two and temporary, carries with it of course no moral taint in a country where the award for bribery is graduated to the amount received, without any reference to moral violation; where the bamboo is the standard of punishment as well for error in judgment or remissness as for crime —only commuted to a fine in honor of official rank; where, as a distinction in favor of the imperial race, the bamboo is softened to the whip and banishment mitigated to the pillory.[1] The highest officers have of course the greatest opportunity to oppress, but their extortions are limited by the venality and mendacity of the agents they are compelled to employ. Inferiors also can carry on a system of exactions if they keep on the right side of those above them. The whole class form a body of men mutually jealous of each other's advance, where every incumbent endeavors to supplant his associate; they all agree in regarding the people as the source of their profits, the sponge which all must squeeze, but differ in the degree to which they should carry on the same plan with each other. Although sprung from the mass of the people, the welfare of the community has little place in their thoughts. Their life is spent in ambitious efforts to rise upon the fall of others, though they do not lose all sense of character or become reckless of the means of advance, for this would destroy their chance of success. The game they play with each other and their imperial master is, however, a harmless one compared with what was

---

[1] *Chinese Repository*, Vol. IV., p. 59.

done in old Rome or in Europe four or five centuries ago, or even lately among the pashas and viziers of the sultans and shahs in Western Asia. To the honor of the Chinese, life is seldom sacrificed for political crime or envious emulation; no officer dreads a bowstring or a poisoned cup from his lord paramount, nor is he on the watch against the dagger of an assassin hired by a vindictive competitor. Whatever heights of favor or depths of umbrage he may experience, the servant of the Emperor of China need not, in unproved cases of delinquency, fear for his life; but he not unfrequently takes it himself from conscious guilt and dread of just punishment.

The names and standing of all officers are published quarterly by permission of government in the *Red Book* (which by an usual coincidence is bound in red), called the "Complete Record of the Girdle Wearers" (*Tsin Shin Tsiuen Shu*), comprised in four volumes, 12mo, to which are added two others of the Army and Bannermen. This publication was first issued at the command of Wanlih, of the Ming dynasty, about 1580, and mentions the native province of each person, whether Chinese, Manchu, Mongol, or enrolled Chinese, describes the title of the office, its salary, and gives much general information. The publishers of the book expect that officers will inform them of the changes that take place in their standing, and sometimes omit to mention those who do not thus report themselves.

A memoir of the public life of a high officer in China would present a singular picture of ups and downs, but, on account of their notorious disregard of truth, Chinese documents are unsafe to trust entirely in drawing such a sketch. One of the most conspicuous men in late times was Duke Ho, the premier in the time of Macartney's embassy, who for many years exercised a greater control over the counsels of a Chinese sovereign than is recorded of any other man during the present dynasty. This man was originally a private person, who attracted the notice of the Emperor by his comeliness, and secured it by his zeal in discharging the offices entrusted to him. With but few interruptions he gradually mounted the ladder of promotion, and for some years before Kienlung's death, when the latter's energies had begun to fail from age, was virtual master of the country. Staunton describes him as possessing eminent abilities; "the manners of Hokwăn were not less pleasing than his understanding was penetrating and acute. He seemed indeed to possess the qualities of a perfect statesman."[1] The favorite had gradually filled the highest posts with his friends, and his well-wishers were so numerous in the general and provincial governments that some began to apprehend a rising in his favor when the Emperor died. Kiaking, on coming to the throne, began to take those cautious measures for his removal which showed the great influence he possessed; one of these proceedings was to appoint him superintendent of the rites of mourning, in order, probably, that his official duties might bring him often to the palace. After four years the Emperor drew up sixteen articles of impeachment, most of them frivolous and vexatious, though of more consequence in the eyes of a Chinese prince than they would have been at other courts. One article alleged that he had ridden on horseback up to the palace gate; another, that he had appropriated to his own household the females educated for the imperial harem; a third, that he had detained the reports of officers in time of war from coming to the Emperor's eye, and had appointed his own retainers to office, when they were notoriously incompetent; a fourth, that he had built many apartments of *nan-muh*, a kind of laurel-wood exclusively appropriated to royalty, and imitated regal style in his grounds and establishment; a fifth, that "on the day previous to our Royal Father's announcement of our election as his successor, Hokwăn waited upon us and presented the insignia of the newly conferred rank—thereby betraying an important secret of state, in hopes of obtaining our favor." He was also accused of having pearls and jewels of larger size than those even in the Emperor's regalia. But so far as can be inferred from what was published, this Cardinal Wolsey of China was, comparatively speaking, not cruel in the exercise of his power, and the real cause of his fall was evidently his riches. In the schedule of his confiscated property it was mentioned that besides houses, lands, and other immovable property to an amazing extent, not less

[1] *Embassy to China*, Vol. III., p. 26.

than one hundred and five millions of dollars in bullion and gems were found in his treasury. A special tribunal was instituted for his trial, and he was allowed to become his own executioner, while his constant associate was beheaded. These were the only deaths, the remainder of his relatives and dependents being simply removed and degraded. His power was no doubt too great for the safety of his master if he had proved faithless; but his wealth was too vast for his own security, even had he been innocent. The Emperor, in the edict which contains the sentence, cites as a precedent for his own acts similar condemnation of premiers by three of his ancestors in the present dynasty, but nothing definite is known of their crimes or trials.[1]

Taukwang was more clement, or more fortunate than his father, and upon coming to the throne continued Tohtsin in power; this statesman had held the premiership from 1815 to 1832, with but few interruptions, when he was allowed to retire at the age of seventy-five. He had served under three emperors, having risen step by step from the situation of clerk in one of the offices. His successor, Changling, experienced a far more checkered course, but remained in favor at last, and retired from the premiership in 1836, aged about seventy-nine. He became very popular with his master from his ability in quelling the insurrection of Jehangír in Turkestan in 1827. Even a few such instances of the honor in which an upright, energetic, and wise minister is regarded by prince and people have great influence in encouraging young men to act in the same way.

Few Chinese statesmen have been oftener brought into the notice of western foreigners than Sung, one of the commissioners attached to Lord Macartney's embassy, and a favorite of all its members. His lordship speaks of him then as a young man of high quality, possessing an elevated mind; and adds that "during the whole time of our connection with him he has on all occasions conducted himself toward us in the most friendly and gentleman-like manner." This was in 1793. In 1817 he is mentioned as one of the Cabinet; but not long after, for some unknown reason, he was degraded by Kiaking to the sixth rank, and ap-

[1] *Chinese Repository*, Vol. III., p. 241.

pointed adjutant-general among the Tsakhar Mongols; from thence he memorialized his master respecting the ill conduct of some lamas, who had been robbing and murdering. Sung and his friends opposed the Emperor's going to Manchuria, and were involved in some trouble on this account, the reasons of which it is difficult to understand. He was promoted, however, to be captain-general of Manchuria, but again fell under censure, and on his visit to his paternal estate at Mukden the Emperor took him back to the capital and appointed him to some important office. He soon got into new trouble with the Emperor, who in a proclamation remarks that "Sung is inadequate to the duties of minister of the imperial presence; because, although he formerly officiated as such, he is now upward of seventy years of age, and rides badly on horseback;" he is therefore sent to Manchuria to fill his old office of captain-general. The next year the ex-minister and his adherents were involved in a long trial about the loss of a seal, and he was deprived of his command and directed to retire to his own Banner; the real reasons of this disgrace were probably connected with the change of parties ensuent upon the accession of Taukwang.

Soon afterward Sung was restored to favor and made adjutant at Jeh ho, after having been president of the Censorate for a month. He was allowed to remain there longer than usual, and employed his spare time in writing a book upon the newly acquired territory in Turkestan. In 1824 he was reinstated as president of the Censorate, with admonitions not to confuse and puzzle himself with a multiplicity of extraneous matters. In 1826 he was sent on a special commission to Shansí, and when he returned was honored with a dinner at court on new year's day. He then appears as travelling tutor to the crown-prince, but where his royal highness went for his education does not appear; from this post we find him made president of the Board of Rites, and appointed to inspect the victims for a state sacrifice. He is then ordered to Jeh ho, from whence, in a fit of penitence, or perhaps from fear of a dun, he memorialized the Emperor about a debt of $52,000 he had incurred nearly thirty years before, which he proposed to liquidate by foregoing his salary of $1,000 until the arrears were paid up; the Emperor was in good humor with the old man, and forgave him the whole amount, being assured, he says, of Sung's pure official character. In this memorial, when recounting his services, the aged officer says that he has been twice commander-in-chief and governor of Ílí, governor-general at Nanking, Canton, etc., but had never saved much.

Shortly after this he is recalled from Jeh ho and made *tí-tuh* of Peking, then president of the Board of War; and in a few months he is ordered to proceed across the desert to Cobdo to investigate some affair of importance—a long and toilsome journey of fifteen hundred miles for a man over seventy-five years old. He returned the next year and resumed his post as president of the Board of War, in which capacity he acted as examiner of the students in the Russian College. In 1831 he was made president of the Colonial Office, and later received an appointment as superintendent of the Three Treasuries, but was obliged to resign from ill health. A month's relaxation seems to have wonderfully restored him, for the Emperor, in reply to his petition for employment, expresses surprise that he should so soon be fit for official duties, and plainly intimates his opinion that the disease was all sham, though he accedes to his request so far as to nominate him commander of one of the eight Banners. In 1832 Sung again became involved in intrigues, and was reduced to the third degree of rank; the resignation of Tohtsin and the struggle for the vacant premiership was probably the real reason of this new reverse, though a frivolous accusation of two years' standing was trumped up against him. He was restored again, after a few months' disgrace, at the petition of a beg of a city in Turkestan, which illustrates, by the way, the influence which those princes exert. Old age now began to come upon the courtier in good earnest, and in 1833 he was ordered to retire with the rank and pay of adjutant, which he lived to enjoy only two years. Much of the success of Sung was said to be owing to his having had a daughter in the harem, but his personal character and kindness were evidently the main sources of his enduring influence among all ranks of people and officers; one account says the Manchus almost worshipped him, and beggars clung to his chair in the streets to ask alms. It is wortny of notice that in all his reverses there is no mention made of any severer punishment than degradation or banishment, and in this particular the political life of Sung is probably a fair criterion of the usual fortune of high Chinese statesmen. The leading events in the life of Changling, the successor of Tohtsin, together with a few notices of the governor of Canton in 1833, Lí Hung-pin, are given in the *Repository*.[1]

Commissioners Lin and Kíying became more famous among foreigners than their compeers in the capital, from the parts they acted in the war with England in 1840, but only a few notices of their lives are accessible. Lin Tseh-sü was born in 1785, in Fuhchau, and passed through the literary examinations, becoming a graduate of the second rank at the age of nineteen, and of the third when twenty-six. After filling an office or two in the Imperial Academy, he was sent as assistant literary examiner to Kiangsí in 1816, and during three subsequent years acted as examiner and censor in various places. In 1819 he filled the office of intendant of circuit, in Chehkiang; and after absence on account of health, he was, in 1823, appointed to the post of treasurer of Kiangsu, in the absence of the incumbent. In 1826 he was made overseer of the Yellow River, but hearing of his mother's death, resigned his office to mourn for her. After the period of mourning was finished he went to Peking and received the office of judge in Shensí; but before he had been in it a month he was made treasurer of Kiangsu, and before he could enter upon this new office he heard of his father's death, and was obliged to resign once more. In 1832 he was nominated treasurer in Hupeh, and five months later transferred to the same office in Honan, and six months after that sent to Kiangsu again. Three months after this third transfer he was reinstated overseer of the Yellow River, and within a short time elevated to be governor of Kiangsí, which he retained three years, and acted as governor-general of Liang Kiang two years more. In 1838 he was made governor-general of Hu Kwang; and shortly after

[1] *Chinese Repository*, Vol. IV., pp. 61-66.

this ordered to come to Peking to be admitted to an imperial audience, and by special favor permitted to ride on horseback within the palace.

He was at this audience appointed imperial commissioner to put down the opium trade and manage the affairs of the maritime frontier of Kwantung, receiving at the time such plenipotentiary powers to act for the Emperor as had only once before been committed to a subject since 1644, viz., when Changling was sent to Turkestan to quell the insurrection. Lin's ill success in dealing with the opium trade and its upholders in the British government reflect no discredit on his own ability, for the task was beyond the powers of the Empire; but his fame even now stands high among the Cantonese. One incident showing his kindness to the crew of the Sunda, an English vessel lost on Hainan Island, on their arrival in Canton in October, 1839, while he was fighting their consular officers, gave a good insight into the candor of the man. In December, 1839, he was appointed governor-general of Liang Kiang; but succeeded to that of Liang Kwang in February, 1840. In October of the same year the seals of office were taken away, and he was ordered to return to Peking. He remained, however, till May of the next year to advise with Kíshen in his difficult negotiations with the English. Lin left Canton in May, 1841, leading two thousand troops to defend Ningpo, but this rôle was not his forte. In July, 1842, he was banished to Ĭlí, but the sentence was suspended for a season by giving him a third time the oversight of the Yellow River. However, in 1844 we find him in Ĭlí, holding an inferior appointment and trying to bring waste lands near the Mohammedan cities under cultivation; his zeal was rewarded the next year by a pardon, and the year after that by the high post of governor-general of Shensí and Kansuh, in which region he set himself to work to reform the civil service and increase the revenue. In 1847 the cares of office wore upon him, so that he asked for a furlough and went back to Fuhchau, aged sixty-two. His ambition was not yet satisfied, for he was made governor-general in Yunnan in 1848, but his strength was not equal to its duties, and he again retired in 1849. The young Emperor Hienfung, startled at the rapid rise of the Tai-ping rebels, applied to the aged statesman to help him as he had his father. Lin responded to the call of his sovereign, but death came upon him before he reached Kwangsí, on the 22d of November, 1850, at the age of sixty-seven. More enduring than some of his official acts was the preparation and publication of the *History of Maritime Nations*, with maps, in fifty books, in which he gave his countrymen all the details he could gather of other nations.[1]

Much less is known of the official life of Kíying than of Lin, but the Manchu proved himself superior to the Chinese in trimming his course to meet the inevitable and avoid the rocks his predecessor struck. In 1835 his name is mentioned as president of the Board of Revenue and controller of the Tsung-jin fu. He was detained at the capital as commander-in-chief of the forces there until 1842, when his Majesty sent him to Canton to take the place of Yihshan. He was ordered to stop at Hangchau, however, on his way, and make a report of the condition of affairs; his memorials seem to have had great influence, for he was appointed joint commissioner with Îlípu in April of that year. At the negotiations of Nanking Kíying acted as chief commissioner, and was mainly instrumental in bringing the war to a conclusion. He proceeded to Canton in May, 1843, to succeed Îlípu, and there acted as sole commissioner in negotiating the supplementary treaty and the commercial regulations with the British, returning to the capital in December, 1843. His prudence and vigor had great effect in calming the irritation of the people of Canton. On the arrival of the American plenipotentiary he was vested with full powers to treat with Mr. Cushing, and soon after with the French and Swedish envoys, with all of whom he signed treaties. During the progress of these negotiations Kí Kung died and Kíying succeeded him.

His administration as governor-general continued till January, 1848, when he returned to Peking to receive higher honors from the Emperor. In 1849 he went to Kiangsu to inquire

---

[1] Compare Dr. Bowring in *N. C. Br. R. A. Soc. Journal*, Part III., Art. VII. (Dec., 1852).

into the salt department, and then to Northern Shansí to settle differences with the Mongols. From this period he held various posts in the cabinet and capital, busy in all court intrigues, and rather losing his good name, till he fell into disgrace. In 1856, when the envoys of the four western Powers were at Tientsin, he entered into some underhand dealings against the policy of Kweiliang and Hwashana, and was sent there as joint commissioner. He had hardly entered upon his functions by the presentation of his commission, when he suddenly returned to Peking against the Emperor's will, and was ordered to take poison in the presence of the head of the Clan to avoid the ignominy of a public execution.[1] Few Chinese statesmen in modern times have borne a higher character for prudence, dignity, and intelligence than Kíying, and the confidence reposed in him is creditable to his imperial master. In his demeanor, says Sir Thomas Wade, "there was a combination of dignity and courtesy which more than balanced the deficiencies of a by no means attractive exterior." The portrait of him has been engraved from a native painting made at Canton, and is a good one. It was kindly furnished for this work by J. R. Peters, Jr.

The facts of this man's career are not all known, but his connection by birth with the Clan brought him into an entirely different set of influences from Lin, while his training removed him from the contact with the people which made the other so popular and influential. Both of them were good instances of Chinese statesmen, and their checkered lives as here briefly noticed resemble that of their compeers in the highest grades of official dignity. The sifting which the personnel of the Emperor's employees in all their various grades receive generally brings the cleverest and most trustworthy to the top; no one can come in contact with them in state affairs without an increase of respect for their shrewdness, loyalty, and skill. One observable feature of the Chinese political world is the great age of the high officers, and it is not easy to account for their

---

[1] *Chinese Repository*, passim. Oliphant, *Lord Elgin's Mission to China and Japan*, Chap. XVII. Minister Reed, in *U. S. Dip. Correspondence*, 1857–58.

being kept in their posts, when almost worn out, by a monarch who wished to have efficient men around him, until we learn how little real power he can arbitrarily exert over the details of the branches of his government. It is somewhat explainable on the ground that, as long as the old incumbents are alive, the Emperor, being more habituated to their company and advice, prefers to retain those whose competency has been proven by their service. The patriarch, kept near the Emperor, is moreover a kind of hostage for the loyalty of his following; and the latter, scattered throughout the provinces, can be managed and moved about through him with less opposition: he is, still further, a convenient medium through which to receive the exactions of the younger members of the service, and convey such intimations as are thought necessary. The system of clientelage which existed among the Gauls and Franks is also found in China with some modifications, and has a tendency to link officers to one another in parties of different degrees of power. The Emperor published an order in 1833 against this system of patronage, and it is evident that he would find it seriously interfering with his power were it not constantly broken up by changing the relations of the parties and sending them away in different directions. Peking is almost the only place where the "teacher and pupils," as the patron and client call each other, could combine to much purpose; and the principal safeguard the throne seems to have against intrigues and parties around it lies in the conflicting interests arising among themselves, though a long-established or unscrupulous favorite, as in the cases of Duke Ho and Suhshun in 1855–61, can sometimes manage to engross the whole power of the crown.

Notwithstanding the heavy charges of oppression, cruelty, bribery, and mendacity which are often brought against officers with more or less justice, it must not be inferred that no good qualities exist among them. Thousands of them desire to rule equitably, to clear the innocent and punish the guilty, and exert all the knowledge and power they possess to discharge their functions to the acceptance of their master and their own good name among the inhabitants. Such officers, too, generally rise, while the cruelties of others are visited with degradation. The pasquinades which the people stick up in the streets indicate their sentiments, and receive much more attention than would such vulgar expressions in other countries, because it is almost the only way in which their opinions can be safely uttered. The popularity which upright officers receive acts as an incentive to others to follow in the same steps, as well as a reward to the person himself. The governor of Kwangtung in 1833, Chu, was a very popular officer, and when he obtained leave to resign his station on account of age, the people vied with each other in showing their hearty regret at losing him. The old custom was observed of retaining his boots and presenting him with a new pair at every city he passed through, and many other testimonials of their regard were adopted. On leaving the city of Canton he circulated a few verses, "to console the people and excite them to virtue," for he heard that some of them wept on learning of his departure.

From ancient days, my fathers trod the path
Of literary fame, and placed their names
Among the wise; two generations past,
Attendant on their patrons, they have come
To this provincial city.[1] Here this day
'Tis mine to be imperial envoy;
Thus has the memory of ancestral fame
Ceased not to stimulate this feeble frame.

My father held an office at Lungchau.[2]
And deep imprinted his memorial there;
He was the sure and generous friend
Of learning unencouraged and obscure.
When now I turn my head and travel back
In thought to that domestic hall, it seems
As yesterday, those early happy scenes—
How was he pained if forced to be severe!

---

[1] The Chinese have a great affection for the place of their nativity, and consider a residence in any other province like being in a foreign settlement. They always wish to return thither in life, or have their remains carried and interred there after death.

[2] A district in the province of Kwangsí.

From times remote Kwangtung has been renowned
For wise and mighty men ; but none can stand
Among them, or compare with Kiuh Kiang : [1]
Three idle and inglorious years are past,
And I have raised no monument of fame,
By shedding round the rays of light and truth,
To give the people knowledge. In this heart
I feel the shame, and cannot bear the thought.

But now, in flowered pavilions, in street
Illuminations, gaudy shows, to praise
The gods and please themselves, from year to year
The modern people vie, and boast themselves,
And spend their hard-earned wealth—and all in vain;
For what shall be the end ? Henceforth let all
Maintain an active and a useful life,
The sober husband and the frugal wife.

The gracious statesman,[2] politic and wise,
Is my preceptor and my long-tried friend ;
Called now to separate, spare our farewell
The heartrending words affection so well loves.
That he may still continue to exhort
The people, and instruct them to be wise,
To practice virtue and to keep the laws
Of ancient sages, is my constant hope.

When I look backward o'er the field of fame
Where I have travelled a long fifty years,
The struggle for ambition and the sweat
For gain seem altogether vanity.
Who knoweth not that heaven's toils are close,
Infinitely close ? Few can escape.
Ah! how few great men reach a full old age!
How few unshorn of honors end their days!

Inveterate disease has twined itself
Around me, and binds me in slavery.
The kindness of his Majesty is high [3]
And liberal, admitting no return

---

[1] Kiuh Kiang was an ancient minister of state during the Tang dynasty. His imperial master would not listen to his advice and he therefore retired. Rebellion and calamities arose. The Emperor thought of his faithful servant and sent for him; but he was already dead.

[2] Governor Loo.

[3] In permitting Chu to retire from public life.

Unless a grateful heart; still, still my eyes
Will see the miseries of the people—
Unlimited distresses, mournful, sad,
To the mere passer-by awaking grief.

Untalented, unworthy, I withdraw,
Bidding farewell to this windy, dusty world;
Upward I look to the supremely good—
The Emperor—to choose a virtuous man
To follow me. Henceforth it will be well—
The measures and the merits passing mine;
But I shall silent stand and see his grace
Diffusing blessings like the genial spring.

Ilípu, Kí Kung, the late governor-general of Kwangtung, and Shu, the prefect of Ningpo in 1842, are other officers who have been popular in late years. When Lin passed through Macao in 1839, the Chinese had in several places erected honorary portals adorned with festoons of silk and laudatory scrolls; and when he passed the doors of their houses and shops they set out tables decorated with vases of flowers, "in order to manifest their profound gratitude for his coming to save them from a deadly vice, and for removing from them a dire calamity by the destruction and severe interdiction of opium." Alas, that his efforts and intentions should have been so fruitless!

The *Peking Gazette* frequently contains petitions from old officers describing their ailments, their fear lest they shall not be able to perform their duties, the length of their official service, and requesting leave of absence or permission to retire. It is impossible to regard all the expressions of loyalty in these papers, coming as they do from every class of officers, as heartless and made out according to a prescribed form; but we are too ready to measure them by our own standard and fashion, forgetting that it is not the defects of a system which give the best standard of its value and efficiency. Let us rather, as an honest expression of feeling, quote a few lines from a memorial of Shí, a censor in 1824: "Reflecting within myself that, notwithstanding the decay of my strength, it has still pleased the imperial goodness to employ me in a high office instead of rejecting and discarding me at once, I have been most anxious to effect a cure, in order that, a weak old horse as I am, it might be still in my power, by the exertion of my whole strength, to recompense a ten-thousandth part of the benevolence which restored me to life."[1]

Connected with the triennial schedule of official merits and demerits is the necessity the high officers of state are under of confessing their faults of government; and the two form a peculiar and somewhat stringent check upon their intrigues and malversation, making them, as Le Comte observes, "exceeding circumspect and careful, and sometimes even virtuous against their own inclinations." The confessions reported in the *Peking Gazette* are, however, by no means satisfactory as to the real extent or nature of these acts; most of the confessors are censors, and perhaps it is in virtue of their office that they thus sit in judgment upon themselves. Examples of the crimes mentioned are not wanting. The governor-general of Chihlí requested severe punishment in 1832 for not having discovered a plotting demagogue who had collected several thousand adherents in his and the next provinces; his request was granted. An admiral in the same province demands punishment for not having properly educated his son, as thereby he went mad and wounded several people. Another calls for judgment upon himself because the Empress-dowager had been kept waiting at the palace gate by the porters when she paid her Majesty a visit. One officer accused himself for not being able to control the Yellow River; and his Majesty's cook in 1830 requested punishment for being too late in presenting his bill of fare, but was graciously forgiven. The rarity of these confessions, compared with the actual sins, shows either that they are, like a partridge's doublings, made to draw off attention from the real nest of malversation, or that few officers are willing to undergo the mortification.

The Emperor, in his character of vicegerent of heaven, occasionally imposes the duty of self-confession upon himself. Kiaking issued several public confessions during his reign, but the *Gazette* has not contained many such papers within the last thirty years. These confessions are drawn from him more by

[1] *Chinese Repository*, Vol. IV., p. 71.

natural calamities, such as drought, freshets, epidemics, etc., than by political causes, though insurrections, fires, ominous portents, etc., sometimes induce them. The personal character of the monarch has much to do with their frequency and phraseology. On occasion of a drought in 1817 the Emperor Kiaking said: "The remissness and sloth of the officers of government constitute an evil which has long been accumulating. It is not the evil of a day; for several years I have given the most pressing admonitions on the subject, and have punished many cases which have been discovered, so that recently there appears a little improvement, and for several seasons the weather has been favorable. The drought this season is not perhaps entirely on their (the officers') account. I have meditated upon it, and am persuaded that the reason why the azure Heavens above manifest disapprobation by withholding rain for a few hundred miles only around the capital, is that the fifty and more rebels who escaped are secreted somewhere near Peking. Hence it is that fertile vapors are fast bound, and the felicitous harmony of the seasons interrupted." On the 14th of May, 1818, between five and six o'clock in the evening, a sudden darkness enveloped the capital, attended by a violent wind from the southeast and much rain. During its action two intervals occurred when the sky became a lurid red and the air offensive, terrible claps of thunder startling the people and frightening the monarch. His astrologers could not relieve his forebodings of evil, and he issued a manifesto to explain the matter to his subjects and discharge his own conscience. One sentence is worth quoting: "Calumnious accusations cause the ruin and death of a multitude of innocent people; they alone are capable of provoking a sign as terrible as this one just seen. The wind coming from the southeast is proof enough that some great crime has been committed in that region, which the officials, by neglecting their duties, have ignored, and thereby excited the ire of Heaven." [1]

One of the most remarkable specimens of these papers is a prayer for rain issued by Taukwang, July 24, 1832, on occasion

---

[1] *Annales de la Foi,* No. 6, 1823, pp. 21–24.

of a severe drought at the capital. Before publishing this paper he had endeavored to mollify the anger and heat of heaven by ordering all suspected and accused persons in the prisons of the metropolis to be tried, and their guilt or innocence established, in order that the course of justice might not be delayed, and witnesses be released from confinement. But these vicarious corrections did not avail, and the drought continuing, he was obliged, as high-priest of the Empire, to show the people that he was mindful of their sufferings, and would relieve them, if possible, by presenting the following memorial:

"Kneeling, a memorial is hereby presented, to cause affairs to be heard.

"Oh, alas! imperial Heaven, were not the world afflicted by extraordinary changes, I would not dare to present extraordinary services. But this year the drought is most unusual. Summer is past, and no rain has fallen. Not only do agriculture and human beings feel the dire calamity, but also beasts and insects, herbs and trees, almost cease to live. I, the minister of Heaven, am placed over mankind, and am responsible for keeping the world in order and tranquillizing the people. Although it is now impossible for me to sleep or eat with composure, although I am scorched with grief and tremble with anxiety, still, after all, no genial and copious showers have been obtained.

"Some days ago I fasted, and offered rich sacrifices on the altars of the gods of the land and the grain, and had to be thankful for gathering clouds and slight showers; but not enough to cause gladness. Looking up, I consider that Heaven's heart is benevolence and love. The sole cause is the daily deeper atrocity of my sins; but little sincerity and little devotion. Hence I have been unable to move Heaven's heart, and bring down abundant blessings.

"Having searched the records, I find that in the twenty-fourth year of Kienlung my exalted Ancestor, the Emperor Pure, reverently performed a 'great snow service.' I feel impelled, by ten thousand considerations, to look up and imitate the usage, and with trembling anxiety rashly assail Heaven, examine myself, and consider my errors; looking up and hoping that I may obtain pardon. I ask myself whether in sacrificial services I have been disrespectful? Whether or not pride and prodigality have had a place in my heart, springing forth there unobserved? Whether, from length of time, I have become remiss in attending to the affairs of government, and have been unable to attend to them with that serious diligence and strenuous effort which I ought? Whether I have uttered irreverent words, and have deserved reprehension? Whether perfect equity has been attained in conferring rewards or inflicting punishments? Whether in raising mausolea and laying out gardens I have distressed the people and wasted property? Whether in the appointment of officers I have failed to obtain fit persons, and thereby the acts of government have been petty and vexatious to the people? Whether punishments have been unjustly inflicted or not? Whether the oppressed have found no means of appeal? Whether in persecuting heterodox sects the innocent have not been involved? Whether or not the magistrates have insulted the people and refused to listen to their affairs? Whether, in the successive military operations on the western frontiers, there may not have been the horrors of human slaughter for the sake of imperial rewards? Whether the largesses bestowed on the afflicted southern provinces were properly applied, or the people were left to die in the ditches? Whether the efforts to exterminate or pacify the rebellious mountaineers of Hunan and Kwangtung were properly conducted; or whether they led to the inhabitants being trampled on as mire and ashes? To all these topics to which my anxieties have been directed I ought to lay the plumb-line, and strenuously endeavor to correct what is wrong; still recollecting that there may be faults which have not occurred to me in my meditations.

"Prostrate I beg imperial Heaven (*Hwang Tien*) to pardon my ignorance and stupidity, and to grant me self-renovation; for myriads of innocent people are involved by me, the One man. My sins are so numerous it is difficult to escape from them. Summer is past and autumn arrived; to wait longer will really be impossible. Knocking head, I pray imperial Heaven to hasten and confer gracious deliverance—a speedy and divinely beneficial rain, to save the people's lives and in some degree redeem my iniquities. Oh, alas! imperial Heaven, observe these things. Oh, alas! imperial Heaven, be gracious to them. I am inexpressibly grieved, alarmed, and frightened. Reverently this memorial is presented." [1]

This paper apparently intimates some acknowledgment of a ruling power above, and before a despot like the Emperor of China would place himself in such an equivocal posture before his people, he would assure himself very thoroughly of their sentiments; for its effects as a state paper would be worse than null if the least ridicule was likely to be thrown upon it. In this case heavy showers followed the same evening, and appropriate thanksgivings were ordered and oblations presented before the six altars of heaven, earth, land, and grain, and the gods of heaven, earth, and the revolving year.

The orders of the court are usually transmitted in manuscript, except when some grand event or state ceremony requires a general proclamation, in which cases the document is printed on yellow paper and published in both the Chinese and Manchu languages, encircled with a border of dragons. The governors and their subordinates, imperial commissioners, and collectors of customs are the principal officers in the provinces who pub-

[1] *Chinese Repository*, Vol. I., p. 236.

lish their orders to the people, consisting of admonitions, exhortations, regulations, laws, special ordinances, threatenings, and municipal requirements. Standing laws and local regulations are often superbly carved on tablets of black marble, and placed in the streets to be "held in everlasting remembrance," so that no one can plead ignorance; a custom which recalls the mode of publishing the Twelve Tables at Rome. Several of these monuments, beautifully ornamented, are to be seen at Canton and Macao. The usual mode of publishing the commands of government is to print the document in large characters, and post copies at the door of the offices and in the streets in public places, with the seal of the officer attached to authenticate them. The sheets on which they are printed being common bamboo paper, and having no protection from the weather, are, however, soon destroyed; the people read them as they are thus exposed, and copy them if they wish, but it is not uncommon, too, for the magistrates to print important edicts in pamphlet form for circulation. These placards are written in an official style, differing from common writing as much as that does in English, but not involved or obscure. A single specimen of an edict issued at Canton will suffice to illustrate the form of such papers, and moreover show upon what subjects a Chinese ruler sometimes legislates, and the care he is expected to take of the people.

"Sü and Hwang, by special appointment magistrates of the districts of Nanhai and Pwanyu, raised ten steps and recorded ten times, hereby distinctly publish important rules for the capture of grasshoppers, that it may be known how to guard against them in order to ward off injury and calamity. On the 7th day of the 8th month in the 13th year of Taukwang [September 20, 1833], we received a communication from the prefect of the [department of Kwangchau], transmitting a despatch from their excellencies the governor-general and governor, as follows:

"'During the fifth month of the present year flights of grasshoppers appeared in the limits of Kwangsí, in [the departments of] Liu, Tsin, Kwei, and Wu, and their vicinage, which have already, according to report, been clean destroyed and driven off. We have heard that in the department of Kauchau and its neighborhood, conterminous to Kwangsí, grasshoppers have appeared which multiply with extreme rapidity. At this time the second crop is in the blade (which if destroyed will endamage the people), and it is proper, therefore, immediately, wherever they are found, to capture and drive them off, marshalling the troops to advance and wholly exterminate them. But Kwangtung heretofore has never experienced this calamity, and we apprehend the officers and people do not understand the mode of capture; wherefore we now exhibit in order the most important rules for catching grasshoppers. Let the governor's combined forces be immediately instructed to capture them *secundum artem;* at the same time let orders be issued for the villagers and farmers at once to assemble and take them, and for the magistrate to establish storehouses for their reception and purchase, thus without fail sweeping them clean away. If you do not exert yourselves to catch the grasshoppers, your guilt will be very great; let it be done carefully, not clandestinely delaying, thus causing this misfortune to come upon yourselves, transgressing the laws, and causing us again, according to the exigencies of the case, to promulgate general orders and make thorough examination, etc., etc. Appended hereto are copies of the rules for catching grasshoppers, which from the lieutenant-governor must be sent to the treasurer, who will enjoin it upon the magistrates of the departments, and he again upon the district magistrates.'

"Having received the preceding, besides respectfully transmitting it to the colonel of the department to be straightway forwarded to all the troops under his authority, and also to all the district justices, that they all with united purpose bend their energies to observe, at the proper time, that whenever the grasshoppers become numerous they join their forces and extirpate them, thus removing calamity from the people; we also enjoin upon whomsoever receives this that the grasshoppers be caught according to these several directions, which are therefore here arranged in order as follows:

"'1. When the grasshoppers first issue forth they are to be seen on the borders of large morasses, from whence they quickly multiply and fill large tracts of land; they produce their young in little hillocks of black earth, using the tail to bore into the ground, not quite an inch in depth, which still remain as open holes, the whole somewhat resembling a bee's nest. One grasshopper drops ten or more pellets, in form like a pea, each one containing a hundred or more young. For the young grasshoppers fly and eat in swarms, and this laying of their young is done all at once and in the same spot; the place resembles a hive of bees, and therefore it is very easily sought and found.

"'2. When the grasshoppers are in the fields of wheat and tender rice and the thick grass, every day at early dawn they all alight on the leaves of the grass, and their bodies being covered with dew are heavy and they cannot fly or hop; at noon they begin to assemble for flight, and at evening they collect in one spot. Thus each day there are three periods when they can be caught, and the people and gentry will also have a short respite. The mode of catching them is to dig a trench before them, the broader and longer the better, on each side placing boards, doors, screens, and such like things, one stretched on after another, and spreading open each side. The whole multitude must then cry aloud, and, holding boards in their hands, drive them all into the trench; meanwhile those on the opposite side, provided with brooms and rakes, on seeing any leaping or crawling out, must sweep them back; then covering them with dry grass, burn them all up. Let the fire be first kindled in the trench, and then drive them into it; for if they are only buried up, then many of them will crawl out of the openings and so escape.

"'3. When the swarms of grasshoppers see a row of trees, or a close line of flags and streamers, they usually hover over and settle; and the farmers frequently suspend red and white clothes and petticoats on long poles, or make red and green paper flags, but they do not always settle with great rapidity. Moreover, they dread the noise of gongs, matchlocks, and guns, hearing which they fly away. If they come so as to obscure the heavens, you must let off the guns and clang the gongs, or fire the crackers; it will strike the front ranks with dread, and flying away, the rest will follow them and depart.

"'4. When the wings and legs of the grasshoppers are taken off, and [their bodies] dried in the sun, the taste is like dried prawns, and moreover, they can be kept a long time without spoiling. Ducks can also be reared upon the dried grasshoppers, and soon become large and fat. Moreover, the hill people catch them to feed pigs; these pigs, weighing at first only twenty catties or so, in ten days' time grow to weigh more than fifty catties; and in rearing all domestic animals they are of use. Let all farmers exert themselves and catch them alive, giving rice or money according to the number taken. In order to remove this calamity from your grain, what fear is there that you will not perform this? Let all these rules for catching the grasshoppers be diligently carried into full effect.'

"Wherefore these commands are transcribed that all you soldiers and people may be fully acquainted with them. Do you all then immediately in obedience to them, when you see the proper time has come, sound the gong; and when you see the grasshoppers and their young increasing, straightway get ready, on the one hand seizing them, and on the other announcing to the officers that they collect the troops, that with united strength you may at once catch them, without fail making an utter extermination of them; thus calamity will be removed from the people. We will also then confer rewards upon those of the farmers and people who first announce to the magistrates their approach. Let every one implicitly obey. A special command.

"Promulgated Taukwang, 13th year, 8th month, and 15th day."[1]

The concluding part of an edict affords some room for displaying the character of the promulgator. Among other endings are such as these: "Hasten! hasten! a special edict." "Tremble hereat intensely." "Lay not up for yourselves future repentance by disobedience." "I will by no means eat my words." "Earnestly observe these things." In their state papers Chinese officers are constantly referring to ultimate truths and axioms, and deducing arguments therefrom in a peculiarly national grandiloquent manner, though some of their

[1] *Easy Lessons in Chinese*, pp. 223–227. The effect of these instructions relating to grasshoppers does not appear to have equalled the zeal of the officers composing them; swarms of locusts, however, are in general neither numerous nor devastating in China.

conclusions are preposterous non-sequiturs. Commissioner Lin addressed a letter to the Queen of England regarding the interdiction of opium, which began with the following preamble:

"Whereas, the ways of Heaven are without partiality, and no sanction is allowed to injure others in order to benefit one's self, and that men's natural feelings are not very diverse (for where is he who does not abhor death and love life?)—therefore your honorable nation, though beyond the wide ocean at a distance of twenty thousand *li*, also acknowledges the same ways of Heaven, the same human nature, and has the like perceptions of the distinctions between life and death, benefit and injury. Our heavenly court has for its family all that is within the four seas; and as to the great Emperor's heaven-like benevolence—there is none whom it does not overshadow; even regions remote, desert, and disconnected have a part in his general care of life and well-being."

The edicts furnish almost the only exponents of the intentions of government. They present several characteristic features of the ignorant conceit and ridiculous assumptions of the Chinese, while they betray the real weakness of the authorities in the mixture of argument and command, coaxing and threatening, pervading every paragraph. According to their phraseology, there can possibly be no failure in the execution of every order; if they are once made known, the obedience of the people follows almost as a matter of course; while at the same time both the writer and the people know that most of them are not only perfunctory but nearly useless. The responsibility of the writer in a measure ceases with the promulgation of his orders, and when they reach the last in the series their efficiency has well nigh departed. Expediency is the usual guide for obedience; deceiving superiors and oppressing the people the rule of action on the part of many officials; and their orders do not more strikingly exhibit their weakness and ignorance than their mendacity and conceit. A large proportion of well-meaning officers are sensible too that all their efforts will be neutralized by the half-paid, unscrupulous retainers and clerks in the *yamuns;* and this checks their energy.

It is not easy, without citing many examples accompanied

with particular explanations, to give a just idea of the actual execution of the laws, and show how far the people are secured in life and property by their rulers; and perhaps nothing has been the source of such differing views regarding the Chinese as the predominance writers give either to the theory or the practice of legislation. Old Magaillans has hit this point pretty well when he says: "It seems as if the legislators had omitted nothing, and that they had foreseen all inconveniences that were to be feared; so that I am persuaded no kingdom in the world could be better governed or more happy, if the conduct and probity of the officers were but answerable to the institution of the government. But in regard they have no knowledge of the true God, nor of the eternal rewards and punishments of the other world, they are subject to no remorses of conscience, they place all their happiness in pleasure, in dignity and riches; and therefore, to obtain these fading advantages, they violate all the laws of God and man, trampling under foot religion, reason, justice, honesty, and all the rights of consanguinity and friendship. The inferior officers mind nothing but how to defraud their superiors, they the supreme tribunals, and all together how to cheat the king; which they know how to do with so much cunning and address, making use in their memorials of words and expressions so soft, so honest, so respectful, so humble and full of adulation, and of reasons so plausible, that the deluded prince frequently takes the greatest falsehoods for solemn truths. So that the people, finding themselves continually oppressed and overwhelmed without any reason, murmur and raise seditions and revolts, which have caused so much ruin and so many changes in the Empire. Nevertheless, there is no reason that the excellency and perfection of the laws of China should suffer for the depravity and wickedness of the magistrates."[1]

Magaillans resided in China nearly forty years, and his opinion may be considered on the whole as a fair judgment of the real condition of the people and the policy of their rulers.

---

[1] *A new History of China, containing a description of the most considerable particulars of that Empire, written by* Gabriel Magaillans, *of the Society of Jesus, Missionary Apostolick. Done out of French.* London, 1688, p. 249.

When one is living in the country itself, to hear the complaints of individuals against the extortion and cruelty of their rulers, and to read the reports of judicial murder, torture, and crime in the *Peking Gazette*, are enough to cause one to wonder how such atrocities and oppressions are endured from year to year, and why the sufferers do not rise and throw aside the tyrannous power which thus abuses them. But the people are generally conscious that their rulers are no better than themselves, and that they would really gain nothing by such a procedure, and their desire to maintain as great a degree of peace as possible leads them to submit to many evils, which in western countries would soon be remedied or cause a revolution. In order to restrain the officers in their misrule, Section CCX. of the code ordains that "If any officer of government, whose situation gives him power and control over the people, not only does not conciliate them by proper indulgence, but exercises his authority in a manner so inconsistent with the established laws and approved usages of the Empire, that the sentiments of the once loyal subjects being changed by his oppressive conduct, they assemble tumultuously and openly rebel, and drive him at length from the capital city and seat of his government; such officer shall suffer death."

By the laws of China, every officer of the nine ranks must be previously qualified for duty by a degree; in the ninth are included village magistrates, deputy treasurers, jailers, etc., but the police, local interpreters, clerks, and other attendants on the courts are not considered as having any rank, and most of them are natives of the place where they are employed. The only degradation they can feel is to turn them out of their stations, but this is hardly a palliative of the evils the people suffer from them; the new leech is more thirsty than the old. The cause of many of the extortions the people suffer from their rulers is found in the system of purchasing office, at all times practised in one shape or other, but occasionally resorted to by the government. As the counterpart of this system, that of receiving bribes must be expected therefore to prevail, and being in fact practised by all grades of dignitaries, and sometimes even upheld by them as a "necessary evil," it adds still more to the bad consequences resulting from this mode of obtaining office. Indeed, so far is the practice of "covering the eyes" carried in China, that the people seldom approach their rulers without a gift to make way for them.

One mode taken by the highest ranks to obtain money is to notify inferiors that there are certain days on which presents are expected, and custom soon increases these as much as the case will admit. Subscriptions for objects of public charity or disbursements, such as an inundation, a bad harvest, bursting of dikes, and other similar things which the government must look after, are not unfrequently made a source of revenue to the incumbents by requiring much more than is needed; those who subscribe are rewarded by an empty title, a peacock's feather, or employment in some insignificant formality. The sale of titular rank is a source of revenue, but the government never attempts to subvert or interfere with the well-known channel of attaining office by literary merit, and it seldom confers much real power for money when unconnected with some degree of fitness. The security of its own position is not to be risked for the sake of an easy means of filling its exchequer, yet it is impossible to say how far the sale of office and title is carried. The censors inveigh against it, and the Emperor almost apologizes for resorting to it, but it is nevertheless constantly practised. The government stocks of this description were opened during the late rebellions and foreign wars, as the necessities of the case were a sufficient excuse for the disreputable practice. In 1835 the sons of two of the leading hong-merchants were promoted, in consequence of their donations of $25,000 each to repair the ravages of an inundation; subscribers to the amount of $10,000 and upward were rewarded by an honorary title, whose only privilege is that it saves its possessor from a bambooing, it being the law that no one holding any office can be personally chastised.[1]

Besides the lower officers, the clerks in their employ and the police, who are often taken from the garrison soldiery, are the agents in the hands of the upper ranks to squeeze the people.

---

[1] Compare the *Chinese Repository*, Vol. XVIII., p. 207.

There are many clerks of various duties and grades about all the offices who receive small salaries, and every application and petition to their superiors, going through their hands, is attended by a bribe to pass them up. The military police and servants connected with the offices are not paid any regular salary, and their number is great. In the large districts, like those of Nanhai and Pwanyu, which compose the city of Canton and suburbs, it is said there are about a thousand unpaid police; in the middle-sized ones between three and four hundred, and in the smallest from one to two hundred. This number is increased by the domestics attending high officers as part of their suite, and by their old acquaintances, who make themselves known when there is any likelihood of being employed. Among other abuses mentioned by the censors is that of magistrates appointing their own creatures to fill vacancies until those nominated by his Majesty arrive; like a poor man oppressing the poor, such officers are a sweeping rain. A similar abuse arises when country magistrates leave their posts to go to the provincial capital to dance attendance upon their superiors, and get nominated to a higher place or taken into their service as secretaries, because they will work for nothing; the duties of their vacated offices are meantime usually left undone, and underlings take advantage of their absence to make new exactions. The governor fills vacant offices with his own friends, and recommends them to his Majesty to be confirmed; but this has little effect in consolidating a system of oppression from the constant changes going on. In fact, it is hard to say which feature of the Chinese polity is the least disastrous to good government, these constant changes which neutralize all sympathy with the people on the part of rulers, or on the other hand make it useless for seditious men to try to foment rebellion.

The retinues of high provincial officers contain many dependents and expectant supernumeraries, all subservient to them; among them are the descendants of poor officers; the sons of bankrupt merchants who once possessed influence; dissipated, well bred, unscrupulous men, who lend themselves to everything flagitious; and lastly, fortune-seekers without money, but possessing talents of good order to be used by any one who will hire them. Such persons are not peculiar to China, and their employment is guarded against in the code, but no law is more of a dead letter. Officers of government, too, conscious of their delinquencies, and afraid their posts will soon be taken from them, of course endeavor to make the most of their opportunities, and by means of such persons, who are usually well acquainted with the leading inhabitants of the district, harass and threaten such as are likely to pay well for being left in quiet. It does them little or no good, however, for if they are not removed they must fee their superiors, and if they are punished for their misdeeds they are still more certain of losing their wicked exactions.

In the misappropriation of public funds, and peculation of all kinds in materials, government stores, rations, wages, and salaries, the Chinese officials are skilled experts, and are never surprised at any disclosures.

Another common mode of plundering the people is for officers to collude with bands of thieves, and allow them to escape for a composition when arrested, or substitute other persons for the guilty party in case the real offenders are likely to be condemned. Sometimes these banditti are too strong even for an upright magistrate, and he is obliged to overlook what he cannot remedy; for, however much he may wish to arrest and bring them to justice, his policemen are too much afraid of their vengeance to venture upon attacking them. An instance of this occurred near Canton in 1839, when a boat, containing a clerk of the court and three or four police, came into the fleet of European opium-ships to hunt for some desperate opium smugglers who had taken refuge there. The fellows, hearing of the arrival of the boat, came in the night, and surrounding it took out the crew, bound their pursuers, and burned them alive with the boat in sight of the whole fleet, to whom the desperadoes looked for protection against their justly incensed countrymen.

A censor in 1819, complaining of flagrant neglect in the administration of justice in Chihlí, says: "Among the magistrates are many who, without fear or shame, connive at robbery and deceit. Formerly, horse-stealers were wont to conceal themselves in some secret place, but now they openly bring their plunder to market for sale. When they perceive a person to be weak, they are in the habit of stealing his property and returning it to him for money, while the officers, on hearing it, treat it as a trivial matter, and blame the sufferer for not being more cautious. Thieves are apprehended with warrants on them, showing that when they were sent out to arrest thieves they availed of the opportunity to steal for themselves. And at a village near the imperial residence are very many plunderers concealed, who go out by night in companies of twenty or thirty persons, carrying weapons with them; they frequently call up the inhabitants, break open the doors, and having satisfied themselves with what food and wine they can obtain, they threaten and extort money, which if they cannot procure they seize their clothes, ornaments, or cattle, and depart. They also frequently go to shops, and having broken open the shutters impudently demand money, which if they do not get they set fire to the shop with the torches in their hands. If the master of the house lay hold on a few of them and sends them to the magistrate, he merely imprisons and beats them, and before half a month allows them to run away."[1]

The unpaid retainers about the *yamuns* are very numerous, and are more dreaded than the police; one censor says they are looked upon by the people as tigers and wolves; he effected the discharge of nearly twenty-four thousand of them in the province of Chihlí alone. They are usually continued in their places by the head magistrate, who, when he arrives, being ignorant of the characters of those he must employ, re-engages such as are likely to serve. In cases of serious accusation the clerks frequently subpœna all who are likely to be implicated, and demand a fee for liberating them when their innocence is shown. These myrmidons still fear the anger of their superiors and a recoil of the people so far as to endeavor to save appearances by hushing up the matter, and liberating those

[1] *Chinese Repository*, Vol. IV., p. 218.

unjustly apprehended, with great protestations of compassion. It may be added that, as life is not lightly taken, thieves are careful not to murder or maltreat their victims dangerously, nor do the magistrates venture to take life outright by torture, though their cruelties frequently result in death by neglect or starvation. Money and goods are what both policemen and officials want, not blood and revenge. Parties at strife with each other frequently resort to legal implication to gratify their ill-will, and take a pitiful revenge by egging on the police to pillage and vex their enemy, though they themselves profit nowise thereby.

The evils resulting from a half-paid and venal magistracy are dreadful, and the prospects of their removal very slight. The governor of Chihlí, in 1829, memorialized the Emperor upon the state of the police, and pointed out a remedy for many abuses, one of which was to pay them fair salaries out of the public treasury; but it is plain that this remedy must begin with the monarch, for until an officer is released from sopping his superior he will not cease exacting from his inferiors. Experience has shown the authorities how far it can safely be carried; while many officers, seeing how useless it is to irritate the people, so far as ultimately enriching themselves is concerned, endeavor to restrain their policemen. One governor issued an edict, stating that none of his domestics were allowed to browbeat shopmen, and thus get goods or eatables below the market price, and permitted the seller to collar and bring them to him for punishment when they did so. When an officer of high rank, as a governor, treasurer, etc., takes the seals of his post, he ofttimes issues a proclamation, exhorting the subordinate ranks to do as he means to do—"to look up and embody the kindness of the high Emperor," and attend to the faithful discharge of their duties. The lower officers, in their turn, join in the cry, and a series of proclamations, by turns hortative and mandatory, are echoed from mastiff, spaniel, and poodle, until the cry ends upon the police. Thus the prefect of Canton says: "There are hard-hearted soldiers and gnawing lictors who post themselves at ferries or markets, or rove about the streets, to extort money under various pretexts; or, being intoxicated, they disturb and annoy the people in a hundred ways. Since I came into office here I have repeatedly commanded the inferior magistrates to act faithfully and seize such persons, but the depraved spirit still continues."

A censor, speaking of the police, says: "They no sooner get a warrant to bring up witnesses than they assail both plaintiff and defendant for money to pay their expenses, from the amount of ten taels to several scores. Then the clerks must have double what the runners get; if their demands be not satisfied they contrive every species of annoyance. Then, again, if there are people of property in the neighborhood, they will implicate them. They plot also with pettifogging lawyers to get up accusations against people, and threaten and frighten them out of their money." [1]

One natural consequence of such a state of society and such a perversion of justice is to render the people afraid of all contact with the officers of government and exceedingly selfish in all their intercourse, though the latter trait needs no particular training to develop it in any heathen country. It also tends to an inhuman disregard of the life of others, and chills every emotion of kindness which might otherwise arise; for by making a man responsible for the acts of his neighbors, or by involving a whole village in the crimes of an individual, all sense of justice is violated. The terror of being implicated in any evil that takes place sometimes prevents the people from quenching fires until the superior authorities be first informed, and from relieving the distressed until it is often too late. Hence, too, it not unfrequently happens that a man who has had the ill fortune to be stabbed to death in the street, or who falls down from disease and dies, remains on the spot till the putrescence obliges the neighbors, for their own safety, to remove the corpse. A dead body floating down the river and washing ashore is likely to remain on the banks until it again drifts away or the authorities get it buried, for no unofficial person would voluntarily run the risk of being seen interring it. One censor reports that when he asked the people why they did not remove the loathsome ob-

---

[1] Compare Doolittle, *Social Life of the Chinese*, Vol. I., p. 330.

ject, they said: "We always let the bodies be either buried in the bellies of fishes or devoured by the dogs; for if we inform the magistrates they are sure to make the owner of the ground buy a coffin, and the clerks and assistants distress us in a hundred ways." The usual end of these memorials and remonstrances is that the police are ordered to behave better, the clerks commanded to abstain from implicating innocent people and retarding the course of justice, and their masters, the magistrates, threatened with the Emperor's displeasure in case the grievance is not remedied: after which all goes on as before, and will go on as long as both rulers and ruled are what they are.

The working out of the principle of responsibility accounts for many things in Chinese society and jurisprudence that otherwise appear completely at variance with even common humanity. It makes an officer careless of his duties if he can shift the responsibility of failure upon his inferiors, who, at the same time, he knows can never execute his orders; it renders the people dead to the impulses of relationship, lest they become involved in what they cannot possibly control and hardly know at the time of its commission. Mr. Lindsay states that when he was at Tsungming in 1832 the officers were very urgent that he should go out of the river, and in order to show him the effect of his non-compliance upon others a degraded subaltern was paraded in his sight. "His cap with its gold button was borne before him, and he marched about blindfolded in procession between two executioners, with a small flag on a bamboo pierced through each ear. Before him was a placard with the inscription, 'By orders of the general of Su and Sung: for a breach of military discipline, his ears are pierced as a warning to the multitude.' His offence was having allowed our boat to pass the fort without reporting it."

During the first war with England, fear of punishment induced many of the subordinates to commit suicide when unable to execute their orders, and the same motive impelled their superiors to avoid the wrath of the Emperor in like fashion. The hong-merchants and linguists at Canton, during the old regime, were constantly liable, from the operation of this principle, to exactions and punishments for the acts of their foreign customers. One of them, Sunshing, was put in prison and ruined because Lord Napier came to Canton from Whampoa in the boat of a ship which the unhappy merchant had "secured" several weeks before, and the linguist and pilot were banished for allowing what they could not possibly have hindered even if they had known it.

Having examined in this general manner the various grades of official rank, we come to the people; and a close view will show that this great mass of human beings exhibits many equally objectionable traits, while oppression, want, clannish rivalry, and brigandage combine to keep it in a constant state of turmoil. The subdivisions into tithings and hundreds are better observed in rural districts than in cities, and the headmen of those communities, in their individual and collective character, possess great influence, from the fact that they represent the popular feeling. In all parts of the country this popular organization is found in some shape or other, though, as if everything was somehow perverted, it not unfrequently is an instrument of greater oppression than defence. The division of the people into clans is far more marked in the southern provinces than in those lying north of the Yangtsz', and has had a depressing effect upon their good government. It resembles in general the arrangement of the Scottish clans, as do the evils arising from their dissensions and feuds those which history records as excited among the Highlanders by the rivalry between Campbells and Macgregors.

The eldership of villages has no necessary connection with the clans, for the latter are unacknowledged by the government, but the clan having the majority in a village generally selects the elders from among their number. This system is of very ancient date; its elementary details are given in the *Chau-lí*, one of the oldest works extant in China; Heeren furnishes the same details for India and Raffles for Java, reaching back in their duration to remote antiquity.[1] In the vicinity of Canton the elder

[1] Heeren, *Asiatic Nations*, Vol. II., p. 259. Raffles, *Java*, Vol. II. App. Biot, *L'Instruction publique*, pp. 59, 200.

is elected by a sort of town meeting, and holds his office during good behavior, receives such a salary as his fellow villagers give him, and may be removed to make way for another whenever the principal persons in the village are displeased with his conduct. His duties are limited to the supervision of the police and general oversight of what is done in the village, and to be a sort of agent or spokesman between the villagers and higher authorities; the duties, the power, and the rank of these officers vary almost indefinitely. The preponderance of one clan prevents much strife in the selection of the elder, but the degree of power reposed in his hand is so small that there is probably little competition to obtain the dignity. A village police is maintained by the inhabitants, under the authority of the elder; the village of Whampoa, for instance, containing about eight thousand inhabitants, pays the elder $300 salary, and employs fourteen watchmen. His duties further consist in deciding upon the petty questions arising between the villagers and visiting the delinquents with chastisement, enforcing such regulations as are deemed necessary regarding festivals, markets, tanks, streets, collection of taxes, etc. The system of surveillance is, however, kept up by the superior officers, who appoint excise officers, grain agents, tide-waiters, or some other subordinate, as the case may require, to exercise a general oversight of the headmen.

The district magistrate, with the *siunkien* and their deputies over the hundred, are the officers to whom appeals are carried from the headmen; they also receive the reports of the elders respecting suspicious characters within their limits, or other matters which they deem worthy of reference or remonstrance. A similarity of interests leads the headmen of many villages to meet together at times in a public hall for secret consultation upon important matters, and their united resolutions are generally acted upon by themselves or by the magistrates, as the case may be. This system of eldership, and the influential position the headmen occupy, is an important safeguard the people possess against the extremity of oppressive extortion; while, too, it upholds the government in strengthening the loyalty of those who feel that the only security they possess against theft, and loss of all things from their seditious countrymen, is to uphold the institutions of the land, and that to suffer the evils of a bad magistracy is less dreadful than the horrors of a lawless brigandage.

The customs and laws of clanship perpetuate a sad state of society, and render districts and villages, otherwise peaceful, the scenes of unceasing turmoil and trouble. There are only about four hundred clans in the whole of China, but inasmuch as all of the same surname do not live in the same place, the separation of a clan answers the same purpose as multiplying it. Clannish feelings and feuds are very much stronger in Kwangtung and Fuhkien than in other provinces. As an instance which may be mentioned, the *Gazette* contains the petition of a man from Chauchau fu, in Kwangtung, relating to a quarrel, stating that "four years before, his kindred having refused to assist two other clans in their feuds, had during that period suffered most shocking cruelties. Ten persons had been killed, and twenty men and women, taken captives, had had their eyes dug out, their ears cut off, their feet maimed, and so rendered useless for life. Thirty houses were laid in ruins and three hundred acres of land seized, ten thousand taels plundered, ancestral temples thrown down, graves dug up, dikes destroyed, and water cut off from the fields. The governor had offered a reward of a thousand taels to any one who would apprehend these persons, but for the ten murders no one had been executed, for the police dare not seize the offenders, whose numbers have largely increased, and who set the laws at defiance." This region is notorious for the turbulence of its inhabitants; it adjoins the province of Fuhkien, and the people, known at Canton as *Hoklo*, emigrate in large numbers to the Indian Archipelago or to other provinces. The later *Gazettes* contain still more dreadful accounts of the contests of the clans, and the great loss of life and property resulting from their forays, no less than one hundred and twenty villages having been attacked, and thousands of people killed. These battles are constantly occurring, and the authorities, feeling themselves too weak to put them down, are obliged to connive at them and let the clans fight it out.

Ill will is kept up between the clans, and private revenges gratified, by every personal annoyance that malice can suggest or opportunity tempt. If an unfortunate individual of one clan is met alone by his enemy, he is sure to be robbed or beaten, or both; the boats or the houses of each party are plundered or burned, and legal redress is almost impossible. Graves are defaced and tombstones injured, and on the annual visit to the family sepulchre perhaps a putrid corpse is met, placed there by the hostile clan; this insult arouses all their ire, and they vow deadly revenge. The villagers sally out with such arms as they possess, and death and wounds are almost sure to result before they separate. In Shunteh (a district between Canton and Macao) upward of a thousand men engaged with spears and firearms on one of these occasions, and thirty-six lives were lost; the military were called in to quell the riot. In Tungkwan district, southeast of Canton, thirty-six ringleaders were apprehended, and in 1831 it was reported that four hundred persons had been killed in these raids; only twenty-seven of their kindred appealed to government for redress.

When complaint is made to the prefect or governor, and investigation becomes inevitable, the villagers have a provision to meet the exigencies of the case, which puts the burden of the charges as equally as possible upon the whole clan. A band of "devoted men" are found—persons who volunteer to assume such crimes and run their chance for life—whose names are kept on a list, and they come forward and surrender themselves to government as the guilty persons. On the trial their friends employ witnesses to prove it a justifiable homicide, and magnify the provocation, and if there are several brought on the stand at once they try to get some of them clear by proving an alibi. It not unfrequently happens that the accused are acquitted—seldom that they are executed; transportation or a fine is the usual result. The inducement for persons to run this risk of their lives is security from the clan of a maintenance for their families in case of death, and a reward, sometimes as high as $300, in land or money when they return. This sum is raised by taxing the clan or village, and the imposition falls heavily on the poorer portion of it, who can neither avoid nor easily pay it. This system of substitution pervades all parts of society, and for all misdemeanors. A person was strangled in Macao in 1838 for having been engaged in the opium trade, who had been hired by the real criminal to answer to his name. Another mode of escape, sometimes tried in such cases when the person has been condemned, is to bribe the jailers to report him dead and carry out his body in a coffin; but this device probably does not often answer the end, as the turnkeys require a larger bribe than can be raised. There can be little doubt of the prevalence of the practice, and for crimes of even minor penalty.

To increase the social evils of clanship and systematized thieving, local tyrants occasionally spring up, persons who rob and maltreat the villagers by means of their armed retainers, who are in most cases, doubtless, members of the same clan. One of these tyrants, named *Yeh*, or Leaf, became quite notorious in the district of Tungkwan in 1833, setting at defiance all the power of the local authorities, and sending out his men to plunder and ravage whoever resisted his demands, destroying their graves and grain, and particularly molesting those who would not deliver up their wives or daughters to gratify him. He was arrested through craft by the district magistrate at Canton leaving his office and inducing him, for old acquaintance sake, to return with him to the provincial city; he was there tried and executed by the governor, although it was at the time reported that the Board of Punishments endeavored to save his life because he had been in office at the capital. In order that no attempt should be made to rescue him, he was left in ignorance of his sentence until he was put into the sedan to be carried to execution.

Clannish banditti often supply themselves with firearms, and prowling the country to revenge themselves on their enemies, soon proceed to pillage every one; in disarming them the government is sometimes obliged to resort to contemptible subterfuges, which conspicuously show its weakness and encourage a repetition of the evil. Parties of tramps, called *hakka*, or 'guests,' roam over Kwangtung province, squatting on vacant places along the shores, away from the villages, and forming small clannish communities; as soon as they increase, occupying more and more of the land, they begin to commit petty depredations upon the crops of the inhabitants, and demand money for the privilege of burying upon the unoccupied ground around them. The government is generally unwilling to drive them off by force, because there is the alternative of making them robbers thereby, and they are invited to settle in other waste lands, which they can have free of taxation, and leave those they have cultivated if strictly private property. This practice shows the populousness of the country in a conspicuous manner. To these evils must be also added the large bodies of floating banditti or dakoits, who rove up and down all the watercourses "like sneaking rats" and pounce upon defenceless boats. Hardly a river or estuary in the land is free from these miscreants, and lives and property are annually destroyed by them to a very great amount, especially on the Yangtsz', the Pearl River, and other great thoroughfares.

The popular associations in cities and towns are chiefly based upon a community of interests, resulting either from a similarity of occupation, when the leading persons of the same calling form themselves into guilds, or from the municipal regulations requiring the householders living in the same street to unite to maintain a police and keep the peace of their division. Each guild has an assembly-hall, where its members meet to hold the festival of their patron saint, to collect and appropriate the subscriptions of the members and settle the rent or storage on the rooms and goods in the hall, to discuss all public matters as well as the good cheer they get on such occasions, and to confer with other guilds. The members often go to a great expense in emulating each other in their processions, and some rivalry exists regarding their rights, over which the government keeps a watchful eye, for all popular assemblies are its horror. The shopkeepers and householders in the same street are required to have a headman to superintend the police, watchmen, and beggars within his limits. The rulers are sometimes thwarted in their designs by both these forms of popular assemblies, and they no doubt tend in many ways to keep up a degree of independence and of mutual acquaintance, which compels the respect of the government. The governor of Canton in 1838 endeavored to search all the shops in a particular street, to ascertain if there was opium in them; but the shopmen came in a body at the head of the street, and told the policemen that they would on no account permit their shops to be searched. The governor deemed it best to retire. Those who will not join or agree to what the majority orders in these bodies occasionally experience petty tyranny, but in a city this must be comparatively trifling. Several of the leading men in the city are known to hold meetings for consultation in still more popular assemblies for different reasons of a public and pressing nature. There is a building at Canton called the *Ming-lun Tang*, or "Free Discussion Hall," where political matters are discussed under the knowledge of government, which rather tries to mould than put them down, for the assistance of such bodies, rightly managed, in carrying out their intentions, is considerable, while discontent would be roused if they were forcibly suppressed. In October, 1842, meetings were held in this hall, at one of which a public manifesto was issued, here quoted entire as a specimen of the public appeals of Chinese politicians and orators:

"We have been reverently consulting upon the Empire—a vast and undivided whole! How can we permit it to be severed in order to give it to others? Yet we, the rustic people, can learn to practise a rude loyalty; we too know to destroy the banditti, and thus requite his Majesty. Our Great Pure dynasty has cared for this country for more than two hundred years, during which a succession of distinguished monarchs, sage succeeding sage, has reigned; and we who eat the herb of the field, and tread the soil, have for ages drank in the dew of imperial goodness, and been imbued with its benevolence. The people in wilds far remote beyond our influence have also felt this goodness, comparable to the heavens for height, and been upheld by this bounty, like the earth for thickness. Wherefore peace being now settled in the country, ships of all lands come, distant though they be from this for many a myriad of miles; and of all the foreigners on the south and west there is not one but what enjoys the highest peace and contentment, and entertains the profoundest respect and submission.

"But there is that English nation, whose ruler is now a woman and then a man, its people at one time like birds and then like beasts, with dispositions more fierce and furious than the tiger or wolf, and hearts more greedy than the snake or hog—this people has ever stealthily devoured all the southern barbarians, and like the demon of the night they now suddenly exalt themselves. During the reigns of Kienlung and Kiaking these English barbarians humbly besought entrance and permission to make a present; they also presumptuously requested to have Chusan, but those divine personages, clearly perceiving their traitorous designs, gave them a peremptory refusal. From that time, linking themselves in with traitorous traders, they have privily dwelt at Macao, trading largely in opium and poisoning our brave people. They have ruined lives—how many millions none can tell; and wasted property—how many thousands of millions who can guess! They have dared again and again to murder Chinese, and have secreted the murderers, whom they have refused to deliver up, at which the hearts of all men grieved and their heads ached. Thus it has been that for many years past the English, by their privily watching for opportunities in the country, have gradually brought things to the present crisis.

"In 1838, our great Emperor having fully learned all the crimes of the English and the poisonous effects of opium, quickly wished to restore the good condition of the country and compassionate the people. In consequence of the memorial of Hwang Tsioh-sz', and in accordance to his request, he specially deputed the public-minded, upright, and clear-headed minister, Lin Tseh-sü, to act as his imperial commissioner with plenipotentiary powers, and go to Canton to examine and regulate. He came and took all the stored-up opium and stopped the trade, in order to cleanse the stream and cut off the fountain; kindness was mixed with his severity, and virtue was evident in his laws, yet still the English repented not of their errors, and as the climax of their contumacy called troops to their aid. The censor Hwang, by advising peace, threw down the barriers, and bands of audacious robbers willingly did all kinds of disreputable and villainous deeds. During the past three years these rebels, depending upon their stout ships and effective cannon, from Canton went to Fuhkien, thence to Chehkiang and on to Kiangsu, seizing our territory, destroying our civil and military authorities, ravishing our women, capturing our property, and bringing upon the inhabitants of these four provinces intolerable miseries. His Imperial Majesty was troubled and afflicted, and this added to his grief and anxiety. If you wish to purify their crimes, all the fuel in the Empire will not suffice, nor would the vast ocean be enough to wash out our resentment. Gods and men are alike filled with indignation, and Heaven and Earth cannot permit them to remain.

"Recently, those who have had the management of affairs in Kiangnan have been imitating those who were in Canton, and at the gates of the city they have willingly made an agreement, peeling off the fat of the people to the tune of hundreds of myriads, and all to save the precious lives of one or two useless officers; in doing which they have exactly verified what Chancellor Kin Ying-lin had before memorialized. Now these English rebels are barbarians dwelling in a petty island beyond our domains; yet their coming throws myriads of miles of country into turmoil, while their numbers do not exceed a few myriads. What can be easier than for our celestial dynasty to exert its fulness of power and exterminate these contemptible sea-going imps, just as the blast bends the pliant bamboo? But our highest officers and ministers cherish their precious lives, and civil and military men both dread a dog as they would a tiger; regardless of the enemies of their country or the griefs of the people, they have actually sundered the Empire and granted its wealth; acts more flagitious these than those of the traitors in the days of the Southern Sung dynasty, and the reasons for which are wholly beyond our comprehension. These English barbarians are at bottom without ability, and yet we have all along seen in the memorials that officers exalt and dilate upon their prowess and obstinacy; our people are courageous and enthusiastic, but the officers on the contrary say that they are dispirited and scattered: this is for no other reason than to coerce our prince to make peace, and then they will luckily avoid the penalty due for 'deceiving the prince and betraying the country.' Do you doubt? Then look at the memorial of Chancellor Kin Ying-lin, which says: 'They take the occasion of war to seek for self-aggrandizement;' every word of which directly points at such conduct as this.

"We have recently read in his Majesty's lucid mandate that 'There is no other way, and what is requested must be granted;' and that 'We have conferred extraordinary powers upon the ministers, and they have done nothing but deceive us.' Looking up we perceive his Majesty's clear discrimination and divine perception, and that he was fully aware of the imbecility of his ministers; he remembers too the loyal anger of his people. He has accordingly now temporarily settled all the present difficulties, but it is that, having matured his plans, he may hereafter manifest his indignation, and show to the Empire that it had not fathomed the divine awe-inspiring counsels.

"The dispositions of these rebellious English are like that of the dog or sheep, whose desires can never be satisfied; and therefore we need not inquire whether the peace now made be real or pretended. Remember that when they last year made disturbance at Canton they seized the Square fort, and thereupon exhibited their audacity, everywhere plundering and ravishing. If it had not been that the patriotic inhabitants dwelling in Hwaitsing and other hamlets, and those in Shingping, had not killed their leader and destroyed their devilish soldiers, they would have scrupled at nothing, taking and pillaging the city, and then firing it in order to gratify their vengeance and greediness: can we imagine that for the paltry sum of six millions of dollars they would, as they did, have raised the siege and retired? How to be regretted! That when the fish was in the frying-pan, the Kwangchau fu should come and pull away the firewood, let loose the tiger to return to the mountains, and disarm the people's indignation. Letting the enemy thus escape on one occasion has successively brought misery upon many provinces: whenever we speak of it, it wounds the heart and causes the tears to flow.

"Last year, when the treaty of peace was made, it was agreed that the English should withdraw from beyond Lankeet, that they should give back the forts near there and dwell temporarily at Hongkong, and that thenceforth all military operations were forever to cease. Who would have supposed that before the time stipulated had passed away they would have turned their backs upon this agreement, taken violent possession of the forts at the Bogue with their 'wooden dragons' [*i.e.*, ships of war]—and when they came upon the gates of the City of Rams with their powerful forces, who was there to oppose them? During these three years we have not been able to restore things as at first, and their deceptive craftiness, then confined to these regions, has rapidly extended itself to Kiangnan. But our high and mighty Emperor, preeminently intelligent and discerning [*lit.* grasping the golden mirror and holding the gemmeous balances], consents to demean himself to adopt soothing counsels of peace, and therefore submissively accords with the decrees of Heaven. Having a suspicion that these outlandish people intended to encroach upon us, he has secretly arranged all things. We have respectfully read through all his Majesty's mandates, and they are as clear-sighted as the sun and moon; but those who now manage affairs are like one who, supposing the raging fire to be under, puts himself as much at ease as swallows in a court, but who, if the calamity suddenly reappears, would be as defenceless as a grampus in a fish-market. The law adjudges the penalty of death for betraying the country, but how can even death atone for their crimes? Those persons who have been handed down to succeeding ages with honor, and those whose memories have been execrated, are but little apart on the page of righteous history; let our rulers but remember this, and we think they also must exert themselves to recover their characters. We people have had our day in times of great peace, and this age is one of abundant prosperity; scholars are devising how to recompense the kindness of the government, nor can husbandmen think of forgetting his Majesty's exertions for them. Our indignation was early excited to join battle with the enemy, and we then all urged one another to the firmest loyalty.

"We have heard the English intend to come into Pearl River and make a settlement; this will not, however, stop at Chinese and foreigners merely dwelling together, for men and beasts cannot endure each other; it will be like opening the door and bowing in the thief, or setting the gate ajar and letting the wolf in. While they were kept outside there were many traitors within; how much more, when they encroach even to our bedsides, will our troubles be augmented? We cannot help fearing it will eventuate in something strange, which words will be insufficient to express. If the rulers of other states wish to imitate the English, with what can their demands be waived? Consequently, the unreasonable demands of the English are going to bring great calamity upon the people and deep sorrow to the country. If we do not permit them to dwell with us under the same heaven, our spirits will feel no shame; but if we willingly consent to live with them, we may in truth be deemed insensate.

"We have reverently read in the imperial mandate, 'There must indeed be some persons among the people of extraordinary wisdom or bravery, who can stir them up to loyalty and patriotism or unite them in self-defence; some who can assist the government and army to recover the cities, or else defend passes of importance against the robbers; some who can attack and burn their vessels, or seize and bring the heads of their doltish leaders; or else some with divine presence and wisdom, who can disclose all their silly counsels and get to themselves a name of surpassing merit and ability and receive the highest rewards. We can confer,' etc., etc. We, the people, having received the imperial words, have united ourselves together as troops, and practise the plan of joining hamlets and villages till we have upward of a million of troops, whom we have provisioned according to the scale of estimating the produce of respective farms; and now we are fully ready and quite at ease as to the result. If nothing calls us, then each one will return to his own occupation; but if the summons come, joining our strength in force we will incite each other to effort; our brave sons and brothers are all animated to deeds of arms, and even our wives and daughters, finical and delicate as jewels, have learned to discourse of arms. At first, alas, those who guarded the passes were at ease and careless, and the robbers came unbidden and undesired; but now [if they come], we have only zealously to appoint each other to stations, and suppress the rising of the waves to the stillest calm [*i.e.*, to exterminate them]. When the golden pool is fully restored to peace, and his Majesty's anxiety for the south relieved; when the leviathan has been driven away, then will our anger, comparable to the broad ocean and high heavens, be pacified.

"Ah! We here bind ourselves to vengeance, and express these our sincere intentions in order to exhibit great principles; and also to manifest Heaven's retribution and rejoice men's hearts, we now issue this patriotic declaration. The high gods clearly behold: do not lose your first resolution."[1]

This spirited paper was subsequently answered by the party desirous of peace, but the anti-English feeling prevailed, and the committee appointed by the meeting set the English consulate on fire a few days after, to prevent it being occupied. There were many reasons at the time for this dislike; its further exhibition, however, ended with this attack, and has now pretty much died out with the rising of a new generation.

The many secret associations existing among the people are mostly of a political character, but have creeds like religious sects, and differ slightly in their tenets and objects of worship. They are traceable to the system of clans, which giving the people at once the habit and spirit for associations, are easily made use of by clever men for their own purposes of opposition to government. Similar grievances, as local oppression, hatred of the Manchus, or hope of advantage, add to their numbers and strength, and were they founded on a full acquaintance with the grounds of a just resistance to despotism, they would soon overturn the government; but as out of an adder's egg only a cockatrice can be hatched, so until the people are enlightened with regard to their just rights, no permanent melioration can be expected. It is against that leading feature in the Manchu policy, *isolation*, that these societies sin, which further prompts to systematic efforts to suppress them. The only objection

[1] *Chinese Repository*, Vol. XI., p. 630.

the supreme government seems to have against the religion of the people is that it brings them together; they may be Buddhists, Rationalists, Jews, Mohammedans, or Christians, apparently, if they will worship in secret and apart. On the other hand, the people naturally connect some religious rites with their opposition and cabals in order to more securely bind their members together.

The name of the most powerful of these associations is mentioned in Section CLXII. of the code for the purpose of interdicting it; since then it has apparently changed its designation from the *Pih-lien kiao*, or 'Water-lily sect,' to the *Tien-tí hwui* or *San-hoh hwui*, *i.e.*, 'Triad society,' though both names still exist, the former in the northern, the latter in the maritime provinces and Indian Archipelago; their ramifications take also other appellations. The object of these combinations is to overturn the reigning dynasty, and in putting this prominently forward they engage many to join them. About the beginning of the century a wide-spread rebellion broke out in the northwestern and middle provinces, which was put down after eight years' war, attended with desolation and bloodshed; since that time the Water-lily sect has not been so often spoken of. The Triad society has extended itself along the coasts, but it is not popular, owing more than anything else to its illegality, and the intimidation and oppression employed toward those who will not join it. The members have secret regulations and signs, and uphold and assist each other both in good and bad acts, but, as might be inferred from their character, screening evil doers from just punishment oftener than relieving distressed members. The original designs of the association may have been good, but what was allowable in them soon degenerated into a systematic plan for plunder and aim at power. The government of Hongkong enacted in 1845 that any Chinese living in that colony who was ascertained to belong to the Triad society should be declared guilty of felony, be imprisoned for three years, and after branding expelled the colony. These associations, if they cause the government much trouble by interfering with its operations, in no little degree, through the overbearing conduct of the leaders, uphold it by showing the people what may be expected if they should ever get the upper hand.[1]

The evils of mal-administration are to be learned chiefly from the memorials of censors, and although they may color their statements a little, very gross inaccuracies would be used to their own disadvantage, and contradicted by so many competitors, that most of their statements may be regarded as having some foundation. An unknown person in Kwangtung memorialized the Emperor in 1838 concerning the condition of that province, and drew a picture of the extortions of the lower agents of government that needs no illustrations to deepen its darkness or add force to its complaints. An extract from each of the six heads into which the memorial is divided will indicate the principal sources of popular insurrection in China, besides the exhibition they give of the tyranny of the officers.

In his preface, after the usual laudation of the beneficence and popularity of the monarch, the memorialist proceeds to express his regret that the imperial desires for the welfare of his subjects should be so grievously thwarted by the villany of his officers. After mentioning the calamities which had visited the province in the shape of freshets, insurrections, and conflagrations, he says that affairs generally had become so bad as to compel his Majesty to send commissioners to Canton repeatedly in order to regulate them. "If such as this be indeed the state of things," he inquires, "what wonder is it if habits of plunder characterize the people, or the clerks and under officers of the public courts, as well as village pettifoggers, lay themselves out on all occasions to stir up quarrels and instigate false accusations against the good?" He recommends reform in six departments, under each of which he thus specifies the evils to be remedied:

---

[1] Compare Dr. Milne, in *Transactions R. A. S. of Gr. Brit. and Irel.*, Vol. I., p. 240 (1825). *Journal of the R. A. S.*, Vol. I., p. 93, and Vol. VI., p. 120. *Chinese Repository*, Vol. XVIII., pp. 280–295. A. Wylie, in the *Shanghai Almanac for* 1854. *Notes and Queries on C. and J.*, Vol. III., p. 55. T. T. Meadows, *The Chinese and their Rebellions*, London, 1856. Gustave Schlegel, *Thian Ti Hwui, the Hung-League or Heaven-Earth-League. A Secret Society with the Chinese in China and India*, Batavia, 1866.

First.—In the department of police there is great negligence and delay in the decision of judicial cases. Cases of plunder are very common, most of which are committed by banditti under the designations of Triad societies, Heaven and Earth brotherhoods, etc. These men carry off persons to extort a ransom, falsely assume the character of policemen, and in simulated revenue cutters pass up and down the rivers, plundering the boats of travellers and forcibly carrying off the women. Husbandmen are obliged to pay these robbers an "indemnity," or else as soon as the crops are ripe they come and carry off the whole harvest. In the precincts of the metropolis, where their contiguity to the tribunals prevents their committing depredations in open day, they set fire to houses during the night, and under the pretence of saving and defending the persons and property carry off both of them; hence, of late years, calamitous fires have increased in frequency, and the bands of robbers multiplied greatly. In cases of altercations among the villagers, who can only use their local patois, it rests entirely with the clerks to interpret the evidence; and when the magistrate is lax or pressed with business, they have the evidence pre-arranged and join with bullies and strife-makers to subvert right and wrong, fattening themselves upon bribes extorted under the names of "memoranda of complaints," "purchases of replies," etc., and retarding indefinitely the decision of cases. They also instigate thieves to bring false accusations against the good, who are thereby ruined by legal expenses. While the officers of the government and the people are thus separated, how can it be otherwise than that appeals to the higher tribunals should be increased and litigation and strife prevail?

Second.—Magistrates overrate the taxes with a view to a deduction for their own benefit, and excise officers connive at non-payment. The revenue of Kwangtung is paid entirely in money, and the magistrates, instead of taking the commutation at a regular price of about five dollars for one hundred and fifty pounds of rice, have compelled the people to pay nine dollars and over, because the inundation and bad harvests had raised the price of grain. In order to avoid this extortion the police go to the villagers and demand a douceur, when they will get them off from all payment. But the imperial coffers are not filled by this means, and the people are by and by forced to pay up their arrearages, even to the loss of most of their possessions.

Third.—There is great mismanagement of the granaries, and instead of being any assistance to the people in time of scarcity, they are only a source of peculation for those who are charged with their oversight.

Fourth.—The condition of the army and navy is a disgrace; illicit traffic is not prevented, nor can insurrections be put down. The only care of the officers is to obtain good appointments, and reduce the actual number of soldiers below the register in order that they may appropriate the stores. The cruisers aim only to get fees to allow the prosecution of the contraband traffic, nor will the naval officers bestir themselves to recover the property of plundered boats, but rather become the protectors of the lawless and partakers of their booty. Robberies are so common on the rivers that the traders from the island of Hainan, and Chauchau near Fuhkien, prefer to come by sea, but the revenue cutters overhaul them under pretence of searching for contraband articles, and practise many extortions.

Fifth.—The monopoly of salt needs to be guarded more strictly, and the private manufacture of salt stopped, for thereby the revenue from this source is materially diminished.

Sixth.—The increase of smuggling is so great, and the evils flowing from it so multiplied, that strong measures must be taken to repress it. Traitorous Chinese combine with depraved foreigners to set the laws at defiance, and dispose of their opium and other commodities for the pure silver. In this manner the country is impoverished and every evil arises, the revenues of the customs are diminished by the unnecessary number of persons employed and by the fees they receive for connivance. If all these abuses can be remedied, "it will be seen that when there are men to rule well, nothing can be found beyond the reach of their government."

The chief efforts of officials are directed to put down banditti, and maintain such a degree of peace as will enable them to collect the revenue and secure the people in the quiet possession of their property; but the people are too ready to resist their rulers, and this brings into operation a constant struggle of op posing desires. One side gets into the habit of resisting even the proper requisitions of the officers, who, on their part, endeavor in every way to reimburse their outlay in bribes to their superiors; and the combined action of the two proves an insurmountable impediment to the attainment of even that degree of security a Chinese officer wishes. The general commission of robbery and dakoity, and the prevalence of bands of thieves, therefore proves the weakness of the government, not the insurrectionary disposition of the people. In one district of Hupeh the governor reported in 1828 that "very few of the inhabitants have any regular occupation, and their dispositions are exceedingly ferocious; they fight and kill each other on every provocation. In their villages they harbor thieves who flee from other districts, and sally forth again to plunder." In the northern parts of Kwangtung the people have erected high and strongly built houses to which they flee for safety from the attacks of robbers. These bands sometimes fall upon each other, and the feudal animosities of clanship adding fuel and rage to the rivalry of partisan warfare, the destruction of life and property is great. Occasionally the people zealously assist their rulers to apprehend them, though their exertions depend altogether upon the energy of the incumbent; an officer in Fuhkien is recommended for promotion because he had apprehended one hundred and seventy-three persons, part of a band of robbers which had infested the department for years, and tried and convicted one thousand one hundred and sixty criminals, most or all of whom were probably executed.

In 1821 there were four hundred robbers taken on the borders of Fuhkien; in 1827 two hundred were seized in the south of the province, and forty-one more brought to Canton from the eastward. The governor offered $1,000 reward for the capture of one leader, and $3,000 for another. The judge of the province put forth a proclamation upon the subject in the same year, in which he says there were four hundred and thirty undecided cases of robbery by brigands then on the calendar; and in 1846 there were upward of two thousand waiting his decision, for each of which there were perhaps five or six persons in prison or under constraint until the case was settled. These bands prowl in the large cities and commit great cruelties. In 1830 a party of five hundred openly plundered a rich man's house in the western suburbs of Canton; and in Shunteh, south of the city, $600 were paid for the ransom of two persons carried off by them. The ex-governor, in 1831, was attacked by them near the Mei ling pass on his departure from Canton, and plundered of about ten thousand dollars. The magistrates of Hiangshan district, south of Canton, were ordered by their superiors the same year to apprehend five hundred of the robbers. Priests sometimes harbor gangs in their temples and divide the spoils with them, and occasionally go out themselves on predatory excursions. No mercy is shown these miscreants when they are taken, but the multiplication of executions has no effect in deterring them from crime.

Cruelty to individual prisoners does not produce so much disturbance to the general peace of the community as the forcible attempts of officers to collect taxes. The people have the impression that their rulers exact more than is legal, and consequently consider opposition to the demands of the tax-gatherer as somewhat justifiable, which compels, of course, more stringent measures on the part of the authorities, whose station depends not a little on their punctuality in remitting the taxes. Bad harvests, floods, or other public calamities render the people still more disinclined to pay the assessments. In 1845 a serious disturbance arose near Ningpo on this account, which with unimportant differences could probably be paralleled in every prefecture in the land. The people of Funghwa hien having refused to pay an onerous tax, the prefect of Ningpo seized three literary men of the place, who had been deputed to collect it, and put them in prison; this procedure so irritated the gentry that the candidates at the literary examination which occurred at Funghwa soon afterward, on being assembled at the public hall before the *chíhien*, rose upon him and beat him severely. They were still further incensed against him from having recently detected him in deceitful conduct regarding a petition they had made at court to have their taxes lightened; he had kept the answer and pocketed the difference. He was consequently superseded by another magistrate, and a deputy of the intendant of circuit was sent with the new incumbent to restore order. But the deputy, full of his importance, carried himself so haughtily that the excited populace treated him in the same manner, and he barely escaped with his life to Ningpo. The intendant and prefect, finding matters rising to such a pitch, sent a detachment of twelve hundred troops to keep the peace, but part of these were decoyed within the walls and attacked with such vigor that many of them were made prisoners, a colonel and a dozen privates killed, and two or three hundred wounded or beaten, and all deprived of their arms. In this plight they returned to Ningpo, and, as the distance is not great, apprehensions were entertained lest the insurgents should follow up their advantage by organizing themselves and marching upon the city to seize the prefect. The officers sent immediately to Hangchau for assistance, from whence the governor sent a strong force of ten thousand men to restore order, and soon after arrived himself. He demanded three persons to be given up who had been active in fomenting the resistance, threatening in case of non-compliance that he would destroy the town; the prefect and his deputy from the intendant's office were suspended and removed to another post. These measures restored quiet to a considerable extent.[1]

The existence of such evils in Chinese society would rapidly disorganize it were it not for the conservative influence upon society of early education and training in industry. The government takes care to avail itself of this better element in public opinion, and grounds thereon a basis of action for the establishment of good order. But this, and ten thousand similar instances, only exhibit more strongly how great a work there is to be done before high and low, people and rulers, will understand their respective duties and rights; before they will, on the one hand, pay that regard to the authority of their rulers which is necessary for the maintenance of good order, and, on the other, resist official tyranny in preserving their own liberties.

If the character of the officers, therefore, be such as has been

---

[1] *Missionary Chronicle*, Vol. XIV., p. 140. Smith's *China*, p. 250.

briefly shown—open to bribery, colluding with criminals, sycophantic toward superiors, and cruel to the people; and the constituents of society present so many repulsive features—opposing clans engaged in deadly feuds, bandits scouring the country to rob, policemen joining to oppress, truth universally disregarded, selfishness the main principle of action, and almost every disorganizing element but imperfectly restrained from violent outbreaks and convulsions, it will not be expected that the regular proceedings of the courts and the execution of the laws will prove on examination to be any better than the materials of which they are composed. As civil and criminal cases are all judged by one officer, one court tries nearly all the questions which arise. A single exception is provided for in the code, wherein it is ordered that "in cases of adultery, robbery, fraud, assaults, breach of laws concerning marriage, landed property or pecuniary contracts, or any other like offences committed by or against individuals in the military class—if any of the people are implicated or concerned, the military commanding officer and the civil magistrate shall have a concurrent jurisdiction."[1]

At the bottom of the judicial scale are the village elders. This incipient element of the democratic principle has also existed in India in much the same form; but while its power ended in the local eldership there, in China it is only the lowest step of the scale. The elders give character to the village, and are expected to manage its public affairs, settle disputes among its inhabitants, arrange matters with other villages, and answer to the magistrates on its behalf. The code provides that all persons having complaints and informations address themselves in the first instance to the lowest tribunal of justice in the district, from which the cognizance of the affair may be transferred to the superior tribunals. The statement of the case is made in writing, and the officer is required to act upon it immediately; if the parties are dissatisfied with the award, the judgment of the lower courts is carried up to the superior ones. No case can

[1] For cases of this sort in Cambodia, Rémusat makes mention of a variety of ordeals which curiously resemble those resorted to on the continent of Europe during the Middle Ages. *Nouveaux Mélanges*, Tome I., p. 126.

be carried directly to the Emperor; it must go through the Board of Punishments; old men and women, however, sometimes present petitions to him on his journeys, but such appeals seldom occur, owing to the difficulty of access. The captains in charge of the gates of Peking, in 1831, presented a memorial upon the subject, in which they attribute the number of appeals to the obstinacy of many persons in pressing their cases and the remissness of local officers, so that even women and girls of ten years of age take long journeys to Peking to state their cases. The memorialists recommend that an order be issued requiring the two high provincial officers to adjudicate all cases, either themselves or by a court of errors, and not send the complainants back to the district magistrates. These official porters must have been much troubled with young ladies coming to see his Majesty, or perhaps were advised to present such a paper to afford a text for the Emperor to preach from; to confer such power upon the governor and his associates would almost make them the irresponsible sovereigns of the provinces. Appeals frequently arise out of delay in obtaining justice, owing to the amount of business in the courts; for the calendar may be expected to increase when the magistrate leaves his post to curry favor with his superiors. The almost utter impossibility of learning the truth of the case brought before them, either from the principal parties or the witnesses, must be borne in mind when deciding upon the oppressive proceedings of the magistrates to elicit the truth. Mention is made of one officer promoted for deciding three hundred cases in a year; again of a district magistrate who tried upward of a thousand within the same period; while a third revised and decided more than six hundred in which the parties had appealed. What becomes of the appeals in such cases, or whose decision stands, does not appear; but if such proceedings are common, it accounts for the constant practice of sending appeals back to be revised, probably after a change in the incumbent.

Few or no civil cases are reported in the *Gazette* as being carried up to higher courts, and probably only a small proportion of them are brought before the authorities, the rest being settled by reference. Appeals to court receive attention, and it may be inferred, too, that many of them are mentioned in the *Gazette* in order that the carefulness of the supreme government in revising the unjust decrees against the people should be known through the country, and this additional check to malversation on the part of the lower courts be of some use. Many cases are reported of widows and daughters, sons and nephews, of murdered persons, to whom the revenge of kindred rightly belongs, appealing against the unjust decrees of the local magistrates, and then sent back to the place they came from; this, of course, was tantamount to a *nolle prosequi*. At other times the wicked judges have been degraded and banished. One case is reported of a man who found his way to the capital from Fuhkien to complain against the magistracy and police, who protected a clan by whom his only son had been shot, in consideration of a bribe of $2,000. His case could not be understood at Peking in consequence of his local pronunciation, which indicates that all cases are not reported in writing. One appeal is reported against the governor of a province for not carrying into execution the sentence of death passed on two convicted murderers; and another appellant requests that two persons, who were bribed to undergo the sentence of the law instead of the real murderers, might not be substituted—he, perhaps, fearing their subsequent vengeance.

All officers of government are supposed to be accessible at any time, and the door of justice to be open to all who claim a hearing; and in fact, courts are held at all hours of night and day, though the regular time is from sunrise to noonday. The style of address varies according to the rank; *tajin*, or magnate, for the highest, *ta laoyé*, or great Sir, and *laoyé*, Sir, for the lower grade, are the most common. A drum is said to be placed at the inferior tribunals, as well as before the Court of Representation in Peking, which the plaintiff strikes in order to make his presence known, though from the number of hangers-on about the doors of official residences, the necessity of employing this mode of attracting notice is rare. At the gate of the governor-general's palace are placed six tablets, having appropriate inscriptions for those who have been wronged by wicked officers; for those who have suffered from thieves; for persons falsely accused; for those who have been swindled; for such as have been grieved by other parties; and lastly, for those who have secret information to impart. The people, however, are aware how useless it would be to inscribe their appeals upon these tablets; they write them out and carry them up to his excellency, or to the proper official—seldom forgetting the indispensable present.

Magistrates are not allowed to go abroad in ordinary dress and without their official retinue, which varies for the different grades of rank. The usual attendants of the district magistrates are lictors with whips and chains—significant of the punishments they inflict; they are preceded by two gong-

Mode of Carrying High Officers in Sedan.

bearers, who every few moments strike a certain number of raps to intimate their master's rank, and by two avant-couriers, who howl out an order for all to make room for the great man. A servant bearing aloft a *lo*, or state umbrella (of which a drawing is given on the title-page), also goes before him, further to increase his display and indicate his rank.[1] A subaltern usually runs by the side of his sedan, and his secretary and messengers, seated in more ordinary chairs or following on foot, make up the cortége. The highest officers are carried by eight bearers, others by four, and the lowest by two. Lanterns are used at night and red tablets in the daytime, to indicate his rank. Officers of higher ranks are attended by a few soldiers

[1] Heeren informs us that a similar insignia was used in Persia in early days.

in addition, and in the capital are required to have mounted attendants if they ride in carts; those who bear the sedan are usually in a uniform of their master's devising. The parade and noise seen in the provinces are all hushed in Peking, where the presence of majesty subdues the glory of the officers which it has created. When in court the officer sits behind a desk upon which are placed writing materials; his secretaries, clerks, and interpreters being in waiting, and the lictors with their instruments of punishment and torture standing around. Persons who are brought before him kneel in front of the tribunal. His official seal, and cups containing tallies which are thrown down to indicate the number of blows to be given the culprits, stand upon the table, and behind his seat a *ki-lin*, or unicorn, is depicted on the wall. There are inscriptions hanging around the room, one of which exhorts him to be merciful. There is little pomp or show, either in the office or attendants, compared with our notions of what is usual in such matters among Asiatics. The former is a dirty, unswept, tawdry room, and the latter are beggarly and impertinent.

No counsel is allowed to plead, but the written accusations, pleas, or statements required must be prepared by licensed notaries, who may also read them in court, and who, no doubt, take opportunity to explain circumstances in favor of their client. These notaries buy their situations, and repay themselves by a fee upon the documents; they are the only persons who are analogous to the lawyers in western countries, and most of them have the reputation of extorting largely for their services. Of course there is no such thing as a jury, or a chief justice stating the case to associate judges to learn their opinion; nor is anything like an oath required of the witnesses.

The presiding officer can call in others to assist him in the trial to any extent he pleases. In one Canton court circular it is stated that no less than sixteen officers assisted the governor-general and governor in the trial of one criminal. The report of the trial is as summary as the recital of the bench of judges is minute: "H. E. Gov. Tăng arrived to join the futai in examining a criminal; and at 8 A.M., under a salute of guns, the doors of the great hall of audience were thrown open, and their

PRISONER CONDEMNED TO THE CANGUE, IN COURT.
(His son praying to take his place.)

excellencies took their seats, supported by all the other functionaries assembled for the occasion. The police officers of the judge were then directed to bring forward the prisoner, Yeh A-shun, a native of Tsingyuen hien; he was forthwith brought in, tried, and led out. The futai then requested the imperial death-warrant, and sent a deputation of officers to conduct the criminal to the market-place and there decapitate him. Soon after the officers returned, restored the death-warrant to its place, and reported that they had executed the criminal." The prisoner, or his friends for him, are allowed to appear in every step of the inquiry prior to laying the case before the Emperor, and punishment is threatened to all the magistrates through whose hands it passes if they neglect the appeal; but this extract shows the usage of the courts.

The general policy of officers is to quash cases and repress appeals, and probably they do so to a great degree by bringing extorted confessions of the accused party and the witnesses in proof of the verdict. Governor Lí of Canton issued a prohibition in 1834 against the practice of old men and women presenting petitions—complaining of the nuisance of having his chair stopped in order that a petition might be forced into it, and threatening to seize and punish the presumptuous intruders if they persisted in this custom. He instructs the district magistrates to examine such persons, to ascertain who pushed them forward, and to punish the instigators, observing, "if the people are impressed with a due dread of punishment, they will return to respectful habits." It seems to be the constant effort on the part of the officers to evade the importunities of the injured and shove by justice, and were it not owing to the perseverance of the people, a system of irremediable oppression would soon be induced. But the poor have little chance of being heard against the rich, and if they do appeal they are in most cases remanded to the second judgment of the very officer against whom they complain; and of course as this is equivalent to a refusal from the high grades to right them at all, commotions gradually grow out of it, which are managed according to the exigencies of the case by those who are likely to be involved in their responsibility. The want of an irresistible police to compel obedience has a restraining effect on the rulers, who know that Lynch law may perhaps be retaliated upon them if they exasperate the people too far. A prefect was killed in Chauchau fu some years ago for his cruelty, and the people excused their act by saying that it was done because the officer had failed to carry out the Emperor's good rule, and they would not endure it longer. Amid such enormities it is no wonder if the peaceably disposed part of the community prefer to submit in silence to petty extortions and robberies, rather than risk the loss of all by unavailing complaints.

The code contains many sections regulating the proceedings of courts, and provides heavy punishments for such officers as are guilty of illegalities or cruelty in their decisions, but the recorded cases prove that most of these laws are dead letters. Section CCCCXVI. ordains that "after a prisoner has been tried and convicted of any offence punishable with temporary or perpetual banishment or death, he shall, in the last place, be brought before the magistrate, together with his nearest relations and family, and informed of the offence whereof he stands convicted, and of the sentence intended to be pronounced upon him in consequence; their acknowledgment of its justice or protest against its injustice, as the case may be, shall then be taken down in writing: and in every case of their refusing to admit the justice of the sentence, their protest shall be made the ground of another and more particular investigation." All capital cases must be reviewed by the highest authorities at the metropolis and in the provinces, and a final report of the case and decision submitted to the Emperor's notice. Section CCCCXV. requires that the law be quoted when deciding. The numerous wise and merciful provisions in the code for the due administration of justice only place the conduct of its authorized executives in a less excusable light, and prove how impossible it is to procure an equitable magistracy by mere legal requirements and penalties.

The confusion of the civil and criminal laws in the code, and the union of both functions in the same person, together with the torture and imprisonment employed to elicit a confession, serve as an indication of the state of legislation and jurisprudence. The common sense of a truthful people would revolt against the infliction of torture to get out the true deposition of a witness, and their sense of honor would resist the disgraceful exposure of the cangue for not paying debts. As the want of truth among a people indicates a want of honor, the necessity of more stringent modes of procedure suggests the practice of torture; its application is allowed and restricted by several sections of the code, but in China, as elsewhere, it has always been abused. Torture is practised upon both criminals and witnesses, in court and in prison; and the universal dread among the people of coming before courts, and having anything to do with their magistrates, is owing in great measure to the illegal sufferings they too often must endure. It has also a powerful deterrent effect in preventing crime and disorder. Neither imprisonment nor torture are ranked among the five punishments, but they cause more deaths, probably, among arrested persons than all other means.

Among the modes of torture employed in court, and reported in the *Gazette*, are some revolting to humanity, but which of them are legal does not appear. The clauses under Section I. in the code describe the legal instruments of torture; they consist of three boards with proper grooves for compressing the ankles, and five round sticks for squeezing the fingers, to which may be added the bamboo; besides these no instruments of torture are legally allowed, though other ways of putting the question are so common as to give the impression that some of them at least are sanctioned. Pulling or twisting the ears with roughened fingers, and keeping them in a bent position while making the prisoner kneel on chains, or making him kneel for a long time, are among the illegal modes. Striking the lips with sticks until they are nearly jellied, putting the hands in stocks before or behind the back, wrapping the fingers in oiled cloth to burn them, suspending the body by the thumbs and fingers, tying the hands to a bar under the knees, so as to bend the body double, and chaining by the neck close to a stone, are resorted to when the prisoner is contumacious. One magistrate is accused of having fastened up two criminals to boards by nails driven through their palms; one of them tore his hands loose and was nailed up again, which caused his death; using beds of iron, boiling water, red hot spikes, and cutting the tendon Achilles are also charged against him, but the Emperor exonerated him on account of the atrocious character of the criminals. Compelling them to kneel upon pounded glass, sand, and salt mixed together, until the knees become excoriated, or simply kneeling upon chains is a lighter mode of the same infliction. Mr. Milne mentions seeing a wretch undergoing this torture, his hands tied behind his back to a stake held in its position by two policemen; if he swerved to relieve the agony of his position, a blow on his head compelled him to resume it. The agonies of the poor creature were evident from his quivering lips, his pallid and senseless countenance, and his tremulous voice imploring relief, which was refused with a cold, mocking command, "Suffer or confess."[1]

Flogging is one of the five authorized punishments, but it is used more than any other means to elicit confession; the bamboo, rattan, cudgel, and whip are all employed. When death ensues the magistrate reports that the criminal died of sickness, or hushes it up by bribing his friends, few of whom are ever allowed access within the walls of the prison to see and comfort the sufferers. From the manner in which such a result is spoken of it may be inferred that immediate death does not often take place from torture. A magistrate in Sz'chuen being abused by a man in court, who also struck the attendants, ordered him to be put into a coffin which happened to be near, when suffocation ensued; he was in consequence dismissed the service, punished one hundred blows, and transported three years. One check on outrageous torture is the fear that the report of their cruelty will come to the ears of their superiors, who are usually ready to avail of any mal-administration to get an officer removed, in order to fill the post. In this case, as in other parts of Chinese government, the dread of one evil prevents the commission of another.

The five kinds of punishment mentioned in the code are from ten to fifty blows with the lesser bamboo, from fifty to

[1] W. C. Milne, *Life in China*, London, 1857, p. 99.

one hundred with the greater, transportation, perpetual banishishment, and death, each of them modified in various ways. The small bamboo weighs about two pounds, the larger two and two-thirds pounds. Public exposure in the *kia*, or cangue, is considered rather as a kind of censure or reprimand than a punishment, and carries no disgrace with it, nor comparatively much bodily suffering if the person be fed and screened from the sun. The frame weighs between twenty and thirty pounds, and is so made as to rest upon the shoulders without chafing the neck, but so broad as to prevent the person feeding himself. The name, residence, and offence of the delinquent are written upon it for the information of every passer-by, and a policeman is stationed over him to prevent escape. Branding is applied to deserters and banished persons. Imprisonment and fines are not regarded as legal punishments, but rather correctives; and flogging, as Le Comte says, "is never wanting, there being no condemnation in China without this previous disposition, so that it is unnecessary to mention it in their condemnation; this being always understood to be their first dish." When a man is arrested he is effectually prevented from breaking loose by putting a chain around his neck and tying his hands.

Mode of Exposure in the Cangue.

Most punishments are redeemable by the payment of money if the criminal is under fifteen or over seventy years of age, and a table is given in the code for the guidance of the magistrate in such cases. An act of grace enables a criminal condemned even to capital punishment to redeem himself, if the offence be not one of wilful malignity; but better legislation would have shown the good effects of not making the punishments so severe. It is also ordered in Section XVIII., that "any offender under sentence of death for a crime not excluded from the contingent benefit of an act of grace, who shall have infirm parents or grandparents alive over seventy years of age, and no other male child over sixteen to support them, shall be recommended to the mercy of his Majesty; and if only condemned to banishment, shall receive one hundred blows and redeem himself by a fine." Many atrocious laws may be forgiven for one such exhibition of regard for the care of decrepid parents. Few governments exhibit such opposing principles of actions as the Chinese: a strange blending of cruelty to prisoners with a maudlin consideration of their condition, and a constant effort to coax the people to obedience while exercising great severity upon individuals, are everywhere manifest. One who has lived in the country long, however, knows well that they are not to be held in check by rope-yarn laws or whimpering justices, and unless the rulers are a terror to evil-doers, the latter will soon get the upper hand. Dr. Field well considers this point in his interesting notes describing his visit to a *yamun* at Canton.[1] The general prosperity of the Empire proves in some measure the equity of its administration.

Banishment and slavery are punishments for minor official delinquencies, and few officers who live long in the Emperor's employ do not take an involuntary journey to Mongolia, Turkestan, or elsewhere, in the course of their lives. The fates and conduct of banished criminals are widely unlike; some doggedly serve out their time, others try to ingratiate themselves with their masters in order to alleviate or shorten the time of service, while hundreds contrive to escape and return to their homes, though this subjects them to increased punishment. Persons banished for treason are severely dealt with if they return without leave, and those convicted of crime in their

---

[1] Dr. H. M. Field, *From Egypt to Japan*, Chap. XXIV., passim. New York, 1877. *Chinese Repository*, Vol. IV., pp. 214, 260.

place of banishment are increasingly punished; one man was sentenced to be outlawed for an offence at his place of banishment, but seeing that his aged mother had no other support than his labor, the Emperor ordered that a small sum should be paid for her living out of the public treasury. Whipping a man through the streets as a public example to others is frequenty practised upon persons detected in robbery, assault, or some other minor offences. The man is manacled, and one policeman goes before him carrying a tablet, on which are

Publicly Whipping a Thief through the Streets.

written his name, crime, and punishment, accompanied by another holding a gong. In some cases little sticks bearing flags are thrust through his ears, and the lictor appointed to oversee the fulfilment of the sentence follows the executioner, who strikes the criminal with his whip or rattan as the rap on the gong denotes that the appointed number is not yet complete.

Decapitation and strangling are the legal modes of executing criminals, though Kí Kung having taken several incendiaries at Canton, in 1843, who were convicted of firing the city for purposes of plunder, starved them to death in the public squares of the city. The least disgraceful mode of execution is strangulation, which is performed by tying a man to a post and tightening the cord which goes round his neck by a winch; the infliction is very speedy, and apparently less painful than hanging. The least crime for which death is awarded appears to be a third and aggravated theft, and defacing the branding inflicted for former offences. Decollation is considered more disgraceful than strangling, owing to the dislike the Chinese have of dissevering the bodies which their parents gave them entire. There are two modes of decapitation, that of simple decollation being considered, again, as less disgraceful than being "cut into ten thousand pieces," as the phrase *ling chih* has been rendered. The military officer who superintends the execution is attended by a guard, to keep the populace from crowding upon the limits and prevent resistance on the part of the prisoners. The bodies are given up to the friends, except when the head is exposed as a warning in a cage where the crime was committed. If no one is present to claim the corpse it is buried in the public pit. The criminals are generally so far exhausted that they make no resistance, and submit to their fate without a groan—much more, without a dying speech to the spectators. In ordinary cases the executions are postponed until the autumnal assize, when the Emperor revises and confirms the sentences of the provincial governors; criminals guilty of extraordinary offences, as robbery attended with murder, arson, rape, breaking into fortifications, highway robbery, and piracy, may be immediately beheaded without reference to court, and as the expense of maintenance and want of prison room are both to be considered, it is the fact that criminals condemned for one or other of these crimes comprise the greater part of the unreferred executions in the provinces.

It is impossible to ascertain the number of persons executed in China, for the life of a condemned criminal is thought little of; in the court circular it is merely reported that "the execution of the criminals was completed," without mentioning their crimes, residences, or names. At the autumnal revises at Peking the number sentenced is given in the *Gazette;* 935 were sentenced in 1817, of which 133 were from the province of

Kwangtung; in 1826 there were 581; in 1828 the number was 789, and in the next year 579 names were marked off, none of whose crimes, it is inferrible, are included in the list of offences mentioned above. The condemnations are sent from the capital by express, and the executions take place immediately. Most of the persons condemned in a province are executed in its capital, and to hear of the death of a score or more of felons on a single day is no uncommon thing. The trials are more speedy than comports with our notions of justice, and the executions are performed in the most summary manner. It is reported on one occasion that the governor-general of Canton ascended his judgment-seat, examined three prisoners brought before him, and having found them guilty, condemned them, asked himself for the death-warrant (for he temporarily filled the office of governor), and, having received it, had the three men carried away in about two hours after they were first brought before him. A few days after he granted the warrant to execute a hundred bandits in prison. During the terrible rebellion in Kwangtung, in 1854–55, the prisoners taken by the Imperialists were usually transported to Canton for execution. In a space of fourteen months, up to January, 1856, about eighty-three thousand malefactors suffered death in that city alone, besides those who died in confinement; these men were arrested and delivered to execution by their countrymen, who had suffered untold miseries through their sedition and rapine.

When taken to execution the prisoners are clothed in clean clothes.[1] A military officer is present, and the criminals are brought on the ground in hod-like baskets hanging from a pole borne of two, or in cages, and are obliged to kneel toward the Emperor's residence, or toward the death-warrant, which indicates his presence, as if thanking their sovereign for his care. The list is read aloud and compared with the tickets on the prisoners; as they kneel, a lictor seizes their pinioned hands and jerks them upward so that the head is pushed down horizontally, and a single down stroke with the heavy hanger severs

[1] Persons who commit suicide also dress themselves in their best, the common notion being that in the next world they will wear the same garments in which they died.

it from the neck. In the slow and ignominious execution, or *ling chih*, the criminal is tied to a cross and hacked to pieces; the executioner is nevertheless often hired to give the coup-de-grace at the first blow. It is not uncommon for him to cut out the gall-bladder of notorious robbers and sell it, to be eaten as a specific for courage. There is an official executioner besides the real one, the latter being sometimes a criminal taken out of the prisons.

Probably the number of persons who suffer by the sword of the executioner is not one-half of those who die from the effects of torture and privations in prisons. Not much is known of the internal arrangement of the *hells*, as prisons are called; they seem to be managed with a degree of kindness and attention to the comfort of the prisoners, so far as the intentions of government are concerned, but the cruelties of the turnkeys and older prisoners to exact money from the new comers are terrible. In Canton there are jails in the city under the control of four different officers, the largest covering about an acre, and capable of holding upward of five hundred prisoners. Since it is the practice of distant magistrates to send their worst prisoners up to the capital, these jails are not large enough, and jail distempers arise from over-crowding; two hundred deaths were reported in 1826 from this and other causes, and one hundred and seventeen cases in 1831. Private jails were hired to accommodate the number, and one governor reports having found twenty-two such places in Canton where every kind of cruelty was practised. The witnesses and accusers concerned in appellate causes had, he says, also been brought up to the city and imprisoned along with the guilty party, where they were kept months without any just reason. In one case, where a defendant and plaintiff were imprisoned together, the accuser fell upon the other and murdered him. Sometimes the officer is unable from press of business to attend to a case, and confines all the principals and witnesses concerned until he can examine them, but the government takes no means to provide for them during the interval, and many of the poorer ones die. No security or bail is obtainable on the word of a witness or his friends, so that if unable to fee the jailers he is in nearly as bad a case as the criminal. Extending bail to an accused criminal is nearly unknown, but female prisoners are put in charge of their husbands or parents, who are held responsible for their appearance. The constant succession of criminals in the provincial head prison renders the posts of jailers and turnkeys very lucrative. The letters of the Roman Catholic missionaries from China during the last century, found in the *Lettres Édifiantes* and *Annales de la Foi*, contain many sad pictures of the miseries of prison life there.

The prisons are arranged somewhat on the plan of a large stable, having an open central court occupying nearly one-fourth of the area, and small cribs or stalls covered by a roof extending nearly around it, so contrived that each company of prisoners shall be separated from its neighbors on either side night and day, though more by night than by day. The prisoners cook for themselves in the court, and are secured by manacles and gyves, and a chain joining the hands to the neck; one hand is liberated in the daytime in order to allow them to take care of themselves. Heinous criminals are more heavily ironed, and those in the prisons attached to the judge's office are worse treated than the others. Each criminal should receive a daily ration of two pounds of rice, and about two cents with which to buy fuel, but the jailer starves them on half this allowance if they are unable to fee him; clothing is also scantily provided, but those who have money can procure almost every convenience. Each crib full of criminals is under the control of a turnkey, who with a few old offenders spends much time torturing newly arrived persons to force money from them, by which many lose their lives, and all suffer far more in this manner than they do from the officers of government. Well may the people call their prisons hells, and say, when a man falls into the clutches of the jailers or police, "the flesh is under the cleaver."

There are many processes for the recovery of debts and fulfilment of contracts, some legal and others customary, the latter depending upon many circumstances irrelevant to the merits of the case. The law allows that debtors be punished by bambooing according to the amount of the debt. A creditor often resorts to illegal means to recover his claim, which give rise to many excesses; sometimes he quarters himself upon the debtor's family or premises, at others seizes him or some of his family and keeps them prisoners, and, in extreme cases, sells them. Unscrupulous debtors are equally skilful and violent in eluding, cheating, and resisting their incensed creditors, according as they have the power. They are liable, when three months have expired after the stipulated time of payment, to be bambooed, and their property attached. In most cases, however, disputes of this sort are settled without recourse to government, and if the debtor is really without property, he is not imprisoned till he can procure it. The effects of absconding debtors are seized and divided by those who can get them. Long experience, moreover, of each other's characters has taught them, in contracting debts, to have some security at the outset, and therefore in settling up there is not so much loss as might be supposed considering the difficulty of collecting debts. Accusations for libel, slander, breach of marriage contract, and other civil or less criminal offences are not all brought before the authorities, but are settled by force or arbitration among the people themselves and their elders.

The nominal salaries of Chinese officers have already been stated (p. 294). It is a common opinion among the people that on an average they receive about ten times their salaries; in some cases they pay thirty, forty and more thousand dollars beforehand for the situation. One encouragement to the harassing vexations of the official secretaries and police is the dislike of the people to carry their cases before officers who they know are almost compelled to fleece and peel them; they think it cheaper and safer to bear a small exaction from an underling than run the risk of a greater from his master.

If the preventives against popular violence which the supreme government has placed around itself could be strengthened by an efficient military force, its power would be well secured indeed; but then, as in Russia, it would probably become, by degrees, an intolerable tyranny. The troops are, in fact, everywhere present, ostensibly to support the laws, protect the innocent, and punish the guilty; such of them as are employed by the authorities as guards and policemen are, on the whole, efficient and courteous, though miserably paid, while the regiments in garrison are contemptible to both friend and foe.

The efficacy of the system of checks upon the high courts and provincial officers is increased by their intrigues and conflicting ambition, and long experience has shown that the Emperor's power has little to fear from proconsular rebellion. The inefficiency of the army is a serious evil to the people in one respect, for more power in that arm would repress banditti and pirates; while the sober part of the community would coöperate in a hearty effort to quell them. The greatest difficulty the Emperor finds in upholding his authority lies in the general want of integrity in the officers he employs; good laws may be made, but he has few upright agents to execute them. This has been abundantly manifested in the laws against opium and gambling; no one could be found to carry them into execution, though everybody assented to their propriety.

The chief security on the side of the people against an unmitigated oppression such as now exists in Turkey, besides those already pointed out, lies as much as anywhere in their general intelligence of the true principles on which the government is founded and should be executed. With public opinion on its side the government is a strong one, but none is less able to execute its designs when it runs counter to that opinion, although those designs may be excellent and well intended. Elements of discord are found in the social system which would soon effect its ruin were they not counteracted by other influences, and the body politic goes on like a heavy, shackly, lumbering van, which every moment threatens a crashing, crumbling fall, yet goes on still tottering, owing to the original goodness of its construction. From the enormous population of this ancient van, it is evident that any attempt to remodel it must seriously affect one or the other of its parts, and that when once upset it may be impossible to reconstruct it in its original form. There is encouragement to hope that the general intelligence and shrewdness of the government and people of China, their language, institutions, industry, and love of peace, will all act as powerful conservative influences in working out the changes which cannot now be long delayed; and that she will maintain her unity and industry while going through a thorough reform of her political, social, and religious systems.

It is very difficult to convey to the reader a fair view of the administration of the laws in China. Notwithstanding the cruelty of officers to the criminals before them, they are not all to be considered as tyrants; because insurrections arise, attended with great loss of life, it must not be supposed that society is everywhere disorganized; the Chinese are so prone to falsify that it is difficult to ascertain the truth, yet it must not be inferred that every sentence is a lie; selfishness is a prime motive for their actions, yet charity, kindness, filial affection, and the unbought courtesies of life still exist among them. Although there is an appalling amount of evil and crime in every shape, it is mixed with some redeeming traits; and in China, as elsewhere, good and bad are intermingled. Some of the evils in the social system arise from the operation of the principles of mutual responsibility, while this very feature produces sundry good effects in restraining people who have no higher motive than the fear of injuring the innocent. We hear so much of the shocking cruelties of courts and prisons that the vast number of cases before the bench are all supposed to exhibit the same fatiguing reiteration of suffering, injustice, bribery, and cruelty. One must live in the country to see how the antagonistic principles found in Chinese society act and react upon each other, and are affected by the wicked passions of the heart. Officers and people are bad almost beyond belief to one conversant only with the courtesy, justice, purity, and sincerity of Christian governments and society; and yet we think they are not as bad as the old Greeks and Romans, and have no more injustice or torture in their courts, nor impurity or mendacity in their lives. As in our own land we are apt to forget that the recitals of crimes and outrages which the daily papers bring before our eyes furnish no index of the general condition of society, so in China, where that condition is immeasurably worse, we must be mindful that this is likewise true.

CHAPTER IX.

EDUCATION AND LITERARY EXAMINATIONS.

Among the points relating to the Chinese people which have attracted the attention of students in the history of intellectual development, their long duration and literary institutions have probably taken precedence. To estimate the causes of the first requires much knowledge of the second, and from them one is gradually led onward to an examination of the government, religion, and social life of this people in the succeeding epochs of their existence. The inquiry will reveal much that is instructive, and show us that, if they have not equalled many other nations in the arts and adornments of life, they have attained a high degree of comfort and developed much that is creditable in education, the science of rule, and security of life and property.

Although the powers of mind exhibited by the greatest writers in China are confessedly inferior to those of Greece and Rome for genius and original conceptions, the good influence exerted by them over their countrymen is far greater, even at this day, than was ever obtained by western sages, as Plato, Aristotle, or Seneca. The thoroughness of Chinese education, the purity and effectiveness of the examinations, or the accuracy and excellency of the literature must not be compared with those of modern Christian countries, for there is really no common measure between the two; they must be taken with other parts of Chinese character, and comparisons drawn, if necessary, with nations possessing similar opportunities. The importance of generally instructing the people was acknowledged even before the time of Confucius, and practised to a good degree at an age when other nations in the world had no such system; and although in his day feudal institutions prevailed, and offices and rank were not attainable in the same manner as at present, on the other hand magistrates and noblemen deemed it necessary to be well acquainted with their ancient writings. It is said in the *Book of Rites* (B.C. 1200), "that for the purposes of education among the ancients, villages had their schools, districts their academies, departments their colleges, and principalities their universities." This, so far as we know, was altogether superior to what obtained among the Jews, Persians, and Syrians of the same period.

The great stimulus to literary pursuits is the hope thereby of obtaining office and honor, and the only course of education followed is the classical and historical one prescribed by law. Owing to this undue attention to the classics, the minds of the scholars are not symmetrically trained, and they disparage other branches of literature which do not directly advance this great end. Every department of letters, except jurisprudence, history, and official statistics, is disesteemed in comparison; and the literary graduate of fourscore will be found deficient in most branches of general learning, ignorant of hundreds of common things and events in his national history, which the merest schoolboy in the western world would be ashamed not to know in his. This course of instruction does not form well-balanced minds, but it imbues the future rulers of the land with a full understanding of the principles on which they are to govern, and the policy of the supreme power in using those principles to consolidate its own authority.

Centralization and conservatism were the leading features of the teachings of Confucius which first recommended them to the rulers, and have decided the course of public examinations in selecting officers who would readily uphold these principles. The effect has been that the literary class in China holds the functions of both nobles and priests, a perpetual association, *gens æterna in qua nemo nascitur*, holding in its hands public opinion and legal power to maintain it. The geographical isolation of the people, the nature of the language, and the absence of a landed aristocracy, combine to add efficiency to this system; and when the peculiarities of Chinese character, and the nature of the class-books which do so much to mould that character, are considered, it is impossible to devise a better plan for insuring the perpetuity of the government, or the contentment of the people under that government.

It was about A.D. 600, that Taitsung, of the Tang dynasty, instituted the present plan of preparing and selecting civilians by means of study and degrees, founding his system on the facts that education had always been esteemed, and that the ancient writings were accepted by all as the best instructors of the manners and tastes of the people. According to native historians, the rulers of ancient times made ample provision for the cultivation of literature and promotion of education in all its branches. They supply some details to enable us to understand the mode and the materials of this instruction, and glorify it as they do everything ancient, but probably from the want of authentic accounts in their own hands, they do not clearly describe it. The essays of M. Édouard Biot on the *History of Public Instruction in China*, contains well-nigh all the information extant on this interesting subject, digested in a very lucid manner. Education is probably as good now as it ever was, and its ability to maintain and develop the character of the people as great as at any time; it is remarkable how much it really has done to form, elevate, and consolidate their national institutions. The Manchu monarchs were not at first favorably disposed to the system of examinations, and frowned upon the literary hierarchy who claimed all honors as their right; but the next generation saw the advantages and necessity of the *concours*, in preserving its own power.

Boys commence their studies at the age of seven with a teacher; for, even if the father be a literary man he seldom instructs his sons, and very few mothers are able to teach their offspring to read. Maternal training is supposed to consist in giving a right direction to the morals, and enforcing the obedience of the child; but as there are few mothers who do more than compel obedience by commands, or by the rod, so there are none who can teach the infantile mind to look up to its God in prayer and praise.

Among the many treatises for the guidance of teachers, the

Siao Hioh, or 'Juvenile Instructor,' is regarded as most authoritative. When establishing the elements of education, this book advises fathers to "choose from among their concubines those who are fit for nurses, seeking such as are mild, indulgent, affectionate, benevolent, cheerful, kind, dignified, respectful, and reserved and careful in their conversation, whom they will make governesses over their children. When able to talk, lads must be instructed to answer in a quick, bold tone, and girls in a slow and gentle one. At the age of seven, they should be taught to count and name the cardinal points; but at this age the sexes should not be allowed to sit on the same mat nor eat from the same table. At eight, they must be taught to wait for their superiors, and prefer others to themselves. At ten, the boys must be sent abroad to private tutors, and there remain day and night, studying writing and arithmetic, wearing plain apparel, learning to demean themselves in a manner becoming their age, and acting with sincerity of purpose. At thirteen, they must attend to music and poetry; at fifteen, they must practise archery and charioteering. At the age of twenty, they are in due form to be admitted to the rank of manhood, and learn additional rules of propriety, be fathful in the performance of filial and fraternal duties, and though they possess extensive knowledge, must not affect to teach others. At thirty, they may marry and commence the management of business. At forty, they may enter the service of the state; and if their prince maintains the reign of reason, they must serve him, but otherwise not. At fifty, they may be promoted to the rank of ministers; and at seventy, they must retire from public life."

Another injunction is, "Let children always be taught to speak the simple truth; to stand erect and in their proper places, and listen with respectful attention." The way to become a student, "is, with gentleness and self-abasement, to receive implicitly every word the master utters. The pupil, when he sees virtuous people, must follow them, when he hears good maxims, conform to them. He must cherish no wicked designs, but always act uprightly; whether at home or abroad, he must have a fixed residence, and associate with the benevolent, carefully regulating his personal deportment, and controlling the feelings of his heart. He must keep his clothes in order. Every morning he must learn something new, and rehearse the same every evening." The great end of education, therefore, among the ancient Chinese, was not so much to fill the head with knowledge, as to discipline the heart and purify the affections. One of their writers says, "Those who respect the virtuous and put away unlawful pleasures, serve their parents and prince to the utmost of their ability, and are faithful to their word; these, though they should be considered unlearned, we must pronounce to be educated men." Although such terms as purity, filial affection, learning, and truth, have higher meanings in a Christian education than are given them by Chinese masters, the inculcation of them in any degree and so decided a manner does great credit to the people, and will never need to be superseded —only raised to a higher grade.[1]

In intercourse with their relatives, children are taught to attend to the minutest points of good breeding; and are instructed in everything relating to their personal appearance, making their toilet, saluting their parents, eating, visiting, and other acts of life. Many of these directions are trivial even to puerility, but they are none too minute in the ideas of the Chinese, and still form the basis of good manners, as much as they did a score of centuries ago; and it can hardly be supposed that Confucius would have risked his influence upon the grave publication of trifles, if he had not been well acquainted with the character of his countrymen. Yet nothing is trifling which conduces to the growth of good manners among a people, though it may not have done all that was wished.[2]

Rules are laid down for students to observe in the prosecution of their studies, which reflect credit on those who set so high a standard for themselves. Dr. Morrison has given a synopsis of a treatise of this sort, called the 'Complete Collection of Family Jewels,' and containing a minute specification of

---

[1] Compare Du Halde, *Description de l'Empire de la Chine*, Tome II., pp. 365-384; A. Wylie, *Notes*, p. 68; *Chinese Repository*, Vols. V., p. 81, and VI., pp. 185, 393, and 562; *China Review*, Vol. VI., pp. 120, 195, 253, 328, etc.; *New Englander*, May, 1878.

[2] *Chinese Repository*, Vol. IV., pp. 83-87, 306-316.

duties to be performed by all who would be thorough students. The author directs the tyro to form a fixed resolution to press forward in his studies, setting his mark as high as possible, and thoroughly understanding everything as he goes along. "I have always seen that a man who covets much and devotes himself to universal knowledge, when he reads he presumes on the quickness and celerity of his genius and perceptions, and chapters and volumes pass before his eyes, and issue from his mouth as fluently as water rolls away; but when does he ever apply his mind to rub and educe the essence of a subject? In this manner, although much be read, what is the use of it? Better little and fine, than much and coarse." He also advises persons to have two or three good volumes lying on their tables, which they can take up at odd moments, and to keep commonplace books in which they can jot down such things as occur to them. They should get rid of distracting thoughts if they wish to advance in their studies; as "if a man's stomach has been filled by eating greens and other vegetables, although the most precious dainties with exquisite tastes should be given him, he cannot swallow them, he must first get rid of a few portions of the greens; so in reading, the same is true of the mixed thoughts which distract the mind, which are about the dusty affairs of a vulgar world." The rules given by these writers correspond to those laid down among ourselves, in such books as Todd's *Manual for Students*, and reveal the steps which have given the Chinese their intellectual position.[1]

For all grades of scholars, there is but one mode of study; the imitative nature of the Chinese mind is strikingly exhibited in the few attempts on the part of teachers to improve upon the stereotyped practice of their predecessors, although persons of as original minds as the country affords are constantly engaged in education. When the lad commences his studies, an impressive ceremony takes place—or did formerly, for it seems to have fallen into desuetude: the father leads his son to the teacher, who kneels down before the name of some one or other of the ancient sages, and supplicates their blessing upon his

[1] Morrison's *Chinese Dictionary*, Vol. I., Part I., pp. 749–758.

pupil; after which, seating himself, he receives the homage and petition of the lad to guide him in his lessons.[1] As is the case in Moslem countries, a present is expected to accompany this initiation into literary pursuits. In all cases this event is further marked by giving the lad his *shu ming* or 'book name,' by which he is called during his future life. The furniture of the school merely consists of a desk and a stool for each pupil, and an elevated seat for the master, for maps, globes, blackboards, diagrams, etc., are yet to come in among its articles of furniture. In one corner is placed a tablet or an inscription on the wall, dedicated to Confucius and the god of Letters; the sage is styled the 'Teacher and Pattern for All Ages,' and incense is constantly burned in honor of them both.

The location of school-rooms is usually such as would be considered bad elsewhere, but by comparison with other things in China, is not so. A mat shed which barely protects from the weather, a low, hot upper attic of a shop, a back room in a temple, or rarely a house specially built for the purpose, such are the school-houses in China. The chamber is hired by the master, who regulates his expenses and furnishes his apartment according to the number and condition of his pupils; their average number is about twenty, ranging between ten and forty in day schools, and in private schools seldom exceeding ten. The most thorough course of education is probably pursued in the latter, where a well-qualified teacher is hired by four or five persons living in the same street, or mutually related by birth or marriage, to teach their children at a stipulated salary. In such cases the lads are placed in bright, well-aired apartments, superior to the common school-room. The majority of teachers have been unsuccessful candidates for literary degrees, who having spent the prime of their days in fruitless attempts to attain office, are unfit for manual labor, and unable to enter on mercantile life. In Canton, a teacher of twenty boys receives from half a dollar to a dollar per month from each pupil; in country villages, three, four or five dollars a year are given, with the addition, in most cases, of a small present of eatables

---

[1] This custom obtains also in Bokhara.

from each scholar three or four times a year. Private tutors receive from $150 to $350 or more per annum, according to particular engagement. There are no boarding-schools, nor anything answering to infant schools; nor are public or charity schools established by government, or by private benevolence for the education of the poor.

The first hours of study are from sunrise till ten A.M., when the boys go to breakfast; they reassemble in an hour or more, and continue at their books till about five P.M., when they disperse for the day. In summer, they have no lessons after dinner, but an evening session is often held in the winter, and evening schools are occasionally opened for mechanics and others who are occupied during the day. When a boy comes into school in the morning, he bows reverentially before the tablet of Confucius, salutes his teacher, and then takes his seat. The vacations during the year are few; the longest is before new year, at which time the engagement is completed, and the school closes, to be reöpened after the teacher and parents have made a new arrangement. The common festivals, of which there are a dozen or more, are regarded as holydays, and form very necessary relaxations in a country destitute of the rest of the Sabbath. The requisite qualifications of a teacher are gravity, severity, and patience, and acquaintance with the classics; he has only to teach the same series of books in the same fashion in which he learned them himself and keep a good watch over his charge.

When the lads come together at the opening of the school, their attainments are ascertained; the teacher endeavors to have his pupils nearly equal in this respect, but inasmuch as they are all put to precisely the same tasks, a difference is not material. If the boys are beginners, they are brought up in a line before the desk, holding the *San-tsz' King*, or 'Trimetrical Classic,' in their hands, and taught to read off the first lines after the teacher until they can repeat them without help. He calls off the first four lines as follows:

Jin chí tsu, sing pun shen;
Sing siang kin, sih siang yuen;

when his pupils simultaneously cry out:

Jin chí tsu, sing pun shen;
Sing siang kin, sih siang yuen.

Mispronunciations are corrected until each can read the lesson accurately; they are then sent to their seats to commit the sounds to memory. As the sounds are all entire words (not letters, nor syllables, of which they have no idea), the boys are not perplexed, as ours are, with symbols which have no meaning. All the children study aloud, and when one is able to recite the task, he is required to *back* it—come up to the master's desk, and stand with his back toward him while rehearsing it.

The *San-tsz' King* was compiled by Wang Pih-hao of the Sung dynasty (A. D. 1050) for his private school. It contains ten hundred and sixty-eight words, and half that number of different characters, arranged in one hundred and seventy-eight double lines. It has been commented upon by several persons, one of whom calls it "a ford which the youthful inquirer may readily pass, and thereby reach the fountain-head of the higher courses of learning, or a passport into the regions of classical and historical literature." This hornbook begins with the nature of man, and the necessity and modes of education, and it is noticeable that the first sentence, the one quoted above, which a Chinese learns at school, contains one of the most disputed doctrines in the ancient heathen world:

> "Men at their birth, are by nature radically good;
> Though alike in this, in practice they widely diverge.
> If not educated, the natural character grows worse;
> A course of education is made valuable by close attention.
> Of old, Mencius' mother selected a residence,
> And when her son did not learn, cut out the [half-wove] web.
> To nurture and not educate is a father's error;
> To educate without rigor shows a teacher's indolence.
> That boys should not learn is an unjust thing;
> For if they do not learn in youth, what will they do when old?
> As gems unwrought serve no useful end,
> So men untaught will never know what right conduct is."

The importance of filial and fraternal duties are then inculcated by precept and example, to which succeeds a synopsis of the various branches of learning in an ascending series, under several heads of numbers; the three great powers, the four seasons and four cardinal points, the five elements and five constant virtues, the six kinds of grain and six domestic animals, the seven passions, the eight materials for music, nine degrees of kindred, and ten social duties. A few extracts will exhibit the mode in which these subjects are treated.

"There are three powers,—heaven, earth, and man.
There are three lights,—the sun, moon, and stars.
There are three bonds,—between prince and minister, justice;
Between father and son, affection; between man and wife, concord.

Humanity, justice, propriety, wisdom, and truth,—
These five cardinal virtues are not to be confused.
Rice, millet, pulse, wheat, sorghum, millet grass,
Are six kinds of grain on which men subsist.

Mutual affection of father and son, concord of man and wife;
The older brother's kindness, the younger one's respect;
Order between seniors and juniors, friendship among associates;
On the prince's part regard, on the minister's true loyalty;—
These ten moral duties are ever binding among men."

To this technical summary succeed rules for a course of academical studies, with a list of the books to be learned, and the order of their use, followed by a synopsis of the general history of China, in an enumeration of the successive dynasties. The work concludes with incidents and motives to learning drawn from the conduct of ancient sages and statesmen, and from considerations of interest and glory. The examples cited are curious instances of pursuit of knowledge under difficulties, and form an inviting part of the treatise.

"Formerly Confucius had young Hiang Toh for his teacher;
Even the sages of antiquity studied with diligence.
Chau, a minister of state, read the Confucian Dialogues,
And he too, though high in office, studied assiduously.
One copied lessons on reeds, another on slips of bamboo;
These, though without books, eagerly sought knowledge.
[To vanquish sleep] one tied his head [by the hair] to a beam, and another pierced his thigh with an awl;
Though destitute of instructors, these were laborious in study.
One read by the glowworm's light, another by reflection from snow;

These, though their families were poor, did not omit to study.
One carried faggots, and another tied his books to a cow's horn,
And while thus engaged in labor, studied with intensity.
Su Lau-tsiuen, when he was twenty-seven years old
Commenced close study, and applied his mind to books;
This man, when old, grieved that he commenced so late;
You who are young must early think of these things.
Behold Liang Hau, at the ripe age of eighty-two,
In the imperial hall, amongst many scholars, gains the first rank;
This he accomplished, and all regarded him a prodigy;
You, my young readers, should now resolve to be diligent.
Yung, when only eight years old, could recite the Odes;
And Pí, at the age of seven, understood the game of chess;
These displayed ability, and all deemed them to be rare men;
And you, my hopeful scholars, ought to imitate them.
Tsai Wăn-kí could play upon stringed instruments;
Sié Tau-wăn, likewise, could sing and chant;
These two, though girls, were bright and well informed;
You, then, my lads, should surely rouse to diligence.
Liu Ngan of Tang, when only seven years old,
Proving himself a noble lad, was able to correct writing:
He, though very young, was thus highly promoted.
You, young learners, strive to follow his example,
For he who does so, will acquire like honors.
"Dogs watch by night; the cock announces the morning;
If any refuse to learn, how can they be esteemed men?
The silkworm spins silk, the bee gathers honey;
If men neglect to learn, they are below the brutes.
He who learns in youth, to act wisely in mature age,
Extends his influence to the prince, benefits the people,
Makes his name renowned, renders his parents honorable;
Reflects glory on his ancestors, and enriches his posterity.
Some for their offspring, leave coffers filled with gold;
While I to teach children, leave this one little book.
Diligence has merit; play yields no profit;
Be ever on your guard! Rouse all your energies!"

These quotations illustrate the character of the *Trimetrical Classic*, and show its imperfections as a book for young minds. It is a syllabus of studies rather than a book to be learned, and ill suited to entice the boy on in his tasks by giving him mental food in an attractive form. Yet its influence has been perhaps as great as the classics during the last four dynasties, from its general use in primary schools, where myriads of lads have "backed" it who have had no leisure to study much more, and when they had crossed this ford could travel no farther. The boy commences his education by learning these maxims; and by the time he has got his degree—and long before, too—the highest truths and examples known in the land are more deeply impressed on his mind than are ever Biblical truths and examples on graduates of Yale, Oxford, Heidelberg or the Sorbonne. Well was it for them that they had learned nothing in it which they had better forget, for its deficiencies, pointed out by Bridgman in his translation, should not lead us to overlook its suggestive synopsis of principles and examples. The commentary explains them very fully, and it is often learned as thoroughly as the text. Many thousands of tracts containing Christian truths written in the same style and with the same title, have been taught with good effect in the mission schools in China.[1]

The next hornbook put into the boy's hands is the *Pih Kia Sing*, or 'Century of Surnames.' It is a list of the family or clan names commonly in use. Its acquisition also gives him familiarity with four hundred and fifty-four common words employed as names, a knowledge, too, of great importance lest mistakes be made in choosing a wrong character among the scores of homophonous characters in the language. For instance, out of eighty-three common words pronounced *kí*, six only are clan names, and it is necessary to have these very familiar in the daily intercourse of life. The nature of the work forbids its being studied, but the usefulness of its contents probably explains its position in this series.[2]

The third in the list is the *Tsien Tsz' Wăn*, or 'Millenary Classic,' unique among all books in the Chinese language, and whose like could not be produced in any other, in that it consists

---

[1] Compare Dr. Morrison in the *Horæ Sinicæ*, pp. 122–146; B. Jenkins, *The Three-Character Classic, romanized according to the Shanghai dialect*, Shanghai, 1860. The Classic has also been translated into Latin, French, German, Russian, and Portuguese. For the Trimetrical Classic of the Tai-ping régime see a version in the *North China Herald*, No. 147, May 21, 1853, by Dr. Medhurst; also a translation by Rev. S. C. Malan, of Balliol College, Oxford. London, 1856.

[2] E. C. Bridgman in the *Chinese Repository*, Vol. IV., p. 152. *Livre de Cent familles*, Perny, *Dict.*, App., No. XIV., pp. 156 ff.

of just a thousand characters, no two of which are alike in form or meaning. The author, Chau Hing-tsz', flourished about A.D. 550, and according to an account given in the history of the Liang dynasty, wrote it at the Emperor's request, who had ordered his minister Wang Hí-chí to write out a thousand characters, and give them to him, to see if he could make a connected ode with them. This he did, and presented his performance to his majesty, who rewarded him with rich presents in token of his approval. Some accounts (in order that so singular a work might not want for corresponding wonders) add that he did the task in a single night, under the fear of condign punishment if he failed, and the mental exertion was so great as to turn his hair white. It consists of two hundred and fifty lines, in which rhyme and rhythm are both carefully observed, though there is no more poetry in it than in a multiplication table. The contents of the book are similar but more discursive than those of the *Trimetrical Classic.* Up to the one hundred and second line, the productions of nature and virtues of the early monarchs, the power and capacities of man, his social duties and mode of conduct, with instructions as to the manner of living, are summarily treated. Thence to the one hundred and sixty-second line, the splendor of the palace, and its high dignitaries, with other illustrious persons and places, are referred to. The last part of the work treats of private and literary life, the pursuits of agriculture, household government, and education, interspersed with some exhortations, and a few illustrations. A few disconnected extracts from Dr. Bridgman's translation[1] will show the mode in which these subjects are handled. The opening lines are,

> "The heavens are sombre ; the earth is yellow ;
> The whole universe [at the creation] was one wide waste ; "

after which it takes a survey of the world and its products, and Chinese history, in a very sententious manner, down to the thirty-seventh line, which opens a new subject.

---

[1] *Chinese Repository*, Vol. IV., p. 229.

"Now this our human body is endowed
With four great powers and five cardinal virtues:
Preserve with reverence what your parents nourished,—
How dare you destroy or injure it?
Let females guard their chastity and purity,
And let men imitate the talented and virtuous.
When you know your own errors then reform;
And when you have made acquisitions do not lose them.
Forbear to complain of the defects of other people,
And cease to brag of your own superiority.
Let your truth be such as may be verified,
Your capacities, as to be measured with difficulty.
"Observe and imitate the conduct of the virtuous,
And command your thoughts that you may be wise.
Your virtue once fixed, your reputation will be established;
Your habits once rectified, your example will be correct.
Sounds are reverberated in the deep valleys,
And the vacant hall reëchoes all it hears;
So misery is the penalty of accumulated vice,
And happiness the reward of illustrious virtue.
"A cubit of jade stone is not to be valued,
But an inch of time you ought to contend for.
"Mencius esteemed plainness and simplicity;
And Yu the historian held firmly to rectitude.
These nearly approached the golden medium,
Being laborious, humble, diligent, and moderate.
Listen to what is said, and investigate the principles explained:
Watch men's demeanor, that you may distinguish their characters.
Leave behind you none but purposes of good;
And strive to act in such a manner as to command respect.
When satirized and admonished examine yourself,
And do this more thoroughly when favors increase.
"Years fly away like arrows, one pushing on the other;
The sun shines brightly through his whole course.
The planetarium keeps on revolving where it hangs;
And the bright moon repeats her revolutions.
To support fire, add fuel; so cultivate the root of happiness,
And you will obtain eternal peace and endless felicity."

The commentary on the *Thousand Character Classic* contains many just observations and curious anecdotes to explain this book, whose text is so familiar to the people at large that its lines or characters are used as labels instead of figures, as they take up less room. If Western scholars were as familiar with the acts and sayings of King Wăn, of Su Tsin, or of Kwan Chung, as they are with those of Sesostris, Pericles, or Horace, these incidents and places would naturally enough be deemed more interesting than they now are. But where the power of genius, or the vivid pictures of a brilliant imagination, are wanting to illustrate or beautify a subject, there is comparatively little to interest Europeans in the authors and statesmen of such a distant country and remote period.[1]

The fourth in this series, called *Yiu Hioh Shi-tieh*, or 'Odes for Children,' is written in rhymed pentameters, and contains only thirty-four stanzas of four lines. A single extract will show its character, which is, in general, a brief description and praise of literary life, and allusion to the changes of the season, and the beauties of nature.

> It is of the utmost importance to educate children;
> Do not say that your families are poor,
> For those who can handle well the pencil,
> Go where they will, need never ask for favors.
>
> One at the age of seven, showed himself a divinely endowed youth,
> 'Heaven,' said he, 'gave me my intelligence:
> Men of talent appear in the courts of the holy monarch,
> Nor need they wait in attendance on lords and nobles.
>
> 'In the morning I was an humble cottager,
> In the evening I entered the court of the Son of Heaven:
> Civil and military offices are not hereditary,
> Men must, therefore, rely on their own efforts.
>
> 'A passage for the sea has been cut through mountains,
> And stones have been melted to repair the heavens;
> In all the world there is nothing that is impossible;
> It is the heart of man alone that is wanting resolution.
>
> 'Once I myself was a poor indigent scholar,
> Now I ride mounted in my four-horse chariot,
> And all my fellow-villagers exclaim with surprise.'
> Let those who have children thoroughly educate them.

The examples of intelligent youth rising to the highest offices of state are numerous in all the works designed for beginners,

---

[1] Compare *Das Tsiän dsü wen, oder Buch von Tausend Wörtern, aus dem Schinesischen, mit Berücksichtigung der Koraischen und Japanischen Uebersetzung, ins Deutsche übertragen*, Ph. Fr. de Siebold, *Nippon*, Abh. IV., pp. 165-191; B. Jenkins, *The Thousand-Character Classic, romanized*, etc. Shanghai, 1860; *Thsien-Tseu-Wen, Le Livre des Mille Mots*, etc., par Stanislas Julien (with Chinese text), Paris, 1864; *China Review*, Vol. II., pp. 182 ff.

and stories illustrative of their precocity are sometimes given in toy-books and novels. One of the most common instances is here quoted, that of Confucius and Hiang Toh, which is as well known to every Chinese as is the story of George Washington barking the cherry-tree with his hatchet to American youth.

"The name of Confucius was Yu, and his style Chungní; he established himself as an instructor in the western part of the kingdom of Lu. One day, followed by all his disciples, riding in a carriage, he went out to ramble, and on the road, came across several children at their sports; among them was one who did not join in them. Confucius, stopping his carriage, asked him, saying, 'Why is it that you alone do not play?' The lad replied, 'All play is without any profit; one's clothes get torn, and they are not easily mended; above me, I disgrace my father and mother; below me, even to the lowest, there is fighting and altercation; so much toil and no reward, how can it be a good business? It is for these reasons that I do not play.' Then dropping his head, he began making a city out of pieces of tile.

"Confucius, reproving him, said, 'Why do you not turn out for the carriage?' The boy replied, 'From ancient times till now it has always been considered proper for a carriage to turn out for a city, and not for a city to turn out for a carriage.' Confucius then stopped his vehicle in order to discourse of reason. He got out of the carriage, and asked him, 'You are still young in years, how is it that you are so quick?' The boy replied, saying, 'A human being, at the age of three years, discriminates between his father and his mother; a hare, three days after it is born, runs over the ground and furrows of the fields; fish, three days after their birth, wander in rivers and lakes; what heaven thus produces naturally, how can it be called brisk?'

"Confucius added, 'In what village and neighborhood do you reside, what is your surname and name, and what your style?' The boy answered, 'I live in a mean village and in an insignificant land; my surname is Hiang, my name is Toh, and I have yet no style.'

"Confucius rejoined, 'I wish to have you come and ramble with me; what do you think of it?' The youth replied, 'A stern father is at home, whom I am bound to serve; an affectionate mother is there, whom it is my duty to cherish; a worthy elder brother is at home, whom it is proper for me to obey, with a tender younger brother whom I must teach; and an intelligent teacher is there from whom I am required to learn. How have I leisure to go a rambling with you?'

"Confucius said, 'I have in my carriage thirty-two chessmen; what do you say to having a game together?' The lad answered, 'If the Emperor love gaming, the Empire will not be governed; if the nobles love play, the government will be impeded; if scholars love it, learning and investigation will be lost and thrown by; if the lower classes are fond of gambling, they will utterly lose the support of their families; if servants and slaves love to game, they will get a cudgelling; if farmers love it, they miss the time for ploughing and sowing; for these reasons I shall not play with you.'

"Confucius rejoined, 'I wish to have you go with me, and fully equalize the Empire; what do you think of this?' The lad replied, 'The Empire cannot be equalized; here are high hills, there are lakes and rivers; either there are princes and nobles, or there are slaves and servants. If the high hills be levelled, the birds and beasts will have no resort; if the rivers and lakes be filled up, the fishes and the turtles will have nowhere to go; do away with kings and nobles, and the common people will have much dispute about right and wrong; obliterate slaves and servants, and who will there be to serve the prince! If the Empire be so vast and unsettled, how can it be equalized?'

"Confucius again asked, 'Can you tell, under the whole sky, what fire has no smoke, what water no fish; what hill has no stones, what tree no branches; what man has no wife, what woman no husband; what cow has no calf, what mare no colt; what cock has no hen, what hen no cock; what constitutes an excellent man, and what an inferior man; what is that which has not enough, and what which has an overplus; what city is without a market, and who is the man without a style?'

"The boy replied, 'A glowworm's fire has no smoke, and well-water no fish; a mound of earth has no stones, and a rotten tree no branches; genii have no wives, and fairies no husbands; earthen cows have no calves, nor wooden mares any colts; lonely cocks have no hens, and widowed hens no cocks; he who is worthy is an excellent man, and a fool is an inferior man; a winter's day is not long enough, and a summer's day is too long; the imperial city has no market, and little folks have no style.'

"Confucius inquiring said, 'Do you know what are the connecting bonds between heaven and earth, and what is the beginning and ending of the dual powers? What is left, and what is right; what is out, and what is in; who is father, and who is mother; who is husband, and who is wife. [Do you know] where the wind comes from, and from whence the rain? From whence the clouds issue, and the dew arises? And for how many tens of thousands of miles the sky and earth go parallel?'

"The youth answering said, 'Nine multiplied nine times make eighty-one, which is the controlling bond of heaven and earth; eight multiplied by nine makes seventy-two, the begining and end of the dual powers. Heaven is father, and earth is mother; the sun is husband, and the moon is wife; east is left, and west is right; without is out, and inside is in; the winds come from Tsang-wu, and the rains proceed from wastes and wilds; the clouds issue from the hills, and the dew rises from the ground. Sky and earth go parallel for ten thousand times ten thousand miles, and the four points of the compass have each their station.'

"Confucius asking, said, 'Which do you say is the nearest relation, father and mother, or husband and wife?' The boy responded, 'One's parents are near; husband and wife are not [so] near.'

"Confucius rejoined, 'While husband and wive are alive, they sleep under the same coverlet; when they are dead they lie in the same grave; how then can you say that they are not near?' The boy replied, 'A man without a wife is like a carriage without a wheel; if there be no wheel, another one is made, for he can doubtless get a new one; so, if one's wife die, he seeks again, for he also can obtain a new one. The daughter of a worthy family must certainly marry an honorable husband; a house having ten rooms always has a plate and a ridgepole ; three windows and six lattices do not give the light of a single door ; the whole host of stars with all their sparkling brilliancy do not equal the splendor of the solitary moon : the affection of a father and mother—alas, if it be once lost ! '

"Confucius sighing, said, 'How clever ! how worthy ! ' The boy asking the sage said, 'You have just been giving me questions, which I have answered one by one ; I now wish to seek information ; will the teacher in one sentence afford me some plain instruction ? I shall be much gratified if my request be not rejected.' He then said, 'Why is it that mallards and ducks are able to swim ; how is it that wild geese and cranes sing ; and why are firs and pines green through the winter ?' Confucius replied, 'Mallards and ducks can swim because their feet are broad ; wild geese and cranes can sing because they have long necks ; firs and pines remain green throughout the winter because they have strong hearts.' The youth rejoined, 'Not so ; fishes and turtles can swim, is it because they all have broad feet ? Frogs and toads can sing, is it because their necks are long ? The green bamboo keeps fresh in winter, is it on account of its strong heart ?'

"Again interrogating, he said, 'How many stars are there altogether in the sky ?' Confucius replied, 'At this time inquire about the earth ; how can we converse about the sky with certainty ?' The boy said, 'Then how many houses in all are there on the earth ?' The sage answered, 'Come now, speak about something that's before our eyes ; why must you converse about heaven and earth ?' The lad resumed, 'Well, speak about what's before our eyes—how many hairs are there in your eyebrows ?'

"Confucius smiled, but did not answer, and turning round to his disciples called them and said, 'This boy is to be feared ; for it is easy to see that the subsequent man will not be like the child.' He then got into his carriage and rode off."[1]

Next in course to this rather trifling primer comes the *Hiao King*, or 'Canons of Filial Duty,' a short tractate of only 1,903 characters, which purports to be the record of a conversation held between Confucius and his disciple Tsăng Tsan on the principles of filial piety. Its authenticity has been disputed by critics, but their doubts are not shared by their countrymen, who commit it to memory as the words of the sage. The legend is that a copy was discovered in the wall of his dwelling, and compared with another secreted by Yen Chí at the burning of the books; from the two Liu Hiang chose eighteen of the chapters contained in it as alone genuine, and in this shape it has since remained. The sixth section of the Imperial Catalogue is entirely devoted to writers on the *Hiao King*, one of whom was

---

[1] *Chinese Repository*, Vol. X., p. 614.

Yuentsung, an emperor of the Tang dynasty (A.D. 733). Another comment was published in 32 volumes in Kanghi's reign, discussing the whole subject in one hundred chapters. Though it does not share in critical eyes the confidence accorded to the nine classics, the brevity and subject matter of this work have commended it to teachers as one of the best books in the language to be placed in the hands of their scholars; thus its influence has been great and enduring. It has been translated by Bridgman, who regards the first six sections as the words of Confucius, while the other twelve contain his ideas. Two quotations are all that need be here given to show its character.

SECTION I.—*On the origin and nature of filial duty.*—Filial duty is the root of virtue, and the stem from which instruction in the moral principle springs. Sit down, and I will explain this to you. The first thing which filial duty requires of us is, that we carefully preserve from all injury, and in a perfect state, the bodies which we have received from our parents. And when we acquire for ourselves a station in the world, we should regulate our conduct by correct principles, so as to transmit our names to future generations, and reflect glory on our parents. This is the ultimate aim of filial duty. Thus it commences in attention to parents, is continued through a course of services rendered to the prince, and is completed by the elevation of ourselves. It is said in the *Book of Odes*,

> Ever think of your ancestors;
> Reproducing their virtue.

SECTION V.—*On the attention of scholars to filial duty.*—With the same love that they serve their fathers, they should serve their mothers; and with the same respect that they serve their fathers, they should serve their prince; unmixed love, then, will be the offering they make to their mothers; unfeigned respect the tribute they bring to their prince; while toward their fathers both these will be combined. Therefore they serve their prince with filial duty and are faithful to him; they serve their superiors with respect and are obedient to them. By constant obedience and faithfulness toward those who are above them, they are enabled to preserve their stations and emoluments, and to offer the sacrifices which are due to their deceased ancestors and parents. Such is the influence of filial piety when performed by scholars. It is said in the *Book of Odes*,

> When the dawn is breaking, and I cannot sleep,
> The thoughts in my breast are of our parents.[1]

[1] Compare Père Cibot in *Mémoires concernant les Chinois*, Tome IV., pp. 1 ff.; Dr. Legge, *The Sacred Books of China*, Part I. *The Shû-king, Religious Portions of the Shih-king, the Hsiâo-king*, Oxford, 1879; *Asiatic Journal*, Vol. XXIX., pp. 302 ff., 1839.

The highest place in the list of virtues and obligations is accorded to filial duty, not only in this, but in other writings of Confucius and those of his school. "There are," to quote from another section, "three thousand crimes to which one or the other of the five kinds of punishment is attached as a penalty; and of these no one is greater than disobedience to parents. When ministers exercise control over the monarch, then there is no supremacy; when the maxims of the sages are set aside, then the law is abrogated; and so those who disregard filial duty are as though they had no parents. These three evils prepare the way for universal rebellion."

This social virtue has been highly lauded by all Chinese writers, and its observance inculcated upon youth and children by precept and example. Stories are written to show the good effects of obedience, and the bad results of its contrary sin, which are put into their hands, and form also subjects for pictorial illustration, stanzas for poetry, and materials for conversation. The following examples are taken from a toy-book of this sort, called the *Twenty-four Filials*, one of the most popular collections on the subject.

"During the Chau dynasty there lived a lad named Tsăng Tsan (also Tsz'-yu), who served his mother very dutifully. Tsăng was in the habit of going to the hills to collect fagots; and once, while he was thus absent, many guests came to his house, toward whom his mother was at a loss how to act. She, while expecting her son, who delayed his return, began to gnaw her fingers. Tsăng suddenly felt a pain in his heart, and took up his bundle of fagots in order to return home; and when he saw his mother, he kneeled and begged to know what was the cause of her anxiety. She replied, 'there have been some guests here, who came from a great distance, and I bit my finger in order to arouse you to return to me.'

"In the Chau dynasty lived Chung Yu, named also Tsz'-lu, who, because his family was poor, usually ate herbs and coarse pulse; and he also went more than a hundred *li* to procure rice for his parents. Afterward, when they were dead, he went south to the country of Tsu, where he was made commander of a hundred companies of chariots; there he became rich, storing up grain in myriads of measures, reclining upon cushions, and eating food served to him in numerous dishes; but sighing, he said, 'Although I should now desire to eat coarse herbs and bring rice for my parents, it cannot be!'

"In the Chau dynasty there flourished the venerable Lai, who was very obedient and reverential toward his parents, manifesting his dutifulness by exerting himself to provide them with every delicacy. Although upward of seventy years of age, he declared that he was not yet old; and usually dressed himself in parti-colored embroidered garments, and like a child would playfully stand by the side of his parents. He would also take up buckets of water, and try to carry them into the house; but feigning to slip, would fall to the ground, wailing and crying like a child: and all these things he did in order to divert his parents.

"During the Han dynasty lived Tung Yung, whose family was so very poor that when his father died he was obliged to sell himself in order to procure money to bury his remains. After this he went to another place to gain the means of redeeming himself; and on his way he met a lady who desired to become his wife, and go with him to his master's residence. She went with him, and wove three hundred pieces of silk, which being completed in two months, they returned home; on the way, having reached the shade of the cassia tree where they before met, the lady bowed and ascending, vanished from his sight.

"During the Han dynasty lived Ting Lan, whose parents both died when he was young, before he could obey and support them; and he reflected that for all the trouble and anxiety he had caused them, no recompense had yet been given. He then carved wooden images of his parents, and served them as if they had been alive. For a long time his wife would not reverence them; but one day, taking a bodkin, she in derision pricked their fingers. Blood immediately flowed from the wound; and seeing Ting coming, the images wept. He examined into the circumstances, and forthwith divorced his wife.

"In the days of the Han dynasty lived Koh Kü, who was very poor. He had one child three years old; and such was his poverty that his mother usually divided her portion of food with this little one. Koh says to his wife, 'We are so poor that our mother cannot be supported, for the child divides with her the portion of food that belongs to her. Why not bury this child? Another child may be born to us, but a mother once gone will never return.' His wife did not venture to object to the proposal; and Koh immediately dug a hole of about three cubits deep, when suddenly he lighted upon a pot of gold, and on the metal read the following inscription: 'Heaven bestows this treasure upon Koh Kü, the dutiful son; the magistrate may not seize it, nor shall the neighbors take it from him.'

"Măng Tsung, who lived in the Tsin dynasty, when young lost his father. His mother was very sick; and one winter's day she longed to taste a soup made of bamboo sprouts, but Măng could not procure any. At last he went into the grove of bamboos, clasped the trees with his hands, and wept bitterly. His filial affection moved nature, and the ground slowly opened, sending forth several shoots, which he gathered and carried home. He made a soup with them, of which his mother ate and immediately recovered from her malady

"Wu Măng, a lad eight years of age, who lived under the Tsin dynasty, was very dutiful to his parents. They were so poor that they could not afford to furnish their bed with mosquito-curtains; and every summer's night, myriads of mosquitos attacked them unrestrainedly, feasting upon their flesh and blood. Although there were so many, yet Wu would not drive them away, lest they should go to his parents, and annoy them. Such was his affection."[1]

[1] *Chinese Repository*, Vol. VI., p. 131.

The last book learned before entering on the classics has had almost as great an influence as any of them, and none of the works of later scholars are so well calculated to show the ideas of the Chinese in all ages upon the principles of education, intercourse of life, and rules of conduct as this; precepts are illustrated by examples, and the examples referred back to precepts for their moving cause. This is the *Siao Hioh*, or "Juvenile Instructor," and was intended by Chu Hí, its author, as a counterpart of the *Ta Hiao*, on which he had written a commentary. It has had more than fifty commentators, one of whom says, "We confide in the *Siao Hioh* as we do in the gods, and revere it as we do our parents." It is divided into two books, the "fountain of learning," and "the stream flowing from it," arranged in 20 chapters and 385 short sections. The first book has four parts and treats of the first principles of education; of the duties we owe our kindred, rulers, and fellow-men, of those we owe ourselves in regard to study, demeanor, food, and dress; and lastly gives numerous examples from ancient history, beginning with very early times down to the end of the Chau dynasty, B.C. 249, confirmatory of the maxims inculcated, and the good effects resulting from their observance. The second book contains, in its first part, a collection of wise sayings of eminent men who flourished after B.C. 200, succeeded by a series of examples of distinguished persons calculated to show the effects of good principles; both designed to establish the truth of the teachings of the first book. One or two quotations, themselves extracted from other works, will suffice to show something of its contents.

"Confucius said, 'Friends must sharply and frankly admonish each other, and brothers must be gentle toward one another.'"

"Tsz'-kung, asking about friendship, Confucius said, 'Faithfully to inform and kindly to instruct another is the duty of a friend; if he is not tractable, desist; do not disgrace yourself.'"

"Whoever enters with his guests, yields precedence to them at every door; when they reach the innermost one, he begs leave to go in and arrange the seats, and then returns to receive the guests; and after they have repeatedly declined he bows to them and enters. He passes through the right door, they through the left. He ascends the eastern, they the western steps. If a guest be of a lower grade, he must approach the steps of the host, while the latter must repeatedly decline this attention; then the guest may return to the western steps, he ascending, both host and guest must mutually yield precedence: then the host must ascend first, and the guests follow. From step to step they must bring their feet together, gradually ascending—those on the east moving the right foot first, those on the west the left."

The great influence which these six school-books have had is owing to their formative power on youthful minds, a large proportion of whom never go beyond them (either from want of time, means, or desire), but are really here furnished with the kernel of their best literature.

The tedium of memorizing these unmeaning sounds is relieved by writing the characters on thin paper placed over copy slips. The writing and the reading lessons are the same, and both are continued for a year or two until the forms and sounds of a few thousand characters are made familiar, but no particular effort is taken to teach their meanings. It is after this that the teacher goes over the same ground, and with the help of the commentary, explains the meaning of the words and phrases one by one, until they are all understood. It is not usual for the beginner to attend much to the meaning of what he is learning to read and write, and where the labor of committing arbitrary characters is so great and irksome, experience has probably shown that it is not wise to attempt too many things at once. The boy has been familiarizing himself with their shapes as he sees them all the time around him, and he learns what they mean in a measure before he comes to school. The association of form with ideas, as he cons his lesson and writes their words, gradually strengthens, and results in that singular interdependence of the eye and ear so observable among the scholars of the far East. They trust to what is read to help in understanding what is heard much more than is the case in phonetic languages. No effort is made to facilitate the acquisition of the characters by the boys in school by arranging them according to their component parts; they are learned one by one, as boys are taught the names and appearance of minerals in a cabinet. The effects of a course of study like this, in which the powers of the tender mind are not developed by proper nourishment of truthful knowledge, can hardly be otherwise than to stunt the genius, and drill the fac ulties of the mind into a slavish adherence to venerated usage and dictation, making the intellects of Chinese students like the trees which their gardeners so toilsomely dwarf into pots and jars—plants, whose unnaturalness is congruous to the insipidity of their fruit.

The number of years spent at school depends upon the means of the parents. Tradesmen, mechanics, and country gentlemen endeavor to give their sons a competent knowledge of the usual series of books, so that they can creditably manage the common affairs of life. No other branches of study are pursued than the classics and histories, and what will illustrate them, meanwhile giving much care and practice to composition. No arithmetic or any department of mathematics, nothing of the geography of their own or other countries, of natural philosophy, natural history, or scientific arts, nor the study of other languages, are attended to. Persons in these classes of society put their sons into shops or counting-houses to learn the routine of business with a knowledge of figures and the style of letter-writing; they are not kept at school more than three or four years, unless they mean to compete at the examinations. Working men, desirous of giving their sons a smattering, try to keep them at their books a year or two, but millions must of course grow up in utter ignorance. It is, however, an excellent policy for a state to keep up this universal honor paid to education where the labor is so great and the return so doubtful, for it is really the homage paid to the principles taught.

Besides the common schools, there are grammar or high schools and colleges, but they are far less effective. In Canton, there are fourteen grammar schools and thirty colleges, some of which are quite ancient, but most of them are neglected. Three of the largest contain each about two hundred students and two or three professors. The chief object of these institutions is to instruct advanced scholars in composition and elegant writing; the tutors do a little to turn attention to general literature, but have neither the genius nor the means to make many advances. In rural districts students are encouraged to meet at stated times in the town-house, where the headman, or deputy of the *sz'* or township, examines them on themes previously proposed by him.[1] In large towns, the local officers, assisted by the gentry and graduates, hold annual examinations of students, at which premiums are given to the best essayists. At such an examination in Amoy in March, 1845, there were about a thousand candidates, forty of whom received sums varying from sixty to sixteen cents

One of the most notable, as well as the most ancient of collegiate institutions, is the *Kwoh-tsz' Kien*, or 'School for the Sons of the State,' whose extensive buildings in Peking, now empty and dilapidated, show how much easier it is to found and plan a good thing than to maintain its efficiency. This state school originated as early as the Chau dynasty, and the course of study as given in the *Ritual of Chau* was much the same three thousand years ago as at present. Its officers consisted of a rector, usually a high minister of state, aided by five councillors, two directors, two proctors, two secretaries, a librarian, two professors in each of the six halls, and latterly five others for each of the colleges for Bannermen. These halls are named Hall of the Pursuit of Wisdom, the Sincere of Heart, of True Virtue, of Noble Aspiration, of Broad Acquirements, and the Guidance of Nature. The curriculum was not intended to go beyond the classics and the six liberal arts of music, charioteering, archery, etiquette, writing, and mathematics; but as if to encourage the professors to "seek out by wisdom concerning all things that are done under heaven," as Solomon advises, they were told to take their students to the original sources of strategy, astronomy, engineering, music, law, and the like, and points out the defects and merits of each author. The *Kwoh-tsz' Kien* possesses now only the husk of its ancient goodness; and if its professors were not honored, and made eligible to be distinct magistrates after three years' term, the buildings would soon be left altogether empty. Instead of reviving and rearranging it, the Chinese Government

---

[1] *Chinese Repository*, Vol. IV., p. 414. See also Vol. VI., pp. 229–241; Vol. IV., pp. 1–10; Vol. XI., pp. 545–557; and Vol. XIII., pp. 626–641, for further notices of the modes and objects of education; Biot, *Essai sur l'Histoire de l'Instruction Publique en Chine*, and his translation of the *Chao-li*, Vol. II., p. 27, Paris, 1851. *Chinese Recorder*, September, 1871.

has wisely supplanted it by a new college with its new professors and new course of studies—the *Tung-wăn Kwan* mentioned on p. 436. Native free schools, established by benevolent persons in city or country, are not uncommon, and serve to maintain the literary spirit; some may not be very long-lived, but others take their place. In Peking, each of the Banners has its school, and so has the Imperial Clan; retired officials contribute to schools opened for boys connected with their native districts living in the capital. Such efforts to promote education are expected from those who have obtained its high prizes.

How great a proportion of the people in China can read, is a difficult question to answer, for foreigners have had no means of learning the facts in the case, and the natives never go into such inquiries. More of the men in cities can read than in the country, and more in some provinces than in others. In the district of Nanhai, which forms part of the city of Canton, an imperfect examination led to the belief that nearly all the men are able to read, except fishermen, agriculturists, coolies, boat-people, and fuelers, and that two or three in ten devote their lives to literary pursuits. In less thickly settled districts, not more than four- or five-tenths, and even less, can read. In Macao, perhaps half of the men can read. From an examination of the hospital patients at Ningpo, one of the missionaries estimated the readers to form not more than five per cent. of the men; while another missionary at the same place, who made inquiry in a higher grade of society, reckoned them at twenty per cent. The villagers about Amoy are deplorably ignorant; one lady who had lived there over twenty years, writes that she had never found a woman who could read, but these were doubtless from among the poorer classes. It appears that as one goes north, the extent and thoroughness of education diminishes. Throughout the Empire the ability to understand books is not commensurate with the ability to read the characters, and both have been somewhat exaggerated. Owing to the manner in which education is commenced—learning the forms and sounds of characters before their meanings are understood—it comes to pass that many persons can call over the names of the characters while they do not comprehend in the least the sense of what they read. They can pick out a word here and there, it may be a phrase or a sentence, but they derive no clearer meaning from the text before them than a lad, who has just learned to scan, and has proceeded half through the Latin Reader, does from reading Virgil; while in both cases an intelligent audience, unacquainted with the facts, might justly infer that the reader understood what he was reading as well as his hearers did. Moreover, in the Chinese language, different subjects demand different characters; and although a man may be well versed in the classics or in fiction, he may be easily posed by being asked to explain a simple treatise in medicine or in mathematics, in consequence of the many new or unfamiliar words on every page. This is a serious obstacle in the way of obtaining a general acquaintance with books. The mind becomes weary with the labor of study where its toil is neither rewarded by knowledge nor beguiled by wit; consequently, few Chinese are well read in their natural literature. The study of books being regarded solely as the means wherewith to attain a definite end, it follows naturally that when a cultivated man has reached his goal he should feel little disposed to turn to these implements of his profession for either instruction or pleasure.

Wealthy or official parents, who wish their sons to compete for literary honors, give them the advantages of a full course in reading and rhetoric under the best masters. Composition is the most difficult part of the training of a Chinese student, and requires unwearied application and a retentive memory. He who can most readily quote the classics, and approach the nearest to their terse, comprehensive, energetic diction and style, is, *cæteris paribus*, most likely to succeed; while the man who can most quickly throw off well rhythmed verses takes the palm from all competitors. In novels, the ability to compose elegant verses as fast as the pencil can fly is usually ascribed to the hero of the plot. How many of those who intend to compete for degrees attend at the district colleges or high schools is not known, but they are resorted to by students about the time of the examinations in order to make the acquaintance of those who are to compete with them. No public examinations take place in either day or private schools, nor do parents often visit them, but rewards for remarkable proficiency are occasionally conferred. There is little gradation of studies, nor are any diplomas conferred on students to show that they have gone through a certain course. Punishments are severe, and the rattan or bamboo hangs conspicuously near the master, and its liberal use is considered necessary: "To educate without rigor, shows the teacher's indolence," is the doctrine, and by scolding, starving, castigation, and detention, the master tries to instil habits of obedience and compel his scholars to learn their task.

Notwithstanding the high opinion in which education is held, the general diffusion of knowledge, and the respect paid to learning in comparison with mere title and wealth, the defects of the tuition here briefly described, in extent, means, purposes, and results, are very great. Such, too, must necessarily be the case until new principles and new information are infused into it. Considered in its best point of view, this system has effected all that it can in enlarging the understanding, purifying the heart, and strengthening the minds of the people; but in none of these, nor in any of the essential points at which a sound education aims (as we understand the matter), has it accomplished half that is needed. The stream never rises even as high as its source, and the teachings of Confucius and Mencius have done all that is possible to make their countrymen thinking, useful, and intelligent men.

Turn we now from this brief sketch of primary education among the Chinese, to a description of the mode of examining students and conferring the degrees which have been made the passport to office, and learn what are the real merits of the system. Persons from almost every class of society may become candidates for degrees under the certificates of securities, but none are eligible for the second diploma who have not already received the first. It therefore happens that the republican license apparently allowed to well-nigh every subject, in reality reserves the prizes for the few most talented or wealthy persons in the community. A majority of the clever, learned, ambitious, and intelligent spirits in the land look forward to these examinations as the only field worthy of their efforts, and where they are most likely to find their equals and friends. How much better for the good of society, too, is this arena than the camp or the feudal court, the tournament or the monastery!

There are four regular literary degrees, with some intermediate steps of a titular sort. The first is called *siu-tsai*, meaning 'flowering talent,' because of the promise held out of the future success of the scholar; it has often been rendered 'bachelor of arts' as its nearest equivalent. The examinations to obtain it are held under the supervision of the *chihien* in a public building belonging to the district situated near his yamun; and the chief literary officer, called *hioh-ching*, 'corrector of learning,' or *kiao-yu*, 'teacher of the commands,' has the immediate control. When assembled at the hall of examination, the district magistrate, the deputy chancellor, and prefect, having prepared the lists of the undergraduates and selected the themes, allow only one day for writing the essays. The number of candidates depends upon the population and literary spirit of the district; in the districts of Nanhai and Pwanyu, upward of two thousand persons competed for the prize in 1832, while in Hiangshan not half so many came together. The rule for apportioning them was at first according to the annual revenue. When the essays are handed in, they are looked over by the board of examiners, and the names of the successful students entered on a roll, and pasted upon the walls of the magistrate's hall; this honor is called *hien ming*, *i.e.*, 'having a name in the village.' Out of the four thousand candidates referred to above, only thirteen in one district, and fourteen in the other, obtained a name in the village; the entire population of these two districts is not much under a million and a half. Many of the competitors at this primary tripos are unable to finish their essays in the day, others make errors in writing, and others show gross ignorance, all of which so greatly diminish their numbers, that only those who stand near the head of the list of *hien ming* do really or usually enter on the next trial before the prefect. But all have had an equal chance, and few complain that their performances were disregarded, for they can try as often as they please.

Those who pass the first examination are entered as candidates for the second, which takes place in the chief town of the department before the literary chancellor and the prefect, assisted by a literary magistrate called *kiao-shao*, 'giver of instructions;' it is more rigorous than that held before the *chihien*, though similar to it in nature. The prefect arranges the candidates from each district by themselves according to their standing on their several lists, and it is this vantage ground which makes the first trial in one's native place so important to the ambitious scholar. The themes on which they have tested their scholarship are published for the information of friends and the other examiners. If the proportion given above of successful candidates at the district examinations hold for each district, there would not be more than two hundred students assembled at the prefect's hall, but the number is somewhat increased by persons who have purchased the privilege; still the second trial is made among a small number in proportion to the first, and yet more trifling when compared with the amount of population. The names of the successful students at the second trial are exposed on the walls of the office, which is called *fu ming*, *i.e.*, 'having a name in the department,' and these only are eligible as candidates for the third trial. In addition to their knowledge of the classics, the candidates at this trial are often required to write off the text of the *Shing Yu*, or 'Sacred Edict,' from memory, as this work consists of maxims for the guidance of officers. The literary chancellor exercises a superintendence over the previous examinations, and makes the circuit of the province to attend them in each department, twice in three years. There are various ranks among these educational officials, corresponding to the civilians in the province; transfers are occasionally made from one service to the other, and the oversight of the latter is always given at the examinations wherever they are held. Most of the literary officers, however, remain in their own line, as it is highly honorable and more permanent. At the third trial in the provincial capital, he confers the first degree of *siu-tsai* upon those who are chosen out of the whole list as the best scholars.

There are several classes of bachelors, depending somewhat on the manner in which they obtained their degree; those who get it in the manner here described take the precedence. The possession of this degree protects the person from corporeal punishment, raises him above the common people, renders him a conspicuous man in his native place, and eligible to enter the triennial examination for the second degree. Those who have more money than learning, purchase this degree for sums varying from $200 up to $1,000, and even higher; in later years, according to the necessities of the government, diplomas have been sold as low as $25 to $50, but such men seldom rise. They are called *kien-săng*, and, as might be supposed, are looked upon somewhat contemptuously by those who have passed through the regular examinations, and "won the battle with their own lance." A degree called *kung-săng* is purchased by or bestowed upon the *siu-tsai*, but is so generally recognized that it has almost become a fifth degree, which does not entitle them to the full honors of a *kü-jin*. What proportion of scholars are rewarded by degrees is not known, but it is a small number compared with the candidates. A graduate of considerable intelligence at Ningpo estimated the number of *siu-tsai* in that city at four hundred, and in the department at nearly a thousand. In Canton City, the number of *shin-kin*, or gentry, who are allowed to wear the sash of honor, and have obtained literary degrees, is not over three hundred; but in the whole province there are about twelve thousand bachelors in a population of nineteen millions. Those who have not become *siu-tsai* are still regarded as under the oversight of the *kiao-yu* and others of his class, who still receive their essays; but the body of provincial *siu-tsai* are obliged to report themselves and attend the prefectural tripos before the chancellor, under penalty of losing all the privileges and rank obtained. This law brings them before those who may take cognizance of misdeeds, for these men are often very oppressive and troublesome to their countrymen. The graduates in each district are placed under the control of a chief, whose power is almost equal to the deputy chancellor's; from them are taken the two securities required by each applicant to enter the tripos.

The candidates for *siu-tsai* are narrowly examined when they enter the hall, their pockets, shoes, wadded robes, and ink-stones, all being searched, lest precomposed essays or other aids to composition be smuggled in. When they are all seated in the hall in their proper places, the wickets, doors, windows, and other entrances are all guarded, and pasted over with strips of paper. The room is filled with anxious competitors arranged in long seats, pencil in hand, and ready to begin. The theme is given out, and every one immediately writes off his essay, carefully noting how many characters he erases in composing it, and hands it up to the board of examiners; the whole day is allotted to the task, and a signal-gun announces the hour when the doors are thrown open, and the students can disperse. A man is liable to lose his acquired honor of *siu-tsai* if at a subsequent inspection he is found to have discarded his studies, and he is therefore impelled to pursue them in order to maintain his influence, even if he does not reach the next degree.[1]

Since the first degree is sometimes procured by influence and money, it is the examination for the second, called *kü-jin*, or 'promoted men,' held triennially in the provincial capitals before two imperial commissioners, that separates the candidates into students and officers, though all the students who receive a diploma by no means become officers. This examination is held at the same time in all the eighteen provincial capitals, viz., on the 9th, 12th, and 15th days of the eighth moon, or about the middle of September; while it is going on, the city appears exceedingly animated, in consequence of the great number of relatives and friends assembled with the students. The persons who preside at the examination, besides the imperial commissioners, are ten provincial officers, with the futai at their head, who jointly form a board of examiners, and decide upon the merits of the essays. The number of candidates who entered the lists at Canton in the years 1828 and 1831 was 4,800; in 1832 there were 6,000, which is nearer the usual number. In the largest provinces it reaches as many as 7,000, 8,000, and upward.

Previous to entering the *Kung Yuen*, each candidate has given in all the necessary proofs and particulars, which entitle

---

[1] *Chinese Repository*, Vol. II., p. 249; Vol. XVI., pp. 67–72. Doolittle, *Social Life of the Chinese*, Vol. I., pp. 376–443. Dr. Martin, *The Chinese*.

INTERIOR OF KUNG YUEN, OR 'EXAMINATION HALL,' PEKING.

him to a cell, and receives the ticket which designates the one he is to occupy. He enters the night before, and is searched to see that no manuscript essay, "skinning paper," or miniature edition of the classics, is secreted on his person. If anything of the sort is discovered, he is punished with the cangue, degraded from his first degree, and forbidden again to compete at the examination; his father and tutor are likewise punished. Some of the pieces written for this purpose are marvels of penmanship, and the most finished compositions; one set contained an essay on every sentence in the Four Books, each of the sheets covered with hundreds of characters, and the paper so thin that they could be easily read through it. The practice is, however, quite common, notwithstanding the penalties, and one censor requested a law to be passed forbidding small editions to be printed, and booksellers' shops to be searched for them.

The general arrangement of the examination halls in all the provincial capitals is alike. A description of that at Canton, given on page 166, is typical of them all.

The Hall at Peking, situated on the eastern side, not far from the observatory, contains ten thousand cells, and these do not always suffice for the host which assembles. The Hall at Fuhchau is equally large; each cell is a little higher than a man's head, and is open on but one side—letting in more rain and wind during inclement days than is comfortable. Confinement in these cramped cells is so irksome as to frequently cause the death of aged students, who are unable to sustain the fatigue, but who still enter the arena in hopes of at last succeeding. Cases have occurred where father, son, and grandson, appeared at the same time to compete for the same prize. Dr. Martin[1] found that out of a list of ninety-nine successful competitors for the second degree, sixteen were over forty years of age, one sixty-two, and one eighty-three. The average age of the whole number was over thirty—while in comparison with like statistics for the third degree, a proportionate increase might be looked for. The unpleasantness of the strait cell is much increased by the smoke arising from the cooking, and by the heat of the weather. All ser-

[1] *The Chinese*, p. 50.

vants are provided by government, but each candidate takes in the rice and fuel which he needs, together with cakes, tea, candles, bedding, etc., as he can afford; no one can go in with him. The enclosure presents a bustling scene during the examination, and its interest intensifies until the names of the successful scholars are published. Should a student die in his cell, the body is pulled through a hole made in the wall of the enclosure, and left there for his friends to carry away. Whenever a candidate breaks any of the prescribed regulations of the contest, his name and offence are reported, and his name is "pasted out" by placarding it on the outer door of the hall, after which he is not allowed to enter until another examination comes around. More than a hundred persons are thus "pasted out" each season, but no heavy disgrace seems to attach to them in consequence.

On the first day after the doors have been sealed up, four themes are selected by the examiners from the Four Books, one of which subjects must be discussed in a poetical essay. The minimum length of the compositions is a hundred characters, and they must be written plainly and elegantly, and sent in without any names attached. In 1828, the acumen of four thousand eight hundred candidates was exercised during the first day on these themes: "Tsăng-tsz' said, 'To possess ability, and yet ask of those who do not; to know much, and yet inquire of those who know little; to possess, and yet appear not to possess; to be full, and yet appear empty.'"—"He took hold of things by the two extremes, and in his treatment of the people maintained the golden medium." "A man from his youth studies eight principles, and when he arrives at manhood, he wishes to reduce them to practice."—The fourth essay, to be written in pentameters, had for its subject, "The sound of the oar, and the green of the hills and water." Among the themes given out in 1843, were these: "He who is sincere will be intelligent, and the intelligent man will be faithful."—"In carrying out benevolence, there are no rules." In 1835, one was, "He acts as he ought, both to the common people and official men, receives his revenue from Heaven, and by it is protected and highly esteemed." Among other more practical texts are the following: "Fire-arms began with the use of rockets in the Chau dynasty; in what book do we first meet with the word for cannon? Is the defence of Kaifung fu its first recorded use? Kublai khan, it is said, obtained cannon of a new kind; from whom did he obtain them? When the Ming Emperors, in the reign of Yungloh, invaded Cochinchina, they obtained a kind of cannon called the weapons of the gods; can you give an account of their origin?"

The three or five themes (for the number seems to be optional) selected from the Five Classics are similar to these, but as those works are regarded as more recondite than the Four Books, so must the essayists try to take a higher style. An officer goes around to gather in the papers, which are first handed to a body of scholars in waiting, who look them over to see if the prescribed rules have all been observed, and reject those which infringe them. The rest are then copied in red ink, to prevent recognition of the handwriting, and the original manuscripts given to the governor. The copies are submitted to another class of old scholars for their criticism, each of whom marks the essays he deems best with a red circle, and these only are placed in the hands of the chancellors sent from Peking for their decision. The examining board are aided by twelve scholars of repute, to each of whom forty or fifty essays are given to read. The students are dismissed during the night of the ninth day, and reassemble before sunrise of the eleventh; all whose essays were rejected on the first review are refused entrance to their cells. At the second tripos, five themes are given out from the Five Classics, and everything proceeds as before in respect to the disposal of the manuscripts. The students are liberated early on the thirteenth as before by companies, under a salute and music as they leave the great door; their number has been much reduced by this time. On the next morning the roll is called, and those who answer to their names for the last struggle are furnished with five themes for essays, one for poetry, taken from the classics or histories, upon doubtful matters of government, or such problems as might arise in law and finance. These questions take even a more extended range, including topics relating to the laws, history, geography, and customs of the Empire in former times, doubtful points touching the classical works, and the interpretation of obscure passages, and biographical notices of statesmen. It is forbidden, however, to discuss any points relating to the policy of the present family, or the character and learning of living statesmen; but the conduct of their rulers is now and then alluded to by the candidates. Manuals of questions on such subjects as candidates are examined in, are commonly exposed for sale in shops about the time of these examinations.[1] By noon of the sixteenth day of the eighth moon, all the candidates throughout the Empire have left their halls, and the examination is over.

The manner in which subjects are handled may be readily illustrated by introducing an essay upon this theme: "When persons in high stations are sincere in the performance of relative and domestic duties, the people generally will be stimulated to the practice of virtue." It is a fair specimen of the jejune style of Chinese essayists, and the mode of reasoning in a circle which pervades their writings.

"When the upper classes are really virtuous, the common people will inevitably become so. For, though the sincere performance of relative duties by superiors does not originate in a wish to stimulate the people, yet the people do become virtuous, which is a proof of the effect of sincerity. As benevolence is the radical principle of all good government in the world, so also benevolence is the radical principle of relative duties amongst the people. Traced back to its source, benevolent feeling refers to a first progenitor; traced forward, it branches out to a hundred generations yet to come. The source of personal existence is one's parents, the relations which originate from Heaven are most intimate; and that in which natural feeling blends is felt most deeply. That which is given by Heaven and by natural feeling to all, is done without any distinction between noble or ignoble. One feeling pervades all. My thoughts now refer to him who is placed in a station of eminence, and who may be called a good man. The good man who is placed in an eminent station, ought to lead forward the practice of virtue; but the way to do so is to begin with his own relations, and perform his duties to them.

"In the middle ages of antiquity, the minds of the people were not yet dissipated—how came it that they were not humble and observant of relative duties, when they were taught the principles of the five social relations? This having been the case, makes it evident that the enlightening of the people must depend entirely on the cordial performance of immediate relative duties. The person in an eminent station who may be called a good man, is he who appears at the head of all others in illustrating by his practice the relative duties.

---

[1] Biot, *Essai sur l'Instruction en Chine*, p. 603.

In ages nearer to our own, the manners of the people were not far removed from the dutiful; how came it that any were disobedient to parents, and without brotherly affection, and that it was yet necessary to restrain men by inflicting the eight forms of punishment? This having been the case, shows that in the various modes of obtaining promotion in the state, there is nothing regarded of more importance than filial and fraternal duties. The person in an eminent station who may be called a good man, is he who stands forth as an example of the performance of relative duties.

"The difference between a person filling a high station and one of the common people, consists in the department assigned them, not in their relation to Heaven: it consists in a difference of rank, not in a difference of natural feeling; but the common people constantly observe the sincere performance of relative duties in people of high stations. In being at the head of a family and preserving order amongst the persons of which it is composed, there should be sincere attention to politeness and decorum. A good man placed in a high station says, 'Who of all these are not related to me, and shall I receive them with mere external forms?' The elegant entertainment, the neatly arranged tables, and the exhilarating song, some men esteem mere forms, but the good man esteems that which dictates them as a divinely instilled feeling, and attends to it with a truly benevolent heart. And who of the common people does not feel a share of the delight arising from fathers, and brothers, and kindred? Is this joy resigned entirely to princes and kings?

"In favors conferred to display the benignity of a sovereign, there should be sincerity in the kindness done. The good man says, 'Are not all these persons whom I love, and shall I merely enrich them by largesses?' He gives a branch as the sceptre of authority to a delicate younger brother, and to another he gives a kingdom with his best instructions. Some men deem this as merely extraordinary good fortune, but the good man esteems it the exercise of a virtue of the first order, and the effort of inexpressible benevolence. But have the common people no regard for the spring whence the water flows, nor for the root which gives life to the tree and its branches? Have they no regard for their kindred? It is necessary both to reprehend and to urge them to exercise these feelings. The good man in a high station is sincere in the performance of relative duties, because to do so is virtuous, and not on account of the common people. But the people, without knowing whence the impulse comes, with joy and delight are influenced to act with zeal in this career of virtue; the moral distillation proceeds with rapidity, and a vast change is effected.

"The rank of men is exceedingly different; some fill the imperial throne, but every one equally wishes to do his utmost to accomplish his duty; and success depends on every individual himself. The upper classes begin and pour the wine into the rich goblet; the poor man sows his grain to maintain his parents; the men in high stations grasp the silver bowl, the poor present a pigeon; they arouse each other to unwearied cheerful efforts, and the principles implanted by Heaven are moved to action. Some things are difficult to be done, except by those who possess the glory of national rule; but the kind feeling is what I myself possess, and may increase to an unlimited degree.

The prince may write verses appropriate to his vine bower; the poor man can think of his gourd shelter; the prince may sing his classic odes on fraternal regards; the poor man can muse on his more simple allusions to the same subject, and asleep or awake indulge his recollections; for the feeling is instilled into his nature. When the people are aroused to relative virtues, they will be sincere; for where are there any of the common people that do not desire to perform relative duties? But without the upper classes performing relative duties, this virtuous desire would have no point from which to originate, and therefore it is said, 'Good men in high stations, as a general at the head of his armies, will lead forward the world to the practice of social virtues.'"

The discipline of mind and memory which these examinations draw out furnishes a grade of intellect which only needs the friction and experience of public life to make statesmen out of scholars, and goes far to account for the influence of Chinese in Asia. The books studied in preparation for such trials must be remembered with extraordinary accuracy, though we may wish they contained more truth and better science. The following are among the questions proposed in 1853, and must be taken as an average: "In the Han dynasty, there were three commentators on the *Yih King*, whose explanations, and divisions into chapters and sentences were all different: can you give an account of them?"—"Sz'ma Tsien took the classics and ancient records in arranging his history according to their facts; some have accused him of unduly exalting the Taoists and thinking too highly of wealth and power. Pan Ku is clear and comprehensive, but on Astronomy and the Five Elements, he has written more than enough. Give examples and proof of these two statements."—"Chin Shao had admirable abilities for historical writings. In his *San Kwoh Chí* he has depreciated Chu-koh Liang, and made very light of Ĭ and Ĭ, two other celebrated characters. What does he say of them?" This kind of question involves a wide range of reading within the native literature, though it of course contracts the mind to look upon that literature as containing all that is worth anything in the world.

Twenty-five days are allowed for the examining board to decide on the essays; and few tasks can be instanced more irksome to a board of honest examiners than the perusal of between fifty and seventy-five thousand papers on a dozen subjects, through which the most monotonous uniformity must necessarily run, and out of which they have to choose the seventy or eighty best —for the number of successful candidates cannot vary far from this, according to the size of the province. The examiners, as has already been described, are aided by literary men in sifting this mass of papers, which relieves them of most of the labor, and secures a better decision. If the number of students be five thousand, and each writes thirteen essays, there will be sixty-five thousand papers, which allots two hundred and sixty essays for each of the ten examiners. With the help of the assistants who are intrusted with their examination, most of the essays obtain a reading, no doubt, by some qualified scholar. There is, therefore, no little sifting and selection, so that when at the last the commissioners choose three rolls of essays and poems from each of the sessions belonging to the same scholar, to pass their final judgment, the company of candidates likely to succeed has been reduced as small in proportion as those in Gideon's host who lapped water. One of the examining committee, in 1832, who sought to invigorate his nerves or clear his intellect for the task by a pipe of opium, fell asleep in consequence, and on awaking, found that many of the essays had caught fire and been consumed. It is generally supposed that hundreds of them are unread, but the excitement of the occasion, and the dread on the part of the examining board to irritate the body of students, act as checks against gross omissions. Very trivial errors are enough to condemn an essay, especially if the examiners have not been gained to look upon it kindly. Section LII. of the code regulates the conduct of the examiners, but the punishments are slight. One candidate, whose essay had been condemned without being read, printed it, which led to the punishment of the examiner, degradation of the graduate, and promulgation of a law forbidding this mode of appealing to the public. Another essay was rejected because the writer had abbreviated a single character.

When the names of the successful wranglers are known, they are published by a crier at midnight, on or before the tenth of the ninth moon; at Canton, he mounts the highest tower, and, after a salute, announces them to the expectant city; the next morning, lists of the lucky scholars are hawked about the streets, and rapidly sent to all parts of the province. The proclamation which contains their names is pasted upon the governor's office under a salute of three guns; his excellency comes out and bows three times towards the names of the *promoted men*, and retires under another salute. The disappointed multitude must then rejoice in the success of the few, and solace themselves with the hope of better luck next time; while the successful ones are honored and feasted in a very distinguished manner, and are the objects of flattering attention from the whole city. On an appointed day, the governors, commissioners, and high provincial officers banquet them all at the futai's palace; inferior officers attend as servants, and two lads, fantastically dressed, and holding fragrant branches of the olive (*Olea fragrans*) in their hands grace the scene with this symbol of literary attainments. The number of A.M., licentiates, or *kü-jin*, who triennially receive their degrees in the Empire, is upwards of thirteen hundred: the expense of the examinations to the government in various ways, including the presents conferred on the graduates, can hardly be less than a third of a million of taels. Besides the triennial examinations, special ones are held every ten years, and on extraordinary occasions, as a victory, a new reign, or an imperial marriage. One was granted in 1835 because the Empress-dowager had reached her sixtieth year.

The third degree of *tsin-sz'*, 'entered scholars,' or doctors, is conferred triennially at Peking upon the successful licentiates who compete for it, and only those among the *kü-jin*, who have not already taken office, are eligible as candidates. On application at the provincial treasury, they are entitled to a part of their travelling expenses to court, but it doubtless requires some interest to get the mileage granted, for many poor scholars are detained from the metropolitan examination, or must beg or borrow in order to reach it. The procedure on this trial is the same as in the provinces, but the examiners are of higher rank; the themes are taken from the same works, and the essays are but little else than repetitions of the same train of thought and argument. After the degrees are conferred upon all who are deemed worthy, which varies from one hundred and fifty to four hundred each time, the doctors are introduced to the Emperor, and do him reverence, the three highest receiving rewards from him. At this examination, candidates, instead of being promoted, are occasionally degraded from their acquired standing for incompetency, and forbidden to appear at them again. The graduates are all inscribed upon the list of candidates for promotion, by the Board of Civil Office, to be appointed on the first vacancy; most of them do in fact enter on official life in some way or other by attaching themselves to high dignitaries, or getting employment in some of the departments at the capital. One instance is recorded of a student taking all the degrees within nine months; and some become *hanlin* before entering office. Others try again and again, till gray hairs compel them to retire. There are many subordinate offices in the Academy, the Censorate, or the Boards, which seem almost to have been instituted for the employment of graduates, whose success has given them a partial claim upon the country. The Emperor sometimes selects clever graduates to prepare works for the use of government, or nominates them upon special literary commissions;[1] It can easily be understood that no small address in managing and appeasing such a crowd of disciplined active minds is required on the part of the bureaucracy, and only the long experience of many generations of the graduates could suffice to keep the system so vigorous as it is.

The fourth and highest degree of *hanlin* is rather an office than a degree, for those who attain it are enrolled as members of the Imperial Academy, and receive salaries. The triennial examination for this distinction is held in the Emperor's palace, and is conducted on much the same plan as all preceding ones, though being in the presence of the highest personages in the Empire, it exceeds them in honor.[2] Manchus and Mongols

---

[1] *Chinese Repository*, Vol. IX., p. 541; Vol. III., p. 118.

[2] See Morrison's *Chinese Dictionary*, Vol. I., Part I., pp. 759–779, for the laws and usages of the several trials. Also Doolittle's *Social Life*, Vol. I., Chaps. XV., XVI., and XVII.; Biot, *Essai sur l'Histoire de l'Instruction Publique en Chine;* W. A. P. Martin, *The Chinese*, pp. 39 ff.; *Journal Asiatique*, Tomes III., pp. 257 and 321, IV., p. 3, and VII. (3d Series, 1839), pp. 32–81; *Journal Asiatic Soc. Bengal*, Vol. XXVIII., No. 1, 1859; *Journal N. C. Br. R. As. Soc.*, New Series, Vol. VI., pp. 129 ff.; *China Review*, Vol. II., p. 309.

compete at these trials with the Chinese, but many facts show that the former are generally favored at the expense of the latter; the large proportion of men belonging to these races filling high offices indicates who are the rulers of the land. The candidates are all examined at Peking; one instance is recorded of a Chinese who passed himself off for a Manchu, but afterward confessed the dissimulation; the head of the division was tried in consequence of his oversight. It is the professed policy of the government to discourage literary pursuits among them, in order to maintain the ancient energy of the race; but where the real power is lodged in the hands of civilians, it is impossible to prevent so powerful a component of the population from competing with the others for its possession.

The present dynasty introduced examinations and gradations among the troops on the same principles as obtain in the civil service; nothing more strikingly proves the power of literary pursuits in China, than this vain attempt to harmonize the profession of arms in all its branches with them. Their enemies were, however, no better disciplined and equipped than they themselves were. Candidates for the first degree present themselves before the district magistrate, with proper testimonials and securities. On certain days they are collected on the parade-grounds, and exhibit their skill in archery (on foot and in the saddle), in wielding swords and lifting weights, graduated to test their muscle. The successful men are assembled afterward before the prefect; and again at a third trial before the literary chancellor, who at the last tripos tests them on their literary attainments, before giving them their degrees of *siu-tsai*. The number of successful military *siu-tsai* is the same as the literary. They are triennially called together by the governor at the provincial capital to undergo further examination for *kü-jin* in four successive trials of the same nature. These occasions are usually great gala days, and three or four scores of young warriors who carry off prizes at these tournaments receive honors and degrees in much the same style as their literary compeers. The trials for the highest degree are held at Peking; and the long-continued efforts in this service generally obtain for the young men posts in the body-guard of the governors or staff appointments. The forty-nine successful candidates out of several thousands at the triennial examination for *kü-jin* in Canton, November, 1832, all hit the target on foot six times successively, and on horseback six times; once with the arrow they hit a ball lying on the ground as they passed it at a gallop; and all were of the first class in wielding the iron-handled battle-axe, and lifting the stone-loaded beam. The candidates are all persons of property, who find their own horses, dresses, arms, etc., and are handsomely dressed, the horses, trimmings, and accoutrements in good order—the arrows being without barbs, to prevent accidents. One observer says, "the marks at which they fired, covered with white paper, were about the height of a man and somewhat wider, placed at intervals of fifty yards; the object was to strike these marks successively with their three arrows, the horses being kept at full speed. Although the bull's-eye was not always hit, the target was never missed: the distance did not exceed fifteen or twenty feet."[1]

Since military honors depend so entirely on personal skill, it may partly account for the inferior rank the graduates hold in comparison with civilians. No knowledge of tactics, gunnery, engineering, fortifications, or even letters in general, seems to be required of them; and this explains the inefficiency of the army, and the low estimation its officers are held in. Sir J. Davis mentions one military officer of enormous size and strength, whom he saw on the Pei ho, who had lately been promoted for his personal prowess; and speaks of another attached to the guard on one of the boats, who was such a foolish fellow that none of the civilians would associate with him.[2] All the classes eligible to civil promotion can enter the lists for military honors; the Emperor is present at the examination for the highest, and awards prizes, such as a cap decorated with a peacock's feather; but no system of prizes or examinations can supply the want of knowledge and courage. Military distinctions not being much sought by the people, and conferring but

[1] Ellis, *Embassy to China*, p. 87; *Chinese Repository*, Vol. XVI., p. 62; Vol. IV., p. 125.

[2] Davis, *Sketches*, Vol. I., pp. 99, 101.

little emolument or power, do not stand as high in public estimation as the present government wishes. The selection of officers for the naval service is made from the land force, and a man is considered quite as fit for that branch after his feats of archery, as if the trials had been in yacht-sailing or manning the yards.

Such is the outline of the system of examinations through which the civil and military services of the Chinese government are supplied, and the only part of their system not to be paralleled in one or other of the great monarchies of past or present times; though the counterpart of this may have also existed in ancient Egypt. "It is the only one of their inventions," as has been remarked, "which is perhaps worth preserving, and has not been adopted by other countries, and carried to greater perfection than they were equal to." But such a system would be unnecessary in an enlightened Christian country, where the people, pursuing study for its own sake, are able and willing to become as learned as their rulers desire without any such inducement. Nor would they submit to the trammels and trickery attendant on competition for office; the ablest politicians are by no means found among the most learned scholars. The honor and power of official position have proved to be ample stimulus and reward for years of patient study. Not one in a score of graduates ever obtains an office, not one in a hundred of competitors ever gets a degree; but they all belong to the literary class, and share in its influence, dignity, and privileges. Moreover, these books render not only those who get the prizes well acquainted with the true principles on which power should be exercised, but the whole nation—gentry and commoners—know them also. These unemployed *literati* form a powerful middle class, whose members advise the work-people, who have no time to study, and aid their rulers in the management of local affairs. Their intelligence fits them to control most of the property, while few acquire such wealth as gives them the power to oppress. They make the public opinion of the country, now controlling it, then cramping it; alternately adopting or resisting new influences, and sometimes successfully thwarting the acts of officials, when the rights of the people are in danger of encroachment; or at other times combining with the authorities to repress anarchy or relieve suffering.

This class has no badge of rank, and is open to every man's highest talent and efforts, but its complete neutralization of hereditary rights, which would have sooner or later made a privileged oligarchy and a landed or feudal aristocracy, proves its vitalizing, democratic influence. It has saved the Chinese people from a second disintegration into numerous kingdoms, by the sheer force of instruction in the political rights and duties taught in the classics and their commentaries. While this system put all on equality, human nature, as we know, has no such equality. At its inception it probably met general support from all classes, because of its fitness for the times, and soon the resistance of multitudes of hopeful students against its abrogation and their consequent disappointment in their life-work aided its continuance. As it is now, talent, wealth, learning, influence, paternal rank, and intrigue, each and all have full scope for their greatest efforts in securing the prizes. If these prizes had been held by a tenure as slippery as they are at present in the American Republic, or obtainable only by canvassing popular votes, the system would surely have failed, for "the game would not have been worth the candle." But in China the throne gives a character of permanency to the government, which opposes all disorganizing tendencies, and makes it for the interest of every one in office to strengthen the power which gave it to him. This loyalty was remarkably shown in the recent rebellion, in which, during the eighteen years of that terrible carnage and ruin, not one imperial official voluntarily joined the Tai-pings, while hundreds died resisting them.

There is no space here for further extracts from the classics which will adequately show their character. They would prove that Chinese youth, as well as those in Christian lands, are taught a higher standard of conduct than they follow. The former are, however, drilled in the very best moral books the language affords; if the Proverbs of Solomon and the New Testament were studied as thoroughly in our schools as the

Four Books are in China, our young men would be better fitted to act their part as good and useful citizens.

In this way literary pursuits have taken precedence of warlike, and no unscrupulous Cæsar or Napoleon has been able to use the army for his own aggrandizement. The army of China is contemptible, certainly, if compared with those of Western nations, and its use is rather like a police, whose powers of protection or oppression are exhibited according to the tempers of those who employ them. But in China the army has not been employed, as it was by those great captains, to destroy the institutions on which it rests; though its weakness and want of discipline often make it a greater evil than good to the people. But had the military waxed strong and efficient, it would certainly have become a terror in the hands of ambitious monarchs, a drain on the resources of the land, perhaps a menace to other nations, or finally a destroyer of its own. The officials were taught, when young, what to honor in their rulers; and, now that they hold those stations, they learn that discreet, upright magistrates do receive reward and promotion, and experience has shown them that peace and thrift are the ends and evidence of good government, and the best tests of their own fitness for office.

Another observable result of this republican method of getting the best-educated men into office is the absence of any class of slaves or serfs among the population. Slavery exists in a modified form of corporeal mortgage for debt, and thousands remain in this serfdom for life through one reason or another. But the destruction of a feudal baronage involved the extinction of its correlative, a villein class, and the oppression of poor debtors, as was the case in Rome under the consuls. Only freemen are eligible to enter the *concours*, but the percentage of slaves is too small to influence the total. To this cause, too, may, perhaps, to a large degree, be ascribed the absence of anything like caste, which has had such bad effects in India.

The system could not be transplanted; it is fitted for the genius of the Chinese, and they have become well satisfied with its workings. Its purification would do great good, doubtless, if the mass of the people are to be left in their present state of ignorance, but their elevation in knowledge would, ere long, revolutionize the whole. There can be no doubt as to the important and beneficial results it has accomplished, with all its defects, in perpetuating and strengthening the system of government, and securing to the people a more equitable and vigorous body of magistrates than they could get in any other way. It offers an honorable career to the most ambitious, talented, or turbulent spirits in the country, which demands all their powers; and by the time they enter upon office, those aspirations and powers have been drilled and molded into useful service, and are ever after devoted to the maintenance of the system they might otherwise have wrecked. Most of the real benefits of Chinese education and this system of examinations are reached before the conferment of the degree of *kü-jin*. These consist in diffusing a general respect and taste for letters among the people; in calling out the true talent of the country to the notice of the rulers in an honorable path of effort; in making all persons so thoroughly acquainted with the best moral books in the language that they cannot fail to exercise some salutary restraint; in elevating the general standard of education so much that every man is almost compelled to give his son a little learning in order that he may get along in life; and finally, through all these influences, powerfully contributing to uphold the existing institutions of the Empire.

From the intimate knowledge thus obtained of the writings of their best minds, Chinese youth learn the principles of democratic rule as opposed to personal authority; and from this instruction it has resulted that no monarch has ever been able to use a standing army to enslave the people, or seize the proceeds of their industry for his own selfish ends. Nothing in Chinese politics is more worthy of notice than the unbounded reverence for the Emperor, while each man resists unjust taxation, and joins in killing or driving away oppressive officials. Educated men form the only aristocracy in the land; and the attainment of the first degree, by introducing its owner into the class of *gentry*, is considered ample compensation for all the expense and study spent in getting it. On the whole, it may safely be asserted that these examinations have done more to maintain the stability, and explain the continuance, of the Chinese government than any other single cause.

The principal defects and malversations in the system can soon be shown. Some are inherent, but others rather prove the badness of the material than of the system and its harmonious workings. One great difficulty in the way of the graduated students attaining office according to their merits is the favor shown to those who can buy nominal and real honors. Two censors, in 1822, laid a document before his Majesty, in which the evils attendant on selling office are shown; viz., elevating priests, highwaymen, merchants, and other unworthy or uneducated men, to responsible stations, and placing insurmountable difficulties in the way of hard-working, worthy students reaching the reward of their toil. They state that the plan of selling offices commenced during the Han dynasty, but speak of the greater disgrace attendant upon the plan at the present time, because the avails all go into the privy purse instead of being applied to the public service; they recommend, therefore, a reduction in the disbursements of the imperial establishment. Among the items mentioned by these oriental Joseph Humes, which they consider extravagant, are a lac of taels (100,000) for flowers and rouge in the seraglio, and 120,000 in salaries to waiting-boys; two lacs were expended on the gardens of Yuenming, and almost half a million of taels upon the parks at Jeh ho, while the salaries to officers and presents to women at Yuenming were over four lacs. "If these few items of expense were abolished," they add, "there would be a saving of more than a million of taels of useless expenditure; talent might be brought forward to the service of the country, and the people's wealth be secured."

In consequence of the extensive sale of offices, they state that more than five thousand *tsin-sz'* doctors, and more than twenty-seven thousand *kü-jin* licentiates, are waiting for employment; and those first on the list obtained their degrees thirty years ago, so that the probability is that when at last employed, they will be too old for service, and be declared superannuated in the first examination of official merits and demerits. The rules to be observed at the regular examinations are strict, but no questions are asked the buyers of office; and they enter, too, on their duties as soon as the money is paid. The censors quote three sales, whose united proceeds amounted to a quarter of a million of taels, and state that the whole income from this source for twenty years was only a few lacs. Examples of the flagitious conduct of these purse-proud magistrates are quoted in proof of the bad results of the plan. "Thus the priest Siang Yang, prohibited from holding office, bought his way to one; the intendant at Ningpo, from being a mounted highwayman, bought his way to office; besides others of the vilest parentage. But the covetousness and cruelty of these men are denominated purity and intelligence; they inflict severe punishments, which make the people terrified, and their superiors point them out as possessing decision: these are our able officers!"

After animadverting on the general practice "of all officers, from governor-generals down to village magistrates, combining to gain their purposes by hiding the truth from the sovereign," and specifying the malversations of Tohtsin, the premier, in particular, they close their paper with a protestation of their integrity. "If your Majesty deems what we have now stated to be right, and will act thereon in the government, you will realize the designs of the souls of your sacred ancestors; and the army, the nation, and the poor people, will have cause for gladness of heart. Should we be subjected to the operation of the hatchet, or suffer death in the boiling caldron, we will not decline it."

These censors place the proceeds of "button scrip" far too low, for in 1826, the sale produced about six millions of taels, and was continued at intervals during the three following years. In 1831, one of the sons of Howqua was created a *kü-jin* by patent for having subscribed nearly fifty thousand dollars to repair the dikes near Canton; and upon another was conferred the rank and title of "director of the salt monopoly" for a lac of taels toward the war in Turkestan. Neither of these persons ever held any office of power, nor probably did they expect it; and such may be the case with many of those who are satisfied with the titles and buttons, feathers and robes, which their money procures. The sale of office is rather accepted as a State necessity which does not necessarily bring tyrants upon the bench; but when, as was the case in 1863, Peiching, head of the Examining Board at Peking, fraudulently issued two or three diplomas, his execution vindicated the law, and deterred similar tampering with the life-springs of the system. During the present dynasty, military men have been frequently appointed to magistracies, and the detail of their offices intrusted to needy scholars, which has tended, still further, to disgust and dishearten the latter from resorting to the literary arena.

The language itself of the Chinese, which has for centuries aided in preserving their institutions and strengthening national homogeneity amid so many local varieties of speech, is now rather in the way of their progress, and may be pointed to as another unfortunate feature which infects this system of education and examination; for it is impossible for a native to write a treatise on grammar about another language in his own tongue, through which another Chinese can, unaided, learn to speak that language. This people have, therefore, no ready means of learning the best thoughts of foreign minds. Such being the case, the ignorance of their first scholars as regards other races, ages, and lands has been their misfortune far more than their fault, and they have suffered the evils of their isolation. One has been an utter ignorance of what would have conferred lasting benefit resulting from the study of outside conceptions of morals, science, and politics. Inasmuch as neither geography, natural history, mathematics, nor the history or languages of other lands forms part of the curriculum, these men, trained alone in the classics, have naturally grown up with distorted views of their own country. The officials are imbued with conceit, ignorance, and arrogance as to its power, resources, and comparative influence, and are helpless when met by greater skill or strength. However, these disadvantages, great as they are and have been, have mostly resulted naturally from their secluded position, and are rapidly yielding to the new influences which are acting upon government and people. To one contemplating this startling metamorphosis, the foremost wish, indeed, must be that these causes do not disintegrate their ancient economies too fast for the recuperation and preservation of whatever is good therein.

Another evil is the bribery practised to attain the degrees. By certain signs placed on the essays, the examiner can easily pick out those he is to approve; $8,000 was said to be the price of a bachelor's degree in Canton, but this sum is within the reach of few out of the six thousand candidates. The poor scholars sell their services to the rich, and for a certain price will enter the hall of examination, and personate their employer, running the risk and penalties of a disgraceful exposure if detected; for a less sum they will drill them before examination, or write the essays entirely, which the rich booby must commit to memory. The purchase of forged diplomas is another mode of obtaining a graduate's honors, which, from some discoveries made at Peking, is so extensively practised, that when this and other corruptions are considered, it is surprising that any person can be so eager in his studies, or confident of his abilities, as ever to think he can get into office by them alone. In 1830, the *Gazette* contained some documents showing that an inferior officer, aided by some of the clerks in the Board of Revenue, during the successive superintendence of twenty presidents of the Board had sold twenty thousand four hundred and nineteen forged diplomas; and in the province of Nganhwui, the writers in the office attached to the Board of Revenue had carried on the same practice for four years, and forty-six persons in that province were convicted of possessing them. All the principal criminals convicted at this time were sentenced to decapitation, but these cases are enough to show that the real talent of the country does not often find its way into the magistrate's seat without the aid of money; nor is it likely that the tales of such delinquencies often appear in the *Gazette*. Literary chancellors also sell bachelors' degrees to the exclusion of deserving poor scholars; the office of the *hiohching* of Kiangsí was searched in 1828 by a special commission, and four lacs of taels found in it; he hung himself to avoid further punishment, as did also the same dignitary in Canton in 1833, as was supposed, for a similar cause. It is in this way, no doubt, that the ill-gotten gains of most officers return to the general circulation.

Notwithstanding these startling corruptions, which seem to involve the principle on which the harmony and efficiency of the whole machinery of state stand, it cannot be denied, judging from the results, that the highest officers of the Chinese government do possess a very respectable rank of talent and knowledge, and carry on the unwieldy machine with a degree of integrity, patriotism, industry, and good order which shows that the leading minds in it are well chosen. The person who has originally obtained his rank by a forged diploma, or by direct purchase, cannot hope to rise or to maintain even his first standing, without some knowledge and parts. One of the three commissioners whom Kíying associated with himself in his negotiations with the American minister in 1844, was a supernumerary *chíhien* of forbidding appearance, who could hardly write a common document, but it was easy to see the low estimation the ignoramus was held in. It may therefore be fairly inferred that enough large prizes are drawn to incite successive generations of scholars to compete for them, and thus to maintain the literary spirit of the people. At these examinations the superior minds of the country are brought together in large bodies, and thus they learn each others views, and are able to check official oppressions with something like a public opinion. In Peking the concourse of several thousands, from the remotest provinces, to compete at or assist in the triennial examinations, exerts a great and healthy influence upon their rulers and themselves. Nothing like it ever has been seen in any other metropolis.

The enjoyment of no small degree of power and influence in their native village, is also to be considered in estimating the rewards of studious toil, whether the student get a diploma or not; and this local consideration is the most common reward attending the life of a scholar. In those villages where no governmental officer is specially appointed, such men are almost sure to become the headmen and most influential persons in the very spot where a Chinese loves to be distinguished. Graduates are likewise allowed to erect flag-staffs, or put up a red sign over the door of their houses showing the degree they have obtained, which is both a harmless and gratifying reward of study; like the additions of *Cantab.* or *Oxon.*, D.D. or LL.D., to their owner's names in other lands.

The fortune attending the unsuccessful candidates is various. Thousands of them get employment as school-teachers, pettifogging notaries, and clerks in the public offices, and others who are rich return to their families. Some are reduced by degrees to beggary, and resort to medicine, fortune-telling, letter-writing, and other such shifts to eke out a living. Many turn their attention to learning the modes of drawing up deeds and forms used in dealings regarding property; others look to aiding military men in their duties, and a few turn authors, and thus in one way or another contrive to turn their learning to account.

During the period of the examinations, when the students are assembled in the capital, the officers of government are careful not to irritate them by punishment, or offend their *esprit de corps*, but rather, by admonitions and warnings, induce them to set a good example. The personal reputation of the officer himself has much to do with the influence he exerts over the students, and whether they will heed his *caveats*. One of the examiners in Chehkiang, irritated by the impertinence of a bachelor, who presumed upon his immunity from corporeal chastisement, twisted his ears to teach him better manners; soon after, the student and two others of equal degree were accused before the same magistrate for a libel, and one of them beaten forty strokes upon his palms. At the ensuing examination, ten of the *siu-tsai*, indignant at this unauthorized treatment, refused to appear, and all the candidates, when they saw who was to preside, dispersed immediately. In his memorial upon the matter, the governor-general recommends both this officer, and another one who talked much about the affair and produced a great effect upon the public mind, to be degraded, and the bachelors to be stripped of their honors. A magistrate of Honan, having punished a student with twenty blows, the assembled body of students rose and threw their caps on the ground, and walked off, leaving him alone. The prefect of Canton, in 1842, having become obnoxious to the citizens from the part he took in ransoming the city when surrounded by the British forces, the students refused to receive him as their examiner, and when he appeared in the hall to take his seat, drove him out of the room by throwing their ink-stones at him; he soon after resigned his station. Perhaps the *siu-tsai* are more impatient than the *kü-jin* from being better acquainted with each other, and being examined by local officers, while the *kü-jin* are overawed by the rank of the commissioners, and, coming from distant parts of a large province, have little mutual sympathy or acquaintance. The examining boards, however, take pains to avoid displeasing any gathering of graduates.

We have seen, then, in what has been of necessity a somewhat cursory *resumé*, the management and extent of an institution which has opened the avenues of rank to all, by teaching candidates how to maintain the principles of liberty and equality they had learned from their oft-quoted 'ancients.' All that these institutions need, to secure and promote the highest welfare of the people—as they themselves, indeed, aver—is their faithful execution in every department of government; as we find them, no higher evidence of their remarkable wisdom can be adduced, than the general order and peace of the land. When one sees the injustice and oppressions in law courts, the feuds and deadly fights among clans, the prevalence of lying, ignorance, and pollution among commoners, and the unscrupulous struggle for a living going on in every rank of life, he wonders that universal anarchy does not destroy the whole machine. But 'the powers that be are ordained of God.' The Chinese seem to have attained the great ends of human government to as high a degree as it is possible for man to go without the knowledge of divine revelation. That, in its great truths, its rewards, its hopes, and its stimulus to good acts has yet to be received among them. The course and results of the struggle between the new and the old in the land of Sinim will form a remarkable chapter in the history of man.

With regard to female education, it is a singular anomaly among Chinese writers, that while they lay great stress upon maternal instruction in forming the infant mind, and leading it on to excellence, no more of them should have turned their attention to the preparation of books for girls, and the establishment of female schools. There are some reasons for the absence of the latter to be found in the state of society, notable among which must stand, of course, the low position of woman in every oriental community, and a general contempt for the capacity of the female mind. It is, moreover, impossible to procure many qualified schoolmistresses, and to this we must add the hazard of sending girls out into the streets alone, where they would run some risk of being stolen. The principal stimulus for boys to study—the hope and prospect of office—is taken away from girls, and Chinese literature offers little to repay them for the labor of learning it in addition to all the domestic duties which devolve upon them. Nevertheless, education is not entirely confined to the stronger sex; seminaries for young women are not at all uncommon in South China, and it is not unusual to find private tutors giving instruction to young ladies at their houses.[1] Though this must be regarded as a comparative statement, and holding much more for the southern than for the northern provinces, on the other hand, it may be asserted that literary attainments are considered creditable to a woman, more than is the case in India or Siam; the names of authoresses mentioned in Chinese annals would make a long list. Yuen Yuen, the governor-general of Canton, in 1820, while in office, published a volume of his deceased's daughter's poetical effusions; and literary men are usually desirous of having their daughters accomplished in music and poetry, as well as in composition and classical lore. Such an education is considered befitting their station, and reflecting credit on the family.

One of the most celebrated female writers in China is Pan Hwui-pan, also known as Pan Chao, a sister of the historian Pan Ku, who wrote the history of the former Han dynasty. She was appointed historiographer after his death, and completed his unfinished annals; she died at the age of seventy, and was honored by the Emperor Ho with a public burial, and

---

[1] Archdeacon Gray, *China*, Vol. I., p. 167.

the title of the Great Lady Tsao. About A.D. 80, she was made preceptress of the Empress, and wrote the first work in any language on female education; it was called *Nü Kiai* or *Female Precepts*, and has formed the basis of many succeeding books on female education. The aim of her writings was to elevate female character, and make it virtuous. She says, "The virtue of a female does not consist altogether in extraordinary abilities or intelligence, but in being modestly grave and inviolably chaste, observing the requirements of virtuous widowhood, and in being tidy in her person and everything about her; in whatever she does to be unassuming, and whenever she moves or sits to be decorous. This is female virtue." Instruction in morals and the various branches of domestic economy are more insisted upon in the writings of this and other authoresses, than a knowledge of the classics or histories of the country.

One of the most distinguished Chinese essayists of modern times, Luhchau, published a work for the benefit of the sex, called the *Female Instructor;* an extract from his preface will show what ideas are generally entertained on female education by Chinese moralists.

"The basis of the government of the Empire lies in the habits of the people, and the surety that their usages will be correct is in the orderly management of families, which last depends chiefly upon the females. In the good old times of Chau, the virtuous women set such an excellent example that it influenced the customs of the Empire—an influence that descended even to the times of the Ching and Wei states. If the curtain of the inner apartment gets thin, or is hung awry [*i.e.*, if the sexes are not kept apart], disorder will enter the family, and ultimately pervade the Empire. Females are doubtless the sources of good manners; from ancient times to the present this has been the case. The inclination to virtue and vice in women differs exceedingly; their dispositions incline contrary ways, and if it is wished to form them alike, there is nothing like education. In ancient times, youth of both sexes were instructed. According to the *Ritual of Chau*, 'the imperial wives regulated the law for educating females, in order to instruct the ladies of the palace in morals, conversation, manners, and work; and each led out her respective classes, at proper times, and arranged them for examination in the imperial presence.' But these treatises have not reached us, and it cannot be distinctly ascertained what was their plan of arrangement. . . . .

"The education of a woman and that of a man are very dissimilar. Thus, a man can study during his whole life; whether he is abroad or at home, he can always look into the classics and history, and become thoroughly acquainted with the whole range of authors. But a woman does not study more than ten years, when she takes upon her the management of a family, where a multiplicity of cares distract her attention, and having no leisure for undisturbed study, she cannot easily understand learned authors; not having obtained a thorough acquaintance with letters, she does not fully comprehend their principles; and like water that has flowed from its fountain, she cannot regulate her conduct by their guidance. How can it be said that a standard work on female education is not wanted! Every profession and trade has its appropriate master; and ought not those also who possess such an influence over manners [as females] to be taught their duties and their proper limits? It is a matter of regret, that in these books no extracts have been made from the works of Confucius in order to make them introductory to the writings on polite literature; and it is also to be regretted that selections have not been made from the commentaries of Ching, Chu, and other scholars, who have explained his writings clearly, as also from the whole range of writers, gathering from them all that which was appropriate, and omitting the rest. These are circulated among mankind, together with such books as the *Juvenile Instructor;* yet if they are put into the hands of females, they cause them to become like a blind man without a guide, wandering hither and thither without knowing where he is going. There has been this great deficiency from very remote times until now.

"Woman's influence is according to her moral character, therefore that point is largely explained. First, concerning her obedience to her husband and to his parents; then in regard to her complaisance to his brothers and sisters, and kindness to her sisters-in-law. If unmarried, she has duties toward her parents, and to the wives of her elder brothers; if a principal wife, a woman must have no jealous feelings; if in straitened circumstances, she must be contented with her lot; if rich and honorable, she must avoid extravagance and haughtiness. Then teach her, in times of trouble and in days of ease, how to maintain her purity, how to give importance to right principles, how to observe widowhood, and how to avenge the murder of a relative. Is she a mother, let her teach her children; is she a step-mother, let her love and cherish her husband's children; is her rank in life high, let her be condescending to her inferiors; let her wholly discard all sorcerers, superstitious nuns, and witches; in a word let her adhere to propriety and avoid vice.

"In conversation, a female should not be froward and garrulous, but observe strictly what is correct, whether in suggesting advice to her husband, in remonstrating with him, or teaching her children, in maintaining etiquette, humbly imparting her experience, or in averting misfortune. The deportment of females should be strictly grave and sober, and yet adapted to the occasion; whether in waiting on her parents, receiving or reverencing her husband, rising up or sitting down, when pregnant, in times of mourning, or when fleeing in war, she should be perfectly decorous. Rearing the silkworm and working cloth are the most important of the employments of a female; preparing and serving up the food for the household, and setting in order the sacrifices, follow next, each of which must be attended to; after them, study and learning can fill up the time." [1]

The work thus prefaced, is similar to Sprague's *Letters to a Daughter*, rather than to a text-book, or a manual intended to be read and obeyed rather than recited by young ladies. Happy would it be for the country, however, if the instructions given by this moralist were followed; it is a credit to a pagan, to write such sentiments as the following: "During infancy, a child ardently loves its mother, who knows all its traits of goodness: while the father, perhaps, cannot know about it, there is nothing which the mother does not see. Wherefore the mother teaches more effectually, and only by her unwise fondness does her son become more and more proud (as musk by age becomes sourer and stronger), and is thereby nearly ruined."—"Heavenly order is to bless the good and curse the vile; he who sins against it will certainly receive his punishment sooner or later: from lucid instruction springs the happiness of the world. If females are unlearned, they will be like one looking at a wall, they will know nothing: if they are taught, they will know, and knowing they will imitate their examples."

It is vain to expect, however, that any change in the standing of females, or extent of their education, will take place until influences from abroad are brought to bear upon them—until the same work that is elswhere elevating them to their proper place in society by teaching them the principles on which that elevation is founded, and how they can themselves maintain it, is begun. The Chinese do not, by any means, make slaves of their females, and if a comparison be made between their condition in China and other modern unevangelized countries, or even with ancient kingdoms or Moslem races, it will in many points acquit them of much of the obloquy they have received on this behalf.

There are some things which tend to show that more of the sex read and write sufficiently for the ordinary purposes of life, than a slight examination would at first indicate. Among these may be mentioned the letter-writers compiled for their use, in which instructions are given for every variety of note and epis-

---

[1] *Chinese Repository*, Vol. IX., p. 542.

tle, except, perhaps, love letters. The works just mentioned, intended for their improvement, form an additional fact. A Manchu official of rank, named Sin-kwăn, who rose to be governor of Kiangsí in Kiaking's reign, wrote a primer in 1838, for girls, called the *Nü-rh Yü*, or '*Words for Women and Girls*.' It is in lines of four characters, and consists of aphorisms and short precepts on household management, behavior, care of children, neatness, etc., so written as to be easily memorized. It shows one of the ways in which literary men interest themselves, in educating youth, and further that there is a demand for such books. A few lines from this primer will exhibit its tenor

Vile looks should never meet your eye,
Nor filthy words defile your ear;
Ne'er look on men of utterance gross,
Nor tread the ground which they pollute.
Keep back the heart from thoughts impure,
Nor let your hands grow fond of sloth;
Then no o'ersight or call deferred
Will, when you're pressed, demand your time

In all your care of tender babes,
Mind lest they're fed or warmed too much;
The childish liberty first granted
Must soon be checked by rule and rein;
Guard them from water, fire, and fools;
Mind lest they're hurt or maimed by falls.
All flesh and fruits when ill with colds
Are noxious drugs to tender bairns—
Who need a careful oversight,
Yet want some license in their play.
Be strict in all you bid them do,
For this will guard from ill and woe.

The pride taken by girls in showing their knowledge of letters is evidence that it is not common, while the general respect in which literary ladies are held proves them not to be so very rare; though for all practical good, it may be said that half of the Chinese people know nothing of books. The fact that female education is so favorably regarded is encouraging to those philanthropic persons and ladies who are endeavoring to establish female schools at the mission stations, since they have not prejudice to contend with in addition to ignorance.

CHAPTER X.

STRUCTURE OF THE CHINESE LANGUAGE.

It might reasonably be inferred, judging from the attention paid to learning, and the honors conferred upon its successful votaries, that the literature of the Chinese would contain much to repay investigation. Such is not the case, however, to one already acquainted with the treasures of Western science, and, in fairness, such a comparison is not quite just. Yet it has claims to the regard of the general student, from its being the literature of so vast a portion of the human species, and the result of the labors of its wisest and worthiest minds during many successive ages. The fact that it has been developed under a peculiar civilization, and breathes a spirit so totally different from the writings of Western sages and philosophers, perhaps increases the curiosity to learn what are its excellences and defects, and obtain some criteria by which to compare it with the literature of other Asiatic or even European nations. The language in which it is written—one peculiarly mystical and diverse from all other media of thought—has also added to its singular reputation, for it has been surmised that what is "wrapped up" in such complex characters must be pre-eminently valuable for matter or elegant for manner, and not less curious than profound. Although a candid examination of this literature will disclose its real mediocrity in points of research, learning, and genius, there yet remains enough to render it worthy the attention of the oriental or general student.

Some of its peculiarities are owing to the nature of the language, and the mode of instruction, both of which have affected the style and thoughts of writers: for, having, when young, been taught to form their sentences upon the models of antiquity, their efforts to do so have moulded their thoughts in the same channel. Imitation, from being a duty, soon became a necessity. The Chinese scholar, forsaking the leadings of his own genius, soon learned to regard his models as not only being all truth themselves, but as containing the sum total of all things valuable. The intractable nature of the language, making it impossible to study other tongues through the medium of his own, moreover tended to repress all desire in the scholar to become acquainted with foreign books; and as he knew nothing of them or their authors, it was easy to conclude that there was nothing worth knowing in them, nothing to repay the toil of study, or make amends for the condescension of ascertaining. The neighbors of the Chinese have unquestionably been their inferiors in civilization, good government, learning, and wealth; and this fact has nourished their conceit, and repressed the wish to travel, and ascertain what there was in remoter regions. In judging of the character of Chinese literature, therefore, these circumstances among others under which it has risen to its present bulk, must not be overlooked; we shall conclude that the uniformity running through it is perhaps owing as much to the isolation of the people and servile imitation of their models, as to their genius: each has, in fact, mutually acted upon and influenced the other.

The "homoglot" character of the Chinese people has arisen more from the high standard of their literature, and the political institutions growing out of its canonical books (which have impelled and rewarded the efforts of students to master the language), than from any one other cause. This feature offers a great contrast to the polyglot character which the Romans possessed even to the last, and suggests the cause and results as interesting topics of inquiry. The Egyptian, Jewish, Syriac, Greek, and Latin languages had each its own national literature, and its power was enough to retain these several nations attached to their own mother tongue, while the Gauls, Iberians, and other subject peoples, having no books, took the language and literature of their rulers and conquerors. Thus the kingdom, "part iron and part clay," fell apart as soon as the grasp of Rome was weakened; while the tendency in China always has been to reunite and homologate.

In this short account of the Chinese tongue, it will be sufficient to give such notices of the origin and construction of the characters, and of the idioms and sounds of the written and spoken language, as shall convey a general notion of all its parts, and to show the distinction between the spoken and written media, and their mutual action. They are both archaic, because the symbols prevented all inflexion and agglutination in the sounds, and all signs to indicate what part of speech each belonged to. They are like the ten digits, containing no vocable and imparting their meaning more to the eye than the ear.

Chinese writers, unable to trace the gradual formation of their characters (for, of course, there could be no intelligible historical data until long after their formation), have ascribed them to Hwangtí, one of their primeval monarchs, or even earlier, to Fuh-hí, some thirty centuries before Christ; as if they deemed writing to be as needful to man as clothes or marriage, all of which came from Fuh-hí. A mythical personage, Tsang-kieh, who flourished about B.C. 2700, is credited with the invention of symbols to represent ideas, from noticing the marking on tortoise-shell, and thence imitating common objects in nature.

The Japanese have tried to attach their *kana* to the Chinese characters to indicate the case or tense, but the combination looks incongruous to an educated Chinese. We might express, though somewhat crudely, analogous combinations in English by endeavoring to write 1-*ty*, 1-*ness*, 1-*ted*, for *unity*, *oneness*, *united*, or 3-1 *God* for *triune God*.

At this crisis, when a medium for conveying and giving permanency to ideas was formed, Chinese historians say: "The heavens, the earth, and the gods, were all agitated. The inhabitants of hades wept at night; and the heavens, as an expression of joy, rained down ripe grain. From the invention of writing, the machinations of the human heart began to operate; stories false and erroneous daily increased, litigations and imprisonments sprang up; hence, also, specious and artful language, which causes so much confusion in the world. It was for these reasons that the shades of the departed wept at night. But from the invention of writing, polite intercourse and music proceeded; reason and justice were made manifest; the relations of social life were illustrated, and laws became fixed. Governors had laws to which they might refer; scholars had authorities to venerate; and hence, the heavens, delighted, rained down ripe grain. The classical scholar, the historian, the mathematician, and the astronomer can none of them do without writing; were there no written language to afford proof of passing events, the shades might weep at noonday, and the heavens rain down blood."[1] This singular myth may, perhaps, cover a genuine fact worthy of more than passing notice—indicating a consentaneous effort of the early settlers on the Yellow River to substitute for the purpose of recording laws and events something more intelligible than the knotted cords previously in use. Its form presents a curious contrast to the personality of the fable of Cadmus and his invention of the Greek letters.

The date of the origin of this language, like that of the letters of Western alphabets, is lost in the earliest periods of postdiluvian history, but there can be no doubt that it is the most ancient language now spoken, and along with the Egyptian and cuneiform, among the oldest written languages used by man. The Ethiopic and Coptic, the Sanscrit and Pali, the Syriac, Aramaic, and Pehlvic, have all become dead languages; and the Greek, Latin, and Persian, now spoken, differ so much

---

[1] Professor H. A. Sayce, of Oxford, in reference to a suggested possible connection between the Chinese and primitive Accadian population of Chaldea, says in a letter to the London *Times*: "I would mention one fact which may certainly be considered to favor it. The cuneiform characters of Babylonia and Assyria are, as is well known, degenerated hieroglyphics, like the modern Chinese characters. The original hieroglyphics were invented by the Accadians before they descended into Babylonia from the mountains of Elam, and I have long been convinced that they were originally written in vertical columns. In no other way can I explain the fact that most of the pictures to which the cuneiform characters can be traced back stand upon their sides. There is evidence to show that the inventors of the hieroglyphics used papyrus, or some similar vegetable substance, for writing purposes before the alluvial plain of Babylonia furnished them with clay, and the use of such a writing material will easily account for the vertical direction in which the characters were made to run."

from the ancient style, as to require special study to understand the books in them: while during successive eras, the written and spoken language of the Chinese has undergone few alterations, and done much to deepen the broad line of demarkation between them and other branches of the human race. The fact, then, that this is the only living language which has survived the lapse of ages is, doubtless, owing to its ideographic character and its entire absence of sound as an integral factor of any symbol. Their form and meaning were, therefore, only the more strongly united because each reader was at liberty to sound them as he pleased or had been taught by local instructors. He was not hindered, on account of his local *brogue*, from communicating ideas with those who employed the same signs in writing. Upon the subsequent rise of a great and valuable literature, the maintenance of the written language was the chief element of national life and integrity among those peoples who read and admired the books. Nor has this language, like those of the Hebrews, the Assyrians, and others already mentioned, ever fallen into disuse and been supplanted by the sudden rise and physical or intellectual vigor of some neighboring community speaking a *patois*. For we find that alphabetic languages, whose words represent at once meaning and sound, are as dependent upon local dialects as is the Chinese tongue upon its symbols; consequently, when in the former case the sounds had so altered that the meanings were obscured, the mode of writing was likely to be changed. The extent of its literature and uses made of it were then the only safeguard of the written forms; while as men learned to read books they became more and more prone to associate sense and form, regarding the sound as traditionary. We have, in illustration of this, to look no further than to our own language, whose cumbersome spelling is in a great measure resulting from a dislike of changing old associations of sense and form which would be involved in the adoption of a phonetic system.

The Chinese have had no inducement, at any stage of their existence, to alter the forms of their symbols, inasmuch as no nation in Asia contiguous to their own has ever achieved a literature which could rival theirs; no conqueror came to impose his tongue upon them ; their language completely isolated them from intellectual intercourse with others. This isolation, fraught with many disadvantages in the contracted nature of their literature, and the reflux, narrowing influence on their minds, has not been without its compensations. A national life of a unique sort has resulted, and to this self-nurtured language may be traced the origin of much of the peace, industry, population, and healthy pride of the Chinese people.

The Chinese have paid great and praiseworthy attention to their language, and furnished us with all needed books to its study. Premising that the original symbols were ideographic, the necessities of the case compelled their contraction as much as possible, and soon resulted in arbitrary signs for all common uses. Their symbols varied, indeed, at different times and in different States; it was not until a genuine literature appeared and its readers multiplied that the varients were dropped and uniformity sought. The original characters of this language are derived from natural or artificial objects, of which they were at first the rude outlines. Most of the forms are preserved in the treatises of native philologists, where the changes they have gradually undergone are shown. The number of objects chosen at first was not great; among them were symbols for the sun, moon, hills, animals, parts of the body, etc. ; and in drawing them the limners seem to have proposed nothing further than an outline sketch, which, by the aid of a little explanation, would be intelligible. Thus the picture  would probably be recognized by all who saw it as representing the *moon ;* that of 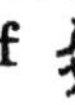 as a *fish ;* and so of others. It is apparent that the number of pictures which could be made in this manner would bear no proportion to the wants and uses of a language, and therefore recourse must soon be had to more complicated symbols, to combining those already understood, or to the adoption of arbitrary or phonetic signs. All these modes have been more or less employed.

Chinese philologists arrange all the characters in their language into six classes, called *luh shu*, or ‘six writings.’ The first, called *siang hing*, morphographs, or ‘imitative symbols,’ are those in which a plain resemblance can be traced between the original form and the object represented; they are among the first characters invented, although the six hundred and eight placed in this class do not include all the original symbols. These pristine forms have since been modified so much that the resemblance has disappeared in most of them, caused chiefly by the use of paper, ink, and pencils, instead of the iron style and bamboo tablets formerly in use for writing; circular strokes being more distinctly made with an iron point upon the hard wood than with a hair pencil upon thin paper; angular strokes and square forms, therefore, gradually took the place of round or curved ones, and contracted characters came into use in place of the original imitative symbols. In this class such characters as the following are given:

tortoise, chariot, child, elephant, deer, vase, hill, eye.

altered to

龜 車 子 象 鹿 壺 山 目

kwei, chi, tsz', siang, luh, hu, shan, muh.

The second class, only one hundred and seven in number, is called *chí sz'*, *i.e.*, 'symbols indicating thought.' They differ from the preceding chiefly in that the characters are formed by combining previously formed symbols in such a way as to indicate some idea easily deducible from their position or combination, and pointing out some property or relative circumstance belonging to them. Chinese philologists consider these two classes as comprising all the symbols in the language, which depict objects either in whole or in part, and whose meaning is apparent from the resemblance to the object, or from the position of the parts. Among those placed in this class are,

 moon half appearing, signifies evening; now written 夕
 sun above the horizon, denotes morning; now written 旦
 something in the mouth, meaning sweet; now written 甘

The third class, amounting to seven hundred and forty characters, is called *hwui i*, *i.e.*, 'combined ideas,' or ideographs, and comprises characters made up of two or three symbols to form a single idea, whose meanings are deducible either from their position, or supposed relative influence upon each other. Thus the union of the sun and moon, 明 *ming*, expresses brightness; 閑 *kien*, a piece of wood in a doorway, denotes obstruction; two trees stand for a forest, as 林 *lin;* and three for a thicket, as 森 *săn;* two men upon the ground conveys the idea of sitting; a *mouth* in a *door* signifies to ask; *man* and *words* means truth and to believe; *heart* and *death* imports forgetfulness; *dog* and *mouth* means to bark; *woman* and *broom* denotes a wife, referring to her household duties; *pencil* and *to speak* is a book, or to write. But in none of these compounded characters is there anything like that perfection of picture writing stated by some writers to belong to the language, which will enable one unacquainted with the meaning of the separate symbols to decide upon the signification of the combined group. On the contrary it is in most cases certain that the third idea made by combining two already known symbols, usually required more or less explanation to fix its precise meaning, and remove the doubt which would otherwise arise. For instance, the combination of the sun and moon might as readily mean a solar or lunar eclipse, or denote the idea of time, as brightness. A piece of wood in a doorway would almost as naturally suggest a *threshold* as an *obstruction;* and so of others. A straight line in a doorway would more readily suggest a closed or bolted door, which is the signification of 閂 *shan*, anciently written 閂; but the idea intended to be conveyed by these combinations would need prior explanation as much as the primitive symbol, though it would thenceforth readily recur to mind when noticing the construction.

It is somewhat singular that the opinion should have obtained so much credence, that their meanings were easily deducible from their shape and construction. It might almost be said, that not a single character can be accurately defined from a mere inspection of its parts; and the meanings now given of some of those which come under this class are so arbitrary and far-fetched, as to show that Chinese characters have not been formed by rule and plummet more than words in other languages. The mistake which Du Ponceau so learnedly combats arose, probably, from confounding *sound* with *construction*, and inferring that, because persons of different nations, who used this as their written language, could understand it when written, though mutually unintelligible when speaking, that it addressed itself so entirely to the eye, as to need no previous explanation.

The fourth class, called *chuen chu*, 'inverted significations,' includes three hundred and seventy-two characters, being such as by some inversion, contraction, or alteration of their parts, acquire different meanings. This class is not large, but these and other modifications of the original symbols to express abstract and new ideas show that those who used the language either saw at once how cumbrous it would become if they went on forming imitative signs, or else that their invention failed, and they resorted to changes more or less arbitrary in characters already known to furnish distinctive signs for different ideas. Thus *yu* 又 the *hand*, turning toward the right means the right; inclined in the other direction, as *tso* 𠂇 it means the left. The *heart* placed beneath *slave*, 怒 signifies anger; *threads obstructed*, as 𢇍, means to sunder; but turned the other way, as 㡭, signifies continuous.

The fifth class, called *kiai shing*, *i.e.*, 'uniting sound symbols,' or phonogram, contains twenty-one thousand eight hundred and ten characters, or nearly all in the language. They are formed of an imitative symbol united to one which merely imparts its sound to the compound; the former usually partakes more or less of the new idea, while the latter loses its own meaning, and gives only its name. In this respect, Chinese characters are superior to the Arabic numerals, inasmuch as combinations like 25, 101, etc., although conveying the same meaning to all nations using them, can *never* indicate sound. This plan of forming new combinations by the union of symbols expressing idea and sound, enables the Chinese to increase the number of characters without multiplying the original symbols; but these compounds, or *lexigraphs*, as Du Ponceau calls them, do not increase very rapidly. In Annam they have become so numerous in the course of years that the Chinese books made in that country are hard to read. The probable mode in which this arose can best be explained by a case which occurred at Canton in 1832. Immature locusts were to be described in a proclamation, but the word *nan*, by which they were called, was not contained in any dictionary. It would be sufficient to designate this insect to all persons living where it was found by selecting a well-understood character, like 南 *south*, having the exact sound *nan*, by which the insect itself was called, and joining it to the determinative symbol *chung* 虫 insect. It would then signify, to every one who knew the sound and meaning of the component parts, the *insect nan;* and be read *nan*, 蝻 meaning this very insect to the people in Kwangtung. If this new combination was carried to a distant part of the country, where the insect itself was unknown, it would convey no more information to the Chinese who *saw* the united symbol, than the sounds *insect nan* would to an Englishman who *heard* them; to both persons a meaning must be given by describing the insect. If, however, the people living in this distant region called the phonetic part of the new character by another sound, as *nam*, *nem*, or *lam*, they would attach another name to the new compound, but the people on the spot would, perhaps, not understand them when they spoke it by that name. If they wrote it, however, both would give it the same signification, but a different sound.

In this way, the thousands of characters under this class have probably originated. But this rule of sounding them according to the phonetic part is not in all cases certain; for in the lapse of time, the sounds of many characters have changed, while those of the parts themselves have not altered; in other cases, the parts have altered, and the sounds remained; so that now only a great degree of probability as to the correct sound can be obtained by inspecting the component parts. The similarity in sound between most of the characters having the same phonetic part is a great assistance in reading Chinese, though very little in understanding it, and has had much influence in keeping the sounds unchanged.

There are a few instances of an almost inadvertent arrival at a true syllabic system, by which the initial consonant of one part, when joined to the final vowel of the other, gives the sound of the character; as *ma* and *fi*, in the character 靡, when united in this way, make *mi*. The meanings of the components are *hemp* and *not*, that of the compound is *extravagant*, *wasteful*, etc., showing no relation to the primary signification. The number of such characters is very small, and the syllabic composition here noticed is probably fortuitous, and not intentional.

The sixth class, called *kia tsié*, *i.e.*, 'borrowed uses,' includes metaphoric symbols and combinations, in which the meaning is deduced by a somewhat fanciful accommodation; their number is five hundred and ninety-eight. They differ but little from the second class of indicative symbols. For instance, the symbol 字 or 字, meaning a written character, is composed of a *child* under a *shelter*—characters being considered as the well-nurtured offspring of hieroglyphics. The character for *hall* means also *mother*, because she constantly abides there. The word for *mind* or *heart* is *sin* 心, originally intended to represent that organ, but now used chiefly in a metaphorical sense. Chinese grammarians find abundant scope for the display of their fancy in explaining the etymology and origin of the characters, but the aid which their researches give toward understanding the language as at present used is small. This classification under six heads is modern, and was devised as a means of arranging what existed already, for they confess that their characters were not formed according to fixed rules, and have gradually undergone many changes.

The total number in the six classes is twenty-four thousand two hundred and thirty-five, being many less than are found in Kanghi's Dictionary, which amount to forty-four thousand four hundred and forty-nine; but in the larger sum are included the obsolete and synonymous characters, which, if deducted, would reduce it to nearly the same number. It is probable that the total of really different characters in the language sanctioned by good usage, does not vary greatly from twenty-five thousand, though authors have stated them at from fifty-four thousand four hundred and nine, as Magaillans does, up to two hundred and sixty thousand eight hundred and ninety-nine, as Montucci. The Chinese editor of the large lexicon on which Dr. Morrison founded his Dictionary, gives it as his opinion that there are fifty thousand characters, including synonyms and different forms; and taking in every variety of tones given to the words, and sounds for which no characters exist, that there are five thousand different words. But even the sum of twenty-five thousand different characters contains thousands of unusual ones which are seldom met with, and which, as is the case with old words in English, are not often learned.

The burden of remembering so many complicated symbols, whose form, sound, and meanings are all necessary to enable the student to read and write intelligibly, is so great that the result has been to diminish those in common use, and increase their meanings. This course of procedure really occurs in most languages, and in the Chinese greatly reduces the labor of acquiring it. It may be safely said, that a good knowledge of ten thousand characters will enable one to read any work in Chinese, and write intelligibly on any subject; and Prémare says a good knowledge of four or five thousand characters is sufficient for all common purposes, while two-thirds of that number might in fact suffice. The troublesome ones are either proper names or technics peculiar to a particular science. The nine canonical works contain altogether only four thousand six hundred and one *different* characters, while in the Five Classics alone there are over two hundred thousand words. The entire number of different characters in the code of laws translated by Staunton is under two thousand.

The invention of printing and the compilation of dictionaries have given to the form of modern characters a greater degree of certainty than they had in ancient times. The variants of some of the most common ones were exceedingly numerous before this period; Callery gives forty-two different modes of writing *pao*, 'precious;' and forty-one for writing *tsun*, 'honorable;' showing the absence of an acknowledged standard, and the slight intercourse between learned men. The best mode of arranging the characters so as to find them easily, has been a subject of considerable trouble to Chinese lexicographers, and the various methods they have adopted renders it difficult to consult their dictionaries without considerable previous knowledge of the language. In some, those having the same sound are grouped together, so that it is necessary to know what a character is called before it can be found; and this arrangement has been followed in vocabularies designed principally for the use of the common people. One well-known vocabulary used at Canton, called the *Făn Yun*, or 'Divider of Sounds,' is arranged on this plan, the words being placed under thirty-three orders, according to their terminations. Each order is subdivided into three or four classes according to the tones, and all the characters having the same tone and termination are placed together, as *kam*, *lam*, *tam*, *nam*, etc. As might be supposed, it requires considerable time to find a character whose tone is not exactly known; and even with the tone once mastered, the uncertainty is equally troublesome if the termination is not familiar: for singular as it may seem to those who are acquainted only with phonetic languages, a Chinese can, if anything, more readily distinguish between two words ♯*ming* and ♭*ming*, whose tones are unlike, than he can between ♯*ming* and ♯*meng*, ♯*ming* or ♯*bing*, where the initial or final differs a little, and the tones are the same.

An improvement on this plan of arrangement was made by adopting a mode of expressing the sounds of Chinese characters introduced by the Buddhists, in the *Yuh Pien*, published A.D. 543, and ever since used in all dictionaries. This takes the initial of the sound of one character and the final of another, and combines them to indicate the sound of the given character; as from *li*-en and y-*ing* to form *ling*. There are thirty-six characters chosen for the initial consonants, and thirty-eight for the final sounds, but the student is perplexed by the different characters chosen in different works to represent them.[1] The inhabitants of Amoy use a small lexicon called the *Shih-wu Yin*, or 'Fifteen Sounds,' in which the characters are classified

[1] Biot has a brief note upon the methods employed by native scholars for studying pronunciation. *Essai sur l'instruction en Chine*, p. 597.

on this principle, by first arranging them all under fifty finals, and then placing all those having the same termination in a regular series under fifteen initials. Supposing a new character, *chien*, is seen, whose sound is given, or the word is heard in conversation and its meanings are wanted, the person turns to the part of the book containing the final *ien*, which is designated perhaps by the character *kien*, and looks along the initials until he comes to *ch*, which is indicated by the character *chang*. In this column, all the words in the book read or spoken *chien*, os whatever tone they may be, are placed together according to their tones; and a little practice readily enables a person speaking the dialect to use this manual. It is, however, of little or no avail to persons speaking other dialects, or to those whose vernacular differs much from that of the compiler, whose own ear was his only guide. Complete dictionaries have been published on the phonetic plan, the largest of which, the *Wu Ché Yun Fu*, is arranged with so much minuteness of intonation as to puzzle even the best educated natives, and consequently abridge its usefulness as an expounder of words.

The unfitness of either of these modes of arrangement to find an unknown character, led to another classification according to their composition, by selecting the most prominent parts of each character as its key, or radical, and grouping those together in which the same key occurred. This plan was adopted subsequently to that of arranging the characters according to the sounds, about A.D. 543, when their number was put at five hundred and forty-two; they were afterward reduced to three hundred and sixty, and toward the close of the Ming dynasty finally fixed at two hundred and fourteen in the *Tsz' Lui*. It is now in general use from the adoption of the abridged dictionary, the *Kanghi Tsz' Tien*; though this number could have been advantageously reduced, as has been shown by Gonçalves, its universal adoption, more than anything else, renders it the best system. All characters found under the same radical are placed consecutively, according to the number of strokes necessary to write them, but no regularity is observed in placing those having the same number of strokes. The term *primitive* has been technically applied to the remaining part of the character, which, though perhaps no older than the radical, is conveniently denoted by this word. The characters selected for the radicals are all common ones, and among the most ancient in the language; they are here grouped according to their meanings in order to show something of the leading ideas followed in combination.

Corporal.—Body, corpse, head, hair, down, whiskers, face, eye, ear, nose, mouth, teeth, tusk, tongue, hand, heart, foot, hide, leather, skin, wings, feathers, blood, flesh, talons, horn, bones.

Biological.—Man, woman, child; horse, sheep, tiger, dog, ox, hog, hog's head, deer; tortoise, dragon, reptile, mouse, toad; bird, gallinaceous fowls; fish; insect.

Botanical.—Herb, grain, rice, wheat, millet, hemp, leeks, melon, pulse, bamboo, sacrificial herb; wood, branch, sprout, petal.

Mineral.—Metal, stone, gems, salt, earth.

Meteorological.—Rain, wind, fire, water, icicle, vapor, sound; sun, moon, evening; time.

Utensils.—A chest, a measure, a mortar, spoon, knife, bench, couch, crockery, clothes, tiles, dishes, napkin, net, plough, vase, tripod, boat, carriage, pencil; bow, halberd, arrow, dart, ax, musical reed, drum, seal.

Descriptives.—Black, white, yellow, azure, carnation, sombre; color; high, long, sweet, square, large, small, strong, lame, slender, old, fragrant, acrid, perverse, base, opposed.

Actions.—To enter, to follow, to walk slowly, to arrive at, to stride, to walk, to run, to reach to, to touch, to stop, to fly, to overspread, to envelop, to encircle, to establish, to overshadow, to adjust, to distinguish, to divine, to see, to eat, to speak, to kill, to fight, to oppose, to stop, to embroider, to owe, to compare, to imitate, to bring forth, to use, to promulge.

Miscellaneous.—A desert, cave, field, den, mound, hill, valley, rivulet, cliff, retreat. A city; roof, gate, door, portico. One, two, eight, ten. Demon; an inch, mile; without, not, false; a scholar, statesman, letters; art, wealth; motion; self, myself, father; a point; again; wine; silk; joined hands; a long journey; print of a bear's foot; a surname; classifier of cloth.

The number of characters found under each of these radicals in Kanghí's Dictionary varies from five up to one thousand three hundred and fifty-four. The radical is not uniformly placed, but its usual position is on the left of the primitive. Some occur on the top, others on the bottom; some inclose the primitive, and many have no fixed place, making it evident that no uniform plan was adopted in the original construction. They must be thoroughly learned before the dictionary can be readily used.

and some practice had before a character can be quickly found.[1] The groups occurring under a majority of the radicals are more or less natural in their general meaning, a feature of the language which has already been noticed (page 375). Some of the radicals are interchanged, and characters having the same meaning sometimes occur under two or three different ones—variations which seem to have arisen from the little importance of a choice out of two or three similar radicals. Thus the same word *tsien*, 'a small cup,' is written under the three radicals *gem*, *porcelain*, and *horn*, originally, no doubt, referring to the material for making it. This interchange of radicals adds greatly to the number of duplicate forms, which are still further increased by a similar interchange of primitives having the same sound. These two changes very seldom occur in the same character, but there are numerous instances of synonymous forms under almost every radical, arising from an interchange of primitives, and also under analogous radicals caused by their reciprocal use. Thus, from both these causes, there are, under the radical *ma*, 'a horse,' one hundred and eighteen duplicate forms, leaving two hundred and ninety-three different words; of the two hundred and four characters under *niu*, 'an ox,' thirty-nine are synonymous forms; and so under other radicals. These characters do not differ in meaning more than *favor* and *favour*, or *lady* and *ladye*; they are mere variations in the form of writing, and though apparently adding greatly to the number of characters, do not seriously increase the difficulty of learning the language.

Variants of other descriptions frequently occur in books, which needlessly add to the labor of learning the language. Ancient forms are sometimes adopted by pedantic writers to show their learning, while ignorant and careless writers use abridged or vulgar forms, because they either do not know the correct form, or are heedless in using it. When such is the case, and the character cannot be found in the dictionary, the reader is entirely at fault, especially if he be a foreigner, though in China itself he would not experience much difficulty

[1] *Easy Lessons in Chinese*, pp. 3–29; *Chinese Repository*, Vol. III., pp. 1–37

where the natives were at hand to refer to. Vulgar forms are very common in cheap books and letters, which are as unsanctioned by the dictionaries and good usage, as cockney phrases or miner's slang are in pure English. They arise, either from a desire on the part of the writer to save time by making a contracted form of few strokes instead of the correct character of many strokes; or he uses common words to express an energetic vulgar phrase, for which there are no authorized characters, but which will be easily understood phonetically by his readers. These characters would perchance not be understood at all outside of the range of the author's dialect, because the phrase itself was new; their individual meaning, indeed, has nothing to do with the interpretation of the sentence, for in this case they are merely signs of sound, like words in other languages, and lose their lexigraphic character. For instance, the words *kia-fí* for coffee, *kap-tan* for captain, *mí-sz'* for *Mr*, etc., however they were written, would be intelligible to a native of Canton if they expressed those sounds, because he was familiar with the words themselves; but a native of Shensí would not understood them, because, not knowing the things intended, he would naturally refer to the characters themselves for the meaning of the phrase, and thus be wholly misled. In such cases, the characters become mere syllables of a phonetic word. Foreign names are often transliterated by writers on geography or history, and their recognition is no easy task to their readers.[1]

In addition to the variations in the forms of characters, there are six different styles of writing them, which correspond to black-letter, script, italic, roman, etc., in English. The first is called *Chuen shu* (from the name of the person who invented it), which foreigners have styled the *seal character*, from its use in seals and ornamental inscriptions. It is next to the picture hieroglyphics, the most ancient fashion of writing, and has undergone many changes in the course of ages. It is studied by those who cut seals or inscriptions, but no books are ever printed in it.

---

[1] One may gain some idea of this difficulty by referring to the geographical names contained in the Russo-Chinese Treaty, quoted on page 215.

1 書有六體曰篆曰隸曰楷曰行曰艸曰宋

2 書有六躰曰篆曰隸曰楷曰行曰艸曰宋

3 書有六體曰篆曰隸曰楷曰行曰草曰宋

4 書有六體曰篆曰隸曰楷曰行曰草曰宋

5 書有六體曰篆曰隸曰楷曰行曰草曰宋

6 書有六體曰篆曰隸曰楷曰行曰草曰宋

The second is the *li shu*, or style of official attendants, which was introduced about the Christian era, as an elegant style to be employed in engrossing documents. It is now seen in prefaces and formal inscriptions, and requires no special study to read it, as it differs but slightly from the following.

The third is the *kiai shu*, or pattern style, and has been gradually formed by the improvements in good writing. It is the usual form of Chinese characters, and no man can claim a literary name among his countrymen if he cannot write neatly and correctly in this style.

The fourth is called *hing shu*, or running hand, and is the common hand of a neat writer. It is frequently used in prefaces and inscriptions, scrolls and tablets, and there are books prepared in parallel columns having this and the pattern style arranged for school-boys to learn to write both at the same time. The running hand cannot be read without a special study; and although this labor is not very serious when the language of books is familiar, still to become well acquainted with both of them withdraws many days and months of the pupil from progress in acquiring knowledge to learning two modes of writing the same word.

The fifth style is called *tsao tsz'*, or plant character, and is a freer description of running hand than the preceding, being full of abbreviations, and the pencil runs from character to character, without taking it from the paper, almost at the writer's fancy. It is more difficult to read than the preceding, but as the abbreviations are somewhat optional, the *tsao tsz'* varies considerably, and more or less resembles the running hand according to the will of the writer. The fancy of the Chinese for a "flowing pencil," and a mode of writing where the elegance and freedom of the caligraphy can be admired as much or more than the style or sentiment of the writing, as well as the desire to contract their multangular characters as much as possible, has contributed to introduce and perpetuate these two styles of writing. How much all these varieties of form superadd to the difficulty of learning the mere apparatus of knowledge need hardly be stated.

The sixth style is called *Sung shu*, and was introduced under the Sung dynasty in the tenth century, soon after printing on wooden blocks was invented. It differs from the third style, merely in a certain squareness and angularity of stroke, which transcribers for the press only are obliged to learn. Of these six forms of writing, the pattern style and running hand are the only two which the people learn to any great extent, although many acquire the knowledge of some words in the seal character, and the running hand of every person, especially those engaged in business, approaches more or less to the plant character. But foreigners will seldom find time or inclination to learn to write more than one form, to be able to read and communicate on all occasions.

Besides these styles, there are fanciful ones, called 'tadpole characters,' in imitation of various objects;[1] the Emperor Kienlung brought together thirty-two of them in an edition of his poem, the *Elegy upon the City of Mukden.*[2]

All the strokes in the characters are reduced to eight elementary ones, which are contained in the single character

永 *yung*, 'eternal.'

A dot, a line, a perpendicular, a hook, a spike, a sweep, a stroke, a dash-line.

Each of these is subdivided into many forms in copy-books, having particular names, with directions how to write them, and numerous examples introduced under each stroke.[3]

---

[1] The writer has an edition of the *Thousand Character Classic*, containing each couplet of eight words in a different form of character, making one hundred and twenty-five styles of type—too grotesque to be imitated, and probably never actually in use.

[2] See page 193. In order that the Manchu portion of this famous poem might not appear inferior to the Chinese, the Emperor ordered thirty-two varieties of Manchu characters to be *invented* and published in like manner with the others. Rémusat, *Mélanges*, Tome II., p. 59. Père Amiot, *Éloge de la Ville de Moukden. Trad. en françois.* Paris, 1770.

[3] *Chinese Chrestomathy*, Chap. I., Secs. 5 and 6, where the rules for writing Chinese are given in full with numerous examples; *Easy Lessons in Chinese*, p. 59; *Chinese Repository*, Vol. III., p. 37.

The Chinese regard their characters as highly elegant, and take unwearied pains to learn to write them in a beautiful, uniform, well-proportioned manner. Students are provided with a painted board upon which to practise with a brush dipped in blackened water. The articles used in writing, collectively called *wan fang sz' pao*, or 'four precious things of the library,' are the pencil, ink, paper, and ink-stone. The best pencils are made of the bristly hair of the sable and fox, and cheaper ones from the deer, cat, wolf and rabbit; camel's hair is not used. A combination of softness and elasticity is required, and those who are skilled in their use discern a difference and an excellence altogether imperceptible to a novice. The hairs are laid in a regular manner, and when tied up are brought to a delicate tip; the handle is made of the twigs of a bamboo cultivated for the purpose. The ink, usually known as India ink, is made from the soot of burning oil, pine, fir, and other substances, mixed with glue or isinglass, and scented. It is formed into oblong cakes or cylinders, inscribed with the maker's name, the best kinds being put up in a very tasteful manner. A singular error formerly obtained credence regarding this ink, that it was inspissated from the fluid found in the cuttle-fish. When used, the ink is rubbed with water upon argillite, marble, or other stones, some of which are cut and ground in a beautiful manner. Chinese paper is made from bamboo, by triturating the woody fibre to a pulp in mortars after the pieces have been soaked in ooze, and then taking it up in moulds; the pulp is sometimes mixed with a little cotton fibre. Inferior sorts are made entirely from cotton refuse; and in the North, where the bamboo does not grow, the bark of the *Broussonetia*, or paper mulberry, furnishes material for a tough paper used for windows, wrappings, and account books, etc. Bamboo paper has no sizing in it, and is a frail material for preserving valuable writings, as it is easily destroyed by insects, mildew, or handling.[1]

In the days of Confucius, pieces of bamboo pared thin, palm

---

[1] *Journal Asiatic Soc. Bengal*, Vol. III. (Sept., 1834), p. 477. S. Julien in the *Revue de l'Orient et de l'Algerie*, XX., p. 74, 1856.

leaves, and reeds, were all used for writing upon with a sharp stick or stile. About the third century before Christ, silk and cloth were employed, and hair pencils made for writing. Paper was invented about the first century, and cotton-paper may have been brought from India, where it was in use more than a hundred years before. India ink was manufactured by the seventh century; and the present mode of printing upon blocks was adopted from the discovery of Fungtau in the tenth century, of taking impressions from engraved stones. In the style of their notes and letters, the Chinese show both neatness and elegance; narrow slips of tinted paper are employed, on which various emblematic designs are stamped in water lines, and enclosed in fanciful envelopes. It is common to affix a cipher instead of the name, or to close with a periphrasis or sentence well understood by the parties, and thereby avoid any signature; this, which originated, no doubt, in a fear of interception and unpleasant consequences, has gradually become a common mode of subscribing friendly epistles.

The mode of printing is so well fitted for the language that few improvements have been made in its manipulations, while the cheapness of books brings them within reach of the poorest. Cutting the blocks, and writing the characters, form two distinct branches of the business; printing the sheets, binding the volumes, and publishing the books, also furnish employment to other craftsmen. The first step is to write the characters upon thin paper, properly ruled with lines, two pages being cut upon one block, and a heavy double line surrounding them. The title of the work, chapter, and paging are all cut in a central column, and when the leaf is printed it is folded through this column so as to bring the characters on the edge and partly on both pages. Marginal notes are placed on the top of the page; comments, when greatly extended, occupy the upper part, separated from the text by a heavy line, or when mere scholia, are interlined in the same column in characters of half the size. Sometimes two works are printed together, one running through the volume on the upper half of the leaves, and separated from that occupying the lower half by a heavy line. Illustrations usually occupy separate pages at the commencement of the book, but there are a few works with woodcuts of a wretched description, inserted in the body of the page. In books printed by government, each page is sometimes surrounded with dragons, or the title page is adorned in red by this emblem of imperial authority.

When the leaf has been written out as it is to be printed, it is turned over and pasted upon the block, face downward. The wood usually used by blockcutters is pear or plum; the boards are half or three-fourths of an inch thick, and planed for cutting on both sides. The paper, when dried upon the board, is carefully rubbed off with the wetted finger, leaving every character and stroke plainly delineated. The cutter then, with his chisels, cuts away all the blank spots in and around the characters, to the depth of a line or more, after which the block is ready for the printer, whose machinery is very simple. Seated before a bench, he lays the block on a bed of paper so that it will not move nor chafe. The pile of paper lies on one side, the pot of ink before him, and the pressing brush on the other. Taking the ink brush, he slightly rubs it across the block twice in such a way as to lay the ink equably over the surface; he then places a sheet of paper upon it, and over that another, which serves as a tympanum. The impression is taken with the fibrous bark of the gomuti palm; one or two sweeps across the block complete the impression, for only one side of the paper is printed. Another and cheaper method in common use for publishing slips of news, court circulars, etc., consists in cutting the characters in blocks of hard wax, from which as many as two hundred impressions can often be taken before they become entirely illegible. The ink is manufactured from lampblack mixed with vegetable oil; the printers grind it for themselves.

The sheets are taken by the binder, who folds them through the middle by the line around the pages, so that the columns shall register with each other, he then collates them into volumes, placing the leaves evenly by their folded edge, when the whole are arranged, and the covers pasted on each side. Two pieces of paper stitch it through the back, the book is trimmed, and sent to the bookseller. If required, it is stitched firmly with thread, but this part, as well as writing the title on the bottom edges of the volume, and making the pasteboard wrapper, are usually deferred till the taste of a purchaser is ascertained. Books made of such materials are not as durable as European volumes, and those who can afford the expense frequently have valuable works inclosed in wooden boxes. They are printed of all sizes between small *sleeve* editions (as the Chinese call 24 and 32 mos) up to quartos, twelve or fourteen inches square, larger than which it is difficult to get blocks.

The price varies from one cent—for a brochure of twenty-five or thirty pages—to a dollar and a half a volume. It is seldom higher save for illustrated works. A volume rarely contains more than a hundred leaves, and in fine books their thickness is increased by inserting an extra sheet inside of each leaf. At Canton or Fuhchau, the *History of the Three States*, bound in twenty-one volumes 12mo, printed on white paper, is usually sold for seventy-five cents or a dollar per set. Kanghí's Dictionary, in twenty-one volumes 8vo, on yellow paper, sells for four dollars; and all the nine classics can be purchased for less than two. Books are hawked about the streets, circulating libraries are carried from house to house upon movable stands, and booksellers' shops are frequent in large towns. No censorship, other than a prohibition to write about the present dynasty, is exercised upon the press; nor are authors protected by a copyright law. Men of wealth sometimes show their literary taste by defraying the expense of getting the blocks of extensive works cut, and publishing them. Pwan Sz'-ching, a wealthy merchant at Canton, published, in 1846, an edition of the *Pei Wăn Yun Fu*, in one hundred and thirty thick octavo volumes, the blocks for which must have cost him more than ten thousand dollars. The number of good impressions which can be obtained from a set of blocks is about sixteen thousand, and by retouching the characters, ten thousand more can be struck off.

The disadvantages of this mode of printing are that other languages cannot easily be introduced into the page with the Chinese characters; the blocks occupy much room, are easily spoiled or lost; and are incapable of correction without much expense. It possesses some compensatory advantages peculiar to the Chinese and its cognate languages, Manchu, Corean, Japanese, etc., all of which are written with a brush and have few or no circular strokes. Its convenience and cheapness, coupled with the low rate of wages, will no doubt make it the common mode of printing Chinese among the people for a long time.

The honor of being the first inventor of movable types undoubtedly belongs to a Chinese blacksmith named Pí Shing, who lived about A.D. 1000, and printed books with them nearly five hundred years before Gutenberg cut his matrices at Mainz. They were made of plastic clay, hardened by fire after the characters had been cut on the soft surface of a plate of clay in which they were moulded. The porcelain types were then set up in a frame of iron partitioned off by strips, and inserted in a cement of wax, resin, and lime to fasten them down. The printing was done by rubbing, and when completed the types were loosened by melting the cement, and made clean for another impression.

This invention seems never to have been developed to any practical application in superseding block-printing. The Emperor Kanghí ordered about two hundred and fifty thousand copper types to be engraved for printing publications of the government, and these works are now highly prized for their beauty. The cupidity of his successors led to melting these types into cash, but his grandson Kienlung directed the casting of a large font of lead types for government use.

The attention of foreigners was early called to the preparation of Chinese movable types, especially for the rapid manufacture of religious books, in connection with missionary work. The first fonts were made by P. P. Thoms, for the E. I. Company's office at Macao in 1815, for the purpose of printing Morrison's Dictionary. The characters were cut with chisels on blocks of type metal or tin, and though it was slow work to cut a full font, they gradually grew in numbers and variety till they served to print over twenty dictionaries and other works, designed to aid in learning Chinese, before they were destroyed by fire in 1856. A small font had been cast at Serampore in 1815, and in 1838, the Royal Printing Office at Paris had obtained a set of blocks engraved in China, from which thick castings were made and the separate types obtained by sawing the plates. M. Le Grand, a type-founder in Paris, about the year 1836, prepared an extensive font of type with comparatively few matrices, by casting the radical and primitive on separate bodies; and the plan has been found, within certain limits, to save so much expense and room that it has been adopted in other fonts.

These experiments in Europe showed the feasibility of making and using Chinese type to any extent, but their results as to elegance and accuracy of form were not satisfactory, and proved that native workmen alone could meet the native taste. Rev. Samuel Dyer of the London Mission at Singapore began in 1838, under serious disadvantages, for he was not a practical printer, to cut the matrices for two complete fonts. He continued at his self-appointed task until his death in 1844, having completed only one thousand eight hundred and forty-five punches. His work was continued by R. Cole, of the American Presbyterian Missions, a skilful mechanic in his line, and in 1851 he was able to furnish fonts of two sizes with four thousand seven hundred characters each. Their form and style met every requirement of the most fastidious taste, and they are now in constant use.

While Mr. Dyer's fonts were suspended by his death, an attempt was made by a benevolent printer, Herr Beyerhaus of Berlin, to make one of an intermediate size on the Le Grand principle of divisible types; his proposal was taken up by the Presbyterian Board of Missions in New York, and after many delays a beautiful font was completed and in use about 1859. At this time, Mr. W. Gamble of that Mission in Shanghai, carried out his plan of making matrices by the electrotype process, and completed a large font of small pica type in about as many months as Dyer and Beyerhaus had taken years. By means of these various fonts books are now printed in many parts of China, in almost any style, and type foundries cast in whatever quantities are needed. The government has opened an extensive printing office in Peking, and its example will encourage native booksellers to unite typography with xylographic printing. More than this as conducing to the diffusion of knowledge among the people is the stimulus these cheap fonts of type have given to the circulation of newspapers in all the ports; but for their convenient and economical use Chinese newspapers could not have been printed at all. It will be quite within the reach of native workmen, who are skilled in electrotyping, stereotyp ing, and casting type, to make types of all sizes and styles for their own books, as the growing intelligence of the people creates a demand for illustrated and scientific publications, as well as cheap ones.[1]

Nothing has conduced more to a misapprehension of the nature of the Chinese language than the way in which its phonetic character has been spoken of by different authors. Some, describing the primitive symbols, and the modifications they have undergone, have conveyed the impression that the whole language consisted of hieroglyphic or ideographic signs, which depicted ideas, and conveyed their meaning entirely to the eye, irrespective of the sound. For instance, Rémusat says, "The character is not the delineation of the sound, nor the sound the expression of the character;" forgetting to ask himself how or when a character in any language ever delineated a sound. Yet every Chinese character is sounded as much as the words in alphabetic languages, and some have more than one to express their different meanings; so that, although the character could not delineate the sound of the thing it denoted, the sound is the expression of the character. Others, as Mr. Lay,[2] have dissected the characters, and endeavored to trace back some analogy in the meanings of all those in which the same primitive is found, and by a sort of analysis, to find out how much of the signification of the radical was infused into the primitive to form the present meaning. His plan, in general terms, is to take all the characters containing a certain primitive, and find out how much of the meaning of that primitive is contained in each one; then he reconstructs the series by defining the primitive, incidentally showing the intention of the framers of the characters in choos-

[1] *Chinese Repository*, Vol. III., pp. 246–252, 528; Vol. XIV., p. 124; *Missionary Recorder*, January, 1875.

[2] *Chinese as They Are*, Chap. XXXIV.

ing that particular one, and apportioning so much of its aggregate meaning to each character as is needed, and adding the meaning of the radical to form its whole signification. If we understand his plan, he wishes to construct a formula for each group containing the same primitive, in which the signification of the primitive is a certain function in that of all the characters containing it; to add up the total of their meanings, and divide the amount among the characters, allotting a quotient to each one. Languages are not so formed, however, and the Chinese is no exception. Some of Mr. Lay's statements are correct, but his theory is fanciful. It is impossible to decide what proportion was made by combining a radical and a primitive with any reference to their meanings, according to Mr. Lay's theory, and how many of them were simply phonetic combinations; probably nine-tenths of the compound characters have been constructed on the latter principle.

The fifth class of syllabic symbols were formed by combining the symbolic and syllabic systems, so as to represent sound chiefly, but bearing in the construction of each one some reference to its general signification. The original hieroglyphics contained no sound, *i.e.*, were not formed of phonetic constituents; the object depicted had a name, but there was no clue to it. It was impossible to do both—depict the object, and give its name in the same character. At first, the number of people using these ideographic symbols being probably small, every one called them by the same name, as soon as he knew what they represented, and began to read them. But when the ideas attempted to be written far exceeded in number the symbols, or, what is more likely, the invention of the limmers, recourse was had to the combination of the symbols already understood to express the new idea. This was done in several modes, as noticed above, but the syllabic system needs further explanation, from the extent to which it has been carried. The character 蝻 *nan*, to denote the young of the locust, has been adduced. The same principle would be applied in *reading* every new character, of which the phonetic primitive merely was recognized, although its meaning might not be known. Probably all the characters in the fifth class were sounded in strict accordance with their phonetic primitives when constructed, but usage has changed some of their sounds, and many characters belonging to other classes, apparently containing the same primitive, are sounded quite differently; this tends to mislead those who infer the sound from the primitive. This mode of constructing and naming the characters also explains the reason why there are so few sounds compared with the number of characters; the phonetic primitive perpetuated its name in all its progeny.

More than seven-eighths of the characters have been formed from less than two thousand symbols, and it is difficult to imagine how it could have been used so long and widely without some such method to relieve the memory of the burden of retaining thousands of arbitrary marks. But, until the names and meanings of the original symbols are learned, neither the sound nor sense of the compound characters will be more apparent to a Chinese than they are to any one else; until those are known, their combinations cannot be understood, nor even then the meaning wholly deduced; each character must be learned by itself, just as words in other languages. The sounds given the original symbols doubtless began to vary early after coming into use. Intercommunication between different parts of the country was not so frequent as to prevent local dialects from arising; but however strong the tendency of the spoken monosyllables to coalesce into polysyllables, the intractable symbols kept them apart. It is surprising, too, what a tendency the mind has to trust to the eye rather than to the ear, in getting and retaining the sense of a book; it is shown in many ways, and arises from habit more than any real difficulty in catching the idea *vivâ voce*. If the characters could have coalesced, their names would soon have run together, and been modified as they are in other languages. The classics, dictionaries, and unlimited uses of a written language, maintained the same meaning; but as their sounds must be learned traditionally, endless variations and patois arose. Moreover, as new circumstances and increasing knowledge give rise to new words in all countries, so in China, new scenes and expressions arise requiring to be incorporated into the written language. Originally they were unwritten though well understood sounds; and when first written must be explained, as is the case with foreign words like *tabu*, *ukase*, *vizier*, etc., *ad infin.*, when introduced into English. Different writers might, however, employ different primitives to express the sound, not aware that it had already been written, and hence would arise synonyms; they might use dissimilar radicals, and this as well would increase the modes of writing the sound. But the inconvenience of thus multiplying characters would be soon perceived in the obscurity of the sentence, for if the new character was not in the dictionary, its sound and composition were not enough to explain the meaning. When the language had attained a certain copiousness, the mode of education and the style of literary works compelled scholars to employ such characters only as were sanctioned by good use, or else run the risk of not being understood.

The unwritten sounds, however, could not wait for this slow mode of adoption, but the risk of being misunderstood by using characters phonetically led to descriptive terms, conveying the idea and not the sound. Where alphabetic languages adopt a technic for a new thing, the Chinese make a new phrase. This is illustrated by the terms *Hung-mao jin*, or 'Red Bristled men,' for Englishmen; *Hwa-kí*, or 'Flowery Flag,' for Americans; *Sí-yang*, or 'Western Ocean,' for Portuguese, etc., used at Canton, instead of the proper names of those countries. Cause and effect act reciprocally upon each other in this instance; the effect of using unsanctioned characters to express unwritten sounds, is to render a composition obscure, while the restriction to a set of characters compels their meaning to be sufficiently comprehensive to include all occasions. Local, unwritten phrases, and unauthorized characters, are so common, however, owing to the partial communication between distant parts of so great a country and mass of people, that it is evident, if this bond of union were removed by the substitution of an alphabetical language, the Chinese would soon be split into many small nations. However desirable, therefore, might be the introduction of a written language less difficult of acquisition, and more flexible, there are some reasons for wishing it to be delayed until more intelligence is diffused and juster principles of government obtain. When the people themselves feel the need of it, they will contrive some better medium for the promotion of knowledge.

The monosyllabic sound of the primitive once imparted to the ideophonous compound, explains the existence of so many characters having the same sound. When these various characters were presented to the eye of the scholar, no trouble was felt in recognizing their sense and sound, but confusion was experienced in speaking. This has been obviated in two ways. One is by repeating a word, or joining two of similar meanings but of different sounds, to convey a single idea; or else by adding a classifying word to express its nature. Both these modes do in fact form a real dissyllable, and it would appear so in an alphabetical language. The first sort of these *hien-hioh sz'*, or 'clam-shell words,' as they are called, are not unfrequent in books, far more common in conversation and render the spoken more diffuse than the written language—more so, perhaps, than is the case in other tongues. Similar combinations of three, four, and more characters occur, especially where a foreign article or term is translated, but the genius of the language is against the use of polysyllables. Such combinations in English as *household*, *house-warming*, *housewife*, *house-room*, *houseleeks*, *hot-house*, *wood-house*, *household-stuff*, etc., illustrate these dissyllables in Chinese; but they are not so easily understood. Such terms as *understand*, *courtship*, *withdraw*, *upright*, etc., present better analogies to the Chinese compounds. In some the real meaning is totally unlike either of the terms, as *tungkia* (lit. 'east house'), for master; *tungsí* (lit. 'east west'), for thing; *kungchu* (lit. 'lord ruler'), for princess, etc. The classifiers partake of the nature of adjectives, and serve not only to sort different words, but the same word when used in different senses. They correspond to such words in English as *herd*, *fleet*, *troop*, etc. To say a fleet of cows, a troop of ships, or a herd of soldiers, would be ridiculous only in English, but a similar misapplication would confuse the sense in Chinese.

The other way of avoiding the confusion of homophonous monosyllables, which, notwithstanding the "clam-shell words," and the extensive use of classifiers, are still liable to misapprehension, is by accurately marking its right *shing* or tone, but as nothing analogous to them is found in European languages, it is rather difficult to describe them. At Canton there are eight arranged in an upper and lower series of four each; at Peking there are only four, at Nanking five, and at Swatow seven. The Chinese printers sometimes mark the *shing* on certain ambiguous characters, by a semicircle put on one corner: but this is rarely done, as every one who can read is supposed to know how to speak, and consequently to be familiar with the right tone. These four tones are called *ping*, *shang*, *kü*, and *jih*, meaning, respectively, the *even*, *ascending*, *departing*, and *entering* tone. They are applied to every word, and have nothing to do either with accent or emphasis; in asking or answering, entreating or refusing, railing or flattering, soothing or recriminating, they remain ever the same. The unlettered natives, even children and females, who know almost nothing of the distinctions into four, five, seven, or eight *shing*, observe them closely in their speech, and detect a mispronunciation as soon as the learned man. A single illustration of them will suffice. The *even* tone is the natural expression of the voice, and native writers consider it the most important. In the sentence,

"When I asked him, 'Will you let me see it?' he said, 'No, I'll do no such thing,'"

the different cadence of the question and reply illustrate the upper and lower even tone. The *ascending* tone is heard in exclamatory words as *ah! indeed!* It is a little like the crescendo in music, while the *departing tone* corresponds in the same degree to the diminuendo. The drawling tone of repressed discontent, grumbling and eking out a reply, is not unlike the departing tone. The entering tone is nearly eliminated in the northern provinces, but gives a marked feature to speech in the southern; it is an abrupt ending, in the same modulation that the even tone is, but as if broken off; a man about to say *lock*, and taken with a hiccup in the middle so that he leaves off the last two letters, or the final consonant, pronounces the *juh shing*. A few characters have two tones, which give them different meanings; the *ping shing* often denotes the substantive, and the *kü shing*, the verb, but there is no regularity in this respect.

The tones are observed by natives of all ranks, speaking all patois and dialects, and on all occasions. They present a serious difficulty to the adult foreigner of preaching or speaking acceptably to the natives, for although by a proper use of classifiers, observance of idioms, and multiplication of synonyms, he may be understood, his speech will be rude and his words distasteful, if he does not learn the tones accurately. In Amoy and Fuhchau, he will also run a risk of being misunderstood. If the reader, in perusing the following sentence, will accent the italicized syllables, he will have an imperfect illustration of the confusion a wrong intonation produces: "The pre*sent* of that ob*ject* occasioned such a trans*port* as to *ab*stract my mind from all around." In Chinese, however, it is not *accent* upon one of two syllables which must be learned, but the integral tone of a single sound, as much as in the musical octave.

It is unnecessary here to enter into any detailed description or enumeration of the words in the Chinese language. One remarkable feature is the frequency of the termination *ng* preceded by all the vowels, which imparts a peculiar singing character to Chinese speech, as *Kwangtung*, *Yangtsz' kiang*, etc. In a list of sounds in the court dialect, about one-sixth of the syllables have this termination, but a larger proportion of characters are found under those syllables, than the mere list indicates. In Morrison's Dictionary the number of separate words in the court dialect is 411, but if the aspirated syllables be distinguished, there are 533. In the author's *Syllabic Dictionary* the number is 532; Wade reduces the Peking dialect to 397 syllables in one list, and increases it to 420 in another. In the Cantonese there are 707; in the dialect of Swatow, 674; at Amoy, about 900; at Fuhchau, 928; and 660 at Shanghai. All these lists distinguish between aspirated and unaspirated words, as *ting* and *t'ing*, *pa* and *p'a*, which to an English ear are nearly identical. The largest part of the sounds are common to the dialects, but the distinctions are such as to render it easy to detect each when spoken; the court dialect is the most mellifluous of the whole and easiest to acquire. All the consonants in English are found in one or another of the dialects, besides many not occurring in that language, as *bw*, *chw*, *gw*, *jw*, *lw*, *mw*, *nw*, etc. There are also several imperfect vowel sounds not known in any European language, as *hm* or *'m*, *hn* or *'n*, *ng* (a high nasal sound), *sz'*, *'rh*, *ch'*, etc. The phrase *'m 'ng tăk* in the Canton dialect, meaning *cannot be pushed*, or *chain^n mai^n lang*, 'a blind man,' in the Amoy, cannot be so accurately expressed by these or any other letters that one can learn the sound from them. If it is difficult for us to express their sounds by Roman letters, it is still stranger for the Chinese to write English words. For instance, *baptize* in the Canton dialect becomes *pa-pí-tai-sz'*; *flannel* becomes *fat-lan-yin*; *stairs* becomes *sz'-ta-sz'*; *impregnable* becomes *im-pí-luk-na-pu-lí*; etc. Such words as *Washington*, *midshipman*, *tongue*, etc., can be written nearer their true sound, but the indivisible Chinese monosyllables offer a serious obstacle in the way of introducing foreign words and knowledge into the language.

The preceding observations explain how the numerous local variations from the general language found in all parts of China have arisen. Difficult as the spoken language is for a foreigner to acquire, from the brevity of the words and nicety of their tones, the variety of the local pronunciations given to the same character adds not a little to the labor, especially if he be situated where he is likely to come in contact with persons from different places. Amid such a diversity of pronunciation, and where one sound is really as correct as another, it is not easy to define what should constitute a dialect, a patois, or a corruption. A dialect in other languages is usually described as a local variation in pronunciation, or the use of peculiar words and expressions, not affecting the idiom or grammar of the tongue; but in the Chinese, where the written character unites the mass of people in one language, a dialect has been usually regarded by those who have written on the subject, as extending to variations in the idiom, and not restricted to differences in pronunciation and local expressions. According to this definition, there are only four or five dialects (which would in fact be as many languages if they were not united by the written character), but an endless variety of patois or local pronunciations. The Chinese have published books to illustrate the court, Changchau or Amoy, the Canton and Fuhchau dialects. The differences in the idioms and pronunciation are such as to render persons speaking them mutually unintelligible, but do not affect the style of writing, whose idioms are founded upon the usage of the best writers, and remain unchanged.

The court language, the *kwan hwa*, or mandarin dialect, is rather the proper language of the country—*the Chinese language*—than a dialect. It is studied and spoken by all educated men, and no one can make any pretence to learning or accomplishments who cannot converse in it in whatever part of the Empire he may be born. It is the common language throughout the northeastern provinces, especially Honan, Shantung, and Nganhwui, though presenting more or less variations even in them from the standard of the court and capital. This speech is characterized by its soft and mellifluous tones, the absence of all harsh, consonantal endings, and the prevalence of liquids and labials. In parts of the provinces where it is spoken, as the eastern portions of Chehkiang and Kiangsu, gutturals are common, and the initials softened or changed.

This tongue is the most ancient speech now spoken, for stanzas of poetry written twenty-five centuries ago, in the times previous to Confucius, are now read with the same rhymes as when penned. The expressions of the *kwan hwa*, although resembling the written language more than the other dialects, are still unlike it, being more diffuse, and containing many synonyms and particles not required to make the sense clear when it is addressed to the eye. The difference is such in this respect that two well-educated Chinese speaking in the terse style of books would hardly understand each other, and be obliged to use more words to convey their meaning when speaking than they would consider elegant or necessary in an essay. This is, to be sure, more or less the case in all languages, but from the small variety of sounds and their monosyllabic brevity, it is unavoidable in Chinese, though it must not be inferred that the language cannot be written so as to be understood when read off; it can be written as diffusely as it is spoken, but such a style is not considered very elegant. There are books written in the colloquial, however, from which it is not difficult to learn the style of conversation, and such books are among the best to put into the hands of a foreigner when beginning the study.

The local patois of a place is called *tu tan*, or *hiang tan*, *i.e.*, local or village brogue, and there is an interpreter of it attached to almost every officer's court for the purpose of translating the peculiar phrases of witnesses and others brought before him. The term *dialect* cannot, strictly, in its previous definition, be applied to the *tu tan*, though it is usually so called; it is a patois or brogue. The Canton dialect is called by its citizens *pak wa*, 'the plain speech,' because it is more intelligible than the court dialect. It is comparatively easy of acquisition, and differs less from the *kwan hwa*, in its pronunciation and idioms, than that of Amoy and its vicinity; but the diversity is still enough to render it unintelligible to people from the north. A very few books have been written in it, but none which can afford assistance in learning it. A native scholar would consider his character for literary attainments almost degraded if he should write books in the provincial dialects, and forsake the style of the immortal classics. The principal feature in the pronunciation of the Canton dialect which distinguishes it from the general language, is the change of the abrupt vowel terminations, as *loh*, *kiah*, *pih*, into the well-defined consonants *k*, *p*, and *t*, as *lok*, *kap*, *pít*, a change that considerably facilitates the discrimination of the syllables. The idioms of the two cannot well be illustrated without the help of the written character, but the differences between the sounds of two or three sentences may be exhibited: The phrase, *I do not understand what he says*, is in the

Court dialect: *Wo min puh tung teh ta kiang shim mo.*

Canton dialect: *Ngo 'm hiu kü kong măt yé.*

The rice contains sand in it.

Court dialect: *Na ko mí yu sha tsz'.*

Canton dialect: *Ko tik mai yau sha tsoi noi.*

None of the provincial patois differ so much from the *kwan hwa*, and afford so many peculiarities, as those spoken in the province of Fuhkien and eastern portions of Kwangtung. All of them are nasal, and, compared with those spoken elsewhere, harsh and rough. They have a large number of unwritten sounds, and so supply the lack; the same character often has one sound when read and another when spoken; all of them are in common use. This curious feature obliges the foreigner to learn two parallel languages when studying this dialect, so intimate and yet so distinct are the two. The difference between them will be more apparent by quoting a sentence: "He first performed that which was difficult, and afterward imitated what was easier." The corresponding words of the colloquial are placed underneath the reading sounds.

Sien k'i su chi sé lan, ji ho k'i hau chi sé tek.
Tai seng chó i é su é sé oh, ji tui au k'wⁿa i é hau giem é sé tit lióh.

The changes from one into the other are exceedingly various both in sound and idiom. Thus, *bien chien*, 'before one's face,' becomes *bin chan* when spoken; while in the phrase *cheng jit*, 'a former day,' the same word *chien* becomes *cheng* and not *chan*; *bòé chu*, 'pupil of the eye,' becomes *ang a*; *sit hwan*, 'to eat rice,' becomes *chiah puiⁿ*. Their dialect, not less than their trafficking spirit, point out the Amoy people wherever they are met, and as they are usually found along the whole coast and in the Archipelago, and are not understood except by their provincial compatriots, they everywhere clan together and form separate communities. Dr. Medhurst published a dictionary of the Changchau dialect, in which the sounds of the characters are given as they are read. Dr. C. Douglas has gathered a great vocabulary of words and phrases used in the Amoy colloquial, in which he has attempted to reduce everything to the Romanized system of writing, and omitted all the characters.

The dialects of Fuhchau, Swatow, and Canton have been similarly investigated by Protestant missionaries. Messrs. Maclay and Baldwin have taken the former in hand, and their work leaves very little to be desired for the elucidation of that speech. Goddard's vocabulary of the Swatow has no examples; and Williams' *Tonic Dictionary* of the Canton dialect gave no characters with the examples. This deficiency was made up in Lobscheid's rearrangement of it under the radicals.

The extent to which the dialects are used has not been ascertained, nor the degree of modification each undergoes in those parts where it is spoken; for villagers within a few miles, although able to understand each other perfectly, still give different sounds to a few characters, and have a few local phrases, enough to distinguish their several inhabitants, while towns one or two hundred miles apart are still more unlike. For instance, the citizen of Canton always says *shui* for water, and *tsz'* for child, but the native of Macao says *sui* and *chi* for these two words; and if his life depended upon his uttering them as they are spoken in Canton, they would prove a shibboleth which he could not possibly enunciate. Strong peculiarities of speech also exist in the villages between Canton and Macao which are found in neither of those places. Yet whatever sound they give to a character it has the same tone, and a Chinese would be much less surprised to hear water called ♯*chwui*, than he would to hear it called ♭*shui* in the lower even tone, instead of its proper ascending tone. The tones really approach vowels in their nature more than mere musical inflections; and it is by their nice discrimination, that the people are able to understand each other with less difficulty than we might suppose amidst such a jargon of vocables.

This accurate discrimination in the vowel sounds, and comparative indifference to consonants, which characterize the Chinese spoken languages, has arisen, no doubt, from the monosyllabic nature, and the constant though slight variations the names of characters undergo from the traditionary mode in which they must be learned. There being no integral sound in any character, each and all of them are, of course, equally correct, *per se*; but the various general and local dictionaries have each tended somewhat to fix the pronunciation, just as books and education have fixed the spelling of English words. Nor do the Chinese more than other people learn to pronounce their mother tongue from dictionaries, and the variations are consequently but partially restrained by them. It may truly be said, that no two Chinese speak all words alike, while yet, through means of the universally understood character, the greatest mass of human beings ever collected under one government are enabled to express themselves without difficulty, and carry on all the business and concerns of life.

The grammar of the Chinese language is unique, but those writers who say it has no grammar at all must have overlooked the prime signification of the word. There are in all languages words which denote things, and others which signify qualities; words which express actions done by one or many, already done, doing or to be done; actions absolute, conditional, or ordered. The circumstances of the doer and the subject of the action, make prepositions necessary, as well as other connecting words. Thus the principles of grammar exist in all intelligible speech, though each may require different rules. These rules the Chinese language possesses, and their right application, the proper collocation of words, and use of particles, which supply the place of inflection, constitute a difficult part in its acquisition. It has no etymology, properly speaking, for neither the characters nor their names undergo any change; whether used as verbs or nouns, adjectives or particles, they remain the same. The same word may be a noun, a verb, an adverb, or any part of speech, nor can its character be certainly known till it is placed in a sentence, when its meaning becomes definite. Its grammar, therefore, is confined chiefly to its syntax and prosody. This feature of the Chinese language is paralleled in English by such words as *light*, used as a noun, adjective, and verb; *like*, used as a verb, adjective, and adverb; *sheep* and *deer*, used both in the singular and plural; *read*, used in the past, present, and future tenses; and in all cases without undergoing any change. But what is occasional and the exception in that tongue, becomes the rule in Chinese; nor is there any more confusion in the last than in the first.

A good summary of the principles of Chinese grammar is given by Rémusat, who says that generally,

"In every Chinese sentence, in which nothing is understood, the elements of which it is composed are arranged in the following order: the subject, the verb, the complement direct, and the complement indirect.

"Modifying expressions precede those to which they belong: thus, the adjective is placed before the substantive, subject, or complement; the substantive governed before the verb that governs it; the adverb before the verb, the proposition incidental, circumstantial, or hypothetical, before the principal proposition, to which it attaches itself by a conjunction expressed or understood.

"The relative position of words and phrases thus determined, supplies the place often of every other mark intended to denote their mutual dependence, their character whether adjective or adverbial, positive, conditional, or circumstantial.

"If the subject be understood, it is because it is a personal pronoun, or that it is expressed above, and that the same substantive that is omitted is found in the preceding sentence, and in the same quality of subject, and not in any other.

"If the verb be wanting, it is because it is the substantive verb, or some other easily supplied, or one which has already found place in the preceding sentences, with a subject or complement not the same.

"If several substantives follow each other, either they are in construction with each other, or they form an enumeration, or they are synonyms which explain and determine each other.

"If several verbs succeed each other, which are not synonyms and are not employed as auxiliaries, the first ones should be taken as adverbs or verbal nouns, the subjects of those which follow; or these latter as verbal nouns, the complements of those which precede."

Chinese grammarians divide all words into *shih tsz'* and *hü tsz'*, *i.e.*, essential words and particles. The former are subdivided into *sz' tsz'* and *hwoh tsz'*, *i.e.*, nouns and verbs; the latter into initials or introductory words, conjunctions, exclamations, finals, transitive particles, etc. They furnish examples under each, and assist the student, with model books, in which the principles of the language and all rhetorical terms are explained. The number and variety of grammatical and philological works prove that they have not neglected the elucidation and arrangement of their mother tongue. The rules above cited are applicable to the written language, and these treatises refer entirely to that; the changes in the phraseology of the colloquial do not affect its grammar, however, which is formed upon the same rules.

Although the characters are, when isolated, somewhat indefinite, there are many ways of limiting their meaning in sentences. Nouns are often made by suffixing formative particles, as *nu kí*, 'angry spirit,' merely means *anger; í kí*, 'righteous spirit,' is *rectitude; chin 'rh*, 'needle child,' is a needle, etc.; the suffix, in these cases, simply materializing the word. Gender is formed by distinctive particles, prefixed or suffixed by appropriate words for each gender, or by denoting one gender always by a dissyllabic compound; as *male*-being, for the masculine; horse-*sire*, or horse-*mother*, for stallion or dam; *hero*, *heroine*, *emperor*, *empress*, etc.; and lastly as *wang-hau*, *i.e.*, king-*queen*, for *queen*, while *wang* alone means *king*. Number is formed by prefixing a numeral, as *Yung*, *Tsin*, *two* men; by suffixing a formative, *mun*, *tăng*, and others, as *jin-tăng*, man-*sort*, or men; *ta-mun*, he-*s* or they; by repeating the word, as *jin-jin*, man-man or *men*; *chu-chu*, place-place, or places, *i.e.*, everywhere; and lastly, by the scope of the passage. The nominative, accusative, and vocative cases are commonly known by their position; the genitive, dative, and ablative are formed by appropriate prepositions, expressed or understood. The vocative is common in light reading and historical studies.

Adjectives precede nouns, by which position they are usually determined. Comparisons are made in many ways. *Hau* is *good*, *kăng hau* is *better*, and *chí hau* is *best*; *shih făn hau hau* is *very good*; *hau hau tih* is *pretty good*, etc. The position of an adjective determines its comparison, as *chang yih chih* means *longer by one cubit*; *yih chih chang* is a *cubit long*. The comparison of ideas is made by placing the two sentences parallel to each other; for instance, "Entering the hills and seizing a tiger is easy, opening the mouth and getting men to lean to is difficult," is the way of expressing the comparison, "It is easier to seize a tiger in the hills, than to obtain the good offices of men." The proper use of antithesis and parallelism is considered one of the highest attainments in composition. The numerals are thirteen in number, with the addition of the character 零 *ling* to denote a cipher. All amounts are written just as they are to be read, as *yih peh sz' shih san*, 一百四十三 *i.e.*, 'one hundred four tens three.' They are here introduced, with their pronunciation in three dialects.

	1	2	3	4	5	6	7	8	9	10	100	1,000	10,000
	一	二	三	四	五	六	七	八	九	十	百	千	萬
Court Dialect.	*yih*	*'rh*	*san*	*sz'*	*wu*	*luh*	*tsih*	*pah*	*kiu*	*shih*	*peh*	*tsien*	*wan.*
Canton Dialect.	*yat*	*í*	*sam*	*sz'*	*'ng*	*luk*	*tsàt*	*pat*	*kau*	*shap*	*pak*	*tsín*	*man.*
Fuhkien Dialect.	*it*	*jí*	*sam*	*su*	*ngou*	*liok*	*chit*	*pat*	*kiu*	*sip*	*pek*	*chien*	*ban.*

The Chinese, like the ancient Greeks, enumerate only up to a myriad, expressing sums higher than that by stating how many myriads there are; the notation of 362,447,180 is three myriads, six thousand, two hundred and forty-four myriads, seven thousand, one hundred, and eighty. Pronouns are few in number, and their use is avoided whenever the sense is clear without them. The personal pronouns are three, *wo*, *ní*, and *ta*, but other pronouns can all be readily expressed by adjectives, by collocation, and by participial phrases. The classifiers sometimes partake of the nature of adjective pronouns, but usually are mere distributive or numerical adjectives.

Verbs, or "living characters," constitute the most important part of speech in the estimation of Chinese grammarians, and the *shun tuh*, or easy flow of expression, in their use, is carefully studied. The dissyllabic compounds, called *clam-shell words*, are usually verbs, and are made in many ways; by uniting two similar words, as *kwei-kien* (lit. peep-look), 'to spy;' by doubling the verb, as *kien-kien*, meaning to look earnestly; by prefixing a formative denoting action, as *ta shwui* (lit. strike sleep), 'to sleep;' by suffixing a modifying word, as *grasp-halt*, to grasp firmly; *think-arise*, to cogitate, etc. No part of the study requires more attention than the right selection of these formatives in both nouns and verbs; perfection in the *shun tuh* and use of antitheses is the result only of years of study.

The various accidents of voice, mood, tense, number, and person, can all be expressed by corresponding particles, but the genius of the language disfavors their frequent use. The passive voice is formed by prefixing particles indicative of agency before the active verb, as "The villain *received* my sword's *cutting*," for "The villain was wounded by my sword." The imperative, potential, and subjunctive moods are formed by particles or adjuncts, but the indicative and infinitive are not designated, nor are the number and person of verbs usually distinguished. The number of auxiliaries, particles, adjuncts, and suffixes of various kinds, employed to express what in other languages is denoted by inflections, is really very moderate; and a nice discrimination exhibited in their use indicates the finished scholar.[1]

[1] *Chinese Repository*, Vol. VIII., p. 347.

The greatest defect in the Chinese language is the indistinct manner in which time is expressed; not that there is any want of terms to denote its varieties, but the terseness of expression admired by Chinese writers leads them to discard every unessential word, and especially those relating to time. This defect is more noticed by the foreigner than the native, who has no knowledge of the precision of time expressed by inflection in other languages. Adverbs, prepositions, conjunctions, and interjections are not distinguished by native grammarians; the former are classed with adjectives, and the others are collectively called *hü tsz'*—'empty words.'

No distinction is made between proper and common names, and as every word can be employed as a name it becomes a source of confusion to the translator; in some books a single line drawn on the side of characters denotes the names of persons, and a double line the names of places; important words are denoted by commencing a new line with them, raised one or two characters above the other columns, which answers to capitalizing them. In most books an entire absence of all marks of punctuation, and divisions into sentences and paragraphs, causes needless doubt in the mind of the reader. The great convenience experienced in European languages from the use of capital letters, marks of punctuation, separation into sentences and paragraphs, and the distinction of time, is more plainly seen when a translation is to be made from languages like the Chinese and Japanese, in which they are disregarded. A false taste prevents them from using them; they admire a page of plain characters so much that a student who should punctuate his essay would run a risk of being ridiculed.

It is not easy yet to decide on the best way to adapt the technical words in western science to the genius of this language. The vast terminology in natural history, with the still greater array of scientific names, need not be introduced into it, but can remain in their original Latin and Greek, where Chinese scientists can consult them. New compounds have already been proposed for gases, metals, earths, acids, and other elementary substances, in which the radical and primitive are chosen with reference to their meanings, the latter being more complicated than usual for this purpose. These will gradually get into use as the sciences are studied, and their number will not be troublesomely large.

There are several distinct styles of composition recognized. The *ku wăn*, or the terse antithetic style of the ancient classics, is considered as inimitable and unimprovable, and really possesses the qualities of energy, vivacity, and brevity in a superior degree; the *wăn chang*, or style of elevated composition, adopted in essays, histories, and grave works; and the *siao shwoh*, or colloquial style, used in stories.

If there are serious defects, this language also possesses some striking beauties. The expressive nature of the characters, after their component parts have become familiar, causes much of the meaning of a sentence to pass instantly before the eye, while the energy arising from the brevity attainable by the absence of all inflections and partial use of particles, add a vigor to the style that is hardly reached by any alphabetic language. Dr. Morrison observes that "Chinese fine writing darts upon the mind with a vivid flash, a force and a beauty, of which alphabetic language is incapable." It is also better fitted than any other for becoming a universal medium of communication, and has actually become so to a much greater extent than any other; but the history of its diffusion, and the modifications it has undergone among the five nations who use it, though presenting a curious topic for philological inquiry, is one far too extensive to be discussed here. So general a use of one written language, however, affords some peculiar facilities for the diffusion of knowledge by means of books as introductory to the general elevation of the people using it, and their preparation for substituting an alphabetic language for so laborious and unwieldy a vehicle of thought, which it seems impossible to avoid as Christian civilization and knowledge extend.

It is often asked, is the Chinese language hard to learn? The preceding account of it shows that to become familiar with its numerous characters, to be able to speak the delicately marked tones of its short monosyllables, and to compose in it with perspicuity and elegance, is the labor of years of close application. To do so in Greek, Latin, English, or any settled tongue, is also a toilsome task, and excepting the barren labor of remembering so many different characters, it is not more so in Chinese than in others. But knowledge sufficient to talk intelligibly, to write perspicuously, and read with considerable ease, is not so herculean a task as some suppose, though this degree is not to be attained without much hard study. Moreover, dictionaries, manuals, and translations are now available which materially diminish the labor, and their number is constantly increasing.

The rules for studying it cannot be laid down so that they will answer equally well for all persons. Some readily catch the most delicate inflections of the voice, and imitate and remember the words they hear ; such persons soon learn to speak, and can make themselves understood on common subjects with merely the help of a vocabulary. Others prefer to sit down with a teacher and learn to read, and for most persons this is the best way to begin. At first, the principal labor should be directed to the characters, reading them over with a teacher and learning their form. Commence with the two hundred and fourteen radicals, and commit them to memory, so that they can be repeated and written in their order; then learn the primitives, or at least become familiar with the names and meaning of all the common ones. The aid this preliminary study gives in remembering the formation of characters is worth all the time it takes. Students make a mistake if they begin with the Testament or a tract; they can learn more characters in the same period, and lay a better foundation for acquiring others, by commencing with the radicals and primitives. Meanwhile, they will also be learning sounds and becoming familiar with the tones, which should be carefully attended to as a particular study from the living voice.

When these characters are learned, short sentences or reading lessons selected from good *Chinese* authors, with a translation attached, should be taken up and committed to memory. Phrases may also be learned at the same time, for use in conversation ; an excellent way is to memorize one or two hundred common words, and then practise putting them together in sentences. The study of reading lessons and phrases, with practice in speaking and writing them, will prepare the way for commencing the study of the classics or other native authors. By the time the student has reached this point he needs no further directions; the path he wishes thenceforth to pursue can easily be marked out by himself. It is not amiss here to remark that many persons ardently desirous of fitting themselves soon for preaching or talking to the people, weary their minds and hinder their ultimate progress by too hard study at first upon the dry characters; others come to look upon the written language as less important so long as they can talk rapidly and well, but in the end find that in this, as in every other living tongue, there is no royal road which does not lead them through the grammar and literature.[1]

This sketch of the Chinese language would be incomplete without a notice of the singular jargon which has grown up between the natives and foreigners along the coast, called *pigeon-English.* It has been so long in use as the medium of traffic and household talk that it now bids fair to become an unwritten patois, of which neither the Chinese nor the English will own the parentage. The term *pigeon*, a corruption from *business*, shows, in its transformation, some of the influences which our words must undergo as they pass through the Chinese characters. The foreigners who first settled at Canton had no time nor facilities for learning the dialect, and the traders with whom they bargained soon picked up more foreign words than the former did native. The shopmen ere long formed vocabularies of foreign words obtained from their customers, and wrote the sounds as nearly as possible; these were committed to memory and formed into sentences according to the idioms of their own language, and disregarding all our inflections, in which they had no instruction. Thus the two parties gradually came to understand each other enough for all practical ends; the foreigners were rather pleased to talk

[1] Many aids in learning the general language and all the leading dialects have been prepared in English, French, German, and Portuguese, but several of the early ones, as Morrison, Gonçalves, Medhurst, and Bridgman, are already out of print. The names of all of these may be found most easily in the first volume of M. Cordier's exhaustive *Dictionnaire Bibliographique des ouvrages relatifs à l'Empire chinois*, pp. 725–804. Paris, 1881.

"broken China," as it was not inaptly called, and habit soon made it natural to a new-comer to talk it to the natives, and it obviated all necessity for studying Chinese. The body of the jargon is English, the few Chinese, Portuguese, and Malay words therein imparting a raciness which, with the novelty of the expressions, has of late attracted much attention to this new language. Though apparently without any rules, the natives are very liable to misapprehend what is said to them by their masters or customers, because these rules are not followed, and constant difficulty arises from mutual misunderstanding of this sort. The widening study of Chinese is not likely to do away with this droll lingo at the trade ports, and several attempts have been made to render English pieces into it. On the other hand, in California and elsewhere, the Chinese generally succeed in learning the languages of their adopted countries better than in talking *pigeon-English*, or the similar mongrel vernacular spoken at Macao by the native-born Chinese.

A knowledge of the Chinese language is a passport to the confidence of the people, and when foreigners generally learn it the natives will begin to divest themselves of their prejudices and contempt. As an inducement to study, the scholar and the philanthropist have the prospect of benefiting and informing through it vast numbers of their fellow-men, of imparting to them what will elevate their minds, purify their hearts, instruct their understandings, and strengthen their desire for more knowledge; they have an opportunity of doing much to counteract the tremendous evils of the opium trade by teaching the Chinese the only sure grounds on which they can be restrained, and at the same time of making them acquainted with the discoveries in science, medicine, and arts among western nations.

CHAPTER XI.

CLASSICAL LITERATURE OF THE CHINESE.

The literature contained in the language now briefly described is very ample and discursive, but wanting in accuracy and unenlivened by much variety or humor. The books of the Chinese have formed and confirmed their national taste, which consequently exhibits a tedious uniformity. The unbounded admiration felt for the classics and their immaculate authors, fostered by the examinations, has further tended to this result, and caused these writings to become still more famous from the unequalled influence they have exerted. It may be very readily seen, then, with what especial interest the student of Chinese sociology turns to an investigation of their letters, the immense accumulation of forty centuries. Were its amount and prominence the only features of their literature, these would suffice to make necessary some study thereof; but in addition, continued research may reveal some further qualities of "eloquence and poetry, enriched by the beauty of a picturesque language, preserving to imagination all its colors," which will substantiate the hearty expressions used by Rémusat when first he entered upon a critical examination of its treasures.

In taking a survey of this literature, the *Sz' Ku Tsiuen Shu Tsung-muh*, or 'Catalogue of all Books in the Four Libraries,' will be the best guide, since it embraces the whole range of letters, and affords a complete and succinct synopsis of the contents of the best books in the language. It is comprised in one hundred and twelve octavo volumes, and is of itself a valuable work, especially to the foreigner. The books are arranged into four divisions, viz., Classical, Historical, and Professional writings, and Belles-lettres. This Catalogue contains about 3,440 separate titles, comprising upward of 78,000 books; besides these, 6,764 other works, numbering 93,242 books, have been described in other catalogues of the imperial collections. These lists comprise the bulk of Chinese literature, except novels, Buddhist translations, and recent publications.

The works in the first division are ranged under nine sections; one is devoted to each of the five Classics (with a subsidiary section upon these as a whole), one to the memoir on Filial Duty, one to the Four Books, one to musical works, and the ninth to treatises on education, dictionaries, etc.

At the head of the 'Five Classics' (*Wu King*) is placed the *Yih King*, or 'Book of Changes,' a work which if not—as it has been repeatedly called—*Antiquissimus Sinarum liber*, can be traced with tolerable accuracy to an origin three thousand years ago. It ranks, according to Dr. Legge, third in antiquity among the Chinese classics, or after the *Shu* and portions of the *Shí King*; but if an unbounded veneration for enigmatical wisdom supposed to lie concealed under mystic lines be any just claim for importance, to this wondrous monument of literature may easily be conceded the first place in the estimation of Chinese scholars.

While following Dr. Legge in his recent exposition of this classic,[1] a clearer idea of its subject-matter can hardly be given than by quoting his words stating that "the text may be briefly represented as consisting of sixty-four short essays, enigmatically and symbolically expressed, on important themes, mostly of a moral, social, and political character, and based on the same number of lineal figures, each made up of six lines, some of which are whole and the others divided." The evolution of the eight diagrams from two original principles is ascribed to Fuh-hí (B.C. 3322), who is regarded as the founder of the nation, though his history is, naturally enough, largely fabulous. From the *Liang Ĭ*, or 'Two Principles' (—) (– –), were fashioned the *Sz' Siang*, or 'Four Figures,' by placing these over themselves and each of them over the other, thus:

[1] *The Sacred Books of China. The Texts of Confucianism.* Translated by James Legge. Part II. *The Yi King.* Oxford, 1882.

The same pairs placed in succession under the original lines formed eight trigrams called the

PAH KWA of FUH-HÍ.

☰	☱	☲	☳	☴	☵	☶	☷
kien	*tui*	*lí*	*chin*	*siuen*	*kan*	*kăn*	*kwăn*
Heaven, the Sky.	Water collected, as in a marsh or lake.	Fire, as in lightning; the Sun.	Thunder.	The Wind; Wood.	Water, as in rain, clouds, springs, streams, and defiles. The Moon.	Hills or Mountains.	The Earth.
S.	S.E.	E.	N.E.	S.W.	W.	N.W.	N.
Untiring strength; power.	Pleasure; complacent satisfaction.	Brightness; elegance.	Moving, exciting power.	Flexibility; penetration.	Peril; difficulty.	Resting; the act of arresting.	Capaciousness; submission.

The table furnishes us with the natural objects that these figures are said to represent, the attributes which should seem to be suggested by them, and which, with the application of the eight points of the compass, together form the material for a cabalistic logomancy peculiarly pleasing to Chinese habits of thought. The trigrams furnish, moreover, the state and position, at any given place or time, of the twofold division of the one primordial *kí*, or 'Air,' called *Yang* and *Yin*, and have thus become the source from whence the system of *Fung-shui* is derived and on whose changes it is founded. This substance *kí* answers sufficiently closely to the animated air of the Grecian philosopher Anaximenes; its divisions are a subtle and a coarse principle which, acting and reacting upon each other, produce four *siang*, or 'forms,' and these again combine into eight *kwa*, or trigrams. Fuh-hí is thus said to have arranged the first four of the *Pah Kwa* under the *Yang* (strong or hard) principle, and the last four under the *Yin* (weak or soft) principle; the former indicate vigor or authority, and it is their part to command, while of the latter, representing feebleness or submission, it is the part to obey.

It was probably Wăn Wang, King Wăn, chief of the principality of Chau in 1185 B.C., who when thrown into prison by his jealous suzerain Shau, the tyrant of Shang, arranged and multiplied the trigrams—long before his time used for purposes of divination—into the sixty-four hexagrams as they now occur in the *Yih King*. His was a wholly different disposition, both of names, attributes, and the compass points, from the original trigrams of Fuh-hí; again, he added to them certain social relations of father, mother, three sons, and three daughters, which has ever since been found a convenient addition to the conjuring apparatus of the work. "I like to think," says Dr. Legge, "of the lord of Chau, when incarcerated in Yu-lí, with the sixty-four figures arranged before him. Each hexagram assumed a mystic meaning and glowed with a deep significance. He made it to tell him of the qualities of various objects of nature, or of the principles of human society, or of the condition, actual and possible, of the kingdom. He named the figures each by a term descriptive of the idea with which he had connected it in his mind, and then he proceeded to set that idea forth, now with a note of exhortation, now with a note of warning. It was an attempt to restrict the follies of divination within the bounds of reason. . . . But all the work of King Wăn in the *Yih* thus amounts to no more than sixty-four short paragraphs. We do not know what led his son Tan to enter into his work and complete it as he did. Tan was a patriot, a hero, a legislator, and a philosopher. Perhaps he took the lineal figures in hand as a tribute of filial duty. What had been done for the whole hexagram he would do for each line, and make it clear that all the six lines 'bent one way their precious influence,' and blended their rays in the globe of light which his father had made each figure give forth. But his method strikes us as singular. Each line seemed to become living, and suggested some phenomenon in nature, or some case of human experience, from which the wisdom or folly, the luckiness or unluckiness, indicated by it could be inferred. It cannot be said that the duke carried out his plan in a way likely to interest any one but a *hien shăng* who is a votary of divination and admires the style of its oracles. According to our notions, a framer of emblems should be a good deal of a poet; but those of the *Yih* only make us think of a dryasdust. Out of more than three hundred and fifty, the greater number are only grotesque. We do not recover from the feeling of disappointment till we remember that both father and son had to write 'according to the trick,' after the manner of diviners, as if this lineal augury had been their profession."

Such is the text of the *Yih*. The words of King Wăn and his son are followed by commentaries called the *Shih Yih*, or 'Ten Wings.' These are of a much later period than the text, and are commonly ascribed to Confucius, though it is extremely doubtful if the sage was author of more than the sentences introduced by the oft-repeated formula, "The Master said," occurring in or concluding many chapters of the 'Wings.' Without lingering over the varied contents of these appendices, more than to point out that the fifth and sixth Wings ('Appended Sentences'), known as the 'Great Treatise,' contains for the first time the character *Yih*, or 'Change,' it will be necessary, before leaving this classic, to illustrate its curious nature by means of a single quotation.

XXXI.—THE *HIEN* HEXAGRAM.

Hien indicates that [on the fulfilment of the conditions implied in it] there will be free course and success. Its advantageousness will depend on the being firm and correct, [as] in marrying a young lady. There will be good fortune.

1. The first line, divided, shows one moving his great toes.

2. The second line, divided, shows one moving the calves of his leg. There will be evil. If he abide [quiet in his place] there will be good fortune.

3. The third line, undivided, shows one moving his thighs, and keeping close hold of those whom he follows. Going forward [in this way] will cause regret.

4. The fourth line, undivided, shows that firm correctness which will lead to good fortune and prevent all occasion for repentance. If its subject be unsettled in his movements, [only] his friends will follow his purpose.

5. The fifth line, undivided, shows one moving the flesh along the spine above the heart. There will be no occasion for repentance.

6. The sixth line, divided, shows one moving his jaws and tongue.

An idea of the several commentaries, or 'Wings,' upon such a passage may be gained from the following excerpts. First comes the 'Treatise on the Twan,' or King Wăn's paragraphs; then the 'Treatise on the Symbols,' consisting of observations on Duke Chau's exposition.

From the *Second Wing*.—1. *Hien* is here used in the sense of *Kan*, meaning [mutually] influencing.

2. The weak [trigram] above, and the strong one below; their two influences moving and responding to each other, and thereby forming a union; the repression [of the one] and the satisfaction [of the other]; [with their relative position] where the male is placed below the female—all these things convey the notion of 'a free and successful course [on the fulfilment of the conditions], while the advantage will depend on being firm and correct, as in marrying a young lady, and there will be good fortune.' . . . etc., etc.

Fourth Wing.—[The trigram representing] a mountain and above it that for [the waters of] a marsh form *Hien*. The superior man, in accordance with this, keeps his mind free from preoccupation, and open to receive [the influences of] others.

1. 'He moves his great toe'—his mind is set on what is beyond [himself].

2. Though 'there would be evil, yet if he abide [quiet] in his place there will be good fortune'—through compliance [with the circumstances of his condition and place] there will be no injury.

3. 'He moves his thighs'—he still does not [want to] rest in his place. His will is set on 'following others;' what he holds in his grasp is low.

4. 'Firm correctness will lead to good fortune, and prevent all occasion for repentance'—there has not yet been any harm from [a selfish wish to] influence. 'He is unsettled in his movements'—[his power to influence] is not yet either brilliant or great.

5. 'He [tries to] move the flesh along the spine above the heart'—his aim is trivial.

6. 'He moves his jaws and tongue'—he [only] talks with loquacious mouth.

Sixth Wing ('Appended Sentences').—Chapter I.—1. The eight trigrams having been completed in their proper order, there were in each the [three] emblematic lines. They were then multiplied by a process of addition till the [six] component lines appeared.

2. The strong line and the weak push themselves each into the place of the other, and hence the changes [of the diagrams] take place. The appended explanations attach to every form of them its character [of good or ill], and hence the movements [suggested by divination] are determined accordingly.

3. Good fortune and ill, occasion for repentance or regret, all arise from these movements . . . etc., etc.

The hundreds of fortune-tellers seen in the streets of Chinese towns, whose answers to their perplexed customers are more or less founded on these cabala, indicate their influence among the illiterate; while among scholars, who have long since conceded all divination to be vain, it is surprising to remark the profound estimation in which these inane lines are held as the consummation of all wisdom—the germ, even, of all the truths which western science has brought to light! Each hexagram is supposed to represent, at any given time, six different phases of the primordial *ki*. "As all the good and evil in the world," observes McClatchie, "is attributed by the Chinese philosophers to the purity or impurity of the animated air from which the two-fold soul in man is formed, a certain moral value attaches to each stroke, and the diviner prognosticates accordingly that good or evil luck, as the case may be, will result to the consulter of the oracle with regard to the matter on which he seeks it. Nine is the number of Heaven, or the undivided stroke, and six is the number of Earth, or the divided stroke, and hence each stroke has a double designation. The first stroke, if undivided, is designated 'First-Nine,' but if divided it is designated 'First-Six,' and so on. The second and fifth strokes in each diagram are important, being the centre or medium strokes of their respective lesser diagrams. The fifth stroke, however, is the most important in divination, as it represents that portion of the air which is the especial throne of the imperial power, and is the 'undeflected due medium.' Nothing but good luck can follow if the person divining with the straws obtains this stroke. Tao, or the Divine Reason, which is the supreme soul of the whole Kosmos, animates the air, pervading its six phases, and thus giving power to the diagrams to make known future events to mankind."

Of course anything and everything could be deduced from such a fanciful groundwork, but the Chinese have taken up the discussion in the most serious manner, and endeavored to find the hidden meaning and evolutions of the universe from this curious system. The diagrams have, moreover, supplied the basis for many species of divination by shells, letters, etc., by which means the mass of the people are deluded into the belief of penetrating futurity, and still more wedded to their superstitions. The continued influence of such a work as the *Yih* illustrates the national *penchant* for laws and method, while equally indicating the general indifference to empirical research and the facts deduced from study of natural history. If, from a philosophical standpoint, we consider the barrenness of its results, there is little, indeed, to say for the *Yih King*, save concurrence in Dr. Gustave Schlegel's epithet, "a mechanical play of idle abstractions;" nevertheless, this classic contains in its whimsical dress of inscrutable strokes much of practical wisdom, giving heed to which it is not hard to agree with Dr. Legge in concluding that "the inculcation of such lessons cannot have been without good effect in China during the long course of its history."[1]

The second section of the Imperial Catalogue contains treatises upon the *Shu King*, or 'Book of Records.' This classic,

[1] Some fourteen hundred and fifty treatises on the *Yih*—consisting of memoirs, digests, expositions, etc.—are enumerated in the Catalogue. The foreign literature upon it has heretofore been scant. The only other translations of the classic *in extenso*, besides Dr. Legge's, already quoted, are the *Y-King; Antiquissimus Sinarum liber quem ex latina interpretatione;* P. Regis, *aliorumque ex Soc. Jesu P.P.*, *edidit* Julius Mohl, 2 vols., Stuttgart, 1834–39; and *A Translation of the Confucian Yih King, or the Classic of Change*, by the Rev. Canon McClatchie, Shanghai, 1876 (with Chinese text). Compare further *Notice du livre chinois nommé Y-king, avec des notes, par* M Claude Visdelou, contained in Père Gaubil's *Chou king*, Paris, 1843; *Die verbogenen Alterthümer der Chineser aus dem uralten Buche Yeking untersuchet, von* M. Joh. Heinrich Schuhmacher, Wolfenbüttel, 1763; Joseph Haas, in *Notes and Queries on China and Japan*, Vol. III., 1869; *China Review*, Vols. I., p. 151; IV., p. 257; and V., p. 132.

first in importance as it is in age among the five *King*, consists of a series of documents relating to the history of China from the times of Yao down to King Hiang, of the Chau dynasty (B.C. 2357–627). Its earlier chapters were composed at periods following the events of which they relate, but after the twenty-second century B.C. the *Shu* comes to us, though in a mutilated condition, as the contemporary chronicle of proclamations, addresses, and principles of the early sovereigns. Internal evidence leads to the conclusion that Confucius acted chiefly as editor of documents existing in his day; he probably wrote the preface, but what alterations it received at his hand cannot now be ascertained. When it left his care it contained eighty-one documents in one hundred books, arranged under the five dynasties of Yao, Shun, Hia, Shang, and Chau, the last one coming down to within two hundred and twenty-one years of his own birth. Most of these are lost, and others are doubted by Chinese critics, so that now only forty-eight documents remain, thirty of them belonging to the Chau, with the preface ascribed to Confucius. He showed his estimate of their value by calling the whole *Shang Shu*, or the 'Highest Book,' and we may class their loss with that of other ancient works in Hebrew or Greek literature. The *Shu King* now contains six different kinds of state papers, viz., imperial ordinances, plans drawn up by statesmen as guides for their sovereign, instructions prepared for the guidance of the prince, imperial proclamations and charges to the people, vows taken before Shangtí by the monarch when going out to battle, and, lastly, mandates, announcements, speeches, and canons issued to the ministers of state.[1]

The morality of the *Shu King*, for a pagan work, is extremely good; the principles of administration laid down in it, founded on a regard to the welfare of the people, would, if carried out, insure universal prosperity. The answer of Kaoyao to the

---

[1] Several translations have been made by missionaries. One by P. Gaubil was edited by De Guignes in 1770; a second by Rev. W. H. Medhurst, in 1846; but the most complete by J. Legge, D.D., in 1865, with its notes and text, has brought this *Record* better than ever before to the knowledge of western scholars.

monarch Yu is expressive of a mild spirit: "Your virtue, O Emperor, is faultless. You condescend to your ministers with a liberal ease; you rule the multitude with a generous forbearance. Your punishments do not extend to the criminal's heirs, but your rewards reach to after-generations. You pardon inadvertent faults, however great, and punish deliberate crime, however small. In cases of doubtful crimes you deal with them lightly; of doubtful merit, you prefer the highest estimate. Rather than put to death the guiltless, you will run the risk of irregularity and laxity. This life-loving virtue has penetrated the minds of the people, and this is why they do not render themselves liable to be punished by your officers."[1]

In the counsels of Yu to Shun are many of the best maxims of good government, both for rulers and ruled, which antiquity has handed down in any country. The following are among them: "Yih said, Alas! Be cautious. Admonish yourself to caution when there seems to be no reason for anxiety. Do not fail in due attention to laws and ordinances. Do not find enjoyment in indulgent ease. Do not go to excess in pleasure. Employ men of worth without intermediaries. Put away evil advisers, nor try to carry out doubtful plans. Study that all your purposes may be according to reason. Do not seek the people's praises by going against reason, nor oppose the people to follow your own desires. Be neither idle nor wayward, and even foreign tribes will come under your sway."

The *Shu King* contains the seeds of all things that are valuable in the estimation of the Chinese; it is at once the foundation of their political system, their history, and their religious rites, the basis of their tactics, music, and astronomy. Some have thought that the knowledge of the true God under the appellation of Shangtí is not obscurely intimated in it, and the precepts for governing a country, scattered through its dialogues and proclamations, do their writers credit, however little they may have been followed in practice. Its astronomy has attracted much investigation, but whether the remarks of the commentators are to be ascribed to the times in which they

---

[1] Legge, *The Chinese Classics*, Vol. III. *Shoo King*, p. 59.

themselves flourished, or to the knowledge they had of the ancient state of the science, is doubtful. The careful and candid discussions by Legge in the introduction to his translation furnish most satisfactory conclusions as to the origin, value, and condition of this venerable relic of ancient China. For his scholarly edition of the *Classics* he has already earned the hearty thanks of every student of Chinese literature.[1]

The third of the classics, the *Shí King*, or 'Book of Odes,' is ranked together with the two preceding, while its influence upon the national mind has been equally great; a list of commentators upon this work fills the third section of the Catalogue. These poetical relics are arranged into four parts: The *Kwoh Fung*, or 'National Airs,' numbering one hundred and fifty-nine, from fifteen feudal States; the *Siao Ya*, or 'Lesser Eulogiums,' numbering eighty, and arranged under eight decades; the *Ta Ya*, or 'Greater Eulogiums,' numbering thirty-one, under three decades (both of these were designed to be sung on solemn occasions at the royal court); and the *Sung*, or 'Sacrificial Odes,' numbering forty-one chants connected with the ancestral worship of the rulers of Chau, Lu, and Shang. Out of a total number of three hundred and eleven now extant, six have only their titles preserved, while to a major part of the others native scholars give many various readings.

In the preface to his careful translation Dr. Legge has collected all the important information concerning the age, origin, and purpose of these odes, as furnished by native commentators, whose theory is that "it was the duty of the kings to make themselves acquainted with all the odes and songs current in

[1] *Chinese Repository*, Vol. VIII., p. 385; Vol. IX., p. 573. *Le Chou-king, un des Livres Sacrés des Chinois, qui renferme les Fondements de leur ancienne Histoire*, etc. Traduit par Feu le P. Gaubil. Paris, 1770, in-4. *La Morale du Chou-king ou le Livre Sacré de la Chine.* (The same), Paris, 1851. *Ancient China. The Shoo King, or the Historical Classic: being the most ancient authentic Record of the Annals of the Chinese Empire*, translated by W. H. Medhurst, Sen., Shanghae, 1846. *Nouveau Journal Asiatique*, Tomes V. (1830), p. 401; VI., p. 401, and XIV. (1842), p. 152. *China Review*, Vol. IV., p. 13. Dr. Legge's translation has recently (1879) appeared, without the Chinese text, in Max Müller's series of *Sacred Books of the East*, Vol. III. Richthofen, *China*, Bd. I., pp. 277–365, an exhaustive treatise on the early geography of China, with valuable historical maps.

the different States, and to judge from them of the character of the rule exercised by their several princes, so that they might minister praise or blame, reward or punishment accordingly." These odes and songs seem to have been gathered by Wăn Wang and Duke Chau at the beginning of the Chau dynasty (B.C. 1120), some of them at the capital, others from the feudal rulers in the course of royal progresses through the land, the royal music-master getting copies from the music-masters of the princes. The whole were then arranged, set to music, too, it may be, and deposited for use and reference in the national archives, as well as distributed among the feudatories. Their ages are uncertain, but probably do not antedate B.C. 1719 nor come after 585, or about thirty years before Confucius. Their number was not improbably at first fully up to the three thousand mentioned by the biographers of Confucius, but long before the sage appeared disasters of one kind and another had reduced them to nearly their present condition. What we have is, therefore, but a fragment of various collections made in the early reigns of the Chau sovereigns, which received, perhaps, larger subsequent additions than were preserved to the time of Confucius. He probably took them as they existed in his day, and feeling, possibly, like George Herbert, that

> "A verse may finde him, who a sermon flies,
> And turn delight into a sacrifice,"

did everything he could to extend their adoption among his countrymen. It is difficult to estimate the power they have exerted over the subsequent generations of Chinese scholars—nor has their influence ever tended to debase their morals, if it has not exalted their imagination. They have escaped the looseness of Moschus, Ovid, or Juvenal, if they have not attained the grandeur of Homer or the sweetness of Virgil and Pindar. There is nothing of an epic character in them—nor even a lengthened narrative—and little of human passions in their strong development. The metaphors and illustrations are often quaint, sometimes puerile, and occasionally ridiculous. Their acknowledged antiquity, their religious character, and their illustration of early Chinese customs and feelings form their principal claims to our notice and appreciative study. M. Ed. Biot, of Paris, was the first European scholar who studied them carefully in this aspect, and his articles in the *Journal Asiatique* for 1843 are models of analytic criticism and synthetic compilation, enabling one, as he says, " to contemplate at his ease the spectacle of the primitive manners of society in the early age of China, so different from what was then found in Europe and Western Asia."

An ode referred to the time of Wăn Wang (a contemporary of Saul) contains a sentiment reminding us of Morris' lines beginning "Woodman, spare that tree." It is in Part I., Book II., and is called *Kan-tang*, or the 'Sweet pear-tree.'

1. O fell not that sweet pear-tree!
   See how its branches spread.
Spoil not its shade,
For Shao's chief laid
   Beneath it his weary head.

2. O clip not that sweet pear-tree!
   Each twig and leaflet spare—
'Tis sacred now,
Since the lord of Shao,
   When weary, rested him there.

3. O touch not that sweet pear-tree!
   Bend not a twig of it now;
There long ago,
As the stories show,
   Oft halted the chief of Shao.[1]

The eighth ode in Book III., called *Hiung Chi*, or 'Cock Pheasant,' contains a wife's lament on her husband's absence.

1. Away the startled pheasant flies,
   With lazy movement of his wings;
Borne was my heart's lord from my eyes—
   What pain the separation brings!

2. The pheasant, though no more in view,
   His cry below, above, forth sends.
Alas! my princely lord, 'tis you,—
   Your absence, that my bosom rends.

---

[1] Dr. Legge, *The She King, translated into English verse*, p. 70. London, 1876.

3. At sun and moon I sit and gaze,
In converse with my troubled heart.
Far, far from me my husband stays!
When will he come to heal its smart?

4. Ye princely men, who with him mate,
Say, mark ye not his virtuous way?
His rule is, covet nought, none hate:
How can his steps from goodness stray?[1]

From the same book we translate somewhat freely an example (No. 17) of love-song, or serenade, not uncommon among these odes.

Maiden fair, so sweet, retiring,
At the tryst I wait for thee;
Still I pause in doubt, inquiring
Why thou triflest thus with me.

Ah! the maid so coy, so handsome,
Pledged she with a rosy reed;
Than the reed is she more winsome.
Love with beauty hard must plead!

In the meadows sought we flowers,
These she gave me—beauteous, rare:
Far above the gift there towers
The dear giver—lovelier, fair!

Among the 'Lesser Eulogiums' (Book IV., Ode 5) is one more ambitious in its scope, relating to the completion of a palace of King Siuen, about B.C. 800.

1. On yonder banks a palace, lo! upshoots,
The tender blue of southern hill behind,
Time-founded, like the bamboo's clasping roots;
Its roof, made pine-like, to a point defined.
Fraternal love here bears its precious fruits,
And unfraternal schemes be ne'er designed!

2. Ancestral sway is his. The walls they rear
Five thousand cubits long, and south and west
The doors are placed. Here will the king appear,
Here laugh, here talk, here sit him down and rest.

---

[1] *Ib.*, p. 83.

3. To mould the walls, the frames they firmly tie;
 The toiling builders beat the earth and lime;
The walls shall vermin, storm, and bird defy—
 Fit dwelling is it for his lordly prime.

4. Grand is the hall the noble lord ascends;
 In height, like human form, most reverent, grand;
And straight, as flies the shaft when bow unbends;
 Its tints like hues when pheasant's wings expand.

5. High pillars rise the level court around;
 The pleasant light the open chamber steeps,
And deep recesses, wide alcoves are found,
 Where our good king in perfect quiet sleeps.

6. Laid is the bamboo mat on rush mat square;
 Here shall he sleep; and waking say, "Divine
What dreams are good? For bear and piebald bear,
 And snakes and cobras haunt this couch of mine."

7. Then shall the chief diviner glad reply,
 "The bears foreshow their signs of promised sons.
The snakes and cobras daughters prophesy:
 These auguries are all auspicious ones."

8. Sons shall be his—on couches lulled to rest;
 The little ones enrobed, with sceptres play;
Their infant cries are loud as stern behest,
 Their knees the vermeil covers shall display.
As king hereafter one shall be addressed;
 The rest, our princes, all the States shall sway.

9. And daughters also to him shall be born.
 They shall be placed upon the ground to sleep;
Their playthings tiles, their dress the simplest worn;
 Their part alike from good and ill to keep,
And ne'er their parents' hearts to cause to mourn;
 To cook the food, and spirit-malt to steep.[1]

The last two stanzas indicate the comparative estimate, in ancient days, of boys and girls born into a family; and this estimate, still maintained, has been in a great degree upheld by this authority. Another ode in the 'Greater Eulogies' (Book III., Ode 10) deplores the misery that prevailed about B.C. 780, owing to the interference of women and eunuchs in the govern-

[1] *Id.*, *The She King*, p. 222.

ment. Two stanzas only are quoted, which are supposed to have been specially directed against Pao Sz', a mischief-maker in the court of King Yu, like Agrippina and Pulcheria in Roman and Byzantine annals.

3. A wise man builds the city wall,
   But a wise woman throws it down.
Wise is she? Good you may her call;
   She is an owl we should disown!
To woman's tongue let scope be given
   And step by step to harm it leads.
Disorder does not come from Heaven;
   'Tis woman's tongue disorder breeds.
Women and eunuchs! Never came
   Lesson or warning words from them!

4. Hurtful and false, their spite they wreak;
   And when exposed their falsehood lies—
The wrong they do not own, but sneak
   And say, "No harm did we devise."
"Thrice cent. per cent.!" Why, that is trade!
   Yet 'twould the princely man disgrace.
So public things to wife and maid
   Must not silkworms and looms displace.[1]

There are, however, numerous stanzas among the odes in the 'National Airs' which show their fairer side and go far to neutralize these, giving the same contrasts in female character which were portrayed by King Solomon during the same age.

The versification in a monosyllabic language appears very tame to those who are only familiar with the lively and varied rhythms of western tongues; but the Chinese express more vivacity and cadence in their ballads and ditties when sung than one would infer from these ancient relics when transliterated in our letters. As the young lad has usually committed all the three hundred and five odes to memory before he enters the Examination Hall, their influence on the matter and manner of his own future poetical attempts can hardly be exaggerated. It is shown throughout the thousands of volumes enumerated in the fourth division of the Imperial Catalogue. Most of the

[1] *Id.*, *The She King*, p. 347.

Shí King is written in tetrametres, and nothing can be more simple. They have been most unfortunately likened to the Hebrew Psalms by some of the early missionaries, but neither in manner nor matter is the comparison a happy one. One point of verbal resemblance is noticed by Dr. Legge between the first ode in Part III. and the one hundred and twenty-first psalm, where the last line of a stanza is generally repeated in the first line of the next, a feature something like the repetitions in *Hiawatha*. The rhymes and tones both form an essential part of Chinese poetry, one which can only be imperfectly represented in our language. The following furnishes an example of the general style, to which a literal rendering is subjoined:

1. *Nan yin kiao muh,*	South has stately trees,
Puh k'o hiu sih;	Not can shelter indeed;
Han yin yin nü,	Han has rambling women,
Puh k'o kiu sz'.	Not can solicit indeed.
Han chí kwang í,	Han's breadth be sure,
Puh k'o yung sz';	Not can be dived indeed;
Kiang chí yung í	Kiang's length be sure,
Puh k'o fang sz'.	Not can be rafted indeed.
2. *Kiao kiao tso sin,*	Many many mixed faggots,
Yen í kí chu;	Willingly I cut the brambles;
Chí tsz' yü kwei	Those girls going home,
Yen moh kí ma;	Willingly I would feed their horses;
Han chí kwang í, etc.	Han's breadth be sure, etc.
3. *Kiao kiao tso sin,*	Many many mixed faggots,
Yen í kí lao;	Willingly I cut the artemisia;
Chí tsz' yü kwei	Those girls going home,
Yen moh kí kü.	Willingly I would feed their colts;
Han chí kwang í, etc.	Han's breadth be sure, etc.

The highest range of thought in the odes is contained in Part IV., but the whole collection is worthy of perusal, and through the labors of Dr. Legge has been made more accessible than it was ever before. The amount of native literature extant, illustrative, critical, and philological, referring to the *Book of Odes*[1] is not so large as that on the *Yih King;* but the

[1] A recent German translation of these odes has combined, with much accuracy and a smooth versification, the peculiar adaptability of that tongue to the

fifty-five works quoted in his preface[1] contain enough to indicate their industry and acumen. These works will elevate the character of Chinese scholarship in the opinion of those foreigners who remember the disadvantages of its isolation from the literature of other lands, and the difficulties of a language which rendered that literature inaccessible.[2]

The fourth section in the Catalogue contains the Rituals and a list of their editions and commentators, but only one of the three is numbered among the *King* and used as a text-book at the public examinations. This is the *Lí Kí*, or 'Book of Rites,' the *Mémorial des Rites*, as M. Callery calls it in his translation,[3] and one of the works which has done so much to mold and maintain Chinese character and institutions. It is not superior in any respect to the *Chau Lí* and the *Í Lí*, but owes its influence to its position. They were all the particular objects of Tsin Chí Hwangtí's ire in his efforts to destroy every ancient literary production in his kingdom; the present texts were recovered from their hiding-places about B.C. 135. The *Chau Lí*, or 'Ritual of Chau,' is regarded as the work of Duke Chau (B.C. 1130), who gives the detail of the various offices established under the new dynasty, in which he bore so prominent a part. The sections containing the divisions of the administrative part of the Chinese government of that day have furnished the types for the six boards of the present day and their subdivisions. So far as we now know, no nation then existing could show so methodical and effective a system of national polity.

---

reproduction (in some degree) of sounds so foreign to the language as Chinese. *Shí King. Das kanonische Liederbuch der Chinesen. Uebersetzt von* Victor von Strauss. Heidelberg, 1880.

[1] *The Chinese Classics*, Vol. IV., pp. 172–180. Hongkong, 1871.

[2] Compare *Confucii Chi-king sive Liber Carminum, ex latina* P. Lacharme *interpretatione edidit* J. Mohl, Stuttgart, 1830; *Essai sur le Chi-king, et sur l'ancienne poésie chinoise, par* M. Brosset jeune, Paris, 1828; *Bibliothèque orientale*, Vol. II., p. 247 (1872). *Chi-king, ou Livre des Vers*, Traduction de M. G. Pauthier; *China Review*, Vol. VI., pp. 1 ff. and 166 ff. *Journal N. C. Br. R. As. Soc.*, Vol. XII., pp. 97 ff.

[3] *Li-ki ou Mémorial des Rites, traduit pour la première fois du chinois, et accompagné de notes, de commentaires et du texte original, par* J. M. Callery. Turin et Paris, 1853.

The *Í Lí* is a smaller work, treating of family affairs, and as its name, 'Decorum Ritual,' indicates, contains directions for domestic life, as the other does for state matters. That is in forty-four sections and this is in seven, and both are now accepted as among the most ancient works extant. The former was translated by Ed. Biot,[1] and remains a monument of his scholarship and research.

The *Lí Kí* owes its position among the classics to the belief that Confucius here gives his views on government and manners, although these chapters are not regarded as the same in their integrity as those said to have been found in the walls of his house, and brought to light in the second century B.C. by Kao Tang of Lu, under the name of *Sz' Lí*, or the 'Scholar's Ritual.' In the next century Tai Teh collected all the existing documents relating to the ancient rituals in two hundred and fourteen sections, only a portion of which were then held to have emanated from the sage and recorded by his pupils. His work, in eighty-five sections, is called *Ta Tai Lí*, or the 'Senior Tai's Ritual,' to distinguish it from the *Siao Tai Lí*, or the 'Junior Tai's Ritual,' a work in forty-nine sections, by his nephew, Tai Shing. This is the work now known as the *Lí Kí*, M. Callery's translation of which contains the authorized text of Kanghí according to Fan Tsz'-tăng, in thirty-six sections, with many notes. His translation is wearisome reading from the multitude of parentheses interjected into the text, distracting the attention and weakening its continuity.

Those who have read Abbé Huc's entertaining remarks on the Rites in China will find in these three works the reason and application of their details. In explanation of their importance, M. Callery shows in a few words what a wide field they cover: "Ceremony epitomizes the entire Chinese mind; and, in my opinion, the *Lí Kí* is *per se* the most exact and complete monograph that China has been able to give of itself to other nations. Its affections, if it has any, are satisfied by cere-

---

[1] *Le Tcheou-Li ou Rites des Tcheou, traduit pour la première fois du chinois, par* Feu Édouard Biot. 2 Tomes. Paris, 1851.

mony; its duties are fulfilled by ceremony; its virtues and vices are referred to ceremony; the natural relations of created beings essentially link themselves in ceremonial—in a word, to that people ceremonial is man as a moral, political, and religious being in his multiplied relations with family, country, society, morality, and religion." This explanation shows, too, how meagre a rendering *ceremony* is for the Chinese idea of *lí*, for it includes not only the external conduct, but involves the right principles from which all true etiquette and politeness spring. The state religion, the government of a family, and the rules of society are all founded on the true *lí*, or relations of things. Reference has already been made to this profoundly esteemed work (p. 520), and one or two more extracts will suffice to exhibit its spirit and style, singular in its object and scope among all the bequests of antiquity.

Affection between father and son.

In the Domestic Rules it is said, "Men in serving their parents, at the first cock-crowing, must all wash their hands; rinse their mouth; comb their hair; bind it together with a net; fasten it with a bodkin, forming it into a tuft; brush off the dust; put on the hat, tying the strings, ornamented with tassels; also the waistcoat, frock, and girdle, with the note-sticks placed in it, and the indispensables attached on the right and left; bind on the greaves; and put on the shoes, tying up the strings. Wives must serve their husband's father and mother as their own; at the first cock-crowing, they must wash their hands; rinse their mouth; comb their hair; bind it together with a net; fasten it with a bodkin, forming it into a tuft; put on their frocks and girdles, with the indispensables attached on the right and left; fasten on their bags of perfumery; put on and tie up their shoes. Then go to the chamber of their father and mother, and father-in-law and mother-in-law, and having entered, in a low and placid tone they must inquire whether their dress is too warm or too cool; if the parents have pain or itching, themselves must respectfully press or rub [the part affected]; and if they enter or leave the room, themselves either going before or following, must respectfully support them. In bringing the apparatus for washing, the younger must present the bowl; the elder the water, begging them to pour it and wash; and after they have washed, hand them the towel. In asking and respectfully presenting what they wish to eat, they must cheer them by their mild manner; and must wait till their father and mother, and father-in-law and mother-in-law have eaten, and then retire. Boys and girls, who have not arrived at the age of manhood and womanhood, at the first cock-crowing must wash their hands; rinse their mouth; comb their hair; bind it together with a net; and form it into a tuft;

brush off the dust; tie on their bags, having them well supplied with perfumery; then hasten at early dawn to see their parents, and inquire if they have eaten and drunk; if they have, they must immediately retire; but if not, they must assist their superiors in seeing that everything is duly made ready."

Of reproving parents.

"When his parents are in error, the son with a humble spirit, pleasing countenance, and gentle tone, must point it out to them. If they do not receive his reproof, he must strive more and more to be dutiful and respectful toward them till they are pleased, and then he must again point out their error. But if he does not succeed in pleasing them, it is better that he should continue to reiterate reproof, than permit them to do injury to the whole department, district, village, or neighborhood. And if the parents, irritated and displeased, chastise their son till the blood flows from him, even then he must not dare to harbor the least resentment; but, on the contrary, should treat them with increased respect and dutifulness."

Respect to be paid parents in one's conduct.

"Although your father and mother are dead, if you propose to yourself any good work, only reflect how it will make their names illustrious, and your purpose will be fixed. So if you propose to do what is not good, only consider how it will disgrace the names of your father and mother, and you will desist from your purpose."[1]

These extracts show something of the molding principles which operate on Chinese youth from earliest years, and the scope given in his education to filial piety. From conning such precepts the lad is imbued with a respect for his parents that finally becomes intensified into a religious sentiment, and forms, as he increases in age, his only creed—the worship of ancestors. His seniors, on the other hand, have but to point to the text-books before him as authority for all things they exact, and as being the only possible source of those virtues that conduct to happiness. The position of females, too, has remained, under these dogmas, much the same for hundreds of years. Nor is it difficult to account for the influence which they have had. Those who were most aware of their excellence, and had had some experience in the tortuous dealings of the human heart, as husbands, fathers, mothers, officers, and seniors, were those who had the power to enforce obedience upon wives, children,

---

[1] *Chinese Repository*, Vol. V., pp. 306–312.

daughters, subjects, and juniors, as well as teach it to them. These must wait till increasing years brought about their turn to fill the upper rank in the social system, by which time habit would lead them to exercise their sway over the rising generation in the same manner. Thus it would be perpetuated, for the man could not depart from the way his childhood was trained; had the results been more disastrous, it would have been easy for us to explain why, amid the ignorance, craft, ambition, and discontent found in a populous, uneducated, pagan country, such formal rules had failed of benefiting society to any lasting extent. We must look higher for this result, and acknowledge the degree of wholesome restraint upon the passions of the Chinese which the Author of whatever is good in these tenets has seen fit to confer upon them in order to the preservation of society.

The fifth section contains the *Chun Tsiu*, or 'Spring and Autumn Record,' and its literature. This is the only one of the *King* attributed to Confucius, though whether we have in the *Record*, as it now exists, a genuine compilation of the sage, does not appear to be beyond doubt. His object being to construct a narrative of events in continuation of the *Shu King*, he, with assistance from his pupils, drew up a history of his own country, extending from the reign of Ping Wang to about the period of his birth (B.C. 722 to 480). Inasmuch as the author of this chronicle confined himself to the relation of such facts as he deemed worthy to be recorded, and was not above altering or concealing such details as in his private judgment appeared unworthy of the princes of his dynasty, this history cannot be regarded as exactly in conformity with modern notions of what is desirable in works of this class. That Confucius wished to leave behind him a lasting monument to his own name, as well as a narration of events, we gather from more than one of his utterances: "The superior man is distressed lest his name should not be honorably mentioned after death. My principles do not make way in the world; how shall I make myself known to future ages?" In order, therefore, to insure the preservation of his *chef d'œuvre* to all time, he combines with the annals certain censures and righteous decisions which should render it at once a history and a text-book of moral lessons; and in giving the book to his disciples, "It is by the *Chun Tsiu*," he said, "that after-ages will know me, and also by it that they will condemn me."

The title, "Spring and Autumn," is understood by many Chinese scholars to be a term for chronological annals; in this case the name being explained "because their commendations are life-giving like spring, and their censures life-withering like autumn," or, as we find in the *Trimetrical Classic*, "which by praise and blame separates the good and bad."[1] A closer inspection of the *Chun Tsiu* is sure to prove disappointing; spite of the glowing accounts of Mencius and its great reputation, this history is simply a bald record of incidents whose entire contents afford barely an hour's reading. "Instead of a history of events," writes Dr. Legge, "woven artistically together, we find a congeries of the briefest possible intimations of matters in which the court and State of Lu were more or less concerned, extending over two hundred and forty-two years, without the slightest tincture of literary ability in the composition, or the slightest indication of judicial opinion on the part of the writer. The paragraphs are always brief. Each one is designed to commemorate a fact; but whether that fact be a display of virtue calculated to command our admiration, or a deed of atrocity fitted to awaken our disgust, it can hardly be said that there is anything in the language to convey to us the shadow of an idea of the author's feelings about it. The notices—for we cannot call them narratives—are absolutely unimpassioned. A base murder and a shining act of heroism are chronicled just as the eclipses of the sun are chronicled. So and so took

[1] This somewhat fanciful explanation of the title is from the Han commentators. Dr. Legge (*Classics*, Vol. V., Prolegomena, p. 7) observes that "not even in the work do we find such 'censures' and 'commendations;' and much less are they trumpeted in the title of it." His interpretation that Spring and Autumn are put by synechdoche for all four seasons, *i.e.*, the entire record of the year, appears to be a more natural account. The same writer declares that "the whole book is a collection of riddles, to which there are as many answers as there are guessers." The interesting chapters of his *prolegomena* to this translation, and his judicious criticisms on these early records, should tempt all sinologues to read them throughout.

place; that is all. No details are given; no judgment is expressed."

So imperturbable a recital could hardly have been saved from extinction even by the great reputation of the sage, had it not been for the amplification of Tso, a younger contemporary or follower of Confucius, who filled up the meagre sentences and added both flesh and life to the skeleton. It is possible that the enthusiastic praises of Mencius are due to the fact that he associated the text and commentary as one work. The Chuen of Tso has indeed always been regarded as foremost among the secondary classics; nor is it too much, considering his terse yet vivid and pictorial style, to call its author, as does Dr. Legge, "the Froissart of China."[1] In addition to his purpose of explaining the text of the *Chun Tsiu*, Tso's secondary object was to give a general view of the history of China during the period embraced by that record; unless he had put his living tableaux into the framework of his master, there is grave reason to fear that many most important details relating to the sixth and seventh centuries B.C. would have been forever lost. Two other early commentaries, those of Kung Yang and Kuh Liang, dating from about the second century B.C., occupy a high position in the estimation of Chinese scholars as illustrative of the original chronicle. They do not compare with the *Tso Chuen* either in interest or in authority, though it may be said that a study of the *Chun Tsiu* can hardly be made unless attended with a careful perusal of their contents. It will not be without interest to give an example of the *Record*, followed with elucidations of the text by these three annotators. The second year of Duke Hí of Lu (B.C. 657) runs as follows:

1. In the [duke's] second year, in spring, in the king's first month, we [aided in the] walling of Tsu-kin.
2. In summer, in the fifth month, on Sin-sz', we buried our duchess, Gai Kiang.
3. An army of Yu and an army of Tsin extinguished Hia-yang.

---

[1] The same writer adds, in summing up the merits of the *Tso Chuen*: "It is, in my opinion, the most precious literary treasure which has come down to posterity from the Chow dynasty."—*Classics*, Vol. V., Proleg., p. 35.

4. In autumn, in the ninth month, the Marquis of Tsz', the Duke of Sung an officer of Kiang, and an officer of Hwang, made a covenant in Kwan.
5. In winter, in the tenth month, there was no rain.
6. A body of men from Tsu made an incursion into Ching.

Upon the third entry for this year the *Tso Chuen* enlarges:

Seun Seih, of Tsin, requested leave from the marquis to take his team of Kiuh horses and his *peih* of Chui-keih jade, and with them borrow a way from Yu to march through it and attack Kwoh. "They are the things I hold most precious," said the marquis. Seih replied, "But if you get a way through Yu, it is but like placing them in a treasury outside the State for a time." "There is Kung Che-kí in Yu," objected the duke. "Kung Che-kí," returned the other, "is a weak man, and incapable of remonstrating vigorously. And, moreover, from his youth up he has always been with the Duke of Yu, who is so familiar with him that though he should remonstrate the duke will not listen to him." The marquis accordingly sent Seun Seih to borrow a way through Yu with this message: "Formerly Kí, against right and reason, entered your State from Tien-ling, and attacked the three gates of Ming. It suffered for so doing, all through your grace. Now Kwoh, against right and reason, has been keeping guards about the travellers' lodges, to make incursions from them into my southern borders, and I venture to beg a right of way from you to ask an account of its offence." The Duke of Yu granted the request, and even asked to take the lead in invading Kwoh. Kung Che-kí remonstrated with him, but in vain; and he raised his army for the enterprise. In summer, Lí Kih and Seun Seih brought on the army of Tsin, made a junction with that of Yu, and invaded Kwoh, when they extinguished Hia-yang. The army of Yu is mentioned first, because of the bribes which the duke accepted.

The commentary of Kung Yang says on the same paragraph:

Yu was a small State; why is it that it is here made to take precedence of a great one? To make Yu take the lead in the wickedness.

Why is Yu made to take the lead in the wickedness? Yu received the bribes with which those [who were going to] extinguish the State [of Kwoh] borrowed a way through it, and thus brought on its own ruin.

How did it receive [those] bribes? Duke Hien [of Tsin] gave audience to his great officers, and asked them why it was that he had lain all night without sleeping. One of them advanced and said, "Was it because you did not feel at ease [in your mind]? or was it because your [proper] bedfellow was not by your side?" The duke gave no answer, and then Seun Seih came forward and said, "Was it because Yu and Kwoh were appearing to you?" The duke motioned to him to come [more] forward, and then went with him into an inner apartment to take counsel. "I wish," said he, "to attack Kwoh, but Yu will go to its relief, and if I attack Yu Kwoh will succor it; what is to be done? I wish to consider the case with you." Seun Seih replied, "If you will use my counsel, you shall take Kwoh to-day and Yu to-morrow; why should your lordship be troubled?" "How is this to be accomplished?" asked the duke. "Please let [me go to] Yu," said the other, "with your team of Kiuh horses and your white *peih* of Chui-keih, and you are sure to get [what you want]. It will only be taking your valuable [*peih*] from your inner treasury and depositing it in an outer one; your lordship will lose nothing by it." The duke said, "Yes; but Kung Che-kí is there. What are we to do with him?" Seun Seih replied, "Kung Che-kí is indeed knowing; but the Duke of Yu is covetous, and fond of valuable curios; he is sure not to follow his minister's advice. I beg you, considering everything, to let me go." . . . etc., etc.

The following, as a brief sample of the Kuh Liang commentary, takes up the narrative where we have broken off. There is so much that is similar in these two latter exegeses as to lead to the belief that they were composed with reference to each other.

On this Duke Hien sought [in the way proposed] for a passage [through Yu] to invade Kwoh. Kung Che-kí remonstrated, saying, "The words of the envoy of Tsin are humble, but his offerings are great; the matter is sure not to be advantageous to Yu." The Duke of Yu, however, would not listen to him, but received the offerings and granted the passage through the State. Kung Che-kí remonstrated [again], suggesting that the case was like that in the saying about the lips being gone and the teeth becoming cold; after which he fled with his wife and children to Tsao.

Duke Hien then destroyed Kwoh, and in the fifth year [of our Duke Hí] he dealt in the same way with Yu. Seun Seih then had the horses led forward, while he carried the *peih* in his hand, and said: "The *peih* is just as it was, but the horses' teeth are grown longer!"[1]

Meagre as are the items of the text, they show, together with its copious commentaries, the methodical care of the early Chinese in preserving their ancient records. The hints which these and other books give of their intellectual activity during the eight centuries before Christ, naturally compel a higher estimate of their culture than we have hitherto allowed them.[2]

The sixth section of the Catalogue has already been noticed as comprising the literature of the *Hiao King*.

---

[1] To this the Kung Yang commentator adds: "This he said in joke."

[2] Compare *Tchun Tsieou, Le Printemps & l'Automne, ou Annales de la Principauté de Lou, depuis* 722 *jusqu' en* 481, etc. *Traduites en françois, par* Le Roux Deshauterayes. 1750. Dr. E. Bretschneider, in the *Chinese Recorder*, Vol. IV., pp. 51–52, 1871.

The seventh section contains a list of works written to elucidate the Five Classics as a whole, and if their character for originality of thought, variety of research, extent of illustration, and explanation of obscurities was comparable to their size and numbers, no books in any language could boast of the aids possessed by the *Wu King* for their right comprehension. Of these commentators, Chu Hí of Kiangsí, who lived during the Sung dynasty, has so greatly exceeded all others in illustrating and expounding them, that his explanations are now considered of almost equal authority with the text, and are always given to the beginner to assist him in ascertaining its true meaning.

The eighth section of the Catalogue comprises memoirs and comments upon the *Sz' Shu*, or 'Four Books,' which have been nearly as influential in forming Chinese mind as the *Wu King*. They are by different authors, and since their publication have perhaps undergone a few alterations and interpolations, but the changes either in these or the Five Classics cannot be very numerous or great, since the large body of disciples who followed Confucius, and had copies of his writings, would carefully preserve uncorrupt those which he edited, and hand down unimpaired those which contained his sayings. None of the Four Books were actually written by Confucius himself, but three of them are considered to be a digest of his sentiments; they were arranged in their present form by the brothers Ching, who flourished about eight centuries ago.

The first of the Four Books is the *Ta Hioh*, *i.e.*, 'Superior' or 'Great Learning,' which originally formed one chapter of the *Book of Rites*. It is now divided into eleven chapters, only the first of which is ascribed to the sage, the remainder forming the comment upon them; the whole does not contain two thousand words. The argument of the *Ta Hioh* is briefly summed up in four heads, "the improvement of one's self, the regulation of a family, the government of a state, and the rule of an empire." In the first chapter this idea is thus developed in a circle peculiarly Chinese:

The ancients, who wished to illustrate renovating virtue throughout the Empire, first ordered well their own states. Wishing to order well their states, they first regulated their families. Wishing to regulate their families, they first cultivated their persons. Wishing to cultivate their persons, they first rectified their hearts. Wishing to rectify their hearts, they first sought to be sincere in their thoughts. Wishing to be sincere in their thoughts, they first extended their knowledge to the utmost. Such extension of knowledge lay in the investigation of things. Things being investigated, knowledge became complete: knowledge being complete, their thoughts were sincere: their thoughts being sincere, their hearts were then rectified: their hearts being rectified, their persons were cultivated: their persons being cultivated, their families were regulated: families being regulated, states were rightly governed; and states being rightly governed, the Empire was made tranquil.

From the Son of Heaven to the man of the people, all must consider the cultivation of the person to be the foundation.

The subsequent chapters mainly consist of the terse sayings of ancient kings and authors gathered and arranged by Tsăng and afterward by Chu Hí, designed to illustrate and enforce the teachings of Confucius contained in the first. One quotation only can be given from Chapter X.

In the Declaration of [the Duke of] Tsin, it is said: "Let me have but one minister plain and sincere, not pretending to other abilities, but with a simple upright mind; and possessed of generosity, regarding the talents of others as though he possessed them himself, and where he finds accomplished and perspicacious men, loving them in his heart more than his mouth expresses, and really showing himself able to avail himself of them; such a minister will be able to preserve my descendants and the Black-haired people, and benefits to the kingdom might well be looked for. But if it be, when he finds men of ability, he is jealous and hateful to them; and when he meets accomplished and perspicacious men, he opposes them and will not allow their advancement, showing that he is really not able to avail himself of them; such a minister will not be able to protect my descendants and the Black-haired people. May he not even be pronounced dangerous?"

It will be willingly allowed, when reading these extracts, that, destitute as they were of the high sanctions and animating hopes and promises of the Word of God, these Chinese moralists began at the right place in their endeavors to reform and benefit their countrymen, and that they did not fully succeed was owing to causes beyond their reforming power.

The second of the Four Books is called *Chung Yung*, or the 'Just Medium,' and is, in some respects, the most elaborate treatise in the series. It was composed by Kung Kih, the grandson of Confucius (better known by his style Tsz'-sz'), about ninety years after the sage's death. It once also formed part of the *Lí Kí*, from which it, as well as the *Ta Hioh*, were taken out by Chu Hí to make two of the *Sz' Shu*. It has thirty-three chapters, and has been the subject of numerous comments. The great purpose of the author is to illustrate the nature of human virtue, and to exhibit its conduct in the actions of an ideal *kiun tsz'*, or 'princely man' of immaculate propriety, who always demeans himself correctly, without going to extremes. He carries out the advice of Hesiod:

> "Let every action prove a mean confess'd;
> A moderation is, in all, the best."

True virtue consists in never going to extremes, though it does not appear that by this the sage meant to repress active benevolence on the one hand, or encourage selfish stolidity on the other. *Ching*, or uprightness, is said to be the basis of all things; and *ho*, harmony, the all-pervading principle of the universe; "extend uprightness and harmony to the utmost, and heaven and earth will be at rest, and all things be produced and nourished according to their nature." The general character of the work is monotonous, but relieved with some animated passages, among which the description of the *kiun tsz'*, or princely man, is one. "The princely man, in dealing with others, does not descend to anything low or improper. How unbending his valor! He stands in the middle, and leans not to either side. The princely man enters into no situation where he is not himself. If he holds a high situation, he does not treat with contempt those below him; if he occupies an inferior station, he uses no mean arts to gain the favor of his superiors. He corrects himself and blames not others; he feels no dissatisfaction. On the one hand, he murmurs not at Heaven; nor, on the other, does he feel resentment toward man. Hence, the superior man dwells at ease, entirely waiting the will of Heaven."[1]

Chinese moralists divide mankind into three classes, on these principles: "Men of the highest order, as sages, worthies, philanthropists, and heroes, are good without instruction; men of

[1] Collie's *Four Books*, pp. 6–10.

the middling classes are so after instruction, such as husbandmen, physicians, astrologers, soldiers, etc., while those of the lowest are bad in spite of instruction, as play-actors, pettifoggers, slaves, swindlers, etc." The first are *shing*, or sages; the second are *hien*, or worthies; the last are *yu*, or worthless. Sir John Davis notices the similarity of this triplicate classification with that of Hesiod. The *Just Medium* thus describes the first character:

> It is only the sage who is possessed of that clear discrimination and profound intelligence which fit him for filling a high station; who possesses that enlarged liberality and mild benignity which fit him for bearing with others; who manifests that firmness and magnanimity that enable him to hold fast good principles; who is actuated by that benevolence, justice, propriety, and knowledge which command reverence; and who is so deeply learned in polite learning and good principles as to qualify him rightly to discriminate. Vast and extensive are the effects of his virtue; it is like the deep and living stream which flows unceasingly; it is substantial and extensive as Heaven, and profound as the great abyss. Wherever ships sail or chariots run; wherever the heavens overshadow and the earth sustains; wherever the sun and moon shine, or frosts and dews fall, among all who have blood and breath, there is not one who does not honor and love him.[1]

Sincerity or conscientiousness holds a high place among the attributes of the superior or princely man; but in translating the Chinese terms into English, it is sometimes puzzling enough to find those which will exhibit the exact idea of the original. For instance, sincerity is described as "the origin or consummation of all things; without it, there would be nothing. It is benevolence by which a man's self is perfected, and knowledge by which he perfects others." In another place we read that "one sincere wish would move heaven and earth." The *kiun tsz'* is supposed to possess these qualities. The standard of excellence is placed so high as to be absolutely unattainable by unaided human nature; and though Kih probably intended to elevate the character of his grandfather to this height, and thus hand him down to future ages as a *shing jin*, or 'perfect and holy man,' he has, in the providence of God, done his countrymen great service in setting before them such a character as is

[1] *Ib.*, p. 28.

here given in the *Chung Yung*. By being made a text-book in the schools it has been constantly studied and memorized by generations of students, to their great benefit.

The third of the Four Books, called the *Lun Yu*, or 'Analects of Confucius,' is divided into twenty chapters, in which the collective body of his disciples recorded his words and actions, much in the same way that Boswell did those of Johnson. It has not, however, the merit of chronological arrangement, and parts of it are so sententious as to be obscure, if not almost unintelligible. This work discloses the sage's shrewd insight into the character of his countrymen, and knowledge of the manner in which they could best be approached and influenced. Upon the commencement of his career as reformer and teacher, he contented himself with reviving the doctrines of the "Ancients;" but finding his influence increasing as he continued these instructions, he then—yet always as under their authority—engrafted original ideas and tenets upon the minds of his generation. Had even his loftiest sentiments been propounded as his own, they would hardly have been received in his day, and, perhaps, through the contempt felt for him by his contemporaries, have been lost entirely.

Among the most remarkable passages of the Four Books are the following: Replying to the question of Tsz'-kung, "Is there one word which may serve as a rule of practice for all of one's life?" Confucius said: "Is not *shu* ('reciprocity') such a word? What you do not want done to yourself, do not do to others." In a previous place Tsz'-kung had said: "What I do not wish men to do to me, I also wish not to do to men." Confucius replied: "Tsz', you have not attained to that." The same principle is repeated in the *Chung Yung*, where it is said that the man who does so is not far from the path. Another is quoted in the Imperial Dictionary, under the word *Fuh:* "The people of the west have sages," or "There is a sage (or holy man) among the people of the west," where the object is to show that he did not mean Buddha. As Confucius was contemporary with Ezra, it is not impossible that he had heard something of the history of the Israelites scattered throughout the one hundred and twenty-seven provinces of the Persian monarchy, or of the writings of their prophets, though there is not the least historical evidence that he knew anything of the countries in Western Asia, or of the books extant in their languages.

Some idea of the character of the *Lun Yu* may be gathered from a few detached sentences, selected from Marshman's translation.[1]

Grieve not that men know you not, but be grieved that you are ignorant of men.

Governing with equity resembles the north star, which is fixed, and all the stars surround it.

Have no friends unlike yourself.

Learning without reflection will profit nothing; reflection without learning will leave the mind uneasy and miserable.

Knowledge produces pleasure clear as water; complete virtue brings happiness solid as a mountain; knowledge pervades all things; virtue is tranquil and happy; knowledge is delight; virtue is long life.

Without virtue, both riches and honor seem to me like the passing cloud.

The sage's conduct is affection and benevolence in operation.

The man who possesses complete virtue wishes to fix his own mind therein, and also to fix the minds of others; he wishes to be wise himself, and would fain render others equally wise.

Those who, searching for virtue, refuse to stay among the virtuous, how can they obtain knowledge?

The rich and honorable are those with whom men desire to associate; not obtaining their company in the paths of virtue, however, do not remain in it.

In your appearance, to fall below decency would be to resemble a savage rustic, to exceed it would be to resemble a fop; let your appearance be decent and moderate, then you will resemble the honorable man.

When I first began with men, I heard words and gave credit for conduct; now I hear words and observe conduct.

I have found no man who esteems virtue as men esteem pleasure.

The perfect man loves all men; he is not governed by private affection or interest, but only regards the public good or right reason. The wicked man, on the contrary, loves if you give, and likes if you commend him.

The perfect man is never satisfied with himself. He that is satisfied with himself is not perfect.

He that is sedulous and desires to improve in his studies is not ashamed to stoop to ask of others.

Sin in a virtuous man is like an eclipse of the sun and moon; all men gaze at it, and it passes away; the virtuous man mends, and the world stands in admiration of his fall.

Patience is the most necessary thing to have in this world.

---

[1] *The Works of Confucius; containing the original text, with a Translation*, by J. Marshman. Vol. I. Serampore, 1807.

A few facts respecting the life, and observations on the character, of the great sage of Chinese letters, may here be added, though the extracts already made from his writings are sufficient to show his style. Confucius was born B.C. 551, in the twentieth year of the Emperor Ling (about the date at which Cyrus became king of Persia), in the kingdom of Lu, now included in Yenchau, in the south of Shantung. His father was a district magistrate, and dying when he was only three years old, left his care and education to his mother, who, although not so celebrated as the mother of Mencius, seems to have nurtured in him a respect for morality, and directed his studies. During his youth he was remarkable for a grave demeanor and knowledge of ancient learning, which gained him the respect and admiration of his townsmen, so that at the age of twenty, the year after his marriage, he was entrusted with the duties of a subordinate office in the revenue department, and afterward appointed a supervisor of fields and herds. In his twenty-fourth year his mother deceased, and in conformity with the ancient usage, which had then fallen into disuse, he immediately resigned all his employments to mourn for her three years, during which time he devoted himself to study. This practice has continued to the present day.

His examination of the ancient writings led him to resolve upon instructing his countrymen in them, and to revive the usages of former kings, especially in whatever related to the rites. His position gave him an entry to court in Lu, where he met educated and influential men, and by the time he was thirty he was already in repute among them as a teacher. His own king, Siang, gave him the means of visiting the imperial court at Lohyang. Here, together with his disciples, he examined everything, past and present, with close scrutiny, and returned home with renewed regard for the ancient founders of the House of Chau. His scholars and admirers increased in numbers, and a corresponding extension of fame followed, so that ere long he had an invitation to the court of the prince of Tsí, but on arrival there was mortified to learn that curiosity had been the prevailing cause of the invitation, and not a desire to adopt his principles. He accordingly left him and went home, where the struggles between three rival families carried disorder and misery throughout the kingdom; it was with the greatest difficulty that he remained neutral between these factions. His disciples were from all parts of the land, and public opinion began to be influenced by his example. At length an opportunity offered to put his tenets into practice. The civil strife had resulted in the flight of the rebels, and Lu was settling down into better government, when in B.C. 500 Confucius was made the magistrate of the town of Chung-tu by his sovereign, Duke Ting. He was now fifty years old, and began to carry out the best rule he could in his position as minister of crime. For three years he administered the affairs of State with such a mixture of zeal, prudence, severity, and regard for the rights and wants of all classes, that Lu soon became the envy and dread of all other States. He even succeeded in destroying two or three baronial castles whose chiefs had set all lawful authority at defiance. His precepts had been fairly put in practice, and, like Solomon, his influence in after-ages was increased by the fact of acknowledged success.

It was but little more than an experiment, however; for Duke King of Tsí, becoming envious of the growing power of his neighbor, sent Ting a tempting present, consisting of thirty horses beautifully caparisoned, and a number of curious rarities, with a score of the most accomplished courtesans he could procure in his territories. This scheme of gaining the favor of the youthful monarch, and driving the obnoxious cynic from his councils, succeeded, and Confucius soon after retired by compulsion into private life. He moved into the dominions of the prince of Wei, accompanied by such of his disciples as chose to follow him, where he employed himself in extending his doctrines and travelling into the adjoining States.

He was at times applauded and patronized, but quite as often the object of persecution and contumely; more than once his life was endangered. He compared himself to a dog driven from his home: "I have the fidelity of that animal, and I am treated like it. But what matters the ingratitude of men? They cannot hinder me from doing all the good that has been appointed me. If my precepts are disregarded, I have the consolation of knowing in my own breast that I have faithfully performed my duty." He sometimes spoke in a manner that showed his own impression to be that heaven had conferred on him a special commission to instruct the world. On one or two occasions, when he was in jeopardy, he said: "If Heaven means not to obliterate this doctrine from the earth, the men of Kwang can do nothing to me." And "as Heaven has produced whatever virtue is in me, what can Hwan Tui do to me?"

In his instructions he improved passing events to afford useful lessons, and some of those recorded are at least ingenious. Observing a fowler one day sorting his birds into different cages, he said, "I do not see any old birds here; where have you put them?" "The old birds," replied the fowler, "are too wary to be caught; they are on the lookout, and if they see a net or cage, far from falling into the snare they escape and never return. Those young ones which are in company with them likewise escape, but only such as separate into a flock by themselves and rashly approach are the birds I take. If perchance I catch an old bird it is because he follows the young ones." "You have heard him," observed the sage, turning to his disciples; "the words of this fowler afford us matter for instruction. The young birds escape the snare only when they keep with the old ones, the old ones are taken when they follow the young; it is thus with mankind. Presumption, hardihood, want of forethought, and inattention are the principal reasons why young people are led astray. Inflated with their small attainments they have scarcely made a commencement in learning before they think they know everything; they have scarcely performed a few common virtuous acts, and straight they fancy themselves at the height of wisdom. Under this false impression they doubt nothing, hesitate at nothing, pay attention to nothing; they rashly undertake acts without consulting the aged and experienced, and thus securely following their own notions, they are misled and fall into the first snare laid for them. If you see an old man of sober years so badly advised as to be taken with the sprightliness of a youth, attached to him, and thinking and acting with him, he is led astray by him and soon taken in the same snare. Do not forget the answer of the fowler."

Once, when looking at a stream, he compared its ceaseless current to the transmission of good doctrine through succeeding generations, and as one race had received it they should hand it down to others. "Do not imitate those isolated men [the Rationalists] who are wise only for themselves; to communicate the modicum of knowledge and virtue we possess to others will never impoverish ourselves." He seems to have entertained only faint hopes of the general reception of his doctrine, though toward the latter end of his life he had as much encouragement in the respect paid him personally and the increase of his scholars as he could reasonably have wished.

Confucius returned to his native country at the age of sixty-eight, and devoted his time to completing his edition of the classics and in teaching his now large band of disciples. He was consulted by his sovereign, who had invited him to return, and one of his last acts was to go to court to urge an attack on Tsí and punish the murder of its duke. Many legends have gathered around him, so that he now stands before his countrymen as a sage and a demigod; yet there is a remarkable absence of the prophetic and the miraculous in every event connected with these later writings. One story is that when he had finished his writings he collected his friends around him and made a solemn dedication of his literary labors to heaven as the concluding act of his life. "He assembled all his disciples and led them out of the town to one of the hills where sacrifices had usually been offered for many years. Here he erected a table or altar, upon which he placed the books; and then turning his face to the north, adored Heaven, and returned thanks upon his knees in a humble manner for having had life and strength granted him to enable him to accomplish this laborious undertaking; he implored Heaven to grant that the benefit to his countrymen from so arduous a labor might not be small. He had prepared himself for this ceremony by privacy, fasting, and prayer. Chinese pictures represent the sage in the attitude of supplication, and a beam of light or a rainbow descending from the sky upon the books, while his scholars stand around in admiring wonder."[1]

A few days before his death he tottered about the house, sighing,

Tai shan, kí tui hu!—Liang muh, kí hwai hu!—Chí jin, kí wei hu!

The great mountain is broken!
The strong beam is thrown down!
The wise man withers like a plant!

He died soon after, B.C. 478, aged seventy-three, leaving a single descendant, his grandson Tsz'-sz, through whom the succession has been transmitted to the present day. During his life the return of the Jews from Babylon, the invasion of Greece by Xerxes, and conquest of Egypt by the Persians took place. Posthumous honors in great variety, amounting to idolatrous worship, have been conferred upon him. His title is the 'Most Holy Ancient Teacher' Kung tsz', and the 'Holy Duke.' In the reign of Kanghí, two thousand one hundred and fifty years after his death, there were eleven thousand males alive bearing his name, and most of them of the seventy-fourth generation, being undoubtedly one of the oldest families in the world. In the *Sacrificial Ritual* a short account of his life is given, which closes with the following pæan:

Confucius! Confucius! How great is Confucius!
Before Confucius there never was a Confucius!
Since Confucius there never has been a Confucius!
Confucius! Confucius! How great is Confucius!

The leading features of the philosophy of Confucius are subordination to superiors and kind, upright dealing with our fellow-men; destitute of all reference to an unseen Power to whom all men are accountable, they look only to this world for their sanctions, and make the monarch himself only partially amenable to a higher tribunal. It would indeed be hard to overestimate the influence of Confucius in his ideal *princely scholar*, and the power for good over his race this conception ever since has exerted. It might be compared to the glorious work of the

[1] *Chinese Repository*, Vol. XI., p. 421. Pauthier, *La Chine*, Paris, 1839, pp. 121–184.

sculptor on the Acropolis of Athens—that matchless statue more than seventy feet in height, whose casque and spear of burnished brass glittered above all the temples and high places of the city, and engaged the constant gaze of the mariner on the near Ægean; guiding his onward course, it was still ever beyond his reach. Like the Athena Promachos to the ancient Attic voyager, so stands the *kiun-tsz'* of Confucius among the ideal men of pagan moralists. The immeasurable influence in after-ages of the character thus portrayed proves how lofty was his own standard, and the national conscience has ever since assented to the justice of the portrait.

From the duty, honor, and obedience owed by a child to his parents, he proceeds to inculcate the obligations of wives to their husbands, subjects to their prince, and ministers to their king, together with all the obligations arising from the various social relations. Political morality must be founded on private rectitude, and the beginning of all real advance was, in his opinion, comprised in *nosce teipsum*. It cannot be denied that among much that is commendable there are a few exceptionable dogmas among his tenets, and Dr. Legge, as has already been seen, reflects severely on his disregard of truth in the *Chun Tsiu* and in his lifetime. Yet compared with the precepts of Grecian and Roman sages, the general tendency of his writings is good, while in adaptation to the society in which he lived, and their eminently practical character, they exceed those of western philosophers. He did not deal much in sublime and unattainable descriptions of virtue, but rather taught how the common intercourse of life was to be maintained—how children should conduct themselves toward their parents, when a man should enter on office, when to marry, etc., etc., which, although they may seem somewhat trifling to us, were probably well calculated for the times and people among whom he lived.[1]

---

[1] Compare Dr. Legge's *Religions of China;* Prof. R. K. Douglas, *Confucianism and Taouism*, London, 1879; S. Johnson, *Oriental Religions: China*, Boston, 1877; *A Systematical Digest of the Doctrines of Confucius, according to the Analects, Great Learning, and Doctrine of the Mean*, etc., by Ernst Faber. Translated from the German by Möllendorff, Hongkong, 1875; *Histoire de Confucius*, par J. Sénamaud, Bordeaux et Paris, 1878.

Had Confucius transmitted to posterity such works as the Iliad, the De Officiis, or the Dialogues of Plato, he would no doubt have taken a higher rank among the commanding intellects of the world, but it may be well doubted whether his influence among his own countrymen would have been as good or as lasting. The variety and minuteness of his instructions for the nurture and education of children, the stress he lays upon filial duty, the detail of etiquette and conduct he gives for the intercourse of all classes and ranks in society, characterize his writings from those of all philosophers in other countries, who, comparatively speaking, gave small thought to the education of the young. The Four Books and the Five Classics would not, so far as regards their intrinsic character in comparison with other productions, be considered as anything more than curiosities in literature for their antiquity and language, were it not for the incomparable influence they have exerted over so many millions of minds; in this view they are invested with an interest which no book, besides the Bible, can claim. The source and explanation of this influence is to be found in their use as text-books in the schools and competitive examinations, and well would it be for Christian lands if their youth had the same knowledge of the writings of Solomon and the Evangelists. Their freedom from descriptions of impurity and licentiousness, and allusions to whatever debases and vitiates the heart, is a redeeming quality of the Chinese classics which should not be overlooked. Chinese literature contains enough, indeed, to pollute even the mind of a heathen, but its scum has become the sediment; and little or nothing can be found in the writings that are most highly prized which will not bear perusal by any person in any country. Every one acquainted with the writings of Hindu, Greek, and Roman poets knows the glowing descriptions of the amours of gods and goddesses which fill their pages, and the purity of the Chinese canonical books in this respect must be considered as remarkable.

For the most part the Chinese, in worshipping Confucius, content themselves with erecting a simple tablet in his honor; to carve images for the cult of the sage is uncommon. The incident represented in the adjoining wood-cut illustrates, however,

Worship of Confucius and his Disciples.

an exception to the prevailing severity of this worship. A certain Wei Kí, a scholar living in the Tang dynasty (A.D. 657), not content, it is said, with giving instruction in the classics, set up the life-size statues of Confucius and his seventy-two disciples in order to incite the enthusiasm of his own pupils. Into this sanctuary of the divinities of learning were wont to come the *savant* Wei and his scholars—among whom were numbered both his grandfather and several of his grandchildren—to prostrate themselves before the ancient worthies. "But of his descendants," concludes the chronicler, "there were many who arose to positions of eminence in the State."

The last of the Four Books is nearly as large as the other three united, and consists entirely of the writings of Mencius, Măng tsz', or Măng fu-tsz', as he is called by the Chinese.[1] This sage flourished upward of a century after the death of his master, and although, in estimating his character, it must not be forgotten that he had the advantages of his example and stimulus of his fame and teachings, in most respects he displayed an originality of thought, inflexibility of purpose, and extensive views superior to Confucius, and must be regarded as one of the greatest men Asiatic nations have ever produced.

Mencius was born B.C. 371,[2] in the city of Tsau, now in the province of Shantung, not far from his master's native district. He was twenty-three years old when Plato died, and many other great men of Greece were his contemporaries. His father died early, and left the guardianship of the boy to his widow, Changshí. "The care of this prudent and attentive mother," to quote from Rémusat, "has been cited as a model for all virtuous parents. The house she occupied was near that

---

[1] It may here be remarked that the terms *tsz'* or *fu-tsz'* do not properly form a part of the name, but are titles, meaning *rabbi* or *eminent teacher*, and are added to the surnames of some of the most distinguished writers, by way of peculiar distinction; and in the words Mencius and Confucius have been Latinized with Măng and Kung, names of the persons themselves, into one word. The names of other distinguished scholars, as Chu fu-tsz', Ching fu-tsz', etc., have not undergone this change into Chufucius, Chingfucius; but usage has now brought the compellation for these two men into universal use as a distinctive title, somewhat like the term *venerable* applied to Bede.

[2] Rémusat, *Nouveaux Mélanges*, Tome II., pp. 115–129.

of a butcher; she observed that at the first cry of the animals that were being slaughtered the little Măng ran to be present at the sight, and that on his return he sought to imitate what he had seen. Fearful that his heart might become hardened, and be accustomed to the sight of blood, she removed to another house which was in the neighborhood of a cemetery. The relations of those who were buried there came often to weep upon their graves and make the customary libations; the lad soon took pleasure in their ceremonies, and amused himself in imitating them. This was a new subject of uneasiness to Changshí; she feared her son might come to consider as a jest what is of all things the most serious, and that he would acquire a habit of performing with levity, and as a matter of routine merely, ceremonies which demand the most exact attention and respect. Again, therefore, she anxiously changed her dwelling, and went to live in the city, opposite to a school, where her son found examples the most worthy of imitation, and soon began to profit by them. I should not have spoken of this trifling anecdote but for the allusion which the Chinese constantly make to it in the common proverb, 'Formerly the mother of Mencius chose out a neighborhood.'" On another occasion her son, seeing persons slaughtering pigs, asked her why they did it. "To feed you," she replied; but reflecting that this was teaching her son to lightly regard the truth, went and bought some pork and gave him.

Mencius devoted himself early to the classics, and probably attended the instructions of noted teachers of the school of Confucius and his grandson Kih. After his studies were completed, at the age of forty, he came forth as a public teacher, and offered his services to the feudal princes of the country. Among others, he was received by Hwui, king of Wei, but, though mnch respected by this ruler, his instructions were not regarded; and he soon perceived that among the numerous petty rulers and intriguing statesmen of the day there was no prospect of restoring tranquillity to the Empire, and that discourses upon the mild government and peaceful virtues of Yao and Shun, King Wăn and Chingtang, offered little to interest persons whose minds were engrossed with schemes of conquest or pleasure. He thereupon accepted an invitation to go to Tsí, the adjoining State, and spent most of his public life there; the records show that he was often called on for his advice by statesmen of many governments. As he went from one State to another his influence extended as his experience showed him the difficulties of good government amidst the general disregard of justice, mercy, and frugality. His own unyielding character and stern regard for etiquette and probity chilled the loose, unscrupulous men of those lawless times. At length he retired to his home to spend the last twenty years of his life in the society of his disciples, there completing the work which bears his name and has made him such a power among his countrymen. He has always been an incentive and guide to popular efforts to assert the rights of the subject against the injustice of rulers, and an encourager to rulers who have governed with justice. His assertion of the proper duties and prerogatives belonging to both parties in the State was prior to that of any western writer; some of his principles of liberal government were taught before their enunciation in Holy Writ. He died when eighty-four years old (B.C. 288), shortly before the death of Ptolemy Soter at the same age.

After his demise Mencius was honored, by public act, with the title of 'Holy Prince of the country of Tsau,' and in the temple of the sages he receives the same honors as Confucius; his descendants bear the title of 'Masters of the Traditions concerning the Classics,' and he himself is called *A-shing*, or the 'Secondary Sage,' Confucius being regarded as the first. His writings are in the form of dialogues held with the great personages of his time, and abound with irony and ridicule directed against vice and oppression, which only make his praises of virtue and integrity more weighty. After the manner of Socrates, he contests nothing with his adversaries, but, while granting their premises, he seeks to draw from them consequences the most absurd, which cover his opponents with confusion.

The king of Wei, one of the turbulent princes of the time, was complaining to Mencius how ill he succeeded in his endeavors to make his people happy and his kingdom flourishing.

"Prince," said the philosopher, "you love war; permit me to draw a comparison from thence: two armies are in presence; the charge is sounded, the battle begins, one of the parties is conquered; half its soldiers have fled a hundred paces, the other half has stopped at fifty. Will the last have any right to mock at those who have fled further than themselves?"

"No," said the king; "they have equally taken flight, and the same disgrace must attend them both."

"Prince," says Mencius quickly, "cease then to boast of your efforts as greater than your neighbors'. You have all deserved the same reproach, and not one has a right to take credit to himself over another." Pursuing then his bitter interrogations, he asked, "Is there a difference, O king! between killing a man with a club or with a sword?" "No," said the prince. "Between him who kills with the sword, or destroys by an inhuman tyranny?" "No," again replied the prince.

"Well," said Mencius, "your kitchens are encumbered with food, your sheds are full of horses, while your subjects, with emaciated countenances, are worn down with misery, or found dead of hunger in the middle of the fields or the deserts. What is this but to breed animals to prey on men? And what is the difference between destroying them by the sword or by unfeeling conduct? If we detest those savage animals which mutually tear and devour each other, how much more should we abhor a prince who, instead of being a father to his people, does not hesitate to rear animals to destroy them. What kind of father to his people is he who treats his children so unfeelingly, and has less care of them than of the wild beasts he provides for?"

On one occasion, addressing the prince of Tsí, Mencius remarked: "It is not the ancient forests of a country which do it honor, but its families devoted for many generations to the duties of the magistracy. Oh, king! in all your service there are none such; those whom you yesterday raised to honor, what are they to-day?"

"In what way," replied the king, "can I know beforehand that they are without virtue, and remove them?"

"In raising a sage to the highest dignities of the State," replied the philosopher, "a king acts only as he is of necessity bound to do. But to put a man of obscure condition over the nobles of his kingdom, or one of his remote kindred over princes more nearly connected with him, demands most careful deliberation. Do his courtiers unite in speaking of a man as wise, let him distrust them. If all the magistrates of his kingdom concur in the same assurance, let him not rest satisfied with their testimony, but if his subjects confirm the story, then let him convince himself; and if he finds that the individual is indeed a sage, let him raise him to office and honor. So, also, if all his courtiers would oppose his placing confidence in a minister, let him not give heed to them; and if all the magistrates are of this opinion, let him be deaf to their solicitations; but if the people unite in the same request, then let him examine the object of their ill-will, and, if guilty, remove him. In short, if all the courtiers think that a minister should suffer death, the prince must not content himself with their opinion merely. If all the high officers entertain the same sentiment, still he must not yield to their convictions; but if the people declare that such a man is unfit to live, then the prince, inquiring himself and being satisfied that the charge is true, must condemn the guilty to death; in such a case, we may say that the people are his judges. In acting thus a prince becomes the parent of his subjects."

The will of the people is always referred to as the supreme power in the State, and Mencius warns princes that they must both please and benefit their people, observing that "if the country is not subdued in heart there will be no such thing as governing it;" and also, "He who gains the hearts of the people secures the throne, and he who loses the people's hearts loses the throne." A prince should "give and take what is pleasing to them, and not do that which they hate." "Good laws," he further remarks, "are not equal to winning the people by good instruction." Being consulted by a sovereign, whether he ought to attempt the conquest of a neighboring territory, he answered: "If the people of Yen are delighted, then take it; but if otherwise, not." He also countenances the dethroning of a king who does not rule his people with a regard to their happiness, and adduces the example of the founders of the Shang and Chau dynasties in proof of its propriety. "When the prince is guilty of great errors," is his doctrine, "the minister should reprove him; if, after doing so again and again, he does not listen, he ought to dethrone him and put another in his place."

His estimate of human nature, like many of the Chinese sages, is high, believing it to be originally good, and that "all men are naturally virtuous, as all water flows downward. All men have compassionate hearts, all feel ashamed of vice." But he says also, "Shame is of great moment to men; it is only the designing and artful that find no use for shame." Yet human nature must be tried by suffering, and to form an energetic and virtuous character a man must endure much; "when Heaven was about to place Shun and others in important trusts, it first generally tried their minds, inured them to abstinence, exposed them to poverty and adversity; thus it moved their hearts and taught them patience." His own character presents traits widely differing from the servility and baseness usually ascribed to Asiatics, and especially to the Chinese; and he seems to have been ready to sacrifice everything to his principles. "I love life, and I love justice," he observes, "but if I cannot preserve both, I would give up life and hold fast justice. Although I love life, there is that which I love more than life; although I hate death, there is that which I hate more than death." And as if referring to his own integrity, he elsewhere says: "The nature of the superior man is such that, although in a high and prosperous situation, it adds nothing to his virtue; and although in low and distressed circumstances, it impairs it in nothing." In many points, especially in the importance he gives to filial duty, his reverence for the ancient books and princes, and his adherence to old usages, Mencius imitated and upheld Confucius; in native vigor and carelessness of the reproaches of his compatriots he exceeded him. Many translations of his work have appeared in European languages, but Legge's[1] is in most respects the best for its comments, and the notices of Men-

---

[1] *Chinese Classics*, Vol II. Hongkong, 1862.

cius' life and times, and a fair estimate of his character and influence.

Returning to the Imperial Catalogue, its ninth section contains a list of musical works, and a few on dancing or posture-making; they hold this distinguished place in the list from the importance attached to music as employed in the State worship and domestic ceremonies.

The tenth section gives the names of philological treatises and lexicons, most of them confined to the Chinese language. though a few are in Manchu. The Chinese government has excelled in the attention it has given to the compilation of lexicons and encyclopædias. The number of works of this sort here catalogued is two hundred and eighteen, the major part issued during this dynasty, and including only works on the general language, none on the dialects. For their extent of quotation, the variety of separate disquisitions upon the form, origin, and composition of characters, and treatises upon subjects connected with the language, they indicate the careful labor native scholars have bestowed upon the elucidation of their own tongue.

One of them, the *Pei Wăn Yun Fu*, or 'Treasury of compared Characters and Sounds,' is so extensive and profound as to deserve a short notice, which cannot be better made than by an extract from the preface of M. Callery to his prospectus to its translation, of which he only issued one livraison. He says the Emperor Kanghí, who planned its preparation, "assembled in his palace the most distinguished literati of the Empire, and laying before them all the works that could be got, whether ancient or modern, commanded them carefully to collect all the words, allusions, forms and figures of speech of every style, of which examples might be found in the Chinese language; to class the principal articles according to the pronunciation of the words; to devote a distinct paragraph to each expression; and to give in support of every paragraph several quotations from the original works. Stimulated by the munificence, as well as the example, of the Emperor, who reviewed the performances of every day, seventy-six literati assembled at Peking, labored with such assiduity, and kept up such an active correspondence with the learned in all parts of the Empire, that at the end of eight years the work was completed (1711), and printed at the public expense, in one hundred and thirty thick volumes." The peculiar nature of the Chinese language, in the formation of many dissyllabic compounds of two or more characters to express a third and new idea, renders such a work as this thesaurus more necessary and useful, perhaps, than it would be in any other language. Under some of the common characters as many as three hundred, four hundred, and even six hundred combinations are noticed, all of which modify its sense more or less, and form a complete monograph of the character, of the highest utility to the scholar in composing idiomatic Chinese. This magnificent monument of literary labor reflects great credit on the monarch who took so much interest in its compilation (as he remarks in his preface), as to devote the leisure hours of every day, notwithstanding his manifold occupations, for eight years, to overlooking the labors of the scholars engaged upon it.

CHAPTER XII.

POLITE LITERATURE OF THE CHINESE.

The three remaining divisions of the Imperial Catalogue comprise lists of Historical, Professional, and Poetical works. The estimate made of their value will depend somewhat on the peculiar line of research of the student, and to give him the means of doing this would require copious extracts from poetical, religious, topographical or moral writings. Those who have studied them the longest, as Rémusat, Julien, Staunton, Pauthier, the two Morrisons, Legge, etc., speak of them with the most respect, whether it arose from a higher appreciation of their worth as they learned more, or that the zealousness of their studies imparted a tinge of enthusiasm to their descriptions. A writer in the *Quarterly Review* gives good reasons for placing the polite literature of the Chinese first for the insight it is likely to give Europeans into their habits of thought. "The Chinese stand eminently distinguished from other Asiatics by their early possession and extensive use of the important art of printing—of printing, too, in that particular shape, the stereotype, which is best calculated, by multiplying the copies and cheapening the price, to promote the circulation of every species of their literature. Hence they are, as might be expected, a reading people; a certain degree of education is common among even the lower classes, and among the higher it is superfluous to insist on the great estimation in which letters must be held under a system where learning forms the very threshold of the gate that conducts to fame, honors, and civil employment. Amid the vast mass of printed books which is the natural offspring of such a state of things, we make no scruple to avow that the circle of their *belles-lettres*, comprised under the heads of drama, poetry, and novels, has always possessed the highest place in our esteem; and we must say that there appears no readier or more agreeable mode of becoming intimately acquainted with a people from whom Europe can have so little to learn on the score of either moral or physical science than by drawing largely on the inexhaustible stores of their ornamental literature."

The second division in the Catalogue, *Sz' Pu*, or 'Historical Writings,' is subdivided into fifteen sections. These writings are very extensive; even their mere list conveys a high idea of the vast amount of labor expended upon them; and it is impossible to withhold respect, at least, to the industry displayed in compilations like the *Seventeen Histories*, in two hundred and seventeen volumes, and its continuation, the *Twenty-two Histories*, a still larger work. Though the entertaining episodes and sketches of character found in Herodotus and other ancient European historians are wanting, there is plenty of incident in court, camp, and social life, as well as public acts and royal biography. The dynastic records became the duty of special officers, and the headings adopted from the Sui, A.D. 590, have since been followed in arranging the historic materials under twelve heads. From the mass of materials digested by careful scholars have been compiled the records now known; they form, with all their imperfections, the best continuous history of any Asiatic people. Popular abridgments are common, among which the *Tung Kien Kang-muh*, or 'General Mirror of History,' and a compiled abridgment of it, the *Kang Kien I Chí*, or 'History made Easy,' are the most useful.

The earliest historian among the Chinese is Sz'ma Tsien,[1] who flourished about B.C. 104, in which year he commenced the *Sz' Kí*, or 'Historical Memoirs,' in one hundred and thirty chapters. In this great work, which, like the Muses of Herodotus in Greek, forms the commencement of credible modern history with the Chinese, the author relates the actions of the Emperors

---

[1] Compare Rémusat, *Nouveaux Mélanges*, Tome II., pp. 130 ff., where there are excellent biographical notices of Sz'ma Tsien and other native historians.

in regular succession and the principal events which happened during their reigns, together with details and essays respecting music, astronomy, religious ceremonies, weights, public works, etc., and the changes they had undergone during the twenty-two centuries embraced in his Memoirs. It is stated by Rémusat that there are in the whole work five hundred and twenty-six thousand five hundred characters, for the Chinese, like the ancient Hebrews, number the words in their standard authors. The *Sz' Kí* is in five parts, and its arrangement has served as a model for subsequent historians, few of whom have equalled its author in the vivacity of their style or carefulness of their research.

The *General Mirror to Aid in Governing*, by Sz'ma Kwang, of the Sung dynasty, in two hundred and ninety-four chapters, is one of the best digested and most lucid annals that Chinese scholars have produced, embracing the period between the end of the Tsin to the beginning of the Sung dynasty (A.D. 313 to 960). Both the historians Sz'ma Tsien and Sz'ma Kwang filled high offices in the State, were both alternately disgraced and honored, and were mixed up with all the political movements of the day. Rémusat speaks in terms of deserved commendation of their writings, and to a notice of their works adds some account of their lives. One or two incidents in the career of Sz'ma Kwang exhibit a readiness of action and freedom in expressing his sentiments which are more common among the Chinese than is usually supposed. In his youth he was standing with some companions near a large vase used to rear gold fish, when one of them fell in. Too terrified themselves to do anything, all but young Kwang ran to seek succor; he looked around for a stone with which to break the vase and let the water flow out, and thus saved the life of his companion. In subsequent life the same common sense was joined with a boldness which led him to declare his sentiments on all occasions. Some southern people once sent a present to the Emperor of a strange quadruped, which his flatterers said was the mythological *kí-lin* of happy omen. Sz'ma Kwang, being consulted on the matter, replied: "I have never seen the *kí-lin*, therefore I cannot tell whether this be one or not. What I do know is that the real *kí-lin* could never be brought hither by foreigners; he appears of himself when the State is well governed."[1] An extension of this great work by Lí Tao, of the Sung dynasty, in five hundred and twenty books, gave their countrymen a fair account of the thirty-six centuries of their national fortunes; and the digest under Chu Hí's direction has made them still more accessible and famous to succeeding ages.

Few works in Chinese literature are more popular than a historical novel by Chin Shau, about A.D. 350, called the *San Kwoh Chi*, or 'History of the Three States;' its scenes are laid in the northern parts of China, and include the period between A.D. 170 and 317, when several ambitious chieftains conspired against the imbecile princes of the once famous Han dynasty, and, after that was overthrown, fought among themselves until the Empire was again reconsolidated under the Tsin dynasty. This performance, from its double character and the long period over which it extends, necessarily lacks that unity which a novel should have. Its charms, to a Chinese, consist in the animated descriptions of plots and counterplots, in the relations of battles, sieges, and retreats, and the admirable manner in which the characters are delineated and their acts intermixed with entertaining episodes. The work opens with describing the distracted state of the Empire under the misrule of Ling tí and Hwan tí, the last two monarchs of the House of Han (147 to 184), who were entirely swayed by eunuchs, and left the administration of government to reckless oppressors, until ambitious men, taking advantage of the general discontent, raised the standard of rebellion. The leaders ordered their partisans to wear yellow head-dresses, whence the rebellion was called that of the Yellow Caps, and was suppressed only after several years of hard struggle by a few distinguished generals who upheld the throne. Among these was Tung Choh, who, gradually drawing to himself all the power in the State, thereby arrayed against himself others equally ambitious and unscrupulous. Disorganization had not yet proceeded so far that all hope of supporting the rightful throne had left the minds of its adher-

[1] *Chinese Repository*, Vol. IX., pp. 210, 274.

ents, among whom was Wang Yun, a chancellor of the Empire, who, seeing the danger of the State, devised a scheme to inveigle Tung Choh to his ruin, which is thus narrated:

One day Tung Choh gave a great entertainment to the officers of government. When the wine had circulated several times, Lü Pu (his adopted son) whispered something in his ear, whereupon he ordered the attendants to take Chang Wăn from the table into the hall below, and presently one of them returned, handing up his head in a charger. The spirits of all present left their bodies, but Tung, laughing, said, "Pray, sirs, do not be alarmed. Chang Wăn has been leaguing with Yuen Shuh how to destroy me; a messenger just now brought a letter for him, and inadvertently gave it to my son; for which he has lost his life. You, gentlemen, have no cause for dread." All the officers replied, "Yes! Yes!" and immediately separated.

Chancellor Wang Yun returned home in deep thought: "The proceedings of this day's feast are enough to make my seat an uneasy one;" and taking his cane late at night he walked out in the moonlight into his rear garden, when standing near a rose arbor and weeping as he looked up, he heard a person sighing and groaning within the peony pavillion. Carefully stepping and watching, he saw it was Tiau Chen, a singing-girl belonging to the house, who had been taken into his family in early youth and taught to sing and dance; she was now sixteen, and both beautiful and accomplished, and Wang treated her as if she had been his own daughter.

Listening some time, he spoke out, "What underhand plot are you at now, insignificant menial?" Tiau Chen, much alarmed, kneeling, said, "What treachery can your slave dare to devise?" "If you have nothing secret, why then are you here late at night sighing in this manner?" Tiau replied, "Permit your handmaid to declare her inmost thoughts. I am very grateful for your excellency's kind nurture, for teaching me singing and dancing, and for the treatment I have received. If my body should be crushed to powder [in your service], I could not requite a myriad to one [for these favors]. But lately I have seen your eyebrows anxiously knit, doubtless from some State affairs, though I presumed not to ask; this evening, too, I saw you restless in your seat. On this account I sighed, not imagining your honor was overlooking me. If I can be of the least use, I would not decline the sacrifice of a thousand lives." Wang, striking his cane on the ground, exclaimed, "Who would have thought the rule of Han was lodged in your hands! Come with me into the picture-gallery." Tiau Chen following in, he ordered his females all to retire, and placing her in a seat, turned himself around and did her obeisance. She, much surprised, prostrated herself before him, and asked the reason of such conduct, to which he replied, "You are able to compassionate all the people in the dominions of Han." His words ended, the tears gushed like a fountain. She added, "I just now said, if I can be of any service I will not decline, though I should lose my life."

Wang, kneeling, rejoined, "The people are in most imminent danger, and the nobility in a hazard like that of eggs piled up; neither can be rescued without your assistance. The traitor Tung Choh wishes soon to seize the throne, and none of the civil or military officers have any practicable means of defence. He has an adopted son, Lü Pu, a remarkably daring and brave man, who, like himself, is the slave of lust. Now I wish to contrive a scheme to inveigle them both, by first promising to wed you to Lü, and then offering you to Tung, while you must seize the opportunity to raise suspicions in them, and slander one to the other so as to sever them, and cause Lü to kill Tung, whereby the present great evils will be terminated, the throne upheld, and the government re-established. All this is in your power, but I do not know how the plan strikes you." Tiau answered, "I have promised your excellency my utmost service, and you may trust me that I will devise some good scheme when I am offered to them."

"You must be aware that if this design leaks out, we shall all be utterly exterminated." "Your excellency need not be anxious, and if I do not aid in accomplishing your patriotic designs, let me die a thousand deaths."

Wang, bowing, thanked her. The next day, taking several of the brilliant pearls preserved in the family, he ordered a skilful workman to inlay them into a golden coronet, which he secretly sent as a present to Lü Pu. Highly gratified, Lü himself went to Wang's house to thank him, where a well-prepared feast of viands and wine awaited his arrival. Wang went out to meet him, and waiting upon him into the rear hall, invited him to sit at the top of the table, but Lü objected: "I am only a general in the prime minister's department, while your excellency is a high minister in his Majesty's court—why this mistaken respect?"

Wang rejoined, "There is no hero in the country now besides you; I do not pay this honor to your office, but to your talents." Lü was excessively pleased. Wang ceased not in engaging him to drink, the while speaking of Tung Choh's high qualities, and praising his guest's virtues, who, on his side, wildly laughed for joy. Most of the attendants were ordered to retire, a few waiting-maids stopping to serve out wine, when, being half drunk, he ordered them to tell the young child to come in. Shortly after, two pages led in Tiau Chen, gorgeously dressed, and Lü, much astonished, asked, "Who is this?"

"It is my little daughter, Tiau Chen, whom I have ordered to come in and see you, for I am very grateful for your honor's misapplied kindness to me, which has been like that to near relatives." He then bade her present a goblet of wine to him, and, as she did so, their eyes glanced to and from each other.

Wang, feigning to be drunk, said: "The child strongly requests your honor to drink many cups; my house entirely depends upon your excellency." Lü requested her to be seated, but she acting as if about to retire, Wang remarked, "The general is my intimate friend; be seated, my child; what are you afraid of?" She then sat down at his side, while Lü's eyes never strayed from their gaze upon her, drinking and looking.

Wang, pointing to Tiau, said to Lü, "I wish to give this girl to you as a concubine, but know not whether you will receive her?" Lü, leaving the table to thank him, said, "If I could obtain such a girl as this, I would emulate the requital dogs and horses give for the care taken of them."

Wang rejoined, "I will immediately select a lucky day, and send her to your house." Lü was delighted beyond measure, and never took his eyes off her, while Tiau herself, with ogling glances, intimated her passion. The feast shortly after broke up, and Lü departed.

The scheme here devised was successful, and Tung Choh was assassinated by his son when he was on his way to depose the monarch. His death, however, brought no peace to the country, and three chieftains, Tsau Tsau, Liu Pí, and Sun Kiuen, soon distinguished themselves in their struggles for power, and afterward divided the Empire into the three States of Wu, Shuh, and Wei, from which the work derives its name. Many of the personages who figure in this work have since been deified, among whom are Liu Pí's sworn brother Kwan Yü, who is now the Mars (*Kwan tí*), and Hwa To, the Esculapius, of Chinese mythology. Its scenes and characters have all been fruitful subjects for the pencil and the pen of artists and poetasters. One commentator has gone so far as to incorporate his reflections in the body of the text itself, in the shape of such expressions as "Wonderful speech! What rhodomontade! This man was a fool before, and shows himself one now!" Davis likens this work to the Iliad for its general arrangement and blustering character of the heroes; it was composed when the scenes described and their leading actors existed chiefly in personal recollection, and the remembrances of both were fading away in the twilight of popular legends.

Among the numerous historians of China, only a few would repay the labor of an entire translation, but many would furnish good materials for extended epitomes. Among these are the *Tso Chuen*, already noticed; the *Anterior Han Dynasty*, by Pan Ku and his sister; the *Wei Shu*, by Wei Shau (A.D. 386–556); and the works of Sz'ma Kwang. In addition to the dynastic histories, numerous similar works classified under the heads of annals and complete records in two sections of this division would furnish much authentic material for the foreign archæologist. The most valuable relic after the *Chun Tsiu*, of a historic character, is the "Bamboo Books," reported to have been found in a tomb in Honan, A.D. 279; it gives a chronological list down to B.C. 299, with incidents interspersed, and bears many internal evidences of genuineness. Legge and Biot have each translated it.[1]

Biographies of distinguished men and women are numerous, and their preparation forms a favorite branch of literary labor. It is noticeable to observe the consideration paid tò literary women in these memoirs, and the praises bestowed upon discreet mothers whose talented children are considered to be the criteria of their careful training. One work of this class is in one hundred and twenty volumes, called *Sing Pu*, but it does not possess the incident and animation which are found in some less formal biographical dictionaries. The *Lieh Nü Chuen*, or 'Memoirs of Distinguished Ladies' of ancient times, by Liu Hiang, B.C. 125, is often cited by writers on female education who wish to show how women were anciently trained to the practice of every virtue and accomplishment. If a Chinese author cannot quote a case to illustrate his position at least eight or ten centuries old, he thinks half its force abated by its youth. Biographical works are almost as numerous as statistical, and afford one of the best sources for studying the national character; some of them, like the lives of Washington or Cromwell in our own literature, combine both history and biography.

Some of the statistical and geographical works mentioned in this division are noticed on p. 49. Among those on the Constitution is the 'Complete Antiquarian Researches' of Ma Twan-lin (A.D. 1275), in three hundred and forty-eight chapters. It forms a most extensive and profound work, containing researches upon every matter relating to government, and extending through a series of dynasties which held the throne nearly forty centuries. Rémusat goes so far as to say: "This excellent work is a library by itself, and if Chinese literature possessed no other, the language would be worth learning for the sake of reading this alone." No book has been more drawn upon by Europeans for information concerning matters relating to Eastern Asia than this; Visdelou and De Guignes took from

[1] Legge's *Chinese Classics*, Vol. III.; *Prolegomena*, Chap. IV. E. Biot in the *Journal Asiatique*, 2e Series, Tomes XII., p. 537, and XIII., pp. 203, 381.

it much of their information relating to the Tartars and Huns; and Pingsé extracted his account of the comets and ærolites from its pages, besides some geographical and ethnographical papers. Rémusat often made use of its stores, and remarks that many parts merit an entire translation, which can be said, indeed, of few Chinese authors. A supplement prepared and published in 1586 by Wang Kí brings it down to that date. A further revision was issued under imperial patronage in 1772, and a final one not long afterward, continuing the narrative to the reign of Kanghí.[1] It elevates our opinion of a nation whose literature can boast of a work like this, exhibiting such patient investigation and candid comparison of authorities, such varied research and just discrimination of what is truly important, and so extensive a mass of facts and opinions upon every subject of historic interest. Although there be no quotations in it from Roman or Greek classic authors, and the ignorance of the compiler of what was known upon the same subjects in other countries disqualified him from giving his remarks the completeness they would otherwise have had, yet when the stores of knowledge from western lands are made known to a people whose scholars can produce such works as this, the *Memoirs* of Sz'ma Tsien, and others equally good, it may reasonably be expected that they will not lack in industry or ability to carry on their researches.

The third division of *Tsz' Pu*, 'Scholastic' or 'Professional Writings,' is arranged under fourteen sections, viz.: Philosophical, Military, Legal, Agricultural, Medical, Mathematical, and Magical writings, works on the Liberal Arts, Collections, Miscellanies, Encyclopædias, Novels, and treatises on the tenets of the Buddhists and Rationalists. The first section is called *Jü Kia Lui*, meaning the 'Works of the Literary Family,' under which name is included those who maintain, discuss, and teach the tenets of the sages, although they may not accept all that Confucius taught. This class of books is worthy of far more examination than foreigners have hitherto given to it, and they

[1] Compare Rémusat, *Mélanges Asiatiques*, Tome II., p. 166; *Chinese Repository*, Vol. IX., p. 143; Wylie's *Notes*, p. 55; Mayer's *Chinese Reader's Manual*, p. 149.

will find that Chinese philosophers have discussed morals, government, cosmogony, and like subjects, with a freedom and acuteness that has not been credited to them.

It was during the Sung dynasty, when Europe was utterly lethargic and unprogressive, that China showed a marvellous mental activity, and received from Ching, Chu, Chau, and their disciples a molding and conservative influence which has remained to this day. An extract from a discussion by Chu Hí will show the way in which he reasons on the *primum mobile.*

Under the whole heaven there is no primary matter (*lì*) without the immaterial principle (*ki*), and no immaterial principle apart from the primary matter. Subsequent to the existence of the immaterial principle is produced primary matter, which is deducible from the axiom that the one male and the one female principle of nature may be dominated *tao* or *logos* (the active principle from which all things emanate); thus nature is spontaneously possessed of benevolence and righteousness (which are included in the idea of *tao*).

First of all existed *tien lì* (the celestial principle or soul of the universe), and then came primary matter; primary matter accumulated constituted *chih* (body, substance, or the accidents and qualities of matter), and nature was arranged.

Should any ask whether the immaterial principle or primary matter existed first, I should say that the immaterial principle on assuming a figure ascended, and primary matter on assuming form descended; when we come to speak of assuming form and ascending or descending, how can we divest ourselves of the idea of priority and subsequence? When the immaterial principle does not assume a form, primary matter then becomes coarse, and forms a sediment.

Originally, however, no priority or subsequence can be predicated of the immaterial principle and primary matter, and yet if you insist on carrying out the reasoning to the question of their origin, then you must say that the immaterial principle has the priority; but it is not a separate and distinct thing; it is just contained in the centre of the primary matter, so that were there no primary matter, then this immaterial principle would have no place of attachment. Primary matter consists, in fact, of the four elements of metal, wood, water, and fire, while the immaterial principle is no other than the four cardinal virtues of benevolence, righteousness, propriety, and wisdom. . . .

Should any one ask for an explanation of the assertion that the immaterial principle has first existence, and after that comes primary matter, I say, it is not necessary to speak thus: but when we know that they are combined, is it that the immaterial principle holds the precedence, and the primary matter the subsequence, or is it that the immaterial principle is subsequent to the primary matter? We cannot thus carry our reasoning; but should we endeavor to form some idea of it, then we may suppose that the primary matter relies on the immaterial principle to come into action, and wherever the primary matter is coagulated, there the immaterial principle is present. For the primary matter can concrete and coagulate, act and do, but the immaterial principle has neither will nor wish, plan nor operation: but only where the primary matter is collected and coagulated, then the immaterial principle is in the midst of it. Just as in nature, men and things, grass and trees, birds and beasts, in their propagation invariably require seed, and certainly cannot without seed from nothingness produce anything; all this, then, is the primary matter, but the immaterial principle is merely a pure, empty, wide-stretched void, without form or footstep, and incapable of action or creation; but the primary matter can ferment and coagulate, collect and produce things. . . .

Should any one ask, with regard to those expressions, "The Supreme Ruler confers the due medium on the people, and when Heaven is about to send down a great trust upon men, out of regard to the people it sets up princes over them;" and, "Heaven in producing things treats them according to their attainments: on those who do good, it sends down a hundred blessings, and on those who do evil, a hundred calamities;" and, "When Heaven is about to send down some uncommon calamity upon a generation, it first produces some uncommon genius to determine it;" do these and such like expressions imply that above the azure sky there is a Lord and Ruler who acts thus, or is it still true that Heaven has no mind, and men only carry out their reasonings in this style? I reply, these three things are but one idea; it is that the immaterial principle of order is thus. The primary matter in its evolutions hitherto, after one season of fulness has experienced one of decay; and after a period of decline it again flourishes; just as if things were going on in a circle. There never was a decay without a revival.

When men blow out their breath their bellies puff out, and when they inhale their bellies sink in, while we should have thought that at each expiration the stomach would fall in, and swell up at each inspiration; but the reason of it is that when men expire, though the mouthful of breath goes out, the second mouthful is again produced, therefore the belly is puffed up; and when men inspire, the breath which is introduced from within drives the other out, so that the belly sinks in. Lau-tsz' said nature is like an open pipe or bag; it moves, and yet is not compelled to stop, it is empty, and still more comes out; just like a fan-case open at both ends. . . .

The great extreme (*tai kih*) is merely the immaterial principle. It is not an independent separate existence; it is found in the male and female principles of nature, in the five elements, in all things; it is merely an immaterial principle, and because of its extending to the extreme limit, is therefore called the *great extreme*. If it were not for it, heaven and earth would not have been set afloat. . . . From the time when the great extreme came into operation, all things were produced by transformation. This one doctrine includes the whole; it was not because this was first in existence and then that, but altogether there is only one great origin, which from the substance extends to the use, and from the subtle reaches to that which is manifest. Should one ask, because all things partake of it, is the great extreme split up and divided? I should reply, that originally there is only one great extreme (*anima mundi*), of which all things partake, so that each one is provided with a great extreme;

just as the moon in the heavens is only one, and yet is dispersed over the hills and lakes, being seen from every place in succession; still you cannot say that the moon is divided.

The great extreme has neither residence, nor form, nor place which you can assign to it. If you speak of it before its development, then previous to that emanation it was perfect stillness; motion and rest, with the male and female principles of nature, are only the embodiment and descent of this principle. Motion is the motion of the great extreme, and rest is its rest, but these same motion and rest are not to be considered the great extreme itself. . . . Should any one ask, what is the great extreme? I should say, it is simply the principle of extreme goodness and extreme perfection. Every man has a great extreme, everything has one; that which Chao-tsz' called the great extreme is the exemplified virtue of everything that is extremely good and perfect in heaven and earth, men and things.

The great extreme is simply the extreme point, beyond which one cannot go; that which is most elevated, most mysterious, most subtle, and most divine, beyond which there is no passing. Lienkí was afraid lest people should think that the great extreme possessed form, and therefore called it the boundless extreme, a principle centred in nothing, and having an infinite extent. . . . It is the immaterial principle of the two powers, the four forms, and the eight changes of nature; we cannot say that it does not exist, and yet no form or corporeity can be ascribed to it. From this point is produced the one male and the one female principle of nature, which are called the dual powers; the four forms and eight changes also proceed from this, all according to a certain natural order, irrespective of human strength in its arrangement. But from the time of Confucius no one has been able to get hold of this idea.[1]

And, it might be added, no one ever will be able to "get hold" thereof. Such discussions as this have occupied the minds and pens of Chinese metaphysicians for centuries, and in their endeavors to explain the half-digested notions of the *Book of Changes*, they have wandered far away from the road which would have led them in the path of true knowledge, namely, the observation and record of the works and operations of nature around them; and one after another they have continued to roll this stone of Sisyphus until fatigue and bewilderment have come over them all. Some works on female education are found in this section, which seems designed as much to include whatever philosophers wrote as all they wrote on philosophy.

The second and third sections, on military and legal subjects,

[1] Translated by Rev. W. H. Medhurst, in the *Chinese Repository*, Vol. XIII., pp. 552, 609 et seq.

contain no writings of any eminence. The isolation of the Chinese prevented them from studying the various forms of government and jurisprudence observed in other countries and ages; it is this feature of originality which renders their legislation so interesting to western students. Among the fourth, on agricultural treatises, is the *Kăng Chih Tu Shí*, or 'Plates and Odes on Tillage and Weaving,' a thin quarto, which was written A.D. 1210, and has been widely circulated by the present government in order "to evince its regard for the people's support." The first half contains twenty-three plates on the various processes to be followed in raising rice, the last of which represents the husbandmen and their families returning thanks to the gods of the land for a good harvest, and offering a portion of the fruits of the earth; the last plate in the second part of the work also represents a similar scene of returning thanks for a good crop of silk, and presenting an offering to the gods. The drawings in this work are among the best for perspective and general composition which Chinese art has produced; probably their merit was the chief inducement to publish the work at governmental expense, for the odes are too brief to contain much information, and too difficult to be generally understood. The *Encyclopedia of Agriculture*, by Sü Kwang-kí, a high officer in 1600, better known as Paul Sü, gives a most elaborate detail of farming operations and utensils existing in the Ming. Other treatises on special topics and crops have been written, but it is the untiring industry of the people which secures to them the best returns from the soil, for they owe very little to science or machinery.

Among the numerous writings published for the improvement and instruction of the people by their rulers, none have been more influential than the *Shing Yu*, or 'Sacred Commands,' a politico-moral treatise, which has been made known to English readers by the translation of Dr. Milne.[1] The groundwork

[1] *The Sacred Edict*, London, 1817; a second edition of this translation appeared in Shanghai in 1870, and another in 1878. Compare Wylie's *Notes*, p. 71; Sir G. T. Staunton's *Miscellaneous Notices*, etc., pp. 1–56 (1812); *Le Saint Edit, Étude de Littérature chinoise*, préparée par A. Théophile Piry, Shanghai, 1879.

consists of sixteen apothegms, written by the Emperor Kanghí, containing general rules for the peace, prosperity, and wealth of all classes of his subjects. In order that none should plead ignorance in excuse for not knowing the Sacred Commands, it is by law required that they be proclaimed throughout the Empire by the local officers on the first and fifteenth day of every month, in a public hall set apart for the purpose, where the people are not only permitted, but requested and encouraged, to attend. In point of fact, however, this *political preaching*, as it has been called, is neglected except in large towns, though the design is not the less commendable. It is highly praiseworthy to monarchs, secure in their thrones as Kanghí and Yungching were, to take upon themselves the teaching of morality to their subjects, and institute a special service every fortnight to have their precepts communicated to them. If, too, it should soon be seen that their designs had utterly failed of all real good results from the mendacity of their officers and the ignorance or opposition of the people, still the merit due them is not diminished. The sixteen apothegms, each consisting of seven characters, are as follows:

1. Pay just regard to filial and fraternal duties, in order to give due importance to the relations of life.
2. Respect kindred in order to display the excellence of harmony.
3. Let concord abound among those who dwell in the same neighborhood, thereby preventing litigations.
4. Give the chief place to husbandry and the culture of the mulberry, that adequate supplies of food and raiment be secured
5. Esteem economy, that money be not lavishly wasted.
6. Magnify academical learning, in order to direct the scholar's progress.
7. Degrade strange religions, in order to exalt the orthodox doctrines.
8. Explain the laws, in order to warn the ignorant and obstinate.
9. Illustrate the principles of a polite and yielding carriage, in order to improve manners.
10. Attend to the essential employments, in order to give unvarying determination to the will of the people.
11. Instruct the youth, in order to restrain them from evil.
12. Suppress all false accusing, in order to secure protection to the innocent.
13. Warn those who hide deserters, that they may not be involved in their downfall.
14. Complete the payment of taxes, in order to prevent frequent urging.
15. Unite the *pao* and *kia*, in order to extirpate robbery and theft.
16. Settle animosities, that lives may be duly valued.

The amplifications of these maxims by Yungching contain much information respecting the theory of his government, and the position of the writer entitles him to speak from knowledge; his amplification of the fourteenth maxim shows their character.

From of old the country was divided into districts, and a tribute paid proportioned to the produce of the land. From hence arose revenues, upon which the expense of the five *li* and the whole charges of government depended. These expenses a prince must receive from the people, and they are what inferiors should offer to superiors. Both in ancient and modern times this principle has been the same and cannot be changed. Again, the expenses of the salaries of magistrates that they may rule our people; of pay to the army that they may protect them; of preparing for years of scarcity that they may be fed; as all these are collected from the Empire, so they are all employed for its use. How then can it be supposed that the granaries and treasury of the sovereign are intended to injure the people that he may nourish himself? Since the establishment of our dynasty till now, the proportions of the revenue have been fixed by an universally approved statute, and all unjust items completely cancelled; not a thread or hair too much has been demanded from the people. In the days of our sacred Father, the Emperor Pious, his abounding benevolence and liberal favor fed this people upward of sixty years. Daily desirous to promote their abundance and happiness, he greatly diminished the revenue, not limiting the reduction to hundreds, thousands, myriads, or lacs of taels. The mean and the remote have experienced his favor; even now it enters the muscles, and penetrates to the marrow. To exact with moderation, diminish the revenue, and confer favors on the multitude, are the virtues of a prince: to serve superiors, and to give the first place to public service and second to their own, are the duties of a people. Soldiers and people should all understand this. Become not lazy and trifling, nor prodigally throw away your property. Linger not to pay in the revenue, looking and hoping for some unusual occurrence to avoid it, nor entrust your imposts to others, lest bad men appropriate them to their own use.

Pay in at the terms, and wait not to be urged. Then with the overplus you can nourish your parents, complete the marriages of your children, satisfy your daily wants, and provide for the annual feasts and sacrifices. District officers may then sleep at ease in their public halls, and villagers will no longer be vexed in the night by calls from the tax-gatherers; on neither hand will any be involved. Your wives and children will be easy and at rest, than which you have no greater joy. If unaware of the importance of the revenue to government, and that the laws must be enforced, perhaps you will positively refuse or deliberately put off the payment, when the magistrates, obliged to balance their accounts, and give in their reports at stated times, must be rigorously severe. The assessors, suffering the pain of the whip, cannot help indulging their rapacious demands on you; knocking and pecking at your doors like hungry hawks, they will devise numerous methods of getting their wants supplied. These nameless ways of spending will probably amount to

more than the sum which ought to have been paid, and that sum, after all, cannot be dispensed with.

We know not what benefit can accrue from this. Rather than give presents to satisfy the rapacity of policemen, how much better to clear off the just assessments! Rather than prove an obstinate race and refuse the payment of the revenue, would it not be better to keep the law? Every one, even the most stupid, knows this. Furthermore, when superiors display benevolence, inferiors should manifest justice; this belongs to the idea of their being one body. Reflect that the constant labors and cares of the palace are all to serve the people. When freshes occur, dikes must be raised to restrain them; if the demon of drought appear, prayer must be offered for rain; when the locusts come, they must be destroyed. If the calamities be averted, you reap the advantage; but if they overwhelm you, your taxes are forborne, and alms liberally expended for you. If it be thus, and the people still can suffer themselves to evade the payment of taxes and hinder the supply of government, how, I ask, can you be easy? Such conduct is like that of an undutiful son. We use these repeated admonitions, only wishing you, soldiers and people, to think of the army and nation, and also of your persons and families. Then abroad you will have the fame of faithfulness, and at home peacefully enjoy its fruits. Officers will not trouble you, nor their clerks vex you—what joy equal to this! O soldiers and people, meditate on these things in the silent night, and let all accord with our wishes.[1]

Wang Yu-pí, a high officer under Yungching, paraphrased the amplifications in a colloquial manner. His remarks on the doctrines of the Buddhists and Rationalists will serve as an illustration; the quotation here given is found under the seventh maxim.

You simple people know not how to discriminate; for even according to what the books of Buddha say, he was the first-born son of the king Fan; but, retiring from the world, he fled away alone to the top of the Snowy Mountains, in order to cultivate virtue. If he regarded not his own father, mother, wife, and children, are you such fools as to suppose that he regards the multitude of the living, or would deliver his laws and doctrines to you? The imperial residence, the queen's palace, the dragon's chamber, and halls of state—if he rejected these, is it not marvellous to suppose that he should delight in the nunneries, monasteries, temples, and religious houses which you can build for him? As to the Gemmeous Emperor, the most honorable in heaven, if there be indeed such a god, it is strange to think he should not enjoy himself at his own ease in the high heavens, but must have you to give him a body of molten gold, and build him a house to dwell in!

All these nonsensical tales about keeping fasts, collecting assemblies, building temples, and fashioning images, are feigned by those sauntering,

[1] *Sacred Edict*, pp. 254–259.

worthless priests and monks to deceive you. Still you believe them, and not only go yourselves to worship and burn incense in the temples, but also suffer your wives and daughters to go. With their hair oiled and faces painted, dressed in scarlet and trimmed with green, they go to burn incense in the temples, associating with the priests of Buddha, doctors of Reason and bare-stick attorneys, touching shoulders, rubbing arms, and pressed in the moving crowd. I see not where the good they talk of doing is; on the contrary, they do many shameful things that create vexation, and give people occasion for laughter and ridicule.

Further, there are some persons who, fearing that their good boys and girls may not attain to maturity, take and give them to the temples to become priests and priestesses of Buddha and Reason, supposing that after having removed them from their own houses and placed them at the foot of grandfather Fuh (Buddha), they are then sure of prolonging life! Now, I would ask you if those who in this age are priests of these sects, all reach the age of seventy or eighty, and if there is not a short-lived person among them?

Again, there is another very stupid class of persons who, because their parents are sick, pledge their own persons by a vow before the gods that if their parents be restored to health, they will worship and burn incense on the hills, prostrating themselves at every step till they arrive at the summit, whence they will dash themselves down! If they do not lose their lives, they are sure to break a leg or an arm. They say to themselves, "To give up our own lives to save our parents is the highest display of filial duty." Bystanders also praise them as dutiful children, but they do not consider that to slight the bodies received from their parents in this manner discovers an extreme want of filial duty.

Moreover, you say that serving Fuh is a profitable service; that if you burn paper money, present offerings, and keep fasts before the face of your god Fuh, he will dissipate calamities, blot out your sins, increase your happiness, and prolong your age! Now reflect: from of old it has been said, "The gods are intelligent and just." Were Buddha a god of this description, how could he avariciously desire your gilt paper, and your offerings to engage him to afford you protection? If you do not burn gilt paper to him, and spread offerings on his altar, the god Fuh will be displeased with you, and send down judgments on you! Then your god Fuh is a scoundrel! Take, for example, the district magistrate. Should you never go to compliment and flatter him, yet, if you are good people and attend to your duty, he will pay marked attention to you. But transgress the law, commit violence, or usurp the rights of others, and though you should use a thousand ways and means to flatter him, he will still be displeased with you, and will, without fail, remove such pests from society.

You say that worshipping Fuh atones for your sins. Suppose you have violated the law, and are hauled to the judgment-seat to be punished; if you should bawl out several thousand times, "O your excellency! O your excellency!" do you think the magistrate would spare you? You will, however, at all risks, invite several Buddhist and Rationalist priests to your houses to recite their canonical books and make confession, supposing that to chant their mummery drives away misery, secures peace, and prolongs happiness and life. But suppose you rest satisfied with merely reading over the sections of these Sacred Commands several thousands or myriads of times without acting conformably thereto; would it not be vain to suppose that his Imperial Majesty should delight in you, reward you with money, and promote you to office?[1]

This ridicule of the popular superstitions has, no doubt, had some effect, repeated as it is in all parts of the country; but since the literati merely tear down and build up nothing, giving the people no substitute for what they take away, but rather, in their times of trouble, doing the things they decry, such homilies do not destroy the general respect for such ceremonies. The *Shing Yu* has also been versified for the benefit of children, and colloquial explanations added, which has further tended to enforce and inculcate its admonitions. The praise bestowed on this work by Johnson, in his *Oriental Religions*, has a good degree of actual usefulness among the people to confirm his observations; yet they are quite used to hearing the highest moral platitudes from their rulers, to whom they would not lend a dollar on their word.

In the fifth section, on medical writings, separate works are mentioned on the treatment of all domestic animals; among them is one on veterinary surgery, whose writers have versified most of their observations and prescriptions. The *Herbal* of Lí Shí-chin, noticed on p. 370, and monographs on special diseases, all show the industry of Chinese physicians to much better advantage than their science. Works on medicine and surgery are numerous, in which the surface of the body is minutely represented in pictures, together with drawings of the mode of performing various operations. Works on judicial astrology, chiromancy, and other modes of divination, on the rules for finding lucky spots for houses, graves, and temples, are exceedingly numerous, a large number of them written by Rationalists.

The eighth section, on art, contains writings on painting, music, engraving, writing, posturing, and archery, and they will doubtless furnish many new points to western artists on the

---

[1] *Sacred Edict*, p. 146.

principles and attainments of the Chinese in these branches when the works have been made better known.

The ninth section, entitled 'Collections' or 'Repertories,' is divided into memoirs on antiques, swords, coins, and bronzes, and presents a field of interesting research to a foreign archæologist likely to reward him. Another division, containing the monographs on tea, bamboo, floriculture, etc., is not so promising.

The tenth section, on philosophical writings, having a tinge of heterodoxy, is a very large one, and offers a rare opportunity of research to those curious to know what China can contribute to moral science. The writings of Roman Catholics and Moslems are included in this long catalogue.

Under the head of encyclopædias, a list of summaries, compends, and treasuries of knowledge is given, which for extent and bulkiness cannot be equalled in any language. Among them is the *Tai Tien*, or 'Great Record' of the Emperor Yungloh (A.D. 1403), in twenty-two thousand eight hundred and seventy-seven chapters, and containing the substance of all classical, historical, philosophical, and scientific writings in the language. Parts of this compilation were lost, and on the accession of the Manchus one-tenth of it was missing; but by means of the unequalled interest on the part of Yungloh in his national literature, three hundred and eighty-five ancient and rare works were rescued from destruction. The *San Tsai Tu*, or 'Plates [illustrative of the] Three Powers' (*i.e.*, heaven, earth, and man, by which is meant the entire universe), in one hundred and thirty volumes, is one of the most valuable compilations, by reason of the great number of plates it contains, which exhibit the ideas of the compilers much better than their descriptions.

The twelfth section, containing novels and tales, called *Siao Shwoh*, or 'Trifling Talk,' gives the titles of but few of the thousands of productions of this class in the language. Works of fiction are among the most popular and exceptionable books the Chinese have, and those which are not demoralizing are, with some notable exceptions, like the *Ten Talented Authors*, generally slighted. The books sold in the streets are chiefly of this class of writings, consisting of tales and stories generally destitute of all intricacy of plot, fertility of illustration, or elevation of sentiment. They form the common mental aliment of the lower classes, being read by those who are able, and talked about by all; their influence is consequently immense. Many of them are written in the purest style, among which a callection called *Liao Chai*, or 'Pastimes of the Study,' in sixteen volumes, is pre-eminent for its variety and force of expression, and its perusal can be recommended to every one who wishes to study the copiousness of the Chinese language. The preface is dated in 1679; most of the tales are short, and few have any ostensible moral to them, while those which are objectionable for their immorality, or ridiculous from their magic whimsies, form a large proportion. A quotation or two will illustrate the author's invention:

A villager was once selling plums in the market, which were rather delicious and fragrant, and high in price; and there was a Tao priest, clad in ragged garments of coarse cotton, begging before his wagon. The villager scolded him, but he would not go off; whereupon, becoming angry, he reviled and hooted at him. The priest said, "The wagon contains many hundred plums, and I have only begged one of them, which, for you, respected sir, would certainly be no great loss; why then are you so angry?" The spectators advised to give him a poor plum and send him away, but the villager would not consent. The workmen in the market disliking the noise and clamor, furnished a few coppers and bought a plum, which they gave the priest. He bowing thanked them, and turning to the crowd said, "I do not wish to be stingy, and request you, my friends, to partake with me of this delicious plum." One of them replied, "Now you have it, why do you not eat it yourself?" "I want only the stone to plant," said he, eating it up at a munch. When eaten, he held the stone in his hand, and taking a spade off his shoulder, dug a hole in the ground several inches deep, into which he put it and covered it with earth. Then turning to the market people, he procured some broth with which he watered and fertilized it; and others, wishing to see what would turn up, brought him boiling dregs from shops near by, which he poured upon the hole just dug. Every one's eyes being fixed upon the spot, they saw a crooked shoot issuing forth, which gradually increased till it became a tree, having branches and leaves; flowers and then fruit succeeded, large and very fragrant, which covered the tree. The priest then approached the tree, plucked the fruit and gave the beholders; and when all were consumed, he felled the tree with a colter—chopping, chopping for a good while, until at last, having cut it off, he shouldered the foliage in an easy manner, and leisurely walked away.

When first the priest began to perform his magic arts, the villager was also among the crowd, with outstretched neck and gazing eyes, and completely forgot his own business. When the priest had gone, he began to look into his wagon, and lo! it was empty of plums; and for the first time he perceived that what had just been distributed were all his own goods. Moreover, looking narrowly about his wagon, he saw that the dashboard was gone, having just been cut off with a chisel. Much excited and incensed he ran after him, and as he turned the corner of the wall, he saw the board thrown down beneath the hedge, it being that with which the plum-tree was felled. Nobody knew where the priest had gone, and all the market folks laughed heartily.

The Rationalists are considered as the chief magicians among the Chinese, and they figure in most of the tales in this work, whose object probably was to exalt their craft, and add to their reputation. Like the foregoing against hardheartedness, the following contains a little sidewise admonition against theft:

On the west of the city in the hamlet of the White family lived a rustic who stole his neighbor's duck and cooked it. At night he felt his skin itch, and on looking at it in the morning saw a thick growth of duck's feathers, which, when irritated, pained him. He was much alarmed, for he had no remedy to cure it; but, in a dream of the night, a man informed him, "Your disease is a judgment from heaven; you must get the loser to reprimand you, and the feathers will fall off." Now this gentleman, his neighbor, was always liberal and courteous, nor during his whole life, whenever he lost anything, had he even manifested any displeasure in his countenance. The thief craftily told him, "The fellow who stole your duck is exceedingly afraid of a reprimand; but reprove him, and he will no doubt then fear in future." He, laughing, replied, "Who has the time or disposition to scold wicked men?" and altogther refused to do so; so the man, being hardly bestead, was obliged to tell the truth, upon which the gentleman gave him a scolding, and his disorder was removed.

Rémusat compares the construction of Chinese novels to those of Richardson, in which the "authors render their characters interesting and natural by reiterated strokes of the pencil, which finally produce a high degree of illusion. The interest in their pages arose precisely in proportion to the stage of my progress; and in approaching to the termination, I found myself about to part with some agreeable people, just as I had duly learned to relish their society." He briefly describes the defects in Chinese romances as principally consisting in long descriptions of trifling particulars and delineations of localities, and the characters and circumstances of the interlocutors, while the thread of the narrative is carried on mostly in a conversational way, which, from its minuteness, soon becomes tedious. The length of their poetic descriptions and prolix display of the wonders of art or the beauties of nature, thrown in at the least hint in the narrative, or moral reflections introduced in the most serious manner in the midst of diverting incidents, like a long-metre psalm in a comedy, tend to confuse the main story and dislocate the unity requisite to produce an effect.

Chinese novels, however, generally depend on something of a plot, and the characters are sometimes well sustained. "Visits and the formalities of polished statesmen; assemblies, and above all, the conversations which make them agreeable; repasts, and the social amusements which prolong them; walks of the admirers of beautiful nature; journeys; the manœuvres of adventurers; lawsuits; the literary examinations; and, in the sequel, marriage, form their most frequent episodes and ordinary conclusions." The hero of these plots is usually a young academician, endowed with an amiable disposition and devotedly attached to the study of classic authors, who meets with every kind of obstacle and ill luck in the way of attaining the literary honors he has set his heart on. The heroine is also well acquainted with letters; her own inclinations and her father's desires are that she may find a man of suitable accomplishments, but after having heard of one, every sort of difficulty is thrown in the way of getting him; which, of course, on the part of both are at last happily surmounted.

The adventures which distinguished persons meet in wandering over the country incognito, and the happy dénouement of their interviews with some whom they have been able to elevate when their real characters have been let out, form the plan of other tales. There is little or nothing of high wrought description of passion, nor acts of atrocious vengeance introduced to remove a troublesome person, but everything is kept within the bounds of probability; and at the end the vicious are punished by seeing their bad designs fail of their end in the rewards and success given those who have done well. In most of the stories whose length and style are such as to entitle them to the name of novel, and which have attained any reputation, the story is not disgraced by anything offensive; it is rather in the shorter tales that decency is violated. Among them the *Hung Lao Mung*, or 'Dreams of the Red Chamber,' is one of the most popular stories, and open not a little to this objection.

The historical novels, of which there are many, would, if translated, prove more interesting to foreign readers than those merely describing manners, because they interweave much information in the story. The *Shui Hu Chuen*, or 'Narrative of the Water Marshes,' and 'The Annals of the Contending States,' are two of the best written; the latter is more credible as a history than any other work in this class.

The fourth division of the Catalogue is called *Tsih Pu*, or 'Miscellanies,' and the works mentioned in it are chiefly poems or collections of songs, occupying nearly one-third of the whole collection. They are arranged in five sections, namely: Poetry of Tsu, Complete Works of Individuals, and General Collections, On the Art of Poetry, and Odes and Songs. The most ancient poet in the language is Yuh Yuen, a talented Minister of State who flourished previous to the time of Mencius, and wrote the *Lí Sao*, or 'Dissipation of Sorrows.' It has been translated into German and French. His name and misfortunes are still commemorated by the Festival of Dragon-boats on the fifth day of the fifth moon. More celebrated in Chinese estimation are the poets Lí Tai-peh and Tu Fu of the Tang dynasty, and Su Tung-po of the Sung, who combined the three leading traits of a bard, being lovers of flowers, wine, and song, and attaining distinction in the service of government.[1] The incidents in the life of the former of these bards were so varied, and his reckless love of drink brought him into so many scrapes, that he is no less famed for his adventures than for his sonnets. The following story is told of him in the 'Remarkable Facts of all Times,' which is here abridged from the translation of T. Pavié:

Lí, called *Tai-peh*, or 'Great-white,' from the planet Venus, was endowed with a beautiful countenance and a well-made person, exhibiting in all his

[1] The second of these, Tu Fu, is a poet of some distinction noticed by Rémusat (*Nouveaux Mélanges*, Tome II., p. 174). He lived in the eighth century A.D., dying of hunger in the year 768. His writings are usually edited with those of Lí Tai-peh.

movements a gentle nobility which indicated a man destined to rise above his age. When only ten years old, he could read the classics and histories, and his conversation showed the brilliancy of his thoughts, as well as the purity of his diction. He was, in consequence of his precocity, called the Exiled Immortal, but named himself the Retired Scholar of the Blue Lotus. Some one having extolled the quality of the wine of Niauching, he straightway went there, although more than three hundred miles distant, and abandoned himself to his appetite for liquor. While singing and carousing in a tavern, a military commandant passed, who, hearing his song, sent in to inquire who it was, and carried the poet off to his own house. On departing, he urged Lí to go to the capital and compete for literary honors, which, he doubted not, could be easily attained, and at last induced him to bend his steps to the capital. On his arrival there, he luckily met the academician Ho near the palace, who invited him to an alehouse, and laying aside his robes, drank wine with him till night, and then carried him home. The two were soon well acquainted, and discussed the merits of poetry and wine till they were much charmed with each other.

As the day of examination approached, Ho gave the poet some advice. "The examiners for this spring are Yang and Kao, one a brother of the Empress, the other commander of his Majesty's body-guard; both of them love those who make them presents, and if you have no means to buy their favor, the road of promotion will be shut to you. I know them both very well, and will write a note to each of them, which may, perhaps, obtain you some favor." In spite of his merit and high reputation, Lí found himself in such circumstances as to make it desirable to avail of the good-will of his friend Ho; but on perusing the notes he brought, the examiners disdainfully exclaimed, "After having fingered his *protégé's* money, the academician contents himself with sending us a billet which merely rings its sound, and bespeaks our attention and favors toward an upstart without degree or title. On the day of decision we will remember the name of Lí, and any composition signed by him shall be thrown aside without further notice." The day of examination came, and the distinguished scholars of the Empire assembled, eager to hand in their compositions. Lí, fully capable to go through the trial, wrote off his essay on a sheet without effort, and handed it in first. As soon as he saw the name of Lí, the examiner Yang did not even give himself time to glance over the page, but with long strokes of his pencil erased the composition, saying, "Such a scrawler as this is good for nothing but to grind my ink!" "To grind your ink!" interrupted the other examiner Kao; "say rather he is only fit to put on my stockings, and lace up my buskins."

With these pleasantries, the essay of Lí was rejected; but he, transported with anger at such a contemptuous refusal at the public examination, returned home and exclaimed, "I swear that if ever my wishes for promotion are accomplished, I will order Yang to grind my ink, and Kao to put on my stockings and lace up my buskins; then my vows will be accomplished." Ho endeavored to calm the indignation of the poet: "Stay here with me till a new examination is ordered in three years, and live in plenty; the examiners will not be the same then, and you will surely succeed." They therefore continued to live as they had done, drinking and making verses.

After many months had elapsed, some foreign ambassadors came to the capital charged with a letter from their sovereign, whom he was ordered to receive and entertain in the hall of ambassadors. The next day the officers handed in their letter to his Majesty's council, who ordered the doctors to open and read it, but they could none of them decipher a single word, humbly declaring it contained nothing but fly-tracks; "your subjects," they added, "have only a limited knowledge, a shallow acquaintance with things; they are unable to read a word." On hearing this, the Emperor turned to the examiner Yang and ordered him to read the letter, but his eyes wandered over the characters as if he had been blind, and he knew nothing of them. In vain did his Majesty address himself to the civil and military officers who filled the court; not one among them could say whether the letter contained words of good or evil import. Highly incensed, he broke out in reproaches against the grandees of his palace: "What! among so many magistrates, so many scholars and warriors, cannot there be found a single one who knows enough to relieve us of the vexation of this affair? If this letter cannot be read, how can it be answered? If the ambassadors are dismissed in this style, we shall be the ridicule of the barbarians, and foreign kings will mock the court of Nanking, and doubtless follow it up by seizing their lance and buckler and join to invade our frontiers. What then? If in three days no one is able to decipher this letter, every one of your appointments shall be suspended; if in six days you do not tell me what it means, your offices shall every one be taken away; and death shall execute justice on such ignorant men if I wait nine days in vain for its explanation, and others of our subjects shall be elevated to power whose virtue and talents will render some service to their country."

Terrified by these words, the grandees kept a mournful silence, and no one ventured a single reply, which only irritated the monarch the more. On his return home, Ho related to his friend Lí everything that had transpired at court, who, hearing him with a mournful smile, replied, "How to be regretted, how unlucky it is that I could not obtain a degree at the examination last year, which would have given me a magistracy; for now, alas! it is impossible for me to relieve his Majesty of the chagrin which troubles him." "But truly," said Ho, suddenly, "I think you are versed in more than one science, and will be able to read this unlucky letter. I shall go to his Majesty and propose you on my own responsibility." The next day he went to the palace, and passing through the crowd of courtiers, approached the throne, saying, "Your subject presumes to announce to your Majesty that there is a scholar of great merit called Lí, at his house, who is profoundly acquainted with more than one science; command him to read this letter, for there is nothing of which he is not capable."

This advice pleased the Emperor, who presently sent a messenger to the house of the academician, ordering him to present himself at court. But Lí offered some objections: "I am a man still without degree or title; I have neither talents nor information, while the court abounds in civil and military officers, all equally famous for their profound learning. How then can you have recourse to such a contemptible and useless man as I? If I presume to accept this behest, I fear that I shall deeply offend the nobles of the palace"—referring especially to the premier Yang and the general Kao. When his reply was announced to the Emperor, he demanded of Ho why his guest did not come when ordered. Ho replied, "I can assure your Majesty that Lí is a man of parts beyond all those of the age, one whose compositions astonish all who read them. At the trial of last year, his essay was marked out and thrown aside by the examiners, and he himself shamefully put out of the hall. Your Majesty now calling him to court, and he having neither title nor rank, his self-love is touched; but if your Majesty would hear your minister's prayer, and shed your favors upon his friend, and send a high officer to him, I am sure he will hasten to obey the imperial will." "Let it be so," rejoined the Emperor; "at the instance of our academician, we confer on Lí Peh the title of doctor of the first rank, with the purple robe, yellow girdle, and silken bonnet; and herewith also issue an order for him to present himself at court. Our academician Ho will charge himself with carrying this order, and bring Lí Peh to our presence without fail."

Ho returned home to Lí, and begged him to go to court to read the letter, adding how his Majesty depended on his help to relieve him from his present embarrassment. As soon as he had put on his new robes, which were those of a high examiner, he made his obeisance toward the palace, and hastened to mount his horse and enter it, following after the academician. Seated on his throne, Hwantsung impatiently awaited the arrival of the poet, who, prostrating himself before its steps, went through the ceremony of salutation and acknowledgment for the favors he had received, and then stood in his place. The Emperor, as soon as he saw Lí, rejoiced as poor men do on finding a treasure, or starvelings on sitting at a loaded table; his heart was like dark clouds suddenly illuminated, or parched and arid soil on the approach of rain. "Some foreign ambassadors have brought us a letter which no one can read, and we have sent for you, doctor, to relieve our anxiety." "Your minister's knowledge is very limited," politely replied Lí, with a bow, "for his essay was rejected by the judges at the examination, and lord Kao turned him out of doors. Now that he is called upon to read this letter from a foreign prince, how is it that the examiners are not charged with the answer, since, too, the ambassadors have already been kept so long waiting? Since I, a student turned off from the trial, could not satisfy the wishes of the examiners, how can I hope to meet the expectation of your Majesty?" "We know what you are good for," said the Emperor; "a truce to your excuses," putting the letter into his hands. Running his eyes over it, he disdainfully smiled, and standing before the throne, read off in Chinese the mysterious letter, as follows:

"Letter from the mighty Ko To of the kingdom of Po Hai to the prince of the dynasty of Tang: Since your usurpation of Corea, and carrying your conquests to the frontiers of our States, your soldiers have violated our territory in frequent raids. We trust you can fully explain to us this matter, and as we cannot patiently bear such a state of things, we have sent our ambassadors to announce to you that you must give up the hundred and sixty-six towns of Corea into our hands. We have some precious things to offer you in compensation, namely, the medicinal plants from the mountains of Tai Peh, and the byssus from the southern sea, gongs of Tsíching, stags from Fuyu, and horses from Sopin, silk of Wuchau, black fish from the river Meito, prunes from

Kiutu, and building materials from Loyu; some of all these articles shall be sent you. If you do not accept these propositions, we shall raise troops and carry war and destruction into your borders, and then see on whose side victory will remain."

After its perusal, to which they had given an attentive ear, the grandees were stupefied and looked at each other, knowing how improbable it was that the Emperor would accept the propositions of Ko To. Nor was the mind of his Majesty by any means satisfied, and after remaining silent for some time, he turned himself to the civil and military officers about him, and asked what means were available to repulse the attacks of the barbarians in case their forces invaded Corea. Scholars and generals remained mute as idols of clay or statues of wood; no one said a word, until Ho ventured to observe, "Your venerable grandfather Taitsung, in three expeditions against Corea, lost an untold number of soldiers, without succeeding in his enterprise, and impoverished his treasury. Thanks to Heaven Kai-su-wăn died, and profiting by the dissensions between the usurper's sons, the glorious Emperor Taitsung confided the direction of a million of veterans to the old generals Lí Sié and Pí Jinkwei, who, after a hundred engagements, more or less important, finally conquered the kingdom. But now having been at peace for a long time, we have neither generals nor soldiers; if we seize the buckler and lance, it will not be easy to resist, and our defeat will be certain. I await the wise determination of your Majesty."

"Since such is the case, what answer shall we make to the ambassadors?" said Hwantsung. "Deign to ask Lí," said the doctor; "he will speak to the purpose." On being interrogated by his sovereign, Lí replied, "Let not this matter trouble your clear mind. Give orders for an audience to the ambassadors, and I will speak to them face to face in their own language. The terms of the answer will make the barbarians blush, and their Ko To will be obliged to make his respects at the foot of your throne." "And who is this Ko To?" demanded Hwantsung. "It is the name the people of Po Hai give to their king after the usage of their country; just as the Hwui Hwui call theirs Kokan; the Tibetans, Tsangpo; the Lochau, Chau; the Holing, Sí-mo-wei: each one according to the custom of his nation."

At this rapid flood of explanations, the mind of the wise Hwantsung experienced a lively joy, and the same day he honored Lí with the title of an academician; a lodging was prepared for him in the palace of the Golden Bell; musicians made the place re-echo with their harmony; women poured out the wine, and young girls handed him the goblets, and celebrated the glory of Lí with the same voices that lauded the Emperor. What a delicious, ravishing banquet! He could hardly keep within the limits of propriety, but ate and drank until he was unconscious of anything, when the Emperor ordered the attendants to carry him into the palace and lay him on a bed.

The next morning, when the gong announced the fifth watch, the Emperor repaired to the hall of audience; but Lí's faculties, on awaking, were not very clear, though the officers hastened to bring him. When all had gone through their prostrations, Hwantsung called the poet near him, but perceiving that the visage of the new-made doctor still bore the marks of his debauch and discovering the discomposure of his mind, he sent into the kitchen for a little wine and some well-spiced fish broth, to arouse the sleepy bard. The servants presently sent it up on a golden tray, and the Emperor seeing the cup was fuming, condescended to stir and cool the broth a long time with the ivory chopsticks, and served it out himself to Lí, who, receiving it on his knees, ate and drank, while a pleasing joy illumined his countenance. While this was going on, some among the courtiers were much provoked and displeased at the strange familiarity, while others rejoiced to see how well the Emperor knew to conciliate the good will of men. The two examiners, Yang and Kao, betrayed in their features the dislike they felt.

At the command of the Emperor, the ambassadors were introduced, and saluted his Majesty by acclamation, whilst Lí Tai-peh, clad in a purple robe and silken bonnet, easy and gracious as an immortal, stood in the historiographer's place before the left of the throne, holding the letter in his hand, and read it off in a clear tone, without mistaking a word. Then turning toward the frightened envoys, he said, "Your little province has failed in its etiquette, but our wise ruler, whose power is comparable to the heavens for vastness, disdains to take advantage of it. This is the answer which he grants you: hear and be silent." The terrified ambassadors fell trembling at the foot of the throne. The Emperor had already prepared near him an ornamented cushion, and taking a jade stone with which to rub the ink, a pencil of leveret's hair bound in an ivory tube, a cake of perfumed ink, and a sheet of flowery paper, gave them to Lí, and seated him on the cushion ready to draw up the answer.

"May it please your Majesty," objected Lí, "my boots are not at all suitable, for they were soiled at the banquet last evening, and I trust your Majesty in your generosity will grant me some new buskins and stockings fit for ascending the platform." The Emperor acceded to his request, and ordered a servant to procure them; when Lí resumed, "Your minister has still a word to add, and begs beforehand that his untoward conduct may be excused; then he will prefer his request." "Your notions are misplaced and useless, but I will not be offended at them; go on, speak," said Hwantsung; to which Lí, nothing daunted, said, "At the last examination, your minister was turned off by Yang, and put out of doors by Kao. The sight of these persons here to-day at the head of the courtiers casts a certain discomposure over his spirits; let your voice deign to command Yang to rub my ink, whilst Kao puts on my stockings and laces up my buskins; then will my mind and wits begin to recover their energies, and my pencil can trace your answer in the language of the foreigners. In transmitting the reply in the name of the Son of Heaven, he will then not disappoint the confidence with which he is honored." Afraid to displease Lí when he had need of him, the Emperor gave the strange order; and while Yang rubbed the ink and Kao put on the buskins of the poet, they could not help reflecting, that this student, so badly received and treated by them, only fit at the best to render such services to them, availed himself now of the sudden favors of the Emperor to take their own words pronounced against him as a text, and revenge himself upon them for past injuries. But what could they do? They could not oppose the sovereign will, and if they did feel chagrined, they did not dare at least to express it. The proverb hath it true:

"Do not draw upon you a person's enmity, for enmity is never appeased; injury returns upon him who injures, and sharp words recoil against him who says them."

The poet triumphed, and his oath was accomplished. Buskined as he desired, he mounted the platform on the carpet and seated himself on the cushion, while Yang stood at his side and rubbed the ink. Of a truth, the disparity was great between an ink-grinder and the magnate who counselled the Emperor. But why did the poet sit while the premier stood like a servant at his side? It was because Lí was the organ of the monarch's words, while Yang, reduced to act the part of an ink-rubber, could not request permission to sit. With one hand Lí stroked his beard, and seizing his pencil in the other, applied it to the paper, which was soon covered with strange characters, well turned and even without a fault or rasure, and then laid it upon the dragon's table. The Emperor gazed at it in amaze, for it was identical with that of the barbarians; not a character in it resembled the Chinese; and as he handed it about among the nobles, their surprise was great. When requested to read it, Lí, placed before the throne, read in a clear loud tone the answer to the strangers:

"The mighty Emperor of the Tang dynasty, whose reign is called Kiayuen, sends his instructions to Ko To of the Po Hai.

"From ancient times the rock and the egg have not hit each other, nor the serpent and dragon made war. Our dynasty, favored by fate, extends its power, and reigns even to the four seas; it has under its orders brave generals and tried soldiers, solid bucklers and glittering swords. Your neighbor, King Hiehlí, who refused our alliance, was taken prisoner; but the people of Putsau, after offering a present of a metal bird, took an oath of obedience.

"The Sinlo, at the southern end of Corea, have sent us praises written on the finest tissues of silk; Persia, serpents which can catch rats; India, birds that can speak; and Rome, dogs which lead horses, holding a lantern in their mouth; the white parrot is a present from the kingdom of Koling, the carbuncle which illumines the night comes from Cambodia, and famous horses are sent by the tribe of Kolí, while precious vases are brought from Níal: in short, there is not a nation which does not respect our imposing power, and does not testify their regard for the virtue which distinguishes us. Corea alone resisted the will of Heaven, but the divine vengeance has fallen heavily upon it, and a kingdom which reckoned nine centuries of duration was overthrown as in a morning. Why, then, do you not profit by the terrible prognostics Heaven vouchsafes you as examples? Would it not evince your sagacity?

"Moreover, your little country, situated beyond the peninsula, is little more than as a province of Corea, or as a principality to the Celestial Empire; your resources in men and horses are not a millionth part those of China. You are like a chafed locust trying to stop a chariot, like a stiff-necked goose which will not submit. Under the arms of our warriors your blood will run a thousand *lí*. You, prince, resemble that audacious one who refused our alliance, and whose kingdom became annexed to Corea. The designs of our sage Emperor are vast as the ocean, and he now bears with your culpable and unreasonable conduct; but hasten to prevent misfortune by repentance, and cheerfully pay the tribute of each year, and you will prevent the shame and opprobrium which will cover you and expose you to the ridicule of your neighbors. Reflect thrice on these instructions."

The reading of this answer filled the Emperor with joy, who ordered Lí to make known its contents to the ambassadors; he then sealed it with the imperial seal. The poet called Kao to put on the boots which he had taken off, and he then returned to the palace of Golden Bells to inform the envoys concerning his sovereign's orders, reading the letter to them in a loud tone, while they heard tremblingly. The academician Ho reconducted them to the gates of the capital, and there the ambassadors asked who it was who had read the imperial instructions. "He is called Lí, and has the title of Doctor of the Hanlin." "But among so many dignitaries, why did the first Minister of State rub his ink, and the general of the guards lace up his buskins?" "Hear," added Ho; "those two personages are indeed intimate ministers of his Majesty, but they are only noble courtiers who do not transcend common humanity, while Doctor Lí, on the contrary, is an immortal descended from heaven on the earth to aid the sovereign of the Celestial Empire. How can any one equal him?" The ambassadors bowed the head and departed, and on their return rendered an account of their mission to their sovereign. On reading the answer of Lí, the Ko To was terrified, and deliberated with his counsellors: "The Celestial Empire is upheld by an immortal descended from the skies! Is it possible to attack it?" He thereupon wrote a letter of submission, testifying his desire to send tribute each year, which was thenceforth allowed.

Lí Tai-peh afterward drowned himself from fear of the machinations of his enemies, exclaiming, as he leaped into the water, "I'm going to catch the moon in the midst of the sea!"

The poetry of the Chinese has been investigated by Sir John Davis, and the republication of his first paper in an enlarged form in 1870, with the versification of Legge's translations of the *Shí King* by his nephew, and two volumes of various pieces by Stent, have altogether given a good variety.[1] Davis explains the principles of Chinese rhythm, touches upon the tones, notices the parallelisms, and distinguishes the various kinds of verse, all in a scholarly manner. The whole subject, however, still awaits more thorough treatment. Artificial poetry, where

---

[1] Davis, *Poetry of the Chinese*, London, 1870; G. C. Stent, *The Jade Chaplet*, London, 1874; *Entombed Alive, and other Verses*, 1878; Le Marquis D'Hervey-Saint-Denys, *Poésies de l'Epoque des Thang*, Paris, 1862. A number of extracts of classical and modern literature will be found in *Confucius and the Chinese Classics*, compiled by Rev. A. W. Loomis, San Francisco, 1867. *China Review*, Vols. I., p. 248, IV., p. 46, and passim.

the sound and jingle is regarded more than the sense, is not uncommon; the great number of characters having the same sound enables versifiers to do this with greater facility than is possible in other languages, and to the serious degradation of all high sentiment. The absence of inflections in the words cripples the easy flow of sounds to which our ears are familiar, but renders such lines as the following more spirited to the eye which sees the characters than to the ear which hears them:

Liang kiang, siang niang, yang hiang tsiang,
Ki ní, pí chí, lí hí mí, etc.

Lines consisting of characters all containing the same radical are also constructed in this manner, in which the sounds are subservient to the meaning. This bizarre fashion of writing is, however, considered fit only for pedants.

The Augustan age of poetry and letters was in the ninth and tenth centuries, during the Tang dynasty, when the brightest day of Chinese civilization was the darkest one of European. No complete collection of poems has yet been translated into any European language, and perhaps none would bear an entire version. The poems of Lí Tai-peh form thirty volumes, and those of Su Tung-po are contained in one hundred and fifteen volumes, while the collected poems of the times of the Tang dynasty have been published by imperial authority in nine hundred volumes. The proportion of descriptive poetry in it is small compared with the sentimental. The longest poem yet turned into English is the *Hwa Tsien Ki*, or 'The Flower's Petal,' by P. P. Thoms, under the title of *Chinese Courtship;* it is in heptameter, and his version is quite prosaic. Another of much greater repute among native scholars, called *Lí Sao*, or 'Dissipation of Sorrows,' dating from about B.C. 314, has been rendered into French by D'Hervey-Saint-Denys.[1]

It is a common pastime for literary gentlemen to try their

[1] *Chinese Courtship. In Verse. To which is added an Appendix treating of the Revenue of China*, etc., etc., by Peter Perring Thoms, London, 1824. Compare the *Quarterly Review* for 1827, pp. 496 ff. *Le Li-Sao, Poème du IIIe Siècle avant notre ère. Traduit du Chinois*, par le Marquis d'Hervey de Saint-Denys, Paris, 1870.

skill in versification; epigrams and pasquinades are usually put into metre, and at the examinations every candidate must hand in his poetical exercise. Consequently, much more attention is paid by such rhymesters to the jingle of the words and artificial structure of the lines than to the elevation of sentiment or copiousness of illustrations; it is as easy for them to write a sonnet on shipping a cargo of tea as to indite a love-epistle to their mistress. Extemporaneous verses are made on every subject, and to illustrate occurrences that are elsewhere regarded as too prosaic to disturb the muse.

Still, human emotions have been the stimulus to their expression in verse among the Chinese as well as other people; and all classes have found an utterance to them. Ribald and impure ditties are sung by street-singers to their own low classes, but such subjects do not characterize the best poets, as they did in old Rome. A piece called 'Chang Liang's Flute' is a fair instance of the better style of songs:

'Twas night—the tired soldiers were peacefully sleeping,
The low hum of voices was hushed in repose;
The sentries, in silence, a strict watch were keeping
'Gainst surprise or a sudden attack of their foes;

When a low mellow note on the night air came stealing,
So soothingly over the senses it fell—
So touchingly sweet—so soft and appealing,
Like the musical tones of an aërial bell.

Now rising, now falling—now fuller and clearer—
Now liquidly soft—now a low wailing cry;
Now the cadences seem floating nearer and nearer—
Now dying away in a whispering sigh.

Then a burst of sweet music, so plaintively thrilling,
Was caught up by the echoes which sang the refrains
In their many-toned voices—the atmosphere filling
With a chorus of dulcet mysterious strains.

The sleepers arouse, and with beating hearts listen;
In their dreams they had heard that weird music before;
It touches each heart—with tears their eyes glisten,
For it tells them of those they may never see more.

In fancy those notes to their childhood's days brought them,
To those far-away scenes they had not seen for years;
To those who had loved them, had reared them, and taught them,
And the eyes of those stern men were wetted with tears.

Bright visions of home through their mem'ries came thronging,
Panorama-like passing in front of their view;
They were *home-sick*—no power could withstand that strange yearning;
The longer they listened the more home-sick they grew.

Whence came those sweet sounds?—who the unseen musician
That breathes out his soul, which floats on the night breeze
In melodious sighs—in strains so elysian
As to soften the hearts of rude soldiers like these?

Each looked at the other, but no word was spoken,
The music insensibly tempting them on:
They must return home. Ere the daylight had broken
The enemy looked, and behold! they were gone.

There's a magic in music—a witchery in it,
Indescribable either with tongue or with pen;
The flute of Chang Liang, in one little minute,
Had stolen the courage of eight thousand men![1]

The following verses were presented to Dr. Parker at Canton by a Chinese gentleman of some literary attainments, upon the occasion of a successful operation for cataract. The original may be considered as a very creditable example of extempore sonnet:

A fluid, darksome and opaque, long time had dimmed my sight,
For seven revolving, weary years one eye was lost to light;
The other, darkened by a film, during three years saw no day,
High heaven's bright and gladd'ning light could not pierce it with its ray.

Long, long I sought the hoped relief, but still I sought in vain,
My treasures lavished in the search, brought no relief from pain;
Till, at length, I thought my garments I must either pawn or sell,
And plenty in my house, I feared, was never more to dwell.

Then loudly did I ask, for what cause such pain I bore—
For transgressions in a former life unatoned for before?
But again came the reflection how, of yore, oft men of worth,
For slight errors, had borne suff'ring great as drew my sorrow forth.

---

[1] Stent's *Jade Chaplet.*

" And shall not one," said I then, " whose worth is but as naught,
Bear patiently, as heaven's gift, what it ordains ?" The thought
Was scarce completely formed, when of a friend the footstep fell
On my threshold, and I breathed a hope he had words of joy to tell.

" I've heard," the friend who enter'd said, " there's come to us of late
A native of the 'Flowery Flag's' far-off and foreign State ;
O'er tens of thousand miles of sea to the Inner Land he's come—
His hope and aim to heal men's pain, he leaves his native home."

I quick went forth, this man I sought, this gen'rous doctor found ;
He gained my heart, he's kind and good ; for, high up from the ground,
He gave a room, to which he came, at morn, at eve, at night—
Words were but vain were I to try his kindness to recite.

With needle argentine he pierced the cradle of the tear.
What fears I felt ! Su Tung-po's words rung threat'ning in my ear:
" Glass hung in mist," the poet says, " take heed you do not shake ;"
(The words of fear rung in my ear), " how if it chance to break ! "

The fragile lens his needle pierced : the dread, the sting, the pain,
I thought on these, and that the cup of sorrow I must drain ;
But then my mem'ry faithful showed the work of fell disease,
How long the orbs of sight were dark, and I deprived of ease.

And thus I thought : " If now, indeed, I were to find relief,
'Twere not too much to bear the pain, to bear the present grief."
Then the words of kindness which I heard sunk deep into my soul,
And free from fear I gave myself to the foreigner's control.

His silver needle sought the lens, and quickly from it drew
The opaque and darksome fluid, whose effect so well I knew ;
His golden probe soon clear'd the lens, and then my eyes he bound,
And laved with water sweet as is the dew to thirsty ground.

Three days thus lay I, prostrate, still ; no food then could I eat ;
My limbs relax'd were stretched as though th' approach of death to meet
With thoughts astray—mind ill at ease—away from home and wife,
I often thought that by a thread was hung my precious life.

Three days I lay, no food had I, and nothing did I feel ;
Nor hunger, sorrow, pain, nor hope, nor thought of woe or weal ;
My vigor fled, my life seemed gone, when, sudden, in my pain,
There came one ray—one glimm'ring ray,—I see,—I live again !

As starts from visions of the night he who dreams a fearful dream,
As from the tomb uprushing comes one restored to day's bright beam,
Thus I, with gladness and surprise, with joy, with keen delight,
See friends and kindred crowd around ; I hail the blessed light.

With grateful heart, with heaving breast, with feelings flowing o'er,
I cried, "O lead me quick to him who can the sight restore!"
To kneel I tried, but he forbade; and, forcing me to rise,
"To mortal man bend not the knee;" then pointing to the skies:—

"I'm but," said he, "the workman's tool; another's is the hand;
Before *his* might, and in *his* sight, men, feeble, helpless, stand:
Go, virtue learn to cultivate, and never thou forget
That for some work of future good thy life is spared thee yet!"

The off'ring, token of my thanks, he refused; nor would he take
Silver or gold—they seemed as dust; 'tis but for virtue's sake
His works are done. His skill divine I ever must adore,
Nor lose remembrance of his name till life's last day is o'er.

Thus have I told, in these brief words, this learned doctor's praise:
Well does his worth deserve that I should tablets to him raise.

In this facility of versification lies one of the reasons for the mediocrity of common Chinese poetry, but that does not prevent its power over the popular mind being very great. Men and women of all classes take great delight in recitation and singing, hearing street musicians or strolling play-actors; and these results, whatever we may judge by our standards, prove its power and suitableness to influence them. One or two additional specimens on different subjects may be quoted, inasmuch as they also illustrate some of the better shades of feeling and sentiment. A more finished piece of poetry is one written about A.D. 370, by Su-Hwui, whose husband was banished. Its talented authoress is said to have written more than five thousand lines, and among them a curious anagram of about eight hundred characters, which was so disposed that it would make sense equally well when read up or down, crosswise, backward, or forward.[1] Nothing from her pen remains

[1] A translation is given in the *Chinese Repository* (Vol. IX., p. 508) of a supposed complaint made by a cow of her sad lot in being obliged to work hard and fare poorly during life, and then be cut up and eaten when dead; the ballad is arranged in the form of the animal herself, and a herdboy leading her, who in his own form praises the happiness of a rural life. This ballad is a Buddhist tractate, and that fraternity print many such on broad-sheets; one common collection of prayers is arranged like a pagoda, with images of Buddha sitting in the windows of each story.

except this ode, interesting for its antiquity as well as sentiment.

ODE OF SU-HWUI.

When thou receiv'dst the king's command to quiet the frontier,
Together to the bridge we went, striving our hearts to cheer—
Hiding our grief. These words I gasped upon that mournful day :
"Forget not, love, my fond embrace, nor tarry long away!"
Ah! Is it true that since that time no message glads my sight ?
Think you that *now* your lone wife's heart even in bright spring delights ?
Our pearly stairs and pleasant yard the foul weeds have o'ergrown ;
Our nuptial room—and couch—and walls—are now with dust o'erstrown.
Whene'er I think of our farewell, my soul with fear grows cold;
My mind resolves what shape I'd take to see thee as of old.
Now as I watch the deep-sea moon, I long her form to be;
Again, the mountain cloud has filled my dull heart with envy.
For deep-sea moon shines year by year upon the land abroad ;
And ye, O mountain clouds, may meet the form of my adored!
Aye, flying here and flying there, seek my beloved's place,
And at ten thousand thousand miles—speed!—gaze on his fair face.
Alas! for *me* the road is long, steep mountain peaks now sever
Our loving souls. I can but weep—O! may't not be forever!
The long reed's leaves had yellow grown when we our farewell said ;
Who then had thought the plum-tree's bough so oft would turn to red ?
The fairy flowers spreading their leaves have met the early spring—
Ah, genial months, what time for love!—But who can ease *my* sting ?
The pendant willows strew the court, for thee I pull them down ;
The falling flowers enrich the earth, none pick these from the ground
And scatter vernal growth, as once, before the ancestral tomb!
Taking the lute of Tsun I strive to chase away the gloom
By thrumming, as I muse of thee, songs of departed friends.
Sending my inmost thoughts away, they reach the northern ends—
Those northern bounds!—how far they seem, o'erpassed the hills and streams
No news, no word from those confines to lighten e'en my dreams!
My dress, my pillow, once so white, are deeply stained with tears ;
My broidered coat with gilded flowers, all spotted now appears.
The very geese and storks to me, when in their passage north,
Seemed by their cries, my distant love, to tear my heartstrings forth.
No more my lute—though thou wert strong, with passion was I wrung;
My grief was its utmost bent—my song was still unsung.
Ah! husband, lord, thy love I feel is stable as the hills ;
'Tis joy to think each hour of this—a balm for countless ills!

I had but woven half my task—I gave it to his Grace:
O grant my husband quick release, I pine for his embrace!

Among the best of Chinese ballads, if regard be had to the character of the sentiment and metaphors, is one on Picking Tea, which the girls and women sing as they collect the leaves.

BALLAD OF THE TEA-PICKER.

I.

Where thousand hills the vale enclose, our little hut is there,
And on the sloping sides around the tea grows everywhere;
And I must rise at early dawn, as busy as can be,
To get my daily labor done, and pluck the leafy tea.

II.

At early dawn I seize my crate, and sighing, Oh, for rest!
Thro' the thick mist I pass the door, with sloven hair half drest;
The dames and maidens call to me, as hand in hand they go,
"What steep do you, miss, climb to-day—what steep of high Sunglo?"

III.

Dark is the sky, the twilight dim still on the hills is set;
The dewy leaves and cloudy buds may not be gathered yet:
Oh, who are they, the thirsty ones, for whom this work we do,
For whom we spend our daily toil in bands of two and two?

IV.

Like fellows we each other aid, and to each other say,
As down we pull the yielding twigs, "Sweet sister, don't delay;
E'en now the buds are growing old, all on the boughs atop,
And then to-morrow—who can tell?—the drizzling rain may drop."

V.

We've picked enow; the topmost bough is bare of leaves; and so
We lift our brimming loads, and by the homeward path we go;
In merry laughter by the pool, the lotus pool, we hie,
When hark! uprise a mallard pair, and hence affrighted fly.

VI.

Limpid and clear the pool, and there how rich the lotus grows,
And only half its opening leaves, round as the coins, it shows—
I bend me o'er the jutting brink, and to myself I say,
"I marvel in the glassy stream, how looks my face to-day?"

VII.

My face is dirty; out of trim my hair is, and awry;
Oh, tell me, where's the little girl so ugly now as I?
'Tis all because whole weary hours I'm forced to pick the tea,
And driving winds and soaking showers have made me what you see!

VIII.

With morn again come wind and rain, and though so fierce and strong,
With basket big, and little hat, I wend my way along;
At home again, when all is picked, and everybody sees
How muddy all our dresses are, and drabbled to the knees.

IX.

I saw this morning through the door a pleasant day set in;
Be sure I quickly dressed my hair and neatly fixed my pin,
And fleetly sped I down the path to gain the wonted spot,
But, never thinking of the mire, my working shoes forgot!

X.

The garden reached, my bow-shaped shoes are soaking through and through;
The sky is changed—the thunder rolls—and I don't know what to do;
I'll call my comrades on the hill to pass the word with speed
And fetch my green umbrella-hat to help me in my need.

XI.

But my little hat does little good; my plight is very sad!
I stand with clothes all dripping wet, like some poor fisher-lad;
Like him I have a basket, too, of meshes woven fine—
A fisher-lad, if I only had his fishing-rod and line.

XII.

The rain is o'er; the outer leaves their branching fibres show;
Shake down the branch, the fragrant scent about us 'gins to blow;
Gather the yellow golden threads that high and low are found—
Oh, what a precious odor now is wafted all around!

XIII.

No sweeter perfume does the wild and fair Aglaia shed,
Throughout Wu-yuen's bounds my tea the choicest will be said;
When all are picked we'll leave the shoots to bud again in spring,
But for this morning we have done the third, last gathering.

XIV.

Oh, weary is our picking, yet do I my toil withhold?
My maiden locks are all askew, my pearly fingers cold;
I only wish our tea to be superior over all,
O'er this one's "sparrow-tongue," and o'er the other's "dragon-ball."

XV.

Oh, for a month I weary strive to find a leisure day;
I go to pick at early dawn, and until dusk I stay;
Till midnight at the firing-pan I hold my irksome place:
But will not labor hard as this impair my pretty face?

XVI.

But if my face be somewhat lank, more firm shall be my mind;
I'll fire my tea that all else shall be my golden buds behind;
But yet the thought arises who the pretty maid shall be
To put the leaves in jewelled cup, from thence to sip my tea.

XVII.

Her griefs all flee as she makes her tea, and she is glad; but oh,
Where shall she learn the toils of us who labor for her so?
And shall she know of the winds that blow, and the rains that pour their wrath,
And drench and soak us thro' and thro', as plunged into a bath?

XVIII.

In driving rains and howling winds the birds forsake the nest,
Yet many a loving pair are seen still on the boughs to rest;
Oh, wherefore, loved one, with light look, didst thou send me away?
I cannot, grieving as I grieve, go through my work to-day.

XIX.

But though my bosom rise and fall, like bucket in a well,
Patient and toiling as I am, 'gainst work I'll ne'er rebel;
My care shall be to have my tea fired to a tender brown,
And let the *flag* and *awl*, well rolled, display their whitish down.[1]

XX.

Ho! for my toil! Ho! for my steps! Aweary though I be,
In our poor house, for working folk, there's lots of work, I see;
When the firing and the drying's done, off at the call I go,
And once again, this very morn, I climb the high Sunglo.

XXI.

My wicker basket slung on arm, and hair entwined with flowers,
To the slopes I go of high Sunglo, and pick the tea for hours;
How laugh we, sisters, on the road; what a merry turn we've got;
I giggle and say, as I point down the way, There, look, there lies our cot!

XXII.

Your handmaid 'neath the sweet green shade in sheltered cot abides,
Where the pendant willow's sweeping bough the thatchy dwelling hides;
To-morrow, if you wish it so, my guests I pray you'll be!
The door you'll know by the fragrant scent, the scent of the firing tea.

---

[1] The *kí*, or 'flag,' is the term by which the leaflets are called when they just begin to unroll; the *tsiang*, or 'awl,' designates those leaves which are still wrapped up and which are somewhat sharp.

XXIII.

Awhile 'tis cold, and then 'tis warm, when I want to fire my tea,
The sky is sure to shift and change—and all to worry me;
When the sun goes down on the western hills, on the eastern there is rain!
And however fair he promises, he promises in vain.

XXIV.

To-day the tint of the western hills is looking bright and fair,
And I bear my crate to the stile,[1] and wait my fellow toiler there;
A little tender lass is she—she leans upon the rail
And sleeps, and though I hail her she answers not my hail.

XXV.

And when at length to my loudest call she murmurs a reply,
'Tis as if hard to conquer sleep, and with half-opened eye;
Up starts she, and with straggling steps along the path she's gone;
She brings her basket, but forgets to put the cover on!

XXVI.

Together trudge we, and we pass the lodge of the southern bowers,
Where the beautiful sea-pomegranate waves all its yellow flowers;
Fain would we stop and pluck a few to deck our tresses gay,
But the tree is high, and 'tis vain to try and reach the tempting spray.

XXVII.

The pretty birds upon the boughs sing songs so sweet to hear,
And the sky is so delicious now, half cloudy and half clear;
While bending o'er her work, each maid will prattle of her woe,
And we talk till our hearts are sorely hurt, and tears unstinted flow.

XXVIII.

Our time is up, and yet not full our baskets to the mouth—
The twigs anorth are fully searched, let's seek them in the south;
Just then by chance I snapped a twig whose leaves were all apair;
See, with my taper fingers now I fix it in my hair.

XXIX.

Of all the various kinds of tea, the bitter beats the sweet,
But for whomever either seeks, for him I'll find a treat;
Though who it is shall drink them, as bitter or sweet they be,
I know not, my friend—but the pearly end of my finger only see!

---

[1] The *ting* is not exactly a stile, being a kind of shed, or four posts supporting a roof, which is often erected by villagers for the convenience of wayfarers, who can stop there and rest. It sometimes contains a bench or seat, and is usually over or near a spring of water.

XXX.

Ye twittering swallows, rise and fall in your flight around the hill,
But when next I go to the high Sunglo, I'll change my gown—I will;
And I'll roll up the cuff and show arm enough, for my arm is fair to see:
Oh, if ever there were a fair round arm, that arm belongs to me!

In the department of plays and dramas, Chinese literature shows a long list of names, few or none of which have ever been heard of away from their native soil. Some of their pieces have been translated by Julien, Bazin, Davis, and others, most of which were selected from the *Hundred Plays of Yuen*. The origin of the present Chinese drama does not date back, according to M. Bazin, beyond the Tang dynasty, though many performances designed to be played and sung in pantomime had been written before that epoch. He cites the names of eighty-one persons, besides mentioning other plays of unknown authors, whose combined writings amount to five hundred and sixty-four separate plays; all of whom flourished during the Mongol dynasty. The plays that have been translated from this collection give a tolerably good idea of Chinese talent in this difficult department; and, generally speaking, whatever strictures may be made upon the management of the plot, exhibition of character, unity of action, or illustration of manners, the tendency of the play is on the side of justice and morality. Père Prémare first translated a play in 1731, under the title of the *Orphan of Chau*,[1] which was taken by Voltaire as the groundwork of one of his plays. *The Heir in Old Age* and the *Sorrows of Han* are the names of two translated by Sir J. F. Davis. The *Circle of Chalk* was translated and published in 1832 by Julien, and a volume of Bazin, aîné, containing the *Intrigues of an Abigail*, the *Compared Tunic*, the *Songstress*, and *Resentment of Tau Ngo*, appeared in 1838, at Paris. None of these pieces exhibit much intricacy of plot, nor would the simple arrangements of Chinese theatres allow much increase to the *dramatis personæ* without confusion. M. Bazin, moreover, translated the *Pí-pa Kí*, or *History of a Lute*,

[1] *Tchao-chi-cou-eulh, ou l'Orphelin de la Maison de Tchao, tragédie chinoise, traduite* par le R. P. de Prémare, Miss. de la Chine, 1755. Julien published a translation of the same, Paris, 1834.

a drama in twenty-four acts, of more pretensions, partaking of the novel as well as the drama; the play is said to have been represented at Peking in 1404, under the Ming dynasty.[1]

Besides plays in the higher walks of the drama, which form the principal part of the performances at theatres, there are by-plays or farces, which, being confined to two or three interlocutors, depend for their attractiveness upon the droll gesticulations, impromptu allusions to passing occurrences, and excellent pantomimic action of the performers. They are usually brought on at the conclusion of the bill, and from the freedom given in them to an exhibition of the humor or wit of the players, are much liked by the people. A single illustration will exhibit the simple range and character of these burlettas.

THE MENDER OF CRACKED CHINAWARE.

DRAMATIS PERSONÆ. { *Niu Chau*........ A wandering tinker.
Wang Niang...... A young girl.

Scene—A Street.

NIU CHAU *enters—across his shoulder is a bamboo, to each end of which are suspended boxes containing the various tools and implements of his trade, and a small stool. He is dressed meanly; his face and head are painted and decorated in a fantastic manner.*

(*Sings*) Seeking a livelihood by the work of my hands,
Daily do I traverse the streets of the city.
(*Speaks*) Well, here I am, a mender of broken jars,
An unfortunate victim of ever changing plans.
To repair old fractured jars
Is my sole occupation and support.
'Tis even so. I have no other employment.

(*Takes his boxes from his shoulder, places them on the ground, sits beside them, and drawing out his fan, continues speaking*)—

A disconsolate old man—I am a slave to inconveniences.
For several days past I have been unable to go abroad,

---

[1] Since the appearance of M. Bazin's *Théâtre Chinois* (Paris, 1838) and Davis' *Sorrows of Han* (London, 1829), there has been astonishingly little done in the study of Chinese plays. Compare, for the rest, an article on this subject by J. J. Ampère, in the *Revue des Deux Mondes*, September, 1838; *The Far East*, Vol. I. (1876), pp. 57 and 90; *Chinese Repository*, Vol. VI., p. 575; *China Review*, Vol. I., p. 26; also Lay's *Chinese as They Are*, and Dr. Gray's *China*, passim. Lieut. Kreitner gives an interesting picture of the Chinese theatre in a country town, together with a few pages upon the drama, of which his party were spectators. *Im fernen Osten*, pp. 595–599.

But, observing this morning a clear sky and fine air,
I was induced to recommence my street wanderings.
(*Sings*) At dawn I left my home,
But as yet have had no job.
Hither and yon, and on all sides,
From the east gate to the west,
From the south gate to the north,
And all over within the walls,
Have I been, but no one has called
For the mender of cracked jars. Unfortunate man!
But this being my first visit to the city of Nanking,
Some extra exertion is necessary;
Time is lost sitting idle here, and so to roam again I go.

(*Shoulders his boxes and stool, and walks about, crying*)—

Plates mended! Bowls mended!
Jars and pots neatly repair'd!

Lady Wang (*heard within*). Did I not hear the cry of the mender of cracked jars?
I'll open the door and look. (*She enters, looking around.*)
Yes, there comes the repairer of jars.

Niu Chau. Pray, have you a jar to mend?
I have long been seeking a job.
Did you not call?

Lady W. What is your charge for a large jar—
And how much for a small one?

Niu Chau. For large jars, one mace five.

Lady W. And for small ones?

Niu Chau. Fifty pair of cash.

Lady W. To one mace five, and fifty pair of cash,
Add nine candareens, and a new jar may be had.

Niu Chau. What, then, will you give?

Lady W. I will give one candareen for either size.

Niu Chau. Well, lady, how many cash can I get for this candareen?

Lady W. Why, if the price be high, you will get eight cash.

Niu Chau. And if low?

Lady W. You will get but seven cash and a half.

Niu Chau. Oh, you wicked, tantalizing thing!
(*Sings*) Since leaving home this morning,
I have met but with a trifler,
Who, in the shape of an old wife,
Tortures and gives me no job;
I'll shoulder again my boxes, and continue my walk,
And never again will I return to the house of Wang.

(*He moves off slowly.*)

Lady W. Jar-mender! return, quickly return; with a loud voice, I entreat you; for I have something on which I wish to consult with you.

Niu Chau. What is it on which you wish to consult me?
Lady W. I will give you a hundred cash to mend a large jar.
Niu Chau. And for mending a small one?
Lady W. And for mending a small one, thirty pair of cash.
Niu Chau. One hundred, and thirty pair!—truly, lady, this is worth consulting about.
Lady Wang, where shall I mend them?
Lady W. Follow me. (*They move toward the door of the house.*)
(*Sings*) Before walks the Lady Wang.
Niu Chau. And behind comes the *pu-kang* (or jar-mender).
Lady W. Here, then, is the place.
Niu Chau. Lady Wang, permit me to pay my respects.
(*Bows repeatedly in a ridiculous manner.*)
We can exchange civilities.
I congratulate you; may you prosper—before and behind.
Lady W. Here is the jar; now go to work and mend it.
(*Takes the jar in his hand and tosses it about, examining it.*)
Niu Chau. This jar has certainly a very appalling fracture.
Lady W. Therefore, it requires the more care in mending.
Niu Chau. That is self-evident.
Lady W. Now, Lady Wang will retire again to her dressing room,
And, after closing the door, will resume her toilet.
Her appearance she will beautify;
On the left, her hair she will comb into a dragon's head tuft,
On the right, she will arrange it tastefully with flowers;
Her lips she will color with blood-red vermilion,
And a gem of chrysoprase will she place in the dragon's head tuft.
Then, having completed her toilet, she will return to the door,
And sit down to look at the jar-mender. (*Exit.*)

(*Niu Chau sits down, straps the jar on his knee, and arranges his tools before him, and as he drills holes for the clamps, sings*)—

Every hole drilled requires a pin,
And every two holes drilled require pins a pair.
As I raise my head and look around,

(*At this moment Lady Wang re-enters, beautifully dressed, and sits down by the door.*)

There sits, I see, a delicate young lady;
Before she had the appearance of an old wife,
Now she is transformed into a handsome young girl.
On the left, her hair is comb'd into a dragon's head tuft;
On the right it is adorn'd tastefully with flowers.
Her lips are like plums, her mouth is all smiles,
Her eyes are as brilliant as the phœnix's; and
She stands on golden lilies, but two inches long.
I look again, another look,—down drops the jar.
(*The jar at this moment falls, and is broken to pieces.*)

(*Speaks*) Heigh-ya! Here then is a dreadful smash!

Lady W. You have but to replace it with another, and do so quickly.

Niu Chau. For one that was broken, a good one must be given.
Had two been broken, then were a pair to be supplied;
An old one being smashed, a new one must replace it.

Lady W. You have destroyed the jar, and return me nothing but words.
Give me a new one, then you may return home,—not before.

Niu Chau. Here upon my knees upon the hard ground, I beg Lady Wang, while she sits above, to listen to a few words. Let me receive pardon for the accident her beauty has occasioned, and I will at once make her my wife.

Lady W. Impudent old man! How presume to think
That I ever can become your wife!

Niu Chau. Yes, it is true, I am somewhat older than Lady Wang,
Yet would I make her my wife.

Lady W. No matter then for the accident, but leave me now at once.

Niu Chau. Since you have forgiven me, I again shoulder my boxes,
And I will go elsewhere in search of a wife.
And here, before high heaven, I swear never again to come near the house of Wang.
You a great lady! You are but a vile ragged girl,
And will yet be glad to take up with a much worse companion.

(*Going away, he suddenly throws off his upper dress, and appears as a handsome young man.*)

Lady W. Henceforth, give up your wandering profession,
And marrying me, quit the trade of a jar-mender.
With the Lady Wang pass happily the remainder of your life.

(*They embrace, and exeunt.*)

Such is the general range and survey of Chinese literature, according to the Catalogue of the Imperial Libraries. It is, take it in a mass, a stupendous monument of human toil, fitly compared, so far as it is calculated to instruct its readers in useful knowledge, to their Great Wall, which can neither protect from its enemies, nor be of any real use to its makers. Its deficiencies are glaring. No treatises on the geography of foreign countries nor truthful narratives of travels abroad are contained in it, nor any account of the languages of their inhabitants, their history, or their governments. Philological works in other languages than those spoken within the Empire are unknown, and must, owing to the nature of the language, remain so until foreigners prepare them. Works on natural history, medicine, and physiology are few and useless, while those on mathematics and the exact sciences are much less popular and useful than they might be; and in the great range of theology, founded on the true basis of the Bible, there is almost nothing. The character of the people has been mostly formed by their ancient books, and this correlate influence has tended to repress independent investigation in the pursuit of truth, though not to destroy it. A new infusion of science, religion, and descriptive geography and history will lead to comparison with other countries, and bring out whatever in it is good.

A survey of this body of literature shows the effect of governmental patronage, in maintaining its character for what appears to us to be a wearisome uniformity. New ideas, facts, and motives must now come from the outer world, which will gradually elevate the minds of the people above the same unvarying channel. If the scholar knows that the goal he strives for is to be attained by proficiency in the single channel of classical knowledge, he cannot be expected to attend to other studies until he has secured the prize. A knowledge of medicine, mathematics, geography, or foreign languages, might, indeed, do the candidate much more good than all he gets out of the classics, but knowledge is not his object; and where all run the same race, all must study the same works. But let there be a different programme of themes and essays, and a wider range of subjects required of the students, and the present system of governmental examinations in China, with all its imperfections, can be made of great benefit to the people, if it is not put to a strain too great for the end in view.

The Chinese are fond of proverbs and aphorisms. They employ them in their writings and conversation as much as any people, and adorn their houses by copying them upon elegant scrolls, carving them upon pillars, and embroidering them upon banners. A complete collection of the proverbs of the Chinese has never been made, even among the people themselves any more than among those of other lands. Davis published, in 1828, a volume called *Moral Maxims*, containing two hundred aphorisms; P. Perny issued an assortment of four hundred and forty-one in 1869; and J. Doolittle collected several hundred proverbs, signs, couplets, and scrolls in his *Vocabulary.* Besides these, a collection of two thousand seven hundred and twenty proverbs was published in 1875 by W. Scarborough, furnished with a good index, and, like the others noted here, with the original text. Davis mentions the *Ming Sin Pao Kien*, or 'Jewelled Mirror for Illumining the Mind,' as containing a large number of proverbs. The *Ku Sz' Kiung Lin*, or 'Coral Forest of Ancient Matters,' is a similar collection; but if that be compared to a dictionary of quotations, this is better likened to a classical dictionary, the notes which follow the sentences leaving the reader in no doubt as to their meaning.

Manuscript lists of sentences suitable for hanging upon doors or in parlors are collected by persons who write them at New Year's, and whose success depends upon their facility in quoting elegant couplets. The following selection will exhibit to some extent this branch of Chinese wisdom and wit:

Not to distinguish properly between the beautiful and ugly, is like attaching a dog's tail to a squirrel's body.

An avaricious man, who can never have enough, is as a serpent wishing to swallow an elephant.

While one misfortune is going, to have another coming, is like driving a tiger out of the front door, while a wolf is entering the back.

The tiger's cub cannot be caught without going into his den.

To paint a snake and add legs. (Exaggeration.)

To sketch a tiger and make it a dog, is to imitate a work of genius and spoil it.

To ride a fierce dog to catch a lame rabbit. (Useless power over a contemptible enemy.)

To attack a thousand tigers with ten men. (To attempt a difficulty with incommensurate means.)

To cut off a hen's head with a battle-axe. (Unnecessary valor.)

To cherish a bad man is like nourishing a tiger; if not well fed he will devour you: or like rearing a hawk; if hungry he will stay by you, but fly away when fed.

To instigate a villain to do wrong is like teaching a monkey to climb trees.

To catch a fish and throw away the net;—not to requite benefits.

To take a locust's shank for the shaft of a carriage;—an inefficient person doing important work.

A pigeon sneering at a roc;—a mean man despising a prince.

To climb a tree to catch a fish, is to talk much and get nothing.

To test one good horse by judging the portrait of another.

A fish sports in the kettle, but his life will not be long.

Like a swallow building her nest on a hut is an anxious statesman.

Like a crane among hens is a man of parts among fools.

Like a sheep dressed in a tiger's skin is a superficial scholar.

Like a cuckoo in a magpie's nest is one who enjoy's another's labor.

To hang on the tail of a beautiful horse. (To seek promotion.)

Do not pull up your stockings in a melon field, or arrange your hat under a peach tree, lest people think you are stealing.

An old man marrying a young wife is like a withered willow sprouting.

Let us get drunk to-day while we have wine; the sorrows of to-morrow may be borne to-morrow.

If the blind lead the blind, they will both go to the pit.

Good iron is not used for nails, nor are soldiers made of good men.

A fair wind raises no storm.

A little impatience subverts great undertakings.

Vast chasms can be filled, but the heart of man is never satisfied.

The body may be healed, but the mind is incurable.

When the tree falls the monkeys flee.

Trouble neglected becomes still more troublesome.

Wood is not sold in the forest, nor fish at the pool.

He who looks at the sun is dazzled, he who hears the thunder is deafened. (Do not come too near the powerful.)

He desires to hide his tracks, and walks on the snow.

He seeks the ass, and lo! he sits upon him.

Speak not of others, but convict yourself.

A man is not always known by his looks, nor the sea measured by a bushel.

Ivory does not come from a rat's mouth.

If a chattering bird be not placed in the mouth, vexation will not sit between the eyebrows.

Prevention is better than cure.

For the Emperor to break the laws is one with the people's doing so.

Doubt and distraction are on earth, the brightness of truth in heaven.

Punishment can oppose a barrier to open crime, laws cannot reach to secret offences.

Wine and good dinners make abundance of friends, but in time of adversity not one is to be found.

Let every man sweep the snow from before his own doors, and not trouble himself about the hoarfrost on his neighbor's tiles.

Better be upright with poverty than depraved with abundance. He whose virtue exceeds his talents is the good man; he whose talents exceed his virtues is the fool.

Though a man may be utterly stupid, he is very perspicuous when reprehending the bad actions of others; though he may be very intelligent, he is dull enough when excusing his own faults: do you only correct yourselves on the same principle that you correct others, and excuse others on the same principles you excuse yourselves.[1]

If I do not debauch other men's wives, my own will not be polluted.

Better not be than be nothing.

The egg fights with the rock—hopeless resistance.

One thread does not make a rope; one swallow does not make a summer.

To be fully fed and warmly clothed, and dwell at ease without learning, is little better than a bestial state.

A woman in one house cannot eat the rice of two. (A wise woman does not marry again.)

Though the sword be sharp, it will not wound the innocent.

Sensuality is the chief of sins, filial duty the best of acts.

Prosperity is a blessing to the good, but to the evil it is a curse.

Instruction pervades the heart of the wise, but cannot penetrate the ears of a fool.

The straightest trees are first felled; the cleanest wells first drunk up.

The yielding tongue endures; the stubborn teeth perish.

The life of the aged is like a candle placed between two doors—easily blown out.

The blind have the best ears, and the deaf the sharpest eyes.

The horse's back is not so safe as the buffalo's. (The politician is not so secure as the husbandman.)

A wife should excel in four things: virtue, speech, deportment, and needlework.

He who is willing to inquire will excel, but the self-sufficient man will fail.

Anger is like a little fire, which if not timely checked may burn down a lofty pile.

Every day cannot be a feast of lanterns.

Too much lenity multiplies crime.

If you love your son, give him plenty of the cudgel; if you hate him, cram him with dainties.

When the mirror is highly polished, the dust will not defile it; when the heart is enlightened with wisdom, impure thoughts will not arise in it.

A stubborn wife and stiffnecked son no laws can govern.

He is my teacher who tells me my faults, my enemy who speaks my virtues.

He has little courage who knows the right and does it not.

To sue a flea, and catch a bite—the results of litigation.

Would you understand the character of a prince, look at his ministers; or the disposition of a man, observe his companions; or that of a father, first mark his son.

The fame of good deeds does not leave a man's door, but his evil acts are known a thousand miles off.

---

[1] The commendation by Lord Brougham of this "admirable precept," as he called it, is cited by Sir J. Davis.

A virtuous woman is a source of honor to her husband, a vicious one disgraces him.

The original tendency of man's heart is to do right, and if well ordered will not of itself be mistaken.

They who respect themselves will be honored, but disesteeming ourselves we shall be despised.

The load a beggar cannot carry he himself begged.

The happy-hearted man carries joy for all the household.

The more mouths to eat so much the more meat.

The higher the rat creeps up the cow's horn the narrower he finds it.

CHAPTER XIII.

ARCHITECTURE, DRESS, AND DIET OF THE CHINESE.

It is a sensible remark of De Guignes,[1] that "the habit we fall into of conceiving things according to the words which express them, often leads us into error when reading the relations of travellers. Such writers have seen objects altogether new, but they are compelled, when describing them, to employ equivalent terms in their own language in order to be understood; while these same terms tend to deceive the reader, who imagines that he sees such palaces, colonnades, peristyles, etc., under these designations as he has been used to, when, in fact, they are quite another thing." The same observation is true of other things than architecture, and of other nations than the Chinese, and this confusion of terms and meanings proves a fruitful source of error in regard to an accurate knowledge of foreign nations, and a just perception of their condition. For instance, the terms *a court of justice*, *a common school*, *politeness*, *learning*, *navy*, *houses*, etc., as well as the names of things, like *razor*, *shoe*, *cap*, *bed*, *pencil*, *paper*, etc., are inapplicable to the same things in England and China; while it is plainly impossible to coin a new word in English to describe the Chinese article, and equally inexpedient to introduce the native term. If, for example, the utensil used by the Chinese to shave with were picked up in Portsmouth by some English navvy who had never seen or heard of it, he would be more likely to call it an oyster-knife, or a wedge, than a razor; while the use to which it is

---

[1] *Voyage à Péking*, Vol. II., p. 173.

applied must of course give it that name, and would, if it were still more unlike the western article. So with other things. The ideas a Chinese gives to the terms *hwangtí*, *kwanfu*, *pao*, *pih*, and *shu*, are very different from those conveyed to an American by the words *emperor*, *magistrate*, *cannon*, *pencil*, and *book*. Since a person can only judge of what he hears or reads by what he knows, it is desirable that when he meets with western names applied to their equivalents in eastern countries, the function of a different civilization, habits, and notions should not be overlooked in the opinion he forms. These remarks are peculiarly applicable to the domestic life of the Chinese, to their houses, diet, dress, and social customs; although careful descriptions may go a good way in conveying just ideas, it cannot be hoped that they will do what the most cursory examination of the object or trait would instantly accomplish.

The notions entertained abroad on these particulars are, it need hardly be remarked, rather more accurate than those the Chinese have of distant countries, and it is scarcely possible that they can lose their conceit in their own civilization and position among the nations so long as such ideas are entertained as the following extract exhibits. Tien Kí-shih, a popular essayist of the last century, thus congratulates himself and his readers: "I felicitate myself that I was born in China, and constantly think how very different it would have been with me if I had been born beyond the seas in some remote part of the earth, where the people, far removed from the converting maxims of the ancient kings, and ignorant of the domestic relations, are clothed with the leaves of plants, eat wood, dwell in the wilderness, and live in the holes of the earth; though born in the world, in such a condition I should not have been different from the beasts of the field. But now, happily, I have been born in the Middle Kingdom. I have a house to live in; have food and drink, and elegant furniture; have clothing and caps, and infinite blessings: truly, the highest felicity is mine." This extract well indicates the isolation of the writer and his race from their fellow-men; among the neighboring nations even the Japanese would have shown him his erroneous view. The seclusion which had been forced upon both these peoples, who closed their doors as the surest possible defence against aggression from foreign traders and sought in this fashion to remove all cause of quarrel, brought with it in time the almost equal dangers of ignorance and inability to understand their true position among the nations of the world.

The architecture of the Chinese suggests, in its general outline and the peculiar concave roof, a canvas tent as its primary *motive*, though there is no further proof than this likeness of its origin. From the palace to the hovel, in temples and in private dwellings, this type everywhere stands confessed,[1] and almost nothing like a dome or cupola, a spire or a turret, is anywhere

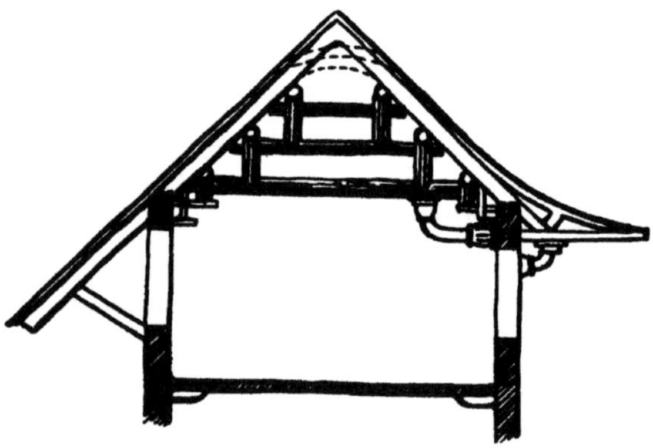

Diagram of Chinese Roof Construction. (From Fergusson.)

found. Few instances occur of an attempt to develop even this simple model into a grand or imposing building. While the Mogul princes in India reared costly mausolea and palaces to perpetuate their memory and the splendor of their reigns, the monarchs of China, with equal or greater resources at command, seldom indulged in this princely pastime, or even attempted the erection of any enduring monument to commemorate their taste or their splendor. Whether it was owing to the absenee of the beautiful and majestic models seen in western countries,

[1] It is said that when Ghengis in his invasion of China took a city, his soldiers immediately set about pulling down the four walls of the houses, leaving the overhanging roofs supported by the wooden columns—by which process they converted them into excellent tents for themselves and their horses.—*Encyclopædia Britannica:* Art. CHINA.

or to ignorance of the mechanical principles of the art, the fact is not the less observable, and the inference as to the advance made by them in knowledge and taste not less just.

Fergusson has no doubt assigned one good reason for this fact, in that "the Chinese never had either a dominant priesthood or a hereditary nobility. The absence of the former class is important, because it is to sacred art that architecture has owed its highest inspiration, and sacred art is never so strongly developed as under the influence of a powerful and splendid hierachy. In the same manner the want of a hereditary nobility is equally unfavorable to domestic architecture of a durable description. Private feuds and private wars were till lately unknown, and hence there are no fortalices or fortified mansions, which by their mass and solidity give such a marked character to a certain class of domestic edifices in the west."[1] These reasons have their weight, but they hardly cover the whole question, whose solution reaches into the well-known inertness of the imaginative faculty in the Chinese mind. It is nevertheless true that there is nothing in the whole Empire worthy to be called an architectural ruin, nothing which can inform us whether previous generations constructed edifices more splendid or more mean than the present.[2]

Dwelling-houses are generally of one story, having neither cellars nor basements, and lighted by lattices opening into a court; they must not equal adjacent temples in height, nor possess the ornaments appropriated to palaces and religious establishments. The common building materials are bricks, adobie or matting for the walls, stone for the foundation, brick tiling for the roof, and wood only for the inner work; stone and wooden houses are not unknown, but are so rare as to attract

---

[1] James Fergusson, *History of Indian and Eastern Architecture*, p. 687; compare also *Mémoires Concernant les Chinois*, where Chinese architecture is treated of in almost every volume.

[2] The foreign literature upon this subject is as yet scant and unimportant. Compare the rare and costly *Designs of Chinese Buildings, Furniture, Dresses, etc., from Originals drawn in China by* Mr. Chambers, London, 1757, folio; J. M. Callery, *De l'Architecture Chinoise*, in the *Revue d'Architecture;* Wm. Simpson, in *Transactions of the Royal Institute of British Architects*, 1873–74, p. 33; *Notes and Queries on China and Japan.*

attention. The high prices of timber and the very partial use of window-glass have both tended to modify and restrict the construction of dwellings. The *ní chuen*, or sifted earth, is a compound of decomposed granite or gravel and lime mixed with water, and sometimes a little oil, of which durable walls are made by pounding it into a solid mass between planks secured at the sides and elevated as the wall rises, or by beating it into large blocks; when stuccoed and protected from the rain this material gradually hardens into stone. In houses of the better sort the stone work of the foundation rises three or four feet above the ground, and sometimes the finished surfaces, great size of the stones and the regularity of their arrangement make one regret that the same skill had not been expended on large edifices. In towns their fronts present no opening except the door, and when the outer walls of several houses join those of gardens and enclosures, the street presents an uninteresting sameness, unrelieved by steps, windows, balconies, porticoes, or front yards. The walls are twenty-five or thirty feet high, usually hollow, or too thin to safely support the roof unaided. In the common buildings a framework of wood is erected on the foundation, which has large stones so arranged as to receive the posts, and on these rests the entire weight of the roof. The brick nogging fills up the intervals, but supports nothing; it is sometimes solid, more frequently merely a face-work, and if the roof becomes leaky or broken a heavy rain will destroy the wall, as it soaks through the courses and washes out the mud within. In the central provinces common walls are often made of small bricks four inches square and one thick, which are laid on their edges in a series of hollows; between the courses a plank sometimes adds greater strength to the wall. These cellular constructions are more durable than would be imagined provided the stucco remains uninjured.

The bricks are the same size as our own, and usually burned to a grayish slate color; they are made by hand, and sell at a price varying from three dollars to eight dollars a thousand. In the sea-coast districts lime is cheaply obtained from shells, but in the interior from limestone calcined by anthracite coal; the people use it pure, only occasionally mixing sand with it for either mortar or stucco. The walls are often stuccoed, and when not thus covered the bricks are occasionally rubbed smooth and pointed with fine cement. In place of a broad cornice the top is frequently relieved by a pretty ornament of moulded work of painted clay figures in *alto relievo*, representing a battle scene, a landscape, clusters of flowers, or some other design, defended from the weather by the projecting eaves. A black painted band, relieved by corners and designs of flowers and scrolls, is a cheap substitute for the carved figures.

The roofs are hipped in some provinces, but rarely in the north. They are steep, and if kept tight will last several years; the grass which is apt to spring up on them is a source of injury, and its growth or removal alike endangers the soundness of the construction. The yellow and green glazed tiles of public buildings add to their beauty, as do the dragon's heads and globes on their ridge-poles; these features, together with the earthen dogs at the corners of temples or official houses, make the structures exceedingly picturesque. In Peking the framework under the wide eaves of palaces is tastefully painted in green and gold, and protected by a netting of copper wire. Roofs are made of earthen tiles laid on coarse clapboarding that rests on the purlines in alternate ridges and furrows. The under layer consists of square thin pieces, laid side by side in ascending rows with the lower edges overlapping; the sides are covered by the semi-cylindrical tiles, which are further protected by a covering of mortar. In the northern provinces the tiles are laid in a course of mud resting on straw over the clapboarding. The workmen begin the tiling at the ridge-pole and finish as they come down to the eaves, so as not to walk over the tiles and crack them; but such roofs easily leak in driving storms. No chimneys are seen; the slope is steep, for quick discharge of rain and snow. Terraces are erected on shops, but balustrades or flat roofs are seldom seen. Occasionally the gable walls rise above the roof in degrees, imparting a singular, bow-like aspect to the edifice. The purlines and ridge-pole extend from wall to wall, and the rafters are slender strips. In all roofs the principal weight rests on the two rows of pillars at the sides, that uphold the plates, and the antefixæ which support the broad eaves far beyond the wall. A series of beams and posts above the plates and tie-beams make the roof very heavy but also secure; curb and mansard roofs are unknown.

The pillars of stone or timber in Chinese temples are often noticeable, owing to their size or length as single pieces. They are, however, unadorned with either capital or carved base, though the shaft may be finely carved and painted, the color decoration being often upon a thick coating of *papier-maché*, laid on to protect the wood. In two-story houses the sleepers of the floor are supported on tie-beams attached to the main posts if they do not rest on the wall. Posts form an element of all Chinese buildings, either to support the roof or the veranda. The entrance is on the sides, and the wall is set back from the outer line of the eaves so as to afford a shelter or porch. Hipped roofs enable the architect to encompass the entire building with a veranda, this being a common arrangement in the southern provinces. A slight ceiling usually conceals the tiling, but the apartment appears lofty owing to the cavity of the roof.

The pavilion is a prominent feature of Chinese architecture, and its ornamentation calls out the best talent of the builder in making his edifice acceptable. One charming specimen of this style at the Emperor's summer palace of Yuen-ming Yuen is already famous, its material being of pure copper; it is about fourteen feet square and twenty high.

Another beautiful structure which well exhibits the pavilion is shown in the adjoining cut. It is the *Pih-yung Kung*, or 'Classic Hall,' built by Kienlung adjacent to the Confucian Temple at Peking (page 74), and devoted to expounding the classics. This lofty building, which may be here seen through an ornamental arch across the court, is perfectly square, covered with a four-sided double roof, whose bright yellow tiles and gilded ball at the apex produce a most brilliant effect in the sunlight. The deep veranda, completely encircling the structure and supported by a score of colored wooden pillars, very ably relieves the dead mass and heavy upper roof of the pavilion

PIH-YUNG KUNG, OR 'CLASSIC HALL,' PEKING.

proper. Around flow the waters of a circular tank, edged with marble balustrades and spanned by four bridges which form the approaches to each of the sides.

The general disposition of a Chinese dwelling of the better sort is that of a series of rooms separated and lighted by intervening courts, and accessible along a covered corridor communicating with each, or by side passages leading through the courts. In cities, where the houses are cramped and the lots irregular in shape, there is more diversity in the arrangement and size of rooms; and in the country establishments of wealthy families, where the gradual increase of the members calls for additional space, the succession of courts and buildings, interspersed with gardens and pools, sometimes renders the whole not a little complicated. The great expense of timber for floors, posts, and sleepers has been the chief reason for retaining the single story, rather than the awkwardness caused by cramping women's feet. No contrivance for warming the rooms by means of chimneys or flues exists, except that found in the *kang*, or brick bed, on which the inmates lie and sit.

The entrance into large mansions in the country is by a triple gate leading through a lawn or garden up to the hall; in towns, a single door, usually elevated a step or two above the street, introduces the visitor into a porch or court. A wall or movable screen is placed inside of the doorway, and the intervening space is occupied by the porter; upon the wall on the left is often seen a shrine dedicated to the gods of the threshold. In the houses of officials, upon this wall is inscribed a list of dignities and offices which the master has held during his life. The door is solidly constructed, and moves upon pivots turning in sockets. Under the projecting eaves hang paper lanterns informing the passer-by of the name and title of the householder, and when lighted at night serving to illumine the street and designate his habitation; for door-plates and numbers are unknown. The roughness of the gate is somewhat concealed by the names or grotesque representations of two tutelar gods, Shintu and Yuhlui, to whom the guardianship of the house is entrusted; while the sides and lintel are embellished with felicitous quotations written upon red paper, or with sign-boards of official rank. The doorkeeper and other servants lodge in small rooms within the gateway, and above the porch is an attic containing one or two apartments, to be reached by a rude stairway.

On passing behind the screen a court, occasionally adorned with flowers or a fancy fish-pool, is crossed before reaching the principal hall. The upper end of the hall is furnished with a high table, on which incense vases, idolatrous utensils, and offerings are placed in honor of the divinities and lares worshipped there, whose tablets and names are on the wall. Sometimes the table merely contains flowers in jars, fancy pieces of white quartz, limestone or jade, or ornaments of various kinds. Before the table is a large couch, with a low stand in its centre, and a pillow for reclining upon. In front of it the chairs are arranged down the room in two rows facing each other, each pair having a small table between them. The floors are made of thick, large tiles of brick or marble, or of hard cement. Even in a bright day the room is dim, and the absence of carpets and fireplaces, and of windows to afford a prospect abroad, renders it cheerless to a foreigner accustomed to his own glazed and loftier houses.

A rear door near the side wall opens either into a kitchen or court, across which are the female apartments, or directly into the latter and the rooms for domestics. Instead of being always rectangular the doors are sometimes made round, leaf-shaped, or semi-circular, and it is thought desirable that they should not open opposite each other, lest evil spirits find their way in from the street. The rear rooms are lighted by skylights when other modes are unavailable, and along the southern sea-coasts the thin laminæ of a species of oyster (*Placuna*) cut into small squares supply the place of window-glass. Commerce is gradually bringing this material into greater use all over the land, though the fear of thieves still limits it. Corean paper is the chief substitute for glass in the north. The kitchen is a small affair, for the universal use of portable furnaces enables the inmates to cook wherever the smoke will be least troublesome. Warming the house, even as far north as Ningpo, is not frequent, as the inmates rely on their quilted and fur garments for protection. The flue of the tiled-brick divan, or *kang*, is connected with a pit lined with brick dug in the floor in front; when the pot of coal is well lighted and placed near the opening, the draft carries the heat into the passages running under the surface, and soon warms the room without much smoke. The pot of burning coal furnishes all the cooking-fire the poor have, and at night the inmates sleep on the warm bricks.

The country establishments of wealthy men furnish the best expression of Chinese ideas of elegance and comfort. In these enclosures the hall of ancestors, library, school-room, and summer-houses are detached and erected upon low plinths, surrounded by a veranda, and frequently decorated with tracery and ornamental carving. Near the rear court are the female apartments and offices, many of the former and the sleeping apartments being in attics. Considerable space is occupied by the quadrangles, which are paved and embellished by fish-pools, flowering shrubs, and other plants. Mr. Fortune describes[1] the house and garden of a gentleman at Ningpo as being connected by rude-looking caverns of rock-work, "and what at first sight appears to be a subterranean passage leading from room to room, through which the visitor passes to the garden. The small courts, of which a glimpse is caught in passing along, are fitted up with rock-work; dwarf trees are planted here and there in various places, and graceful creepers hang down into the pools in front. These being passed, another cavernous passage leads into the garden, with its dwarf trees, vases, ornamented lattices, and beautiful shrubs suddenly opening to the view. By windings and glimpses along the rocky passages into other courts, and hiding the real boundary by masses of shrubs and trees, the grounds are made to appear much larger than they really are."

The houses of the poor are dark, dirty, low, and narrow tenements, where the floor is of earth covered with mats or tiled, and the doorway the only opening, on which a swinging mat conceals the interior. The whole family often sleep, eat, and live in a single room. Pigs, dogs, and hens dispute the space

---

[1] *Wanderings in China*, p. 98.

with children and furniture—if a table and a few trestles and stools, pots and plates, deserve that name. The filthy street without is a counterpart to the gloomy, smoky abode within, and a single walk through the streets and lanes of such a neighborhood is sufficient to reconcile a person to any ordinary condition of life. On the outskirts of the town a still poorer class take up with huts made of mats and thatch upon the ground, through which the rain and wind find free course. It is surprising that people can live and enjoy health, and even be cheerful, as the Chinese are, in such circumstances. Between these hovels and the abodes of the rich is a class of middle houses, consisting of three or four small rooms surrounding a court, each one lodging a family, which uses its portion of the quadrangle.

The best furniture is made of a heavy wood stained to resemble ebony; camphor, elm, pine, aspen, and melia woods furnish cheaper material. Ornamental articles, porcelain vases, copper tripods or pots, stone screens, book-shelves, flowers in pots, etc., show the national taste. Ink sketches of landscapes, gay scrolls inscribed with sentences suspended from the walls, and pretty lanterns relieve the baldness of the room; their combined effect is not destitute of variety and elegance, though there is a lack of *comfort*. Partitions are sometimes fancifully made of lattice-work, with openings neatly arranged for the reception of boxes containing books. The bedrooms are small, poorly ventilated, and seldom visited except at night. A massive bedstead of costly woods, elaborately carved, and supporting a tester for the silk curtains and mosquito-bars, is often shown as the family pride and heirloom; a scroll of fine writing adorns its fringe or valance. Mattresses or feather beds are not used, and the pillow is a hollow square frame of rattan or bamboo. The bed, wardrobe, and toilet usually complete the furniture of the sleeping apartments of the Chinese; but if this is also the sitting room, the bed is rolled up so as often to furnish seats on its boards.

The grounds of the rich are laid out in good style, and were not the tasteful arrangements and diversified shrubbery which would render them charming resorts almost always spoiled by general bad keeping—neglect and ruin, if not nastiness and offals, being often visible—they would please the most fastidious. The necessity of having a place for the women and children to recreate themselves is one reason for having an open enclosure, even if it be only a plat of flowers or a bed of vegetables. In the imperial gardens the attempt to make an epitome of nature has been highly successful. De Guignes describes their art of gardening as "imitating the beauties and producing the inequalities of nature. Instead of alleys planted symmetrically or uniform grounds, there are winding footpaths, trees here and there as if by chance, woody or sterile hillocks, and deep gulleys with narrow passages, whose sides are steep or rough with rocks, and presenting only a few miserable shrubs. They like to bring together in gardening, in the same view, cultivated grounds and arid plains; to make the field uneven and cover it with artificial rock-work; to dig caverns in mountains, on whose tops are arbors half overthrown, and around which tortuous footpaths run and return into themselves, prolonging, as it were, the extent of the grounds and increasing the pleasure of the walk."

A fish-pond, supplied by a rivulet running wildly through the grounds, forms a pretty feature of such gardens, in which, if there be room, a summer-house is erected on a rocky islet, or on piles over the water, accessible by a rugged causey of rock-work. The nelumbium lily, with its plate-like leaves and magnificent flowers, is a general favorite in such places; carp and other fish are reared in their waters, and gold-fish in small tanks. Whenever it is possible a gallery runs along the sides of the pond for the pleasure and use of the females in the household. A tasteful device in some gardens, which beguiles the visitor's ramble, is a rude kind of shell or pebble mosaic inlaid in the gravelly paths, representing birds, animals, or other figures; the time required to decipher them prolongs the walk, and apparently increases the size of the grounds. The pieces of rock-work are cemented and bound with wire; and in fish-pools, grottos, or causeways this unique ornament has a charming effect, the moss and plants which grow upon it adding rather to its appropriateness.

The wood and mason work is unsubstantial, requiring constant repairs; when new they present a pretty appearance, but both gardens and houses, when neglected, soon fall into a ruinous condition. Some of the principal merchants at Canton, in the former days of the hong monopoly, had cultivated grounds of greater or less extent attached to their establishments. One of them, by way of variety, constructed a summer-house entirely of glass, this wonderful structure being made so that it could be closed and protected with shutters.

The arrangement of shops and warehouses is modified by the uses to which they are applied, but they still resemble dwelling-houses more than is the case with stores in western cities. The rear room of the shop is a small apartment, used for a dormitory, store-room, or workshop, and sometimes for all these purposes together; it is in most cases on an upper floor. Small ones are lighted from the street, but the largest by a skylight, in which cases there is a latticed screen reaching across the room, to secure the inside from the street. The whole shop-front is thrown open by day and closed at night by shutters running in grooves, and secured by heavy cross-bars to a row of posts which fit in sockets in the threshold and lintel. The doorway recedes a foot or two, and the projecting roof serves to protect customers, and such goods as are exposed, from the rain and sun. In small shops there are two counters, a long one running back from the door, and another at right angles to it, reaching partly across the front. The shopman sits within the angle formed by these, and as they are low he can easily serve a customer in the street as well as in the shop. At night the smaller one often forms a lodging place for homeless beggars. The facing of the outer counter is of granite, and in Canton a niche containing a tablet inscribed to the god of wealth is cut in the end, where incense is burned. Another shrine is placed on high within the apartment, dedicated to the deity of the place, whoever he may be.

The loft is much contracted; and that it may not intercept the skylight, it is usually a small chamber reached by a gallery, and lighted in front. Chinese tradesmen do not make much display in exhibiting their goods, and the partial use of glass renders it somewhat unsafe for them to do so. The want of a yard compels them to cook and wash either behind or on top of the building; clerks and workmen usually eat and sleep under the shop roof. In the densest parts of Canton the roofs are covered with a loose framework, on which firewood is piled, clothes washed and dried, and meals cooked; it also affords a sleeping place in summer. In case of fire, however, these lumbered roofs become like so many tinder-boxes, and aid not a little to spread the flames.

The narrowness of the streets in Chinese cities is a source of many inconveniences; few exceed ten or twelve feet in width, and most of those in Canton are less than eight. No large squares having fountains and shrubbery, nor any open spaces except the areas in front of temples relieve the closeness of these lanes. The absence of horses and carriages in southern cities, and a custom of huddling together, a desire to screen the thoroughfare from the sun, and ignorance of the advantages of another mode, are among the leading reasons for making them so contracted; while the difficulty of collecting a mob in them should be mentioned as one point in their favor. In case of fire it is difficult to get access to the burning buildings, and dangerous for the inmates to move or save their property. At all times porters carrying burdens are impeded by the crowd of passengers, who likewise must pass Indian file lest they tilt against the porters. Ventilation is imperfect where the buildings are packed so closely, and the public necessaries and their offal carried through the streets by the scavengers pollute the air. Drainage is very superficial and incomplete; the sewers easily choke up or get broken and exude their contents over the pathway. The ammoniacal and other gases which are generated aggravate the ophthalmic diseases so prevalent; and it is a matter of surprise that the cholera, plague, or yellow fever does not visit the inhabitants of such confined abodes, who breathe so tainted an atmosphere. The peculiar government of cities by means of wards and neighborhoods, each responsible to the officials, combined with the ignorance among all ranks of the principles of hygiene, will account for the evils so patent to one accustomed to the energetic sway of a mayor and board of health in most European cities, who can bring knowledge and power to coöperate for the well-being of all.

The streets are usually paved with slabs of stone laid crosswise, and except near markets and wells are comparatively clean. They are not laid out straight, and some present a singularly irregular appearance from the slight angle which each house makes with its neighbors; it being considered rather unlucky to have them exactly even. The names of the streets are written on the gateways crossing them, whenever they are marked at all; occasionally, as at Canton, each division makes a separate neighborhood and has its own name; a single long street will thus have five, six, or more names. The general arrangement of a Chinese city presents a labyrinth of streets, alleys, and byways very perplexing to a stranger who has neither plan nor directory to guide him, nor numbers upon the houses and shops to direct him. The sign-boards are hung each side of the door, or securely inserted in stone sockets; some of them are ten or fifteen feet high, and being gaily painted and gilded on both sides with picturesque characters, a succession of them as seen down a street produces a gay effect. The inscriptions simply mention the kind of goods sold, and without half the puffing seen in western cities; accounts sometimes given of the inscriptions on sign-boards in Chinese cities, as "No cheating here," and others, describe the exception and not the rule. The edicts of government, handbills of medicines and the famous doctors who make them, notices offering rewards for children who are lost or slaves escaped, new shops opened, houses to let, or other events, cover blank walls in great variety, printed on red, black, white, or yellow paper; the absence of newspapers leads shopmen to depend more for patronage upon a circle of customers and the distribution of cards than to spend much money in handbills. The shrines of the street gods occur in southern cities, located in niches in the wall, with altars before them.

The temples and assembly-halls are the only public buildings in Chinese cities belonging to the people. Their courts and cloisters, with such gardens, tea-houses, and pools as may be accessible, attract constant crowds, and furnish the only places of common resort. The priests derive no small portion of their income from travellers, and their establishments are consequently made more commodious and extensive than the number of priests or the throng of worshippers require.

The assembly-halls or club-houses form a peculiar feature of Chinese society. There are more than a hundred in Canton and many hundreds in Peking. They are built sometimes by a particular craft as its guildhall, or more commonly erected by persons resorting to the place for trade, study, or amusement, who subscribe to fit up a commodious establishment to accommodate persons coming from the same town. In this way their convenience, assistance, oversight, and general safety are all increased.[1] All buildings pay a ground rent to the government, but no data are available for comparing this tax with that levied in western cities. The government furnishes the owner of the ground with a *hung ki*, or 'red deed,' in testimony of his right to occupancy, which puts him in possession as long as he pays the taxes. There is a record office in the local magistracy of such documents.

Houses are rented on short leases, and the rent collected quarterly in advance; the annual income from real estate is between nine and twelve per cent. The yearly rent of the best shops in Canton is from $150 to $400; there is no system of insuring against fire, which, with the municipal taxes and the difficulty of collecting bad rents, enhances their price. Such kind of property in China is liable to many risks.

The taverns are numerous and adapted for every calling. Though they will not bear comparison with western hotels, they are far in advance of the cheerless khans and caravansaries found in Western Asia. The traveller brings his own bedding, sometimes also his own provision, and when night comes spreads his mat upon the floor or divan and lies down in his clothes. The better sort of travellers order a room for themselves, but officials or rich men go to temples, or hire a boat in which to travel and sleep; this usage takes off the best class of customers. One considerable source of income to innkeepers is the prepa-

---

[1] Compare pp. 76 and 167.

ration of dinners for parties of men, who either come to the house or send to it for so many covers; for when a gentleman invites his friends to an entertainment it is common to serve it up at his warehouse, or at an inn. In towns and cities thousands of men eat in the streets; the number of eating and cooking-stalls produces a most lively impression upon a stranger. This custom has had a good effect in promoting the general courtesy so conspicuous among the people, and is increased by great numbers of street story-tellers. The noisy hilarity of the customers, as they ply their "nimble lads," or chopsticks, and the vociferous cries of the cooks recommending their cakes and dishes, with the steaming savor from the frying-pan and kettles, form only one of the many objects to attract the notice of the foreign observer. Their appearance and the variety of bustling scenes and picturesque novelties presented to him afford constant instruction and entertainment. Those at Canton have been thus described by an eye-witness.

The number of itinerant workmen of one kind or another which line the sides of the streets or occupy the areas before public buildings in Chinese towns is a remarkable feature. Fruiterers, pastrymen, cooks, venders of gimcracks, and wayside shopmen are found in other countries as well as China; but to see a travelling blacksmith or tinker, an itinerant glass-mender, a peripatetic repairer of umbrellas, a locomotive seal-cutter, an ambulatory barber, a migratory banker, a peregrinatory apothecary or druggist, or a walking shoemaker and cobbler, one must travel hitherward. These movable establishments, together with fortune-tellers, herb and booksellers, chiromancers, etc., pretty well fill up the space, so that one often sees both sides of the streets literally lined with the stalls, wares, or tools of persons selling or making something to eat or to wear. The money-changer sits behind a small table, on which his strings of cash are chained, and where he weighs the silver he is to change; his neighbor, the seal-cutter, sits next him near a like fashioned table. The barber has his chest of drawers made to serve for a seat, and if he has not a furnace of his own he heats his water at the cook's or the blacksmith's fire near by, perhaps shaving his friend gratis by way of recompense.

The herbseller chooses an open place where he will not be trampled on, and there displays his simples and his plasters, while the dentist, with a ghastly string of fangs and grinders around his neck, testimonials of his skill, sits over against him, each with his infallible remedy. The book-peddler and chooser of lucky days, and he who searches for stolen goods by divination, arrange themselves on either side, with their tables and stalls, and array of sticks, pencils, signs, and pictures, all trying to "catch a little pigeon." The spectacle-mender and razor-grinder, the cutler and seller of bangles and bracelets,

and the maker of clay puppets or mender of old shoes, are not far off, all plying their callings as busily as if they were in their own shops. Then, besides the hundreds of stalls for selling articles of food, dress, or ornament, there are innumerable hucksters going up and down with baskets and trays slung on their shoulders, each bawling or making his own peculiar note, which, with coolies transporting burdens, chair-bearers carrying sedans, and passengers following one another like a stream, with here and there a woman among them, so fill up the streets that it is no easy matter to navigate one's way. Notwithstanding all these obstructions, it is worthy of note and highly praiseworthy to see these crowds pass and repass with the greatest rapidity in the narrow streets without altercation or disturbance, and seldom with accident.[1]

Streets at the north present a somewhat different, and on the whole a less inviting because less entertaining and picturesque aspect. Their greater width allows carts to pass, and it also offers more room for the garbage, the rubbish, and the noisome sights that are most disgusting, all of which are made worse in rainy weather by the mud through which one flounders. Barrow thus delineates those in Peking: "The multitude of movable workshops of tinkers and barbers, cobblers and blacksmiths, the tents and booths where tea and fruit, rice and other eatables were exposed for sale, with the wares and merchandise arrayed before the doors, had contracted this spacious street to a narrow road in the middle, just wide enough for two little vehicles to pass each other. The processions of men in office attended by their numerous retinues, bearing umbrellas and flags, painted lanterns and a variety of strange insignia of their rank and station, different trains that were accompanying, with lamentable cries, corpses to their graves, and with squalling music, brides to their husbands; the troops of dromedaries laden with coals from Tartary; the wheel-barrows and hand-carts stuffed with vegetables, occupied nearly the whole of this middle space in one continued line. All was in motion. The sides of the streets were filled with an immense concourse of people, buying and selling and bartering their different commodities. The buzz and confused noises of this mixed multitude, proceeding from the loud bawling of those who were crying their wares, the wrangling of others, with every now and then a strange twanging sound like the jarring of a cracked jewsharp (the barber's

---

[1] *Chinese Repository*, Vol. X., p. 473.

signal), the mirth and laughter that prevailed in every group, could scarcely be exceeded. Peddlers with their packs, jugglers and conjurers, fortune-tellers, mountebanks and quack doctors, comedians and musicians, left no space unoccupied."[1]

Shops are closed at nightfall, and persons going abroad carry a lantern or torch. Over the thoroughfares slender towers are erected, where notice of a fire is given and the watches of the night announced by striking a gong. Few persons are met in the streets at night, and the private watch kept by all who are able greatly assists the regular police in preserving order and apprehending thieves. These watchers go up and down their wards beating large bamboos, to let "thieves know they are on the lookout." Considering all things, large Chinese cities are remarkably quiet at night. Beggars find their lodgings in the porches and squares of temples, or sides of the streets, and nestle together for mutual warmth. This class is under the care of a headman, who, in order to collect the poor-tax allowed by law, apportions them in the neighborhoods with the advice of the elders and constables. During the day they go from one door to another and receive their allotted stipend, which cannot be less than one cash to each person. They sit in the doorway and sing a ditty or beat their clap-dishes and sticks to attract attention, and if the shopkeeper has no customers he lets them keep up their cries, for he knows that the longer they are detained so much the more time will elapse before they come again to his shop. Many are blind and all present a sickly appearance, their countenances begrimed with dirt and furrowed by sorrow and suffering. The very difficult question how to assist, restrain, and employ the poor has been usually left to the mercy and wisdom of the municipal officers in the cities; and the results are not on the whole discreditable to their humanity and benevolence. Many persons give the headman a dollar or more per month to purchase exemption from the daily importunity of the beggars, and families about to have a house-warming, marriage, or funeral, as also newly arrived junks, are obliged to fee him to get rid of the clamorous and loathsome crowd.

---

[1] *Travels in China*, p. 96.

When fires occur the officers of government are held responsible; the law being that if ten houses are burned *within the walls*, the highest officer in it shall be fined nine months' pay; if more than thirty, a year's salary; and if three hundred are consumed, he shall be degraded one degree. The governor and other high officers, attended by a few troops, are frequently seen at fires in Canton, as much to prevent thievery as to direct in extinguishing the flames. The engines are hurried through the narrow streets at a fearful rate; those who carry away property are armed with swords to defend it, and usually add to the crash of the burning houses by loud cries. The police do not hesitate to pull down houses if the fire can thereby be sooner extinguished, but there is no organized body of firemen, nor any well-arranged system of operations in such cases, though conflagrations are ordinarily soon under control. Cruel men often take the opportunity at such times to steal and carry off defenceless persons, especially young girls.

At Canton the usage is general of levying a bonus on the owners of the houses adjacent to the burnt district, whose dwellings were saved by the exertions of the firemen, the appraisement decreasing as the distance increases; the sum is divided among the firemen. The householders thus saved also employ priests to erect an altar near by, whereon to perform a service, and "return thanks for Heaven's mercy." On the whole, the fire control in China is superior to that in Turkey, where the firemen pay themselves for their efforts by extortions practised upon house-owners.

The pagoda is a building considered as so peculiar to the Chinese that a landscape or painting relating to China without a pagoda perched on a hill—like one of Egyptian scenery destitute of a pyramid—would be considered deficient. The term *pagoda* is used in its proper sense by most of the French and Portuguese writers to denote a temple for idols, but in English books it has always been appropriated to the polygonal towers seen throughout the country. Some confusion has arisen in consequence of applying the account of an immense temple full of idols to these towers. The English use is the most definite in China, although its misapplication is indefensible if we regard its derivation.

The form of the Chinese *tah* is probably derived from the spire on the top of the Hindu dagoba, as its name is doubtless taken from the first syllable; but their purpose has so long been identified with the geomantic influences which determine the luck of a place that the people do not associate them with Buddhism. Mr. Milne explains this in his remark that "the presence of such an edifice not only secures to the site the protection of heaven, if it already bears evidence of enjoying it, but represses any evil influences that may be native to the spot, and imparts to it the most salutary and felicitous omens."[1] Those in the southern and central provinces seldom contain idols of any pretensions. They are ascended by stairways built in the thick walls on alternate sides of the stories. In the north there is another kind, designed to contain a *shé-lí*, or relic of Buddha, having a large room near the base for worshipping the idol placed in it, but otherwise entirely solid and nearly uniform in size to the top; the stories are merely numerous narrow projections, like eaves or string courses, on which hundreds of small images are sometimes placed. These structures more nearly resemble the Indian *dagoba* than the other kind, and are always connected with a monastery, while those are not uniformly so placed, though under a priestly oversight.

No town is considered complete without a pagoda, and many large cities have several; there must be nearly two thousand in the Empire, some of which are quite celebrated. It is rare to see a new one, and the ruinous condition of most of them indicates the weakness of the faith which erected them. They vary in height from five to thirteen stories, and are mostly built in so solid a manner that they are likely to remain for centuries. One at Hangchau is octagonal, each face twenty-eight feet wide and the wall at the base eighteen feet thick; the top is reached by a spiral stairway between the walls; a covered gallery on the outside of each story affords resting-places and ever-changing views to the visitor; it is one hundred and seventy feet high, and was built during the Sung dynasty, in the twelfth century. The prospect from its summit is superb; the pic-

[1] *Life in China*, p. 453.

turesque combination of sea and shore, land and water, city and country, wilderness, gardens, and hills, with many historical and religious associations interesting to a native, make it one of the most charming landscapes in China.

Sir John Davis visited one near Lintsing chau in Shantung, in very good repair, inhabited by Buddhist priests, and containing two idols; each of its nine stories was inscribed with *Ometo Fuh*, in large characters. It was erected since the completion of the Grand Canal. A winding stairway of near two hundred steps conducted to the top, about one hundred and fifty feet from the ground, from whence an extensive view was obtained of the surrounding country. The basement was excellently built of granite, and all the rest of glazed brick, beautifully joined and cemented.

The objects in building these structures being of a mixed nature, sometimes geomantic and sometimes religious, their materials, size, and structure vary considerably. There are two inside of Canton, and three near the Pearl River, below the city; fifteen others occur in the prefecture. Suchau has two, Ningpo one, Fuhchau two, and Peking six in and out of the walls. One of those at Canton was built by the Moslems about a thousand years ago, a plain brick tower nearly two hundred feet high, from which the faithful were probably called to prayers in the adjacent mosque. Fergusson's remarks upon Chinese architecture would probably have been modified had the writer enjoyed a wider range of observation and a fuller knowledge of the designs of native builders. They are, however, the conclusions of a competent observer, and the position he gives to the pagoda among the tower-like buildings of the world, arising from its peculiar form, its divisions, and its apparent uselessness, will be generally accepted as just.

Mr. Milne, in his interesting work, has a good account of pagodas; he shows that while their model is of Hindu origin, and has been carefully followed since the first one was erected (about A.D. 250) at Nanking, the popular geomantic ideas connected with their octagonal form and great height have gradually increased and influenced their location. The Buddhists seem themselves to have lost their ancient confidence in the protection of the *shé-li* (or *saina*) supposed to be built in them. The number of Indian words transliterated in Chinese accounts of these edifices further proves their foreign origin. For convenience and accuracy in describing them, it would be best to restrict the term *pagoda* to the hollow octagonal towers, the word *dagoba* to the solid ones covering the relics, and *tope* to the erections over priests when buried.

Pagodas are sometimes made of cast iron; those hitherto observed are in the central provinces. One exists in Chehkiang province, nearly fifty feet high and of nine stories. The octagonal pieces forming the walls are each single castings, as are also the plates forming the roof. The whole structure, including the base and spire, was made of twenty pieces of iron. Its interior is filled with brick, probably with the design to strengthen it against storms. The ignorance of the Chinese of later days of the Hindu origin of pagodas has led to their regarding those now in existence as of native design, and appropriated by the Buddhists for their own ends. Most of them are falling to ruins; and the assurances held out by the geomancers that the pagoda will act like an electric tractor to draw down every felicitous omen from above, so that fire, water, wood, earth, and metal will be at the service of the people, the soil productive, trade prosperous, and the natives submissive and happy, all fail to call out funds for repairing them.[1]

The dull appearance of a Chinese city when seen from a distance is unlike that of European cities, in which spires, domes, and towers of churches and cathedrals, halls, palaces, and other public buildings relieve the uniformity of rows of dwellings. In China, temples, houses, and palaces are nearly of one height; their sameness being only partially relieved by trees mingled with pairs of tall flag-staffs with frames near their tops, which at a distance rather suggest the idea of dismantled gallows. Nature, however, charms and delights, and few countries present more beautiful landscapes; even the tameness of the works of man serves as a foil for the diversified beauties of the cultivated landscape.

---

[1] *Voyages à Peking*, Tome II., p. 79; Davis' *Sketches*, Vol. I., p. 213; Fergusson, *Indian and Eastern Architecture*, 1876, p. 695; Milne's *Life in China*, p. 429 seq.; *Chinese Repository*, Vol. XIX., pp. 535–540.

A Chinese usually prefers to travel by water, and in the southeastern provinces it may be said that vehicles solely designed for carrying travellers or goods do not exist, for the carts and wheelbarrows which are met with are few and miserably made. But north of the Yangtsz' River, all over the Great Plain carts and wheelbarrows form the chief means of travel and transportation. The high cost of timber and the bad roads compel the people to make these vehicles very rude and strong, having axles and wheels able to bear the strains or upsets which befall them. Carts for goods are drawn by three or four horses

Wheelbarrows Used for Travelling.

usually driven tandem, and fastened by long traces to the axletree, one remaining within the thills. The common carts, drawn by one or two mules, are oblong boxes fastened to an axle, covered with cotton cloth, and cushioned to alleviate the jolting; the passengers get in and out at the front, where the driver sits close to the horse. In Peking the members of the imperial clan and family are allowed to use carts having the wheel behind the body; their ranks are further indicated by a red or yellow covering, and a greater or less number of outriders to escort them. The wheelbarrow is in great use for short distances throughout the same region. The position of the wheel in the centre enables the man to propel a heavy load readily. When on a good road, and aided by a donkey, the larger varieties of barrow carry easily a burden of a ton's weight; two men are necessary to maintain the balance and guide the rather top-heavy vehicle.

Where travelling by water is impossible, sedan chairs are used to carry passengers, and coolies with poles and slings transport their luggage and goods. There are two kinds of sedan, neither of them designed for reclining like the Indian *palky*. The light one is made of bamboo, and so narrow that the sitter is obliged to lean forward as he is carried; the large one, called *kiao*, is, whether viewed in regard to lightness, comfort, or any other quality associated with such a mode of carriage, one of the most convenient articles found in any country. Its use is subject to sumptuary laws, and forbidden to the common people unless possessing some kind of rank. In Peking only the highest officials ride in them, with four bearers. In other cities two chairmen manage easily enough to maintain a gait of four miles an hour with a sedan upon their shoulders. Goods are carried upon poles, and however large or heavy the package may be, the porters contrive to subdivide its weight between them by means of their sticks and slings. The number of persons who thus gain a livelihood is great, and in cities they are employed by headmen, who contract for work just as carmen do elsewhere; when unengaged by overseers, parties station themselves at corners and other public places, ready to start at a beck, after the manner of *Dienstmänner* in German cities. In the streets of Canton groups of brawny fellows are often seen idling away their time in smoking, gambling, sleeping, or jeering at the wayfarers; and, like the husbandmen mentioned in the parable, if one ask them why they stand there all the day idle? the answer will be, "Because no man hath hired us."

The chair-bearers form a distinct guild in cities, and the establishments where sedans and their bearers are to be hired suggest a comparison with the livery stables of western cities; the men, in fact, are nicknamed at Canton *mo mí ma*, 'tailless horses.' A vehicle used sometimes by the Emperor and high officers consists of an open chair set upon poles, so made that the incumbent can be seen as well as see around him. It undergoes' many changes in different parts of the country, as it is both cheap and light and well fitted for traversing mountainous regions.

In the construction and management of their river craft the Chinese excel. As boats are intended to be the residences of those who navigate them, regard is had to this in their arrangement. Only a part of the fleets of boats seen on the river at Canton are intended for transportation, a large number being designed for fixed residences, and perhaps half of them are permanently moored. They are not obliged to remain where they station themselves, but the boats and their inmates are both under the supervision of a water police, who register them and point out the position they may occupy. Barges for families, those in which oil, salt, fuel, or other articles are sold, lighters, passage-boats, flower-boats, and other kinds, are by this means grouped together, and more easily found. It was once ascertained that there were eighty-four thousand boats registered as belonging to the city of Canton, but whether all remained near the city and did not go to other parts of the district, or whether old ones were erased from the register when broken up, was not determined. It is not likely, however, that at one time this number of boats ever lay opposite the city. No one who has been at Canton can forget the noisy, animating sight the river offers, nor failed to have noticed the good-humored carefulness with which boats of every size pass each other without collision.

It is difficult to describe the many kinds of craft found on Chinese waters without the assistance of drawings. They are furnished with stern sculls moving upon a pivot, and easily propelling the boat. Large boats are furnished with two or three of these, which, when not in use, are conveniently hauled in upon the side. They are provided with oars, the loom and blade of which are fastened by withs, and work through a band attached to a stake; the rower stands up and pushes his oar with the same motion as that employed by the Venetian gondolier. Occasionally an oarsman is seen rowing with his feet. The mast in some large cargo boats consists of two sticks, resting on the gunwales, joined at top, and so arranged as to be hoisted from the bow; in those designed for residences no provision is made for a mast. Fishing boats, lighters, and seagoing craft have one or two permanent masts. In all, except the smallest, a wale or frame projects from the side, on which the boatmen walk when poling the vessel. The sails in the south are woven of strips of matting, sewed into a single sheet, and provided with yards at the top and bottom; the bamboo ribs crossing it serve to retain the hoops that run on the mast, and enable the boatmen to haul them close on the wind. A driver is sometimes placed on the taffrail, and a small foresail near the bow, but the mainsail is the chief dependence. No Chinese boat has a bowsprit, and very few are coppered, or have two decks, further than an orlop in the stern quarter in which to stow provisions; no dead-lights give even a glimmer to these recesses, which are necessarily small.

The internal arrangement of dwelling-boats is simple. The better sort are from sixty to eighty feet long, and about fifteen wide, divided into three rooms; the stem is sharp, and upholds a platform on which, when they are moored alongside, it is easy to pass from one boat to another. Each one is secured by ropes to large hawsers which run along the whole line at the bow and stern. The room nearest the bow serves for a lobby to the principal apartment, which occupies about half the body of the boat; the two are separated by trellis bulkheads, but the sternmost room, or sleeping apartment, is carefully screened. Cooking and washing are performed on a high stern framework, which is admirably contrived, by means of furnaces and other conveniences above and hatches and partitions below deck, to serve all these purposes, contain all the fuel and water necessary, and answer for a sleeping place as well. By means of awnings and frameworks the top of the boat also subserves many objects of work or pleasure. The window-shutters are movable, fitted for all kinds of weather and for flexibility of arrangement, meeting all the demands of a family and the particular service of a vessel; nothing can be more ingenious.

The handsomest of these craft are called *hwa ting*, or flower-boats, and are let to parties for pleasure excursions on the river;

a large proportion of them are also the abodes of public women. The smaller sorts at Canton are generally known as *tankia* boats; they are about twenty-five feet long, contain only one room, and are fitted with moveable mats to cover the whole vessel; they are usually rowed by women. In these "egg-houses" whole families are reared, live, and die; the room which serves for passengers by day is a bedroom by night; a kitchen at one time, a washroom at another, aud a nursery always.

As to this custom of living upon the water, we have an interesting testimony of its practice so far back as the fourteenth century, from the letter of a Dominican Friar in 1330. "The realm of Cathay," writes the missionary, "is peopled passing well. . . . . And there be many great rivers and great sheets of water throughout the Empire; insomuch that a good half of the realm and its territory is under water. And on these waters dwell great multitudes of people because of the vast population that there is in the said realm. They build wooden houses upon boats, and so their houses go up and down upon the waters; and the people go trafficking in their houses from one province to another, whilst they dwell in these houses with all their families, with their wives and children, and all their household utensils and necessaries. And so they live upon the waters all the days of their life. And there the women be brought to bed, and do everything else just as people do who dwell upon dry land."[1]

It is unnecessary to particularize the various sorts of lighters or *chop-boats* found along the southern coast, the passenger boats plying from town to town along the hundreds of streams, and the smacks, revenue cutters, and fishing craft to be seen in all waters, except to call attention to their remarkable adaptation for the ends in view. The best sorts are made in the southern provinces; those seen at Tientsin or Niuchwang suffer by comparison for cleanliness, safety, and speed, owing partly to the high price of wood and the less use made of them for dwellings. On the head waters of the River Kan the boats are of a peculiarly light construction, with upper works entirely of

[1] Yule, *Cathay and the Way Thither*, Vol. I., p. 243.

matting, and the hull like a crescent, well fitted to encounter the rapids and rocks which beset their course.

Besides these various kinds the revenue service employs a narrow, sharp-built boat, propelled by forty or fifty rowers, armed with swivels, spears, boarding-hooks, and pikes, and lined on the sides with a menacing array of rattan shields painted with tigers' heads. Smugglers have similarly made boats, and now and then imitate the government boats in their appearance, which, on their part, often compete with them in smuggling. In 1863 the imperial government was induced to adopt a national flag for all its own vessels, which will no doubt gradually extend to merchant craft. It is triangular in shape, and has a dragon with the head looking upward. It is usual for naval officers to exhibit long yellow flags with their official titles at full length; the vessels under them are distinguished by various pennons. Junks carry a great assortment of flags, triangular and square, of white, red, and other colors, most of them bearing inscriptions. The number of governmental boats and war junks, and those used for transporting the revenue and salt, is proportionately very small; but if all the craft found on the rivers and coasts of China be included, their united tonnage perhaps equals that of all other nations put together. The dwellers on the water near Canton are not, as has been sometimes said, debarred from living ashore. A boat can be built cheaper than a brick house, and is equally comfortable; it is kept clean easier, pays no ground-rent, and is not so obnoxious to fire and thieves. Most of them are constructed of fir or pine and smeared with wood oil; the seams are caulked with rattan shavings and paid over with a cement of oil and gypsum. The sailing craft are usually flat-bottomed, sharp forward, and guided by an enormous rudder which can be hoisted through the open stern sheets when in shallow waters. The teak-wood anchors have iron-bound flukes, held by coir or bamboo hawsers—now often replaced by iron chain and grapnel.[1]

[1] Compare an article by W. F. Mayers in *Notes and Queries on C. and J.*, Vol. I., pp. 170–173 (with illustrations); Mrs. Gray, *Fourteen Months in Canton*, passim; Dr. Edkins in *Journal N. C. Br. R. A. Soc.*. Vol. XI., p. 123; Doolittle, *Vocabulary*, Part III., No. LXVIII; Engineer J. W. King in *The United Service*, Vol. II., p. 382 (Phila., 1880).

The old picturesque junk, with its bulging hull, high stern, and great eyes on the bow, is rapidly disappearing before steamers. Its original model is said to be a huge sea monster; the teeth at the cutwater and top of the bow define its mouth, the long boards on each side of the bow form the armature of the head, the eyes being painted on them, the masts and sails are the fins, and the high stern is the tail frisking aloft. The cabins look more like niches in a sepulchre than the accommodations for a live passenger. The crew live upon deck most of the time, and are usually interested in the trade of the vessel or an adventure of their own. The hold is divided into watertight compartments, a contrivance that has its advantages when the vessel strikes a rock, but prevents her carrying a cargo comparable to her size. The great number of passengers which have been stowed in these vessels entailed a frightful loss of life when they were wrecked. In February, 1822, Capt. Pearl, of the English ship Indiana, coming through Gaspar Straits, fell in with the cargo and crew of a wrecked junk, and saved one hundred and ninety-eight persons (out of one thousand six hundred with whom she had left Amoy), whom he landed at Pontianak; this humane act cost him $55,000.[1]

Among secondary architectural works deserving notice are bridges and honorary portals. There is good reason for supposing that the Chinese have been acquainted with the arch from very early times, though they make comparatively little use of it. Certain bridges have pointed arches, others have semicircular, and others approach the form of a horse-shoe, the transverse section of an ellipse, or even like the Greek Ω, the space being widest at the top. In some the arch is high for the accommodation of boats passing beneath; and where no heavy wains or carriages cross and jar the fabric, it can safely be made light. A graceful specimen of this class is the structure seen in the illustration on page 754. This bridge, though serving no practical purpose, is one of the greatest ornaments about the Emperor's summer palace of Yuen-ming Yuen. The material is marble; its summit is reached by forty steps rising abruptly

---

[1] *Chinese Repository*, Vol. VI., p. 149.

from the causeway, and impracticable, of course, for any but pedestrians.

The balustrades and paving of the long marble bridges near Peking and Hangchau, some of them adorned with statues of elephants, lions, and other animals, present a pleasing effect, while their solidity and endurance of freshes running over the top at times attest the skill of the architects. Wooden bridges furnish means for crossing small streams in all parts of the land; when the river is powerful, or the rise and fall of the tide great,

Bridge in Wan-shao Shan Gardens, near Peking.

it is crossed on boats fastened together, with contrivances for drawing out two or three in the centre when the passing craft demand a passage. At Tientsin, Ningpo, and other cities, this means of crossing entails little delay in comparison to its cheapness. Some of the bridges in and about Peking are beautiful structures; their erection, however, presented no difficult problem, while that at Fuhchau was a greater feat of engineering. It is about four hundred yards long and five wide, consisting of nearly forty solid buttresses of hewn stone placed at unequal distances and joined by slabs of granite; some of these slabs are three feet square and forty-five feet long. They support a granite pavement. The bridge was formerly lined with shops, which the increased traffic has caused to be removed. Another similar bridge lies seven miles north of it on the River Min, and a third of equal importance at the city of Chinchew, north of Amoy. Some of the mountain streams and passes in the west and north are crossed by rope bridges of ingenious construction, and by chain suspension bridges.

Mr. Lowrie describes a bridge at Changchau, near Amoy, and these structures are more numerous in the eastern provinces than elsewhere. "It is built on twenty-five piles of stone about thirty feet apart, and perhaps twenty feet each in height. Large round beams are laid from pile to pile, and smaller ones across in the simplest and rudest manner; earth is then placed above these and the top paved with brick and stone. One would suppose that the work had been assigned to a number of different persons, and that each one had executed his part in such manner as best suited his own fancy, there being no regularity whatever in the paving. Bricks and stone were intermingled in the most confused manner, and the railing was here wood and there stone. We were particularly struck with the length of some of the granite stones used in paving the bridge; one was eight, another eleven, and three others eighteen paces, or about forty-five feet long, and two broad. The bridge averaged eight or ten feet in width, and about half its length on both sides was occupied by shops." [1]

A causeway of ninety arches crosses a feeder of the Grand Canal near Hangchau. The stones for the arch in one bridge noticed by Barrow were cut so as to form a segment of the arch, and at each end were mortised into transverse blocks of stone stretching across the bridge; they decreased in length from ten feet at the spring of the arch to three at the vertex, and the summit stone was mortised, like the rest, into two transverse blocks lying next to it.[2] The tenons were short, and the dis-

[1] *Chinese Repository*, Vol. XII., p. 528; Medhurst's *Hohkeën Dictionary*, Introduction pp. XXII, XXIII.

[2] Barrow's *Travels*, p. 338.

position of the principal pieces such that a bridge built in this way would not support great weights or endure many ages. The mode of placing the pieces can be seen in the cut. In other instances the stones are laid in the same manner as in Europe; many small bridges over creeks and canals have cambered or straight arches. When one of these structures falls into ruins or becomes dangerous, the people seldom bestir themselves to repair the damage, preferring to wait for the government; they thereby lose the benefit of self-dependence and action.

Bridge showing the mode of Mortising the Arch.

It is singular how the term *triumphal arch* came to be applied to the *pai-fang* and *pai-lau*, or honorary portals or tablets, of the Chinese; for a triumph was perhaps never heard of in that country, and these structures are never arched. They consist merely of a broad gateway flanked with two smaller ones, and suggest a turnpike gate with side-ways for foot passengers rather than a triumphal monument. They are scattered in great numbers over the provinces, and are erected in honor of distinguished persons, or by officers to commemorate their parents, by special favor from the Emperor. Some are put up in honor of women who have distinguished themselves for their chastity and filial duty, or to widows who have refused a second marriage. Permission to erect them is considered a high honor, and perhaps the term *triumphal* was given them from this circumstance. The economical and peaceful nature of such honors conferred upon distinguished men in China is most characteristic; a man is allowed to build a stone gateway to himself or his parents, and the Emperor furnishes the inscription, or perhaps sends with it a patent of nobility. Their general arrangement is exhibited in the title-page of this work; the two characters, *shing chí*, at the top, meaning 'sacred will,' intimate that it was erected by his Majesty's permission.

Some of the *pai-lau* are elaborately ornamented with carved work and inscriptions; and as a protection to the frieze a ponderous covering of tiles projects over the top, which, however, exposes the structure to injury from tempests. They are placed in conspicuous places in the outskirts of towns, and in the streets before temples or near government edifices. Travellers looking for what they had read about have sometimes strangely mistaken the gateways at the heads of streets or the entrance to temples for the honorary portals.[1] Those built of stone are fastened by mortises and tenons in the same manner as the wooden ones; they seldom exceed twenty or twenty-five feet in height. The skill and taste displayed in the symmetry and carving upon some of them are creditable; but as the man in whose honor it is erected is, generally speaking, "the architect of his own fame," he prudently considers the worth of that commodity, and makes an inferior structure to what would have been done if his fellow-subjects, "deeply sensible of the honor," had come together to appoint a committee and open a subscription list for the purpose. Among the numerous *pai-lau* in and near Peking, two or three deserve mention for their beauty. One lies in the Confucian Temple in front of the *Pih-yung Kung*, and is designed to enhance the splendor of its approach by presenting, as it were, a frame before its façade. It is built of stone and overlaid with square encaustic tiles of many hues.

---

[1] *Encyclopædia Americana*, Art. CANTON.

The arrangement of the colors, the carving on the marble, and the fine proportions of the structure render it altogether one of the most artistic objects in China. Another like it is built in the Imperial Park, but the position is not so advantageous. Fergusson points out the similarity between these *pai-lau* and certain Hindu gateways, and claims that India furnished the model. The question of priority is hardly susceptible of proof; but his fancy that a large *pai-lau* in a street of Amoy presented a simulated coffin on it above the principal cornice, leads us to suspect that he was looking for what was never in the builder's mind.

The construction of forts and towers presents little worthy of observation, since there is no other evidence of science than what the erection of lines of massive stone wall displays. The port-holes are too large for protection and the parapet too slight to resist modern missiles. The Chinese idea of a fortification is a wall along the water's edge, with embrasures and battlements, and a plain wall landward without port-holes or parapets, enclosing an area in which a few houses accommodate the garrison and ammunition. Some erected at the junction of streams are pierced on all sides; others are so unscientifically planned that the walls can be scaled at angles where not a single gun can be brought to bear. The towers are rectangular edifices of brick on a stone foundation, forty feet square and fifty or sixty high, to be entered by ladders through a door half way up the side.

The forts in the neighborhood of Canton, probably among the best in the Empire, are all constructed without fosse, bastion, glacis, or counter-defence of any kind. Both arrangement and placement are alike faulty: some are square and approachable without danger; others circular on the outer face but with flank or rear exposed; others again built on a hillside like a pound, so that the garrison, if dislodged from the battlements, are forced to fly up the slope in full range of their enemy's fire. The gate is on the side, unprotected by ditch, drawbridge, or portcullis, and poorly defended by guns upon the walls or in the area behind. In general the points chosen for their forts display a misapprehension of the true principles of defence, though some may be noted as occupying commanding positions.

In recent times mud defences and batteries of sand-bags have proved a much safer defence than such buildings against ships and artillery, and show the aptitude of the people to adopt practical things. Though not particularly resolute on the field, the Chinese soldier stands well to his guns when behind a fortification of whose strength he is assured. The forts which have recently been constructed under supervision of European engineers are rapidly taking the place of native works in all parts of the country.

Dress, like other things, undergoes its changes in China, and fashions alter there as well as elsewhere, but they are not as rapid or as striking as among European nations. The full costume of both sexes is, in general terms, commodious and graceful, combining all the purposes of warmth, beauty, and ease which could be desired, excepting always the shaven crown and braided queue of the men and the crippled feet of the women, in both of which fashions they have not less outraged nature than deformed themselves. On this point different tastes exist, and some prefer the close-fitting dress of Europeans to the loose robes of Asiatics; but when one has become in a measure habituated to the latter, one is willing to allow the force of the criticism that the European male costume is "a mysterious combination of the inconvenient and the unpicturesque: hot in summer and cold in winter, useless for either keeping off rain or sun, stiff but not plain, bare without being simple, not durable, not becoming, and not cheap." The Chinese dress has remained, in its general style, the same for centuries; and garments of fur or silk are handed down from parent to child without fear of attracting attention by their antique shapes. The fabrics most worn are silk, cotton, and grass-cloth for summer, with the addition of furs and skins in winter; woollen is used sparingly, and almost wholly of foreign manufacture.

The principal articles of dress are inner and outer tunics of various lengths made of cotton or silk, reaching below the loins or to the feet; the lapel on the right side folds over the breast and fits close about the neck, which is left uncovered. The sleeves are much wider and longer than the arms, have no cuffs or facings, and in common cases serve for pockets. A Chinese, instead of saying "he pocketed the book," would say "he sleeved it." In robes of ceremony the end of the sleeve resembles a horse's hoof, and good breeding requires the hand to be kept in a position to exhibit the cuff when sitting. In warm weather one upper garment is deemed sufficient; in winter a dozen can be put on without discommodity, and this number is sometimes

Barber's Establishment, showing also the Dress of the Common People.

actually seen upon persons engaged in sedentary employments, or on those who sit in the air. Latterly, underwear of flannel has become common among the better dressed, who like the knitted fabric so close-fitting and warm. The lower limbs are comparatively slightly protected; a pair of loose trousers, covered to the knee by cloth stockings, is the usual summer garment; tight leggings are pulled over both in winter and attached to the girdle by loops; and as the trousers are rather voluminous and the tunic short, the excess shows behind from under these leggings in a rather unpleasant manner. Gentlemen and officers always wear a robe with the skirt opened at the sides, which conceals this intermission of the under apparel. The colors preferred for outer garments are various hues of buff, purple, or blue.

The shoes are made of silk or cotton, usually embroidered for women's wear in red and other colors. The soles are of felt, sometimes of paper inside a rim of felt, and defended on the bottom by hide. These shoes keep the feet dry and unchilled on the tiles or ground, so that a Chinese may be said really to carry the floor of his house under his feet instead of laying it on the ground. The thick soles render it necessary for ease in walking to round up their ends, which constrains the toes into an elevated position so irksome that all go slipshod who conveniently can do so. The cost of a cotton suit need not exceed five dollars, and a complete silken one, of the gayest colors and best materials, can easily be procured for twenty-five or thirty. Quilted cotton garments are exceedingly common, and are so made as to protect the whole person from the cold and obviate the need of fires. In the north dressed sheepskin robes furnish bedding as well as garments, and their durability will long make them more desirable than woven fabrics.

The ancient Chinese wore the hair long, bound upon the top of the head, somewhat after the style of the Lewchewans; and taking pride in its glossy black, called themselves the *black-haired race*. But in 1627 the Manchus, then in possession of only Liautung, issued an order that all Chinese under them should adopt their coiffure as a sign of allegiance, on penalty of death; the fashion thus begun by compulsion is now followed from choice. The fore part of the head is shaved to the crown and the hair braided in a single plait behind. Laborers often wind it about the head or knot it into a ball out of the way when barebacked or at work. The size of the queue can be enlarged by permitting an additional line of hair to grow; the appearance it gives the wearer is thus described by Mr. Downing, and the quotation is not an unfair specimen of the remarks of travellers upon China: "At the hotel one of the waiters was dressed in a peculiar manner about the head. Instead of the hair being shaved in front, he had it cut round the top of the forehead about an inch and a half in length. All the other part was turned as usual and plaited down the back. This thin semi-circular ridge of hair was then made to stand bolt upright, and as each hair was separate and stiff as a bristle, the whole looked like a very fine-toothed comb turned upward. This I imagined to be the usual way of dressing the head by single unengaged youths, and of course must be very attractive." Thus what the wearer regarded as ill-looking, and intended to braid in as soon

Tricks Played with the Queue.

as it was long enough, is here taken as a device for beautifying himself in the eyes of those he never saw or cared to see.

The people are vain of a long thick queue, and now and then play each other tricks with it, as well as use it as a ready means for correction; but nothing irritates them more than to cut it off. Men and women oftener go bareheaded than covered, warding off the sun by means of a fan; in winter felt or silk skull-caps, hoods, and fur protect them from cold. Laborers shelter themselves from rain under an umbrella hat and a grotesque thatch-work of leaves neatly sewn upon a coarse network—very effectual for the purpose. In illustration of the remark at the beginning of this chapter, it might be added that if they were not worn on the head such hats would be called trays, so unlike are they to the English article of that name. The formal head-dress is the conical straw or felt hat so peculiar to this nation, usually covered with a red fringe of silk or hair.

The various forms, fabrics, colors, and ornaments of the dresses worn by grades of officers are regulated by sumptuary laws. Citron-yellow distinguishes the imperial family, but his Majesty's apparel is less showy than many of his courtiers, and in all that belongs to his own personal use there is an appearance of disregard of ornament. The five-clawed dragon is figured upon the dress and whatever pertains to the Emperor, and in certain things to members of his family. The monarchs of China formerly wore a sort of flat-topped crown, shaped somewhat like a Cantab's cap, and having a row of jewels pendent from each side. The summer bonnet of officers is made of finely woven straw covered with a red fringe; in winter it is trimmed with fur. A string of beads hanging over an embroidered robe, a round knob on the cap, thick-soled satin boots, two or three pouches for fans or chopsticks, and occasionally a watch or two hanging from the girdle, constitute the principal points of difference between the official and plebeian costume. No company of men can appear more splendid than a large party of officers in their winter robes made of fine, lustrous crapes, trimmed with rich furs and brilliant with gay embroidery. In winter a silk or fur spencer is worn over the robe, and forms a handsome and warm garment. Lambskins are much used, and the downy coats of unyeaned lambs, which, with the finer furs and the skins of hares, wild cats, rabbits, foxes, wolves, otter, squirrels, etc., are worn by all ranks. Some years ago a lad used to parade the streets of Canton, who presented an odd appearance in a long spencer made of a tiger's skin. The Chinese like strong contrasts in the colors of their garments, sometimes wearing yellow leggings underneath a light blue robe, itself set off by a purple spencer.

The dress of women is likewise liable to few fluctuations, and all ranks can be sure that the fashion will last as long as the gown. The garments of both sexes among the common people resemble each other more than in Western Asia. The tunic or short gown is open in front, buttoning around the neck and under the arm, reaching to the knee, like a smock-frock in its general shape. The trousers among the lower orders are usually worn over the stockings, both being covered, on ceremonial occasions, by a petticoat reaching to the feet. Laboring women, whose feet are left their natural size, go barefoot or slipshod in the warm latitudes, but cover their feet carefully farther north. Both sexes have a paucity of linen in their habiliments—if not a shiftless, the Chinese certainly are a shirtless race, and such undergarments as they have are not too often washed.

The head-dress of married females is becoming and even elegant. The copious black hair is bound upon the head in an oval-formed knot, which is secured in its place and shape by a broad pin placed lengthwise on it, and fastened by a shorter one thrust across and under the bow. The hair is drawn back from the forehead into the knot, and elevated a little in front by combing it over the finger; in order to make it lie smooth the locks are drawn through resinous shavings moistened in warm water, which also adds an extra gloss, at the cost, however, of injury to the hair. In front of the knot a tube is often inserted, in which flowers can be placed. The custom of wearing them is nearly universal, fresh blossoms being preferred when obtainable, and artificial at other times. Having no covering on the head there is more opportunity than in the west to display pretty devices in arranging the hair. A widow is known by her white flowers, a maiden by one or two plaits instead of a knot, and so on; in their endless variety of form and ornament, Chinese women's head-dresses furnish a source of constant study. Mr. Stevens tells us that the animated appearance of the dense crowd which assembled on the bridge and banks of the river at Fuhchau when he passed in 1835, was still more enlivened by the flowers worn by the women.

Matrons wear an embroidered fillet on the forehead, an inch or more wide, pointed between the eyebrows, and covering the front of the hair though not concealing the baldness which often comes on early from the resinous bandoline used. This fillet is embroidered, or adorned with pearls, a favorite ornament with

PROCESSION OF LADIES TO AN ANCESTRAL TEMPLE.

Chinese ladies. The women along the Yangtsz' River wear a band of fur around the head, which relieves their colorless complexions. A substitute for bonnets is common in summer, consisting of a flat piece of straw trimmed with a fringe of blue cloth. The hair of children is unbound, but girls more advanced allow the side locks to reach to the waist and plait a tress down the neck; their coarse hair does not curl, and the beautiful luxuriance of curls and ringlets seen in Europe is entirely unknown. False hair is made use of by both sexes, the men being particularly fond of eking out their queues to the fullest length. Gloves are not worn, the long sleeves being adequate for warmth; in the north the ears are protected from freezing by ear-tabs lined with fur, and often furnished with a tiny looking-glass on the outside.

The dress of gentlewomen, like that of their husbands, is regulated by sumptuary laws, but none of these prevent their costumes from being as splendid as rich silks, gay colors, and beautiful embroidery can make them. The neck of the robe is protected by a stiff band, and the sleeves are large and long, just the contrary of the common style, which being short allows the free use and display of a well-turned arm. The official embroidery allowed to the husband is changed to another kind on his wife's robe indicative of the same rank. No belt or girdle is seen, nor do stays compress the waist to its lasting injury. One of the prettiest parts of a lady's dress is the petticoat, which appears about a foot below the upper robe covering the feet. Each side of the skirt is plaited about six times, and in front and rear are two pieces of buckram to which they are attached; the plaits and front pieces are stiffened with wire and lining. Embroidery is worked upon these two pieces and the plaits in such a way that as the wearer steps the action of the feet alternately opens and shuts them on each side, disclosing a part or the whole of two different colored figures, as may be seen in the illustration. The plaits are so contrived that they are the same when seen in front or from behind, and the effect is more elegant when the colors are well contrasted. In order to produce this the plaits close around the feet, unlike the wider skirt of western ladies.

Ornaments are less worn by the Chinese than other Asiatic nations. The men suspend a string of fragrant beads together with the tobacco-pouch from the jacket lapel, or occasionally wear seal-rings, finger-rings, and armlets of strass, stone, or glass. They are by law prohibited from carrying weapons of any sort. The women wear bangles, bracelets, and ear-rings of glass, stone, and metal; most of these appendages are regarded more as amulets to ward off evil influences than mere ornaments. Felicitous charms, such as aromatic bags, old coins, and rings, are attached to the persons of children, and few adults venture to go through life without some preservative of this kind; no sacred thread or daub of clay, as in India, is known, however, nor any image of a saint or other figurine, as in Romish countries. The queer custom of wearing long nails is practised by comparatively few; and although a man or woman with these appendages would not be deemed singular, it is not regarded as in good taste by well-bred persons. Pedantic scholars wear them more than other professions, in order to show that they are above manual labor; but the longest set the writer ever saw was, oddly enough, on a carpenter's fingers, who thereby showed that he was not obliged to use his tools. Fine ladies protect theirs with silver sheaths.

The practice of compressing the feet, so far as investigation has gone, is more an inconvenient than a dangerous custom, for among the many thousands of patients who have received aid in the missionary hospitals, few have presented themselves with ailments chargeable to this source. A difference of opinion exists respecting its origin. Some accounts state that it arose from a desire thereby to remove the reproach of the club feet of a popular empress, others that it gradually came into use from the great admiration of and attempt to imitate delicate feet, and others that it was imposed by husbands to keep their wives from gadding.[1] Its adoption was gradual, however it may have commenced, and not without resistance. It is practised

[1] It is recorded that Hau-Chu, of the Chin dynasty, in the year A.D. 583 ordered Lady Yao to bind her feet so as to make them look like the new moon; and that the evil fashion has since prevailed against all subsequent prohibitions.—*Notes and Queries on China and Japan*, Vol. II., pp. 27 and 43.

by all classes of society except the Manchus and Tartars, poor as well as rich (for none are so poor as not to wish to be fashionable); and so habituated does one become to it after a residence in the country, that a well-dressed lady with large feet seems to be denationalized. There is no certain age at which the operation must be commenced, but in families of easy circumstances the bandages are put on before five; otherwise not until betrothment, or till seven or eight years old. The whole operation is performed, and the shape maintained, by bandages, which are never permanently removed or covered by stockings; iron or wooden shoes are not used, the object being rather to prevent the feet growing than to make them smaller.

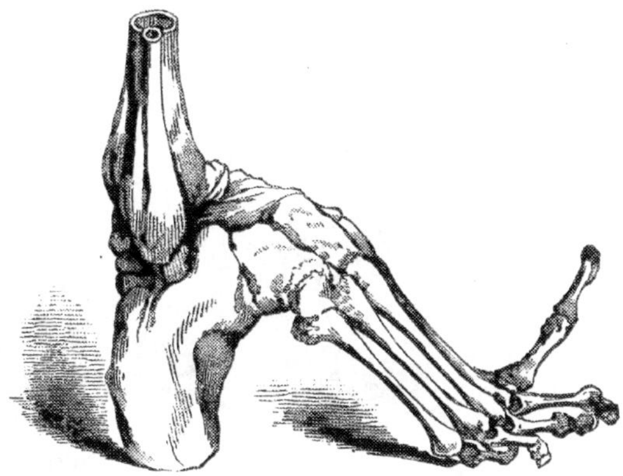

Appearance of the Bones of a Foot when Compressed.

A good account of the effects of this practice is given in a paper contained in the *Transactions of the Royal Society of London*, written by Dr. Cooper, detailing the appearances presented on dissection. The foot belonged to a person in low life; it was five and one-fourth inches long, which is full eighteen lines over the most fashionable size. The big toe was bent upward and backward on the foot, and the second twisted under it and across, so that the extremity reached the inner edge of the foot. The third toe somewhat overlapped the second, but lying less obliquely, and reaching to the first joint of the great toe. The ball of the great toe, much flattened, separated these two from the fourth and fifth toes. The fourth toe stretched obliquely inward under the foot, but less so than the little toe, which passed under and nearly across the foot, and had been bound down so strongly as to bend the tarsal bone. The dorsum of the foot was much curved, and a deep fissure crossed the sole and separated the heel and little toe, as if the two ends of the foot had been forced together; this was filled for three inches with a very condensed cellular tissue; the instep was three and one-half inches high. The heel-bone, which naturally forms a considerable angle with the ankle, was in a direct line with the leg-bones; and the heel itself was large and flat, covered with a peculiarly dense integument, and forming, with the end of the metatarsal bone of the great toe and the two smallest toes bent under the sole, the three points of taction in walking. When the operation is begun earlier, and the bones are more flexible, four of the toes are bent under the foot and only the big toe laid upon the top. The development of the muscles of the calf being checked, the leg tapers from the knee downward, though there is no particular weakness in the limb. The appearance of the deformed member when uncovered is shocking, crushed out of all proportion and beauty, and covered with a wrinkled and lifeless skin like that of a washerwoman's hand. It is surprising how the circulation is kept up in the member without any pain or wasting away; the natural supposition would be that if any nutriment was conveyed to it, there would be a disposition to grow until maturity was attained, and consequently constant pain ensue, or else that it would be destroyed or mortify for want of nourishment.

Feet of Chinese Ladies.

The gait of these victims of fashion can be imitated by a person walking on the heels. Women walking alone swing their arms and step quick and short, elderly women availing themselves, when practicable, of an umbrella, or leaning upon the shoulder of a lad or maid for support—literally making a walking-stick of them. The pain is said to be severe at first, and a recurrence now and then is felt in the sole; but the evident freedom from distress exhibited in the little girls who are seen walking or playing in the streets, proves that the amount of suffering and injurious effects upon life and health are perhaps not so great as has been imagined. The case is different when the girl is not victimized until ten or more years old. The toes are then bent under and the foot forced into the smallest compass; the agony arising from the constrained muscles and excoriated flesh is dreadful, while, too, the shape of the member is, even in Chinese eyes, a burlesque upon the beautiful littleness so much desired.

The opinion prevails abroad that only the daughters of the rich or learned pay this price to Dame Fashion. A greater proportion is indeed found among the well-to-do classes, and in the southern provinces near the rivers the unfashionables form perhaps half of the whole; for those who dwell in boats, and all who in early life may have lived on the water or among the farmsteads, and slave girls sold in infancy for domestics, are usually left in the happy though low-life freedom of nature. Close observation in the northern provinces show general adoption of the usage among the poor, whose feet are not, however, usually so small as in the south. Foreigners, on their arrival at Canton or Fuhchau, seeing so many women with natural feet on the boats and about the streets, wonder where the "little-footed Celestials" they had heard of were, the only specimens they see being a few crones by the wayside mending clothes. Across the Mei ling range the proportion increases. All the women who came to the hospital at Chusan in 1841, to the number of eight hundred or one thousand, had their feet more or less cramped; and some of them walked several miles to the hospital and home again the same day. Although the operation may be less painful than has been represented, the people are so much accustomed to it that most men would refuse to wed a woman whose feet were of the natural size; and a man who should find out that his bride had large feet when he expected small ones would be exonerated if he instantly sent her back to her parents. The *kin lien*, or 'golden lilies,' are desired as the mark of gentility; the hope of rising to be one of the upper ten, and escaping the roughness and hard work attached to the lower class, goes far

Shape of a Lady's Shoe.

to strengthen even children to endure the pain and loss of freedom consequent on the practice. The secret of the prevalence of the cruel custom is the love of ease and praise; and not till the principles of Christianity extend will it cease. In Peking, where the Manchus have shown the advantages nature has over fashion, the example of their women for two hundred and fifty years, aided by the earnest efforts of the great Emperor Kanghí, has not had the least effect in inducing Chinese ladies to give it up. The shoes are made of red silk and prettily embroidered; but no one acquainted with Chinese society would say that "if a lady ever breaks through the prohibition against displaying her person, she presents her feet as the surest darts with which a lover's heart can be assailed!"[1]

Cosmetics are used by females to the serious injury of the skin. On grand occasions the face is entirely bedaubed with white paint, and rouge is added to the lips and cheeks, giving a singular starched appearance to the physiognomy. A girl thus beautified has no need of a fan to hide her blushes, for they cannot be seen through the paint, her eye being the only index of emotion. The eyebrows are blackened with charred sticks, and arched or narrowed to resemble a nascent willow leaf, or the moon when first seen—as in the ballad translated by Mr. Stent, which pictures the beauty as possessing

> Eyebrows shaped like leaves of willows
> Drooping over "autumn billows;"
> Almond shaped, of liquid brightness,
> Were the eyes of Yang-kuei-fei.[2]

A belle is described as having cheeks like the almond flower, lips like a peach's bloom, waist as the willow leaf, eyes bright as dancing ripples in the sun, and footsteps like the lotus flower. Much time and care is bestowed, or said to be, by females upon their toilet, but if those in the upper classes have anything like

---

[1] Murray's *China*, Vol. II., p. 266. Compare the *Chinese Repository*, Vol. III., p. 537; *Rec. de Mém. de Médecine milit.* (Paris), 1862–63–64 passim; *Chinese Recorder*, Vols. I., II., and III. passim (mostly a series of articles on this subject by Dr. Dudgeon); *The Far East*, February, 1877, p 27.

[2] *The Jade Chaplet*, p. 121.

the variety of domestic duties which their sisters in common life perform, they have little leisure left for superfluous adorning. If dramas give an index of Chinese manners and occupations, they do not convey the idea that most of the time of well-bred ladies is spent in idleness or dressing.

At his toilet a Chinese uses a basin of tepid water and a cloth, and it has been aptly remarked that he never appears so dirty as when trying to clean himself. Shaving is done by the barber, for no man can shave the top of his head. Whiskers are never worn, even by the very few who have them, and mustaches are not considered proper for a man under forty. Snuff bottles and tobacco pipes are carried and used by both sexes, but the practice of chewing betel-nut is confined to the men, who, however, take much pains to keep their teeth white. Among ornamental articles of dress, in none do they go to so much expense and style as in the snuff bottle, which is often carved from stone, amber, agate, and other rare minerals with most exquisite taste. Snuff is put on the thumb-nail with a spoon fastened to the stopper—a more cleanly way than the European mode of "pinching."[1]

The articles of food which the Chinese eat, and the mode and ceremonies attending their feasts, have aided much in giving them the odd character they bear abroad, though uncouth or unsavory viands form an infinitesimal portion of their food, and ceremonious feasts not one in a thousand of their repasts. Travellers have so often spoken of birdsnest soup, canine hams, and grimalkin fricassees, rats, snakes, worms, and other culinary novelties, served up in equally strange ways, that their readers get the idea that these articles form as large a proportion of the food as their description does of the narrative. In general, the diet of the Chinese is sufficient in variety, wholesome, and

---

[1] On Chinese costume, see Wm. Alexander, *The Costume of China*, illustrated, London, 1805; *Mœurs et Coutumes des Chinois et leurs costumes en couleur*, par J. G. Grohmann, Leipzig; Breton, *China: Its Costume, Arts, etc.*, 4 vols., translated from the French, London, 1812; another translation is from Auguste Borget, *Sketches of China and the Chinese*, London, 1842; *Illustrations of China and its People. A series of two hundred photographs, with letterpress descriptive of the places and people represented*, by J. Thompson, London, 1874, 4 vols. quarto.

well cooked, though many of the dishes are unpalatable to a European from the vegetable oils used in their preparation, and the alliaceous plants introduced to savor them. In the assortment of dishes, Barrow has truly said that "there is a wider difference, perhaps, between the rich and the poor of China than in any other country. That wealth, which if permitted would be expended in flattering the vanity of its possessors, is now applied to the purchase of dainties to pamper the appetite."

The proportion of animal food is probably smaller among the Chinese than other nations on the same latitude, one platter of fish or flesh, and sometimes both, being the usual allowance on the tables of the poor. Rice, maize, Italian millet, and wheat furnish most of the cereal food; the first is emphatically the staff of life, and considered indispensable all over the land. Its long use is indicated in the number of terms employed to describe it and the variety of allusions to it in common expressions. To *take a meal* is *chih fan*, 'eat rice;' and the salutation equivalent to *how d'ye?* is *chih kwo fan?* 'have you eaten rice?' The grain is deprived of its skin by wooden pestles worked in a mortar by levers, either by a water-wheel or more commonly by oxen or men. It is cleaned by rubbing it in an earthen dish scored on the inside, and steamed in a shallow iron boiler partly filled with water, over which a basket or sieve containing the rice is supported on a framework; a wooden dish fits over the whole and confines the steam. By this process the kernels are thoroughly cooked without forming a pasty mass, as is too often the result when boiled by cooks in Christian countries. Bread, vegetables, and other articles are cooked in a similar manner; four or five sieves, each of them full and nicely fitting into each other, are placed upon the boiler and covered with a cowl; in the water beneath, which supplies the steam, meats or other things are boiled at the same time. Wheat flour is boiled into cakes, dumplings, and other articles, but not baked into bread. Maize, buckwheat, oats, and barley are not ground, but the grain is cooked in various ways, alone or mixed with other dishes. Italian millet, or canary-seed (*Setaria*), furnishes a large amount of nutritious cereal food in the north; the flour is yellow and sweet, and boiled or baked for eating, often seasoned with jujube plums in the cakes. Its cultivation is easy, and its prolific crop makes up in a measure for the small seeds; ten thousand kernels have been counted on one spike in a good season.

The Chinese have a long list of culinary vegetables, and much of their agriculture consists in rearing them. Leguminous and cruciferous plants occupy the largest part of the kitchen garden; more than twenty sorts of peas and beans are cultivated, some for camels and horses, but mostly for men. *Soy* is made by boiling the beans and mixing water, salt, and wheat, and producing fermentation by yeast; its quality is inferior to the foreign. Another more common condiment, called bean curd or bean jam, is prepared by boiling and grinding black beans and mixing the flour with water, gypsum, and turmeric. The consumption of cabbage, broccoli, kale, cauliflower, cress, colewort, and other cruciferous plants is enormous; a great variety of modes are adopted for cooking, preserving, and improving them. The leaves and stems of many plants besides these are included in the variety of greens, and a complete enumeration of them would form a curious list. Lettuce, sow thistle (*Sonchus*), spinach, celery, dandelion, succory, sweet basil, ginger, mustard, radishes, artemisia, amaranthus, tacca, pig weed (*Chenopodium*), burslane, shepherd's purse, clover, ailantus, and others having no English names, all furnish green leaves for Chinese tables. Garlics, leeks, scallions, onions, and chives are eaten by all classes, detected upon all persons, and smelt in all rooms where they are eating or cooking. Carrots, gourds, squashes, cucumbers, watermelons, tomatoes, turnips, radishes, brinjals, pumpkins, okers, etc., are among the list of garden vegetables; the variety of cucurbitaceous plants extends to nearly twenty. Most of these vegetables are inferior to the same articles in the markets of western cities, where science has improved their size or flavor. Several aquatic plants increase the list, among which the nelumbium covers extensive marshes in the eastern and northern provinces, otherwise unsightly and barren. The root is two or three feet long, and pierced longitudinally with several holes; when boiled it is of a yellowish color and sweetish taste, not unlike a turnip. Taro is used less than the nelumbium, and so are the water-caltrops (*Trapa*) and water-chestnuts. The taste of water-caltrops when boiled resembles that of new cheese; water-chestnuts are the round roots of a kind of sedge, and resemble that fruit in color more than in taste, which is mealy and crisp. The sweet potato is the most common tuber; although the Irish potato has been cultivated for scores of years it has not become a common vegetable among the people, except on the borders of Mongolia.

The catalogue of fruits comprises most of those occurring elsewhere in the tropic and temperate zones, and China is probably the earliest home of the peach, plum, and pear. The pears are large and juicy, sometimes weighing eight or ten pounds; the white and strawberry pear are equal to any western variety. The apples are rather dry and insipid. The peaches, plums, quinces, and apricots are better, and offer many good varieties. Cherries are almost unknown. The orange is the common fruit at the south, and the baskets, stalls, and piles of this golden fruit, mixed with and heightened by contrast with other sorts and with vegetables, which line the streets of Canton and Amoy in winter, present a beautiful sight. Many distinct species of Citrus, as the lemon, kumquot, pumelo, citron, and orange, are extensively cultivated. The most delicious is the *chu-sha kih*, or 'mandarin orange;' the skin, when ripe, is of a cinnabar red color, and adheres to the pulp by a few loose fibres. The citron is more prized for its fragrance than taste, and the thick rind is now and then made more abundant by cutting it into strips when growing, each of which becomes a roundish end like a finger, whence the name of *Fuh shao*, or 'Buddha's hand,' given it. It will remain uncorrupt for two or three months, diffusing an agreeable perfume.

Chapter VI. contains brief notices of other fruits. The banana and persimmon are common, and several varieties are enumerated of each; the plantain is eaten raw and cooked, and forms a large item in the subsistence of the poor. The pomegranate, carambola or tree gooseberry, mango, custard-apple, pine-apple, rose-apple, bread-fruit, fig, guava, and olive, some of them as good and others inferior to what are found in other countries, increase the list. The *whampe*, *lichi*, *lungan*, or 'dragon's eyes,' and *loquat*, are the native names of four indigenous fruits at Canton. The whampe (*Cookia*) resembles a grape in size and a gooseberry in taste; the loquat or *pebo* (*Eriobotrya*) is a kind of medlar. The líchí looks like a strawberry in size and shape; the tough, rough red skin encloses a sweet watery pulp of a whitish color surrounding a hard seed. Grapes are plenty and cheap; in the northern cities they are preserved during the winter, and even till May, by constant care in regulating the temperature.

Chestnuts, walnuts, ground-nuts, filberts (*Torreya*), almonds, and the seeds of the salisburia and nelumbium, are the most common nuts. The Chinese date (*Rhamnus*) has a sweetish, acidulous flesh; the olive is salted or pickled; the names of both these fruits are given them because of a resemblance to the western sorts, for neither the proper date nor olive grows in China. A pleasant sweetmeat, like cranberry, is made from the seeds of the arbutus (*Myrica*), and another still more acid from a sort of haw, both of them put up for exportation.

Preserved fruits are common, and the list of sweetmeats and delicacies is increased by the addition of many roots, some of which are preserved in syrup and others as comfits. Ginger, nelumbium roots, bamboo shoots, the common potato, and other vegetables are thus prepared for export as well as domestic consumption. The natives consume enormous quantities of pickles of an inferior quality, especially cabbages and onions, but foreigners consider them detestable. The Chinese eat but few spices; black pepper is used medicinally as a tea, and cayenne pepper when the pod is green.

Oils and fats are in universal use for cooking; crude lard or pork fat, castor oil, sesamum oil, and that expressed from two species of Camellia and the ground-nut, are all employed for domestic and culinary purposes. The Chinese use little or no milk, butter, or cheese; the comparatively small number of cattle raised and the consequent dearness of these articles may have caused them to fall into disuse, for they are all common among the Manchus and Mongols. A Chinese table seems ill furnished to a foreigner when he sees neither bread, butter, nor milk upon it, and if he express his disrelish of the oily dishes or alliaceous stews before him, the Chinese thinks that he delivers a sufficient retort to his want of taste when he answers, "You eat cheese, and sometimes when it can almost walk." Milk is used a little, and no one who has lived in Canton can forget the prolonged mournful cry of *ngao nai!* of the men hawking it about the streets late at night. Women's milk is sold for the sustenance of infants and superannuated people, the idea being prevalent that it is peculiarly nourishing to aged persons.[1]

Sugar is grown only in Formosa and the three southern provinces, which supply the others; neither molasses nor rum are manufactured from it. No sugar is expressed from sorghum stalks, nor do the Chinese know that it contains syrup. The tobacco is milder than the American plant; it is smoked and not chewed or made into cigars, though these are being imported from Manila in steadily increasing quantities, and find favor among many of the wealthier Chinese; snuff is largely used. The betel-nut is a common masticatory, made up of a slice of the nut and the fresh leaf of the betel-pepper with a little lime rubbed on it. The common beverages are tea and arrack, both of which are taken warm; cold water is not often drunk, cold liquids of any kind being considered unwholesome. The constant practice of boiling water before drinking, in preparing tea, doubtless tends to make it less noxious, when the people are not particular as to its sources. Coffee, chocolate, and cocoa are unknown, as are also beer, cider, porter, wine, and brandy.

The meats consumed by the Chinese comprise, perhaps, a greater variety than are used in other countries; while, at the same time, very little land is appropriated to rearing animals for food. Beef is not a common meat, chiefly from a Buddhistic prejudice against killing so useful an animal. Mutton in the southern provinces is poor and dear compared with its ex-

---

[1] Dr. Hobson mentions a case at Shanghai where he was called upon to examine a child well-nigh dead with spurious hydrocephalus. Upon investigation he found that the nurse, "a young healthy-looking woman, with breasts full of milk to overflowing," had "been in the habit of selling her milk in small cupfuls to old persons, under the idea of its highly nutritive properties, and was actually poisoning the child dependent on it." The nurse being promptly changed, the infant recovered almost immediately.—*Journal N. C. Br. R. A. Soc.* New Series, Vol. I., p. 51.

cellence and cheapness north of the Yangtsz' River, where the greater numbers of Mohammedans cause a larger demand for it. The beef of the buffalo and the mutton of the goat are still less used; pork is consumed more than all other kinds, and no meat can be raised so economically. Hardly a family so poor that it cannot possess a pig; the animals are kept even on the boats and rafts, to consume and fatten upon what others leave. Fresh pork probably constitutes more than half of the meat eaten by the Chinese; hams are tolerably plenty, and a dish called "golden hams," from the amber appearance of the joint, makes a conspicuous object in feasts. Horseflesh, venison, wild boar, and antelope are now and then seen, but in passing through the markets mutton, pork, fowls, and fish are the viands which everywhere meet the eye.

A few kittens and puppies are sold alive in cages, mewing and yelping as if in anticipation of their fate, or from pain caused by the pinching and handling they receive at the hands of dissatisfied customers. Those intended for the table are usually fed upon rice, so that if the nature of their food be considered, their flesh is far more cleanly than that of the omnivorous hog; few articles of food have, however, been so identified abroad with the tastes of the people as kittens, puppies, and rats have with the Chinese. American school geographies often contain pictures of a market-man carrying baskets holding these unfortunate victims of a perverse taste (as we think), or else a string of rats and mice hanging by their tails to a stick across his shoulders, which almost necessarily convey the idea that such things form the usual food of the people. Travellers hear beforehand that the Chinese devour everything, and when they arrive in the country straightway inquire if these animals are eaten, and hearing that such is the case, perpetuate the idea that they form the common articles of food. However commonly live kittens and puppies or dressed dogs may be exposed for sale, one may live in a city like Canton or Fuhchau for many years and never see rats offered for food, unless he hunts up the people who sell them for medicine or aphrodisiacs; in fact, they are not so easily caught as to be either common or cheap. A peculiar prejudice in favor of black dogs and cats exists among natives of the south; these animals invariably command a higher price than others, and are eaten at midsummer in the belief that the meat ensures health and strength during the ensuing year.

Rats and mice are, no doubt, eaten now and then, and so are many other undesirable things, by those whom want compels to take what they can get; but to put these and other strange eatables in the front of the list gives a distorted idea of the everyday food of the people. There are perhaps half a dozen restaurants in Canton city where dog's-meat appears upon the *menu;* it is, however, by no means an inexpensive delicacy.[1] The flesh of rats is eaten by old women as a hair restorative.

The blood of ducks, pigs, and sheep is used as food, or prepared for medicine and as a paste; it forms an ingredient in priming and some kind of varnish. It is coagulated into cakes for sale, and in cooking is mixed with the meats and sauces. The blood of all animals is eaten without repugnance so far as concerns religious scruples, except in the case of Buddhist priests.

Frogs are caught in a curious manner by tying a young jumper lately emerged from tadpole life to a line and bobbing him up and down in the grass and grain of a rice field, where the old croakers are wont to harbor. As soon as one of them sees the young frog sprawling and squirming he makes a plunge at him and swallows him whole, whereupon he is immediately conveyed to the frog-fisher's basket, losing his life, liberty, and lunch together, for the bait is rescued from his maw and used again as long as life lasts.

Poultry, including chickens, geese, and ducks, are everywhere raised; of the three the geese are the best flavored, but all of them are reared cheaply and supply a large portion of the poor with the principal meat they eat. The eggs of fowls and ducks are hatched artificially, and every visitor to Canton remembers the duck-boats in which those birds are hatched and reared and carried up and down the river seeking for pasture along its muddy banks. Sheds are erected for hatching, in which are

[1] Archdeacon Gray, *China*, Vol. II., p. 76.

a number of high baskets well lined to retain the heat. Each one is placed over a fireplace, so that the heat shall be conveyed to the eggs through the tile in its bottom and retained in the basket by a close cover. When the eggs are brought a layer is put into the bottom of each basket, and a fire kept in the room at a uniform heat of about 80° F. After four or five days they are examined in a strong light, to separate the addled ones; the others are put back in the baskets and the heat kept up for ten days longer, when they are all placed upon shelves in the centre of the shed and covered with cotton and felt for fourteen days. At the end of the twenty-eighth day the shells are broken to release the inmates, which are sold to those who rear them. Pigeons are raised to a great extent; their eggs form an ingredient in soups. Wild and water fowl are caught in nets or shot; the wild duck, teal, grebe, wild goose, plover, snipe, heron, egret, partridge, pheasant, and ortolan or rice bird are all procurable at Canton, and the list could be increased elsewhere.

If the Chinese eat many things which are rejected by other peoples, they are perfectly omnivorous with respect to aquatic productions; here nothing comes amiss; all waters are vexed with their fisheries. Their nets and other contrivances for capturing fish display great ingenuity, and most of them are admirably adapted to the purpose. Rivers, creeks, and stagnant pools, the great ocean and the little tank, mountain lakes and garden ponds, tubs and rice fields, all furnish their quota to the sustenance of man, and tend to explain, in a great degree, the dense population. The right to fish in running streams and natural waters is open to all, while artificial reservoirs, as ponds, pools, tanks, tubs, etc., are brought into available use; near tide-water the rice grounds are turned into fish-ponds in winter if they will thereby afford a more profitable return. The inhabitants of the water are killed with the spear, caught with the hook, scraped up by the dredge, ensnared by traps, and captured by nets; they are decoyed to jump into boats by painted boards, and frightened into nets by noisy ones, taken out of the water by lifting nets and dived for by birds—for the cormorant seizes what his owner could not easily reach. In short, every possible way of catching or rearing fish is practised in one part of the country or another. Tanks are placed in the streets, with water running through them, where carp or perch are reared until they become so large they can hardly turn round in their pens; eels and water-snakes of every color and size are fed in tubs and jars until customers carry them off.

King-crabs, cuttle-fish, sharks, sting-rays, gobies, tortoises, turtles, crabs, prawns, crawfish, and shrimps add to the variety. The best fish in the Canton market are the garoupa or rock cod, pomfret, sole, mackerel, bynni carp or mango fish, and the polynemus, erroneously called salmon. Carp and tench of many kinds, herring, shad, perch, mullet, and bream, with others less common at the west, are found in great abundance. They are usually eaten fresh, or merely opened and dried in the sun, as stock-fish. Both salt and fresh-water shell-fish are abundant. The oysters are not so well flavored as those on the Atlantic coast of America; the crabs and prawns are excellent, but the clams, mussels, and other fresh-water species are less palatable. Insect food is confined to locusts and grasshoppers, grubs and silk-worms; the latter are fried to a crisp when cooked. These and water-snakes are decidedly the most repulsive things the Chinese eat.

Many articles of food are sought after by this sensual people for their supposed aphrodisiac qualities, and most of the singular productions brought from abroad for food are of this nature. The famous birdsnest soup is prepared from the nest of a swallow (*Collocalia esculenta*) found in caves and damp places in some islands of the Indian Archipelago; the bird macerates the material of the nest from seaweed (*Gelidium* chiefly) in the crop, and constructs it by drawing the food out in fibres, which are attached to the damp stone with the bill. The nest has the same shape as those which chimney swallows build, and holds the young against the cliffs; they rarely exceed three or four inches in the longest diameter. The operation of cleaning is performed by picking away each morsel of dirt or feathers from the nest, and involves considerable labor. After they come forth perfectly free from impurities they are stewed with pigeons' eggs, spicery, and other ingredients into a soup; when cooked they resemble isinglass, and the dish depends upon sauces and seasoning for most of its taste. The biche-de-mer, tripang, or sea-slug, is a marine substance procured from the Polynesian Islands; it is sought after under the same idea of its invigorating qualities, and being cheaper than the birdsnest is a more common dish; when cooked it resembles pork-rind in appearance and taste. Sharks' fins and fish-maws are imported and boiled into gelatinous soups that are nourishing and palatable; and the sinews, tongues, palates, udders, and other parts of different animals are sought after as delicacies. A large proportion of the numerous made dishes seen at great feasts consists of such odd articles, most of which are supposed to possess some peculiar strengthening quality.

The art of cooking has not reached any high degree of perfection. Like the French, it is very economical, and consists of stews and fried dishes more than of baked or roasted. Salt is proportionately dear from its preparation being a government monopoly, and this has led to a large use of onions for seasoning. The articles of kitchen furniture are few and simple; an iron boiler, shaped like the segment of a sphere, for stewing or frying, a portable earthen furnace, and two or three different shaped earthenware pots for boiling water or vegetables constitute the whole establishment of thousands of families. A few other utensils, as tongs, ladles, forks, sieves, mills, etc., are used to a greater or less extent, though the variety is quite commensurate with the simple cookery. Both meats and vegetables, previously hashed into mouthfuls, are stewed or fried in oil or fat; they are not cooked in large joints or steaks for the table of a household. Hogs are baked whole for sacrifices and for sale in cook-shops, but before being eaten are hashed and fried again. Cutting the food into small pieces secures its thorough cooking with less fuel than it would otherwise require, and is moreover indispensable for eating with chopsticks. Two or three vegetables are boiled together, but meat soups are seldom seen; and the immense variety of puddings, pastry, cakes, pies, custards, ragouts, creams, etc., made in western lands is almost unknown in China.[1]

---

[1] *Mémoires conc. les Chinois*, Tome XI., pp. 78 ff. C. C. Coffin in the *Atlantic Monthly*, 1869, p. 747. Doolittle's *Vocabulary*, Part III., No. XVIII. M. Henri Cordier in the *Journal des Débats*, Nov. 19, 1879. *Notes and Queries on C. and J.*, Vol. II., pp. 11 and 26.

CHAPTER XIV.

SOCIAL LIFE AMONG THE CHINESE.

The preceding chapter, in a measure, exhibits the attainments the Chinese have reached in the comforts and elegances of living. These terms, as tests of civilization, however, are so comparative that it is rather difficult to define them; for the notions which an Englishman, an Egyptian, and a Chinese severally might have of comfort and elegance in the furniture and arrangement of their houses are almost as unlike as their languages. If Fisher's *Views of China* be taken as a guide, one can easily believe that the Chinese need little from abroad to better their condition in these particulars; while if one listen to the descriptions of some persons who have resided among them, it will be concluded that they possess neither comfort in their houses, civility in their manners, nor cleanliness in their persons. In passing to an account of their social life, this variety of tastes should not be overlooked; and if some points appear objectionable when taken alone, a little further examination will, perhaps, show that they form part of a system which requires complete reconstruction before it could be happily and safely altered.

The observations of a foreigner upon Chinese society are likely to be modified by his own feelings, and the way in which he has been treated by natives there; but their behavior to him might be very unlike what would be deemed good breeding among themselves. If a Chinese feared or expected something from a foreigner, he would act toward him more politely than if the contrary were the case; on the one hand better, on the other worse, than he would toward one of his own countrymen in like circumstances. In doing so, it may be remarked with regret that he would only imitate the conduct of a host of foreigners who visit China, and whose coarse remarks, rude actions, and general supercilious conduct toward the natives ill comport with their superior civilization and assumed advantages. One who looked at the matter reasonably would not expect much true politeness among a people whose conceit and ignorance, selfishness and hauteur, were nearly equal; nor be surprised to find the intercourse between the extremes of society present a strange mixture of brutality and commiseration, formality and disdain. The separation of the sexes modifies and debases the amusements, even of the most moral, leads the men to spend their time in gambling, devote it to the pleasures of the table, or dawdle it away when the demands of business, study, or labor do not arouse them. Political parties, which exert so powerful an influence upon the conduct of men in Christian countries, leading them to unite and communicate with each other for the purpose of watching or resisting the acts of government, do not exist; and where there is a general want of confidence, such institutions as insurance companies, savings or deposit banks, corporate bodies to build a railroad or factory, and associations of any kind in which persons unite their funds and efforts to accomplish an object, are not to be expected; they do not exist in China, nor did they in Rome or ancient Europe. Nor will any one expect to hear that literary societies or voluntary philanthropic associations are common. These, as they are now found in the west, are the products of Christianity alone, and we must wait for the planting of the tree before looking for its fruit. The legal profession, as distinct from the possession of office, is not an occupation in which learned men can obtain an honorable livelihood; the priesthood is confined to monasteries and temples, and its members do not enter into society; while the practice of medicine is so entirely empirical and strange that the few experienced practitioners are not enough to redeem the class. These three professions, which elsewhere do so much to elevate society and guide public opinion, being wanting, educated men have no stimulus to draw them out into independent action. The competition for literary degrees and official rank, the eager pursuit of trade, or the dull routine of mechanical and agricultural labor, form the leading avocations of the Chinese people. Unacquainted with the intellectual enjoyments found in books and the conversation of learned men, and having no educated taste, as we understand that term (while, too, he cannot find such a thing as virtuous female society), the Chinese resorts to the dice-box, the opium-pipe, or the brothel for his pleasures, though even there with a loss of character among his peers.

The separation of the sexes has many bad results, only partially compensated by some conservative ones. Woman owes her present elevation at the west to Christianity, not only in the degree of respect, support, freedom from servile labor, and education which she receives, but also in the reflex influences she exerts of a purifying, harmonizing, and elevating character. Where the requirements of the Gospel exert no force, her rights are more or less disregarded, and if she become as debased as the men, she can exert little good influence even upon her own family, still less upon the community. General mixed society can never be maintained with pleasure unless the better parts of human nature have the acknowledged preëminence, and where she, who imparts to it all its gracefulness and purity, is herself uneducated, unpolished, and immodest, the common sense of mankind sees its impropriety. By advocating the partition of the sexes, legislators and moralists in China have acted as they best could in the circumstances of the case, and by preventing the evils beyond their remedy, provided the best safeguards they could against general corruption. In her own domestic circle a Chinese female, in the character and duties of daughter, wife, or mother, finds as much employment, and probably as many enjoyments, as the nature of her training has fitted her for. She does not hold her proper place in society simply because she has never been taught its duties or exercised its privileges.

In ordinary cases the male and female branches of a household are strictly kept apart; not only the servants, but even brothers and sisters do not freely associate after the boys commence their studies. At this period of life, or even earlier, an anxious task devolves upon parents, which is to find suitable partners for their children. Betrothment is entirely in their hands, and is conducted through the medium of a class of persons called *mei-jin*, or go-betweens, who are expected to be well acquainted with the character and circumstances of the parties. Mothers sometimes contract their unborn progeny on the sole contingency of a difference of sex, but the usual age of forming these engagements is ten, twelve, or older, experience having shown that the casualties attending it render an earlier period undesirable.

There are six ceremonies which constitute a regular marriage, though their details vary much in different parts of the Empire: 1. The father and elder brother of the young man send a go-between to the father and brother of the girl, to inquire her name and the moment of her birth, that the horoscope of the two may be examined, in order to ascertain whether the proposed alliance will be a happy one. 2. If the eight characters[1] seem to augur aright, the boy's friends send the *mei-jin* back to make an offer of marriage. 3. If that be accepted, the second party is again requested to return an assent in writing. 4. Presents are then sent to the girl's parents according to the means of the parties. 5. The go-between requests them to choose a lucky day for the wedding. 6. The preliminaries are concluded by the bridegroom going or sending a party of friends with music to bring his bride to his own house. The match-makers contrive to multiply their visits and prolong the negotiations, when the parties are rich, to serve their own ends.

In Fuhkien parents often send pledges to each other when their children are mere infants, and registers containing their names and particulars of nativity are exchanged in testimony of the contract. After this has been done it is impossible to retract the engagement, unless one of the parties becomes a leper or is disabled. When the children are espoused older, the boy sometimes accompanies the go-between and the party carrying the presents to the house of his future mother-in-law, and receives from her some trifling articles, as melon-seeds, fruits, etc., which

---

[1] Compare p. 628.

he distributes to those around. Among the presents sent to the girl are fruits, money, vermicelli, and a ham, of which she gives a morsel to each one of the party, and sends its foot back. These articles are neatly arranged, and the party bringing them is received with a salute of fire-crackers.

From the time of engagement until marriage a young lady is required to maintain the strictest seclusion. Whenever friends call upon her parents she is expected to retire to the inner apartments, and in all her actions and words guard her conduct with careful solicitude. She must use a close sedan whenever she visits her relations, and in her intercourse with her brothers and the domestics in the household maintain great reserve. Instead of having any opportunity to form those friendships and acquaintances with her own sex which among ourselves become a source of so much pleasure at the time and advantage in after life, the Chinese maiden is confined to the circle of her relations and her immediate neighbors. She has few of the pleasing remembrances and associations that are usually connected with school-day life, nor has she often the ability or opportunity to correspond by letter with girls of her own age. Seclusion at this time of life, and the custom of crippling the feet, combine to confine women in the house almost as much as the strictest laws against their appearing abroad; for in girlhood, as they know only a few persons except relatives, and can make very few acquaintances after marriage, their circle of friends contracts rather than enlarges as life goes on. This privacy impels girls to learn as much of the world as they can, and among the rich their curiosity is gratified through maid-servants, match-makers, pedlers, visitors, and others. Curiosity also stimulates young ladies to learn something of the character and appearance of their intended husbands, but the rules of society are too strict for young persons to endeavor to form a personal attachment, though it is not impossible for them to *see* each other if they wish, and there are, no doubt, many contracts suggested to parents by their children.

The office of match-maker is considered honorable, and both men and women are employed to conduct nuptial negotiations. Great confidence is reposed in their judgment and veracity, and as their employment depends somewhat upon their tact and character, they have every inducement to act with strict propriety in their intercourse with families. The father of the girl employs their services in collecting the sum agreed upon in the contract, which, in ordinary circumstances, varies from twenty-five to forty dollars, increasing to a hundred and over according to the condition of the bridegroom; until that is paid the marriage does not take place. The presents sent at betrothment are sometimes costly, consisting of silks, rice, cloths, fruits, etc.; the bride brings no dower, but both parents frequently go to expenses they can ill afford when celebrating the nuptials of their children, as the pride of family stimulates each party to make undue display.

The principal formalities of a marriage are everywhere the same, but local customs are observed in some regions which are quite unknown and appear singular elsewhere. In Fuhkien, when the lucky day for the wedding comes, the guests assemble in the bridegroom's house to celebrate it, where also sedans, a band of music, and porters are in readiness. The courier, who acts as guide to the chair-bearers, takes the lead, and in order to prevent the onset of malicious demons lurking by the road, a baked hog or large piece of pork is carried in front, that the procession may safely pass while these hungry souls are devouring the meat. Meanwhile the bride arrays herself in her best dress and richest jewels. Her girlish tresses have already been bound up, and her hair arranged by a matron, with due formality; an ornamental and complicated head-dress made of rich materials, not unlike a helmet or corona, often forms part of her coiffure. Her person is nearly covered by a large mantle, over which is an enormous hat like an umbrella, that descends to the shoulders and shades the whole figure. Thus attired she takes her seat in the red gilt marriage sedan, called *hwa kiao*, borne by four men, in which she is completely concealed. This is locked by her mother or some other relative, and the key given to one of the bridemen, who hands it to the bridegroom or his representative on reaching his house.

The procession is now rearranged, with the addition of as many red boxes and trays to contain the wardrobe, kitchen utensils, and the feast, as the means of the family or the extent of her paraphernalia require. As the procession approaches the bridegroom's house the courier hastens forward to announce its coming, whereupon the music strikes up, and fire-crackers salute her until she enters the gate. As she approaches the door the bridegroom conceals himself, but the go-between brings forward a young child to salute her, while going to seek the closeted bridegroom. He approaches with becoming gravity and opens the sedan to hand out his bride, she still retaining the hat and mantle; they approach the ancestral tablet, which they reverence with three bows, and then seat themselves at a table upon which are two cups of spirits. The go-between serves them, though the bride can only make the motions of drinking, as the large hat completely covers her face. They soon retire into a chamber, where the husband takes the hat and mantle from his wife, and sees her, perhaps, for the first time in his life. After he has considered her for some time, the guests and friends enter the room to survey her, when each one is allowed to express an opinion; the criticisms of the women are severest, perhaps because they remember the time they stood in her unpleasant position. This cruel examination being over, she is introduced to her husband's parents, and then salutes her own. Such are some of the customs among the Fuhkienese. Other usages followed in marriages and betrothals have been carefully described by Doolittle, with particular reference to the same people, and by Archdeacon John H. Gray, alluding to other parts of the Empire.[1]

The bridegroom, previous to the wedding, receives a new name or "style," and is formally capped by his father in presence of his friends, as an introduction to manhood. He invites the guests, sending two red cakes with each invitation, and to him each guest, a few days before the marriage, returns a present or a sum of money worth about ten or fifteen cents, nominally equal to the expenses he will be considered as occasioning. Another invitation is sent the day after to a feast, and the bride also calls on the ladies who attended her wedding,

[1] *Social Life of the Chinese*, Chapters II. and III.; *China*, Chap. VII.; also *Fourteen Months in Canton*, by Mrs Gray.

from whom she receives a ring or some other article of small value. The gentlemen also make the bridegroom a present of a pair of lanterns to hang at his gateway. On the night of the wedding they sometimes endeavor to get into the house when the pair is supposed to be asleep, in order to carry off some article, which the bridegroom must ransom at their price.

Among the poor the expenses of a wedding are much lessened by purchasing a young girl, whom the parents bring up as a daughter until she is marriageable, and in this way secure her services in the household. A girl already affianced is for a like reason sometimes sent to the boy's parents, that they may support her. In small villages the people call upon a newly married couple near the next full moon, when they are received standing near the bedside. The men enter first and pay their respects to the bride, while her husband calls the attention of his visitors to her charms, praises her little feet, her beautiful hands, and other features, and then accompanies them into the hall, where they are regaled with refreshments. After the men have retired the women enter and make their remarks upon the lady, whose future character depends a good deal upon the manner in which she conducts herself. If she shows good temper, her reputation is made. Many a prudent woman on this occasion says not a word, but suffers herself to be examined in silence in order that she may run no risk of offending.[1] Far different is this introduction to married life from the bridal tour and cordial greetings of friends which ladies receive in western lands during the honeymoon!

The bridal procession is a peculiar feature of Chinese social life. It varies in its style, nature of the ornaments, and the whole get-up in all parts of the land, but is always as showy as the means of the parties will allow. It is composed of bearers of lanterns and official tablets, musicians, relatives of the bride and groom and their personal friends, framed stands with roofs carried on thills to hold the bride's effects, all centering around her sedan. In Peking such a procession will sometimes be stretched out half a mile, and the sedan borne by a dozen or

[1] *Chinese Repository*, Vols. IV., p. 568, and X., pp. 65-70; *Annales de la Foi*, No. XL., 1835.

more bearers. The coolies are dressed in red, and they and their burdens are usually provided by special shopmen, who purvey on such occasions. The tablets of literary rank held by members of the family, wooden dragons' heads, titular lanterns, and other official insignia are borne in state, an evidence of its high standing. In some places an old man, elegantly dressed, heads the procession, bearing a large umbrella to hold over the bride when she enters and leaves her sedan; behind him come bearers with lanterns, one of which carries the inscription, "The phœnixes sing harmoniously." To these succeed the music and the honorary tablets, titular flags, state umbrella, etc., and two stout men as executioners dressed in a fantastic manner, wearing long feathers in their caps, and lictors, chain-bearers, and other emblems of office. Parties of young lads, prettily dressed and playing on drums, gongs, and flutes, or carrying lanterns and banners, occasionally form a pleasing variety in the train, which is continued by the trays and covered tables containing the bride's trousseau, and ended with the sedan containing herself.

The ceremonies attending her reception at her husband's house are not uniform. In some parts she is lifted out of the sedan, over a pan of charcoal placed in the court, and carried into the bed-chamber; in other places she enters and leaves her sedan on rugs spread for her use, and walks into the chamber. After a brief interval she returns into the hall, bearing a tray of betel-nut for the guests, and then worships a pair of geese brought in the train with her husband, this bird being an emblem of conjugal affection. On returning to her chamber the bridegroom follows her and takes off the red veil, after which they pledge each other in wine, the cups being joined by a thread. While there a matron who has borne several children to one husband comes in to pronounce a blessing upon them and make up the nuptial bed. The assembled guests then sit down to the feast and ply the *sin lang*, 'new man' or bridegroom, pretty well with liquor; the Chinese on such occasions do not, however, often overpass the rules of sobriety. The *sin fujin*, 'new lady' or bride, and her mother-in-law also attend to those of her own sex who are present in other apartments, but among the poor a pleasanter sight is now and then seen in all the guests sitting at one table.

In the morning the pair worship the ancestral tablets and salute all the members of the family; among the poor this important ceremony occurs very soon after the pair have exchanged their wine-cups. The pledging of the bride and groom in a cup of wine, and their worship of the ancestral tablets and of heaven and earth, are the important ceremonies of a wedding after the procession has reached the house. Marriages are celebrated at all hours, though twilight and evening are preferred; the spring season, or the last month in the year, are regarded as the most felicitous nuptial periods. From the way in which the whole matter is conducted there is some room for deception by sending another person in the sedan than the one betrothed, or the man may mistake the name of the girl he wishes to marry. Mr. Smith mentions one of his acquaintances, who, having been captivated with a girl he saw in the street, sent a go-between with proposals to her parents, which were accepted; but he was deeply mortified on receiving his bride to find that he had mistaken the number of his charmer, and had received the fifth daughter instead of the fourth.

The Chinese do not marry another woman with these observances while the first one is living, but they may bring home concubines with no other formality than a contract with her parents, though it is considered somewhat discreditable for a man to take another bedfellow if his wife have borne him sons, unless he can afford each of them a separate establishment. It is not unfrequent for a man to secure a maid-servant in the family with the consent of his wife by purchasing her for a concubine, especially if his occupation frequently call him away from home, in which case he takes her as his travelling companion and leaves his wife in charge of the household. The fact that the sons of a concubine are considered as legally belonging to the wife induces parents to betroth their daughters early, and thus prevent their entering a man's family in this inferior capacity. The Chinese are sensible of the evils of a divided household, and the laws place its control in the hands of the wife. If she have no sons of her own, she looks out for a likely boy among her clansmen to adopt, knowing that otherwise her husband will probably bring a concubine into the family. It is difficult even to guess at the extent of polygamy, for no statistics have been or can be easily taken. Among the laboring classes it is rare to find more than one woman to one man, but tradesmen, official persons, landholders, and those in easy circumstances frequently take one or more concubines; perhaps two-fifths of such families have them. Show and fashion lead some to increase the number of their women, though aware of the discord likely to arise, for they fully believe their own proverb, that "nine women out of ten are jealous." Yet it is probably true that polygamy finds its greatest support from the women themselves. The wife seeks to increase her own position by getting more women into the house to relieve her own work and humor her fancies. The Chinese illustrate the relation by comparing the wife to the moon and the concubines to the stars, both of which in their appropriate spheres wait upon and revolve around the sun.

If regard be had to the civilization of the Chinese and their opportunities for moral training, the legal provisions of the code to protect females in their acknowledged rights and punish crimes against the peace and purity of the family relation reflect credit upon their legislators. In these laws the obligation of children to fulfil the contract made by their parents is enforced, even to the annulling of an agreement made by a son himself in ignorance of the arrangements of his parents. The position of the *tsí*, or wife taken by the prescribed formalities, and that of the *tsieh*, or women purchased as concubines, are accurately defined, and the degradation of the former or elevation of the latter so as to interchange their places, or the taking of a second *tsí*, are all illegal and void. The relation between the two is more like that which existed between Sarah and Hagar in Abraham's household, or Zilpah and Bilhah and their mistresses in Jacob's, than that indicated by our terms first and second wife, of which idea the Chinese words contain no trace. The degrees of unlawful marriages are comprehensive, extending even to the prohibition of persons having the same *sing*, or family name, and to two brothers marrying sisters. The laws forbid the marriage of a brother's widow, of a father's or grandfather's wife, or a father's sister, under the penalty of death; and the like punishment is inflicted upon whoever seizes the wife or daughter of a freeman and carries them away to marry them.

These regulations not only put honor upon marriage, but render it more common among the Chinese than almost any other people, thereby preventing a vast train of evils. The tendency of unrestrained desire to throw down the barriers to the gratification of lust must not be lost sight of; and as no laws on this subject can be effectual unless the common sense of a people approve of them, the Chinese, by separating the sexes in general society, have removed a principal provocation to sin, and by compelling young men to fulfil the marriage contracts of their parents have also provided a safeguard against debauchery at the age when youth is most tempted to indulge, and when indulgence would most strongly disincline them to marry at all. They have, moreover, provided for the undoubted succession of the inheritance by disallowing more than one *wife*, and yet have granted men the liberty they would otherwise take, and which immemorial usage in Asiatic countries has sanctioned. They have done as well as they could in regulating a difficult matter, and better, on the whole, perhaps, than in most other unchristianized countries. If any one supposes, however, that because these laws exist sins against the seventh commandment are uncommon in China, he will be as mistaken as those who infer that because the Chinese are pagans nothing like modesty, purity, or affection exists between the sexes.

When a girl "spills the tea"—that is, loses her betrothed by death—public opinion honors her if she refuse a second engagement; and instances are cited of young ladies committing suicide rather than contract a second marriage. They sometimes leave their father's house and live with the parents of their affianced husband as if they had been really widows. It is considered derogatory for widows to marry; though it may be that the instances quoted in books with so much praise only indicate how rare the practice is in reality. The widow is occasionally sold for a concubine by her father-in-law, and the grief and contumely of her degradation is enhanced by separation from her children, whom she can no longer retain. Such cases are, however, not common, for the impulses of maternal affection are too strong to be thus trifled with, and widows usually look to their friends for support, or to their own exertions if their children be still young; they are assisted, too, by their relatives in this laudable industry and care. It is a lasting stigma to a son to neglect the comfort and support of his widowed mother. A widower is not restrained by any laws, and weds one of his concubines or whomsoever he chooses; nor is he expected to defer the nuptials for any period of mourning for his first wife.

The seven legal reasons for divorce, viz., barrenness, lasciviousness, jealousy, talkativeness, thievery, disobedience to her husband's parents, or leprosy, are almost nullified by the single provision that a woman cannot be put away whose parents are not living to receive her back again. Parties can separate on mutual disagreement, but the code does not regulate the alimony; and a husband is liable to punishment if he retain a wife convicted of adultery. If a wife merely elopes she can be sold by her husband, but if she marry while absent she is to be strangled; if the husband be absent three years a woman must state her case to the magistrates before presuming to remarry.

In regard to the general condition of females in China the remark of De Guignes is applicable, that "though their lot is less happy than that of their sisters in Europe, their ignorance of a better state renders their present or prospective one more supportable; happiness does not always consist in absolute enjoyment, but in the idea which we have formed of it."[1] She does not feel that any injustice is done her by depriving her of the right of assent as to whom her partner shall be; her wishes and her knowledge go no farther than her domestic circle, and where she has been trained in her mother's apartments to the various duties and accomplishments of her sex, her removal to a husband's house brings to her no great change.

This, however, is not always the case, and the power accorded to the husband over his wife and family is often used with great tyranny. The young wife finds in her new home little of the

---

[1] *Voyages à Peking*, Tome II., p. 283.

sympathy and love her sisters in Christian lands receive. Her mother-in-law is not unfrequently the source of her greatest trials, and demands from her both the submission of a child and the labor of a slave, which is not seldom returned by disobedience and bitter revilings. If the husband interfere she has less likelihood of escaping his exactions; though in the lower walks of life his cruelty is restrained by fear of losing her and her services, and in the upper diverted by indifference as to what she does, in the pursuit of other objects. If the wife behave well till she herself becomes a mother and a mother-in-law, then the tables are turned; from being a menial she becomes almost a goddess. Luhchau, a writer on female culture, mentions the following indirect mode of reproving a mother-in-law: "Loh Yang travelled seven years to improve himself, during which time his wife diligently served her mother-in-law and supported her son at school. The poultry from a neighbor's house once wandered into her garden, and her mother-in-law stole and killed them for eating. When she sat down to table and saw the fowls she would not dine, but burst into tears, at which the old lady was much surprised and asked the reason. 'I am much distressed that I am so poor and cannot afford to supply you with all I wish I could, and that I should have caused you to eat flesh belonging to another.' Her parent was affected by this, and threw away the dish."

The evils attending early betrothment induce many parents to defer engaging their daughters until they are grown, and a husband of similar tastes can be found; for even if the condition of the families in the interval of betrothment and marriage unsuitably change, or the lad grows up to be a dissipated, worthless, or cruel man, totally unworthy of the girl, still the contract must be fulfilled, and the worst party generally is most anxious for it. The unhappy bride in such cases often escapes from her present sufferings and dismal prospects by suicide. A case occured in Canton in 1833 where a young wife, visiting her parents shortly after marriage, so feelingly described her sufferings at the hands of a cruel husband to her sisters and friends that she and three of her auditors joined their hands together and drowned themselves in a pond, she to escape present misery and they to avoid its future possibility. Another young lady, having heard of the worthless character of her intended, carried a bag of money with her in the sedan, and when they retired after the ceremonies were over thus addressed him: "Touch me not; I am resolved to abandon the world and become a nun. I shall this night cut off my hair. I have saved $200, which I give you; with the half you can purchase a concubine, and with the rest enter on some trade. Be not lazy and thriftless. Hereafter, remember me." Saying this, she cut off her hair, and her husband and his kindred, fearing suicide if they opposed her, acquiesced, and she returned to her father's house.[1] Such cases are common enough to show the dark side of family life, and young ladies implore their parents to rescue them in this or some other way from the sad fate which awaits them. Sometimes girls become skilled in female accomplishments to recommend themselves to their husbands, and their disappointment is the greater when they find him to be a brutal, depraved tyrant. A melancholy instance of this occurred in Canton in 1840, which ended in the wife committing suicide. Her brother had been a scholar of one of the American missionaries, and took a commendable pride in showing specimens of his sister's exquisite embroidery, and not a few of her attainments in writing, which indicated their reciprocal attachment. The contrary happens too, sometimes, where the husband finds himself compelled to wed a woman totally unable to appreciate or share his pursuits, but he has means of alleviating or avoiding such misalliances which the weaker vessel has not. On the whole, as we have said, one must admit that woman holds a fairly high position in China. If she suffers from the brutality of her husband, the tyranny of her mother-in-law, or the overwork of household, field, or loom, she is as often herself blameworthy for indolence, shiftlessness, gadding, and bad temper. The instances which are given by Gray[2] in his account of marital atrocities prove the length to which a man will wreak his rage on the helpless; but they are the exception to the general testi-

---

[1] *Chinese Repository*, Vol. I., p. 293. [2] *China*, Chap. VII.

mony of the people themselves. So far as general purity of society goes, one may well doubt whether such abominable conduct as is legalized among Mormons in Utah is any improvement on the hardships of woman among the Chinese.

Pursuing this brief account of the social life of the Chinese, the right of parents in managing their children comes into notice. It is great, though not unlimited, and in allowing them very extensive power, legislators have supposed that natural affection of the parents, a desire to continue the honorable succession of the family, together with the influence of proper education, were as good securities against paternal cruelty and neglect as any laws which could be made. Fathers give their sons the *ju ming*, or 'milk name,' about a month after birth. The mother, on the day appointed for this ceremony, worships and thanks the goddess of Mercy, and the boy, dressed and having his head shaved, is brought into the circle of assembled friends, where the father confers the name and celebrates the occasion by a feast. The milk name is kept until the lad enters school, at which time the *shu ming*, or 'school name,' is conferred upon him, as already mentioned. The *shu ming* generally consists of two characters, selected with reference to the boy's condition, prospects, studies, or some other event connected with him; sometimes the milk name is continued, as the family have become accustomed to it. Such names as *Ink-grinder*, *Promising-study*, *Opening-olive*, *Entering-virtue*, *Rising-advancement*, etc., are given to young students at this time. Though endearing or fanciful names are often conferred, it is quite as common to vilify very young children by calling them *dog*, *hog*, *puppy*, *flea*, etc., under the idea that such epithets will ward off the evil eye. Girls have only their milk and marriage names; the former may be *a flower*, *a sister*, *a gem*, or such like; the latter are terms like *Emulating the Moon*, *Orchis Flower*, *the Jasmine*, *Delicate Perfume*, etc. A mere number at Canton, as *A-yat*, *A-sam*, *A-luk* (No. 1, No. 3, No. 6), often designates the boys till they get their book names.[1]

[1] Doolittle's *Handbook*, Vol. III., p. 660, gives a list of names collected at Fuhchau, which are applicable to other provinces.

The personal names of the Chinese are written contrariwise to our own, the *sing*, or surname, coming first, then the *ming*, or given name, and then the complimentary title; as Liang Wăn-tai siensăng, where *Liang*, or 'Millet,' is the family name, *Wăn-tai*, or 'Terrace of Letters,' the given name, and *siensăng*, Mr. (*i.e.*, Master), or 'Teacher.' A few of the surnames are double, as *Sz'ma Tsien*, where Sz'ma is the family name and Tsien the official title. A curious idea prevails among the people of Canton, that foreigners have no surname, which, as Pliny thought of the inhabitants of Mt. Atlas, they regard as one of the proofs of their barbarism; perhaps this notion came by inference from the fact that the Manchus write only their given name, as Kíshen, Kíying, Îlípu, etc. When writing Chinese names in translations and elsewhere, some attention should be paid to these particulars; the names of Chinese persons and places are constantly appearing in print under forms as singular as would be *Williamhenryharrison*, *Rich-Ard-Ox-Ford*, or *Phila Del-phia-city* in English. The name being in a different language, and its true nature unknown to most of those who write it, accounts for the misarrangement.

In Canton and its vicinity the names of people are abbreviated in conversation to one character, and an *A* prefixed to it; —as *Tsinteh*, called *A-teh* or *A-tsin.* In Amoy the *A* is placed after, as *Chin-a;* in the northern provinces no such usage is known. Some families, perhaps in imitation of the imperial precedent, distinguish their members from others in the clan by adopting a constant character for the first one in the *ming*, or given name; thus a family of brothers will be named Lin Tung-pei, Lin Tung-fung, Lin Tung-peh, where the word *Tung* distinguishes this sept of the clan Lin from all others. There are no characters exclusively appropriated to proper names or different sexes, as George, Agnes, etc., all being chosen out of the language with reference to their meanings. Consequently, a name is sometimes felt to be incongruous, as Naomi, when saluted on her return to Bethlehem, felt its inappropriateness to her altered condition, and suggested a change to Mara. Puns on names and sobriquets are common, from the constant contrast of the sounds of the characters with circumstances suggesting a comparison or a play upon their meanings; sly jokes are also played when writing the names of foreigners, by choosing such characters as will make a ridiculous meaning when read according to their sense and not their sound.

When a man marries he adopts a third name, called *tsz'*, or 'style,' by which he is usually known through life; this is either entirely new or combined from previous names. When a girl is married her family name becomes her given name, and the given name is disused, her husband's name becoming her family name. Thus *Wa Salah* married to *Wei San-wei* drops the *Salah*, and is called *Wei Wa shí, i.e.*, Mrs. Wei [born of the clan] Wa, though her husband or near relatives sometimes retain it as a trivial address. A man is frequently known by another compellation, called *pieh tsz'*, or 'second style,' which the public do not presume to employ. When a young man is successful in attaining a degree, or enters an office, he takes a title called *kwan ming*, or 'official name,' by which he is known to government. The members or heads of licensed mercantile companies each have an official name, which is entered in their permit, from whence it is called among foreigners their *chop name*. Each of the heads of the co-hong formerly licensed to trade with foreigners at Canton had such an official name. Besides these various names, old men of fifty, shopkeepers, and others take a *hao*, or 'designation;' tradesmen use it on their signboards as the name of their shop, and not unfrequently receive it as their personal appellation. Of this nature are the appellations of the tradesmen who deal with foreigners, as *Cutshing*, *Chanlung*, *Linchong*, etc., which are none of them the names of the shopmen, but the designation of the shop. It is the usual way in Canton for foreigners to go into a shop and ask "Is Mr. Wanglik in?" which would be almost like one in New York inquiring if Mr. Alhambra or Mr. Atlantic-House was at home, though it does not sound quite so ridiculous to a Chinese. The names taken by shopkeepers allude to trade or its prospects, such as *Mutual Advantage*, *Obedient Profit*, *Extensive Harmony*, *Rising Goodness*, *Great Completeness*, etc.; the names of the partners as such are not employed to form the firm. Besides this use of the *hao*, it is also employed as a brand upon goods; the terms *Hoyuen*, *Kinghing*, *Yuenkí*, meaning 'Harmonious Springs,' 'Cheering Prospects,' 'Fountain's Memorial,' etc., are applied to particular parcels of tea, silk, or other goods, just as brands are placed on lots of wine, flour, or pork. This is called *tsz'-hao*, or 'mark-designation,' but foreigners call both it and the goods it denotes a *chop*.

When a man dies he receives another and last, though not necessarily a new name in the hall of ancestors; upon emperors and empresses are bestowed new ones, as *Benevolent*, *Pious*, *Discreet*, etc., by which they are worshipped and referred to in history, as *that* designation which is most likely to be permanent.

In their common intercourse the Chinese are not more formal than is considered to be well-bred in Europe; it is on extraordinary or official occasions that they observe the precise etiquette for which they are famous. The proper mode of behavior toward all classes is perhaps more carefully inculcated upon youth than it is in the west, and habit renders easy what custom demands. The ceremonial obeisance of a court or a levee, or the salutations proper for a festival, are not carried into the everyday intercourse of life; for as one chief end of the formalities prescribed for such times is to teach due subordination among persons of different rank, they are in a measure laid aside with the robes which suggested them. True politeness, exhibited in an unaffected regard for the feelings of others, cannot, we know, be taught by rules; but a great degree of urbanity and kindness is everywhere shown, whether owing to the naturally placable disposition of the people or to the effects of their early instruction in the forms of politeness. Whether in the crowded and narrow thoroughfares, the village green, the market, the jostling ferry, or the thronged procession—wherever the people are assembled promiscuously, good humor and courtesy are observable; and when altercations do arise wounds or serious injuries seldom ensue, although from the furious clamor one would imagine that half the crowd were in danger of their lives.

Chinese ceremonial requires superiors to be honored according to their station and age, and equals to depreciate themselves while lauding those they address. The Emperor, considering himself as the representative of divine power, exacts the same prostration which is paid the gods; and the ceremonies which are performed in his presence partake, therefore, of a religious character, and are not merely particular forms of etiquette, which may be altered according to circumstances. There are eight gradations of obeisance, commencing with "the lowest form of respect, called *kung shao*, which is merely joining the hands and raising them before the breast. The next is *tso yih*, bowing low with the hands thus joined. The third is *ta tsien*, bending the knee as if about to kneel; and *kwei*, an actual kneeling, is the fourth. The fifth is *ko tao* (*kotow*), kneeling and striking the head on the ground, which when thrice repeated makes the sixth, called *san kao*, or 'thrice knocking.' The seventh is the *luh kao*, or kneeling and knocking the head thrice upon the ground, then standing upright and again kneeling and knocking the head three times more. The climax is closed by the *san kwei kiu kao*, or thrice kneeling and nine times knocking the head. Some of the gods of China are entitled to the *san kao*, others to the *luh kao*, while the Emperor and Heaven are worshipped by the last. The family now on the throne consider this last form as expressing in the strongest manner the submission and homage of one state to another."[1] The extreme submission which the Emperor demands is partaken by and transferred to his officers of every grade in a greater or less degree; the observance of these forms is deemed, therefore, of great importance, and a refusal to render them is considered to be nearly equivalent to a rejection of their authority.

Minute regulations for the times and modes of official intercourse are made and promulgated by the Board of Rites, and to learn and practise them is one indispensable part of official duty. In court the master of ceremonies stands in a conspicuous place, and with a loud voice commands the courtiers to rise and kneel, stand or march, just as an orderly sergeant directs the drill of

---

[1] *Memoir of Dr. Morrison*, Vol. II., p. 142.

recruits. The same attention to the ritual is observed in their mutual intercourse, for however much an inferior may desire to dispense with the ceremony, his superior will not fail to exact it. In the salutations of entrée and exit among officers these forms are particularly conspicuous, but when well acquainted with each other, and in moments of conviviality, they are in a great measure laid aside; but the juxtaposition of art and nature among them, at one moment laughing and joking, and the next bowing and kneeling to each other as if they had never met, sometimes produces amusing scenes to a foreigner. The entire ignorance and disregard of these forms by foreigners unacquainted with the code leaves a worse impression upon the natives at times, who ascribe such rudeness to hauteur and contempt.

Without particularizing the tedious forms of official etiquette, it will be sufficient to describe what is generally required in good society. Military men pay visits on horseback; civilians and others go in sedans or carts; to walk is not common. Visiting cards are made of vermilioned paper cut into slips about eight inches long and three wide, and are single or folded four, six, eight, or more times, according to the position of the visitor. If he is in recent mourning, the paper is white and the name written in blue ink, but after a stated time this is indicated by an additional character. The simple name is stamped on the upper right corner, or if written on the lower corner, with an addition thus, "Your humble servant (*lit.*, 'stupid younger brother') Pí Chí-wăn bows his head in salutation." On approaching the house his attendant hands a card to the doorkeeper, and if he cannot be received, instead of saying "not at home," the host sends out to "stay the gentleman's approach," and the card is left. If contrariwise the sedan is carried through the doorway into the court, where he comes forth to receive his guest; as the latter steps out each one advances just so far, bowing just so many times, and going through the ceremonies which they mutually understand and expect, until both have taken their seats at the head of the hall, the guest sitting on the left of the host, and his companions, if he have any, in the chairs on each side. The inquiries made after the mutual welfare of friends and each other are couched in a form of studied laudation and depreciation, which when literally translated seem somewhat affected, but to them convey no more than similar civilities do among ourselves—in truth, perhaps not so much of sincere good-will. For instance, to the remark, "It is a long time since we have met, sir," the host replies (literally), "How presume to receive the trouble of your honorable footsteps; is the person in the chariot well?"—which is simply equivalent to, "I am much obliged for your visit, and hope you enjoy good health."

Tea and pipes are always presented, together with betel-nut or sweetmeats on some occasions, but it is not, as among the Turks, considered disrespectful to refuse them, though it would be looked upon as singular. If the guest inquire after the health of relatives he should commence with the oldest living, and then ask how many sons the host has; but it is not considered good breeding for a formal acquaintance to make any remarks respecting the mistress of the house. If the sons of the host are at home they are generally sent for, and make their obeisance to their father's friend by coming up before him and performing the *kotow* as rapidly as possible, each one making haste, as if he did not wish to delay him. The guest raises them with a slight bow, and the lads stand facing him at a respectful distance. He will then remark, perhaps, if one of them happen to be at his studies, that "the boy will perpetuate the literary reputation of his family" (*lit.*, 'he will fully carry on the fragrance of the books'); to which his father rejoins, "The reputation of our family is not great (*lit.*, 'hills and fields' happiness is thin'); high expectations are not to be entertained of him; if he can only gain a livelihood it will be enough." After a few such compliments the boys say *shao pei*, 'slightly waiting on you,' *i.e.*, pray excuse us, and retire. Girls are seldom brought in, and young ladies never.

The periphrases employed to denote persons and thus avoid speaking their names in a measure indicate the estimation in which they are held. For instance, "Does the honorable great man enjoy happiness?" means "Is your father well?" "Distinguished and aged one what honorable age?" is the mode of asking how old he is; for among the Chinese, as it seems to have been among the Egyptians, it is polite to ask the names and ages of all ranks and sexes. "The old man of the house," "excellent honorable one," and "venerable great prince," are terms used by a visitor to designate the father of his host. A child terms his father "family's majesty," "old man of the family," "prince of the family," or "venerable father." When dead a father is called "former prince," and a mother "venerable great one in repose;" and there are particular characters to distinguish deceased parents from living. The request, "Make my respects to your mother"—for no Chinese gentleman ever asks to *see* the ladies—is literally, "Excellent-longevity hall place in my behalf wish repose," the first two words denoting she who remains there. Care should be taken not to use the same expressions when speaking of the relatives of the guest and one's own; thus, in asking, "How many worthy young gentlemen [sons] have you?" the host replies, "I am unfortunate in having had but one boy," literally, "My fate is niggardly; I have only one little bug." This runs through their whole Chesterfieldian code. A man calls his wife *tsien nui*, *i.e.*, 'the mean one of the inner apartments,' or 'the foolish one of the family;' while another speaking of her calls her "the honorable lady," "worthy lady," "your favored one," etc.

Something of this is found in all oriental languages; to become familiar with the right application of these terms in Chinese, as elsewhere in the east, is no easy lesson for a foreigner. In their salutations of ceremony they do not, however, quite equal the Arabs, with their kissing, bowing, touching foreheads, stroking beards, and repeated motions of obeisance. The Chinese seldom embrace or touch each other, except on unusual occasions of joy or among family friends; in fact, they have hardly a common word for a kiss. When the visitor rises to depart he remarks, "Another day I will come to receive your instructions;" to which his friend replies, "You do me too much honor; I rather ought to wait on you to-morrow." The common form of salutation among equals is for each to clasp his own hands before his breast and make a slight bow, saying, *Tsing! Tsing!* *i.e.*, 'Hail! Hail!' This is repeated by both at the same time, on meeting as well as separating.[1] The formalities of leave-taking correspond to those of receiving, but if the parties are equal, or nearly so, the host sees his friend quite to the door and into his sedan.

Officers avoid meeting each other, especially in public, except when etiquette requires them. An officer of low rank is obliged to stop his chair or horse, and on his feet to salute his superior, who receives and returns the civility without moving. Those of equal grades leave their places and go through a mock struggle of deference to get each first to return to it. The common people never presume to salute an officer in the streets, nor even to look at him very carefully. In his presence, they speak to him on their knees, but an old man, or one of consideration, is usually requested to rise when speaking, and even criminals with gray hairs are treated with respect. Officers do not allow their inferiors to sit in their presence, and have always been unwilling to concede this to foreigners; those of the lowest rank consider themselves far above the best of such visitors, but this affectation of rank is already passing away. The converse, of not paying them proper respect, is more common among a certain class of foreigners.

Children are early taught the forms of politeness toward all ranks. The duties owed by younger to elder brothers are peculiar, the firstborn having a sort of birthright in the ancestral worship, in the division of property, and in the direction of the family after the father's decease. The degree of formality in the domestic circle inculcated in the ancient *Book of Rites* is never observed to its full extent, and would perhaps chill the affection which should exist among its members, did not habit render it easy and proper; and the extent to which it is actually carried depends a good deal upon the education of the family. In forwarding presents it is customary to send a list with the note, and if the person deems it proper to decline some of them, he marks on the list those he takes and returns the rest; a douceur is always expected by the bearer, and needy fellows some-

---

[1] *Chinese Chrestomathy*, Chap. V., Sec. 12, p. 182. This phrase is the origin of the word *chinchin*, so often heard among the Chinese.

times pretend to have been sent with some insignificant present from a grandee in hopes of receiving more than its equivalent as a cumshaw from the person thus honored. De Guignes mentioned one donor who waited until the list came back, and then sent out and purchased the articles which had been marked and sent them to his friend.

Travellers have so often described the Chinese formal dinners, that they have almost become one of their national traits in the view of foreigners; so many of these banquets, however, were given by or in the name of the sovereign, that they are hardly a fair criterion of usual private feasts. The Chinese are both a social and a sensual people, and the pleasures of the table form a principal item in the list of their enjoyments; nor are the higher delights of mental recreation altogether wanting, though this part of the entertainment is according to their taste and not ours. Private meals and public feasts among the higher classes are both dull and long to us, because ladies do not participate; but perhaps we judge more what our own tables would be without their cheerful presence, while in China each sex is of the opinion that the meal is more enjoyable without interference from the other.

An invitation to dinner is written on a slip of red paper like a visiting-card, and sent some days before. It reads, "On the — day a trifling entertainment will await the light of your countenance. Tsau San-wei's compliments." Another card is sent on the day itself, stating the hour of dinner, or a servant comes to call the guests. The host, dressed in his cap and robes, awaits their arrival, and after they are all assembled, requests them to follow his example and lay aside their dresses of ceremony. The usual way of arranging guests is by twos on each side of small uncovered tables, placed in lines; an arrangement as convenient for serving the numerous courses which compose the feast, and removing the dishes, as was the Roman fashion of reclining around a hollow table; it also allows a fair view of the musical or theatrical performances. On some occasions, in the sunny south, however, a single long or round table is laid out in a tasteful manner, having pyramids of cakes alternating with piles of fruits and dishes of preserves, all covered more or less with flowers, while the table itself is partly hidden from view by nosegays and leaves. If the party be large, ten minutes or more are consumed by the host and guests going through a tedious repetition of requests and refusals to take the highest seats, for not a man will sit down until he sees the host occupying his chair.

On commencing, the host, standing up, salutes his guests, in a cup, apologizing for the frugal board before them, his only desire being to show his respects to them. At a certain period in the entertainment, they reply by simultaneously rising and drinking his health. The Western custom of giving a sentiment is not known; and politeness requires a person when drinking healths to turn the bottom of the tiny wine-cup upward to show that it is drained. Glass dishes are gradually becoming cheap and common among the middle class, but the table furniture still mainly consists of porcelain cups, bowls, and saucers of various sizes and quality, porcelain spoons shaped like a child's pap-boat, and two smooth sticks made of bamboo, ivory, or wood, of the size of quills, well known as the *chop-sticks*, from the native name *kwai tsz'*, *i.e.*, 'nimble lads.' Grasping these implements on each side of the forefinger, the eater pinches up from the dishes meat, fish, or vegetables, already cut into mouthfuls, and conveys one to his mouth. The bowl of rice or millet is brought to the lips, and the contents shovelled into the mouth in an expeditious manner, quite suitable to the name of the tools employed. Less convenient than forks, chopsticks are a great improvement on fingers, as every one will acknowledge who has seen the Hindus throw the balls of curried rice into their mouths.

The succession of dishes is not uniform; soups, meats, stews, fruits, and preserves are introduced somewhat at the discretion of the major-domo, but the end is announced by a bowl of plain rice and a cup of tea. The fruit is often brought in after a recess, during which the guests rise and refresh themselves by walking and chatting, for three or four hours are not unfrequently required even to taste all the dishes. It is not deemed impolite for a guest to express his satisfaction with the good fare before him, and exhibit evidences of having stuffed himself to repletion; nor is it a breach of manners to retire before the dinner is ended. The guests relieve its tedium by playing the game of *chai mei*, or morra (the *micare digitis* of the old Romans), which consists in showing the fingers to each other across the table, and mentioning a number at the same moment; as, if one opens out two fingers and mentions the number four, the other instantly shows six fingers, and repeats that number. If he mistake in giving the complement of ten, he pays a forfeit by drinking a cup. This convivial game is common among all ranks, and the boisterous merriment of workmen or friends at their meals is frequently heard as one passes through the streets in the afternoon.[1] The Chinese generally have but two meals a day, breakfast at nine and dinner at four, or thereabouts.

The Chinese are comparatively a temperate people. This is owing principally to the universal use of tea, but also to taking their arrack very warm and at their meals, rather than to any notions of sobriety or dislike of spirits. A little of it flushes their faces, mounts into their heads, and induces them when flustered to remain in the house to conceal the suffusion, although they may not be really drunk. This liquor is known as toddy, arrack, saki, tsiu, and other names in Eastern Asia, and is distilled from the yeasty liquor in which boiled rice has fermented under pressure many days. Only one distillation is made for common liquor, but when more strength is wanted, it is distilled two or three times, and it is this strong spirit alone which is rightly called *samshu*, a word meaning 'thrice fired.' Chinese moralists have always inveighed against the use of spirits, and the name of Ĭ-tih, the reputed inventor of the deleterious drink, more than two thousand years before Christ, has been handed down with opprobrium, as he was himself banished by the great Yu for his discovery.

The *Shu King* contains a discourse by the Duke of Chau on the abuse of spirits. His speech to his brother Fung, B.C. 1120, is the oldest temperance address on record, even earlier than the words of Solomon in the Proverbs. "When your reverend

---

[1] Compare the *China Review*, Vol. IV., p. 400.

father, King Wăn, founded our kingdom in the western region, he delivered announcements and cautions to the princes of the various states, their officers, assistants, and managers of affairs, morning and evening, saying, 'For sacrifices spirits should be employed. When Heaven was sending down its [favoring] commands and laying the foundations of our people's sway, spirits were used only in the great sacrifices. [But] when Heaven has sent down its terrors, and our people have thereby been greatly disorganized, and lost their [sense of] virtue, this too can be ascribed to nothing else than their unlimited use of spirits; yea, further, the ruin of the feudal states, small and great, may be traced to this one sin, the free use of spirits.' King Wăn admonished and instructed the young and those in office managing public affairs, that they should not habitually drink spirits. In all the states he enjoined that their use be confined to times of sacrifices; and even then with such limitations that virtue should prevent drunkenness."[1]

The general and local festivals of the Chinese are numerous, among which the first three days of the year, one or two about the middle of April to worship at the tombs, the two solstices, and the festival of dragon-boats, are common days of relaxation and merry-making, only on the first, however, are the shops shut and business suspended. Some persons have expressed their surprise that the unceasing round of toil which the Chinese laborer pursues has not rendered him more degraded. It is usually said that a weekly rest is necessary for the continuance of the powers of body and mind in man in their full activity, and that decrepitude and insanity would oftener result were it not for this relaxation. The arguments in favor of this observation seem to be deduced from undoubted facts in countries where the obligations of the Sabbath are acknowledged, though where the vast majority cease from business and labor, it is not easy for a few to work all the time even if they wish, owing to the various ways in which their occupations are involved with those of others; yet, in China, people who appa-

---

[1] *Chinese Repository*, Vol. XV., p. 433. *Book of Records*, Part V., Book X., Legge's translation; also Medhurst's and Gaubil's translations.

rently tax themselves uninterruptedly to the utmost stretch of body and mind, live in health to old age. A few facts of this sort incline one to suppose that the Sabbath was designed by its Lord as a day of rest for man from a constant routine of relaxation and mental and physical labor, in order that he might have leisure for attending to the paramount duties of religion, and not alone as a day of relaxation and rest, without which they could not live out all their days. Nothing like a seventh day of rest, or religious respect to that interval of time, is known among the Chinese, but they do not, as a people, exercise their minds to the intensity, or upon the high subjects common among Western nations, and this perhaps is one reason why their yearly toil produces no disastrous effects. The countless blessings which flow from an observance of the fourth commandment can be better appreciated by witnessing the wearied condition of the society where it is not acknowledged, and whoever sees such a society can hardly fail to wish for its introduction.

Converts to Christianity in China, who are instructed in its strict observance, soon learn to prize it as a high privilege; and its general neglect among the native Roman Catholics has removed the only apparent difference between them and the pagans. The former prime minister of China once remarked that among the few really valuable things which foreigners had brought to China, the rest of the Sabbath day was one of the most desirable; he often longed for a quiet day.[1]

The return of the year is an occasion of unbounded festivity and hilarity, as if the whole population threw off the old year with a shout, and clothed themselves in the new with their change of garments. The evidences of the approach of this chief festival appear some weeks previous. The principal streets are lined with tables, upon which articles of dress, furniture, and fancy are disposed for sale in the most attractive manner. Necessity compels many to dispose of certain of their treasures or superfluous things at this season, and sometimes exceedingly curious bits of bric-a-brac, long laid up in families, can be pro-

[1] Nevius, *China and the Chinese*, pp. 399–408.

cured at a cheap rate. It is customary for superiors to give their dependents and employees a present, and for shopmen to send an acknowledgment of favors to their customers; one of the most common gifts among the lower classes is a pair of new shoes. Among the tables spread in the streets are many provided with pencils and red paper of various sizes, on which persons write sentences appropriate to the season in various styles, to be pasted upon the doorposts and lintels of dwellings and shops,[1] or suspended from their walls. The shops also put on a most brilliant appearance, arrayed in these papers interspersed among the *kin hwa*, or 'golden flowers,' which are sprigs of artificial leaves and flowers made in the southern cities of brass tinsel and fastened upon wires; the latter are designed for an annual offering in temples, or to place before the household tablet. Small strips of red and gilt paper, some bearing the word *fuh*, or 'happiness,' large and small vermilion candles, gaily painted, and other things used in idolatry, are likewise sold in great quantities, and with the increased throng impart an unusually lively appearance to the streets. Another evident sign of the approaching change is the use of water upon the doors, shutters, and other woodwork of houses and shops, washing chairs, utensils, clothes, etc., as if cleanliness had not a little to do with joy, and a well-washed person and tenement were indispensable to the proper celebration of the festival. Throughout the southern rivers all small craft, tankia-boats, and lighters are beached and turned inside out for a scrubbing.

A still more praiseworthy custom attending this season is that of settling accounts and paying debts; shopkeepers are kept busy waiting upon their customers, and creditors urge their debtors to arrange these important matters. No debt is allowed to overpass new year without a settlement or satisfactory arrangement, if it can be avoided; and those whose liabilities altogether exceed their means are generally at this season obliged to wind up their concerns and give all their available property into the hands of their creditors. The consequences of this general pay-

---

[1] A like custom existed among the Hebrews, now continued in the modern *mezuzaw*. Deut. vi. 9. Jahn's *Archæology*, p. 38.

day are a high rate of money, great resort to the pawnbrokers, and a general fall in the price of most kinds of produce and commodities. Many good results flow from the practice, and the conscious sense of the difficulty and expense of resorting to legal proceedings to recover debts induces all to observe and maintain it, so that the dishonest, the unsuccessful, and the wild speculator may be sifted out from amongst the honest traders.

De Guignes mentions one expedient to oblige a man to pay his debts at this season, which is to carry off the door of his shop or house, for then his premises and person will be exposed to the entrance and anger of all hungry and malicious demons prowling around the streets, and happiness no more revisit his abode; to avoid this he is fain to arrange his accounts. It is a common practice among devout persons to settle with the gods, and during a few days before the new year, the temples are unusually thronged by devotees, both male and female, rich and poor. Some persons fast and engage the priests to intercede for them that their sins may be pardoned, while they prostrate themselves before the images amidst the din of gongs, drums, and bells, and thus clear off the old score. On new year's eve the streets are full of people hurrying to and fro to conclude the many matters which press upon them. At Canton, some are busy pasting the five slips upon their lintels, signifying their desire that the five blessings which constitute the sum of all human felicity (namely, longevity, riches, health, love of virtue, and a natural death) may be their favored portion. Such sentences as "May the five blessings visit this door," "May heaven send down happiness," "May rich customers ever enter this door," are placed above them; and the doorposts are adorned with others on plain or gold sprinkled red paper, making the entrance quite picturesque. In the hall are suspended scrolls more or less costly, containing antithetical sentences carefully chosen. A literary man would have, for instance, a distich like the following:

May I be so learned as to secrete in my mind three myriads of volumes:
May I know the affairs of the world for six thousand years.

A shopkeeper adorns his door with those relating to trade:

May profits be like the morning sun rising on the clouds.
May wealth increase like the morning tide which brings the rain.
Manage your occupation according to truth and loyalty.
Hold on to benevolence and rectitude in all your trading.

The influence of these mottoes, and countless others like them which are constantly seen in the streets, shops, and dwellings throughout the land, is inestimable. Generally it is for good, and as a large proportion are in the form of petition or wish, they show the moral feeling of the people.

Boat-people in Kwangtung and Fuhkien provinces are peculiarly liberal of their paper prayers, pasting them on every board and oar in the boat, and suspending them from the stern in scores, making the vessel flutter with gaiety. Farmers stick theirs upon barns, trees, wattles, baskets, and implements, as if nothing was too insignificant to receive a blessing. The house is arranged in the most orderly and cleanly manner, and purified with religious ceremonies and lustrations, firing of crackers, etc., and as the necessary preparations occupy a considerable portion of the night, the streets are not quiet till dawn. In addition to the bustle arising from business and religious observances, which marks this passage of time, the constant explosion of firecrackers, and the clamor of gongs, make it still more noisy. Strings of these crackling fireworks are burned at the doorposts, before the outgoing and incoming of the year, designed to expel and deter evil spirits from the house. The consumption is so great as to cover the streets with the fragments, and farmers come the week after into Canton city and sweep up hundreds of bushels for manure.

The first day of the year is also regarded as the birthday of the entire population, for the practice among the Hebrews of dating the age from the beginning of the year, prevails also in China; so that a child born only a week before new year, is considered as entering its second year on the first day of the first month. This does not, however, entirely supersede the observance of the real anniversary, and parents frequently make a solemnity of their son's birthday. A missionary thus describes the celebration of a son's sixth birthday at Ningpo. "The little fellow was dressed in his best clothes, and his father had brought gilt paper, printed prayers, and a large number of bowls of meats, rice, vegetables, spirits, nuts, etc., as an offering to be spread out before the idols. The ceremonies were performed in the apartment of the *Tao Mu,* or 'Bushel Mother,' who has special charge of infants before and after birth. The old abbot was dressed in a scarlet robe, with a gilt image of a serpent fastened in his hair; one of the monks wore a purple, another a gray robe. A multitude of prayers, seemingly a round of repetitions, were read by the abbot, occasionally chanting a little, when the attendants joined in the chorus, and a deafening clamor of bells, cymbals, and wooden blocks, added force to their cry; genuflexions and prostrations were repeatedly made. One part of the ceremony was to pass a live cock through a barrel, which the assistants performed many times, shouting some strange words at each repetition; this act symbolized the dangers through which the child was to pass in his future life, and the priests had prayed that he might as safely come out of them all, as the cock had passed through the barrel. In conclusion, some of the prayers were burned and a libation poured out, and a grand symphony of bell, gong, drum, and block, closed the scene."[1]

A great diversity of local usages are observed at this period in different parts of the country. In Amoy, the custom of "surrounding the furnace" is generally practised. The members of the family sit down to a substantial supper on new year's eve, with a pan of charcoal under the table, as a supposed preservative against fires. After the supper is ended, the wooden lamp-stands are brought out and spread upon the pavement with a heap of gold and silver paper, and set on fire after all demons have been warned off by a volley of fire-crackers. The embers are then divided into twelve heaps, and their manner of going out carefully watched as a prognostic of the kind of weather to be expected the ensuing year. Many persons wash their bodies in warm water, made aromatic by the infusion of leaves, as a

---

[1] *Presbyterian Missionary Chronicle*, 1846.

security against disease; this ceremony, and ornamenting the ancestral shrine, and garnishing the whole house with inscriptions, pictures, flowers, and fruit, in the gayest manner the means of the family will allow, occupy most of the night.

The stillness of the streets and the gay inscriptions on the closed shops on new year's morning present a wonderful contrast to the usual bustle and crowd, resembling the Christian Sabbath. The red papers of the doors are here and there interspersed with the blue ones, announcing that during the past year death has come among the inmates of the house; a silent but expressive intimation to passers that some who saw the last new year have passed away. In certain places, white, yellow, and carnation colored papers are employed, as well as blue, to distinguish the degree of the deceased kindred. Etiquette requires that those who mourn remain at home at this period. By noontide the streets begin to be filled with well-dressed persons, hastening in sedans or afoot to make their calls; those who cannot afford to buy a new suit hire one for this purpose, so that a man hardly knows his own domestics in their finery and robes. The meeting of friends in the streets, both bound on the same errand, is attended with particular demonstrations of respect, each politely struggling who shall be most affectedly humble. On this day parents receive the prostrations of their children, teachers expect the salutations of their pupils, magistrates look for the calls of their inferiors, and ancestors of every generation, and gods of various powers are presented with the offerings of devotees in the family hall or public temple. Much of the visiting is done by cards, on which is stamped an emblematic device representing the three happy wishes—of children, rank, and longevity; a common card suffices for distant acquaintances and customers. It might be a subject of speculation whether the custom of visiting and renewing one's acquaintances on new year's day, so generally practised among the Dutch and in America, was not originally imitated from the Chinese; but as in many other things, so in this, the westerns have improved upon the easterns, in calling upon the ladies. Persons, as they meet, salute each other with

Kung-hí! Kung-hí! 'I respectfully wish you joy!'—or *Sin-hí! Sin-hí!* 'May the new joy be yours,' either of which, from its use at this season, is quite like the *Happy New Year!* of Englishmen.

Toward evening, the merry sounds proceeding from the closed doors announce that the sacrifice provided for presentation before the shrines of departed parents is cheering the worshippers; while the great numbers who resort to gambling-shops show full well that the routine of ceremony soon becomes tiresome, and a more exciting stimulus is needed. The extent to which play is now carried is almost indescribable. Jugglers, mountebanks, and actors also endeavor to collect a few coppers by amusing the crowds. Generally speaking, however, the three days devoted to this festival pass by without turmoil, and business and work then gradually resume their usual course for another twelvemonth.

The festival of the dragon-boats, on the fifth day of the fifth month, presents a very different scene wherever there is a serviceable stream for its celebration. At Canton, long, narrow boats, holding sixty or more rowers, race up and down the river in pairs with huge clamor, as if searching for some one who had been drowned. This festival was instituted in memory of the statesman Küh Yuen, about 450 B.C., who drowned himself in the river Mih-lo, an affluent of Tungting Lake, after having been falsely accused by one of the petty princes of the state. The people, who loved the unfortunate courtier for his fidelity and virtues, sent out boats in search of the body, but to no purpose. They then made a peculiar sort of rice-cake called *tsung*, and setting out across the river in boats with flags and gongs, each strove to be first on the spot of the tragedy and sacrifice to the spirit of Küh Yuen. This mode of commemorating the event has been since continued as an annual holiday. The bow of the boat is ornamented or carved into the head of a dragon, and men beating gongs and drums, and waving flags, inspirit the rowers to renewed exertions. The exhilarating exercise of racing leads the people to prolong the festival two or three days, and generally with commendable good humor, but their eagerness to beat often breaks the boats, or leads them into so much danger that the magistrates sometimes forbid the races in order to save the people from drowning.[1]

The first full moon of the year is the feast of lanterns, a childish and dull festival compared with the two preceding. Its origin is not certainly known, but it was observed as early as A.D. 700. Its celebration consists in suspending lanterns of different forms and materials before each door, and illuminating those in the hall, but their united brilliancy is dimness itself compared with the light of the moon. At Peking, an exhibition of transparencies and pictures in the Board of War on this evening attracts great crowds of both sexes if the weather be good. Magaillans describes a firework he saw, which was an arbor covered with a vine, the woodwork of which seemed to burn, while the trunk, leaves, and clusters of the plant gradually consumed, yet so that the redness of the grapes, the greenness of the leaves, and natural brown of the stem were all maintained until the whole was burned. The feast of lanterns coming so soon after new year, and being somewhat expensive, is not so enthusiastically observed in the southern cities. At the capital this leisure time, when public offices are closed, is availed of by the jewellers, bric-a-brac dealers, and others to hold a fair in the courts of a temple in the Wai Ching, where they exhibit as beautiful a collection of carvings in stone and gems, bronzes, toys, etc., as is to be seen anywhere in Asia. The respect with which the crowds of women and children are treated on these occasions reflects much credit on the people.

In the manufacture of lanterns the Chinese surely excel all other people; the variety of their forms, their elegant carving, gilding, and coloring, and the laborious ingenuity and taste displayed in their construction, render them among the prettiest ornaments of their dwellings. They are made of paper, silk, cloth, glass, horn, basket-work, and bamboo, exhibiting an infinite variety of shapes and decorations, varying in size from a small hand-light, costing two or three cents, up to a magnificent chandelier, or a complicated lantern fifteen feet in diameter, contain-

---

[1] Compare Morrison's Dictionary under *Tsung;* Doolittle, *Social Life*, Vol. II., pp. 55–60; *Notes and Queries on China and Japan*, Vol. II., p. 157.

ing several lamps within it, and worth three or four hundred dollars. The uses to which they are applied are not less various than the pains and skill bestowed upon their construction are remarkable. One curious kind is called the *tsao-ma-tăng*, or 'horse-racing lantern,' which consists of one, two, or more wire frames, one within the other, and arranged on the same principle as the smoke-jack, by which the current of air caused by the flame sets them revolving. The wire framework is covered with paper figures of men and animals placed in the midst of appropriate scenery, and represented in various attitudes; or, as Magaillans describes them, "You shall see horses run, draw chariots and till the earth; vessels sailing, kings and princes go in and out with large trains, and great numbers of people, both afoot and a horseback, armies marching, comedies, dances, and a thousand other divertissements and motions represented."

One of the prettiest shows of lanterns is seen in a festival observed in the spring or autumn by fisherman on the southern coasts to propitiate the gods of the waters. An indispensable part of the procession is a dragon fifty feet or more long, made of light bamboo frames of the size and shape of a barrel, connected and covered with strips of colored cotton or silk; the extremities represent the gaping head and frisking tail. This monster symbolizes the ruler of the watery deep, and is carried through the streets by men holding the head and each joint upon poles, to which are suspended lanterns; as they follow each other their steps give the body a wriggling, waving motion. Huge models of fish, similarly lighted, precede the dragon, while music and fireworks—the never-failing warning to lurking demons to keep out of the way—accompany the procession, which presents a very brilliant sight as it winds in its course through the dark streets. These sports and processions give idolatry its hold upon a people; and although none of them are required or patronized by government in China as in other heathen countries, most of the scenes and games which please the people are recommended by connecting with them the observances or hopes of religion and the merrymaking of the festive board.

In the middle of the sixth moon lanterns are hung from the

top of a pole placed on the highest part of the house. A single small lantern is deemed sufficient, but if the night be calm, a greater display is made by some householders, and especially in boats, by exhibiting colored glass lamps arranged in various ways. The illumination of a city like Canton when seen from a high spot is made still more brilliant by the moving boats on the river. On one of these festivals at Canton, an almost total eclipse of the moon called out the entire population, each one carrying something with which to make a noise, kettles, pans, sticks, drums, gongs, guns, crackers, and what not to frighten away the dragon of the sky from his hideous feast. The advancing shadow gradually caused the myriads of lanterns to show more and more distinctly and started a still increasing clamor, till the darkness and the noise were both at their climax; silence gradually resumed its sway as the moon recovered her fulness.

The Chinese are fond of processions, and if marriages and funerals be included, have them more frequently than any other people. Livery establishments are opened in every city and town where processions are arranged and supplied with everything necessary for bridal and funeral occasions as well as religious festivals. Not only are sedans, bands of music, biers, framed and gilded stands for carrying idols, shrines, and sacrificial feasts, red boxes for holding the bride's trousseau, etc., supplied, but also banners, tables, stands, curiosities, and uniforms in great variety. The men and boys required to carry them and perform the various parts of the ceremony are hired, a uniform hiding their ragged garments and dirty limbs. Guilds often go to a heavy expense in getting up a procession in honor of their patron saint, whose image is carried through the streets attended by the members of the corporation dressed in holiday robes and boots. The variety and participators of these shows are exceedingly curious and characteristic of the people's taste. Here are seen splendid silken banners worked with rich embroidery, alternating with young girls bedizened with paint and flowers, and perched on high seats under an artificial tree or apparently almost in the air, resting upon frames on men's shoulders; bands of music; sacrificial meats and fruits adorned with flowers; shrines, images, and curious rarities laid out upon red pavilions;

boys gaily dressed in official robes and riding upon ponies, or harnessed up in a covered framework to represent horses, all so contrived and painted that the spectator can hardly believe they are not riding Lilliputian ponies no bigger than dogs. A child standing in a car and carrying a branch on its shoulder, on one twig of which stands another child on one foot or a girl holding a plate of cakes in her hand, on the top of which stands another miss on tiptoe, the whole borne by coolies, sometimes add to the diversion of the spectacle and illustrate the mechanical skill of the exhibitors. Small companies dressed in a great variety of military uniforms, carrying spears, shields, halberds, etc., now and then volunteer for the occasion, and give it a more martial appearance. The carpenters at Canton are famous for their splendid processions in honor of their hero, Lu Pan, in which also other craftsmen join; for this demi-god corresponds to the Tubal-cain of Chinese legends, and is now regarded as the patron of all workmen, though he flourished no longer ago than the time of Confucius. Besides these festivities and processions, there are several more strictly religious, such as the annual mass of the Buddhists, the supplicatory sacrifice of farmers for a good crop, and others of more or less importance, which add to the number of days of recreation.

Theatrical representations constitute a common amusement, and are generally connected with the religious celebration of the festival of the god before whose temple they are exhibited. They are got up by the priests, who send their neophytes around with a subscription paper, and then engage as large and skilful a band of performers as the funds will allow. There are few permanent buildings erected for theatres, for the Thespian band still retains its original strolling character, and stands ready to pack up its trappings at the first call. The erection of sheds for playing constitutes a separate branch of the carpenter's trade; one large enough to accommodate two thousand persons can be put up in the southern cities in a day, and almost the only part of the materials which is wasted is the rattan which binds the posts and mats together. One large shed contains the stage, and three smaller ones before it enclose an area, and are furnished with rude seats for the paying spectators. The subscribers' bounty is acknowledged by pasting red sheets containing their names and amounts upon the walls of the temple. The purlieus are let as stands for the sale of refreshments, for gambling tables, or for worse purposes, and by all these means the priests generally contrive to make gain of their devotion.[1]

Parties of actors and acrobats can be hired cheaply, and their performances form part of the festivities of rich families in their houses to entertain the women and relatives who cannot go abroad to see them. They are constituted into separate corporations or guilds, and each takes a distinguishing name, as the 'Happy and Blessed company,' the 'Glorious Appearing company,' etc.

The performances usually extend through three entire days, with brief recesses for sleeping and eating, and in villages where they are comparatively rare, the people act as if they were bewitched, neglecting everything to attend them. The female parts are performed by lads, who not only paint and dress like women, but even squeeze their toes into the "golden lilies," and imitate, upon the stage, a mincing, wriggling gait. These fellows personate the voice, tones, and motions of the sex with wonderful exactness, taking every opportunity, indeed, that the play will allow to relieve their feet by sitting when on the boards, or retiring into the green-room when out of the acts. The acting is chiefly pantomine, and its fidelity shows the excellent training of the players. This development of their imitative faculties is probably still more encouraged by the difficulty the audience find to understand what is said; for owing to the differences in the dialects, the open construction of the theatre, the high falsetto or recitative key in which many of the parts are spoken, and the din of the orchestra intervening between every few sentences, not one quarter of the people hear or understand a word.

The scenery is very simple, consisting merely of rudely painted mats arranged on the back and sides of the stage, a few tables, chairs, or beds, which successively serve for many

---

[1] Gray's *China* (Vol. II., p. 273) contains a cut of a mat theatre from a native drawing. See also Doolittle, *Social Life*, Vol. II., pp. 292–299.

uses, and are brought in and out from the robing-room. The orchestra sits on the side of the stage, and not only fill up the intervals with their interludes, but strike a crashing noise by way of emphasis, or to add energy to the rush of opposing warriors. No falling curtain divides the acts or scenes, and the play is carried to its conclusion without intermission. The dresses are made of gorgeous silks, and present the best specimens of ancient Chinese costume of former dynasties now to be seen. The imperfections of the scenery require much to be suggested by the spectator's imagination, though the actors themselves supply the defect in a measure by each man stating what part he performs, and what the person he represents has been doing while absent. If a courier is to be sent to a distant city, away he strides across the boards, or perhaps gets a whip and cocks up his leg as if mounting a horse, and on reaching the end of the stage cries out that he has arrived, and there delivers his message. Passing a bridge or crossing a river are indicated by stepping up and then down, or by the rolling motion of a boat. If a city is to be impersonated, two or three men lie down upon each other, when warriors rush on them furiously, overthrow the wall which they formed, and take the place by assault. Ghosts or supernatural beings are introduced through a wide trap-door in the stage, and, if he thinks it necessary, the impersonator cries out from underneath that he is ready, or for assistance to help him up through the hole.

Mr. Lay describes a play he saw, in which a medley of celestial and terrestrial personages were introduced. "The first scene was intended to represent the happiness and splendor of beings who inhabit the upper regions, with the sun and moon and the elements curiously personified playing around them. The man who personated the sun held a round image of the sun's disk, while the female who acted the part of the moon had a crescent in her hand. The actors took care to move so as to mimic the conjunction and opposition of these heavenly bodies as they revolve round in their apparent orbs. The Thunderer wielded an axe, and leaped and dashed about in a variety of extraordinary somersaults. After a few turns the monarch, who had been so highly honored as to find a place, through the partiality of a mountain nymph, in the abodes of the happy, begins to feel that no height of good fortune can secure a mortal against the common calamities of this frail life. A wicked courtier disguises himself in a tiger's skin, and in this garb imitates the animal itself. He rushes into the retired apartments of the ladies, frightens them out of their wits, and throws the heir-apparent into a moat. The sisters hurry into the royal presence, and casting themselves on the ground divulge the sad intelligence that a tiger has borne off the young prince, who it appears was the son of the mountain nymph aforesaid. The loss the bereaved monarch takes so much to heart, that he renounces the world and deliberates about the nomination of a successor. By the influence of a crafty woman he selects a young man who has just sense enough to know that he is a fool. The settlement of the crown is scarcely finished when the unhappy king dies, and the blockhead is presently invested with the crown, but instead of excelling in his new preferment the lout bemoans his lot in the most awkward strains of lamentation, and cries, 'O dear! what shall I do?' with such piteous action, and yet withal so truly ludicrous, that the spectator is at a loss to know whether to laugh or to weep. The courtier who had taken off the heir and broken the father's heart finds the new king an easy tool for prosecuting his traitorous purposes, and the state is plunged into the depths of civil discord at home and dangerous wars abroad.

"In the sequel a scene occurred in which the reconciliation of this court and some foreign prince depends upon the surrender of a certain obnoxious person. The son-in-law of the victim is charged with the letter containing this proposal, and returns to his house and disguises himself for the sake of concealment. When he reaches the court of the foreign prince he discovers that he has dropped the letter in changing his clothes, and narrowly escapes being taken for a spy without his credentials. He hurries back, calls for his garments, and shakes them one by one in an agony of self-reproach, but no letter appears. He sits down, throwing himself with great violence upon the chair, with a countenance inexpressibly full of torture and despair: reality could have added nothing to the imitation. But while every eye was riveted upon him, he called the servant-maid and inquired if she knew anything about the letter; she replied she overheard her mistress reading a letter whose contents were so and so. The mistress had taken her seat at a distance from him and was nursing her baby; and the instant he ascertained the letter was in her possession, he looked toward her with such a smile upon his cheek, and with a flood of light in his eye, that the whole assembly heaved a loud sigh of admiration; for the Chinese do not applaud by clapping and stamping, but express their feelings by an ejaculation that is between a sigh and a groan. The aim of the husband was to wheedle his wife out of the letter, and this smile and look of affection were merely the prelude; for he takes his chair, places it beside her, lays one hand softly on her shoulder, and fondles the child with the other in a style so exquisitely natural and so completely English, that in this dramatic picture it was seen that nature fashioneth men's hearts alike. His addresses were, however, ineffectual, and her father's life was not sacrificed."[1]

The morals of the Chinese stage, so far as the sentiments of the pieces are concerned, are better than the acting, which sometimes panders to depraved tastes, but no indecent exposure, as of the persons of dancers, is ever seen in China. The audience stand in the area fronting the stage, or sit in the sheds around it; the women present are usually seated in the galleries. The police are at hand to maintain order, but the crowd, although in an irksome position, and sometimes exposed to a fierce sun, is remarkably peaceable. Accidents seldom occur on these occasions, but whenever the people are alarmed by a crash, or the stage takes fire, loss of life or limb generally ensues. A dreadful destruction took place at Canton in May, 1845, by the conflagration of a stage during the performances, by which more than two thousand lives were sacrificed; the survivors had occasion to remember that fifty persons had been killed many years before in the same place, and while a play was going on, by the falling of a wall.[2]

Active, manly plays are not popular in the south, and instead

---

[1] *Chinese as They Are*, p. 114. [2] *Chinese Repository*, Vol. XIV., p. 335.

of engaging in a ball-game or regatta, going to a bowling alley or fives' court, to exhibit their strength and skill, young men lift beams headed with heavy stones, like huge dumb-bells, to prove their muscle, or kick up their heels in a game of shuttlecock. The out-door amusements of gentlemen consist in flying kites, carrying birds on perches and throwing seeds high in the air for them to catch, sauntering through the fields, or lazily boating on the water. Pitching coppers, fighting crickets or quails, tossing up several balls at once, kicking large leaden balls against each other, snapping sticks, chucking stones, or guessing the number of seeds in an orange, are plays for lads.

Gambling is universal. Hucksters at the roadside are provided with a cup and saucer, and the clicking of their dice is heard at every corner. A boy with but two cash prefers to risk their loss on the throw of a die to simply buying a cake without trying the chance of getting it for nothing. Gaming-houses are opened by scores, their keepers paying a bribe to the local officers, who can hardly be expected to be very severe against what they were brought up in and daily practise; and women, in the privacy of their apartments, while away their time at cards and dominoes. Porters play by the wayside when waiting for employment, and hardly have the retinue of an officer seen their superiors enter the house, than they pull out their cards or dice and squat down to a game. The most common game of luck played at Canton is called *fan tan*, or 'quadrating cash.' The keeper of the table is provided with a pile of bright large cash, of which he takes a double handful, and lays them on the table, covering the pile with a bowl. The persons standing outside the rail guess the remainder there will be left after the pile has been divided by four, whether one, two, three, or nothing, the guess and stake of each person being first recorded by a clerk; the keeper then carefully picks out the coins four by four, all narrowly watching his movements. Cheating is almost impossible in this game, and twenty people can play at it as easily as two. Chinese cards are smaller and more numerous than our own; but the dominoes are the same.

Combats between crickets are oftenest seen in the south,

where the small field sort is common. Two well-chosen combatants are put into a basin and irritated with a straw until they rush upon each other with the utmost fury, chirruping as they make the onset, and the battle seldom ends without a tragical result in loss of life or limb. Quails are also trained to mortal combat; two are placed on a railed table, on which a handful of millet has been strewn, and as soon as one picks up a kernel the other flies at him with beak, claws, and wings, and the struggle is kept up till one retreats by hopping into the

Boys Gambling with Crickets.

hand of his disappointed owner. Hundreds of dollars are occasionally betted upon these cricket or quail fights, which, if not as sublime or exciting, are certainly less inhuman than the pugilistic fights and bull-baits of Christian countries, while both show the same brutal love of sport at the expense of life.

A favorite amusement is the flying of kites. They are made of paper and silk, in imitation of birds, butterflies, lizards, spectacles, fish, men, and other objects; but the skill shown in flying them is more remarkable than the ingenuity displayed in their construction. The ninth day of the ninth moon is a festival devoted to this amusement all over the land. Doolittle describes them as sometimes resembling a great bird, or a serpent thirty feet long; at other times the spectator sees a group of hawks hovering around a centre, all being suspended by one strong cord, and each hawk-kite controlled and moved by a separate line. On this day he estimates that as many as thirty thousand people assemble on the hills around Fuhchau to join

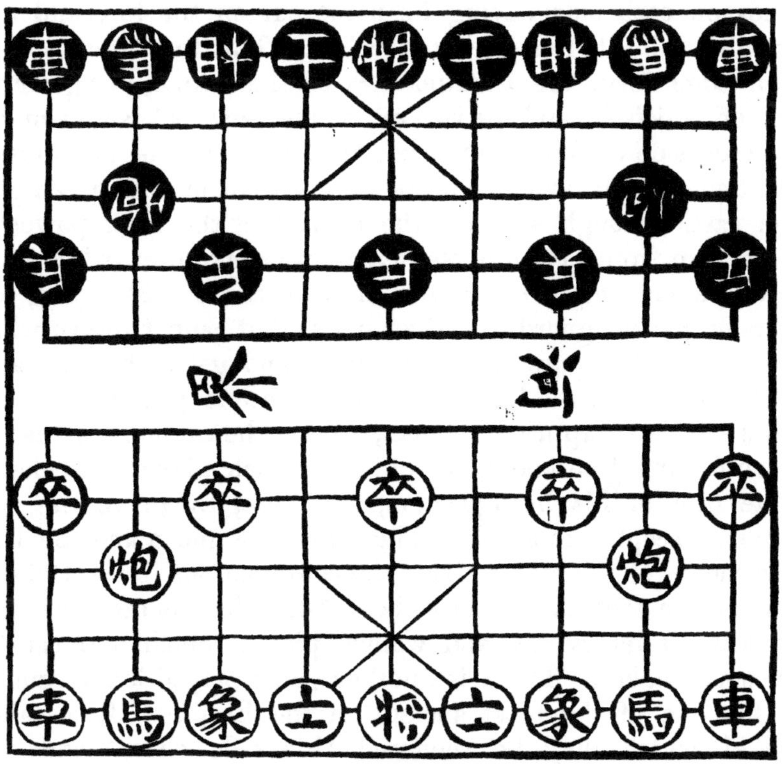

Chinese Chess-board.

in this amusement if the weather be propitious. Many of the kites are cut adrift under the belief that, as they float off, they carry away with them all impending disasters.

The Chinese game of chess is very ancient, for Wu Wang (B.C. 1120) is the reputed inventor, and its rules of playing are so unlike the Indian game as to suggest an independent origin, which is confirmed by the peculiar feature of the *kiai ho*, or river, running across the board. There are seventy-two squares, of which eight are run together to form the river, leaving thirty-two on each side; but as the men stand on the intersection of the lines, there are ninety positions for the sixteen pieces used by each player, or twenty-six more than in the European game. The pieces are arranged for playing as in the diagram above.

The pieces are like chequer-men in shape, each of the seven kinds on each side having its name cut on the top, and distinguished by its red or black colors. The four squares near each edge form the headquarters of the *tsiang*, or 'general,' out of which he and his two *sz'*, or 'secretaries,' cannot move. On each side of the headquarters are two elephants, two horses, and two chariots, whose powers are less than our bishop, knight, and castle, though similar; the chariot is the most powerful piece. In front of the horses stand two cannoniers, which capture like our knight but move like our castle. Five *pao*, soldiers or pawns, guard the river banks, but cannot return when once across it in pursuit of the enemy, and get no higher value when they reach the last row. Each piece is put down in the point where it captured its man, except the cannoniers; as the general cannot be taken, the object of each player is to checkmate him in his headquarters, therefore, by preventing his moving except into check. The want of a queen and the limited moves of the men restrict the combinations in the Chinese game more than in western chess, but it has its own elements of skill. Literary men and women play it much, and usually for small stakes. There is another game played less frequently but one of the most ancient in the Empire. It is called *wei-kí*, which may be rendered 'blockade chess,' and was common in the days of the sages, perhaps even earlier than chess. The board contains three hundred and twenty-four squares, eighteen each way, and the number of pieces is three hundred, though both the number of points and of pieces may be less than this size of the full game. The pieces are black and white and stand on the crossings of the lines, three hundred and sixty-one in number. The object of the opponents is to surround each other's men and take up the crossings they occupy, or neutralize their power over those near them.

Each player puts down a piece anywhere on the board, and continues to do so alternately, capturing his adversary's positions until all the crossings are occupied and the game is ended.[1]

If this sketch of the customs and amusements of the Chinese in their social intercourse and public entertainments is necessarily brief, it is perhaps enough to exhibit their character. Dr. Johnson has well remarked that no man is a hypocrite in his amusements. The absence of some of the violent and gladiatorial sports of other countries, and of the adjudication of doubtful questions by ordeals or duels; the general dislike of a resort to force, their inability to cope with enemies of vastly less resources and numbers, and the comparative disesteem of warlike achievements, all indicate the peaceful traits of Chinese character. Duels are unknown, assassinations are infrequent, betting on horse-races is still to begin, and running amuck à la Malay is unheard of. When two persons fall out upon a matter, after a vast variety of gesture and huge vociferation of opprobrium, they will blow off their wrath and separate almost without touching each other. Some contrarieties in their ideas and customs from those practised among ourselves have frequently been noticed by travellers, a few of which are grouped in the following sketch:

On asking the boatman in which direction the harbor lay, I was answered west-north, and the wind, he said, was west-south; he still further perplexed my ideas as to our course by getting out his compass and showing me that the needle pointed south. It was really a needle as to size, weight, and length, about an inch and a half long, the south end of it painted red, and all the time quivering on the pivot. His boat differed from our vessels, too, in many ways: the cooking was done in the stern and the passengers were all accommodated in the bow, while the sailors slept on deck and had their kits stowed in lockers amidships.

On landing, the first object that attracted my attention was a military officer wearing an embroidered petticoat, who had a string of beads around his neck and a fan in his hand. His insignia of rank was a peacock's feather pointing downward instead of a plume turning upward; he had a round knob or button on the apex of his sugar-loaf cap, instead of a star on his breast or epaulettes on his shoulders; and it was with some dismay that I saw him mount his horse on the right side. Several scabbards hung from his belt, which

---

[1] *Temple Bar*, Vol. XLIX., p. 45.

I naturally supposed must be dress swords or dirks; but on venturing near through the crowd I was undeceived by seeing a pair of chopsticks and a knife-handle sticking out of one, and soon his fan was folded up and put in the other. I therefore concluded that he was going to a dinner instead of a review. The natives around me shaved the hair from the front half of their heads and let it grow long behind: many of them did not shave their faces, and others employed their leisure in diligently pulling the straggling hairs down over their mouths. We arrange our toilets differently, thought I; but could easily see the happy device of chopsticks, which enabled these gentlemen to put their food into the mouth endwise under this natural fringe. A group of hungry fellows, around the stall of a travelling cook, further exhibited the utility of these *kwai-tsz'*, or 'nimble lads' (as I afterward learned chopsticks were called), for each had put his bowl of rice to his lips, and was shovelling in the contents till the mouth would hold no more. "We keep our bowls on the table," said I, "do our cooking in the house, and wait for customers to come there instead of travelling around after them;" but these chopsticks serve for knife, fork, and spoon in one.

On my way to the hotel I saw a group of old people and graybeards. A few were chirruping and chuckling to larks or thrushes, which they carried perched on a stick or in cages; others were catching flies or hunting for crickets to feed them, while the remainder of the party seemed to be delightfully employed in flying fantastic paper kites. A group of boys were gravely looking on and regarding these innocent occupations of their seniors with the most serious and gratified attention. A few of the most sprightly were kicking a shuttlecock back and forth with great energy, instead of playing rounders with bat and ball as boys would do.

As I had come to the country to reside for some time, I made inquiries respecting a teacher, and happily found one who understood English. On entering he stood at the door, and instead of coming forward and shaking my hands, he politely bowed and shook his own, clasping them before his breast. I looked upon this mode as an improvement on our custom, especially when the condition of the hands might be doubtful, and requested him to be seated. I knew that I was to study a language without an alphabet, but was not prepared to see him begin at what I had always considered to be the end of the book. He read the date of its publication, "the fifth year, tenth month, and first day." "We arrange our dates differently," I observed, and begged him to read—which he did, from top to bottom, and proceeding from right to left. "You have an odd book here," remarked I, taking it up; "what is the price?" "A dollar and eight-thirds," said he, upon which I counted out three dollars and two-thirds and went on looking at it. The paper was printed only on one side; the running title was on the edge of the leaves instead of the top of the page, the paging was near the bottom, the number and contents of the chapters were at their ends, the marginal notes on the top, where the blank was double the size at the foot, and a broad black line across the middle of each page, like that seen in some French newspapers, separated the two works composing the volume, instead of one being printed after the other. The back was open and the sewing outside, and the name neatly written on the bottom edge. "You have given me too much," said he, as he handed me back two dollars and one-third, and then explained that eight-thirds meant eight divided by three, or only three-eighths. A small native vocabulary which he carried with him had the characters arranged according to the termination of their sounds, *ming*, *sing*, *king*, being all in a row, and the first word in it being *seen*. "Ah! my friend," said I, "English won't help me to find a word in that book; please give me your address." He accordingly took out a red card, big as a sheet of paper, on which was written Ying San-yuen in large characters, and pointed out the place of his residence, written on the other side. "I thought your name was Mr. Ying; why do you write your name wrong end first?" "It is you who are in the wrong," replied he; "look in your yearly directory, where alone you write names as they should be written, putting the honored family name first."

I could only say, "Customs differ;" and begged him to speak of ceremony, as I gave him back the book. He commenced, "When you receive a distinguished guest, do not fail to place him on your left, for that is the seat of honor; and be careful not to uncover the head, as that would be an unbecoming act of familiarity." This was a little opposed to my established notions; but when he reopened the volume and read, "The most learned men are decidedly of the opinion that the seat of the human understanding is in the belly," I cried out, "Better say it is in the feet!" and straightway shut up the book, dismissing him for another day; for this shocked all my principles of correct philosophy, even if King Solomon was against me.

On going abroad I met so many things contrary to my early notions of propriety that I readily assented to a friend's observation, that the Chinese were our antipodes in many things besides geographical position. "Indeed," said I, "they are so; I shall expect shortly to see a man walking on his head. Look! there's a woman in trousers and a party of gentlemen in petticoats; she is smoking and they are fanning themselves." However, on passing them I saw that the latter had on tight leggings. We soon met the steward of the house dressed in white, and I asked him what merry-making he was invited to; with a look of concern he told me he was returning from his father's funeral. Instead of having crape on his head he wore white shoes, and his dress was slovenly and neglected. My companion informed me that in the north of China it was common for rich people at funerals to put a white harness on the mules and shroud the carts in coarse cotton; while the chief mourners walked next to the bier, making loud cryings and showing their grief by leaning on the attendants. The friends rode behind and the musicians preceded the coffin—all being unlike our sable plumes and black crapes.

We next went through a retired street, where we heard sobbing and crying inside a court, and I inquired who was dead or ill. The man, suppressing a smile, said, "It is a girl about to be married, who is lamenting with her relatives and fellows as she bids adieu to the family penates and lares and her paternal home. She has enough to cry about, though, in the prospect of going to her mother-in-law's house."

I thought, after these unlucky essays, I would ask no more questions, but use my eyes instead. Looking into a shop, I saw a stout fellow sewing lace on a bonnet for a foreign lady; and going on to the landing-place, behold, all the ferry-boats were rowed by women, and from a passage-boat at the wharf I saw all the women get out of the bow to go ashore. "What are we coming to next?" said I; and just then saw a carpenter take his foot-rule out of his stocking to measure some timber which an apprentice was cutting with a saw whose blade was set nearly at right angles with the frame. Before the door sat a man busily engaged in whitening the thick soles of a pair of cloth shoes. "That's a shoewhite, I suppose," said I; "and he answers to the shoeblacks in New York, who cry 'Shine! shine!'" "Just so," said my friend; "and beyond him see the poor wretch in *chokey*, with a board or cangue around his neck for a shirt-collar; an article of his toilet which answers to the cuffs with which the lads in the Tombs there are garnished instead of bracelets. In the prisons in this land, instead of cropping the hair of a criminal, as with us, no man is allowed to have his head shaved."

In the alleys called streets, few of them ten feet wide, the signs stood on their ends or hung from the eaves; the counters of the shops were next the street, the fronts were all open, and I saw the holes for the upright bars which secured the shop at night. Everything was done or sold in the streets or markets, which presented a strange medley. The hogs were transported in hampers on the shoulders of coolies, to the evident satisfaction of the inmates, and small pigs were put into baskets carried in slings, while the fish were frisking and jumping in shallow tubs as they were hawked from door to door.

A loud din led us to look in at an open door to see what was going on, and there a dozen boys were learning their tasks, all crying like auctioneers; one lad reciting his lesson out of Conufcius turned his back to the master instead of looking him in the face, and another who was learning to write put the copy-slip under the paper to imitate it, instead of looking at it as our boys would do.

We next passed a fashionable lady stepping out of her sedan chair. Her head was adorned with flowers instead of a bonnet, her hands gloveless, and her neck quite bare. Her feet were encased in red silk pictured shoes not quite four inches long; her plaited, embroidered petticoat was a foot longer than her gown, and her waist was not to be seen. As she entered the court-yard, leaning on the shoulder of her maid to help her walk on those cramped feet, my friend observed, "There you see a good example of a live walking-stick."

A little after we met one of his acquaintances accompanying a prettily carved coffin, and he asked who was dead.

"No man hab catchee die," replied the Celestial; "this one piecy coffin I just now gib my olo fader. He likee-too much counta my numba one ploper; s'pose he someteem catchee die, can usee he."

"So fashion, eh?" rejoined my friend; "how muchee plice can catchee one alla same same for that?"

"I tinky can get one alla same so fashion one tousan dollar, so; this hab first chop hansom, lo."

"Do you call that gibberish English or Chinese?" I asked; for the language sounded no less strange than the custom of presenting a coffin to a living father differed from my preconceived notions of filial duty.

"That's the purest pigeon-English," replied he; "and you must be the Jack Downing of Canton to immortalize it."

"Come, rather let us go home, for soon I shall hardly be able to tell where or who I am in this strange land." [1]

In summing up the moral traits of Chinese character—a far more difficult task than the enumeration of its oddities—we must necessarily compare them with that perfect standard given us from above. While their contrarieties indicate a different external civilization, a slight acquaintance with their morals proves tneir similarity to their fellow-men in the lineaments of a fallen and depraved nature. Some of the better traits of their character have been marvellously developed. They have attained, by the observance of peace and good order, to a high degree of security for life and property; the various classes of society are linked together in a remarkably homogeneous manner by the diffusion of education in the most moral books in their language and a general regard for the legal rights of property. Equality of competition for office removes the main incentive to violence in order to obtain posts of power and dignity, and industry receives its just reward of food, raiment, and shelter with a uniformity which encourages its constant exertion. If any one asks how they have reached this point, we would primarily ascribe it to the blessing of the Governor of the nations, who has for His own purposes continued one people down to the present time from remote antiquity. The roots of society among them have never been broken up by emigration or the overflowing conquest of a superior race, but have been fully settled in a great regard for the family compact and deep reverence for parents and superiors. Education has strengthened and disseminated the morality they had, and God has blessed their filial piety by fulfilling the first commandment with promise and making their days long in the land which He has given them. Davis lays rather too much stress upon geographical and climatic causes in accounting for their advancement in these particulars, though their isolation has no doubt had much to do with their security and progress.

When, however, these traits have been mentioned, the Chinese are still more left without excuse for their wickedness, since

---

[1] *Chinese Repository*, Vol. X., p. 106; *New York Christian Weekly*, 1878.

being without law, they are a law unto themselves; they have always known better than they have done. With a general regard for outward decency, they are vile and polluted in a shocking degree; their conversation is full of filthy expressions and their lives of impure acts. They are somewhat restrained in the latter by the fences put around the family circle, so that seduction and adultery are comparatively infrequent, the former may even be said to be rare; but brothels and their inmates occur everywhere on land and on water. One danger attending young girls going abroad alone is that they will be stolen for incarceration in these gates of hell. By pictures, songs, and aphrodisiacs they excite their sensuality, and, as the Apostle says, "receive in themselves that recompense of their error which is meet."

More uneradicable than the sins of the flesh is the falsity of the Chinese, and its attendant sin of base ingratitude; their disregard of truth has perhaps done more to lower their character than any other fault. They feel no shame at being detected in a lie (though they have not gone quite so far as not to know when they do lie), nor do they fear any punishment from their gods for it. On the other hand, the necessity of the case compels them, in their daily intercourse with each other, to pay some regard to truth, and each man, from his own consciousness, knows just about how much to expect. Ambassadors and merchants have not been in the best position to ascertain their real character in this respect; for on the one side the courtiers of Peking thought themselves called upon by the mere presence of an embassy to put on some fictitious appearances, and on the other, the integrity and fair dealing of the hong merchants and great traders at Canton is in advance of the usual mercantile honesty of their countrymen. A Chinese requires but little motive to falsify, and he is constantly sharpening his wits to cozen his customer—wheedle him by promises and cheat him in goods or work. There is nothing which tries one so much when living among them as their disregard of truth, and renders him so indifferent as to what calamities may befall so mendacious a race; an abiding impression of suspicion toward everybody rests upon the mind, which chills the warmest wishes for their welfare and thwarts many a plan to benefit them. Their better traits diminish in the distance, and patience is exhausted in its daily proximity and friction with this ancestor of all sins. Mr. Abeel mentions a case of deceit which may serve as a specimen.

Soon after we arrived at Kulang su, a man came to us who professed to be the near relation and guardian of the owners of the house in which we live, and presented a little boy as the joint proprietor with his widowed mother. From the appearance of the house and the testimony of others we could easily credit his story that the family were now in reduced circumstances, having not only lost the house when the English attacked the place, but a thousand dollars besides by native robbers; we therefore allowed him a small rent, and gave the dollars to the man, who put them into the hands of the child. The next month he made his appearance, but our servant, whom we had taken to be peculiarly honest for a heathen, suggested the propriety of inquiring whether the money was ever given to those for whom it was professedly received; and soon returned with the information that the mother had heard nothing of the money, the man who received it not living in the family, but had now sent a lad to us who would receive it for her, and who our servants assured us would give it to the proper person. A day or two afterward our cook whispered to me that our *honest* servant, who had taken so much pains to prevent all fraud in the matter, had made the lad give him one-half of the money for his disinterestedness in preventing it from falling into improper hands; and further examination showed us that this very cook had himself received a good share to keep silent.

Thieving is exceedingly common, and the illegal exactions of the rulers, as has already been sufficiently pointed out, are most burdensome. This vice, too, is somewhat restrained by the punishments inflicted on criminals, though the root of the evil is not touched. While the licentiousness of the Chinese may be in part ascribed to their ignorance of pure intellectual pleasures and the want of virtuous female society, so may their lying be attributed partly to their truckling fear of officers, and their thievery to the want of sufficient food or work. Hospitality is not a trait of their character; on the contrary, the number and wretched condition of the beggars show that public and private charity is almost extinct; yet here too the sweeping charge must be modified when we remember the efforts they make to sustain their relatives and families in so densely peopled a country. Their avarice is not so distinguishing a feature as their love of money, but the industry which this desire induces or presupposes is the source of most of their superiority to their neighbors. The politeness which they exhibit seldom has its motive in good-will, and consequently, when the varnish is off, the rudeness, brutality, and coarseness of the material is seen; still, among themselves this exterior polish is not without some good results in preventing quarrels, where both parties, fully understanding each other, are careful not to overpass the bounds of etiquette.

On the whole, the Chinese present a singular mixture: if there is something to commend, there is more to blame; if they have some glaring vices, they have more virtues than most pagan nations. Ostentatious kindness and inbred suspicion, ceremonious civility and real rudeness, partial invention and servile imitation, industry and waste, sycophancy and self-dependence, are, with other dark and bright qualities, strangely blended. In trying to remedy the faults of their character by the restraints of law and the diffusion of education, they have no doubt hit upon the right mode; and their shortcomings show how ineffectual both must be until the Gospel comes to the aid of ruler and subject in elevating the moral sense of the whole nation. Female infanticide in some parts openly confessed, and divested of all disgrace and penalties everywhere; the dreadful prevalence of all the vices charged by the Apostle Paul upon the ancient heathen world; the alarming extent of the use of opium (furnished, too, under the patronage, and supplied in purity by the power and skill of Great Britain from India), destroying the productions and natural resources of the people; the universal practice of lying and dishonest dealings; the unblushing lewdness of old and young; harsh cruelty toward prisoners by officers, and tyranny over slaves by masters—all form a full unchecked torrent of human depravity, and prove the existence of a kind and degree of moral degradation of which an excessive statement can scarcely be made, or an adequate conception hardly be formed.

END OF VOLUME I.

For Product Safety Concerns and Information please contact our EU representative GPSR@taylorandfrancis.com Taylor & Francis Verlag GmbH, Kaufingerstraße 24, 80331 München, Germany

Batch number: 10725818

Printed by Printforce, the Netherlands